Psychological and Behavioral Examinations in Cyber Security

John McAlaney
Bournemouth University, UK

Lara A. Frumkin
Open University, UK

Vladlena Benson
University of West London, UK

A volume in the Advances in Digital Crime,
Forensics, and Cyber Terrorism (ADCFCT) Book
Series

Published in the United States of America by
    IGI Global
    Information Science Reference (an imprint of IGI Global)
    701 E. Chocolate Avenue
    Hershey PA, USA 17033
    Tel: 717-533-8845
    Fax: 717-533-8661
    E-mail: cust@igi-global.com
    Web site: http://www.igi-global.com

Library of Congress Cataloging-in-Publication Data

Names: McAlaney, John, 1979- editor. | Frumkin, Lara Anne, 1972- editor. |
  Benson, Vladlena, 1976- editor.
Title: Psychological and behavioral examinations in cyber security / John
  McAlaney, Lara A. Frumkin, and Vladlena Benson, editors.
Description: Hershey : Information Science Reference, [2018]
Identifiers: LCCN 2017026831| ISBN 9781522540533 (hardcover) | ISBN
  9781522540540 (ebook)
Subjects: LCSH: Electronic commerce--Psychological aspects. | Decision
  making--Psychological aspects. | Computer networks--Security networks. |
  Cyberspace--Security measures.
Classification: LCC HF5548.32 .P79 2018 | DDC 658.4/78--dc23 LC record available at https://lccn.loc.gov/2017026831

This book is published in the IGI Global book series Advances in Digital Crime, Forensics, and Cyber Terrorism (ADCF-CT) (ISSN: 2327-0381; eISSN: 2327-0373)

Advances in Digital Crime, Forensics, and Cyber Terrorism (ADCFCT) Book Series

Bryan Christiansen
Tactical Systems, LLC, USA
Agnieszka Piekarz
Independent Researcher, Poland

ISSN:2327-0381
EISSN:2327-0373

MISSION

The digital revolution has allowed for greater global connectivity and has improved the way we share and present information. With this new ease of communication and access also come many new challenges and threats as cyber crime and digital perpetrators are constantly developing new ways to attack systems and gain access to private information.

The **Advances in Digital Crime, Forensics, and Cyber Terrorism (ADCFCT) Book Series** seeks to publish the latest research in diverse fields pertaining to crime, warfare, terrorism and forensics in the digital sphere. By advancing research available in these fields, the **ADCFCT** aims to present researchers, academicians, and students with the most current available knowledge and assist security and law enforcement professionals with a better understanding of the current tools, applications, and methodologies being implemented and discussed in the field.

COVERAGE

- Computer virology
- Watermarking
- Crime scene imaging
- Mobile Device Forensics
- Criminology
- Digital Surveillance
- Encryption
- Cyber terrorism
- Information warfare
- Global Threat Intelligence

IGI Global is currently accepting manuscripts for publication within this series. To submit a proposal for a volume in this series, please contact our Acquisition Editors at Acquisitions@igi-global.com or visit: http://www.igi-global.com/publish/.

Titles in this Series

For a list of additional titles in this series, please visit: www.igi-global.com/book-series

Combating Internet-Enabled Terrorism Emerging Research and Opportunities
Emily Stacey (Swansea University, UK)
Information Science Reference • copyright 2017 • 133pp • H/C (ISBN: 9781522521907) • US $115.00 (our price)

Combating Security Breaches and Criminal Activity in the Digital Sphere
S. Geetha (VIT University, Chennai, India) and Asnath Victy Phamila (VIT University, Chennai, India)
Information Science Reference • copyright 2016 • 309pp • H/C (ISBN: 9781522501930) • US $205.00 (our price)

National Security and Counterintelligence in the Era of Cyber Espionage
Eugenie de Silva (University of Leicester, UK & Virginia Research Institute, USA)
Information Science Reference • copyright 2016 • 308pp • H/C (ISBN: 9781466696617) • US $200.00 (our price)

Handbook of Research on Civil Society and National Security in the Era of Cyber Warfare
Metodi Hadji-Janev (Military Academy "General Mihailo Apostolski", Macedonia) and Mitko Bogdanoski (Military Academy "General Mihailo Apostolski", Macedonia)
Information Science Reference • copyright 2016 • 548pp • H/C (ISBN: 9781466687936) • US $335.00 (our price)

Cybersecurity Policies and Strategies for Cyberwarfare Prevention
Jean-Loup Richet (University of Nantes, France)
Information Science Reference • copyright 2015 • 472pp • H/C (ISBN: 9781466684560) • US $245.00 (our price)

New Threats and Countermeasures in Digital Crime and Cyber Terrorism
Maurice Dawson (University of Missouri–St. Louis, USA) and Marwan Omar (Nawroz University, Iraq)
Information Science Reference • copyright 2015 • 368pp • H/C (ISBN: 9781466683457) • US $200.00 (our price)

Handbook of Research on Digital Crime, Cyberspace Security, and Information Assurance
Maria Manuela Cruz-Cunha (Polytechnic Institute of Cavado and Ave, Portugal) and Irene Maria Portela (Polytechnic Institute of Cávado and Ave, Portugal)
Information Science Reference • copyright 2015 • 602pp • H/C (ISBN: 9781466663244) • US $385.00 (our price)

The Psychology of Cyber Crime Concepts and Principles
Gráinne Kirwan (Dun Laoghaire Institute of Art, Design and Technology, Ireland) and Andrew Power (Dun Laoghaire Institute of Art, Design and Technology, Ireland)
Information Science Reference • copyright 2012 • 372pp • H/C (ISBN: 9781613503508) • US $195.00 (our price)

701 East Chocolate Avenue, Hershey, PA 17033, USA
Tel: 717-533-8845 x100 • Fax: 717-533-8661
E-Mail: cust@igi-global.com • www.igi-global.com

Editorial Advisory Board

Table of Contents

Detailed Table of Contents

Chapter 1
Online Decision Making: Online Influence and Implications for Cyber Security 1
> *Helen Joanne Wall, Edge Hill University, UK*
> *Linda K. Kaye, Edge Hill University, UK*

The growth in computer-mediated communication has created real challenges for society; in particular, the internet has become an important resource for "convincing" or persuading a person to make a decision. From a cybersecurity perspective, online attempts to persuade someone to make a decision has implications for the radicalisation of individuals. This chapter reviews multiple definitions and theories relating to decision making to consider the applicability of these to online decision making in areas such as buying behaviour, social engineering, and radicalisation. Research investigating online decision making is outlined and the point is made that research examining online research has a different focus than research exploring online decision making. The chapter concludes with some key questions for scholars and practitioners. In particular, it is noted that online decision making cannot be explained by one single model, as none is sufficient in its own capacity to underpin all forms of online behaviour.

Chapter 2
Human Factors Leading to Online Fraud Victimisation: Literature Review and Exploring the Role of Personality Traits 26
> *Jildau Borwell, The National Police of the Netherlands, The Netherlands*
> *Jurjen Jansen, Open University of the Netherlands, The Netherlands & NHL University of*
> *   Applied Sciences, The Netherlands & Dutch Police Academy, The Netherlands*
> *Wouter Stol, Open University of the Netherlands, The Netherlands & NHL University of*
> *   Applied Sciences, The Netherlands & Dutch Police Academy, The Netherlands*

With the advent of the internet, criminals gained new tools to commit crimes. Crimes in which the use of connected information technologies is essential for the realisation of the offence are defined as cybercrimes. The human factor is often identified as the weakest link in the information security chain, and it is often the behaviour of humans that leads to the success of cybercrimes. In this chapter, end-user characteristics are studied that may predict cybercrime victimisation. This is done by means of a review of the literature and by a study on personality traits. More specifically, personality traits from the big five are tested on victims of three different types of online fraud, phishing, Microsoft fraud, and purchasing fraud, and are compared with norm groups of the Dutch population. This chapter ends with implications for online fraud prevention and possibilities to advance the study of cyber victimisation.

Chapter 3

A great deal of research has been devoted to the exploration and categorization of threats posed from malicious attacks from current employees who are disgruntled with the organisation, or are motivated by financial gain. These so-called "insider threats" pose a growing menace to information security, but given the right mechanisms, they have the potential to be detected and caught. In contrast, human factors related to aspects of poor planning, lack of attention to detail, and ignorance are linked to the rise of the accidental or unintentional insider. In this instance there is no malicious intent and no prior planning for their "attack," but their actions can be equally as damaging and disruptive to the organisation. This chapter presents an exploration of fundamental human factors that could contribute to an individual becoming an unintentional threat. Furthermore, key frameworks for designing mitigations for such threats are also presented, alongside suggestions for future research in this area.

Technical advances in cyber-attack attribution continues to show incremental improvement. A growing interest in the role of the human in perception management, and decision-making suggest that other aspects of human cognition may be able to help inform attribution, and other aspects of cyber security such as defending and training. Values shape behaviors and cultural values set norms for groups of people. Therefore, they should be considered when modeling behaviors. The lack of studies in this area requires exploration and foundational work to learn the limits of this area of research. This chapter highlights some of the findings of some of the recent studies.

The internet provides an ever-expanding, valuable resource for entertainment, communication, and commerce. However, this comes with the simultaneous advancement and sophistication of cyber-attacks, which have serious implications on both a personal and commercial level, as well as within the criminal justice system. Psychologically, such attacks offer an intriguing, under-exploited arena for the understanding of the decision-making processes leading to online fraud victimisation. In this chapter, the authors focus on approaches taken to understand response behaviour surrounding phishing emails. The chapter outlines how approaches from industry and academic research might work together to more effectively understand and potentially tackle the persistent threat of email fraud. In doing this, the authors address alternative methodological approaches taken to understand susceptibility, key insights drawn from each, how useful these are in working towards preventative security measures, and the usability of each approach. It is hoped that these can contribute to collaborative solutions.

Chapter 6

This chapter begins with a brief review of the literature that highlights what psychology research and practice can offer to cybersecurity education. The authors draw on their wide-ranging inter-disciplinary teaching experience, and in this chapter, they discuss their observations gained from teaching psychological principles and methods to undergraduate and postgraduate cybersecurity students. The authors pay special attention to the consideration of the characteristics of cybersecurity students so that psychology is taught in a way that is accessible and engaging. Finally, the authors offer some practical suggestions for academics to help them incorporate psychology into the cybersecurity curriculum.

Across many online contexts, internet users are required to make judgments of trustworthiness in the systems or other users that they are connecting with. But how can a user know that the interactions they engage in are legitimate? In cases where trust is manipulated, there can be severe consequences for the user both economically and psychologically. In this chapter, the authors outline key psychological literature to date that has addressed the question of how trust develops in online environments. Specifically, three use cases in which trust relationships emerge are discussed: crowdfunding, online health forums, and online dating. By including examples of different types of online interaction, the authors aim to demonstrate the need for advanced security measures that ensure valid trust judgments and minimise the risk of fraud victimisation.

As the front end of the digitized commercial world, corporations, marketers, and advertisers are under the spotlight for taking advantage of some part of the big data provided by consumers via their digital presence and digital advertising. Now, collectors and users of that data have escalated the level of their asymmetric power with scope and depth of the instant and historical data on consumers. Since consumers have lost the ownership (control) over their own data, their reaction ranges from complete opposition to voluntary submission. This chapter investigates psychological and societal reasons for this variety in consumer behavior and proposes that a contractual solution could promote a beneficial end to all parties through transparency and mutual power.

Sheryl Prentice, Lancaster University, UK
Paul J. Taylor, Lancaster University, UK

It has long been recognised that terrorists make use of the internet as one of many means through which to further their cause. This use of the internet has fuelled a large number of studies seeking to understand terrorists' use of online environments. This chapter provides an overview of current understandings of online terrorist behavior, coupled with an outline of the qualitative and quantitative approaches that can and have been adopted to research this phenomenon. The chapter closes with a discussion of the contentious issue of ethics in online terrorism research. The aim of the chapter is to equip readers with the necessary knowledge and skills to conduct their own research into terrorists' online behavior, taking best ethical practices into consideration when doing so.

Rami Mohammed Baazeem, Jeddah University, Saudi Arabia

Religion plays a major role in shaping individual behaviour, especially in the religious countries. This chapter sheds light on the effect of religiosity on the intention to use technology and privacy and will use Saudi Arabia as an example. Using the unified theory of acceptance and use of technology (UTAUT) will help explain the intention to use technology. Thus, it clarifies that the intention to use technology is affected by the user behaviour. The user's behaviour is shaped by their religious beliefs which also affect their privacy views. A systematic review of the privacy literature shows that there is a lack of study on the effect of the religious beliefs on privacy. After reading this chapter, policy makers and managers will understand that religious belief should be considered when making new laws and regulations.

Helen Thackray, Bournemouth University, UK
John McAlaney, Bournemouth University, UK

This chapter provides a brief introduction to hacktivism and social protest online and highlights some of the socio-psychological and cognitive factors that can lead to individuals taking part in hacktivism groups. Hacktivism is an ill-defined area which some claim as a legitimate form of protest in the online world and others regard as illegal hacking; there is truth to both arguments, and those who believe it should be protected will continue to work for it to be recognised. The chapter explains how the depth of social ties and influence are still being examined, and whilst cognitive biases are recognised, strategies to mitigate and combat the vulnerability they present are still being developed.

This chapter attempts to synthesize the mainstream theories of radicalization and the cyber-psychological and behavioral approaches with a view to identifying individuals' radicalization online. Based on the intersections of those two fields, this chapter first elaborates how radical groups use cyberspace with a specific concentration on the so-called cyber caliphate claimed by the Islamic State of Iraq and al-Sham (ISIS). Second, it revisits mainstream theories of radicalization and specifies the psychological and behavioral facets of the radicalization processes proposed by those theories. Following that, it integrates theories of radicalization with cyber-psychological and behavioral explanations of online radicalization to reveal how ISIS's use of cyberspace attracts individuals and facilitates online radicalization.

Chapter 13

Recent studies have shown that, despite being equipped with highly secure technical controls, a broad range of cyber security attacks were carried out successfully on many organizations to reveal confidential information. This shows that the technical advancements of cyber defence controls do not always guarantee organizational security. According to a recent survey carried out by IBM, 55% of these cyber-attacks involved insider threat. Controlling an insider who already has access to the company's highly protected data is a very challenging task. Insider attacks have great potential to severely damage the organization's finances as well as their social credibility. Hence, there is a need for reliable security frameworks that ensure confidentiality, integrity, authenticity, and availability of organizational information assets by including the comprehensive study of employee behaviour. This chapter provides a detailed study of insider behaviours that may hinder organization security. The chapter also analyzes the existing physical, technical, and administrative controls, their objectives, their limitations, insider behaviour analysis, and future challenges in handling insider threats.

Chapter 14

Data objects having low value like insurance or data-entry forms are shared between a client and rural business process outsourcing (RBPO) organisations for tasks like translation, proofreading, and data entry. These data objects are first decomposed into smaller parts and then assigned to RBPO users. Each user in a RBPO has access to only a few parts of a complete data object which he can leak to unauthorised users. But since the value of these parts is low, there is not enough incentive for the user to leak them. Such scenarios need good-enough security models that can provide reasonable security to an aggregate number of parts of low value data objects. In this chapter, the authors study the secure data assignment and leakage in RBPO by modeling it in the form of an optimisation problem. They discuss different scenarios of object decomposition and sharing, penalty assignment, and data leakage in the context of RBPO. They use LINGO toolbox to run their model and present insights.

With the advancement of technology and internet connectivity, the potential for alternative methods of research is vast. Whilst pen-and-paper questionnaires and laboratory studies still prevail within most scientific disciplines, many researchers are selecting more contemporary methods for undertaking research. This chapter provides an overview of a number of key online research methodologies to highlight their role in scientific investigation. In particular, it suggests how these may function to enhance our understanding of psychological issues, particularly within areas relating to cybersecurity.

The chapter presents an overview of emerging issues in the psychology of human behaviour and the evolving nature of cyber threats. It reflects on the role of social engineering as the entry point of many sophisticated attacks and highlights the relevance of the human element as the starting point of implementing cyber security programmes in organisations as well as securing individual online behaviour. Issues associated with the emerging trends in human behaviour research and ethics are presented for further discussion. The chapter concludes with a set of open research questions warranting immediate academic attention to avoid the exponential growth of information breaches in the future.

Foreword

Introductions to books such as this one very often include proclamations that "this is a timely volume", to the extent that the phrase becomes something of a cliché. In this case, however, it is absolutely true. The themes and topics covered by this book bear directly on our understanding of, and reactions to, events that have an ongoing, significant and sustained impact on the world in which we live.

Formal definitions of 'cyber security' typically revolve around systems, standards, technologies and processes for protecting computer systems, networks and the data they contain from unauthorised access or malicious attacks. Such a definition may imply that cyber security is somewhat of a dry, technically focused enterprise, mainly of concern to computer scientists and industry professionals. That is a long way from the truth: cyber security, and security violations, have profound implications for all of us.

We now live in a world where all manner of devices, services and the people who use them are networked and vulnerable to electronic attack. These range from obvious targets like traditional computer and telecommunications systems, to nuclear reactors, children's toys and domestic appliances. All may be threatened or exploited in different ways. As our reliance on communication technologies and networked devices inexorably grows, cyber security will become more and more critical to society.

At the time when this book was being written, various aspects of cyber security were rarely far from the headlines. Businesses and public services including hospitals, were crippled by ransomware attacks. Online fraud was rampant, with costs to economies and individuals that are hard to quantify. In a number of countries, there were allegations that foreign states had hacked political campaign organisations, resulting in the theft and publication of emails for political purposes. There were accusations of meddling in multiple elections by electronic means. There were frequent concerns about online influence leading to political and religious extremism, and the use of telecommunications and networks by terrorists, criminals and national security agencies. Loss, theft, and publication of personal information were depressingly frequent, ranging from the personal photos of celebrities to very large scale losses of personal data and breaches of confidentiality by public and private organisations. Whether directly or indirectly, issues such as these touched all of our lives.

In any technical field, there is a tendency to prioritise technical approaches to solving problems. However, hardware and software engineering can only ever be part of the solution to cyber security. Since the days of the earliest computer hackers, it has been known that the human element is among the weakest components in any system. The use of 'social engineering' techniques (manipulating people in various ways to gain access to secure computer systems) was, and remains, a key weapon in the arsenal of those who seek to illegitimately access or attack the systems, services and infrastructure underpinning many aspects of modern life.

Humans will always interact with any information system at some level, and human behaviour thus becomes a part of the system. And of course, a human actor is always the instigator of any attack upon a system. It is therefore imperative to understand how people interact with the technologies at hand, and what individual behaviours may introduce vulnerabilities. For example, what factors might make some individuals or organisations more susceptible to malicious influence? How do psychological phenomena and information technologies mediate, underpin or facilitate such processes of influence? What can be done to protect individuals, groups and systems from such attacks? These questions are clearly in the domain of psychology and the behavioural sciences. Without considering them, no approach to cyber security can ever be successful.

This collection of chapters deals with several key themes around the intersection of psychology and cyber security. One of the areas explored is individual decision making in online environments, which leads to the considerations of privacy protection behaviour, trust formation and individual cyber security concerns affecting consumer behaviour and ultimately victimisation. Next, a number of phenomena relevant to cyber security on a global level are addressed. In particular, this volume investigates how culture and religion might impact upon security, arguing that cyber security measures and technology acceptance are affected by individual cultural differences. The discussion delves into the issues connected to online radicalisation and cyber terrorism reflecting the currency of this volume in light of the recent attacks worldwide and the pressing need to bring this phenomenon to an end. Cyber security professionals often say that we can never achieve a perfect cyber security posture. The risk of cyber security threats rather is said to be minimised through the application of protective mechanisms and security controls. The discussion of cyber security will not be complete without addressing two key elements in this: how can we educate and motivate individuals to behave in a way that reduces risk?

Drawing on up-to-date research findings, each chapter addresses key practical and theoretical issues in a variety of important applied contexts. The questions addressed here are not just of academic interest; they have critical implications for the security of our society. Taken together, these chapters provide an excellent overview of current research and thinking across a broad spectrum of cyber security-related issues and behavioural phenomena. They will prove a valuable resource both for those working in the behavioural sciences, and those with a more technical focus. It is only by different disciplines working together across that boundary that risk can be reduced and security enhanced.

Tom Buchanan
University of Westminster, UK

Preface

Researchers in a variety of disciplines turn to psychology to help understand human behaviour and decision making. Psychology has a long history of understanding human behaviour, thoughts and actions. By applying that research and theoretical knowledge to the topic of cyber security, academics and practitioners may be able to better understand why and when people engage in cyberattacks. Such knowledge is useful to those in law enforcement and policy. It is also crucial to those working in organisations who try to keep their companies safe.

Threats can come from inside the organisation or from outside. Insider threats pose a particularly difficult challenge as one has to monitor who may be a threat and to some extent why they are a threat at any given time. To know that, we must rely on psychology to help us analyse human behaviour. Without a foundation in how to better understand human behaviour, we could be at a loss to predict who may be an inside threat.

Outside threats are in some ways easier to understand and many cyber threats originating outside an organisation require no assistance from insiders. There is only so much technology can do to keep corporations safe. As good as the technology is, humans are adept thinkers and will be able to navigate a way around most security systems. That is not to say that anyone could do so, but those who have a knack for it and are so inclined could breach the security. Those who are less skilled but equally as motivated, may be able to pay someone to breach the organisation's security.

Concepts such as trust and relationship development are relevant to this work. Psychology has long studied these ideas and can contribute a significant literature to them. For example, in trust studies, psychological research has investigated how the concept is developed, and how it is fostered. It looks at what leads to a breakdown in trust in dyads as well as in larger group settings. Through this sort of research, we may be able to apply it and develop a greater understanding towards how hacking groups are formed and rely on each other to breach a security wall. We may also use it to try to mitigate such violations by developing interventions to build trust within an organisation or between the organisation and potential outside hackers.

Similarly, we may rely on psychological research in relationship development. We could look at how relationships are created and who wants to be part of certain relationships. We could look for weaknesses in relationships and what holds people together. Understanding why certain people are drawn to others, what motivates groups to form and to have a particular agenda, is all crucial in considering security of cyber systems.

Aspects of disinhibition and anonymity in the online setting need to be considered as well. Disinhibition has been studied in psychology since at least the 1960s. Addressing what increases people's chances of acting in a particular circumstance or failing to act in others is not new to the field. What is new, however, is looking to see how that research and those findings may be applied to the online environment. What features about individual differences may increase someone's chances of using the internet to engage or encourage terrorism? What might make an individual think about why s/he should use online media for a social protest or choose to protest in a more traditional way, or not at all? Theories and research in social psychology have studied why people may be inhibited or disinhibited to act in certain ways; these book chapters are able to use that foundation as a cornerstone to better explore how the human agent is relevant in cyber security.

Anonymity is an interesting concept to consider both in psychology and cyber security. We know from psychology that in large groups when people feel that they cannot be identified (that is, they are anonymous) they are more likely to engage in risky behaviour. It is possible, therefore, that we would expect that sort of behaviour in the online environment where identity may be protected. The importance of this to cyber security is not to be considered lightly. If techno-savvy people can protect their identity, this leaves a vulnerable online environment rife for infiltration. Infiltration could come from multiple sources as many of these chapters attest to. The insider threat, especially if the culprit could remain anonymous, is undoubtedly of concern. The hackers or those who are simply interested in breaching cyber security for the thrill of it with low risk of getting caught may feel a challenge waiting. Engaging in social protest again with a low cost as the methods of finding the perpetrator are not well established could lead to those with only minor grievances to consider violating the security wall. More structured groups who wish to see a corporation's downfall are able to spend the time, effort and energy to develop a well-planned security breach. They may be able to call on outsiders to help, again as the prospect of remaining unknown is substantial.

Ethics is another area where psychology has spent a fair amount of time trying to consider how to understand human behaviour from a theoretical perspective whilst also ensuring that human rights are not violated. In doing so it provides a good cornerstone to address cyber security from multiple angles. First, by considering the research that has been done to understand human behaviour, someone looking at violations of cyber security can rely on solid design with ethical guidelines fully considered. From the organisation's viewpoint, second, a foundation in psychology can help to guide strict approaches to prevent breaches while still mainly an ethically appropriate approach to employees and those who use and interact with the organisation. Third, company may consider, again ethically, how to prevent security breaches whilst maintaining a usable online platform.

Using these concepts as well as other aspects that are cornerstones of psychological research we can see how it is a crucial field to consider when looking at cyber security. Human behaviour is at fault for a number of security violations, especially if the technology becomes more and more robust. Relying on well evidenced and well researched concepts within human behaviour, we see how the human element is a base to understand and mitigate intrusions in cyber security.

This book covers a variety of topics and addresses different challenges that have emerged in response to changes in the ways in which it is possible to study various areas of decision making, behaviour and human interaction in relation to cyber security.

Each of the chapters brings its own contribution on how psychology furthers our understanding of cyber security. The innovative chapters link a strong foundation in human behaviour research with application to a topic of crucial importance in today's world. By looking at the chapters (see descriptions below) it should be clear how this topic is of the utmost importance in today's world. Understanding cyber security and breaches in it can only help to make all of us safer. Looking at ways to protect our finances, our images stored online and companies protected data, helps us all. Considering research on psychology and cultural identity may help us in understanding who and in what circumstances someone may decide to encroach on secure systems.

In a world as complex and fast moving technologically as one in which we find ourselves, a reference book such as this is a must. It provides the foundation of understanding aspects of human behaviour coupled with an area of real concern criminologically. It is necessary at this juncture of technology and human behaviour to understand who, when and why people might breach security systems. Who are the players most likely to do this and what can the authorities, policymakers and organisations themselves do to mitigate these threats? When are breaches likely to take place? Does it happen when political tensions rise and those prone to engaging in terrorism might increase? Does it happen when employees become disgruntled? How about when people want to set themselves a challenge to see if they can violate a security system? There are numerous questions about why these intrusions may happen at this particular time and in particular places. Culture, decision making, spotting vulnerabilities, etc. all make for an online system that is rife to be breached. In today's society, we cannot take a lax approach to our security nor to leaving human behaviour to the academics. We must join forces to make sure that we all stay safe, and continue to understand, before the violators do, what cyber vulnerabilities we have exposed.

This book was written with a large audience in mind. First, it was created for the practitioner. When understanding your own organisation and how to protect it, we thought a base in human behaviour would be relevant. If human behaviour and a century of research in this field is ignored, we are not using our collective knowledge to help society today.

Second, this book is addressed to the policymaker. Knowing what the risks are from the organisational perspective interwoven with research is crucial when considering applications of academe. Policymakers often do not have the luxury of reading the latest research in a field before needing to consider the political agenda. Hopefully this book gives a summary of relevant literature when contemplating cyber security.

Third, this book was conceived for the academic and researcher. These chapters show how theoretical work in psychology can be applied to a timely and real world problem. As much as researchers enjoy studying concepts to support or refute theory, to do so and see it have great impact in the broader community is pleasing. This book exemplifies how such work can provide said impact. Reading the chapters provides a trail map of concepts in psychology being applied to keeping us all safe in the cyberworld.

Finally, technology developers should read this book. Those who work in the field of cyber security undeniably see the thin line that is walked between staying secure and keeping cyber systems free. We all want systems that allow as many people to use them as possible and to keep our lives as simple as they can be. But, creating a banking system for people to use from the comfort of their home, while it may keep our lives simpler as we do not need to go to the bank during opening hours, is not useful if our finances are at risk. A fine balance must be found by our technology counterparts to ensure that social groups may use online fora without posing a risk for terrorist attacks. If the technologists can find that happy medium, we are in as safe and user friendly a world as possible. The problem of course is that that line often moves and the technologists may use this book to better understand how human behaviour can change and shift over time, providing them a stronger foundation for which to understand where that line is moving to next.

Below is a brief summary of the chapters in this book. They range across topics as you will see but hopefully gives a flavour of how psychology can contribute to this field. As both psychology and cyber security are vast, it does not attempt to be an exhaustive book. Yet, it should give a strong foundation on understanding a range of relevant topics from decision making, cognitive bias, terrorism, social media and guidance on how to do one's own study in an ethically appropriate way.

Chapter 1, "Online Decision Making: Online Influence and Implications for Cyber Security," addresses the challenges of understanding the differences between decision making that is performed online and research that uses an online forum alone. This chapter looks at how computer mediated communication impacts on how we make decisions online. Developing perspectives on decision making, and the applicability of the theories to the online environment is considered, with issues such as buying behaviour to radicalisation being addressed. This chapter encourages joint thinking from the practitioner and the researcher. It offers the idea that multiple models and perspectives are needed to understand how CMC influences our capacity to make decisions in the online forums.

Chapter 2, "Human Factors Leading to Online Fraud Victimisation: Literature Review and Exploring the Role of Personality Traits," highlights the role human behaviour has as the weakest link in cyber security. This literature review explores the role of personality traits, seeks an explanation for online fraud victimisation, and does so from a criminological and psychological perspective. First, a review of the literature in this area is presented. More specifically, the routine activity approach and the Big Five personality traits are discussed and applied to online fraud. Second, a novel empirical study on personality traits is presented, in which the influence of the Big Five personality traits on online fraud victimisation is assessed. This chapter ends by presenting implications for online fraud prevention as well as possibilities to advance the study of cyber victimisation.

Chapter 3, "The 'Human Factor' in Cyber Security: Exploring the Accidental Insider," describes the threat posed by members of an organisation. These threats may come from disgruntled employees or more innocuously from ignorance. Either way, they pose a potentially serious threat to information security. This chapter discussing aspects of the insider threat as well as the human factors that may contribute to one becoming a threat. Methods to detect and mitigate the threats are presented here.

Chapter 4, "Cyber + Culture: Exploring the Relationship," highlights some of the findings of a selection of recent studies on the relationship between national culture and specific cyber behaviours. The goal of this work was to understand the ongoing problem of attribution in cyber security as advances in technology is showing improvement in cyber-attack attribution, albeit slowly. Interest in the psychological research of decision making and the role of the human in perception management lead to the belief that behaviour may be able to ward off some cyber-attacks by defending and training users. In modelling behaviours related to cyber security, one needs to consider the role of culture in values which shape behaviours. This chapter crucially contributes to an area of research that is lacking by providing foundational work in this field.

Chapter 5, "Examinations of Email Fraud Susceptibility: Perspectives From Academic Research and Industry Practice," covers issues associated with the positive and negative sides of the internet being used for entertainment, commerce and communication. The potential for human advancement in this venue is substantial but so is the risk of increasingly sophisticated cyber-attacks. These undoubtedly could have serious personal and commercial implications. From a psychological viewpoint the attacks offer an insight into the decision making processes which may lead to being a victim of online fraud. The authors use their chapter to attempt to understand responses to phishing emails whilst exploring how industry and academic research might collaborate to better address email fraud threats. Various methods to understand susceptibility and considering preventable security measures are used to try to develop integrative solutions.

Chapter 6, "Introducing Psychological Concepts and Methods to Cyber Security Students," discusses the role and impact of psychology research on cyber security education. By using both prior cross-disciplinary teaching experience and observations of teaching psychological principles and methods to undergraduate and postgraduate cyber security students, the authors have compiled information about their experiences. There is a strong focus on making the material accessible and engaging. Suggestions as to how to integrate psychological into the cyber security curriculum completes the chapter.

Chapter 7, "The Role of Psychology in Understanding Online Trust," addresses the challenges of trusting people in the online environment. The authors discuss the manipulation of trust and the sometimes dire economic and psychological consequences. Literature on developing trust online is reviewed and several case studies describe trust relationships. Crowdfunding, online health forums and online dating help us to understand the need for stronger security measures which can increase trust judgments and minimise the risk of falling prey to fraud online.

Chapter 8, "Volunteered Surveillance," addresses the issues of data collection, data ownership, digital tracking, digital privacy, cyber security and ad-blocking in modern society through managerial, psychological and behavioural lenses. As technology advances more parties gain access to private data relying on "agree or leave" contracts, forcing individuals to give up ownership of their own behavioural patterns. These data are then commonly used for commercial purposes in forms of advertising, targeted marketing or more. Consumers on the other hand, seem to react to this in a very broad spectrum ranging from ad-blocking software to voluntary data submission. This chapter analyses why and how these reactions happen and propose solutions that could be beneficial to all parties included. This is a very novel macro concern and requires institutionalised oversight of all concerned stakeholders; governments, digital service providers and publishers, advertisers, self-regulatory organisations in related sectors and non-governmental organisations protecting consumers.

Chapter 9, "Psychological and Behavioral Examinations of Online Terrorism," presents mixed method research results on how terrorists use the internet to further their agendas. Several studies have investigated how terrorists use the online environment and the chapter first explores current knowledge about the online behaviour of terrorists. It follows on to describe how qualitative and quantitative combined studies can be used to consider how to conduct research in this area. After that a serious discussion is given to the difficult area of ethics in this field of research. The chapter closes by imparting information to the reader about the skills and knowledge necessary to undertake one's own research in this arena along with consideration of the ethics around such work.

Chapter 10, "The Role of Religiosity in Technology Acceptance: The Case of Privacy in Saudi Arabia," covers issues associated with how religion affects user behaviour and the acceptance of emerging technology. Religiosity is used to measure individual beliefs; this chapter explains how Islam influences user behaviour and intention to use technology. Saudi Arabia, as an example of a hardline Islamic nation according to the author of this chapter, is used for the discussions of privacy and technology influence in a single religion country. The chapter presents conclusions on how religion influences people's behaviour, privacy perceptions and acceptance technology.

Chapter 11, "Groups Online: Hacktivism and Social Protest," reviews the broadly defined topic of hacktivism. It offers up the proviso that it can be viewed as a legitimate form of online protest or one of illegal hacking. Additionally, there are those who feel that there is truth to both arguments, and believe it is imperative to protect those who engage in hacktivism. These counter definitions make it difficult to understand how to bridge the gap in assessing motivations. The authors give a brief introduction to hacktivism and online social protest online. In particular, the socio-psychological and cognitive factors possibly providing the foundation for individuals to take part in hacktivism groups are addressed. Within the socio-psychological arena, the authors consider the concepts of social ties and influence. These are subfields that are important to address when looking at how individuals join, form and remain in groups. The subfield of cognitive biases is important as well and biases are examined in light of how people think and process information given the biases we each hold. Conclusions are drawn with strategies to mitigate and support vulnerabilities considering hacktivism and social protest.

Chapter 12, "A Cyber-Psychological and Behavioral Approach to Online Radicalization," addresses the challenges of bringing mainstream theories of radicalisation and cyberpsychology together with a goal towards understanding who might become radicalised. The chapter uses Islamic State of Iraq and al-Sham (ISIS) as a case study to understand how radicalised groups use cyberspace. By using academic theory, the chapter considers behavioural aspects of the radicalisation process. It also reviews how those theories are relevant in explaining, facilitating and attracting people online to a radicalisation pathway.

Chapter 13, "Insider Attack Analysis in Building Effective Cyber Security for an Organization," provides a detailed study on how behaviours from those inside may hinder security of the organisation. A number of recent studies had shown that even though there are highly advanced and secure technical controls, several cyber-attacks were carried out across multiple organisations yielding the release of confidential information. It should be clear then that technical advancements of cyber defences are not impenetrable to organisational security. Insiders often have the advantage of being a trusted party when engaging in cyber-attacks and monitoring said insiders is very challenging. The insider has the potential to cause problems to the social credibility of the organisation as well as damage its financial stability. The author reviews behaviours of insiders who may pose a cyber security threat to an organisation and provides some guidance for reliable security frameworks.

Chapter 14, "A Study of Good-Enough Security in the Context of Rural Business Process Outsourcing," presents insights using scenarios of object decomposition and sharing. By looking at low value data objects such as insurance or data-entry forms the chapter is able to explore how information is shared between a client and Rural Business Process Outsourcing (RBPO) organisations. Such sharing is usually across tasks like translation, proof-reading and data entry. These data objects are decomposed into smaller parts before being sent to the RBPO allowing for each RBPO user to only access a few parts of a complete data object. Nevertheless, this information could be leaked to unauthorised users which would breach the data security. As the value of these parts is low there is little incentive for them to truly be leaked. Here is where the idea of a good enough security system comes in. The good enough model should provide reasonable security to a group of low value data objects. This chapter describes the work of secure data assignment and leakage in RBPO. By modelling this work as an optimisation problem, the authors are able to review object decomposition scenarios in light of sharing, penalty assignment and data leakage.

Chapter 15, "Online Research Methods," opens the discussion on the use of more contemporary approaches to data collection than traditional pen and paper questionnaires. Although the traditional methods are still more readily used, various online methodologies may enhance scientific investigation and understandings of particular phenomena. The chapter explores how these could be potentially useful in understanding psychological issues related to a range of cyber security problems.

Chapter 16, "Emerging Threats for the Human Element and Countermeasures in Current Cyber Security Landscape," presents an overview of emerging issues in psychology of human behaviour and the evolving nature of cyber threats. The chapter reflects on the role of social engineering as the entry point of many sophisticated attacks and highlights the relevance of the human element as the starting point of implementing cyber security programmes in organisations as well as securing individual online behaviour. Issues associated with the emerging trends in human behaviour research and ethics are presented for further discussion. The chapter concludes with a set of open research questions warranting immediate academic attention to avoid the exponential growth of information breaches in the future.

This publication addresses the emerging importance of digital psychology and the opportunities offered by cyber researchers. We hope that experts from all areas of research, information systems, psychology, sociology, human resources, leadership, strategy, innovation, law, finance and others, will find this book useful in their practice.

John McAlaney
Bournemouth University, UK

Vladlena Benson
University of West London, UK

Lara A. Frumkin
Open University, UK

Acknowledgment

First and foremost, we would like to thank our families for their patience and unresolved support during numerous late nights and weekends spent working on this book. It was a long and difficult journey for them. We would like to express our gratitude to Professors Jonathan Loo and Shanyu Tang for their valuable insights when steering this project through its final (and lengthy) stages. We would like to thank Professors Tom Buchanan and Debi Ashenden for deeming the subject of the book interesting and the project worthwhile.

We wish to thank many people who saw us through this book; to all those who provided support, talked things over, read, wrote, offered comments, and assisted in the editing, proofreading and design.

We would like to thank the IGI project team for enabling us to publish this book.

Chapter 1
Online Decision Making:
Online Influence and Implications for Cyber Security

Helen Joanne Wall
Edge Hill University, UK

Linda K. Kaye
Edge Hill University, UK

ABSTRACT

The growth in computer-mediated communication has created real challenges for society; in particular, the internet has become an important resource for "convincing" or persuading a person to make a decision. From a cybersecurity perspective, online attempts to persuade someone to make a decision has implications for the radicalisation of individuals. This chapter reviews multiple definitions and theories relating to decision making to consider the applicability of these to online decision making in areas such as buying behaviour, social engineering, and radicalisation. Research investigating online decision making is outlined and the point is made that research examining online research has a different focus than research exploring online decision making. The chapter concludes with some key questions for scholars and practitioners. In particular, it is noted that online decision making cannot be explained by one single model, as none is sufficient in its own capacity to underpin all forms of online behaviour.

INTRODUCTION

Understanding online decision making is becoming increasingly important within cybersecurity concerns given the mass information and access available to the general population. In previous generations, the Internet was primarily inhabited by computer scientists or programmers. However, the evolution of Web 2.0 and its capabilities of permitting user-generated platforms such as social networking sites, has subsequently meant access and content-generation is available to the masses. As such, the monitoring and auditing of online content is a substantial task, resulting in much online content, regardless of its authenticity, being accessible to the masses. Resultantly, online users face a wealth of content, upon which they

DOI: 10.4018/978-1-5225-4053-3.ch001

are required to make a number of decisions (e.g., is this content harmful?; should I trust this website?; how secure is this online payment system?; who is the source of this content and are they trustworthy? etc). Understanding online decision making is therefore becoming an increasingly demanding issue and requires exploration in the context of its relationship to cybersecurity. As an example, ongoing work is being invested in respect of fake news detection as well as preventative measures for this (Farajtabar et al., 2017; Shu, Silva, Wang, Tang & Liu, 2017). The recency of this agenda highlights the currency of these issues in contemporary society.

Moreover, the accessibility afforded by online technologies has been shown to offer numerous benefits to individuals ranging from increasing educational provision (Attwell, 2007; Cook, Levinson, Garside, Dupras, Erwin, & Montori, 2008) to improving physical and mental health support (Eysenbach, 2001; Kalichman, Benotsch, Weinhardt, Austin, Luke, & Cherry, 2003). However, the growth in Computer Mediated Communication (CMC) has also created real challenges for society; in particular, the Internet has become an important resource for 'convincing' or persuading a person to make a decision to do (or not do) something. Although concepts such as persuasion and decision making refer to distinct processes this Chapter considers the interplay between these related concepts. This Chapter will begin by defining decision making and outlining some evidence surrounding decision making across a range of online contexts. The second half of the chapter considers related theories of persuasion and attitude and behaviour change and discusses the factors that have been shown to influence attitude and behaviour change online. The chapter concludes by acknowledging that research investigating online decision making is broad in scope and often tends to have a different focus to offline research.

DEFINITION AND MODELS OF DECISION MAKING

Decision making has been the topic of considerable research attention and has been studied across a variety of disciplines such as management science, medicine, economics and psychology. Numerous definitions exist but in its simplest terms decision making has been defined as the selection of a particular course of action (Chick, Pardon, Reyna & Goldman, 2012). For instance, people choose which school/university to send their children to, which political party to vote for, and which football team to support, out of a range of possible alternatives. On the web, people also need to make decisions such as whether to visit a website, click on a 'pop up', and even whether or not reply to another's Facebook post. From a commercial perspective, online decision making has been defined as a concept that describes the cognitive processes that occur in the mind of customers before they make a decision on the web (Ullmann-Margalit, 2006), such as whether to order a mobile phone.

Numerous theories exist on decision making (see Beresford & Sloper, 2008 for a detailed overview); however, as the main focus here is to outline evidence on the factors associated with online decision making interested readers are directed to Janis and Mann (1977; Mintz, 2016; Plous, 1993) for a more exhaustive theoretical overview. Beresford and Sloper (2008) note that theories regarding decision making tend to be either normative theories of cognition or more descriptive theories of cognition. Normative theories tend to be concerned with how people should reason (Over, 2004) such as probabilistic theories outlined next. In contrast, the more descriptive theories aim to describe how people reason when making decisions. Early mathematical models defined the decision-making processes in terms of probabilities of outcomes and selecting the best course of action (Chick et al., 2012). Specifically, three perspectives have tended to dominate the literature on decision making: i) Multi-attribute Utility; ii) Maximised Subjective Expected Utilities; iii) and Bayes' Theorem.

Multi Attribute Utility

In this model, decision making refers to mathematical approaches that aid a decision maker when comparing alternatives (Pratt, 1964; Meyer, 2010), such as when a person has to decide between two or more options. Here the decision is based on the attributes of the options. As noted by Amichai-Hamburger (2005), it is a mathematical model that is applied to help people to make the correct decision, often under uncertainty. Imagine deciding on which mobile phone to purchase – each alternative device will have certain attributes such as aesthetic appearance, camera quality, storage space, and battery life. When applying this model, weights are allocated to each attribute depending on its importance to the decision and then the alternatives are scored The attribute is then multiplied by the importance of the weight designated to it as some alternatives may get a high score but be less important in the final decision. Thus, the final score helps to determine the utility of all of the alternatives (see Amichai-Hamburger, 2005). In sum, the model assigns values to each alternative so that individuals can weight alternatives by attributes and rank the decision outcomes. These types of principles have been shown to be useful in evaluating mobile phone alternatives (Işıklar, & Büyüközkan, 2007; see Wallenius, Dyer, Fishburn, Steuer, Zionts, & Deb, K, 2008 for detailed overview).

Maximised Subjective Expected Utilities

Similar to the Multi Attribute Utility model, the Maximised Subject Expected Utilities model acknowledges that individuals choose alternatives that have the maximum expected utility. Specifically, Amachai-Hamburger (2005) notes that utilities and values can be different for different people; therefore, this model involves determining whether additional information is available and what the cost may be. For example, one might weigh up the cost of new information and evaluate the gain to come from not having it versus having it (Edwards & Fasolo, 2001). According to this model, decision makers select the alternative that has the maximum expected utility (Amichai-Hamburger, 2005). A study by Bauer and Hein (2006) utilised this general line of reasoning and explored the factors affecting consumers' decisions about whether or not to adopt a new remote access technology. They found that perceived risks in Internet banking appeared to be responsible for hesitation to adopt the technology and they also found that older consumers were less likely to bank online irrespective of their individual risk tolerances[1].

Bayes' Theorem

This is a normative model of decision making (cf., Duda & Hart, 1973) based on conditional probability. Essentially the model posits that we can make a prediction about the probability of one event occurring given another event and this can aid in making decisions. As noted by Amichai-Hamburger, 2005, p. 235), it has the following formula:

P (A \ B) = P (A Ç B) / P(B).

Put simply, the above formula asserts that if a person has a belief about an event and that event has a known probability distribution (Prior; P(E)), and individuals also have additional information with known reliability (Likelihoods; P(I \ E)), then the initial belief can be revised (Posterior; P (E \ I)) (see Amachai-Hamburger, 2005 and Duda & Hart, 1973 for a more detailed overview). Numerous studies exist that have utilised the basic principles of this theory in computer help systems. For instance, a study by Huang and Bian (2009) looked at personalised recommendations for tourist attractions over the Internet and found that the system could recommend tourist attractions to a user by taking into account the travel behaviour of both the user and of other users (see also Zhang, Chen, Xiang, Zhou, & Xiang, 2013 for similar study).

Decision Biases and Alternative 'Models' of Decision Making

Although the above models of decision making have been well examined offline there are alternative ways to conceptualise decision making online. In contrast to economic models of decision making based on probabilities, the psychological perspective of decision making suggests that each decision we make, such as whether or not to purchase something, can be dependent upon context. Recall that the Maximum Subjective Expected Utilities theory above states that we can assign values to alternatives, yet, it has also been acknowledged that the values we attach to certain options may differ in terms of prior experiences, mood and even the options that are available (Carmon, Wertenbroch, & Zeelenberg, 2003). Of course, context has also been shown to be important in the online world with numerous studies outlining how measured outcomes can be different on other platforms such as Facebook (Wall, Kaye & Malone, 2016) and Twitter.

Moreover, there is often an assumption that when people make decisions they aim to make the most optimal and 'correct' decision Muth (1961; Lucas, 1971), but a number of studies have shown that this is not always the case. Indeed, it appears that sometimes our decisions are not based on rational choices such as the weighting of alternative options and assessment of probabilities, more specifically, our decisions can be biased by factors such as framing effects (McKenzie, 2004). A "framing effect" happens when equivalent descriptions of a problem lead decision outcomes to differ (McKenzie, 2004). A study by O'Neill, Hancock, Zivkov, Larson and Law (2016) examined team decision making using different communication media and decision frames. Findings suggested that when tasks were framed as having a demonstrably correct solution, virtual teams were at a disadvantage whereas face-to-face (FtF) teams were more effective on all decision behaviours. For the present discuss of decision making and decision-making theories it is important to note that framing effects create significant implications for the "Rationality Debate" in psychology (e.g., Shafir & LeBoeuf 2002). That is, if the way in which a problem is framed can led to different decision outcomes some have suggested that these effects are taken as evidence for incoherence in human decision making (McKenzie, 2004; Sher & McKenzie, 2008). Therefore, it is important to consider alternative models of decision making before reviewing the evidence in online decision making.

Relatedly, when a decision appears complex or a person is overloaded with information, a number of heuristics may be used to make processing more manageable (Muscanell, Guadagno, & Murphy, 2014). The influence of such heuristics and other cognitive biases when making decisions has received substantial support (Kahneman, 2011). Work of Tversky and Kahneman (1981) shows that people generally do not make rational decisions. It is well known, for example, that individuals often find it difficult to evaluate the full range of alternatives in depth and aim to reduce effort related to decision making

(Shugan 1980). In response, people tend to employ alternative processes to reach decisions (Payne 1982, Payne et al. 1988). These alternative, and arguably, broader ways to think about 'decision making' will be outlined briefly in this section.

Individual Differences in Online Decision Making

When considering the alternative explanations for decision-making, it is important to note that this may often be underpinned by other factors, such as individual variations. That is, evidence suggests that when making decisions online, people vary in the extent to which they engage in systematic evaluation. In relation to website trust, Sillence, Briggs, Harris, and Fishwick (2006) proposed a 3-stage model whereby individuals first engage in heuristic-based processing which focuses on website design and layout (Stage 1), followed by a second and more systematic processing of website content (Stage 2) with the third and final stage of interaction with the website and longer-term use. A study by Rains and Karmikel (2009) also revealed that judgements of website credibility varied depending on expertise. They showed that consumers based their assessments of website credibility on attractiveness whereas experts tended to be influenced by variables related to the quality and content of information.

Additionally, there are some interesting gender differences to note in respect that it has been found that women find it more difficult to trust impersonal decision aids like personalized mobile recommendations compared to men, as their shopping decisions tend to be more emotionally driven (Awad & Ragowsky, 2008). Contrastingly, men seem to value additional personalization-based services more than women, with women being shown to be more critical towards recommendations on smartphone applications (Awad & Ragowsky, 2008). As such, the role of emotions in the decision-making process appear to be important and are not readily acknowledged by the aforementioned more rational perspectives which attempt to explain decision making. Nevertheless, whilst emotions have been shown to operate in the decision-making process (Dillard & Nabi, 2006), there remains a limited understanding of the underlying mechanisms (i.e., the why) in terms of *when* emotions, such as fear appeals, are most effective (Ruiter, Kessels, Peters, & Kok, 2014) in persuading a person to make a particular decision. Indeed, when people feel emotionally vulnerable or distressed, they have been shown to have a much narrower focus of attention (Fredrickson & Branigan, 2005; Tice, Bratslavsky, & Baumeister, 2001). Clearly, this presents some debate about the applicability of the aforementioned "rationale" theories to all behaviours involving decision making, and implies that there are additional factors to consider within this issue. As well as emotions, other social factors may also be important, discussed next.

Functional Perspective

Making decisions is not always an individual task and often groups are tasked with making decisions. A "functional perspective" of decision making has emerged in the study of group decision-making quality (Cragan & Wright, 1990) and has received empirical attention in offline settings (Barge & Hirokawa, 1989; Gouran & Hirokawa, 1996; Hirokawa, 1985, 1988, 1994). Although it constitutes a dominant paradigm in the group decision making literature, it has been applied much less to online research. The functional perspective asserts that group communication is important in decision making as it "represents the means by which group members attempt to meet the requisites for successful group decision making" (Gouran & Hirokawa, 1983, p. 170). Gouran and Hirokawa (1996) notes that the effectiveness of decision making appears to be dependent on four factors: i) a suitable understanding of the problematic situation; ii) a suitable understanding of the necessities for an effective choice; iii) a suitable valuation of alternative choices such as the positive qualities; and, iv) a suitable assessment of the negative qualities of alternative choices. In FtF groups it has been shown that the four requirements are predictive of the effectiveness of the decision (Hirokawa, 1985; 1988). In contrast, synchronous text-based CMC appears to reduce the likelihood that groups will work through the four requirements. It appears that CMC introduces structural factors which alter the extent to which the critical functions of group decision making are achieved (Gouran & Hirokawa, 1996). However, it is important to note that CMC can vary considerably in the way in which it operates for communication and group-based tasks. That is, the asynchronicity of many CMC platforms bring about a further variable which may impact upon the extent to which online decision making is realised in group-based contexts. As such, exploring online decision making, and associated processes, is greatly more complex due to these variations as well as other functionalities which afford far more diversity in group-based communication compared to FtF contexts. One such theory which can go some way to explain group-based decision-making online and how this may vary from offline, is that of the de-individuation model, which posits that many online group environments may deindividuate users and limit the availability of social cues and visual identity, which results in more polarized decisions being made compared to in FtF group contexts (Lea, 1991; Lea & Spears, 1991; Postmes, Spears, & Lea, 1998). This theory is derived from the more general theory of social identity theory (Tajfel, 1978, 1979; Tajfel & Turner, 1979), in which an individual's identity is largely shaped by their affiliation to a given social group. The notion of deindividuation develops from this theory in respect of the Social Identity Model of Deindividuation Effects (SIDE) model whereby, particularly online, a group member can become anonymous within a given social group (Postmes, 2007). This therefore can result in a loss of individual identity, and promote stronger group identity which may be an additional force which facilitates intergroup conflict and polarization (Sunstein, 2001). This may be particularly problematic in the context of radicalisation whereby an individual may become integrated into a radicalised group via online means and adhere to radicalised behaviour as they may perceive a lack of identifiability and accountability for their actions. However, this does not necessarily explain how group decision making may be more (or less) successful in different types of online environments, particularly those which are not anonymous, and how synchronicity of platform may play a role here.

DECISION MAKING ONLINE

As previously discussed, there are numerous decision-making models (see Beresford & Sloper, 2008 for an excellent overview). Interestingly, Amachai-Hamburger (2005) notes that studies that examine decision making in online settings tend to either compare decision making between on and offline contexts and/or explore decision making outcomes. That is, studies relating to online decisions tend to be less focused on the cognitive strategies being implemented as part of the decision-making process (i.e., models) and more interested in how the nature of online communication and the different online platforms influence the specific decision and decision outcome. For example, studies have examined how satisfied users are or how long they take to reach a decision online versus offline (Liu, Fang, Wan, & Zhou, 2016). Other studies have compared results of decision making tasks based on whether they occur online or offline (FtF) (Jonassen & Kwon, 2001; Dietz-Uhler & Bishop-Clark, 2001). One example comes from Hall, Bernhardt and Dodd (2015) which examined older adults on and offline use of online health information and medical decision making. Differences in the frequency of heath sources sought were found between users and nonusers with the former preferring a more self-reliant approach and the latter preferring a physician-related approach. The next section of this Chapter will now review some of the existing studies on decision making online.

Decision Making: FtF vs CMC

There has been a wealth of research conducted which has compared FtF versus online behaviours, to explore the extent to which one context may be more (or less) influential than the other towards decision-making outcomes. This research has largely focused on customer satisfaction and behaviour in e-commerce (Goodrich & de Mooij, 2013; Ho, Lin & Chen, 2012; Kohli, Devaraj & Mahmood, 2014; Senecal, Kalczynski, & Nantel, 2005; Shankar, Smith & Rangaswamy, 2003). Although there are other studies focusing on other forms of online behaviour, including information seeking (Cotton & Gupta, 2004; Hall, Bernhardt & Dodd, 2015), there is very little evidence which points to decision making process and outcomes beyond commerce. In the case of shopping behaviour, it has been noted that online shopping may be more impactful on tangible outcomes, due to functionalities such as grouping and "sorting" information (Shankar et al., 2003), which may proffer greater opportunities for relative thinking to a greater extent than traditional shopping contexts. Indeed, relative thinking serves a role in the way in which we process information and make decisions. For instance, when making financial decisions, we tend to focus on relative price differences, rather than the individual prices themselves. Additionally, online shopping also includes functionalities including personalised recommendations and peer options (ratings or star reviews) (Häubl & Trifts, 2000; Meuter, Ostrom, Roundtree, & Bitner, 2000), which, in line with the aforementioned discussion regarding social-based influence, also enables more persuasive systems for decision making in commercial contexts when online compared to offline (Brown & Reingen, 1987). As such, these differences in the availability of relevant information is said to result in consumers investing more cognitive effort into their decision making when online, as they are better informed of the options and thus realise the benefits this may bring (Johnson & Payne, 1985). Previous studies have applied existing models of consumer behaviour as a framework for exploring the process of these behaviours online (Darley, Blankson & Luethge, 2010). Specifically, the adapted version of Engel, Kollat and Blackwell's (EKB) model is a comprehensive model of consumer behavior which posits that consumer behaviour is a dynamic ongoing process (Engel, Blackwell, & Miniard, 1986; Engel, Kollat, & Blackwell 1978) and recognises external factors such as social, individual, economic and online environments and their role in the process stages of online purchasing behaviour. This provides a helpful and comprehensive framework through which to understand some decision making which occurs online although is restricted to those commercial purchasing behaviours.

Specific factors which have been explored in relation to online decision making (for online purchasing) include; consumer perceived trust risk, as well as online privacy and security concerns and quality of website (Kim, Ferrin & Rao, 2008). Clearly there are factors here which are relevant only to online forms of purchasing, highlighting the potential challenges associated with applying existing decision-making models to online contexts. Additionally, there is much less theoretical underpinning which can explain decision making in other forms of online interactions such as in social networking sites or through email, which are more interactional rather than transactional in nature. With this in mind, to explore these more interactional forms of CMC, the conceptual underpinning tends to focus more on persuasive influence rather than decision making, which will be discussed subsequently.

HOW DOES THE INTERNET INFLUENCE A PERSON TO DECIDE TO ENGAGE WITH RADICALISATION?

In the context of Cybersecurity, radicalisation is a prominent issue, given its potential devastating societal impacts. Radicalisation has been defined in different ways and has been suggested to involve a shift in a person's attitudes and behaviour (Schmid, 2013); therefore, it would seem appropriate to discuss theories of attitude and behaviour change when considering online decision making. In line with the definition of decision making presented at the beginning of this chapter (i.e., deciding on a particular outcome/alternative), radicalisation appears to 'work' by offering an alternative and attractive worldview for individuals to be a part of, which may be particularly appealing for those who feel marginalised and alienated in society (Lyons, 2015). The next section will consider how people become lured into terrorist activities online; in other words, what factors lead people to decide to join terrorist networks?

Numerous studies classify the Internet as an accelerant of the radicalisation process (Bergin, 2009), because it allows people to connect in an instantaneous manner. Facebooks 'group' function has been said to be important when recruiting new members (Torok, 2010). Specifically, terrorist organisations appear to create Facebook groups designed to garner support from people (Torok, 2010) and then slowly introduce jihadist material once group members have increased in numbers. Indirect support for the power of the Internet in influencing people to become engaged in terrorist organisations comes from studies which have examined political action. Indeed, political blogs and web sites tend to attract those who are already politically active; therefore, social network sites may be bringing in new voters, particularly the young, to get involved in the political process (Toronto Star, 2008).

When considering some of the reasons why people make the decision to join terrorist groups, the Internet appears to play a critical role. It has been shown to generate social ties that are needed for recruitment and radicalisation and has been shown to strengthen a sense of identity through the phenomenon of "group polarization" (McCauley & Moskalenko, 2008). Precht (2007) notes that members of certain radicalizing groups tend to disseminate their radicalisation via continual discussion, and if young people discover these online communications and form connections with similar others, then their radicalisation may develop. Moreover, shy individuals may benefit from the access that the Internet provides (Torok, 2010; Yeap & Park, 2010).

Further to this, the Internet has been described as an 'echo chamber' (Ramakrishna, 2010; Saddiq, 2010; Stevens & Neumann, 2009) or a 'mental reinforcement activity' (Silber & Bhatt, 2007). The consensus in the literature appears to be that the Internet enables people to gain easier access to content that they are interested in – something not as easy offline when people tend to come face to face with people with opposing viewpoints. (Briggs & Strugnell, 2011; Shetret, 2011). Moreover, the Internet can give the illusion of 'strength in numbers' (Saddiq, 2010).

Persuasion and Decision Making: The Relationship Between Attitudes and Behaviour

This chapter has outlined a number of findings regarding the factors that influence decision making illustrating that decision making is not always a straight forward process. This next section will outline related theories of attitude and behaviour change and theories of persuasion. Persuasive communication has been defined as "any message that is intended to shape, reinforce, or change the responses of another, or others" (Cialdini, 2001; Fogg, 2002). Substantive research has identified some key factors that affect attitude and behavioural change in offline settings (e.g., attractiveness; Petty, & Briñol, 2015; Rifon, Jiang, & Kim, 2016; likeability; Tormala, & Briñol, 2015). In contrast, less is known about persuasion in online environments, particularly for young adults (18– 34 years old) who are the most frequent users of YouTube (Lenhart & Madden, 2007; Purcell, 2013; YouTube, 2013) and use the Internet a great deal. This is particularly pertinent when considering the increased numbers of teenagers being lured into terrorist activities (Baumert, Buesa, & Lynch, 2013; Quayle, & Taylor, 2011; Silke, 2008). The focus of this next section is to outline relevant theories of persuasion and attitude and behaviour change and to present evidence from the online arena on the factors that shape attitude and behaviour change online.

Theory of Reasoned Action

The Theory of Reasoned Action (TRA) (Ajzen & Fishbein, 1980) is particularly influential in the field of decision-making regarding health-related behaviour and assumes that in most cases individuals can decide whether or not to perform a behaviour. TRA posits that the main driver of behaviour is the person's intention, which are derived from two cognitive processes: the person's attitude towards the behaviour and his/her perceived social norms regarding the behaviour (i.e., 'subjective norm') (Ajzen & Fishbein, 1980). Attitude is assumed to be determined by the person's belief about, and evaluation of, the outcomes of an action (note how this is similar to the general definition of direct messaging). Similar to theories of persuasion, TRA recognises that behaviour occurs in the context of social influences which exert pressure to perform (or not perform) a certain behaviour. Another influence on behavioural intention is the subjective norm (i.e., beliefs that people who are important to us think that we should/not perform the behaviour) and the person's motivation to comply with these opinions.

Theory of Planned Behaviour

Ajzen (1988) proposed an extension of TRA – the Theory of Planned Behaviour (TPB) because the TRA mistakenly assumed that most behaviours of interest are those where the person has the resources, skills and opportunities to engage in their desired action; therefore, the concept of perceived control was added to the model. A person's perceived behavioural control reflects his/her beliefs about factors that may inhibit or promote the performance of the behaviour. Meta-analyses of studies applying TPB conclude that it accounts for considerable proportions of the variance in intentions across a range of behaviours (39-41 per cent) and a somewhat lower proportion of variance in behaviour (27-34 per cent) (Armitage & Conner, 2001; Godin & Kok, 1996 – cited in de Wit & Stroebe, 2004). Numerous support has been gathered for this theory (Ajzen, 2011; Armitage & Conner, 2001) and it has also been the subject of debate as true experimental tests of the TPB with full factorial designs tend to inconclusive. TRA and TPB have been applied to a wide range of decisions in online contexts (Hansen, Jensen, & Solgaard, 2004; Yousafzai, Foxall, & Pallister, 2010).

Perceived behavioural control reflects the perceived ease or difficulty of performing the behaviour and is conceptually similar to self-efficacy. Self-efficacy has been defined as an individual's belief in his/her ability to perform a certain behaviour (Bandura 1977). It affects a person's attitudes, health choices and even the level of effort that people tend to invest in goal setting (Bandura 2004). According to Bandura, there are four major sources of self-efficacy: mastery experiences, vicarious experiences (e.g. role modelling), verbal persuasion (e.g. feedback) and psychological responses. Mastery experiences refer to personal experiences, whereas vicarious experiences refer to another person, similar to oneself, who has successfully performed particular tasks or behaviours. Verbal persuasion refers to prompts about a person's ability to master the given tasks or behaviours. Psychological responses refer to a person's somatic and emotional states, which a person relies on when making judgments about her/his ability to master the given tasks or behaviours (Bandura 1994, p 71–72).

A number of studies have utilised the tenets of TPB online. Goodman, Morrongiello and Meckling (2016) conducted a randomized control trial, grounded in TPB, evaluating the efficacy of an online intervention targeting vitamin d intake and status and knowledge in young adults. Factors including past behaviour, behavioural expectations, norms, perceived behavioural control, and intentions lead to changes in behaviour (i.e., vitamin D intake). The intervention group watched a video, received online information and tracked intake of vitamin D using a mobile application for 12 weeks. Findings revealed that whilst participating in an intervention did not improve vitamin D status, it led to increased vitamin D intake, knowledge and perceived importance of supplementation. A study by Jackson, Ingram, Boyer, Robillard, and Huhns (2016) also applied the TPB and examined the effectiveness of a mobile application intervention in young college students. The aim was to decrease sexual health risk behaviour. Although they did not find change in intention from pre-test to post-test they did find increases in knowledge. A third example comes from Spook, Paulussen, Kok, and van Empelen (2016) who evaluated a serious self-regulated game intervention for overweight related behaviours. They adopted a theory driven approach to behaviour and attitude change as they measured numerous behavioural outcome measures such as dietary intake, physical activity, barriers to health intake, determinants of intake and self-efficacy and found that although the pilot intervention did not show any favourable effects on intake there was reassuring evidence to show that the intervention may contribute to changing dietary intake and behaviours.

Elaboration Likelihood Model

The Elaboration Likelihood Model (ELM) (Petty & Cacioppo, 1986) represents a general theory of attitude change and outlines two routes to persuasion; central and peripheral. The former involves careful examination of content, such as content about an intervention, which can be cognitively demanding and requires sufficient ability and motivation to process all of the content. When people are not able to process all of the message content thoroughly via the central route, people tend to process content via the peripheral route. The peripheral route to persuasion depends on heuristic cues such as attitudes towards the source (e.g. if the persuader tells us something is bad we may be more likely to think it is bad). Essentially, this model suggests that the effectiveness of persuasive techniques can depend on depth of information processing. Evidence suggests that when making decisions to change a behaviour central processing can be more likely to encourage lasting behaviour change than peripheral processing (see Petty & Cacioppo, 1986).

In the case of central route persuasion (also known as systematic processing) people focus on message content and make decisions about their attitude on a topic based on things such as quality of argument. Evidence has shown that people are more likely to engage in central processing if a topic is important to them personally and if they have the ability to engage in systematic processing and also if the argument is well written (Chaiken et al., 1996). In contrast, when using the peripheral route to persuasion individuals are more likely to use decision cues or rules of thumb (i.e., heuristics) in order to help them make decisions about their attitude on a particular topic. For instance, one may be more persuaded by the quantity of arguments as opposed to the quality, and the perceived credibility of the persuader has also been shown to be influential, particularly when people know little about a topic or do not have the ability to engage in more systematic processing (i.e., processing vis the central route) (Petty & Cacioppo, 1984; see also Amichai-Hamburger, 2005). It is not always a case of one or the other type of processing and individuals can engage in both types of processing in certain situations (Amichai-Hamburger, 2005).

PERSUASION

Online research has tended to look at interactive and non-interactive persuasion. One of the earlier studies on this topic was conducted by Matheson and Zana (1989) who examined the impact of self-awareness on persuasion. They predicted that communication modalities (FtF vs. online) would influence processing whereby those online would experience greater private self-awareness and thus process a persuasive message using the systematic route. Participants in their study completed two decision making problems with a partner, wrote a short paragraph on a designated topic, and read persuasive communication and filled out an attitude measure and measures of private and public self-awareness. Findings revealed no differences in attitude change across communication modality; however, differences in private self-awareness were found. Specifically, those who participated online experienced increased private self-awareness and authors concluded that those in the online condition were more likely to have engaged in more systematic processing.

Sagarin, Britt, Heider, Wood and Lynch (2003) looked at the impact of persuasive adverts which were placed at the edge of the computer screen whilst participants completed various anagram exercises. These adverts were both persuasive and distracting yet participants reported not attending to them. Evidence also suggests that studies using non interactive persuasive methods such as 'pop ups' suggest that when there is no communication between targets of influence and influence agent (i.e., in this case the pop up) people tend to respond similarly to how participants respond in offline studies asking people to read persuasive communication – i.e., there is a tendency toward central processing of messages. However, the evidence on online interpersonal persuasion appears to be different and has relevance for online radicalisation.

Studies on interpersonal persuasion online explore how the persuasion process is shaped by the features of online communication (Amachia-Hamburger, 2005). In two substantive studies by Guadagno and Cialdini (2002) the impact of an influence agent in either FtF discussion or non-anonymous email was investigated. Specifically, the influence agent presented strong or weak arguments as part of a discussion. Results showed that strong arguments were more persuasive than weak arguments, as one might expect. An interesting interaction effect emerged whereby females reported less attitude change when the discussion occurred over email than FtF. Authors surmised that this was due to females' desire for bonding with the influence agent, which was reduced in the online condition and thus recued the impact of the online influence agent. Other work by Guadagno and Cialdini (2002; cited in Amachia-Hamburger, 2005) suggests that in same-sex interactions, women appear to struggle to persuade another female to change their attitude over email unless there is commonality between them whereas for males communication modality appears to be much less important.

Cialdini (2001) notes that there are many tendencies to comply with another's request, which can be explained in terms of six principles of persuasion: scarcity, reciprocation, commitment, consensus, liking and authority (see Table 1). Amichai-Hamburger (2005) notes that these principles serve as decision heuristics that assist in decision making.

Table 1. Cialdini's six principles of persuasion (2001)

1. Scarcity	Valuing more of scarce items
2. Reciprocation	Feeling obliged to return a favour
3. Commitment	Tendency to align with earlier commitments
4. Consensus (high vs. low number of likes, comments)	Tendency to comply with a persuasive message if others have also complied
5. Liking	Propensity to say 'yes' to people we like and the tendency to be influenced by someone who is similar to us
6. Authority (information vs. emotional)	Inclination to comply more with a request made by a legitimate authority

Influence agents tend to use decision heuristics to gain compliance (i.e., consensus) from targets of influence and this next section will outline some evidence from the online arena.

A study by Dubrovsky, Kiesler and Sethna investigated the role of expertise and status (i.e. authority) on decision making in FtF and CMC. In their study they asked groups to discuss two topics in either CMC or FtF. Group members consisted of a high-status member such as a graduate student and also three low status group member consisting of undergraduate students. One of the topics was a topic where only the high-status member was an expert whilst the second topic was a topic where the low status members were more knowledgeable. Interesting differences emerged suggesting that status was less salient in CMC relative to FtF. Specifically, they found that in FtF interactions the high-status member was more likely to have more influence and engaged in greater discussion over the rest of the group whereas in CMC interactions status cue effects were somewhat reduced as both high and low status members were just as likely to be first in expressing their views (e.g., often speaking at the same time).

In line with models of persuasion, other studies have applied "nudge" techniques online in an attempt to change people's attitudes, behaviours and decisions and have employed various metrics to determine the effect of such attitude/behaviour change approaches. Zhang and Xu (2016) conducted a study into the impact of a ''social'' nudge (i.e., % of users on this app that approve the different types of data permissions) versus a "frequency" nudge. Interestingly, findings differed in opposing ways whereby the social nudge created positive feelings whereas the frequency nudge created negative feelings such as reduced comfort level in sharing data with the app.

Other online techniques that have been shown to be influential for behaviour change are the use of warning messages and are much more direct than priming (see Wogalter et al., 2012, pp. 868-894; Christin, Egelman, Vidas, & Grossklags, 2012). Some research has concluded that browser warnings overall do not have positive effects (Egelman & Schechter, 2013; Egelman, Cranor, & Hong, 2008; Xiao & Benbasat, 2015). Moreover, in relation to security features and how they inform people to make decisions such as whether to open up a browser or download a pdf, another persuasion tactic – that of social proof (i.e., tendency to look to others for cues on how to behave) has been explored (Cialdini & Goldstein, 2004). Research by Das, Kramer, Dabbish, and Hong (2014) has supported the notion that observing others do something leads to increased levels of that specific behaviour as they experimented on Facebook and found that showing people the number of their friends that used security features lead to 37% more viewers to explore the promoted security features compared to raising awareness about security issues (see Junger et al., 2017 for a detailed review).

When considering the factors that influence an individual to become radicalised it is important to examine evidence on the techniques of persuasion. Many techniques of persuasion exist and Ferreira and Lensini (2015) have integrated key principles which they have termed the Principles of Persuasion in Social Engineering (PPSE). These are authority, social proof, liking, commitment, reciprocation and distraction. In terms of ' authority', studies conducted on the importance of the internet on 'authority' have tended to focus on religious authority. In terms of authority, a recent study conducted by Campbell (2010) examined Christian blogs and found that online religious authorities more often endorsed tradition. During the process of indoctrination a religious authority posing as a "spiritual sanctioner" has been shown to increase the power of influence on the individual (Aly & Strieger, 2010). This finding appears to be supported as Winter (2017) reported that the recruitment of an individual into a terrorist organisation is not complete without the existence of an *enlister* (Winter, 2016).

Research on the principle of conformity has been linked to reinforcing the normalisation of extremist beliefs. More specifically, researchers exploring group polarisation (i.e., like-minded people joining together and echoing similar views thereby reinforcing attitudes) have noted that online opinions are amplified due to polarising (Torok, 2010). Sabouni, Cullen and Armitage (2017) comment that once a person with a need to belong interacts with an extremist online, there will be a gradual normalisation of the extremist views (Torok, 2011).

The principle of 'liking' also forms part of the PPSE and appears to be relevant to online decision making, particularly in relation to radicalisation. Neo, Dillon, Shi, Tan, Wang and Gomes (2016) note that online extremists use the phenomenon of liking by allowing socially deprived individuals to become a part of their tightly knit group. Torok (2010) and Baumert et al. (2013) state that marginalised individuals and those with a need to belong appear to be a primary target for online radicalisation. The persuasion principle of reciprocation is the mutual exchange of an act with an act of like value. In terms of online radicalisation, giving a socially deprived individual access to join an extremist network may be interpreted as an act of kindness to which they then reciprocate such as spreading the group's ideology. The individual concerned then decides to join and then adapts their ideology, which can be a big commitment; thus, various forms of reciprocation that follow may be the individuals attempt to demonstrate consistency – thereby supporting their original decision to join (Sabouni et al., 2017). This particular principle is largely similar to the underpinning properties of Social Exchange Theory whereby an individual is more likely to reciprocate a behaviour if he/she has received rewards for a similar behaviour previously (Homans, 1974). As such probability of behaviour is largely based on a cost-benefit analysis.

The influence principle of distraction, although not part of Cialdini's model, forms part of the integrated model (i.e., PPSE) and works by creating strong emotional responses that intensify the emotional state of the individual. In terms of radicalisation, distraction is often accomplished by focusing the targets attention on one thing to cause them to overlook another and if the distraction is strong enough it may cause the distortion of logical facts and may end up altering their entire belief system (Hadnagy, 2010; Winter, 2016). Given that YouTube is the most common platform for spreading radical ideas, Haider (2015) notes that one way to achieve distraction is via frequent posts on YouTube. For example, the graphic content exhibited by many videos posted online can impact an individual's emotional state. In support, Neo et al. (2016) note that online posts by Islamic extremists that have used such distractors are videos containing news about conflict driven areas, reports about discriminatory attacks against Muslims and stories about group victories. Therefore, distraction appears to be a form of influence that may be used to encourage people to decide to engage in terrorism via using distraction to consume the target with the concept of the Muslim community being disadvantaged and them not belonging to the host society (Haider, 2015). Taken together, Sabouni et al. (2017) concludes that extremists appear to exploit target personality and emotion by utilising persuasion methods such as those outlined above, to increase the targets receptiveness to the attack. Most prominently being a sense of alienation from society (Neo et al. 2016) online extremists appear to affirm the need to belong in individuals who feel alienated from the rest of society by allowing them to access their group.

The Concept of Social Engineering and Cyber Attacks

When considering the topic of persuasion and the role of the Internet in attitude and behaviour change, the concept of Social engineering is important to discuss. Social engineering has been defined as 'The science of using social interaction as a means to persuade an individual or an organization to comply with a specific request from an attacker where either the social interaction, the persuasion or the request involves a computer-related entity' (Mouton, Leenen, Malan, & Venter, 2014) or non-computing context. More generally, the science of social engineering is the general term of manoeuvring individuals to perform acts that may or may not be in their best interest (Hadnagy, 2010). The recent NHS cyber-attack (Graham, 2017) is a prime example of the need for an increased understanding into the factors that affect people's disclosure of private information. Indeed, many cyberattacks begin with users who unknowingly or mistakenly disclose personal information to attackers such as being sent a link via a phishing email with a request to fill in personal details (Hong, 2012; Purkait, 2012). The success of these types of attacks can often depend on whether a persons is duped, or willing, to disclose information.

Similar to the notion of persuasion, social engineering attackers rely on human error by exploiting psychology and also behavioural weaknesses (Luo, Brody, Seeazzu & Burd, 2011) – there are many social engineering principles that have been used to manipulate different people, indeed many techniques of persuasion and information have been noted but, as noted by Graham (2017), often the numerous factors outlined did not have clear factors or tended to be discipline bound. In support, a recent article by Ingram (2017) notes that ISIS appear to draw on pragmatic functions in their online messages to convince and persuade its audience to engage in rational choice decision making i.e., decisions based on a cost-benefit balance of options. ISIS also appears to draw on perceptual factors by playing upon identity crisis and solution constructs to shape how its audiences perceive and judge the world (see Ingram, 2017). The central narrative of this type of message seems to be that: ISIS are protectors of Sunnis (the in group identity) whereas ISIS's enemies are evil others (out group identity) that are responsible for Sunni crises to which ISIS are the only hope for solutions (Ingram, 2017). ISIS appear to disseminate this type of messaging as a means to convince its audiences to engage in identity-choice decision-making (i.e., choices made in accordance with one's identity). Numerus other narratives tend to be employed such as value-reinforcing messages or dichotomy-reinforcing messages (Ingram, 2017) The former is designed to reinforce the in group's positive values and actions and the others negative values and actions. The latter (i.e., dichotomy-reinforcing messaging) tends to either accentuate the contrast between in and out group attributes or demonstrate how solutions are required to address crises. By highlighting these dualities, Ingram notes that dichotomy-reinforcing messages appear to be used to both generate sociopolitical anxieties in the audience and provide readers with clear choices between the in group or others.

Numerous intervention approaches have been applied online to try to reduce, and ultimately stop, the occurrence of cyber-attacks. Some studies have applied the concept of 'priming' to the online world and produced differing results. For example, a study by Parsons, McCormac, Pattinson and Jerram (2015) revealed that explicitly priming participants so that they were aware that the aims of the study was to recognise phishing emails resulted in better performance relative to a control group that was unaware of study aims. Importantly, other studies have not found support for priming effectiveness (Grazioli &Wang, 2001; Zhang & Xu, 2016; Hong, 2012). The results of Junger (2017) are in line with this trend.

CONCLUSION

This chapter has considered multiple definitions and theories and research relating to decision making to consider the applicability of these to online decision making. The breadth and complexity of these has been acknowledged; in particular, research investigating online decision making is broad in scope and often tends to have a different focus to offline research. It was noted that normative theories tend to be concerned with how people should reason whereas descriptive theories tend to describe how people actually reason. These distinctions and breadth of empirical work associated with these distinctions highlighted the potential challenges associated with applying existing decision-making models to online contexts. Specifically, we note that online behaviours are vast and diverse, as well as there being many variations in online platforms themselves. This raises substantial challenges when applying specific decision-making models across these disparate environments. That is, we note that more rational models may be more relevant when underpinning online behaviours which may be more transactional (online purchasing) or informational (comparing hotel prices) in nature, whereas persuasion theories may be better suited for more interactional or social behaviours (e.g., joining networks, "Liking" or sharing group pages). Indeed, it appears that across studies, these theories have seemingly been applied in these ways, yet no commentary to date accounts for the vast distinctions in this regard. Online decision making cannot be explained by one single model, as none is sufficient in its own capacity to underpin all forms of online behaviour and how they occur in varying contexts, which can differ in factors such as synchronicity and social affordances, for example. Further, there remains a lack of theoretical explanation as to how online decision making translates into real world behaviours (and vice versa), particularly in the context of radicalisation. Although the models may account for factors and processes which are relevant in one context or another, there is scant conceptual knowledge of how these decision-making behaviours may be fluid between online and offline contexts. This presents key practical challenges when attempting to apply decision making models to online contexts, particularly given the diversity of the behaviours which may be afforded within virtual environments. We outline a number of key questions below which challenge the current thinking of online decision making, to present an agenda for future conceptual and empirical work.

CHAPTER QUESTIONS

1. When does decision making start online? E.g., becoming radicalised is unlikely to happen instantaneously; therefore, the decision to become involved in terrorism may be a lengthy process shaped by numerous factors beyond the scope of traditional, rational probability based models with increasing complexity online.
2. Does the applicability of different decision-making models vary depending on the specific online behaviour? I.e., more transaction-based behaviours (e.g., online shopping) or informational (e.g., comparing online hotel prices) may be better explained by models such as consumer models of

decision marking. However, more interactional-based behaviours (responding to comments on Social Network Sites) may be better explained using alternative models such persuasive influence.

3. In the context of radicalisation, online decision-making should be acknowledged in light of its potential influence on real-world behaviours. To what extent are decision-making models sufficient to underpin the transitions of behaviours between online and offline contexts?

4. What behavioural indicators are evident to help practitioners detect decision-making online, and how does this vary for different virtual contexts?

REFERENCES

Ajzen, I. (1991). The theory of planned behavior. *Organizational Behavior and Human Decision Processes*, *50*(2), 179–211. doi:10.1016/0749-5978(91)90020-T

Ajzen, I., & Fishbein, M. (1980). *Understanding attitudes and predicting social behaviour*. Academic Press.

Amichai-Hamburger, Y. (Ed.). (2013). *The social net: Understanding our online behavior*. OUP Oxford. doi:10.1093/acprof:oso/9780199639540.001.0001

Armitage, C. J., & Conner, M. (2001). Efficacy of the theory of planned behaviour: A meta-analytic review. *British Journal of Social Psychology*, *40*(4), 471–499. doi:10.1348/014466601164939 PMID:11795063

Attwell, G. (2007). Personal Learning Environments-the future of eLearning? *Elearning Papers, 2*(1), 1-8.

Awad, N. F., & Ragowsky, A. (2008). Establishing trust in electronic commerce through online word of mouth: An examination across genders. *Journal of Management Information Systems*, *24*(4), 101–121. doi:10.2753/MIS0742-1222240404

Bandura, A. (1977). Self-efficacy: Toward a unifying theory of behavioural change. *Psychological Review*, *84*(2), 191–215. doi:10.1037/0033-295X.84.2.191 PMID:847061

Bandura, A. (1994). Social cognitive theory and exercise of control over HIV infection. In Preventing AIDS (pp. 25-59). Springer US. doi:10.1007/978-1-4899-1193-3_3

Bandura, A. (2004). Health promotion by social cognitive means. *Health Education & Behavior*, *31*(2), 143–164. doi:10.1177/1090198104263660 PMID:15090118

Barge, J. K., & Hirokawa, R. Y. (1989). Toward a communication competency model of group leadership. *Small Group Behavior*, *20*(2), 167–189. doi:10.1177/104649648902000203

Bauer, K., & Hein, S. E. (2006). The effect of heterogeneous risk on the early adoption of Internet banking technologies. *Journal of Banking & Finance*, *30*(6), 1713–1725. doi:10.1016/j.jbankfin.2005.09.004

Baumert, T., Buesa, M., & Lynch, T. (2013). The impact of terrorism on stock markets: The Boston bombing experience in comparison with previous terrorist events. *Institute of Industrial and Financial Analysis Complutense University of Madrid*, *88*, 1–24.

Beresford, B., & Sloper, P. (2008). *Understanding the dynamics of decision-making and choice: A scoping study of key psychological theories to inform the design and analysis of the Panel Study*. York, UK: Social Policy Research Unit, University of York.

Bergin, A. E. (2009). *Changing frontiers in the science of psychotherapy*. Aldine Transaction.

Blackwood, L. M., Hopkins, N. P., & Reicher, S. D. (2012). *Divided by a common language?: conceptualising identity, discrimination, and alienation*. Restoring Civil Societies.

Blau, P. M. (1964). *Social exchange theory*. Academic Press.

Briggs, R., & Strugnell, A. (2011). *Radicalisation: The role of the internet*. Policy Planners' Network Working Paper. London: Institute for Strategic Dialogue.

Brown, J. J., & Reingen, P. H. (1987). Social ties and word of mouth referral behavior. *The Journal of Consumer Research, 14*(3), 350–362. doi:10.1086/209118

Carmon, Z., Wertenbroch, K., & Zeelenberg, M. (2003). Option attachment: When deliberating makes choosing feel like losing. *The Journal of Consumer Research, 30*(1), 15–29. doi:10.1086/374701

Christin, N., Egelman, S., Vidas, T., & Grossklags, J. (2011, February). It's all about the Benjamins: An empirical study on incentivizing users to ignore security advice. In *International Conference on Financial Cryptography and Data Security* (pp. 16-30). Springer.

Cialdini, R. B. (2001). The science of persuasion. *Scientific American, 284*(2), 76–81. doi:10.1038/scientificamerican0201-76 PMID:11285825

Cialdini, R. B., & Goldstein, N. J. (2004). Social influence: Compliance and conformity. *Annual Review of Psychology, 55*(1), 591–621. doi:10.1146/annurev.psych.55.090902.142015 PMID:14744228

Cook, D. A., Levinson, A. J., Garside, S., Dupras, D. M., Erwin, P. J., & Montori, V. M. (2008). Internet-based learning in the health professions: A meta-analysis. *Journal of the American Medical Association, 300*(10), 1181–1196. doi:10.1001/jama.300.10.1181 PMID:18780847

Cotton, S. R., & Gupta, S. S. (2004). Characteristics of online and offline health information seekers and factors that discriminate between them. *Social Science & Medicine, 59*(9), 1795–1806. doi:10.1016/j.socscimed.2004.02.020 PMID:15312915

Cragan, J. F., & Wright, D. W. (1990). Small group communication research of the 1980s: A synthesis and critique. *Communication Studies, 41*(3), 212–236. doi:10.1080/10510979009368305

Cullen, H. D. (1997). *A Comparison of the Decision Quality of Group Decisions Made in a Face-to-Face Environment with Decisions Made Using a Distributed Group Decision Support System (No. AFIT/GIR/LAS/97D-13)*. Air Force Inst of Tech Wright-Patterson AFB OH.

Darley, W. K., Blankson, C., & Luethge, D. J. (2010). Toward an integrated framework for online consumer behavior and decision making process: A review. *Psychology and Marketing, 27*(2), 94–116. doi:10.1002/mar.20322

Das, S., Kramer, A. D., Dabbish, L. A., & Hong, J. I. (2014). Increasing security sensitivity with social proof: A large-scale experimental confirmation. In *Proceedings of the 2014 ACM SIGSAC conference on computer and communications security* (pp. 739-749). ACM. doi:10.1145/2660267.2660271

Dietz-Uhler, B., & Bishop-Clark, C. (2001). The use of computer-mediated communication to enhance subsequent face-to-face discussions. *Computers in Human Behavior, 17*(3), 269–283. doi:10.1016/S0747-5632(01)00006-1

Dillard, J. P., & Nabi, R. L. (2006). The persuasive influence of emotion in cancer prevention and detection messages. *Journal of Communication, 56*(1), S123–S139. doi:10.1111/j.1460-2466.2006.00286.x

Dubrovsky, V. J., Kiesler, S., & Sethna, B. N. (1991). The equalization phenomenon: Status effects in computer-mediated and face-to-face decision-making groups. *Human-Computer Interaction, 6*(2), 119–146. doi:10.1207/s15327051hci0602_2

Duda, R. O., & Hart, P. E. (1973). *Pattern classification and scene analysis*. New York: John Wiley and Sons.

Edwards, W., & Fasolo, B. (2001). Decision technology. *Annual Review of Psychology, 52*(1), 581–606. doi:10.1146/annurev.psych.52.1.581 PMID:11148318

Egelman, S., & Schechter, S. (2013, April). The importance of being earnest (in security warnings). In *International Conference on Financial Cryptography and Data Security* (pp. 52-59). Springer Berlin Heidelberg. doi:10.1007/978-3-642-39884-1_5

Egelman, S., Cranor, L. F., & Hong, J. (2008, April). You've been warned: an empirical study of the effectiveness of web browser phishing warnings. In *Proceedings of the SIGCHI Conference on Human Factors in Computing Systems* (pp. 1065-1074). ACM. doi:10.1145/1357054.1357219

Engel, J. F., Blackwell, R. D., & Miniard, P. W. (1986). *Consumer behaviour*. Hinsdale, IL: Dryden.

Engel, J. F., Kollat, D. T., & Blackwell, R. D. (1978). *Consumer behavior*. Hinsdale, IL: Dryden.

Eysenbach, G. (2001). What is e-health? *Journal of Medical Internet Research, 3*(2), e20. doi:10.2196/jmir.3.2.e20 PMID:11720962

Farajtabar, M., Yang, J., Ye, X., Xu, H., Trivedi, R., Khalil, E., . . . Zha, H. (2017). *Fake News Mitigation via Point Process Based Intervention*. Retrieved September 15, 2017 from http://proceedings.mlr.press/v70/farajtabar17a/farajtabar17a.pdf

Fogg, B. J. (2002). Persuasive technology: Using computers to change what we think and do. *Ubiquity, 5*.

Fredrickson, B. L., & Branigan, C. (2005). Positive emotions broaden the scope of attention and thought-action repertoires. *Cognition and Emotion, 19*(3), 313–332. doi:10.1080/02699930441000238 PMID:21852891

Gibson, C. B., Huang, L., Kirkman, B. L., & Shapiro, D. L. (2014). Where global and virtual meet: The value of examining the intersection of these elements in twenty-first-century teams. *Annual Review of Organizational Psychology and Organizational Behavior, 1*(1), 217–244. doi:10.1146/annurev-orgpsych-031413-091240

Godin, G., & Kok, G. (1996). The theory of planned behavior: A review of its applications to health-related behaviors. *American Journal of Health Promotion, 11*(2), 87–98. doi:10.4278/0890-1171-11.2.87 PMID:10163601

Goodman, S., Morrongiello, B., & Meckling, K. (2016). A randomized, controlled trial evaluating the efficacy of an online intervention targeting vitamin D intake, knowledge and status among young adults. *The International Journal of Behavioral Nutrition and Physical Activity, 13*(1), 116. doi:10.1186/s12966-016-0443-1 PMID:27836017

Goodman, S., Morrongiello, B., Simpson, J. R., & Meckling, K. (2015). Vitamin D intake among young Canadian adults: Validation of a mobile vitamin D calculator app. *Journal of Nutrition Education and Behavior, 47*(3), 242–247. doi:10.1016/j.jneb.2014.11.006 PMID:25959447

Goodrich, K., & de Mooij, M. (2013). How 'social' are social media? A cross-cultural comparison of online and offline purchase decision influences. *Journal of Marketing Communications, 20*(1-2), 103–116. doi:10.1080/13527266.2013.797773

Gouran, D. S., & Hirokawa, R. Y. (1983). The role of communication in decision-making groups: A functional perspective. *Communications in Transition*, 168-185.

Gouran, D. S., & Hirokawa, R. Y. (1996). *Functional theory and communication in decision making and problem-solving groups. An expanded view. In Communication and group decision making* (pp. 55–80). Thousand Oaks, CA: Sage.

Graham, C. (2017). *NHS cyber-attack: Everything you need to know about "biggest ransomware" offensive in history*. The Telegraph.

Grazioli, S., & Wang, A. (2001). Looking without seeing: understanding unsophisticated consumers' success and failure to detect Internet deception. *ICIS 2001 Proceedings*, 23.

Guadagno, R. E., & Cialdini, R. B. (2002). Online persuasion: An examination of gender differences in computer-mediated interpersonal influence. *Group Dynamics, 6*(1), 38–51. doi:10.1037/1089-2699.6.1.38

Guéguen, N., & Jacob, C. (2002). Solicitation by e-mail and solicitor's status: A field study of social influence on the web. *Cyberpsychology & Behavior, 5*(4), 377–383. doi:10.1089/109493102760275626 PMID:12216702

Hall, A. K., Bernhardt, J. M., & Dodd, V. (2015). Older adults' use of online and offline sources of health information and constructs of reliance and self-efficacy for medial decision making. *Journal of Health Communication, 20*(7), 751–758. doi:10.1080/10810730.2015.1018603 PMID:26054777

Hansen, T., Jensen, J. M., & Solgaard, H. S. (2004). Predicting online grocery buying intention: A comparison of the theory of reasoned action and the theory of planned behavior. *International Journal of Information Management, 24*(6), 539–550. doi:10.1016/j.ijinfomgt.2004.08.004

Häubl, G., & Tifts, V. (2000). Consumer Decision Making in Online Shopping Environments: The Effects of Interactive Decision Aids. *Marketing Science, 19*(1), 4–21. doi:10.1287/mksc.19.1.4.15178

Hirokawa, R. Y. (1985). Discussion procedures and decision-making performance. *Human Communication Research, 12*(2), 203–224. doi:10.1111/j.1468-2958.1985.tb00073.x

Hirokawa, R. Y. (1988). Group Communication and Decision-Making Performance A Continued Test of the Functional Perspective. *Human Communication Research, 14*(4), 487–515. doi:10.1111/j.1468-2958.1988.tb00165.x

Ho, C., Lin, M., & Chen, H. (2012). Web users' behavioural patterns of tourism information search: From online to offline. *Tourism Management, 33*(6), 1468–1482. doi:10.1016/j.tourman.2012.01.016

Homans, G. C. (1974). *Social Behaviour: Its Elementary Forms*. New York: Harcourt Brace Jovanovich, Inc.

Hong, J. (2012). The state of phishing attacks. *Communications of the ACM, 55*(1), 74–81. doi:10.1145/2063176.2063197

Huang, Y., & Bian, L. (2009). A Bayesian network and analytic hierarchy process based personalized recommendations for tourist attractions over the Internet. *Expert Systems with Applications, 36*(1), 933–943. doi:10.1016/j.eswa.2007.10.019

Işıklar, G., & Büyüközkan, G. (2007). Using a multi-criteria decision making approach to evaluate mobile phone alternatives. *Computer Standards & Interfaces, 29*(2), 265–274. doi:10.1016/j.csi.2006.05.002

Jackson, D. D., Ingram, L. A., Boyer, C. B., Robillard, A., & Huhns, M. N. (2016). Can Technology Decrease Sexual Risk Behaviors among Young People? Results of a Pilot Study Examining the Effectiveness of a Mobile Application Intervention. *American Journal of Sexuality Education, 11*(1), 41–60. doi:10.1080/15546128.2015.1123129

Janis, I. L., & Mann, L. (1977). *Decision making: A psychological analysis of conflict, choice, and commitment*. Free Press.

Johnson, E. J., & Payne, J. W. (1985). Effort and accuracy in choice. *Management Science, 31*(4), 395–414. doi:10.1287/mnsc.31.4.395

Jonassen, D. H., & Kwon, H. II. (2001). Communication patterns in computer mediated versus face-to face group problem solving. *Educational Technology Research and Development, 49*(1), 35–51. doi:10.1007/BF02504505

Junger, M., Montoya, L., & Overink, F. J. (2017). Priming and warnings are not effective to prevent social engineering attacks. *Computers in Human Behavior, 66*, 75–87. doi:10.1016/j.chb.2016.09.012

Kahneman, D. (2011). *Thinking, Fast and Slow*. Farrar, Straus and Giroux.

Kalichman, S. C., Benotsch, E. G., Weinhardt, L., Austin, J., Luke, W., & Cherry, C. (2003). Health-related Internet use, coping, social support, and health indicators in people living with HIV/AIDS: Preliminary results from a community survey. *Health Psychology, 22*(1), 111–116. doi:10.1037/0278-6133.22.1.111 PMID:12558209

Kaptein, M., Markopoulos, P., De Ruyter, B., & Aarts, E. (2015). Personalizing persuasive technologies: Explicit and implicit personalization using persuasion profiles. *International Journal of Human-Computer Studies, 77*, 38–51. doi:10.1016/j.ijhcs.2015.01.004

Karni, E., & Vierø, M.-L. (2014). *Awareness of Unawareness: A Theory of Decision Making in the Face of Ignorance*. Queen's Economics Department Working Paper, No. 1322.

Kim, D. J., Ferrin, D. L., & Rao, H. R. (2008). A trust-based consumer decision-making model in electronic commerce: The role of trust, perceived risk, and their antecedents. *Decision Support Systems*, *44*(2), 544–564. doi:10.1016/j.dss.2007.07.001

Kohli, R., Devaraj, S., & Mahmood, A. (2014). Understanding Determinants of Online Consumer Satisfaction: A Decision Process Perspective. *Journal of Management Information Systems*, *21*(1), 115–136. doi:10.1080/07421222.2004.11045796

Lea, M., & Spears, R. (1991). Computer-mediated communication, de-individuation and group decision-making. *International Journal of Man-Machine Studies*, *34*(2), 283–301. doi:10.1016/0020-7373(91)90045-9

Lenhart, A., & Madden, M. (2007). *Teens, Privacy & Online Social Networks: How teens manage their online identities and personal information in the age of MySpace*. Academic Press.

Liu, Q. X., Fang, X. Y., Wan, J. J., & Zhou, Z. K. (2016). Need satisfaction and adolescent pathological internet use: Comparison of satisfaction perceived online and offline. *Computers in Human Behavior*, *55*, 695–700. doi:10.1016/j.chb.2015.09.048

Lucas, R. E. Jr, & Prescott, E. C. (1971). Investment under uncertainty. *Econometrica*, *39*(5), 659–681. doi:10.2307/1909571

Lyons, S. L. (2015). *The Psychological Foundations of Homegrown Radicalization: An Immigrant Acculturation Perspective* (Doctoral dissertation).

Matheson, K., & Zanna, M. P. (1989). Persuasion as a function of self-awareness in computer mediated communication. *Social Behaviour*.

McCauley, C., & Moskalenko, S. (2008). Mechanisms of political radicalization: Pathways toward terrorism. *Terrorism and Political Violence*, *20*(3), 415–433. doi:10.1080/09546550802073367

McKenzie, C. R. (2004). Framing effects in inference tasks—and why they are normatively defensible. *Memory & Cognition*, *32*(6), 874–885. doi:10.3758/BF03196866 PMID:15673176

Meuter, M. L., Ostrom, A. L., Roundtree, R. I., & Bitner, M. J. (2000). Self-service technologies: Understanding customer satisfaction with technology-based service encounters. *Journal of Marketing*, *64*(3), 50–64. doi:10.1509/jmkg.64.3.50.18024

Meyer, J. (2010). Representing risk preferences in expected utility based decision models. *Annals of Operations Research*, *176*(1), 179–190. doi:10.1007/s10479-008-0381-7

Mintz, A. (Ed.). (2016). *Integrating Cognitive and Rational Theories of Foreign Policy Decision Making: The Polyheuristic Theory of Decision*. Springer.

Morrongiello, B., Simpson, J. R., & Meckling, K. (2015). Vitamin D intake among youngCanadian adults: Validation of a mobile vitamin D calculator app. *Journal of Nutrition Education and Behavior*, *47*(3), 242–247. doi:10.1016/j.jneb.2014.11.006 PMID:25959447

Mouton, F., Leenen, L., Malan, M. M., & Venter, H. S. (2014, July). Towards an ontological model defining the social engineering domain. In *IFIP International Conference on Human Choice and Computers* (pp. 266-279). Springer Berlin Heidelberg. doi:10.1007/978-3-662-44208-1_22

Muscanell, N. L., Guadagno, R. E., & Murphy, S. (2014). Weapons of influence misused: A social influence analysis of why people fall prey to internet scams. *Social and Personality Psychology Compass*, *8*(7), 388–396. doi:10.1111/spc3.12115

Muth, J. F. (1961). Rational expectations and the theory of price movements. *Econometrica*, *29*(3), 315–335. doi:10.2307/1909635

Christin, N., Egelman, S., Vidas, T., & Grossklags, J. (2012). It's all about the Benjamins: an empirical study on incentivizing users to ignore security advice. In *Proceedings of the 15th international conference on Financial Cryptography and Data Security, FC'11* (pp 16–30). Springer-Verlag. doi:10.1007/978-3-642-27576-0_2

O'Neill, T. A., Hancock, S. E., Zivkov, K., Larson, N. L., & Law, S. J. (2016). Team Decision Making in Virtual and Face-to-Face Environments. *Group Decision and Negotiation*, *25*(5), 995–1020. doi:10.1007/s10726-015-9465-3

Over, D. (2004). Rationality and the normative/descriptive distinction. Blackwell handbook of judgment and decision making, 3-18.

Parsons, K., McCormac, A., Pattinson, M., Butavicius, M., & Jerram, C. (2015). The design of phishing studies: Challenges for researchers. *Computers & Security*, *52*, 194–206. doi:10.1016/j.cose.2015.02.008

Payne, J. W. (1982). Contingent decision behavior. *Psychological Bulletin*, *92*(2), 382–402. doi:10.1037/0033-2909.92.2.382

Payne, J. W., Bettman, J. R., & Johnson, E. J. (1988). Adaptive strategy selection in decision making. *Journal of Experimental Psychology. Learning, Memory, and Cognition*, *14*(3), 534–552. doi:10.1037/0278-7393.14.3.534

Petty, R. E., & Briñol, P. (2015). Emotion and persuasion: Cognitive and meta cognitive processes impact attitudes. *Cognition and Emotion*, *29*(1), 1–26. doi:10.1080/02699931.2014.967183 PMID:25302943

Petty, R. E., & Cacioppo, J. T. (1986). The elaboration likelihood model of persuasion. *Advances in Experimental Social Psychology*, *19*, 123–205. doi:10.1016/S0065-2601(08)60214-2

Plous, S. (1993). *The psychology of judgment and decision making*. Mcgraw-Hill Book Company.

Postmes, T. (2007). The psychological dimensions of collective action, online. In. A. Joinson, K. McKenna, T, Postmes, & U. Reips. (Eds.), The Oxford Handbook of Internet Psychology (pp. 165-184). Oxford, UK: Oxford University Press.

Postmes, T., Spears, R., & Lea, M. (1998). Breaching or building social boundaries? SIDE effects of computer-mediated communication. *Communication Research*, *25*(6), 689–715. doi:10.1177/009365098025006006

Pratt, J. W. (1964). Risk Aversion in the Small and in the Large. *Econometrica*, *32*(1/2), 122–136. doi:10.2307/1913738

Precht, T. (2007). *Home grown terrorism and Islamist radicalisation in Europe. From conversion to terrorism.* Academic Press.

Purcell, M. (2013). Youtube and you. *Library Media Connection, 31*(4), 14–16.

Purkait, S. (2012). Phishing counter measures and their effectiveness–literature review. *Information Management & Computer Security, 20*(5), 382–420. doi:10.1108/09685221211286548

Quayle, E., & Taylor, M. (2011). Social networking as a nexus for engagement and exploitation of young people. *Information Security Technical Report, 16*(2), 44–50.

Rains, S. A., & Karmikel, C. D. (2009). Health information-seeking and perceptions of website credibility: Examining Web-use orientation, message characteristics, and structural features of websites. *Computers in Human Behavior, 25*(2), 544–553. doi:10.1016/j.chb.2008.11.005

Rifon, N. J., Jiang, M., & Kim, S. (2016). Don't hate me because I am beautiful: Identifying the relative influence of celebrity attractiveness and character traits on credibility. In *Advances in Advertising Research* (Vol. 6, pp. 125–134). Springer Fachmedien Wiesbaden. doi:10.1007/978-3-658-10558-7_11

Ruiter, R. A., Kessels, L. T., Peters, G. J. Y., & Kok, G. (2014). Sixty years of fear appeal research: Current state of the evidence. *International Journal of Psychology, 49*(2), 63–70. doi:10.1002/ijop.12042 PMID:24811876

Saddiq, M. A. (2010). *Whither e-jihad: evaluating the threat of internet radicalisation.* Academic Press.

Sagarin, B. J., Britt, M. A., Heider, J. D., Wood, S. E., & Lynch, J. E. (2003). *Bartering Our Attention: The Distraction and Persuasion Effects of On-Line Advertisements.* Cognitive Technology.

Salam, A., Rao, R., & Pegels, C. (1998). An investigation of consumer-perceived risk on electronic commerce transactions: The role of institutional trust and economic incentive in a social exchange framework. *AMCIS 1998 Proceedings*, 114.

Schmid, A. P. (2013). Radicalisation, de-radicalisation, counter-radicalisation: A conceptual discussion and literature review. *ICCT Research Paper, 97*, 22.

Senecal, S., Kalczynski, P. J., & Nantel, J. (2005). Consumers' decision-making process and their online shopping behavior: A clickstream analysis. *Journal of Business Research, 58*(11), 1599–1608. doi:10.1016/j.jbusres.2004.06.003

Shafir, E., & LeBoeuf, R. A. (2002). Rationality. *Annual Review of Psychology, 53*(1), 491–517. doi:10.1146/annurev.psych.53.100901.135213 PMID:11752494

Shankar, V., Smith, A. K., & Rangaswamy, A. (2003). Customer satisfaction and loyalty in online and offline environments. *International Journal of Research in Marketing, 20*(2), 153–175. doi:10.1016/S0167-8116(03)00016-8

Shiau, W. L., & Luo, M. M. (2012). Factors affecting online group buying intention and satisfaction: A social exchange theory perspective. *Computers in Human Behavior, 28*(6), 2431–2444. doi:10.1016/j.chb.2012.07.030

Sher, S., & McKenzie, C. R. (2008). Framing effects and rationality. *The probabilistic mind: Prospects for Bayesian cognitive science*, 79-96.

Shetret, L. (2011). *Use of the Internet for Counter-Terrorist Purposes*. Center on Global Counterterrorism Cooperation. Retrieved May 25, 2017 from, http://www.globalct.org/wpcontent/uploads/2011/02/LS_policybrief_119.pdf

Shu, K., Silva, A., Wang, S., Tang, J., & Liu, H. (2017). Fake news detection on socialmedia. A data mining perspective. *Proceedings of SIGKDD Explorations Newsletter*, *19*(1), 22–36.

Shugan, S. M. (1980). The cost of thinking. *The Journal of Consumer Research*, *7*(2), 99–111. doi:10.1086/208799

Silber, M. D., Bhatt, A., & Analysts, S. I. (2007). *Radicalization in the West: The homegrown threat*. New York: Police Department.

Silke, A. (2008). Research on terrorism. *Terrorism Informatics. Knowledge Management and Data Mining for Homeland Security*, 27-50.

Sillence, E., Briggs, P., Harris, P., & Fishwick, L. (2006). A framework for understanding trust factors in web-based health advice. *International Journal of Human-Computer Studies*, *64*(8), 697–713. doi:10.1016/j.ijhcs.2006.02.007

Spook, J., Paulussen, T., Kok, G., & van Empelen, P. (2016). Evaluation of a serious self-regulation game intervention for overweight-related behaviors ("Balance It"): A pilot study. *Journal of Medical Internet Research*, *18*(9), e225. doi:10.2196/jmir.4964 PMID:27670222

Stevens, T., & Neumann, P. R. (2009). *Countering online radicalisation: A strategy for action*. International Centre for the Study of Radicalisation and Political Violence.

Sunstein, C. R. (2001). Why they hate us: The role of social dynamics. *Harv. JL & Pub. Pol'y*, *25*, 429.

Tajfel, H. (1978). *Differentiation between social groups*. London: Academic Press.

Tajfel, H. (1979). Individuals and groups in social psychology. *The British Journal of Social and Clinical Psychology*, *18*, 183–190. doi:10.1111/j.20448260.1979.tb00324.x

Tajfel, H., & Turner, J. (1979). An integrative theory of inter-group conflict. In J. A. Williams & S. Worchel (Eds.), *The social psychology of inter-group relations* (pp. 33–47). Belmont, CA: Wadsworth.

Tauber, E. M. (1972). Why do people shop? *Journal of Marketing*, *36*(4), 46–49. doi:10.2307/1250426

Tice, D. M., Bratslavsky, E., & Baumeister, R. F. (2001). Emotional distress regulation takes precedence over impulse control: If you feel bad, do it! *Journal of Personality and Social Psychology*, *80*(1), 53–67. doi:10.1037/0022-3514.80.1.53 PMID:11195891

Torok, R. (2010). *"Make A Bomb In Your Mums Kitchen": Cyber Recruiting And Socialisation of 'White Moors' and Home Grown Jihadists*. Academic Press.

Toronto Star. (2008, February 4). How Obama using tech to triumph. *Toronto Star*, p. B1.

Tversky, A., & Kahneman, D. (1981). *Evidential impact of base rates (No. TR-4).* Stanford Univ CA Dept of Psychology. doi:10.21236/ADA099501

Ullmann-Margalit, E. (2006). Big decisions: Opting, converting, drifting. *Royal Institute of Philosophy, 58*(Supplement), 157–172. doi:10.1017/S1358246106058085

Van Kleek, M., Liccardi, I., Binns, R., Zhao, J., Weitzner, D. J., & Shadbolt, N. (2017, May). Better the devil you know: Exposing the data sharing practices of apps. In *Proceedings of the 2017 CHI Conference on Human Factors in Computing Systems* (pp. 5208-5220). ACM. doi:10.1145/3025453.3025556

Wallenius, J., Dyer, J. S., Fishburn, P. C., Steuer, R. E., Zionts, S., & Deb, K. (2008). Multiple criteria decision making, multiattribute utility theory: Recent accomplishments and what lies ahead. *Management Science, 54*(7), 1336–1349. doi:10.1287/mnsc.1070.0838

Wogalter, M. S., Laughery, K. R., & Mayhorn, C. B. (2012). Warnings and hazard communications. Handbook of human factors and ergonomics, 4.

Xiao, B., & Benbasat, I. (2015). Designing warning messages for detecting biased online product recommendations: An empirical investigation. *Information Systems Research, 26*(4), 793–811. doi:10.1287/isre.2015.0592

Yeap, S. Y., & Park, J. (2010). *Countering internet radicalisation: A holistic approach.* Academic Press.

Yousafzai, S. Y., Foxall, G. R., & Pallister, J. G. (2010). Explaining internet banking behavior: Theory of reasoned action, theory of planned behavior, or technology acceptance model? *Journal of Applied Social Psychology, 40*(5), 1172–1202. doi:10.1111/j.1559-1816.2010.00615.x

Zhang, B., & Xu, H. (2016, February). Privacy nudges for mobile Applications: Effects on the creepiness emotion and privacy attitudes. In *Proceedings of the 19th ACM conference on computer-supported cooperative work & social computing* (pp. 1676-1690). ACM. doi:10.1145/2818048.2820073

Zhang, J., Chen, C., Xiang, Y., Zhou, W., & Xiang, Y. (2013). Internet traffic classification by aggregating correlated naive bayes predictions. *IEEE Transactions on Information Forensics and Security, 8*(1), 5–15. doi:10.1109/TIFS.2012.2223675

ENDNOTE

[1]   An additional theory is Social Exchange Theory (SET; Blau, 1964). SET posits that people and organizations interact to maximize their rewards and minimize their costs (Salam, Rao, & Pegels, 1998). Individuals typically expect reciprocal benefits, such as trust, economic return, personal affection, and gratitude when they act according to social norms. A recent study by Shiao and Luo (2012) explored the factors affecting online group buying intention and satisfaction and adopted a SET perspective. Their findings were in line with earlier research by (Tauber, 1972), which suggested that shoppers engage in online group shopping for economic incentives, product novelty, and the fulfillment provided by social interaction.

Chapter 2
Human Factors Leading to Online Fraud Victimisation:
Literature Review and Exploring the Role of Personality Traits

Jildau Borwell
The National Police of the Netherlands, The Netherlands

Jurjen Jansen
Open University of the Netherlands, The Netherlands & NHL University of Applied Sciences, The Netherlands & Dutch Police Academy, The Netherlands

Wouter Stol
Open University of the Netherlands, The Netherlands & NHL University of Applied Sciences, The Netherlands & Dutch Police Academy, The Netherlands

ABSTRACT

With the advent of the internet, criminals gained new tools to commit crimes. Crimes in which the use of connected information technologies is essential for the realisation of the offence are defined as cybercrimes. The human factor is often identified as the weakest link in the information security chain, and it is often the behaviour of humans that leads to the success of cybercrimes. In this chapter, end-user characteristics are studied that may predict cybercrime victimisation. This is done by means of a review of the literature and by a study on personality traits. More specifically, personality traits from the big five are tested on victims of three different types of online fraud, phishing, Microsoft fraud, and purchasing fraud, and are compared with norm groups of the Dutch population. This chapter ends with implications for online fraud prevention and possibilities to advance the study of cyber victimisation.

DOI: 10.4018/978-1-5225-4053-3.ch002

INTRODUCTION

Society is digitising, and with it there has been a broadening of the opportunities that people have in many respects, for instance, when it comes to maintaining social contacts and making government services more accessible. The digital revolution, however, is also expanding the range of opportunities that delinquents have for targeting their victims (Bossler & Holt, 2009; Van Wilsem, 2011). The internet is being used to create new kinds of crime, and many traditional crimes can now be carried out in new and simpler ways (Bossler & Holt, 2010; Pyrooz, Dec, & Moule Jr, 2015). Crimes in which the use of connected information technologies is essential for the realisation of the offence are defined here as cybercrimes. A particular kind of cybercrime that is the focus of this chapter is online fraud – deception with the aim of financial gain whereby information technology is essential to its implementation (Stol, Leukfeldt, & Klap, 2012).

Although online fraud always has a digital component, the human aspect of this kind of offence is also crucial (Parrish, Baily, & Courtney, 2009; Wiederhold, 2014). Fraudsters generally target vulnerable, human characteristics as opposed to relying on breaches in technology. They also use deception to get their hands on sensitive information (Parrish et al., 2009) or to persuade people to make fraudulent purchases (Van Wilsem, 2013). Victims participate actively in the offence, as it were, because they themselves give the fraudsters the information they need, for instance, to access their bank accounts (Jansen & Leukfeldt, 2015). This means that people are the 'weakest link' in this type of crime. That said, not everyone responds to 'fake' e-mails, telephone calls or advertisements. Most people ignore them or delete them immediately (Jones, Towse, & Race, 2015; Parrish et al., 2009). This raises the question of what makes some people respond to the tactics that fraudsters use, and with that fall victim to online fraud, while others do not. In this chapter, an explanation for victimisation is first sought in the routine activity approach (Cohen & Felson, 1979). As will become evident, this approach offers no consensus for what makes a person run an increased risk of falling victim to online fraud. For this reason, the researchers go on to approach the explanation for victimisation from the perspective of personality traits. A better understanding of online fraud victimisation is needed to enhance cyber security.

THE RELEVANCE OF THE HUMAN FACTOR IN EXPLAINING CYBER VICTIMISATION

The rising threat that cybercrime poses has increased the urgency to gain an understanding of online fraud victimisation (NCSC, 2015). The opportunities that the internet offers are multiplying, and society is increasingly adjusting to the idea that these opportunities should be used (Pratt, Holtfreter, & Reisig, 2010). Moreover, the rise in these options is going hand in hand with a decline in the number of analogue alternatives available (NCSC, 2015). As a consequence, people are becoming more dependent on the internet, which in turn is exacerbating their vulnerability (Choi, 2008; Furnell, Bryant, & Phippen, 2007). If we are to steer future developments in the field of information technology in the right direction when it comes to safety and security, then it is essential that we have a good understanding of online fraud and what makes people fall victim to it. The knowledge emanating from this chapter can help various organisations, like the police, banks and commercial companies, both on- and offline, to arrive at more effective, behaviour-oriented preventive measures.

Preventing online fraud is important because this kind of cybercrime can have many adverse consequences. Those who fall victim to online fraud can experience negative social and psychological consequences through their victimisation. For instance, their faith in humanity and their sense of security may diminish. They may also experience stress and feel powerless in the face of this victimisation (Van Wilsem, 2013). In addition, the negative financial consequences of online fraud for citizens as well as the corporate sector and government authorities are considerable (Bernaards, Monsma, & Zinn, 2012; Bloem & Harteveld, 2012). Furthermore, online fraud can lead to a loss of consumer confidence in online activities. Given that the internet is part of the critical infrastructure for social and financial processes (Bernaards et al., 2012), it is crucial that trust in the internet is safeguarded. Ultimately, a weakening of critical infrastructures can lead to social disruption (Van der Hulst & Neve, 2008).

Effective prevention of online fraud on the part of the victim is only achievable if we have a thorough understanding of the problem. Falling victim to online fraud may well be down to various personal and environmental factors. However, not much is known about the factors associated with online fraud victimisation and the factors that may help to explain it (Ngo & Paternoster, 2011). To the extent that research has been conducted into these aspects, it is often lacking in theoretical substantiation (Bossler & Holt, 2010; Van Wilsem, 2013). The support that has been found for the theories applied, like the routine activity approach – which is discussed below – is not strong (Bossler & Holt, 2010; Jansen & Leukfeldt, 2016). In addition to this, relatively speaking, a lot of attention is paid to the technical aspects of online fraud (Bossler & Holt, 2009). This is despite the fact that a psychological approach, based on insight into human nature that this discipline offers, may make a significant contribution to understanding and explaining online fraud victimisation (Wiederhold, 2014).

THE ROUTINE ACTIVITY APPROACH

The routine activity approach is a commonly used explanatory model for online fraud victimisation (Bossler & Holt, 2009; Bullée, 2017; Choi, 2008; Ngo & Paternoster, 2011; Pratt et al., 2010; Van Wilsem, 2013). From the perspective of this approach, the prediction is that victimisation is dependent on a motivated perpetrator, a suitable target and the absence of capable guardians in a convergence of time and space (Cohen & Felson, 1979). The theory focuses on a daily routine that renders a person more, or conversely less, suitable for victimisation (Bossler & Holt, 2009). Internet users expose themselves to cyber criminals unintentionally through, for instance, visiting certain websites, communicating on internet forums and entering their personal data on websites (Jansen, Leukfeldt, Van Wilsem, & Stol, 2013).

Components from the acronym VIVA are often used to determine whether someone is a suitable target (Sutton, 2009). VIVA stands for value, inertia, visibility and accessibility. 'Value' means that perpetrators are interested in wealthy individuals. Some cybercrime studies have, for example, found a correlation between falling victim to identity theft and households with higher incomes (Harrell & Langton, 2013). In terms of online fraud, inertia is often not addressed because it refers to the volume of data and technological specifications of computer systems (Yar, 2005). Thus, inertia might play a role in more technically oriented types of cybercrime. 'Visibility' can be defined as online activities. According to the theory, people who are often online, open attachments from unknown sources, click on pop-ups, do internet banking, buy via web shops, and use outdated antivirus software are more susceptible to online fraud victimisation (Choi, 2008; Hutchings & Hayes, 2009; Ngo & Paternoster, 2011; Pratt et al., 2010). Conclusively, accessibility can be defined as weaknesses in software that can be exploited by perpetrators to attack users. An example of this is the 'WannaCry' ransomware attack in May 2017 (Hern & Gibbs, 2017).

The various aspects of the routine activity approach have been researched, as outlined above, but the research findings differ (Bossler & Holt, 2009; Ngo & Paternoster, 2011; Wijn, Van den Berg, Wetzer, & Broekman, 2016). One possible reason for the differing research findings is that the studies based on the routine activity approach vary in their design. For instance, different studies included different variables or investigated different types of cybercrime, and in some cases small sample sizes were used (Jansen et al., 2017). The lack of explanatory power offered by the routine activity approach may also be due to the 'dragnet method' that fraudsters usually use (Leukfeldt, 2015). With this method, victims are not selected on the basis of their routine activities; rather, attempts are made to reach as many people as possible until someone 'bites'. Moreover, 'high-risk behaviour', like being online a lot, is now commonplace, meaning that victims can no longer be differentiated in this respect (Wijn et al., 2016). Jansen and Leukfeldt (2016) concluded therefore that the way in which the routine activity approach has been applied to online fraud thus far is not appropriate for explaining victimisation based on the individual factors that make someone a suitable target. Perhaps other ways of measuring routine activities or other predictive variables, like personality traits, go further in giving substance to the term 'suitable target'.

PERSONALITY TRAITS

Considering that victims of online fraud actively participate in the offence to which they fall victim (Jansen & Leukfeldt, 2015), personality traits are a potential factor in explaining victimisation. The fact is that personality traits are stable patterns of behaviour that affect the way people process information and react to situations (Johnston, Warkentin, McBride, & Carter, 2016; Parks-Leduc, Feldman, & Bardi, 2014). This makes it probable that these traits are also associated with behaviour that leads to online fraud victimisation (Wijn et al., 2016). Some authors even go so far as to argue that certain people have a 'victim personality' that makes them more vulnerable to fraud (Halevi, Lewis, & Memon, 2013).

Prior research has shown that personality traits have an impact on the extent to which employees comply with security policies (Johnston et al., 2016; McBride, Carter, & Warkentin, 2012), on how safe someone's internet behaviour is (Wijn et al., 2016), on fear of computers (cyberphobia), and on the importance attached to the privacy of information (Korzaan & Boswell, 2008). Also, some studies carried out theoretical or empirical research into the correlation between personality traits and online fraud victimisation (Jones et al., 2015; Parrish et al., 2009). In these studies, the theoretical substantiations are convincing and the empirical findings provide grounds for optimism.

It is impossible to describe abstract concepts like personality and personality traits comprehensively. At most, they can be approached metaphorically using a model or a theory (Howard & Howard, 1995). There are various models that attempt to map out personality, for instance, the Myers-Briggs Type Indicator (MBTI), the DISC – which stands for dominance, influence, steadiness and conscientiousness – and the Big Five personal traits (Cattell & Mead, 2008; Jones & Hartley, 2013; McCrae & Costa, 1989). In this chapter, the researchers have chosen to elaborate the Big Five in greater detail to investigate personality traits in relation to online fraud victimisation. The Big Five is the leading theoretical model and the most widely used measurement method in personality research (Cattell & Mead, 2008; Jones & Hartley, 2013). The model has been tested and corroborated in a wide range of research settings, for instance, in employment situations, in developmental psychology, and in more general psychological research (Cattell & Mead, 2008; Johnston et al., 2016; De Raad & Perugini, 2002). The Big Five has also been applied in research related to cybercrime victimisation (Jones et al., 2015; Parrish et al., 2009), albeit to a limited degree.

The Big Five distinguishes the following five bipolar dimensions: neuroticism, extraversion, openness, altruism and conscientiousness. These attributes are explained below and applied to online fraud victimisation.

Neuroticism, whereby people who score high are more likely to experience negative emotions and are less able to cope with frustration and stress, while people who have low scores are more emotionally stable (Burger, De Caluwé, & Jansen, 2010; Hoekstra & De Fruyt, 2014). A high neuroticism-score may go hand in hand with fear of computers, leading to risk-averse behaviour on the internet and being online less often (Korzaan & Boswell, 2008). This may lead to a reduced risk of victimisation among these people. Their fear also means that, compared to people who score low for neuroticism, they gain less experience when it comes to technology (Parrish et al., 2009). Some services are no longer available offline, forcing people more or less to go online. Thus people who score high for neuroticism are more likely to fall victim to online fraud due to their lack of experience with the technology and the risk-assessment skills that this experience brings. These people are also less good at detecting lies and deception, and are less able to resist people who try to persuade them to do something (Halevi et al., 2013). This makes them more vulnerable to the social engineering techniques that often accompany online fraud. Also, these people are less able to differentiate between the various types of offers that they deal with (Halevi et al., 2013), which increases their susceptibility to purchasing fraud, for instance. Those who score low for neuroticism apparently have more self-control. This means that it is easier for them to resist temptation and impulses (Howard & Howard, 1995), and this reduces their chances of falling victim to online fraud. Also, people who score low are more sensitive to risks related to information security (Johnston et al., 2016), which may mean that they are less likely to fall victim. Even though not all studies find that neuroticism has a significant effect on online fraud victimisation (Modic & Lea, 2011), most studies lead to the prediction that online fraud victims will score high for the neuroticism personality dimension.

Extraversion, whereby people who score high are outward going, energetic and optimistic, and people who score low are more introverted, reserved and less optimistic (Burger et al., 2010; Hoekstra & De Fruyt, 2014; De Raad & Perugini, 2002). People who score high for extraversion may be more vulnerable to online fraud victimisation because they have a more positive attitude, and with that they tend to trust people more (Forgas & East, 2008). This means that they may be more inclined to be taken in by social engineering techniques. That they approach the unknown with confidence and carelessness (Hoekstra & De Fruyt, 2014; Johnston et al., 2016; De Raad & Perugini, 2002) is linked to this. As opposed to this, those who score low for extraversion are more inclined to feel negative emotions. This makes them more sceptical and more reflective, which means that they may be more likely to detect fraud attempts (Forgas & East, 2008). People who score high for extraversion generally ignore poor outcomes and focus on benefits (Johnston et al., 2016; Modic & Lea, 2011). They take greater risks, which in turn increases the chances of them misjudging fraudsters. In addition, people who score high for extraversion apparently have less self-control and with that are more impulsive, which increases the risk of online fraud victimisation even more (Modic & Lea, 2011). This applies particularly to types of online fraud, such as purchasing fraud, given that impulsive people do more online buying and pay less attention to certain conditions (Van Wilsem, 2013). It is also likely that people who are inclined to be impulsive may be more likely to respond to fake e-mails or advertisements, for instance. Taking these things into consideration, the prediction is that online fraud victims would score high for extraversion.

Openness, whereby people who score high are flexible and curious about new knowledge and experiences, while those who score low are more inclined to be conventional and to have a closed attitude (Burger et al., 2010; Hoekstra & De Fruyt, 2014). Because people with a high score for openness are open to new experiences and are inclined to share information, they may be at higher risk of falling victim to online fraud (Parrish et al., 2009). Also, people who score high seem to be less risk averse (Johnston et al., 2016). Because people who score low for openness are less open to new experiences, they may lack online experience (Modic & Lea, 2011). As a consequence, they may not be as good at recognising attempts at online fraud. Additionally, people who score low for openness are more inclined to accept authority (Hoekstra & De Fruyt, 2014), which in turn increases their vulnerability. After all, people often respond to fraudulent messages because they assume that the messages have come from an organisation with authority, and they want to comply (Jansen & Leukfeldt, 2015). People who score high for openness are more inquisitive and enterprising in nature (Hoekstra & De Fruyt, 2014; Korzaan & Boswell, 2008; Parrish et al., 2009). Because of this, they may get more technological experience, which in turn means that they may be more aware of online risks. Another possibility is that people who are more inquisitive and enterprising are more inclined to react to phishing e-mails, fake advertisements or telephone calls. Finally, people who score high for openness apparently have less self-control, which may increase the risk of online fraud victimisation (Modic & Lea, 2011). However, the findings of the research in which this was predicted pointed to the opposite: it emerged that people who got lower scores for openness were more inclined to react to online fraud attempts. They ignored their feelings, including most probably that 'gut feel' that something was not quite right. Bearing in mind that previous research into the openness dimension points in two different directions, no unequivocal predictions can be formulated about scores for openness among online fraud victims.

Altruism, whereby those who score high for this trait focus on interpersonal relationships and trust, while people who score low have a more antagonistic and egocentric attitude (Burger et al., 2010; Hoekstra & De Fruyt, 2014; De Raad & Perugini, 2002). A high score for altruism would lead to a person being more inclined to trust other people and to do what is asked of them (Parrish et al., 2009). This is linked to being sensitive to authority, which would make them more vulnerable to online fraud (Jones et al., 2015; Parrish et al., 2009). Victims of malware and phishing generally play an active part in the offence, often because they are taken in by social engineering tactics and fail to question these enough (Jansen & Leukfeldt, 2015). This kind of gullibility and inclination to comply is in line with a high score for altruism (McCrae & Costa, 1989; Hoekstra & De Fruyt, 2014; De Raad & Perugini, 2002). Previous research has shown that people who score high are more vulnerable to phishing attacks (Darwish, El Zarka, & Aloul, 2013). Because they are more helpful and expect that others have their interests at heart (Hoekstra & De Fruyt, 2014), their risk of falling victim to online fraud is increased even more. As a result, they will be less likely to have their doubts about the fraudster's intentions. That people who score low for altruism have a more sceptical attitude and critical mind-set (Hoekstra & De Fruyt, 2014) can lead to them being less likely to fall victim to online fraud. However, other research shows that people who score high for altruism are more sensitive to vulnerabilities in information security, which in turn means that they are more inclined to comply with security policies (Johnston et al., 2016). Despite this research, the prediction is that online fraud victims generally score high for altruism based on the arguments given.

Conscientiousness, whereby those who score high for this trait are diligent, conforming and thoughtful, while people who score low try to achieve their goals in a less strict and precise way (Burger et al., 2010; Hoekstra & De Fruyt, 2014; De Raad & Perugini, 2002). People who score high for conscientiousness may run less risk of online fraud victimisation considering that they are less irresponsible and are more inclined to act according to rules and procedures (Parrish et al., 2009). This may be an influencing factor because online fraud such as phishing requires following deviating 'procedures' (Jansen & Leukfeldt, 2015). Also, people who score high apparently carry out security scans on their computers more frequently (Wijn et al., 2016). Additionally, they are more sensitive to risks in information security, which means that they are more inclined to comply with security policies (Johnston et al., 2016). Moreover, they are inclined to analyse the available information properly before they draw conclusions and make decisions (Korzaan & Boswell, 2008). This may make them more aware of the implications of behaviour like sharing information. Self-control is an aspect of conscientiousness, whereby conscientious people are more likely to have self-control (McCrae & John, 1992). Subsequently, people with less self-control run a greater risk of falling victim to online fraud (Van Wilsem, 2013). From the previous studies, the prediction can be deduced that online fraud victims score low for the conscientiousness dimension.

Applying the Big Five personality traits does have some disadvantages. For instance, the five dimensions are intercorrelated, which goes against the model's original conditions. Furthermore, it can be argued that the model does not include enough factors because there are more than five dimensions to a personality. In addition, the Big Five was not based on empiricism, although a great deal of empirical support has been found for it (Cattell & Mead, 2008). Having said that, the five personality dimensions are found repeatedly and consistently, to the extent that some authors speak of the Big Five having the status of a law (Howard & Howard, 1995). Couching their words more cautiously, other authors call the Big Five the best available working hypothesis (De Raad & Perugini, 2002). In this chapter, the authors advocate viewing the Big Five in this way.

AN EXPLORATORY STUDY ON PERSONALITY TRAITS AND VICTIMS OF ONLINE FRAUD

Even though a great deal of exploratory research has been done into explanations for online fraud victimisation, it has produced few clear results thus far. Moreover, a study of the literature has shown that the routine activity approach is not very explanatory when it comes to online fraud. For this reason, the authors advocate further investigation. They suggest that this should be done by studying personality variables. Given that research in the context of online fraud is still in its infancy, the authors decided to add a new study to this chapter. By doing so, a new attempt is made to expand knowledge in this field. The authors demarcate online fraud to encompass three different types, namely 1) phishing, 2) Microsoft fraud and 3) purchasing fraud. The researchers selected these three offences because at the moment these are frequently occurring types of online fraud, as a result of which the offences have many victims. Another reason is because it is plausible that human factors – the theme of this chapter – play a part in these crimes given that these crimes involve deception (Jansen & Leukfeldt, 2015). The definitions of these kinds of online fraud have been included in the appendix.

This exploratory research investigates the extent to which online fraud victims differ from the Dutch population in terms of their personality traits. The main question of the research is therefore as follows:

'To what extent do online fraud victims differ from the Dutch population in terms of their personality traits?'

We also investigate the extent to which there are differences in the research findings for the three different types of online fraud. A principal reason for this is that cybercrimes in previous studies were often studied separately, as a result of which differing predictions can be stated about them. Secondly, the modus operandi for the various cybercrimes differ, which may lead to victims having differing attributes. Previous research has shown that various personality traits lead to various kinds of online vulnerability (Halevi et al., 2013).

Hypotheses Development

Based on what is known from the literature, as described in the previous section, the following predictions are outlined for the personal attributes of victims compared to the Dutch population.

H1: Online fraud victims score high for neuroticism compared to the Dutch population;
H2: Online fraud victims score high for extraversion compared to the Dutch population;
H3: Online fraud victims score neither high nor low for openness compared to the Dutch population;
H4: Online fraud victims score high for altruism compared to the dutch population;
H5: Online fraud victims score low for conscientiousness compared to the Dutch population.

Sample Selection

This study used a survey design. In order to get an adequate response rate, the objective was to select 300 respondents for each type of online fraud (phishing, Microsoft fraud, purchasing fraud). The authors assumed a minimum response rate of 10% ($N = 30$ per type of online fraud), which is a yardstick for an adequate sample size for meaningful statistical analysis.

For victims of phishing and Microsoft fraud, a sample was drawn from a system where national police records are stored (Basisvoorziening Informatie [BVI], in Dutch). Cognos was used to retrieve these kinds of victims from this BVI-database. Cognos is an information portal that can be used to search through police records. Searching for official reports was done using queries. For this, the researchers retrieved official reports from 2015.

The queries are compiled based on the literature on the subject, conversations with an advanced user of Cognos, and search terms used by the Dutch National Police Intelligence Service to select cybercrime offences. For phishing the query comprised one search term: *%phish%*. A range of terms were used for Microsoft fraud: *(malware% OR %virus% OR troja% OR worm% OR spyware OR cryptoware OR ransomware) NOT (%phish% OR %wormer%).*[1] The search term 'wormer' was excluded because this combination of letters occurs in the names of Dutch towns, which would then lead to unintentionally selecting irrelevant reports. The queries produced 642 official reports concerning phishing and 1,760 official reports concerning Microsoft fraud.

For victims of purchasing fraud, data from the police's national internet crime reporting point (Landelijk Meldpunt Internetoplichting [LMIO], in Dutch) was used because official reports of this type of online fraud are most frequently recorded by this reporting point. In order to get these reports the researchers submitted a request with the LMIO. The LMIO then provided all official reports from 2015, excluding those that had been withdrawn. This amounted to 37,886 official reports related to purchasing fraud.

Subsequently, the report files that had been collected (in Microsoft Excel format) were cleaned. This entailed only keeping the first official report from those people who had filed more than one report. Furthermore, informants under the age of 18 were excluded, as were those with invalid dates of birth. Excluding informants under the age of 18 was done for ethical reasons, and because personality traits are still stabilising in persons of that age (Hoekstra & De Fruyt, 2014). Informants residing abroad were also excluded. This resulted in 613 official reports for phishing, 1,579 for Microsoft fraud and 33,866 for purchasing fraud.

The software program 'Research Randomizer' (Urbaniak & Plous, 2015) was subsequently used to assign a random number to each report. After that, the numbers were sorted into chronological order. From the first report number onwards, the report text was read to find out whether the report actually did concern online fraud victimisation. This was done until around 300 reports had been selected. It can only be decided whether a report actually concerns online fraud if the report is read (Montoya, Junger, & Hartel, 2013). Moreover, companies were excluded because the study only encompasses private individuals. Official reports in which victimisation was demonstrably caused by someone else were also excluded. Furthermore, non-Dutch informants were excluded given that the questionnaire was in Dutch.

After reading through all 613 phishing reports, 290 met the criteria. For Microsoft fraud, reading 1,133 registrations led to the selection of 302 informants. For purchasing fraud, reading 524 registrations also led to the selection of 302 informants. Finally, the respondents' citizen service numbers were entered into the BVI-database to find the respondents' most recent address information from the Persons Database (Basisregistratie Personen [BRP], in Dutch). This was done to avoid sending correspondence to the wrong address. For purchasing fraud, 28 addresses of victims were not found because they presumably entered the wrong citizen service number when they filed their reports. For this reason, 28 additional victims were selected from the original database. Of those, five addresses from respondents could again not be retrieved when the citizen service numbers were requested from the BVI-database, leading to 297 valid addresses for victims of purchasing fraud. In total, 889 victims of online fraud remained.

The first author, who works as an investigating officer at the National Police of the Netherlands, gathered this information. The gathering of information for this research project is therefore permitted by the Dutch Police Data Act (Wet politiegegevens [Wpg], in Dutch).

Survey Questionnaire and Procedure

The questionnaire compiled for this research consisted of two sections: 1) questions about personality; and 2) questions about demographic attributes.

The first section consisted of 60 statements from the NEO Five-Factor Inventory-3 (NEO-FFI-3), which were used to measure the respondents' Big Five personality traits (Hoekstra & De Fruyt, 2014). This is an abridged version of the NEO Personality Inventory-3 (NEO-PI-3) in which personality traits are measured using 240 items. The NEO questionnaires are commonly used, researched, improved and maintained across the world. They are also known in the Netherlands for being a reliable way to measure the Big Five traits (Hoekstra & De Fruyt, 2014). Examples from statements on the NEO-FFI-3 are 'I often feel nervous and stressed'; 'Some people think I'm selfish and egotistical'; and 'I work hard to accomplish my goals'. The statements used a 5-point Likert-scale, ranging from 1) 'strongly disagree' to 5) 'strongly agree'. The polarised items were recoded with the effect that a higher item score stands for a higher score for the dimension in question. For each dimension, the items were added to form dimension scores.

In the second part, respondents were asked about their demographics, including gender, age, level of education, income and employment situation. For comparative purposes, this section is based on the measurements used in Statistics Netherlands' Statline.

Ten academic peers pre-tested the questionnaire before it was distributed. Based on this, the researchers decided to make some non-substantive amendments to the questionnaire; these amendments concerned adjusting the questionnaire layout and rewording the introductory text.

The questionnaire was then put online by an agency that designs online surveys. Potential respondents received an invitation letter that was printed on Dutch Police letter heads and formatted in line with the Dutch Police's house style. It contained an explanation of the research project, a link to the online survey and a unique code that gave one-off access to the questionnaire. Two weeks later, prospective respondents who had not yet participated were sent a reminder letter. The police chief of the Northern Netherlands unit, also portfolio holder for the Victim Care Department at the National Police, signed the letters. The intention here was to lend the research additional legitimacy. The survey was online from 21 October to 18 November 2016.

Survey Participants

Invitation letters were sent to 889 victims of online fraud. No invitation letters were returned, which indicates that the invitations ended up with the right people. In total, 385 respondents completed the questionnaire in full, which amounts to a response rate of 43.3%. Table 1 shows the respondent attributes by type of online fraud.

The gender and age of the victims are known from the information in the reports. For this reason, the researchers first checked the extent to which the respondents differed from the original sample in terms of these attributes. The chi-square test showed that the percentage of male respondents (62.6%) did not differ significantly from the percentage of men in the original sample (58.8%), $\chi^2 (1, 385) = 2.29, p = .13$. The age of the respondents did, however, differ significantly. With an average 58.1 years, it was higher than the original sample with its 50.7 years; $t (384) = 9.84, p < .01$.

The researchers also compared the respondent attributes to those of the Dutch population as a whole. The percentage of male respondents (62.6%) differed significantly from the percentage of men in the Dutch population according to Statline (2016a) (49.54%), $\chi^2 (1, 385) = 26.26, p < .01$. As for age, respondents were more likely to belong to the middle categories, and less likely to belong to the youngest and oldest categories compared with the Dutch population (Statline, 2016a) $\chi^2 (3, 385) = 126.05, p < .01$. It should be noted that the first age category in the Statline data begins at 20 years, while this category among the respondents begins at 19 years. For level of education, respondents were more likely to fall into the high category, and less likely to belong to the middle and low categories compared with the Dutch population (Statline, 2016b) $\chi^2 (2, 385) = 84.72, p < .01$. With respect to income levels, respondents were more likely to fall into the higher middle categories, and less likely to fall into the lower categories or the highest income category compared with the Dutch population (Statline, 2016c) $\chi^2 (5, 312) = 29.39, p < .01$. Finally, respondents were more likely to be unemployed and less likely to be working compared with the Dutch population (Statline, 2016d), $\chi^2 (1, 385) = 10.86, p < .01$. It should be noted that Statline bases its calculations for employment on the population aged 15-75 years.

Table 1. Respondent attributes by type of online fraud

Respondent Attribute / Fraud Type	Phishing (N = 150) Count (%)	Microsoft Fraud (N = 161) Count (%)	Purchasing Fraud (N = 74) Count (%)	Total (N = 385) Count (%)
Gender				
Female	56 (37.3%)	64 (39.8%)	24 (32.4%)	144 (37.4%)
Male	94 (62.7%)	97 (60.2%)	50 (67.6%)	241 (62.6%)
Age (years)				
<39	8 (5.3%)	13 (8.1%)	31 (41.9%)	5 (13.5%)
40-64	57 (38.0%)	85 (52.8%)	38 (51.4%)	180 (46.8%)
65-80	78 (52.0%)	58 (36.0%)	5 (6.8%)	141 (36.6%)
>80	7 (4.7%)	5 (3.1%)	-	12 (3.1%)
Education				
Low	43 (28.7%)	28 (17.4%)	21 (28.4%)	5 (23.9%)
Medium	37 (24.7%)	45 (28.0%)	23 (31.1%)	105 (27.3%)
High	70 (46.7%)	88 (54.7%)	30 (40.5%)	188 (48.8%)
Income (euros)				
<10,000	-	5 (3.1%)	6 (8.1%)	11 (2.9%)
10,000-20,000	20 (13.3%)	21 (13.0%)	1 (1.4%)	42 (10.9%)
20,000-30,000	39 (26.0%)	36 (22.4%)	18 (24.3%)	93 (24.2%)
30,000-40,000	25 (16.7%)	21 (13.0%)	13 (17.6%)	59 (15.3%)
40,000-50,000	23 (15.3%)	28 (17.4%)	9 (12.2%)	60 (15.6%)
>50,000	18 (12.0%)	14 (8.7%)	15 (20.3%)	47 (12.2%)
Unknown	25 (16.7%)	36 (22.4%)	12 (16.2%)	73 (19.0%)
Employment situation				
Employed	62 (41.3%)	74 (46.0%)	54 (73.0%)	190 (49.4%)
Not employed	88 (58.7%)	87 (54.0%)	20 (27.0%)	195 (50.6%)

Note: The age of participants ranged between 19-90 years (M = 58.1, SD = 14.7)

Data Analysis

To test the hypotheses, the data on Big Five personality traits were analysed using IBM's SPSS (version 23). The Cronbach's alpha for the personality dimensions are .82 for neuroticism, .72 for extraversion, .76 for openness, .70 for altruism and .75 for conscientiousness. This indicates that the measurements for personality constructs were reliable (> .70). The researchers used the norm groups as measured using NEO-FFI-3 for comparing the respondent attributes with the Dutch population. These norm groups give an overview of the average personality scores within the Dutch population. The norm group scores are based on a representative sample size of 1,715 individuals from the Dutch population in 2012 and 2013 (Hoekstra & De Fruyt, 2014).[2]

Comparisons were made with the average dimension scores for each Big Five dimension using *t*-tests. Analysis of variance (ANOVA) and a Bonferroni post hoc test were carried out to check whether there are differences in personality traits between the victims of the different types of online fraud. Separate *t*-tests were also carried out for each type of online fraud. Each time, a two-tailed test was carried out with a significance level of $\alpha = .05$. Further analyses were not possible because no data were collected from non-victims.

Results

First, the scores that the respondents achieved for personality dimensions were compared with those of the average in the Netherlands. The *t*-tests comparing the average dimension scores of the respondents and the average Dutch person are shown in Table 2.

The respondents' average dimension score for *neuroticism* ($M = 27.8$, $SD = 7.2$) is significantly lower than that of the Dutch population ($M = 34.0$, $SD = 7.5$, $t(384) = -16.71$, $p < .01$). This conflicts with the prediction that online fraud victims would score higher for neuroticism, thus not supporting H1. The respondents' average dimension score for *extraversion* ($M = 40.8$, $SD = 5.7$) is significantly higher than that of the Dutch population ($M = 39.3$, $SD = 5.8$, $t(384) = 5.13$, $p < .01$). This supports the prediction that online fraud victims would score high for extraversion compared to the population, thus supporting H2. For *openness*, no significant difference was found between the respondents' average dimension scores ($M = 38.9$, $SD = 6.6$) and the Dutch population ($M = 38.9$, $SD = 5.7$, $t(384) = -0.04$; $p = .97$). This supports the prediction that online fraud victims would neither score high nor low for openness compared to the Dutch population, thus supporting H3. The victims' average dimension score for *altruism* ($M = 45.0$, $SD = 5.2$) is significantly higher than the average for the Dutch population ($M = 41.1$, $SD = 5.6$, $t(384) = 14.82$, $p < .01$). This is in line with the prediction, thus supporting H4. The respondents' average dimension score for *conscientiousness* ($M = 47.7$, $SD = 5.2$) is also significantly higher than that of the average dimension score for the Dutch population ($M = 43.4$, $SD = 5.7$, $t(384) = 16.22$, $p < .01$). This conflicts with the prediction that online fraud victims would score low for conscientiousness compared to the population, thus not supporting H5.

An ANOVA was carried out to check whether the average dimension scores for victims of the different types of online fraud differed from one another. The results are shown in Table 3. Only the averages in the extraversion dimension differ significantly, $F(2, 385) = 10.18$, $p < .01$. A Bonferroni post hoc test was carried out to ascertain where these differences were to be found. It showed that the average score for extraversion for purchasing fraud victims ($M = 43.2$, $SD = 6.1$) is significantly higher ($p < .01$) than that of the phishing victims ($M = 40.9$, $SD = 5.2$) and of the Microsoft fraud victims ($M = 39.6$, $SD = 5.7$).

Table 2. Average scores for personality dimensions

	N	M (SD) Respondents	M (SD) Population	df	t
Neuroticism	385	27.8 (7.2)	34.0 (7.5)	384	-16.71**
Extraversion	385	40.8 (5.7)	39.3 (5.8)	384	5.13**
Openness	385	38.9 (6.6)	38.9 (5.7)	384	-0.04
Altruism	385	45.0 (5.2)	41.1 (5.6)	384	14.82**
Conscientiousness	385	47.7 (5.2)	43.4 (5.7)	384	16.22**

** $p < .01$

Table 3. Average scores for personality dimensions by type of online fraud

Personality Traits Fraud Type	Phishing (*N* = 150)	Microsoft Fraud (*N* = 161)	Purchasing Fraud (*N* = 74)		
	M (SD)	*M (SD)*	*M (SD)*	*df*	*F*
Neuroticism	27.3 (6.8)	28.7 (7.7)	26.9 (6.8)	2	2.21
Extraversion	40.9 (5.2)	39.6 (5.7)	43.2 (6.1)	2	10.18**
Openness	38.4 (6.4)	39.5 (6.6)	38.6 (6.6)	2	1.18
Altruism	44.6 (5.4)	45.6 (4.9)	44.8 (5.3)	2	1.61
Conscientiousness	48.0 (4.9)	47.3 (5.3)	48.0 (5.7)	2	0.94

**p < .01

Finally, the *t*-tests were repeated to compare the average dimension scores for each type of online fraud separately. As far as phishing and purchasing fraud were concerned, the results were in line with the results for all types of online fraud combined. For the victims of Microsoft fraud there is a deviation, which also differs from the stated predictions. For these victims, the average score for the personality dimension extraversion (*M* = 39.6, *SD* = 5.7) did not differ significantly from the average of the population (*M* = 39.3, *SD* = 5.8, *t* (160) = 0.75; *p* = .45).

DISCUSSION

The results discussed above answer the main research question: 'To what extent do online fraud victims differ from the Dutch population in terms of their personality traits?' As far as the Big Five attributes of neuroticism, extraversion, altruism and conscientiousness are concerned, online fraud victims differ from the Dutch population. The victims scored higher for altruism and conscientiousness, and lower for neuroticism. As far as extraversion is concerned, the victims of phishing and purchasing fraud scored higher than the Dutch population, and there was no difference between the victims of Microsoft fraud and the population. For openness, no difference with the Dutch population was found. The research findings for each Big Five dimension are discussed below. At the end of this chapter, the authors consider the research limitations.

- **Neuroticism:** The prediction was that online fraud victims would score high for neuroticism compared to the Dutch population. The research findings, however, did not confirm this prediction. A possible explanation for this has already been offered. Namely, a high score for neuroticism may lead to fear of computers, with the attendant risk-averse internet behaviour, or avoiding the internet altogether, as a consequence (Korzaan & Boswell, 2008). Also, the expectation was that people who score high for neuroticism would find it difficult to differentiate between the various types of offers that they are faced with (Halevi et al., 2013). Combined with their risk-taking behaviour, this can lead them to not responding to online requests, making them less likely to fall victim to online fraud. People who score high for neuroticism are also inclined to feel concerned or unsafe

(Burger et al., 2010; Hoekstra & De Fruyt, 2014). This may make them more alert and suspicious, reducing their chances of victimisation. Follow-up research is required to test these assumptions.

- **Extraversion:** In line with the prediction, online fraud victims scored high for extraversion compared to the Dutch population. This result matches the stated prediction. This is because people who score high for extraversion tend to be more impulsive (Modic & Lea, 2011). Impulsive people are inclined to do more online buying while paying less attention to certain conditions (Van Wilsem, 2013). Moreover, they tend to take more risks, which leads to increased chances to become victim of cybercrime (Saridakis, Benson, Ezingeard, & Tennakoon, 2016). That said, there was a difference between the various types of online fraud. Purchasing fraud victims scored higher for the extraversion dimension than phishing or Microsoft fraud victims. One finding that did not match the prediction was that the extraversion score that Microsoft fraud victims got did not differ from the score for the Dutch population. An explanation for this may also be sought in extraversion being related to impulsiveness. If someone, for instance, enters information after being approached via a phishing e-mail or responds to fake advertising, this may be viewed as impulsive behaviour. Microsoft fraud involves telephone scamming, whereby the victim is persuaded to download certain software. It can be argued that responding to what can sometimes be prolonged exposure to social engineering cannot be classified as impulsive behaviour. These assumptions should be investigated in future research.

- **Openness:** Consistent with the prediction, no differences were found between the openness scores of online fraud victims and those of the Dutch population. It is possible that several, opposite effects within this personality dimension play a role. After all, the inquisitiveness and inclination to share information that people who score high for openness have may lead to a higher risk of falling victim to online fraud (Burger et al., 2010; Halevi et al., 2013; Parrish et al., 2009). People who score low for openness may also be vulnerable to victimisation because they are inclined to be accepting of authority (Hoekstra & De Fruyt, 2014). Their lack of online experience and being less inclined to be open to new experiences may also contribute to this among those people who score low for openness (Modic & Lea, 2011). Follow-up research is required for testing these assumptions.

- **Altruism:** The predictions stated in the literature for altruism were corroborated. The respondents scored high for this dimension in comparison with the Dutch population. The findings indicate that people who are more altruistic are more likely to go along with the tactics that fraudsters use, as they are inclined to trust people and do what is asked of them (Darwish et al., 2013; Hoekstra & De Fruyt, 2014; Parrish et al., 2009). If they are inclined to attribute authority to fraudsters, then this inclination may have played a part in their victimisation (Jones et al., 2015; Parrish et al., 2009). Further research is required to establish whether these assumptions are correct.

- **Conscientiousness:** The predictions for conscientiousness were not consistent with the findings, given that the scores for online fraud victims were higher rather than lower than those of the Dutch population. One possible explanation is that people who score high for conscientiousness 'do what they have to do', and desist from doing what is not allowed (Burger et al., 2010; Hoekstra & De Fruyt, 2014). It is possible that respondents construed the fraudulent request as 'something that ought to be done', which in turn led to their victimisation. Follow-up research is necessary to demonstrate whether that is actually the case.

CONCLUSION AND FUTURE RESEARCH DIRECTIONS

This chapter has made it clear that explaining victimisation from the perspective of human factors is no mean feat. While the routine activity approach may seem promising, the findings from the literature do not give a clear picture of the risk factors associated with online fraud victimisation. The approach using personality traits as an explanatory factor also seems appropriate, but the literature as well as the study presented above demonstrate that future research is required to clarify in greater detail how these things work. The findings do, however, provide interesting points of departure for prevention.

According to the current study, the attributes that online fraud victims have do differ from those of 'the average Dutch person'. This makes it likely that people who score lower for neuroticism, and higher for extraversion, altruism and conscientiousness, run a greater risk of falling victim to online fraud. This insight offers opportunities for deploying targeted preventive measures. In this, organisations, such as the police and interest groups, can play a part in raising awareness and influencing behaviour. Selecting (i.e., targeting) people who get a particular score for the Big Five personality dimensions may seem like a difficult task. After all, it can hardly be expected from people to complete a questionnaire prior to every online threat so that protective measures or information can then be tailored to suit their personality. However, there is research on the subject that shows that it is possible to find out about a person's personality by looking at what they do on Facebook (Lambiotte & Kosinski, 2014). Additionally, with the help of these insights, communication messages aimed at prevention can be tailored to the preferences of people with certain personality traits, for instance, through their style or the way they communicate. Follow-up research may provide clues about the best way to approach people who score lower for neuroticism, and higher for extraversion, altruism and conscientiousness.

Respondent attributes showed that victims were more likely to be male, highly educated and have a higher middle income. As far as phishing and Microsoft fraud were concerned, most victims were between 65-80 years; for purchasing fraud they were under 64 years old (and working). Targeting people based on these demographic attributes is simpler. Also, selecting people with certain demographic attributes sometimes goes together with selecting people with certain personality traits because there are correlations between these attributes. For instance, scores for neuroticism tend to fall while those for altruism and conscientiousness tend to rise with age (Hoekstra & De Fruyt, 2014). Also, men tend to score lower for neuroticism and higher for extraversion compared to women. Further research into the exact relation between personality traits and demographic attributes is called for. The same applies to other attributes that may be associated with personality and which can be used to target potential victims.

Results from previous research indicate that the recommendations outlined are promising. For instance, there are indications that the effectiveness of interventions to persuade people to comply with security policies differs for people with different personality traits. For instance, sanction certainty is less effective for people who score high for extraversion and openness, while sanction severity is more effective for people who score high for altruism and conscientiousness, and low for neuroticism (Johnston et al., 2016). Other research has shown that women learned more than men from information about avoiding phishing attempts (Sheng, Holbrook, Kumaraguru, Cranor, & Downs, 2010). In addition, conscientious, extravert and open people are generally more motivated to learn (Major, Turner & Fletcher, 2006).

Despite the promising results given in this chapter, future research is necessary to get a more complete impression of the part that human factors play. It would be advisable to carry out studies among victims as well as non-victims of online fraud and other kinds of cybercrime. The sample for this research was drawn from victims who had reported the crime to the police, which limits the generalisability of the findings and makes it difficult to determine the causality between personality traits and online fraud victimisation. It would also be worthwhile carrying out qualitative research to determine this causality, so that the links can be brought to light more precisely and can thus be better understood. Additionally, experimental research is necessary in order to determine the effect of measures on the various groups of potential online fraud victims. The study presented here is a step in determining the part that personality plays in online fraud victimisation. Based on the findings, knowledge about victims of online fraud can be further deepened and broadened. This leads to evolving insights, and thus provides a broader basis for combating this common and harmful form of cybercrime more effectively.

REFERENCES

Bernaards, F., Monsma, E. & Zinn, P. (2012). *High tech crime: Criminaliteitsbeeldanalyse 2012* [High-tech crime: Crime image analysis 2012]. Driebergen: Korps Landelijke Politiediensten.

Bloem, B., & Harteveld, A. (2012). *Horizontale fraude: Verslag van een onderzoek voor het Nationaal dreigingsbeeld 2012 [Horizontal fraud: Research report on the national threat assessment 2012]*. Zoetermeer: Dienst IPOL.

Bossler, A. M., & Holt, T. J. (2009). On-line activities, guardianship, and malware infection: An examination of routine activities theory. *International Journal of Cyber Criminology*, *3*(1), 400–420.

Bossler, A. M., & Holt, T. J. (2010). The effect of self-control on victimization in the cyberworld. *Journal of Criminal Justice*, *38*(3), 227–236. doi:10.1016/j.jcrimjus.2010.03.001

Bullée, J. W. (2017). *Experimental social engineering investigation and prevention*. Enschede, The Netherlands: CTIT. doi:10.3990/1.9789036543972

Burger, Y., De Caluwé, L., & Jansen, P. (2010). *Mensen veranderen: Waarom, wanneer en hoe mensen (niet) veranderen [People change: Why, when and how people change or do not change]*. Deventer: Kluwer.

Cattell, H. E. P., & Mead, A. D. (2008). The sixteen personality factor questionnaire (16PF). In G. J. Boyle, G. Matthews, & D. H. Saklofske (Eds.), *The SAGE handbook of personality theory and assessment* (pp. 135–178). Los Angeles, CA: SAGE Publications.

Choi, K. (2008). Computer crime victimization and integrated theory: An empirical assessment. *International Journal of Cyber Criminology*, *2*(1), 308–333.

Chua, C. E. H., Wareham, J., & Robey, D. (2007). The role of online trading communities in managing internet auction fraud. *Management Information Systems Quarterly*, *31*(4), 759–781.

Cohen, L. E., & Felson, M. (1979). Social change and crime rate trends: A routine activity approach. *American Sociological Review*, *44*(4), 588–608. doi:10.2307/2094589

Darwish, A., El Zarka, A., & Aloul, F. (2013). *Towards understanding phishing victims' profile*. Paper presented at the International Conference of Computer Systems and Industrial Informatics, Bochum, Germany.

De Raad, B., & Perugini, M. (Eds.). (2002). *Big Five assessment*. Göttingen: Hogrefe & Huber Publishers.

Forgas, J. P., & East, R. (2008). On being happy and gullible: Mood effects on skepticism and the detection of deception. *Journal of Experimental Social Psychology, 44*(5), 1362–1367. doi:10.1016/j.jesp.2008.04.010

Furnell, S. M., Bryant, P., & Phippen, A. D. (2007). Assessing the security perceptions of personal internet users. *Computers & Security, 26*(5), 410–417. doi:10.1016/j.cose.2007.03.001

Halevi, T., Lewis, J., & Memon, N. (2013). A pilot study of cyber security and privacy related behavior and personality traits. In *Proceedings of the 22nd International Conference on World Wide Web*. New York, NY: ACM. doi:10.1145/2487788.2488034

Harrell, E., & Langton, L. (2013). *Victims of identity theft, 2012*. Washington, DC: Bureau of Justice Statistics.

Hern, A., & Gibbs, S. (2017). *What is WannaCry ransomware and why is it attacking global computers?* Retrieved from https://www.theguardian.com/technology/2017/may/12/nhs-ransomware-cyber-attack-what-is-wanacrypt0r-20

Hoekstra, H., & De Fruyt, F. (2014). *NEO-PI-3 en NEO-FFI-3 persoonlijkheidsvragenlijsten: Handleiding [NEO-PI-3 and NEO-PI-3 personality questionnaires: Manual]*. Amsterdam: Hogrefe Uitgevers.

Howard, P. J., & Howard, J. M. (1995). *The Big Five quickstart: An introduction to the five-factor model of personality for human resource professionals*. Charlotte, NC: Center for Applied Cognitive Studies.

Hutchings, A., & Hayes, H. (2009). Routine activity theory and phishing victimisation: Who gets caught in the 'net'? *Current Issues in Criminal Justice, 20*(3), 1–20.

Jansen, J., Junger, M., Kort, J., Leukfeldt, R., Veenstra, S., Van Wilsem, J., & Van der Zee, S. (2017). Victims. In R. Leukfeldt (Ed.), *Research agenda: The human factor in cybercrime and cybersecurity*. The Hague, The Netherlands: Eleven International Publishing.

Jansen, J., & Leukfeldt, E. R. (2015). How people help fraudsters steal their money: An analysis of 600 online banking fraud cases. In *Proceedings of the 2015 Workshop on Socio-Technical Aspects in Security and Trust (STAST)*, Washington, DC: IEEE Computer Society. doi:10.1109/STAST.2015.12

Jansen, J., & Leukfeldt, E. R. (2016). Phishing and malware attacks on online banking customers in the Netherlands: A qualitative analysis of factors leading to victimization. *International Journal of Cyber Criminology, 10*(1), 79–91.

Jansen, J., Leukfeldt, E. R., Van Wilsem, J. A., & Stol, W. Ph. (2013). *Onlinegedragingen: Een risico voor hacken en persoonsgerichte cyberdelicten?* (Online behaviour: A risk for hacking and person-oriented cybercrimes?). *Tijdschrift voor Criminologie, 55*(4), 394–408. doi:10.5553/TvC/0165182X2013055004005

Johnston, A. C., Warkentin, M., McBride, M., & Carter, L. (2016). Dispositional and situational factors: Influences on information security policy violations. *European Journal of Information Systems, 25*(3), 231–251. doi:10.1057/ejis.2015.15

Jones, C. S., & Hartley, N. T. (2013). Comparing correlations between four-quadrant and five-factor personality assessments. *American Journal of Business Education, 6*(4), 459–470. doi:10.19030/ajbe.v6i4.7945

Jones, H. S., Towse, J. N., & Race, N. (2015). Susceptibility to email fraud: A review of psychological perspectives, data-collection methods, and ethical considerations. *International Journal of Cyber Behavior, Psychology and Learning, 5*(3), 13–29. doi:10.4018/IJCBPL.2015070102

Korzaan, M. L., & Boswell, K. T. (2008). The influence of personality traits and information privacy concerns on behavioral intentions. *Journal of Computer Information Systems, 48*(4), 15–24.

Lambiotte, R., & Kosinski, M. (2014). Tracking the digital footprints of personality. *Proceedings of the IEEE, 102*(12), 1934–1939. doi:10.1109/JPROC.2014.2359054

Lastdrager, E. E. H. (2014). Achieving a consensual definition of phishing based on a systematic review of the literature. *Crime Science, 3*(1), 1–6. doi:10.1186/s40163-014-0009-y

Leukfeldt, E. R. (2015). Comparing victims of phishing and malware attacks: Unravelling risk factors and possibilities for situational crime prevention. *International Journal of Advanced Studies in Computer Science and Engineering, 4*(5), 26–32.

Major, D. A., Turner, J. E., & Fletcher, T. D. (2006). Linking proactive personality and the Big Five to motivation to learn and development activity. *The Journal of Applied Psychology, 91*(4), 927–935. doi:10.1037/0021-9010.91.4.927 PMID:16834515

McBride, M., Carter, L., & Warkentin, M. (2012). *Exploring the role of individual employee characteristics and personality on employee compliance with cybersecurity policies*. Washington, DC: RTI International.

McCrae, R. R., & Costa, P. T. (1989). Reinterpreting the Myers-Briggs Type Indicator from the perspective of the five-factor model of personality. *Journal of Personality, 57*(1), 17–40. doi:10.1111/j.1467-6494.1989.tb00759.x PMID:2709300

McCrae, R. R., & John, O. P. (1992). An introduction to the five-factor model and its applications. *Journal of Personality, 60*(2), 175–215. doi:10.1111/j.1467-6494.1992.tb00970.x PMID:1635039

Modic, D., & Lea, S. E. G. (2011). *How neurotic are scam victims, really? The Big Five and internet scams*. Paper presented at the 2011 Conference of the International Confederation for the Advancement of Behavioral Economics and Economic Psychology, Exeter, UK.

Montoya, L., Junger, M., & Hartel, P. (2013). How 'digital' is traditional crime? In *Proceedings of the 2013 European Intelligence and Security Informatics Conference (EISIC 2013)*. Washington, DC: IEEE Computer Society. doi:10.1109/EISIC.2013.12

NCSC. (2015). Cybersecuritybeeld Nederland (CSBN) 2015 [Cyber security assessment Netherlands (CSAN) 2015]. The Hague, The Netherlands: National Cyber Security Centre.

NCSC. (2016). *Cyber security assessment Netherlands (CSAN 2016)*. The Hague, The Netherlands: National Cyber Security Centre.

Ngo, F. T., & Paternoster, R. (2011). Cybercrime victimization: An examination of individual and situational level factors. *International Journal of Cyber Criminology, 5*(1), 773–793.

Parks-Leduc, L., Feldman, G., & Bardi, A. (2014). Personality traits and personal values: A meta-analysis. *Personality and Social Psychology Review, 19*(1), 3–29. doi:10.1177/1088868314538548 PMID:24963077

Parrish, J. L., Baily, J. L., & Courtney, J. F. (2009). A personality based model for determining susceptibility to phishing attacks. Decision Sciences Institute.

Pratt, T. C., Holtfreter, K., & Reisig, M. D. (2010). Routine online activity and internet fraud targeting: Extending the generality of routine activity theory. *Journal of Research in Crime and Delinquency*, *47*(3), 267–296. doi:10.1177/0022427810365903

Pyrooz, D. C., Decker, S. H., & Moule, R. K. Jr. (2015). Criminal and routine activities in online settings: Gangs, offenders, and the Internet. *Justice Quarterly*, *32*(3), 471–499. doi:10.1080/07418825.2013.778326

Saridakis, G., Benson, V., Ezingeard, J. N., & Tennakoon, H. (2016). Individual information security, user behaviour and cyber victimisation: An empirical study of social networking users. *Technological Forecasting and Social Change*, *102*, 320–330. doi:10.1016/j.techfore.2015.08.012

Sheng, S., Holbrook, M., Kumaraguru, P., Cranor, L., & Downs, J. (2010). *Who falls for phish? A demographic analysis of phishing susceptibility and effectiveness of interventions*. Paper presented at The SIGCHI Conference on Human Factors in Computing Systems, Atlanta, GA.

Statline. (2016a). *Bevolking: Kerncijfers* [Population: Key figures]. Retrieved from http://statline.cbs.nl/StatWeb/publication/?VW=T&DM=SLNL&PA=37296ned&D1=a&D2=0,10,20,30,40,50,60,(1-1),l&HD=130605-0924&HDR=G1&STB=T.

Statline. (2016b). *Bevolking: Hoogst behaald onderwijsniveau* [Population: Highest attained level of education]. Retrieved from http://statline.cbs.nl/Statweb/publication/?DM=SLNL&PA=82275NED&D1=0&D2=0&D3=0&D4=0-1,4-5&D5=1,7,11&D6=64&VW=T

Statline. (2016c). *Inkomensklassen: Particuliere huishoudens naar diverse kenmerken* [Income brackets: Personal households according to various attributes]. Retrieved from http://statline.cbs.nl/Statweb/publication/?DM=SLNL&PA=70958ned&D1=0&D2=2&D3=1-8&D4=0,68-72,75-76&D5=l&HDR=T,G3,G4,G1&STB=G2&VW=T

Statline. (2016d). *Arbeidsdeelname: Kerncijfers* [Rate of employment: Key figures]. Retrieved from http://statline.cbs.nl/Statweb/publication/?DM=SLNL&PA=82309NED&D1=0-11,13-15,18-23&D2=0&D3=0-3,7-8&D4=0&D5=55-58,60-67&HDR=G4&STB=G1,G2,G3,T&VW=T

Stol, W. Ph., Leukfeldt, E. R., & Klap, H. (2012). Cybercrime en politie: Een schets van de Nederlandse situatie anno 2012 [Cybercrime and the police: A sketch of the situation in the Netherlands anno 2012]. *Justitiële Verkenningen*, *38*(1), 25–39.

Sutton, M. (2009). Product design: CRAVED and VIVA. In B. S. Fisher & S. P. Lab (Eds.), *Encyclopedia of Victimology and Crime Prevention*. Thousand Oaks, CA: Sage.

Urbaniak, G. C., & Plous, S. (2015). Research Randomizer (Version 4.0) [software]. Retrieved via: http://www.randomizer.org/

Van der Hulst, R. C., & Neve, R. J. M. (2008). *High tech crime, soorten criminaliteit en hun daders: Een literatuurinventarisatie [High-tech crime, types of crimes and offenders: An inventory of literature]*. The Hague, The Netherlands: Boom Juridische uitgevers.

Van Wilsem, J. (2011). Worlds tied together? Online and non-domestic routine activities and their impact on digital and traditional threat victimization. *European Journal of Criminology*, 8(2), 115–127. doi:10.1177/1477370810393156

Van Wilsem, J. (2013). 'Bought it, but never got it': Assessing risk factors for online consumer fraud victimization. *European Sociological Review*, 29(2), 168–178. doi:10.1093/esr/jcr053

Wiederhold, B. K. (2014). The role of psychology in enhancing cybersecurity. *Cyberpsychology, Behavior, and Social Networking*, 17(3), 131–132. doi:10.1089/cyber.2014.1502 PMID:24592869

Wijn, R., Van den Berg, H., Wetzer, I. M., & Broekman, C. C. M. T. (2016). Supertargets: Verkenning naar voorspellende en verklarende factoren voor slachtofferschap van cybercriminaliteit [Super targets: Exploration of predictive and explanatory factors for cybercrime victimisation]. Soesterberg: Netherlands Organisation for Applied Scientific Research (TNO).

Yar, M. (2005). The novelty of cybercrime: An assessment in light of routine activity theory. *European Journal of Criminology*, 2(4), 407–427. doi:10.1177/147737080556056

ENDNOTES

[1]   It should be noted that the researchers initially planned to extract general malware victims from the database. However, the query resulted in a large representation of one type of 'malware', namely Microsoft fraud. Therefore, this type of fraud is chosen to adopt in the current study.

[2]   Online fraud victims are also part of the Dutch population. This is not a drawback; the method used only renders it less likely that a difference will be found than if a comparison were to be made between online fraud victims and non-online fraud victims.

Chapter 3
The "Human Factor" in Cybersecurity:
Exploring the Accidental Insider

Lee Hadlington
De Montfort University, UK

ABSTRACT

A great deal of research has been devoted to the exploration and categorization of threats posed from malicious attacks from current employees who are disgruntled with the organisation, or are motivated by financial gain. These so-called "insider threats" pose a growing menace to information security, but given the right mechanisms, they have the potential to be detected and caught. In contrast, human factors related to aspects of poor planning, lack of attention to detail, and ignorance are linked to the rise of the accidental or unintentional insider. In this instance there is no malicious intent and no prior planning for their "attack," but their actions can be equally as damaging and disruptive to the organisation. This chapter presents an exploration of fundamental human factors that could contribute to an individual becoming an unintentional threat. Furthermore, key frameworks for designing mitigations for such threats are also presented, alongside suggestions for future research in this area.

INTRODUCTION

The focus of this current chapter is to examine the impact human factors, including aspects of personality traits or cognitive factors that can serve to influence cybersecurity practices and behaviors. The background against which this exploration is framed is related to the insider threat, more specifically those that have no specific motive or malicious intent. The chapter will begin with an examination of key statistics related to cybercrime in business as well as introducing current concerns related to the 'insider threat'. The typology of the insider threat will be discussed in brief, but then will shift to focus more directly on the notion of an 'accidental insider' – those individuals who have no malicious intent to commit transgressions of cybersecurity, but do so through misjudgment, ignorance and lack of understanding/knowledge.

DOI: 10.4018/978-1-5225-4053-3.ch003

Following on from this, the focus will then turn towards research examining key human factors that could influence the cybersecurity posture of the individual. This includes potential links between psychology traits such as impulsivity, decision-making and conscientiousness and information security. The concluding aspects for the chapter will focus on key techniques and frameworks that have the potential to change the behaviors of end-users. These techniques hopefully move individuals towards better cyber-inoculation, and provide mitigation for the threat from the accidental insider.

BACKGROUND

In a recent report published by the Office of National Statistics (ONS, 2016) it was estimated that online fraud was costing companies an estimated £193bn. Furthermore, the survey also noted that 5.8 million individual incidents of cybercrime had been reported in the year 2015-16; these were split between fraudulent activities (bank/credit card account fraud/advance fee fraud) and computer misuse (distribution of computer viruses/unauthorized access to computers/hacking). The Business Crime Survey (BCS, 2015) also noted a 55% increase in reported online fraud between 2014-15. In the same report, one of the key concerns raised was the growing threat from individuals within the organization, or the so called 'insider threat'. This latter point is mirrored by an apparent realization by researchers within the information security community that, for the most part, the weakest element in the cybersecurity chain is that of the human (Anwar et al., 2016; Nurse, Creese, Goldsmith, & Lamberts, 2011; Sasse, Brostoff, & Weirich, 2001; Sasse & Flechais, 2005).

In the context of the continued fight to protect business and organizations from the threat being posed by information theft and cybercrime a great deal of attention is devoted to improving the existing security infrastructure (Pfleeger & Caputo, 2012). Attempts to enhance network security via technological solutions such firewalls, intrusion detection, and biometric devices provide some legitimate protection against a wide variety of threats. However, these steps make an assumption that all threats to the security of the organization are inward facing, and come from an external source or attacker. Early commentators in the area of cybersecurity noted that one of the biggest barriers to creating effective information security strategies is the human elements within the system (Whitten & Tygar, 1998). From a usability perspective it is noted that, for the most part, security protocols and systems are either too confusing or too difficult for the average end-user to engage in effectively (Whitten & Tygar, 1998; Sasse & Flechais, 2005). Accordingly, Sasse and Flechais (2005) noted that the situation is further complicated by additional aspects related to human factors including:

- A lack of understanding on behalf of employees about the importance of the data, software and systems within an organisation
- Ignorance about the level of risk attached to the assets for which they have direct responsibility for and
- A lack of understanding about how their behaviour could be putting the same assets at risk (Sasse & Flechais, 2005).

EXAMINING THE INSIDER THREAT

Establishing the Concept of 'an Insider'

In any system that incorporates an aspect of human activity the concept of 'insider threat' has the potential to impact on that system. In recent years the concept of insider threat has garnered more attention, presenting a growing concern for the internal security of organizations (Greitzer, Kangas, Noonan, & Dalton, 2010; Greitzer et al., 2016; Keeney, 2005; Probst, Hunker, Gollmann, & Bishop, 2010). In the context of businesses, the threat from an insider is multifaceted and can related to breaches in security, effects on the outward prestige of the company, and related financial loss (CPNI, 2013).

Defining a workable framework for insider threat in the context of cyber systems has proven problematic. Bishop and Gates (2008) noted a great deal of disagreement surrounding the definitions of what constitutes an insider threat. They pointed out that such a lack of consistency has the effect of preventing the development of a clear theoretical framework for investigating such an issue. With this view in mind, Bishop and Gates (2008) suggested that a unified approach would allow clearer and more effective methods for the detection of such threats. Moreover, the problematic nature of this area is further compounded when questions about what should be seen as "inside" and what elements remain "outside" of the threat perimeter are considered.

The label of insider threat makes an erroneous assumption that there is a clearly defined 'inside' within which any particular threat can be clearly encapsulated. The parameters that contribute to the notion of an insider become further blurred when viewed against the backdrop of modern working practices. This is particularly salient in instances where companies are increasingly outsourcing aspects of work to subcontractors or where the use of mobile computing allows any number of external bodies access to systems outside the physical sphere (Bishop & Gates, 2008).

In order to provide a theoretical framework for further discussion, the following section presents a brief overview of the research exploring the malicious insider threat. This is contrasted to threats based on ignorance, lack of education, and awareness, or the commonly referred to accidental or unintentional insider threat.

The Malicious Insider

Much of the research literature on the insider threat focuses on the view that these are individuals who have deep-seated malicious intent, and are conducting covert activities for financial and personal gain. For example, the definition presented by Cappelli, Moore, and Silowash (2012) is:

A current or former employee, contractor, or business partner who has or had authorized access to an organization's network, system, or data and intentionally exceeded or misused that access in a manner that negatively affected the confidentiality, integrity, or availability of the organization's information or information systems. (p. xiii)

The research exploring the underlying psychology of the malicious insider is based, for the most part, on a small number of case studies in which the insider threat has been caught. For example Cappelli,

Moore, and Trzeciak, (2012) explored findings from ten case studies. Other researcher, such as Shaw, Ruby, and Post (1998) had previously identified four core indicators for an individual to becoming an insider threat, these included:

1. **Negative Life Experiences**: In this instance the individual expresses their disgruntlement with set-backs in their life through overt displays of anger which are directed towards both peers and those in positions of authority. The individual also presents a low threshold for frustration which is also overtly manifest through aggressive outburst.

2. **Lack of Social Skills and Isolation**: Insiders are assumed to demonstrate a lack of social skills and also exhibit a tendency for social isolation. There is some suggestion here that an *a priori* lack of social skills may preclude the individual in question to becoming isolated, which in turn may lead them to pursue such interactions in other ways such as through online social networking. This heavy reliance on computer-mediated forms of communication means that such individuals are unable to deal with social/emotional issues encountered in workplace situations effectively. As suggested by Shaw et al. (1998) a combination of these elements could lead to the individual retaining feelings of frustration and disgruntlement. This in turn could be overtly viewed in difficult social interactions with peers and work colleagues as well as what is termed "emotional leakage", outbursts that are of a magnitude that far outweigh the nature of the incident.

3. **Sense of Entitlement:** Insiders are proposed to suffer from a sense of entitlement, usually afforded to them via special privileges or access rights they have been permitted in pursuit of their duties. The individual may possess a special skill set that allows them to leverage such special treatment and may be further manifest through poor treatment of peers whom they may view as inferior. They may also have difficulty in adapting to specific rules or protocols that have been put into place by the organisation, perhaps fitting into the Proprietors category highlighted earlier.

4. **Ethical Flexibility:** This is another area in which insiders are deemed to exhibit some degree of underdevelopment. This notion means that insiders may suffer from an inability to empathize with colleagues or others that would usually prevent an individual from engaging in acts of insider threat. Such immaturity is also linked to a breakdown in the inhibitory processes that control emotional outbursts in aspects such as aggression.

Findings from the CPNI (2013) report added some more specific detail to the personality traits that have been associated with those who have committed insider threat. In the context of the CPNI report insider threat was defined as 'a person who exploits, or has the intention to exploit, their legitimate access to an organisation's assets for unauthorised purposes' (p. 4). This study explored 120 UK-based case studies on insider threat, and collated those key elements that had a significant impact on behaviour as well as others within the environment. These personality traits are summarised as:

- **Immaturity:** The individual is seen to lack in overall life experience and falls into the category of being "high maintenance" in terms of the attention and guidance they require; also have clear difficulties in making critical life decisions.
- **Low Self-Esteem**: Lacks confidence in social situations and has a heavy dependence on recognition and praise from others; finds it hard to cope with adverse social situations, criticism and tasks that fall outside of their comfort zone.

- **Amoral and Unethical**: The individual lacks any clear understanding of morality and shows no remorse for their behaviour, particularly in terms of the effect this may have on others.
- **Superficial**: The majority of insiders lack a clear sense of self and identity, presenting someone that is described as being "hard to know" by peers and colleagues.
- **Restless and Impulsive**: A common element that crops up in a variety of places when discussing the nature of the insider's personality. Individual is seen to require constant stimulation and also is highly hedonistic (the requirement to seek pleasure above all other needs is apparent in someone with a hedonistic personality).
- **Lacks Conscientiousness:** Has a disregard for established rules and practices; clearly neglects workplace duties and responsibilities; poor attention to detail, poor judgement and a lack of focus.
- **Manipulative:** Uses their skills of persuasion to get their own way and will garner relationships that will serve to nurture their own self-interest. Also seen to adopt a social position that aids in serving their own needs, such as being agreeable and compliant to those in position of power.
- **Emotionally Unstable:** Prone to a variety of exaggerated mood swings and overt over reactions to problems; appears to complain about the most trivial of incidents.
- **Evidence of Some Underlying Psychological or Personality Disorder:** The CPNI report is vague about this aspect with little specific details on this aspect of the personality profile for the Insider, or indeed how this aspect was measured in their study.

Further to this, the CPNI report also highlights situational aspects that are evident in the psychosocial environment of the insider. These elements are split into two underlying categories:

- "Lifestyle changes" which are related to a change in personal circumstances and thus a change in experienced levels of stress.
- "Circumstantial vulnerabilities" which in the context of the CPNI report refer to "work, profile or personal issues that could make an individual vulnerable" (p.11).

The CPNI report presents a number of key predictors, based on aspects of the individual's life experiences and psychological factors, viewed as being of critical importance in the development of a potential insider threat. These are:

- **Demonstrating Poor Work Attitude:** A failure to follow accepted protocol or to read important documentation about new procedures or operating instructions.
- **Shows Signs of Being Stressed:** Overt symptoms of stress that include loss of temper, apathy (burnout), increase in nervous habits (ticks, aspects of OCD), problems with memory and concentration, evidence of confusion, difficulty in making decisions.
- **Exploitable or Vulnerable Lifestyle:** Has an element of their lifestyle which allows them to be exploited by an external force or agent e.g. serious financial stress, alcohol abuse, drug addiction, gambling – each of these could lead to a strong desire for financial gain.
- **Exploitable or Vulnerable Work Profile:** The individual's position within the company allows them access to highly prized or sought-after assets which in turn could be marketed for profit
- **Recent Negative Life Events:** A variety of elements could be included here, such as problems at work, loss of status (socially and work), personal injury, bereavement, relationship breakup, financial difficulty or loss.

However, these concepts are only directly applicable to those attacks accompanied by a level of intentionality or direct motive. Other researchers have argued against the overarching label of 'insider threat' and moved towards a more flexible term of insiderness (Bishop, Gollmann, Hunker, & Probst, 2008; Hunker & Probst, 2011). These researchers have argued that insider threat is more adequately represented in the form of a continuum rather than a dichotomy. Hunker and Probst (2011) compared the actions of an accidental insider to that of a 'real insider', with the latter being the group of individuals who exhibit malicious intent in their exploits. This real insider group also poses a great deal of skill and expertise, which could include knowledge related to programming, IT infrastructure and company systems that allow for a more holistic view of the attack landscape. At the opposite end of the continuum there are the accidental or unintentional insiders, who may have limited knowledge of accepted security protocols, their actions are obvious, and they make no direct attempt to cover up their mistakes. It is these 'accidental insiders' who present the focus for this current chapter, alongside an examination of how individual differences could make certain people more prone to lapses in cybersecurity.

The Accidental or Unintentional Insider

In order to account for incidences of unintentional insider threat (UIT; CERT, 2013) a further definition was presented:

An unintentional insider threat is a current or former employee, contractor, or business partner who has or had authorized access to an organization's network, system, or data and who, through action or inaction without malicious intent, causes harm or substantially increases the probability of future serious harm to the confidentiality, integrity, or availability of the organization's information or information systems. (CERT, 2013, p. ix)

This definition for UIT focuses directly on threat as a result of inaction or indeed a specific lack of knowledge on the behalf of the individual alongside the lack of actual intent to cause harm. Thus, the key components to the conceptualization of UIT are elements of human failure or limitations related to human performance (CERT, 2013). This has the potential to include mistakes made though time pressures exerted as a result of a job, the level of task difficulty, a lack of knowledge, and cognitive factors such as inattention (CERT, 2013). Examples of unintentional insider threat presented by CERT (2013) included the accidental disclosure of sensitive information (either via website, email or fax); an individual devolving log-in details (password and username) as a result of social engineering or via malware/spyware; the improper disposal of physical records; and the loss of information through the misplacement of portable equipment including smartphones, USB drives, CDs and hard drives. These random acts are of greater potential concern for organizations as they typically have no motive, no direct intent and no prior indicators upon which to act. Unfortunately, the end result is still the same, and the actions of the unintentional insider can be as damaging as those perpetrated by the malicious attacker.

The concept of UIT presents another perspective from which researchers and security professionals can begin to explore the potential threats presented in any system that incorporates humans. The CERT (2014) report noted that over 40% of computer and organizational security professionals believed accidental insiders were the greatest potential source of risk. However, to date, very few attempts have been made to examine how aspects of human factors serve to influence the potential for UIT. This may be in part due to a lack of research focus or the belief that technical solutions alone can provide the mitigation for such.

The rest of this chapter will focus on exploring how a better understanding of underlying human factors could influence aspects of cybersecurity. The first part will explore research that attempted to develop effective scales in order to assess the individual's adherence to effective cybersecurity principles alongside key psychological traits.

Assessing Information Security Behaviors

A variety of attempts have been made to create effective scales designed to record aspects individual adherence to cybersecurity protocols. For the most part these have been deployed in work-based environments, with a respective gap in scales being developed for younger populations and individuals not in employment. It has also been noted that many previous scales have a very narrow focus and explore just one aspect of cybersecurity such as passwords (Stanton et al. (2005), mobile computing (Mylonas et al., 2013) and specific security features of key applications (Furnell et al., 2006; Parsons, McCormac, Butavicius, Pattinson, & Jerram, 2014).

Siponen, Pahnila, and Mahmood (2010) presented one recent attempt to produce a scale that was designed to explore individual attitudes towards information security. The focus of this study was to examine key reasons why certain employees were more likely to comply with the cybersecurity polices of the organization. Their findings suggested that the existence of social pressure from both peers and superiors within their organization influenced the potential for adherence to such policies. It was noted that if peers and superiors have a positive cybersecurity posture this would in turn permeate throughout the organization to its other members. The individual's self-efficacy in the context of cybersecurity was also shown to be a key determiner in their capacity to engage in effective cyber inoculation. For example, Siponen et al. (2010) present the instance of an individual who unwittingly sends confidential information out through email without encrypting it. According to Siponen et al. (2010) the individual must have the knowledge or capacity to encrypt this information before they can actually engage in that behavior. From this regard, if the individual has no awareness of the security policies of the organization, they cannot align to them, and hence are in danger of contravening them through ignorance and misunderstanding. However later researchers noted that the items used within the scale produced by Siponen et al. (2010) were very basic in nature and had the potential to produce an inherent bias, thus leading to an overall underestimation of the current security issues being faced within organisations (McCormac, Parsons, Zwaans, Butavicius, & Pattinson, 2016).

Egelman and Peer (2015a, 2015b) presented the development of the Security Behavior Intention Scale (SeBIS) that comprised of 16-items designed to assess adherence to information security advice. The SeBIS included 4 key sub-scales that measured attitudes towards password generation, securing digital devices, engaging in proactive awareness and updating software. In their initial testing, the researchers explored the relationship of security behaviors to a variety of psychological constructs. These included:

- **Domain-Specific Risk-Taking Scale** (DoSpeRT; Blais & Weber, 2006):
    - A measure that explores the capacity to engage in risk taking behaviours across five key areas including ethical, financial, health and safety, recreational and social.
- **General Decision-Making Style** (GDMS; Scott & Bruce, 1995):

- A measure for how people approach decision-making in association with five dimensions that include rationality, avoidance, dependence, intuition and spontaneity.
- **Need for Cognition** (NFC; Cacioppo, Petty, & Feng Kao, 1984):
  - This is an individual's preference or tendency to engage in and gain pleasure from cognitively effortful activities.
- **Barratt Impulsiveness Scale** (BIS; Patton, Stanford, & Barratt, 1995):
  - Explores impulsivity on three dimensions related to non-planning, attention and motor impulsiveness.
- **Consideration for Future Consequences** (CFC; Joireman, Shaffer, Balliet, & Strathman, 2012):
  - This scale measures the individual's capacity to consider potential future outcomes for their present actions.

The results from initial testing using the SeBIS demonstrated a variety of relationships with the above measures. Each of the four sub-scales for the SeBIS correlated positively with inquisitiveness as measured by the need for cognition scale. Individuals who exhibit higher levels of NFC are perhaps more questioning details of their daily life which could impact their cybersecurity, and this inquisitiveness leads them to investigate and explore rather than ignore or accept. Similarly, a consideration of the consequences of their actions (as measured through the CFC) also showed positive correlations with the four sub-scales of the SeBIS. The authors of the report suggested that a more active engagement in cybersecurity is linked directly to a capacity to assess how their current decisions may affect their future. This maps well onto the finding that the three subscales of the BIS, which measures impulsivity, were negatively correlated with security sub-scales measured on the SeBIS; those individuals who are quick to act or lack impulse control are those who may quickly respond to a spam email or phishing attack. Aspects of decision-making also demonstrated correlations with a number of sub-scales from the SeBIS. For instance, the rational sub-scale of the GDMS showed a positive correlation with aspects of password protection, general security awareness and updating software. The concept of rationality has been linked to a deliberate and logical approach to decision-making, and it has also been noted that those individuals who have a rational approach to decision-making are more likely to assume a personal responsibility for decision that affect them (Scott & Bruce, 1995). The avoidant decision-making type, typified by an individual who puts off or procrastinates about making decisions was negatively correlated to each of the four sub-scales from the SeBIS. There was an associated link between the dependence style of decision-making and scores on the SeBIS too, with those less likely to need help or assistance in their decision-making having a higher level of overall security awareness. Egelman and Peer (2015b) suggested that those individuals who were more proactive about their security had a less of a capacity to rely on others for information.

In the context of the present discussion the findings from Egelman and Peer (2015a, b) provided one of the first attempts to assess how individual differences could have a direct impact on their cybersecurity behaviors. It would appear that those individuals who are more inquisitive, more rational and less prone to procrastination in decision-making represent those more likely to engage in effective cybersecurity behaviors. The benefits of knowing such information presents the theoretical possibility of system design with such differences in mind. This could potentially allow the implementation of system messages and warnings that are tailored to the individual, hence presenting a more targeted mitigation to poor cybersecurity behaviors.

The SeBIS was later employed in further research by Tischer et al. (2016) who examined the potential for individuals to plug in USB devices that had been littered around a university campus. This strategy is often presented as a key mechanism for infiltration used by social engineers who leave such devices in prominent places in an attempt to gain entry to highly protected systems (Tischer et al., 2016). The pathway to gaining access is via the device, which is usually loaded with malware allowing the social engineer remote access to system once it has been plugged into a networked computer. In contrast to Egelman and Peer's work, Tischer et al. (2016) found that individuals who were more likely to plug in a USB device were no risker when compared to a matched sample. In fact, those individuals who did plug in the USB were more risk averse in all categories apart from that of recreational risk. However it appears that individuals devolve responsibility for their protection of the computer and security measures deployed on it, or are ignorant of the risks attached to poor cybersecurity practices (Tischer et al., 2016). Tischer et al. (2016) also used the SeBIS, but noted that the internal reliability of the scale was found to be much lower than had originally been found in the original research by Egelman and Peer (McCormac et al., 2016).

One of the most recently developed scales designed to explore the information security of individuals is the Human Aspects of Information Security Questionnaire (HAIS-Q; (Parsons et al., 2017, 2014). The HAIS-Q comprises of a variety of items that assess three key elements in the context of cybersecurity; these are knowledge, attitude and behavior. The underlying structure of the HAIS-Q examines these constructs in 5 core areas including password management, email use, Internet use, Social networking, incident reporting, mobile computing and information handling (Parsons et al., 2014). Higher scores on the HAIS-Q indicate a good awareness of information security, whilst a lower score demonstrates lack of knowledge as well as the propensity to engage in potentially risky activities, e.g. sharing passwords. The HAIS-Q has undergone an impressive amount of testing across a broad spectrum of populations establishing a robust test-retest reliability in the process (see Parsons et al., 2017).

In the context of exploring individual differences in security behaviors, the HAIS-Q was paired with key demographic and personality factors in a study by McCormac, Zwaans, et al., (2016). Scores on the HAIS-Q were shown to differ significantly across age groups, with the overall observation being that those in the older age groups demonstrated higher overall scores for information security. In order to assess if this relationship was influenced by age-related differences in risk taking behaviors, the researchers controlled for this and noted that the correlation between age and scores on the HAIS-Q persisted, although were slightly weaker. A gender difference between males and females was also noted, with females presenting significantly higher scores on the HAIS-Q compared to males, although the authors noted that the effect size for such a result was small. So in this instance age and gender both present as potential sources for individual differences in cybersecurity-related behaviors. The unknown element here is if these sources for variance in cybersecurity can be accounted for, and if effective system design could serve to isolate and mitigate the impact from such.

The work by McCormac et al. (2016) also included an exploration of how personality traits and a measure of risk taking were associated with scores on the HAIS-Q. The study used the five-factor model of personality, with the most frequently cited version used being that by John and Srivastava (1999), shown in Table 1.

A significant positive relationship between the personality traits of agreeableness, openness and conscientiousness with scores on the HAIS-Q were observed from the research by McCormac et al. (2016). Furthermore, a negative correlation was noted between risk-taking and scores on the HAIS-Q, with those less likely to engage in risky behaviors having higher overall scores. These findings were

Table 1. The five-factor model of personality as taken from John and Srivastava (1999; p.121)

Factor Name	Description
Extraversion	An energetic approach to the social and material world and incudes traits such as sociability, activity, assertiveness, and positive emotionality.
Agreeableness	Contrasts a prosocial and communal orientation towards others with antagonism and includes traits such as altruism, tender-mindedness, trust and modesty.
Conscientiousness	Socially prescribed impulse control that facilitates task and goal oriented behavior, such as thinking before acting, delaying gratification, following norms and rules, and planning, organizing, and prioritizing tasks.
Neuroticism	Contrasts emotional stability and even-temperedness with negative emotionality, such as feeling anxious, nervous, sad, and tense.
Openness	In contrast to closed-mindedness, describes the breadth, depth, originality, and complexity of an individual's mental and experiential life.

noted as being in partial agreement with previous research (Pattinson et al., 2015) which also found that aspects of agreeableness, conscientiousness and openness served to explain the most variance in information security behaviors (McCormac, Zwaans, et al., 2016).

The research reviewed above provides a wide and somewhat contrasting basis for examining human factors in the context of cybersecurity. It would appear that there is some commonality in the findings that have examined self-reported cybersecurity knowledge, attitudes and behaviors. Predominately, individual differences in aspects of personality have the potential to predict to what level that individual will engage in information security behaviors. It appears that those who are more conscientious, open, agreeable, risk adverse and rational are those more likely to positively engage in effective cybersecurity behaviors. Alongside these personality traits it would also appear that both age and gender also serve as important moderators of active information security behavior further complicating issues.

SOLUTIONS AND RECOMMENDATIONS

Mitigating the threat posed by the accidental insider is, on the face of it, not easily accomplished. There is often an assumption made that those aspects of employee behavior which serve to create a level of risk for the organization relates directly to a lack of understanding (Coventry, Briggs, Jeske, & Van Moorsel, 2014). The sheer scope of information security behavior that need to be enhanced, modified or altered provide a clear challenge for any awareness campaign. The list is long and there is no potential 'one-size fits all' approach which could effectively be applied to bring awareness for just a few of these elements. These aspects can include:

- Regularly updating anti-virus software.
- Using only trusted and secure connections, including Wi-Fi.
- Updating existing software.
- Awareness of physical surroundings (e.g. preventing shoulder surfing).
- Reporting suspicious behaviour.
- Keeping up-to-date with current threats.
- An awareness of trusted sites and services.

- Ensuring passwords are strong enough.
- Limiting the amount of personal information being shared online (Coventry et al., 2014).

In order to overcome these potential deficiencies, Coventry et al. (2014) noted that organizations often implement a wide variety of training schemes in an attempt to educate end-users (Leach, 2003). The effectiveness of these training programs is often limited to a unidirectional process where employees are presented with 'best practice', and behavioral change is attempted through the use of 'expert' advice (Coventry et al., 2014). A recent report produced by the Information Security Forum (ISF, 2014) presented a wide range of reasons as to why security awareness training failed to fully engage the human participant within the process. These key points included:

1. Solutions are not aligned to the business risks.
2. Neither progress nor value is measured.
3. Incorrect assumptions are made about people and their motivations.
4. Unrealistic expectations are set.
5. The correct skills are not deployed.
6. Awareness is just background noise (ISF, 2014: 1).

For many individuals it would appear that awareness training becomes an unnecessary burden that must be completed as part of their daily work lives. If expectations placed on the individual employee are also set too high, and the capacity to deploy the skills they have learned is stifled, there is a potential for both time and resources to be wasted.

The actual way in which such awareness training is conveyed can also have a significant impact on its effectiveness for eliciting a change in behavior. For example, Khan, Alghathbar, Nabi, and Khan (2011) noted that educational/academic presentations and group-based discussions served to enhance the knowledge, attitude, intention to engage and behaviors of those studied. Other forms of communication, such as emails, newsletters, videogames, posters and computer-based training all had limited effectiveness in terms of getting individuals to change their behaviors and engage in more effective security activities (Khan et al., 2011).

A variety of attempts have been made to utilize behavioral change mechanisms in the context of cybersecurity (Coventry et al., 2014; Jeske, Coventry, & Briggs, 2013; Turland, Coventry, Jeske, Briggs, & van Moorsel, 2015). However, it is noted that these attempts are exceptions rather than the norm. Other researchers have pointed out that there is a potential to use aspects of behavioral economics as a mechanism for eliciting behavioral change (Briggs, Jeske, & Coventry, 2016). Behavioral economics is starkly contrasted to the standard economic model in terms of human decision making and behavior, with the latter asserting that an individual is fully rational when engaged in decision making and is always mindful of the consequences for their actions (Briggs et al., 2016). The standard economic model has appeared at be an idealistic view of human information processing and has failed to adequately explain the actual behaviors of individuals in any number of key settings. Behavioral economics on the other hand adopts a more pragmatic approach by highlighting several key principles proposed to account for the irrationality of human behavior. This work was formalized in the work of Thaler and Sunstein (2008), which presented the basis for exploring how predictable deviations from rational processes could in turn be used to 'nudge' an individual towards a more desirable decision (Briggs et al., 2016).

The MINDSPACE framework, originally developed by Dolan et al. (2012) has been used by a variety of researchers to capture the key influencers for behavioral change. These elements are included in Table 2.

Coventry et al. (2014) used the MINDSPACE framework provided by Dolan et al., as a basis for creating a set of behavioral nudges to prevent individuals from choosing insecure wireless networks. The researchers highlighted a series of possible nudges aligned to specific scenarios that could be used in a practical way. For example, in the instance of Messenger, the behavioral nudge was to present a warning message from a trusted provider and not from a generic source. The researchers even suggested the possibility of having a celebrity to provide the warning message, but this may only work if the individual is both well respected and well known. In the final testing of the framework, Coventry et al. (2014) opted to use an affective nudge by changing both the color and order of the available wireless networks. Those wireless networks that were deemed safe and secure appears in green towards the top of the list, with unsecure networks appearing lower down the list in red. Jeske et al. (2014) presented the results of this research, with these affective cues presented as an effective mechanism for helping individuals choose a more secure network. However, the researchers also noted that individual differences in the characteristics of users (such as proficiency with IT and poorer impulse control) also led to poorer security decisions, with nudges presenting an effective mechanism for changing the behavior of those with poor impulse control. To date this represents one of the few published empirical tests of behavioural nudges in an information security context, but focuses rather narrowly on just one element from the MINDSPACE framework.

In a final point, Bada, Sass, and Nurse (2014) suggested a series of key aspects that should be considered when designing cyber security awareness campaigns. These key points included:

1. Security awareness training has to be professionally organized and prepared if it is to work – ad hoc training courses and inconsistency in the messages being conveyed will confuse the end user.
2. The use of fear as an effective strategy to create change is not recommended, and there is potential that it could instil a sense of fear in those who can ill afford to take risks.
3. Security education needs to be targeted and needs to be practical in nature – it needs to give the individual a concrete and achievable goal or action, which is in turn measurable and allows feedback to be provided.

Table 2. The MINDSPACE framework for behavior change

MINDSPACE cue	Behavior
Messenger	We are heavily influenced by who communicates information to us
Incentives	Our responses to incentives are shaped by predictable mental shortcuts such as strongly avoiding losses
Norms	We are strongly influenced by what others do
Defaults	We 'go with the flow' of pre-set options
Salience	Our attention is draw to what is novel and seems relevant to us
Priming	Our acts are often influenced by sub-conscious cues
Affects	Our emotional associations can powerfully shape our actions
Commitments	We seek to be consistent with our public promises, and reciprocate acts
Ego	We act in ways that makes us feel better about ourselves.

(from Dolan et al., 2012, p. 266)

4.   Change needs to be sustainable and continuous – once you have the atmosphere to illicit change, this needs to be exploited and feedback should be provided throughout this period.
5.   Cultural contexts should be considered whenever cyber security awareness campaigns are being designed – there is not a one-size fits all approach that will work, and cultural nuances need to be taken into consideration

FUTURE RESEARCH DIRECTIONS

There are multiple directions in which future research could be taken, and a point that becomes apparent when exploring the available literature in this area is that the contribution human factors can make to cybersecurity is only just gaining a significant focus. A consistent and directed approach to exploring how aspects of human factors can serve to influence (and therefore also be targeted in order to mitigate) risk within any system is inherently important. In a similar way, the actual mechanisms used to bring awareness to individuals for effective cybersecurity behaviors also needs to be researched. The following present some key areas for further research, but the scope of the area is overwhelming and deserves a more in-depth discussion than is currently possible.

Behavioral Nudges and ISA

The work by Dolan et al., (2012) in the development of the MINDSPACE framework for behavioral nudges presents a clear pathway for future exploration. A number of researchers have already noted that affective nudging techniques can serve as key mechanisms for eliciting more effective information security awareness (Coventry et al., 2014; Jeske et al., 2013; Turland et al., 2015). However much of this research does focus solely on the affective elements presented in the MINDSPACE framework, meaning that there is an even greater number of potential routes to follow for influencing behavioral change. It may be the case that using a number of key elements from the MINDSPACE framework could create more effective information security strategies, and by adding or subtracting various components, behavioral changes could be enhanced. It is evident that more detailed empirical research is needed in this area in order for such questions to be answered.

Individual Differences and Information Security

Individual differences in the context of information security and accidental insiderness could also provide another avenue for further research. As reviewed in this current chapter, there has been some clear attempts to highlight how individual differences can serve to influence attitudes and adherence to information security. Aspects such as poor impulse control, knowledge of IT and elements of personality have all been linked to information security behaviors. However, there are a huge amount of potential avenues that have been, to date, left unexplored and would provide a useful metric to not only measure ISA against, but also map potential behavioral nudges onto.

One area that has so far escaped in-depth exploration in the context of human factors in cybersecurity is those elements that lie outside of traditional 'trait based' personality factors. These factors link into the artifacts of modern life, and span a plethora of phenomena associated with the use of digital technology. For instance, there has been some discussion of how aspects such as cyberloafing and Internet addiction could both influence ISA (for example see Hadlington, 2017; Hadlington & Parsons, 2017). The term cyberloafing has also been used to describe a process through which individuals actively engage the use of the companies' Internet access during work hours for non-work related purposes (Ozler & Polat, 2012). Blanchard and Henle (2008) defined the concept of cyberloafing as "employees' voluntary nonwork-related use of company provided email and Internet while working (p. 1068). With the prevalence of cyberloading being noted as being widespread in employment (Malachowski, 2005), exploring how ISA is affected by individuals engaging in cyberloafing provides another useful measure of how accepted social norms in the context of work-based use of information technology impacts on cybersecurity. Further work to expand on these findings, and to examine other associated variables, is deemed critical to move the field forward.

CONCLUSION

As noted in this chapter, exploring the role of the human element within the context of any cybersecurity is complex, multifaceted, and presents a potential conundrum to any security professional attempting to secure systems. The threats from the accidental insider, whether it is through ignorance, lack of attention, or human error is quickly becoming a growing concern to security professionals. Unlike malicious attacks from internal and external agents, the impact that UIT has is far harder to detect and mitigate but is potentially just as damaging. Movements towards a clearer understanding of how crucial aspects related to human factors have been made, but progress in this area is slow, fails to keep up with the constant evolution of the threat landscape, and is lacking a clear theoretical framework. Further work needs to be done in this area if we are to develop a clearer understanding of how human factors interact in the cybersecurity landscape. A focus not just on how these factors impact on business cybersecurity, but also personal cybersecurity is also important, and examining how these two aspects interact would also appear to be an aspect for future research. It is also apparent that current research on mitigating risks suggests that a 'one-size-fits-all' approach to preventing lapses in cybersecurity is not currently working. More work focusing on why mitigating threats from human actors within the system is so difficult would appear to be urgently needed. Aligned to this, appropriate interventions need to be designed from the ground up, with a clear focus on their effectiveness rather than a 'fire and forget' attitude where there is no follow up to explore if they have worked.

REFERENCES

Anwar, M., He, W., Ash, I., Yuan, X., Li, L., & Xu, L. (2016). Gender difference and employees' cybersecurity behaviors. *Computers in Human Behavior*, *69*, 437–443. doi:10.1016/j.chb.2016.12.040

Bada, M., Sass, A. M., & Nurse, J. R. C. (2014). *Cyber Security Awareness Campaigns Why do they fail to change behaviour?* Academic Press.

Bishop, M., & Gates, C. (2008). Defining the insider threat. In *Proceedings of the 4th annual workshop on Cyber security and information intelligence research* (pp. 12–14). New York: ACM Press. doi:10.1145/1413140.1413158

Bishop, M., Gollmann, D., Hunker, J., & Probst, C. W. (2008). Countering insider threats. In *Dagstuhl Seminar Proceedings 08302* (pp. 1–18). Academic Press. Retrieved from http://vesta.informatik.rwth-aachen.de/opus/volltexte/2008/1793/pdf/08302.SWM.1793.pdf

Blais, A.-R., & Weber, E. U. (2006). A Domain-Specific Risk-Taking (DOSPERT) scale for adult populations. *Judgment and Decision Making*, *1*(1), 33–47. doi:10.1037/t13084-000

Briggs, P., Jeske, D., & Coventry, L. (2016). Behaviour change interventions for cybersecurity. In L. Little, E. Sillence, & A. Joinson (Eds.), *Behaviour Change Research and Theory; Psychological and Technological Perspectives*. New York: Academic Press.

Cacioppo, P., Petty, R., & Kao, F. C. (1984). The Efficient Assessment of Need for Cognition. *Journal of Personality Assessment*. doi:10.1001/archpsyc.64.10.1204

Cappelli, D., Moore, A., & Silowash, G. (2012). *Common Sense Guide to Mitigating Insider Threats* (4th ed.). Academic Press. Retrieved from http://www.stormingmedia.us/00/0055/A005585.html

Cappelli, D., Moore, A., & Trzeciak, R. (2012). *The CERT Guide to Insider threats*. Academic Press.

CERT. (2013). *Unintentional insider threats: A foundational study*. Retrieved from http://scholar.google.com/scholar?hl=en&btnG=Search&q=intitle:Unintentional+Insider+Threats+:+A+Foundational+Study#0

CERT. (2014). *Unintentional Insider Threats: Social Engineering*. Retrieved from http://oai.dtic.mil/oai/oai?verb=getRecord&metadataPrefix=html&identifier=ADA592507

Coventry, L., Briggs, P., Jeske, D., & Van Moorsel, A. (2014). SCENE: A structured means for creating and evaluating behavioral nudges in a cyber security environment. Lecture Notes in Computer Science, 8517, 229–239. doi:10.1007/978-3-319-07668-3_23

CPNI. (2013). *CPNI Insider Data Collection Study: Report of Main Findings*. London: CPNI.

Dolan, P., Hallsworth, M., Halpern, D., King, D., Metcalfe, R., & Vlaev, I. (2012). Influencing behaviour: The mindspace way. *Journal of Economic Psychology*, *33*(1), 264–277. doi:10.1016/j.joep.2011.10.009

Egelman, S., & Peer, E. (2015a). Predicting Privacy and Security Attitudes. *Computers and Society: The Newletter of ACM SIGCAS*, *45*(1), 22–28. doi:10.1145/2738210.2738215

Egelman, S., & Peer, E. (2015b). Scaling the Security Wall: Developing a Security Behavior Intentions Scale (SeBIS). *Proceedings of the ACM CHI'15 Conference on Human Factors in Computing Systems*, *1*, 2873–2882. doi:10.1145/2702123.2702249

Greitzer, F., Kangas, L., Noonan, C., & Dalton, A. (2010). *Identifying at-risk employees: A behavioral model for predicting potential insider threats*. Retrieved from http://www.pnl.gov/main/publications/external/technical_reports/PNNL-19665.pdf

Greitzer, F. L., Imran, M., Purl, J., Axelrad, E. T., Leong, Y. M., & Becker, D. E. ... Sticha, P. J. (2016). Developing an ontology for individual and organizational sociotechnical indicators of insider threat risk. *CEUR Workshop Proceedings*, 19–27.

Hadlington, L. (2017). Human factors in cybersecurity; examining the link between Internet addiction, impulsivity, attitudes towards cybersecurity, and risky cybersecurity behaviours. *Heliyon (London), 3*(7), e00346. doi:10.1016/j.heliyon.2017.e00346 PMID:28725870

Hadlington, L., & Parsons, K. (2017). Can Cyberloafing and Internet Addiction Affect Organizational Information Security? *Cyberpsychology, Behavior, and Social Networking, 20*(9), 567–571.

Hunker, J., & Probst, C. (2011). Insiders and insider threats—an overview of definitions and mitigation techniques. *Journal of Wireless Mobile Networks, Ubiquitous Computing and Dependable Applications, 2*(1), 4–27. Retrieved from http://isyou.info/jowua/papers/jowua-v2n1-1.pdf

Information Security Forum. (2014). *From Promoting Awareness to Embedding Behaviours - Secure by choice, not by chance, Abstract.* Author.

Jeske, D., Coventry, L., & Briggs, P. (2013). Nudging whom how : IT proficiency, impulse control and secure behaviour. *CHI Workshop on Personalizing Behavior Change Technologies 2014.*

John, O. P., & Srivastava, S. (1999). Big Five Inventory (Bfi). Handbook of Personality: Theory and Research, 2, 102–138. doi:10.1525/fq.1998.51.4.04a00260

Joireman, J., Shaffer, M. J., Balliet, D., & Strathman, A. (2012). Promotion Orientation Explains Why Future-Oriented People Exercise and Eat Healthy: Evidence From the Two-Factor Consideration of Future Consequences-14 Scale. *Personality and Social Psychology Bulletin, 38*(10), 1272–1287. doi:10.1177/0146167212449362 PMID:22833533

Keeney, M. (2005). *Insider threat study: Computer system sabotage in critical infrastructure sectors.* Retrieved from http://scholar.google.com/scholar?hl=en&btnG=Search&q=intitle:Insider+Threat+St udy+:+Computer+System+Sabotage+in+Critical+Infrastructure+Sectors#0

Khan, B., Alghathbar, K. S., Nabi, S. I., & Khan, M. K. (2011). Effectiveness of information security awareness methods based on psychological theories. *African Journal of Business Management, 5*(26), 10862–10868. doi:10.5897/AJBM11.067

Leach, J. (2003). Improving user security behaviour. *Computers & Security, 22*(8), 685–692. doi:10.1016/S0167-4048(03)00007-5

Malachowski, D. (2005). Wasted Time At Work Costing Companies Billions. *Asian Enterprise*, 14–16.

McCormac, A., Parsons, K., Zwaans, T., Butavicius, M., & Pattinson, M. (2016). *Test-retest reliability and internal consistency of the Human Aspects of Information Security Questionnaire* (HAIS-Q). Academic Press.

McCormac, A., Zwaans, T., Parsons, K., Calic, D., Butavicius, M., & Pattinson, M. (2016). Individual differences and Information Security Awareness. *Computers in Human Behavior, 69*, 151–156. doi:10.1016/j.chb.2016.11.065

Nurse, J. R. C., Creese, S., Goldsmith, M., & Lamberts, K. (2011). Trustworthy and effective communication of cybersecurity risks: A review. *Proceedings - 2011 1st Workshop on Socio-Technical Aspects in Security and Trust, STAST 2011*, 60–68. doi:10.1109/STAST.2011.6059257

Ozler, D. E., & Polat, G. (2012). Cyberloafing phenomenon in organizations: determinants and impacts. *International Journal of eBusiness and eGovernment Studies, 4*(2), 1–15. Retrieved from http://www.sobiad.org/eJOURNALS/journal_IJEBEG/arhieves/2012_2/derya_ergun.pdf

Parsons, K., Calic, D., Pattinson, M., Butavicius, M., McCormac, A., & Zwaans, T. (2017). The human aspects of information security questionnaire (HAIS-Q): Two further validation studies. *Computers & Security, 66*, 40–51. doi:10.1016/j.cose.2017.01.004

Parsons, K., McCormac, A., Butavicius, M., Pattinson, M., & Jerram, C. (2014). Determining employee awareness using the Human Aspects of Information Security Questionnaire (HAIS-Q). *Computers & Security, 42*, 165–176. doi:10.1016/j.cose.2013.12.003

Patton, J. H., Stanford, M. S., & Barratt, E. S. (1995). Patton Factor Structure of the BIS.pdf. *Journal of Clinical Psychology.*

Pfleeger, S. L., & Caputo, D. (2012). Leveraging Behavioral Science to Mitigate Cyber Security Risk Security Risk. *Computers & Security, 31*(4), 597–611. doi:10.1016/j.cose.2011.12.010

Probst, C., Hunker, J., Gollmann, D., & Bishop, M. (2010). *Insider Threats in Cyber Security. Vasa.* New York: Springer. doi:10.1007/978-1-4419-7133-3

Sasse, M., Brostoff, S., & Weirich, D. (2001). Transforming the "weakest link": A Human-Computer Interaction Approach for Usable and Effective Security. *BT Technology Journal, 19*(3), 122–131. doi:10.1023/A:1011902718709

Sasse, M., & Flechais, I. (2005). *Usable Security: Why Do We Need It? How Do We Get It?* Retrieved from http://discovery.ucl.ac.uk/20345/

Scott, S., & Bruce, R. (1995). Decision-making Style: The Development and Assessment of a New Measure. *Educational and Psychological Measurement, 55*(5), 818–831. doi:10.1177/0013164495055005017

Shaw, R., Ruby, K., & Post, J. (1998). The Insider Threat to Information Sytems. *Security Awareness Bulletin*, 2–98.

Siponen, M., Pahnila, S., & Mahmood, M. A. (2010). Compliance with information security policies: An empirical investigation. *Computer, 43*(2), 64–71. doi:10.1109/MC.2010.35

Tischer, M., Durumeric, Z., Foster, S., Duan, S., Mori, A., Bursztein, E., & Bailey, M. (2016). Users Really Do Plug in USB Drives They Find. *IEEE Symposium on Security and Privacy*, 1–14. doi:10.1109/SP.2016.26

Turland, J., Coventry, L., Jeske, D., Briggs, P., & van Moorsel, A. (2015). Nudging Towards security: Developing an Application for Wireless Network Selection for Android Phones. *Proceedings of the 2015 British HCI Conference on - British HCI '15*, 193–201. doi:10.1145/2783446.2783588

Whitten, A., & Tygar, J. D. (1998). *Usability of Security: A Case Study. Computer Science.* Retrieved from http://www.dtic.mil/cgi-bin/GetTRDoc?Location=U2&doc=GetTRDoc.pdf&AD=ADA361032

KEY TERMS AND DEFINITIONS

Cyberloafing: Using work-based IT for non-work, personal purposes.

Insider Threat: A threat to an organisation by a former or current employee who, with malicious intent, deploys an exploit designed to either disrupt normal system functioning or exhort sensitive information for financial again.

Personality: A theoretical psychological construct that has permanence throughout the individual's life span.

Unintentional Insider Threat: The threat posed by a current employee who, without malicious intent, causes a breach in organizational cybersecurity.

Chapter 4
Cyber + Culture:
Exploring the Relationship

Char Sample
US Army Research Laboratory, USA

Jennifer Cowley
US Army Research Laboratory, USA

Jonathan Z. Bakdash
U.S. Army Research Laboratory, USA

ABSTRACT

Technical advances in cyber-attack attribution continues to show incremental improvement. A growing interest in the role of the human in perception management, and decision-making suggest that other aspects of human cognition may be able to help inform attribution, and other aspects of cyber security such as defending and training. Values shape behaviors and cultural values set norms for groups of people. Therefore, they should be considered when modeling behaviors. The lack of studies in this area requires exploration and foundational work to learn the limits of this area of research. This chapter highlights some of the findings of some of the recent studies.

INTRODUCTION

The cybersecurity environment has only recently considered the role of behavioral science in explaining cybersecurity events. This addition of behavioral science disciplines will allow analysts and researchers the opportunity to gain fresh insights into these events. The addition of cultural studies to this mix provides context for these insights (Morgan, Cross & Rendell, 2015; Wang, 2016), thereby adding valuable understanding to the analysis.

Morgan et al. (2015) noted that cultural values and preferences are easily transmitted during the learning process, including copying behaviors when uncertain, rewarding conformist behaviors, and examining social learning, thereby providing an explanation of event evaluation context. Morgan et al. (2015) are not alone in maintaining these views on contextual evaluation. Others (Henrich, Heine & Norenzayan,

DOI: 10.4018/978-1-5225-4053-3.ch004

2010; Hofstede, Hofstede & Minkov, 2010; Nisbett, 2010; Schwartz, 2012; Shewder, 1998) have voiced similar views, and, more recently, Wang (2016) has called attention to the importance of cultural context. The context that culture provides results in actions or outcomes that may seem normal for some (Minkov, 2011) but are viewed as abnormal or incomprehensible for others (Fiske & Taylor, 2013).

Wang (2016) discussed the importance of a cross-discipline approach that requires the understanding of cultural values for psychology, a view shared by Nisbett (2010), Henrich et al. (2010), Hofstede et al. (2010), Schwartz (2012), and Shewder (1998). Other disciplines such as education, business management, and marketing recognize the value of incorporating cultural understanding into the body of knowledge. In recent studies, research into information technology usage has considered the role of culture, and, more recently, cybersecurity studies are considering the importance of cultural values (Almeshekah & Spafford, 2014; Elmasry, Auter & Peuchaud, 2014; Henshel, Sample, Cains & Hoffman, 2016).

Inclusion of cultural analysis in cross-discipline research runs the risk of analysts importing their own cultural views into their analysis (Fiske & Taylor, 2013; Van de Vijer & Leung, 1997). Fiske & Taylor (2013) noted that individuals were better able to detect cultural biases outside of their own cultural group, but they were unable to do so as effectively within their own group. These observations by Fiske & Taylor (2013) along with Minkov (2011) underscore the role of cultural values in human cognition and the difficulty in preventing cultural values from informing analysis. However, this challenge should not discourage researchers, especially in cybersecurity research where the environment includes the global Internet.

Culturally aware observations have not yet been widely incorporated into cybersecurity analysis, where the emphasis relies on technical details, and behavioral science disciplines have not yet been fully integrated. The global participation of different actors implies the need for cultural analysis into cyber behaviors and events. Although the addition of psychology is welcome and needed for cybersecurity analysis, sociology provides context for this analysis.

Recently Wang (2016) called attention to the role of culture in psychological evaluation of findings. We aim to extend theories of cultural psychology to a more applied setting in order to evaluate cyber actors. We have reason to believe that cultural values can be a grouping factor for human behavior in various environments, including the virtual environment that defines cyber. Minkov's (2011) observation that culture influences individual thoughts even when the individual believes in self-determination implies that cultural values can describe and predict human behavior in various environments including the virtual environment. In the virtual environment, the human actors regularly engage in thought, and knowing that culture influences thought, a reasonable expectation that cultural values may influence cyber behaviors deserves further investigation.

Nisbett (2010) documented the East versus West differences in perception and environmental interaction. Henrich et al. (2010) observed that the majority of psychological studies were performed on students who were from Western educated, industrialized, rich and developed (WEIRD) countries, and, of these WEIRD countries, the United States provided the majority of subjects. Therefore, the findings are skewed toward the cultural values of WEIRD students from the United States.

Historically, non-cyber disciplines have assessed the capability of culture to predict or explain human behavior (Hofstede et al., 2010; Nisbett, 2010; Schwartz, 2012), but recently cybersecurity and other computing sciences have begun investigating culture as a potential grouping factor to predict or explain cyber behavior (Henshel et al., 2016; Sample, Cowley, Watson & Maple, 2016; Sample, Cowley,

Hutchinson, 2017; Sample & Karamanian, 2015). Cybersecurity is a global interdisciplinary endeavor. The nature of cybersecurity requires cultural analysis to explain both similarities and difference in cyber events involving groups of actors.

Culture has many definitions, but one common thread that runs through all of these definitions is "shared values" (Hofstede et al., 2010; Matusitz, 2014; Morgan et al., 2015; Nisbett, 2010; Schwartz, 2012). Recognizing that cultural values underlie the decision-making process (Guess, 2004; Guss & Dorner, 2012; Hofstede et al., 2010; Matusitz, 2014; Nisbett, 2010) and that shared cultural values are reflected in problem-solving methods, this group of researchers continues to explore culture's role in behaviors and choices for cyber actors, based on the fact that cyber actors rely on thought in their daily activities.

Although the role of cultural values in thought or cognition has been explored (Guess, 2004; Guss & Dorner, 2012; Schwartz, 2012), the role in online behavior specifically cyber attacker, defender, and victim preferences, is only beginning (Almeshekah & Spafford, 2014; Henshel et al., 2016). Few studies have been done to date and those studies have been specifically targeted, thus the studies did not discuss the findings in a larger context. This effort attempts to take an overview of the work performed to date, discuss the significance of the work, and offer suggestions for future work.

The study of culture in the field of cybersecurity is necessary (Henshel et al., 2016). Culture helps describe patterns of human behavior in the physical world (Hofstede et al., 2010; Minkov, 2011; Nisbett, 2010; Schwartz, 2012) that result in artifacts left behind in the environment. This chapter is intended to introduce the concept of human culture, how culture has been used in other disciplines to group classes of human behaviors, and how this concept is being applied to the field of cybersecurity.

OBTAINING CULTURAL ANALYSIS DATA

Cultural anthropologists use archeology to study the artifacts a particular group of people leaves in an environment. The anthropologist is often unable to interview those people to understand what those artifacts are, so the anthropologist must infer how the artifacts explain the culture of the creator and user. This also applies to, cyber actors, particularly attackers who are oftentimes unavailable for interviews; thus the cyber analyst can use digital artifacts that to provide insights in the behaviors, preferences, and priorities of the cyber actors being studied.

Cultural studies such as anthropology rely on human participants. Attempting to have a global representation of participants can become a costly endeavor. Furthermore, cultural studies must be structured in a manner consistent in preventing the researcher from inserting their own cultural views (Van de Vijer & Leung, 1997), which may possibly influence the participant's response as well as the researcher's analysis (Fiske & Taylor, 2013). These are significant obstacles for research that can result in uncertain or inconsistent outcomes.

The digital environment provides a medium for post-event observation that allows researchers to examine raw online events and the environment in which those events occurred. When attacks occur, the digital environment is treated as a crime scene and thereby allows the attack data to be copied and preserved. The digital copy matches the original data, thereby allowing for multiple investigations while preserving the original data.

Cybersecurity professionals in incident response and forensics typically analyze digital artifacts that were created and left behind on the hosts or in the network traffic in response to events; some of those events involve human interactions. All logged events comprise digital artifacts, and although many of the machine-to-machine events (e.g., periodic broadcasts of status) are easily explained and well understood, the interactions that result from humans-to-machine interactions are understood in technical terms but not in behavioral terms. Behavioral understanding provides an explanation for the events and preferences observed whereas values, particularly cultural values, offer the context for those observations. The purpose of this chapter is to review prior work on characterizing attackers, defenders, and victims and to identify the gaps in the literature that, if addressed, may enable better culture-based predictions of tactical and strategic adversarial maneuvers.

We recognize that the reader might still believe that culture should not be central to cybersecurity. However, culture has been shown to set behavioral norms in the physical world (Nisbett 2010; Minkov 2011; Wang 2016). Matusitz (2014) noted culture's role in cyber terrorism; therefore, the exploration and examination of cultural commonalities in cybersecurity is a logical follow-on.

The digital data that we have used for the various studies discussed in this chapter are publicly available. Although the datasets used are limited in the activity observed, the data is raw, and the volume of data (over 11 million records in the archive) is significant. The use of this raw data allows the researchers to perform their analysis without inadvertently capturing the thoughts of other researchers. Minkov (2011) observed that culture could be studied separately from its host (the human). The observational studies discussed in this chapter reflect the researchers' desire to study culture outside the presence of the host.

The persistent nature of the public digital environment is appealing such that the observable logged data from human activity remains available for future analysis long after the event has occurred. In subsequent sections, we discuss how we have used old data to understand the culture of cyber actors in order to explore behaviors and preferences that statistically associate with national cultural values.

Improving cybersecurity network defenses requires improving the predictive capabilities on where and how the attacker will strike along with identifying probable targets. Once identified, these high-probability targets can allocate defensive resources appropriately. Identifying the adversary, or the adversary's values, should allow for (1) accurate prediction of where this entity will likely penetrate a network to stage an attack and (2) what tactics this entity will use to conduct their entire attack strategy.

The current attacker attribution methods are time consuming and, as new actors, emerge as not scalable. What is needed is a grouping variable across classes of actors that may be a good predictor of the types of strategies and techniques attackers and defenders will use when operating in the cyber environment. Understanding the role of cultural values in cybersecurity events offer the potential to group, predict and counter adversary attack preferences and patterns.

CULTURAL VALUES

Cultural values are not innate they are learned (Hofstede et al., 2010; Matusitz, 2014; Nisbett, 2010; Schwartz, 2012). These values are quickly assimilated into the unconscious thought pattern, thus forming preferences (Matusitz, 2014; Fiske & Taylor, 2013; Evans, 2008; Buchtel & Norenzayan, 2009). Once absorbed into unconscious thought, the subject, as well as those who interact with the subject, rely on these biases. For example, some people joyfully celebrate success, whereas others prefer a more reserved response. These differences in norms become unconscious preferences. The reliance on unconscious preferences can and has resulted in cyber actors using defender biases to their own advantage (Almeshekah & Spafford, 2014).

One fallacious assumption underlying definitions of culture is that cultural coherence and uniformity within a collective (Rathje, 2009)—meaning social conformance to a set of ideas, beliefs, behaviors, etc.—exists to obtain cultural membership. However, sociology and other cultural researchers have contradicted that assumption with empirical evidence (Bhabha, 1997; Hofstede, 1980; Roberts et al, 1995). Another criticism of cultural research is that cultural definitions are often broad, politicized, and incorporate folklore (Rathje, 2009) such that the true semantic meaning of the term is obfuscated. Cultural distinctions tend to be broad, but they provide context for psychological findings.

Cultural values define behavioral norms (Morgan et al., 2015; Wang, 2016). According to Hofstede et al. (2010), values form the core of cultural manifestations. Values inform feelings that, in turn, determine preferences. These norms define acceptable behaviors (Hofstede et al., 2010) and values that act as a playbook for individuals who wish to fit into the larger social group (Minkov, 2011; Wang, 2016). When sufficiently reinforced and fully embedded into the unconscious thought process, cultural values become unconscious biases, so that even when the person believes that they are the master of their own thoughts; they are not, rather they are culturally directed (Hofstede et al., 2010; Minkov, 2011; Nisbett, 2010). Although these cultural values define norms, individuals in all societies may exist outside of the culturally defined norm; therefore, cultural values should not be used exclusively for identification and explanation of individual behaviors (Hofstede et al., 2010).

Examples of values include defining good and evil, beauty, safe and dangerous behaviors, morality, manners, normal, natural, logical and rational, conflict management, and acceptable celebratory behaviors (Hofstede et al., 2010). Each of these values is subjectively defined and form the basis or core of cultural values. Embedded cultural values have the ability to inform decisions even when the subject is removed from the environment (Hofstede et al., 2010; Minkov, 2011; Wang, 2016).

The six dimensions of culture that Hofstede et al. (2010) identified are as follows: power distance index (PDI), individualism versus collectivism (IvC), masculine versus feminine (MvF), uncertainty avoidance (UAI), long-term orientation versus short-term orientation (LvS), and indulgence versus restraint (IvR). These dimensions are quantitatively defined on scales of 0 to 100 for 100 countries. The values associated with each dimension are indicated in Table 1.

Table 1. Cultural values

Dimension	Values
PDI	Low scores represent egalitarian values and flexibility. High scores represent authoritarian values, preferential treatment for "in group" members, and shows of strength.
IvC	Low scores represent collectivist values and community is more important that "self", interdependence encouraged. High scores represent individualist values where self needs prevail over group needs.
MvF	Low scores represent feminine values that include nurturing, supportive behaviors, and lack of pre-defined gender roles. High score represent competitive, aggressive behaviors and strong gender roles.
UAI	Low scores represent curiosity of the unknown, whereas high scores represent fear of the unknown.
LvS	Low scores represent immediate satisfaction and tactical strength. High scores represent delayed satisfaction and strategic and holistic thinking.
IvR	Low scores represent closed societies with the appearance of emotional attachment. High scores represent open societies where tolerance of expression is expected.

Beyond the definition provided for culture, we question whether different types of culture exist and at what granularity. Culture, defined as shared values (Hofstede et al., 2010; Matusitz, 2014; Nisbett, 2010; Schwartz, 2012), is a social phenomenon, so culture must be created socially and is not a singleton phenomenon. However, sociability has many layers of granularity (e.g., between two people, within a family, within a work team, nested within organizational teams, at the organizational level, at the region level, at the nation-state level, at continental level, etc.).

In cybersecurity, much of the threat actors are attributed at that nation-state level in the publicly available sources. Thus, we chose definitions that reflect cultural values defined at the national levels, knowing that additional focus should be aimed at team-level culture of threat actors. We chose national definitions of cultural values as a starting point to address cyber actors who are funded and oftentimes trained through national programs (i.e., state-sponsored universities, national armed forces, other governmental programs). Understanding the interplay between cultural values and the digital artifacts may provide the context needed for modeling and predicting cyber events.

The purpose of this section is not to comprehensively review all research that discusses the predictive capabilities of culture with respect to non-cyber human behavior but to demonstrate that predictive capability exists. For comprehensive meta-analytic reviews of the predictive capability of Hofstede's cultural dimensions, see Kirkman et al. (2006, p. 299). We will briefly review what culture has predicted in past research using any theoretical model of culture and then review what Hofstede's cultural model predicts at the nation state level.

In general, cultural values have predicted emotive human states such as wellness (Arrindell et al., 1997) and interpersonal trust (Doney, Cannon & Mullen, 1998; Huff & Kelley, 2003). Culture can also predict the occurrence of behavior and respective outcomes (Singelis & Brown, 1995) such as ethical decision-making (Vitell, Nwachukwu & Barnes, 1993), educational performance (Aguayo, Herman, Ojeda & Flores, 2011), interpersonal information exchange (Dawar, Parker & Prices, 1996), and the use and acceptance of information technology (Al-Gahtani, Hubona & Wang, 2007). Hofstede's cultural dimensions at the national-level have been related to certain individual preferences and outcomes. For example, Shane's (1995) low uncertainty avoidance cultures were more preferential to innovation within organizations, and high individualist cultures have the lowest level of information-seeking behaviors within their social networks (Zaheer & Zaheer, 1997).

Researchers from the field of aviation have evaluated the effect of culture, whether quantitatively via Hofstede's quantified dimensions or qualitatively on aviation accidents. For example, high individualistic cultures (high IvC) with low uncertainty avoidance (UAI) have relatively low aviation accident rates, in contrast to the highest accident rates from low IvC and low UAI (Soeters & Boer, 2000). Low IvC historically associates with a longer decision-making process (Guess, 2004; Guss & Dorner, 2012). In addition, Hofstede et al. (2010, p. 217) identified (1) a lack of precision or (2) tolerance for ambiguity as characteristics associated with low UAI values. Extending cultural analysis into the cyber domain may reveal similar outcomes, but to date, this are remains understudied (Henshel et al., 2016).

Furthermore, work is inherently social, and *culture* dictates social norms. Nation-state actors sometimes operate in groups, and these groups have shared values that guide their decisions. Guess (2004) examined group decision-making in a synthetic environment and found that cultural values shaped group perception, problem definition and ultimately choices made by the groups (Ibid). When cyber armies engage in their work, a logical assumption would suggest that cultural values may also be in use.

Culture has been implicated as a second-order causal factor behind various aviation accidents (Merritt, 1993; Li & Harris, 2005). We conjecture that the field of cybersecurity is focusing attention on perfecting the cybersecurity tools to mitigate cyber attacks and improve human cyber competencies (via workforce development), at the expense of sociocultural problems at the system level. Thus, cultural values may also partially explain many cyber behaviors, events and preferences. Previous research indicates that attacks reflect cultural values (Sample, 2013; Sample, 2014, but we do not understand whether attack and defense strategies can be culturally profiled.

Cultural Values in Cybersecurity

Consistent with the observation by Hofstede et al. (2010) that computers might be standardized, but the humans who use these computers are not, the research examined revealed patterns of behavior that are consistent with specific cultural values. Precedence for cultural studies in cybersecurity is based on the fact that cybersecurity supports information technology (Von Solms & Van Niekerk, 2013). Using their own mental software, these users shape their interactions with computers. Studies in information technology usage and adoption have shown cultural differences (Elmasry et al., 2014; Sample & Karamanian, 2014; Sample & Karamanian, 2015; Zhao & Jiang, 2011). Because cybersecurity ultimately supports the technology on which it runs, the manner in which users use the technology can follow the same pattern when cyber interactions are involved.

In 2013, Sample inferred a relationship between national culture and computer network attack behaviors (Sample, 2013). This linking of cultural values to cyber behaviors follows a progression of the linking between cultural values and information technology usage (Elmasry et al., 2014; Sample & Karamanian, 2014; Sample & Karamanian, 2015; Zhao & Jiang, 2011). Culture has been shown to influence online behaviors in blogging (Mandl, 2009), technology adoption (Sample & Karamanian, 2014; Sample & Karamanian, 2015), and usage (Al-Gahtani et al., 2007; Sanchez-Franco, Martinez-Lopez & Martin-Velicia, 2009). More recently, culture has been linked to deception behaviors (Almeskah & Spafford, 2014).

Sample's (2013) initial study focused on a particular subset of users: attackers. Henshel et al. (2016) identified three groups of cyber actors of interest: attackers, defenders, and victims. The studies discussed in this chapter will be examined in terms of each of these three cyber actors. The discussion of these studies represents an opportunity to place the findings into the larger context of modeling the actors.

A profile of cultural value dimensions can help to explain and characterize groups of people, but, assuming that cultural values are susceptible to slow evolution, these profiles may also be useful as prediction factors. In other words, knowing the cultural values of attackers, defenders, and victims might predict who will attack and what the outcome could be. Prior research has identified relationships between a profile of cultural values and attackers (Sample et al., 2016, 2017a), defenders (Sample & Karamanian, 2015), and victims (Karamanian, Sample & Kolenko, 2016; Sample, Hutchinson, Karamanian & Maple, 2017b); however, it is not clear whether this profile is mutually exclusive to each type of human in the cyber hack.

STUDIES

As mentioned before, digital artifacts may remain in place long after the event occurrence. Thus, collecting data over time intervals allows the researchers to also look for trends along with cultural commonalities. The fact that this raw data reflects naturally occurring human behavior allows for analysis without interference. Because the researchers prefer to use raw observable data to infer human activity, the study of culture can be observed independent of the host or human (Minkov, 2011).

Only one of the three studies discussed relied on data found at the ICANN website (www.icann.org); the remaining studies relied on subsets of data contained in the Zone-H (www.zone-h.org) archives where the entries were dated from 2005 to 2014. The use of large sets of data in conjunction with Hofstede's operationalized data (www.geert-hofstede.com) allowed for quantitative analysis for each of the studies. The evidence-based quantitative studies allowed the researchers to reduce cultural biases during the analysis phase (Van deVijver & Leung, 1997) and base findings on objective data. The paragraphs that follow summarize the findings from each of these studies.

Methods

The methods used in the studies rely on basic statistical tools used for inference, but not causation. The observational, post-hoc analysis of archived data prevents the researchers from working directly with the subjects, but it allows for exploratory analysis that can be used to determine the existence of a phenomenon or pattern. The studies relied on group comparisons, using the Mann-Whitney-Wilcoxon (MWW) test, or Spearman correlations, both are non-parametric statistical methods chosen due to the distribution of the data (Hollander, Wolfe & Chicken, 2014).

When using the MWW test to compare groups, the cultural values for 100 countries, obtained from Hofstede's website (http://www.geert-hofstede.com) comprised the pool of country data. The list of countries found in the group being examined was extracted from the list of countries, forming two groups (participants and non-participants). These two groups were compared against each other and if the groups were considered statistically different ($p \leq 0.05$) then a finding occurred (Hollander et al., 2014). Although this is an imperfect test because the p-value represents the probability of randomly obtaining this finding. Although our test group was not randomly assembled, this method is appropriate for exploratory inference (Hollander, 2014; Sullivan 2007). The null hypothesis stating that cultural values are not related to the preference being evaluated was the standard test used in the group comparisons.

A second test, the Spearman's correlation was also used when counts of events and population data were collected (Hollander et al., 2014). The more commonly known Pearson's correlation assumes a normal distribution, and in each case the data were not normally distributed. In addition, the non-parametric Spearman's test works on both non-parametric and normally distributed data (Ibid). The resulting r-value was evaluated using Cohen's (1988) measure, which was created to deal with the high rate of type 2 errors in human behavior studies (Cohen, 1988). This modified evaluation of the r-value determines that a correlation is strong when r is ≥ 0.5 and moderate when $0.30 \leq r < 0.5$ (Ibid).

Actors

There are many different actors in the cyber environment. Given the nature of the research in cybersecurity, this chapter discusses observational studies performed on attackers, defenders, and victims (Sample et al., 2017a,b; Sample et al., 2015). Each of these studies represents an example that demonstrates cyber behaviors that are consistent with cultural values for each of the selected actor groups: attacker, victim, and defender.

In 2016, Sample et al. challenged the assertion of a single hacker culture that follows a single play-book dictated by SANS (Martin, Brown, Paller, Kirby & Christey, 2011) in two specific areas. The first challenge showed that the preferences did not follow the order included in the SANS and MITRE (http://cwe.mtre.org/top25/#listing) lists for the year examined. The second, finding, which was not included in the publication even though the data was made available, showed that some attackers appeared to distribute their attack vectors evenly, whereas others appeared to show strong preferences. Due to the small group of countries identified, and the fact that the study examined a single year, the distribution finding is only preliminary and must be examined in a larger context. This finding revealed that short-term oriented societies (median value of 20) seem to possess a more even distribution of attack vectors than their long-term oriented counterparts (median value of 50). This result suggests that further research is needed to explore the relationship between national culture and cybersecurity.

The three studies will be discussed in the remainder of this chapter. Two of the studies examined a large group of website defacement data over a multi-year period of time: one study examined attacker preferences, the next study examined commonalities associated with victims of social engineering attacks. The third study examined defenders at a specific point in time inferring the defenders' security priorities.

Attackers

In 2017, Sample et al. (2017a) presented a larger and longer examination of a small but more diverse group of self-identified attackers, using 267,556 records to examine seven different attack methods. Although many factors can contribute to the attack used, including the victim priorities, an attack preference would also contribute this process. This is because an attacker expects a specific outcome when launching an attack. An unanticipated response results in an attacker spending precious time on the target system, which increases the likelihood of being detected and caught. Thus, when the attacker uses a specific attack method, a preferred attack method (attack vector) is one factor to consider.

This study relied on 10 years of attacks, using attack vectors identified in MITRE Cyber Observables EXpression (CybOX™) (http://cybox.mitre.org) framework (MITRE2), and included the following attack vectors: zero-day (0day), brute force attack (BFA), configuration/administrator error, mail, password sniffing, social engineering, and SQL injection. Each of these attack vectors was represented by a sufficient number of countries (14%–35%) so that comparisons and analysis could be performed with confidence. Table 2 shows the distribution of attack preferences. Table 3 shows the findings of the group comparisons between the attackers and non-attackers by attacking preferences.

Table 2. Attack distribution of self-identified attackers

Vector	No. of Attacks	No. of Countries	No. of Groups
0day	3,410	21	90
BFA	2,927	21	73
Config	16,820	23	167
Mail	1,993	12	70
Password	184,155	19	142
Social	2,758	17	112
SQL	48,752	35	326

Table 3. Cultural comparison results between attackers and non-attackers (p-value)

Vector	PDI	IvC	MvF	UAI	LvS	IvR
0day	0.001	-0.288	0.540	0.702	0.819	**-0.048**
BFA	0.019	0.542	0.005	0.345	-0.449	-0.407
Config	0.002	0.676	0.012	0.776	-0.389	-0.407
Mail	0.039	-0.125	*0.072*	0.146	-0.2878	-0.176
Pass	0.012	0.261	*0.098*	0.140	-0.695	-0.271
Social	0.021	0.817	*0.052*	0.111	-0.482	-0.026
SQL	0.017	0.492	0.172	0.011	-0.500	***-0.080***

The findings showed that when attackers were compared with non-attackers for each of the attack vectors, cultural preferences appeared to emerge. High PDI strongly associated with all vectors, which suggested that authoritarian values explain the behavior more than the preference. However, masculinity associated with brute force, configuration/administrator error, and password sniffing attackers. Of note, brute force attacks, much like their name suggests, are widely seen because all attempts are logged and provide an attacker the opportunity to exhaustively attempt various possibilities. This attack allows the attacker to display their speed and completeness, behaviors that can associate with the masculine behaviors of both aggression and strength as used in conflict resolution (Hofstede et al., 2010, p. 180).

High UAI values associated with SQL injection attacks. SQL injection attacks require the attacker to specifically create and enter a command that causes the server to fail, which then gives the attacker access (Halfond & Orso, 2005; Su & Wasserman, 2006) to the system. This attack requires precision to craft the command, a trait associated with high UAI values (Hofstede et al., 2010, p. 217). If the command is well executed, the resulting logged data trail is considerably smaller than the trail of some of the other attacks examined, showing consistency with the precision associated with high UAI.

Restraint associated with social engineering attackers and 0day attacks. As noted in the study by Sample et al. (2017a), the rise of the bug bounty programs (Just, Premraj & Zimmermann, 2008) may have played a role in the use of 0day attacks. 0day attacks are typically purchased and then saved for a later day when needed. Generally speaking, webservers are typically not considered high-value targets. Mail servers and database servers are generally considered the high-value targets because these servers contain user accounts. 0day attacks, like all attacks, should also be examined with the reason in order to gain further insights.

Social engineering attacks are of particular interest because these attacks are designed to get the target to perform an act that they would not typically do. Thus, the attacker is relying less on technology and more on trust or believability. In addition, the association with restraint is of interest, suggesting that less information may be more believable or that too much information might be less believable.

The findings from this study support the assertion that some attack vectors appear to be more attractive to attackers based on their values, including cultural values. These findings support Hofstede's belief that globalized software is being used by culturally influenced minds (Aguayo et al., 2011). Because this line of research is still new, more studies will be needed to provide a more complete understanding of the influence of cultural values on attackers, behaviors, preferences, and decisions.

Defenders

In 2015, Sample and Karamanian examined Domain Name System (DNS) Security Extensions (DNSSEC)-signed top-level domains (TLDs). DNSSEC, when installed and fully operating, act as a defense against attacks that involve the integrity of DNS data (Arends, Austein, Larson, Massey & Rose, 2005). Attacks, such as DNS cache poisoning and DNS hijacking, can be repelled when DNSSEC, with validation checking, is deployed by the DNS servers on both sides of the communication link (St. Johns, 2007). This defensive action was chosen due to the long-standing implementation of DNSSEC and the variable adoption rate.

The first step in deploying DNSSSEC requires the domain to digitally sign the zone, and the list of signed TLDs is maintained at IANNA (www.ianna.org). DNSSEC key management is generally a manual process; however, the process can be made more efficient by parents managing keys for the child domains. The root domain (.) is the parent of all domains including the TLDs, and the root domain was signed in 2010. The signing of the root domain removed a significant implementation obstacle; however, there are still many TLDs that are not signed. The researchers in this study (Sample & Karamanian, 2015) wondered whether cultural values might be considered.

The act of signing a zone equates with being a good net citizen (Arends et al, 2005), but it does not assure additional security until keys are exchanged. However, signing a zone is indicative of plans to share DNSSEC information with other signed zones since this is required for zone-sharing information (Ibid), and a signed TLD may hold and manage keys for children domains (St. Johns, 2007). This study was focused on TLDs. The findings are shown in Tables 4 and 5. The results from this study revealed that the countries with signed TLD zones were low PDI, individualistic, and long-term oriented.

Victims

Social engineering attacks rely on the target performing an act that is prohibited by policy (i.e., clicking on an embedded e-mail link from an unknown source; sharing an account password). The earlier study of self-identified attackers showed cultural values of restraint and high PDI. Therefore, the researchers wondered whether victims shared specific cultural traits. An earlier study by Saridakis, Benson, Ezin-

Table 4. Cultural values in DNNSEC zone signing (p-value)

Value/Dim	PDI	IVC	M/F	UAI	LvS	IVR
p-value	**-0.0001**	**0.001**	-0.1922	0.4602	**0.0001**	0.4483

Table 5. Correlations between cultural values and DNSSEC zone signing (r-value)

Value/Dim	PDI	IVC	M/F	UAI	LvS	IVR
R	**-0.447**	**0.372**	-0.089	0.010	**0.410**	0.016

gard, and Tennakoon (2015) found that social networking users who relied on those sites for information gathering, a trait that Hofstede et al. (2010) associated with populations in masculine societies were more likely to be victimized in the online environment.

The Sample et al. (2017b) study on the victims of social engineering attacks relied on the collection of 17,074 records for sorting and comparison over the period of 2011–2014. The findings from this study can be viewed in Tables 6 and 7.

The results of this study showed that the social engineering victim countries tended to be individualist (high IvC), long-term oriented (LTO), and egalitarian (low PDI) compared with the non-victim countries. The high IvC that indicates individualism coupled with the low PDI or egalitarian values fits well with the Hofstede et al (2010) and Guess (2004) observations of a higher tolerance for risk in pursuit of reward. The LTO finding suggests that the victims may perceive a potential ongoing relationship with the adversary, bearing in mind that the victim does not know that the adversary is a bad actor at this point in the relationship.

CONCLUSION

Culture can help explain similarities as well as differences (Wang, 2016) within and between groups (attackers, defenders, and victims), so we aimed to statistically describe new relationships. The studies examined contain insights into attacker preferences (Sample et al., 2016, 2017a), defending strategies (Sample & Karamanian, 2015), and victim analysis (Karamanian & Sample, 2015; Sample et al., 2017a). All of the studies were observational in nature and relied on publicly available data. In agreement with Wang's (2016) observation that culture can explain similarities as well as differences, all of the studies were performed with the goal of determining whether statistical similarities existed between the actor groups being studied.

Cultural values appear to be a viable grouping mechanism for cyber behaviors and preferences. Hofstede et al (2010) cautions readers that although cultural values can explain and predict actions in a

Table 6. Cultural values of social engineering victims (p-value)

Year/Dim	PDI	IvC	MvF	UAI	LvS	IvR
2011	**-0.0006385**	**+0.0001918**	+0.398	**+0.02721**	**+0.01847**	+0.9592
2012	**-0.004804**	**+0.003447**	+0.1227	**+0.01759**	**+0.00036632**	*-0.05757*
2013	**-0.01232**	**+0.001298**	*+0.0844*	*+0.06694*	**+0.0007319**	-0.291
2014	**-0.005519**	**+0.002825**	*+0.08041*	*+0.09384*	**+0.03672**	-0.8021

Table 7. Correlations between cultural values and social engineering victims (r-value)

Dataset/Dim	PDI	IvC	MvF	UAI	LvS	IvR
Victims	*-0.3460*	*0.4493*	*-0.3232*	*0.0475*	*0.3763*	*0.0702*

broad sense, these values cannot and should not be used to predict individual behaviors (Ibid). Culture sets norms for groups of people, but individuals can and do deviate from norms in all societies.

Cultural values can provide insights into various cyber actors' behaviors, preferences, and even decisions; however, culture is one piece of a larger puzzle. This piece is a critical piece since it provides context.

REFERENCES

Aguayo, D., Herman, K., Ojeda, L., & Flores, L. Y. (2011). Culture predicts Mexican Americans' college self-efficacy and college performance. *Journal of Diversity in Higher Education, 4*(2), 79–89. doi:10.1037/a0022504

Al-Gahtani, S. S., Hubona, G. S., & Wang, J. (2007). Information technology (IT) in Saudi Arabia: Culture and the acceptance and use of IT. *Information & Management, 44*(8), 681–691. doi:10.1016/j.im.2007.09.002

Almeshekah, M. H., & Spafford, E. H. (2014). Planning and integrating deception into computer security defenses. *Proceedings of the 2014 Workshop on New Security Paradigms Workshop*, 127–138. Retrieved from http://dl.acm.org/citation.cfm?id=2683482

Arends, R., Austein, R., Larson, M., Massey, D., & Rose, S. (2005). *DNS Security Introduction and Requirements*. Internet Engineering Task Force (IETF) RFC 4033.

Arrindell, W. A., Hatzichristou, C., Wensink, J., Rosenberg, E., van Twillert, B., Sedema, J., & Meijer, D. (1997). Dimensions of national culture as predictors of cross-national differences in subjective well-being. *Personality and Individual Differences, 23*(1), 37–53. doi:10.1016/S0191-8869(97)00023-8

Bargh, J., & Morsella, E. (2008). The Unconscious Mind. *Perspectives on Psychological Science, 3*(1), 73–79. doi:10.1111/j.1745-6916.2008.00064.x PMID:18584056

Bhabha, H. K. (1997). The world and the home. *Cultural Politics, 11*, 445–455.

Binford, L. R. (1962). Archaeology as anthropology. *American Antiquity, 28*(02), 217–225. doi:10.2307/278380

Bishop, M., Butler, E., Butler, K., Gates, C., & Greenspan, S. (2012). Forgive and Forget. *21st EICAR Annual Conference Proceedings*, 151–159.

Buchtel, E. E., & Norenzayan, A. (2009). *Thinking across cultures: Implications for dual processes*. J. St. BT Evans & K. Frankish.

Cohen, J. (1988). *Statistical Power Analysis for the Behavioural Sciences* (2nd ed.). Hillsdale, NJ: Lawrence Eribaum Associates.

Dawar, N., Parker, P. M., & Price, L. J. (1996). A cross-cultural study of interpersonal information exchange. *Journal of International Business Studies, 27*(3), 497–516. doi:10.1057/palgrave.jibs.8490142

Doney, P. M., Cannon, J. P., & Mullen, M. R. (1998). Understanding the Influence of National Culture on the Development of Trust. *Academy of Management Review, 23*(3), 601–620.

Elmasry, M. H., Auter, P. I., & Peuchaud, S. R. (2014). *Facebook across culture: A cross-cultural content analysis of Egyptian, Qatari and American student Facebook pages* (PhD Dissertation). The American University in Cairo, Egypt.

Evans, J. S. (2008). Dual-processing accounts of reasoning, judgment, and social cognition. *Annual Review of Psychology, 59*(1), 255–278. doi:10.1146/annurev.psych.59.103006.093629 PMID:18154502

Fiske, S. T., & Taylor, S. E. (2013). *Social cognition: From brains to culture*. Thousand Oaks, CA: Sage. doi:10.4135/9781446286395

Geert-Hofstede. (2015). Retrieved from: http://www.geert-hofstede.com

Geert Hofstede. (n.d.). Retrieved from https://geert-hofstede.com/countries.html

Guess, C. D. (2004). Decision-making in Individualistic and Collectivist Cultures. *Readings in Psychology and Culture, 4.* Retrieved from: http://scholarworks.gvsu.edu/cgi/viewcontent.cgi?article=1032&context=orpc

Guss, C. D., & Dorner, D. (2012). Cultural differences in dynamic decision-making strategies in a non-linear, time-delayed task. *Cognitive Systems Research, 12*(3), 365–376.

Halfond, W. G., & Orso, A. (2005, November). AMNESIA: Analysis and monitoring for neutralizing SQL-infection attacks. *Proceedings of the 20th IEEE/ACM International Conference on Automated Software Engineering*, 174–183. doi:10.1145/1101908.1101935

Henrich, J., Heine, S. J., & Norenzayan, A. (2010). The weirdest people in the world? *Behavioral and Brain Sciences, 33*(3), 61-83.

Henshel, D., Sample, C., Cains, M. G., & Hoffman, B. (2016). Integrating Cultural Factors into Human Factors Framework for Cyber Attackers. *7th Annual Conference on Applied Human Factors and Ergonomics Conference.* doi:10.1007/978-3-319-41932-9_11

Hofstede, G. (1980). *Cultures Consequences: International Differences in Work-Related Values* (Vol. 5). Thousand Oaks, CA: Sage.

Hofstede, G., Hofstede, G. J., & Minkov, M. (2010). *Cultures and Organizations*. New York, NY: McGraw-Hill Publishing.

Hollander, Wolfe, & Chicken. (2014). *Nonparametric statistical methods* (3rd ed.). John Wiley & Sons.

Huff, L., & Kelley, L. (2003). Levels of organizational trust in individualist versus collectivist societies: A seven-nation study. *Organization Science, 14*(1), 81–90. doi:10.1287/orsc.14.1.81.12807

ICANN. (n.d.). Retrieved from http://www.icann.org

Just, S., Premraj, R., & Zimmermann, T. (2008). Towards the next generation of bug tracking systems. *VL/HCC 2008 - IEEE Symposium on Visual Languages and Human-Centric Computing*, 82–85.

Karamanian, A., Sample, C., & Kolenko, M. (2016). Hofstede's cultural markers in successful victim cyber exploitations. *11th International Conference on Cyber Warfare and Security*, 205-213.

Kirkman, B. L., Lowe, K. B., & Gibson, C. B. (2006). A quarter century of culture's consequences: A review of empirical research incorporating Hofstede's cultural values framework. *Journal of International Business Studies*, *37*(3), 285–320. doi:10.1057/palgrave.jibs.8400202

Li, W. C., & Harris, D. (2005). HFACS analysis of ROC Air Force aviation accidents: Reliability analysis and cross-cultural comparison. *International Journal of Applied Aviation Studies*, *5*(1), 65–81.

Mandl, T. (2009). Comparing Chinese and German blogs. *HT '09 Proceedings of the 20th ACM Conference on Hypertext and Hypermedia*, 299–308. Retrieved from http://dl.acm.org/citation.cfm?id=1557964

Martin, B., Brown, M., Paller, A. Kirby, D., & Christey, S. (2011) 2011 CWE/SANS top 25 most dangerous software errors. *Common Weakness Enumeration*, 7515.

Matusitz, J. (2014). The role of intercultural communication in cyberterrorism. *Journal of Human Behavior in the Social Environment*, *24*(7), 775–790. doi:10.1080/10911359.2013.876375

Minkov, M. (2011). *Cultural Differences in a Globalizing World*. Bingley, UK: Emerald Group Publishing Limited.

Morgan, T. H., Cross, C. P., & Rendell, L. E. (2015). *Nothing in human behavior makes sense except in the light of culture: Shared interests of social psychology and cultural evolution. In Evolutionary Perspectives on Social Psychology* (pp. 215–228). Springer International Publishing.

Nisbett, R. (2010). *The geography of thought: how Asians and Westerners think differently... and why*. New York: Simon & Schuster.

Rathje, S. (2009). The definition of culture: An application-oriented overhaul. *Interculture Journal*, 35–59.

Roberts, J. M. Jr, Moore, C. C., Romney, A. K., Barbujani, G., Bellwood, P., Dunnell, R. C., & Terrell, J. (1995). Predicting similarity in material culture among New Guinea Villages from propinquity and language: A log-linear approach. *Current Anthropology*, *36*(5), 769–788. doi:10.1086/204431

Sample, C. (2013). Applicability of Cultural Markers in Computer Network Attack Attribution. *Proceedings of the 12th European Conference on Cyber Warfare and Security*, 361–369.

Sample, C., Cowley, J., & Hutchinson, S. (2017a). Cultural Exploration of Attack Vector Preferences for Self-identified Attackers. *IEEE 11th International Conference on Research Challenges in Information Science*, 305–314. doi:10.1109/RCIS.2017.7956551

Sample, C., Cowley, J., Watson, T., & Maple, C. (2016). Re-thinking threat intelligence. *International Conference on Cyber Conflict (CyCon US)*, 1–9.

Sample, C., Hutchinson, S., Karamanian, A., & Maple, C. (2017b). *Cultural Observations on Social Engineering Victims. 16th ECCWS*, 391–401.

Sample, C., & Karamanian, A. (2015). Culture and Cyber Behaviours: DNS Defending. 14th ECCWS, 233–240.

Sanchez-Franco, M. J., Martinez-Lopez, F. J., & Martin-Velicia, F. A. (2009). Exploring the impact of individualism and uncertainty avoidance in Web-based training: An empirical analysis in European higher education. *Computers & Education*, *52*(3), 588–598. doi:10.1016/j.compedu.2008.11.006

Saridakis, G., Benson, V., Ezingard, J., & Tennakoon, H. (2015). Individual information security, user behaviour and cyber victimization: An empirical study of social networking users. *Technological Forecasting and Social Change*. doi:10/1016/j.techfore.2015.08.012

Schwartz, S. H. (2012). An overview of the Schwartz theory of basic values. *Online Readings in Psychology and Culture*, 2(1). doi:10.9707/2307-0919.1116

Shane, S. (1995). Uncertainty avoidance and the preference for innovation championing roles. *Journal of International Business Studies*, 26(1), 47–68. doi:10.1057/palgrave.jibs.8490165

Shewder, R. A. (1999). Why cultural psychology. *Ethos (Berkeley, Calif.)*, 27(1), 62–73. doi:10.1525/eth.1999.27.1.62

Singelis, T. M., & Brown, W. J. (1995). Culture, self, and collectivist communication linking culture to individual behavior. *Human Communication Research*, 21(3), 354–389. doi:10.1111/j.1468-2958.1995.tb00351.x PMID:12349710

Soeters, J. L., & Boer, P. C. (2000). Culture and flight safety in military aviation. *The International Journal of Aviation Psychology*, 10(2), 111–133. doi:10.1207/S15327108IJAP1002_1

St. Johns, M. (2007). *Automated updates of DNS security (DNSSEC) trust anchors*. Internet Engineering Task Force.

Su, Z., & Wassermann, G. (2006, January). The essence of command injection attacks in web applications. *ACM SIGPLAN Notices*, 41(1), 372–382. doi:10.1145/1111320.1111070

Sullivan, M. (2007). *Statistics: Informed decisions using data*. Upper Saddle River, NJ: Pearson Education Inc.

Van de Vijver, F., & Leung, K. (1997). *Methods and Data Analysis for Cross-Cultural Research* (Vol. 1). Thousand Oaks, CA: Sage.

Vitell, S. J., Nwachukwu, S. L., & Barnes, J. H. (1993). The effects of culture on ethical decision-making: An application of Hofstede's typology. *Journal of Business Ethics*, 12(10), 753–760. doi:10.1007/BF00881307

Von Solms, R., & Van Niekerk, J. (2013). From information security to cyber security. *Computers & Security*, 38, 97–102. doi:10.1016/j.cose.2013.04.004

Wang, Q. (2016). Why we should all be cultural psychologists? Lessons learned from the study of social cognition. *Perspectives on Psychological Science*, 11(5), 583–596. doi:10.1177/1745691616645552 PMID:27694456

Zaheer, S., & Zaheer, A. (1997). Country Effects on Information Seeking in Global Electronic Networks. *Journal of International Business Studies*, 28(1), 77–100. doi:10.1057/palgrave.jibs.8490094

Zhao, C., & Jiang, G. (2011). Cultural differences on visual self-presentation through social networking site profile images. *Proceedings of the ACM SIGCHI Conference on Human Factors in Computing Systems (CHI)*. doi:10.1145/1978942.1979110

Chapter 5
Examinations of Email Fraud Susceptibility:
Perspectives From Academic Research and Industry Practice

Helen S. Jones
University of Dundee, UK

John Towse
Lancaster University, UK

ABSTRACT

The internet provides an ever-expanding, valuable resource for entertainment, communication, and commerce. However, this comes with the simultaneous advancement and sophistication of cyber-attacks, which have serious implications on both a personal and commercial level, as well as within the criminal justice system. Psychologically, such attacks offer an intriguing, under-exploited arena for the understanding of the decision-making processes leading to online fraud victimisation. In this chapter, the authors focus on approaches taken to understand response behaviour surrounding phishing emails. The chapter outlines how approaches from industry and academic research might work together to more effectively understand and potentially tackle the persistent threat of email fraud. In doing this, the authors address alternative methodological approaches taken to understand susceptibility, key insights drawn from each, how useful these are in working towards preventative security measures, and the usability of each approach. It is hoped that these can contribute to collaborative solutions.

INTRODUCTION

In 2016, the rate of malicious emails being sent to users was at its highest in five years. For example, in relation to one specific type of phishing, approximately 1 in every 131 emails contains malware (Verizon, 2017). Despite efforts from experts in the field, email fraud remains one of the most pertinent cyber security threats. The persistence of this threat indicates a need for reconsideration of mitigation methods

DOI: 10.4018/978-1-5225-4053-3.ch005

in place to protect against this, as those currently employed do not seem to be sufficient to counteract it. In line with this, there is also a need to consider the effectiveness of methods used within a research setting to improve our understanding of how users become victims to social engineering attacks, such as phishing emails. It is crucial that there is an alignment between the theoretical knowledge base gained through academic research, and the practical role this has in industry efforts to tackle email fraud.

Research across multiple disciplines has considered how best to address the threat posed by social engineering attacks. Computer science research is often concerned with systems-based approaches to managing fraud through the use of detection algorithms (Islam & Abawajy, 2013; Salah, Alcarez Calero, Zeadally, Al-Mulla, & Alzaabi, 2013) or automated heuristic filters, which detect machine learned patterns (Abu-Nimeh, Nappa, Wang, & Nair, 2007; Garera, Provos, Chew, & Rubin, 2007) to prevent emails from reaching the user. However, simultaneous advancement in the techniques employed by the fraudster means that these solutions are short-lived, as a work around is often found within a short space of time to circumvent such detection algorithms. In addition to this, these machine learning approaches tend to focus more on the detection of generic phishing emails, with detectable anomalies to legitimate email traffic. They may be less suited to the detection of more sophisticated attacks that either employ a hacked account, or are more personalised to appear believable. In these cases, the attacker is targeting what is often considered the systems' weakest link – the human user (Barrett, 2003; Mitnick & Simon, 2002; Schneier, 2000).

As the 'weakest link' in cyber security, the human user and the decision-making processes they employ in email management must be understood in order to address the threat and reduce system vulnerability. Contributions from psychology have considered how various factors can affect email response behaviour, from individual differences amongst users, to the context in which a specific email is read. Unfortunately, such findings are constrained by limitations in conducting fundamental cyber security research from both a practical and an ethical perspective. On the other hand, industry experts in cyber security conduct training exercises and vulnerability tests within organisations without the same constraints that feature within academic research. This chapter will outline how the approaches taken in academia and industry to understand and address issues relating to email decision-making can complement one another. In doing this, the authors aim to highlight the importance of unity between these two approaches, emphasising the need for continued collaboration in future research in order to maximise the effectiveness of efforts made to tackle the persistent threat of email fraud.

EMAIL FRAUD TYPOLOGY

As most internet users will be aware, phishing emails come in all shapes and sizes, covering an array of subjects from sale of Viagra pills to urgent account updates. As such, providing a specific definition of phishing is not straightforward, although one useful example comes from Myers (2007):

Phishing: A form of social engineering in which an attacker, also known as a phisher, attempts to fraudulently retrieve legitimate users' confidential or sensitive credentials by mimicking electronic communications from a trustworthy or public organisation in an automated fashion. (p. 1)

Across the wide array of fraudulent emails in circulation, there are a number of factors that allow for a broad categorisation. Three main types of phishing emails that commonly exist will be outlined.

These are often successful in deceiving thousands of users. A series of specific real world examples will then be outlined to demonstrate how these different approaches and techniques might be incorporated in genuine phishing attacks.

1. **Deceptive Emails:** In the most generic sense, deceptive emails are distributed to thousands of users in an attempt to gather confidential information. This vast distribution only require a small response rate to be economically worthwhile for the fraudster. These emails usually attempt to solicit account information, passwords, or install malicious software. Most often, users are required to download a file, or click a link embedded within the email. Following a link may then ask them to input their login details to a fake website, purporting to come from a genuine organisation. Additional persuasive tactics may be employed in these emails, such as a sense of urgency, leading users to panic about losing access to accounts if they do not act. Empirical evidence demonstrates the impact of time pressure on decision-making, as discussed in more detail below, emphasising the impact that this type of persuasive approach can have on a user.

2. **Spear Phishing:** As opposed to the generic phishing emails that are distributed to many users, spear phishing is a sophisticated social engineering technique that targets an attack towards a specific user or group of users. By accessing information about the recipient from social media and public web pages, or with access to insider knowledge, these emails incorporate personal or particularly relevant information, in order to make an attack more believable.

3. **Whaling:** One specific type of spear phishing attack involves imitation of a senior executive of a company, known as whaling. This acts as a way of convincing an employee to respond and act in a way that benefits the fraudster. For example, they may be asked to transfer money to a fraudulent account, under the premise of a legitimate business transaction. This approach is typically conducted by gaining access to the executive's account to send the email, or through the use of a convincingly similar domain name to that of the company being targeted. The specificity of information incorporated into these emails means users often overlook the minor details that indicate the fraudulent nature of the message.

REAL WORLD CASE STUDIES

Media reports of cyber security attacks are becoming more frequent, as they increase in scale and sophistication. Particular attention is drawn to attacks on large corporations that hold confidential data on thousands, or even millions, of members of the public as customers. The high profile individuals whose response decisions allow access to this data are often scrutinised, in particular when there is substantial financial loss as a result of the attack. Such cases demonstrate the extent of risk associated with user response to email fraud, and also the diversity in approaches taken by the fraudsters to target these organisations.

In late 2013, US store Target was the victim of a substantial data breach, with credit card information for around 110 million customers stolen (Peterson, 2014), and it all began with a malware infected phishing email (Picchi, 2014). By targeting a heating and air conditioning firm that were subcontracted by Target, the fraudsters were able to obtain network credentials and access confidential sales and customer data. Although the financial impact of this case has not been reported, it demonstrates the vulnerability of companies who have a strong obligation to protect confidential customer information.

During the US election campaign in late 2016, thousands of emails from the personal account of John Podesta, campaign chairman for Hilary Clinton, began appearing on the whistle-blowing website WikiLeaks (Smith, 2016). These shed light on relationships and disputes between party members, as well as campaign strategies. As the story evolved, it became apparent that these emails were accessed following a phishing attack purporting to be from Google, which Podesta had responded to even after seeking advice from colleagues about its legitimacy. The email inferred unauthorised access to the account and provided a link for Podesta to change his password in order to ensure security. The success of this attack demonstrates the potential impact of response not only on the user, but also in this case on the integrity of an entire political campaign.

In early 2017, reports hit the headlines of two US companies being victims of a phishing attack that led to over $100 million being transferred to the fraudster over a two-year period (Yuhas, 2017). By posing as an employee of a manufacturing company in Asia that regularly conducted business with the companies, the fraudster convinced employees to set up numerous multi-million dollar transactions. It was later announced that Google and Facebook were the victimised companies (Roberts, 2017), two of the world's biggest technology companies. This targeted attack, using a deceptive cover and mirroring transactions that employees were familiar with organising, demonstrates the level of sophistication that can be achieved.

The case studies outlined here give an insight into the different types and variations on phishing emails, from generic password changes to sophisticated social engineering attacks. These also highlight the differing impacts that these can have on the victim or organisation, from confidential data breaches to extensive financial loss.

BEHAVIOURAL EXAMINATIONS OF SUSCEPTIBILITY IN INDUSTRY

The case studies highlighted above give only a brief snapshot of the degree to which organisations across a range of industry sectors can demonstrate vulnerability to email fraud, with varying magnitude. As such, many organisations acknowledge that there is a need to address cyber security concerns. It is becoming more common for companies to employ cyber security experts to conduct vulnerability testing, and the need for this is increased by the introduction of new regulations on data privacy, such as the EU General Data Protection Regulation. It is possible that this shift in attitude towards engaging with additional security measures may be due to compliance with legislation, rather than a deeper understanding of the risks faced, but regardless it shows a step in the right direction towards addressing ongoing cyber security threats. In this section, the authors will outline the approaches commonly used in an industry setting to assess vulnerability to email fraud, and consider how these can benefit organisations, whilst going on to consider how they may be enhanced by integration with theoretical insights from academic research.

Methods

When engaging cyber security experts to mitigate risk, there are three common routes an organisation can take. On the most basic level, some organisations opt for a vulnerability test, which provides a basic overview of the weaknesses within a system, based on data from an automated scan that picks up common errors and configuration mistakes (Yeo, 2013). This type of testing does not allow experts to examine the data that they could potentially obtain through these vulnerabilities. Instead, it highlights surface-level issues, such as missing security patches, that can be fixed promptly and without occupying the time of company employees. It also does not take into account the vulnerability that can result from employee behaviour online.

In addition to this, many organisations employ a penetration testing team to demonstrate the scale of the vulnerability. This allows information to be gathered about whether they are able to infiltrate the organisation's network and systems, and what extent of data they are able to attain. This can involve: an attack on the physical network, to assess whether the devices used by employees can be hacked; attempts to bypass the security solutions that the organisation currently has in place, such as firewalls; and assessment of the effectiveness of attacks targeted at employees of the company, through user-based vulnerability testing, which will be discussed in more detail later in this section.

One major concern in employing external penetration testers, also known as ethical hackers, is their trustworthiness. The organisation is, in a sense, encouraging these experts to hijack their systems, and as a result giving them access to potentially confidential data. A penetration test can either be conducted externally, testing how easily an organisation can be hacked from outside the network, or internally to assess the risk associated with insider attacks. An organisation must have faith that these ethical hackers will not become malicious, taking advantage of an organisation at its most vulnerable for personal gain. The need for this kind of security testing may outweigh the potential cost, and an organisation often has no choice but to trust the ethical hackers (Duke, 2002).

The nature of a penetration test is dependent on the specific needs of an organisation, who will highlight their main concerns to the testers and allow them to conduct simulated attacks as appropriate. For organisations that are concerned with the risk posed by employee behaviour, a penetration test might involve a behavioural assessment through administration of a simulated phishing attack, designed for the purpose of the investigation. The employees who receive the phishing email are kept unaware of the vulnerability testing being conducted, in order to provide a realistic assessment of response behaviour. The rate of response to the simulated attack informs the organisation of the level of risk faced as a result of human decision-making. However, penetration testing only captures the level of vulnerability within an organisation at the given point in time when an attack is simulated. In reality, the level of vulnerability is likely to vary with contextual and organisational changes within the organisation, but multiple simulated attacks across different contexts would be time consuming and may raise suspicion with employees, impairing the validity of the assessment.

In contrast, a comprehensive cyber risk assessment goes a long way to overcome this issue of context, by considering the specific assets that leave an organisation most vulnerable, the likelihood of an attack on these occurring, the impact that could come from this, and the risk management strategies that would be most effective in addressing it (NIST, 2012). Whilst this type of assessment often incorporates vulnerability and penetration testing, it will also go beyond these to explore the risks posed by associated organisations, and shared data networks. In addition, the risk management strategies that result from such an assessment are continually monitored and updated in line with the transient nature of threats faced by the company, and the varying levels of vulnerability encountered.

These three approaches offer differing, but complimentary, methods for understanding the extent of an organisation's vulnerability. Each has an alternative outcome measure, and as such the decision about which to employ is dependent upon the needs of a specific organisation. The key insights that can be attained through the use of such techniques are outlined in more detail below.

Key Insights and Usability

In relation specifically to assessing vulnerability to phishing emails, the use of actual simulated attacks, in which the recipients are unaware of the artificial nature of the email received, means a naturalistic assessment of susceptibility in the work place can be achieved. Simulated phishing attacks as part of a penetration test usually require specific hypotheses that shape the email stimuli, have certain success criterion that demonstrate vulnerability within employees, and require use of a method that can be replicated in future assessments (Barrett, 2003). The rigour involved in the design and implementation of such a test is akin to an empirical experiment carried out as part of an academic research project. Unlike a research study though, there are fewer limitations on the methods used in order to simulate an attack, "the imagination of the social engineer is the only limit to the types of approaches that they can present and exploit" (Barrett, 2003). These tests demonstrate to organisations that the behaviour of employees can put their organisation at risk during an attack, which often results in additional training on how to detect phishing attacks and reduce vulnerability if an actual attack were to happen.

However, some have argued that there are limitations to the techniques involved with simulated attacks, as well as more broadly with penetration testing, which impair the usefulness of this technique in reducing future user vulnerability within an organisation. It has been noted by experts in the field that the lack of continuity or common taxonomy in the type of simulations conducted (Hudic, et al., 2013) makes replication and comparison of results across organisations difficult, in particular where tailored social engineering attacks are implemented (Barrett, 2003). As mentioned above though, the specific risks faced by an organisation vary dependent on their assets, and also across different contexts. As such, a simulated attack requires an element of tailoring (that has the down side of making it non-replicable) in order to give a valid assessment of vulnerability. It is therefore important to consider the balance of assessment rigour and validity in relation to the specific organisation, in order to optimise the impact and utility of this technique.

As an assessment of an organisation's vulnerability to targeted social engineering attacks, penetration tests are limited by an ethical responsibility to avoid infiltration of third party systems and linked organisations (Barrett, 2003). In this sense, the test may underestimate vulnerability, given the magnitude of additional information that could be gathered from these external sources in order to generate or target an attack that affects the organisation itself. As demonstrated in the earlier Target case study, access to confidential data was breached as a result of someone in a third party organisation with close ties to Target, responding to an email attack. By considering the hypothetical scenarios in which third party organisations might increase vulnerability, a cyber risk assessment also describes the additional risks associated with shared access to confidential data and information systems. This is typically accounted for in the development of a risk mitigation strategy that includes monitoring of changes in who has access to data, and addresses the threat associated with this.

Whilst these methods provide a valuable assessment of vulnerability within a naturalistic environment, and in many cases incorporate actual response behaviour through simulated attacks, they provide little insight into the underlying behavioural processes that influence employee behaviour. In relation to penetration testing, this means that there is no assessment of the context in which an email is received and read, which may have an impact on the response decision, as shown in academic research, discussed in more detail later in this chapter. Whilst risk assessments are designed to consider a broader range of vulnerabilities within the organisation, they still lack the depth to understand why some employees may be more susceptible to attack than others. In cases where individual employees *are* recognised for their demonstration of vulnerability during a simulated attack, this can lead to disciplinary actions (Barrett, 2003) rather than attempts to understand and modify behaviour. Where training is invoked upon employees, this can range from warnings and response instructions, to more informative educational and support programmes. The former has limited success in reducing response behaviour though (Junger, Montoya, & Overink, 2017), whilst the latter is less common due to time constraints and cost of implementation. Instead of encouraging secure behaviour in the future, the use of simulated phishing attacks and training may have an unforeseen effect of employee disgruntlement with the process (Murdoch & Sasse, 2017).

By conducting simulated attacks in the work place, there is an overarching ethical concern that these are in some ways designed to 'catch out' employees. The discontent that results from this means that employees may not acknowledge the benefits that could be elicited through more secure behaviour in the future. Compliance in general is a concern, in relation to risk mitigation strategies that come from a cyber risk assessment also. It is therefore important to consider how such risk mitigation strategies might be informed by our understanding of human behaviour and decision-making processes to better understand both vulnerability, and behaviour change around security protocols. Rather than seeking to punish and patronise employees, this understanding would allow effective user-centric security solutions. This is where insights from academic research might be able to better inform the development of security initiatives taken within industry organisations, in an effort to enhance effective response behaviour surrounding cyber threats.

BEHAVIOURAL EXAMINATIONS OF SUSCEPTIBILITY IN RESEARCH

Psychological approaches from academic research offer an alternative perspective to cyber security behaviour, by attempting to understand the underlying mechanisms that influence behaviour. Focusing on the decisions made by human users, such research has attempted to understand *why* certain users demonstrate a higher level of susceptibility to email fraud. Reports suggest a fraudulent email response rate of approximately 5% (Norton, 2014), meaning that 95% of users who receive the same email do not respond. This may be because some did not see the email, some may have deleted it without reading it, but a large proportion are likely to have read (at least some of) the email and made an explicit decision not to respond. This might be because it was not relevant to them, or because they recognised its fraudulent nature. In all cases, the processes underlying such decisions offer an interesting set of clues that may be eventually help optimise secure online behaviour (Fischer, Lee, & Evans, 2013).

Most research studies are conducted within a controlled environment, allowing the researcher to manipulate various aspects of the stimuli and context in which this is viewed, to understand specific behaviours. However, this also means that the naturalistic assessment of susceptibility is jeopardised in many cases. It is therefore important, for this emerging field of psychology, to understand how this level of experimental control affects decision-making behaviour, and consider ways to enhance the validity of research, whilst maintaining ethical integrity.

Methods

Whilst approaches from industry are most often concerned with the immediate and applied need to manage organisational risk by reducing employee vulnerability, academic research places greater emphasis on identifying conceptual relationships between variables, testing and validating theories of causal processes.

Research has adopted a variety of approaches to assess human behaviour surrounding phishing emails, which perhaps contributes to the lack of consistency. In terms of behavioural assessments of susceptibility, methods have ranged from explicit legitimacy judgments of email stimulus, to simulated attacks whereby participants have given consent to an alternative research study. The use of explicit judgment tasks allows for control of situational influences on response behaviour, such as time pressure (Yan & Gozu, 2010; Jones, Towse, Race, & Harrison, submitted), whilst simulated emails provide a more realistic measure that still allows for some level of control over the stimulus that participants are responding to.

In an explicit judgment task, participants are typically asked to make a decision about the legitimacy of a series of email stimulus, or asked how they would respond to each of these. Yan and Gozu (2012) showed participants a set of 36 emails, all of which were genuine phishing emails, and asked them whether they would 'read' or 'delete' each of these. In this particular task, results may be limited by the use of phishing emails only, meaning that participants who were looking to differentiate between phishing and legitimate emails may have demonstrated an expectancy bias. Alternative versions of this type of task have incorporated a mixture of phishing and legitimate emails (Jones, et al., submitted; Nicholson, Coventry, & Briggs, 2017), allowing for a more representative example of what a participant might see in their own inbox. However, such methodologies are still limited by the explicit nature of the legitimacy judgments, which does not reflect the complexity of the decision-making process that likely occurs in real life. Instead, participants are encouraged to engage in certain behaviours, such as employing more rational decision-making strategies, which results in an artificially high accurate response rate to the email stimulus (Yan & Gozu, 2012; Harrison, Vishwanath, & Rao, 2016).

Alternative approaches to the use of explicit judgment tasks have incorporated a role-play element, whereby participants are asked to interact with and manage the inbox of a fictional employee, and report how they would respond to a series of emails (e.g. Downs, Holbrook, & Cranor, 2007; Hong et al., 2013). This variation on the task allows for an assessment of how users interact with an actual inbox, without being alerted to the nature of the task. However, it is possible that the nature of the task itself, asking participants to make response decisions to a set of emails, may alert them to the purpose of the research. This being said, Parsons et al. (2013) demonstrated that participants showed higher accuracy in a role-play scenario like this when they were aware of the nature of the task, compared to participants who were only told the purpose of the study after completing that task. This difference in response behaviour suggests that the naïve participants were not alerted to the purpose of the study whilst completing it. This study raises an important point about the accuracy of response rates seen in lab-based studies of email behaviour though, demonstrating that making explicit judgments may elicit an artificially low level of susceptibility. However, there is little evidence to indicate how this artificial response behaviour relates to real world susceptibility.

An additional limitation to such lab-based assessments of response behaviour is the lack of consequence associated with responding, in comparison to real life. When responding through a simulated account, the participant has nothing to lose in choosing to respond or not respond. This is in contrast to a genuine attack within industry, where an error in judgment can lead to data leaks, espionage, and financial loss. Within the lab environment on the other hand, participants may receive a reward for accurate responses, but the consequences for inaccurate responses do not equate. As it stands, lab-based studies provide an ethically sound alternative to simulated attacks, but with potentially limited validity.

One way of addressing the uncertainty in the validity of judgment tasks as a measure of susceptibility is to consider working with past victims of email fraud (e.g. Button, Nicholls, Kerr, & Owen, 2014; Modic & Lea, 2011; Whitty & Buchanan, 2012). Typically, this research is conducted in a qualitative capacity, gathering insights into the decision-making processes that led to victimisation. This methodology provides a sample that has self-evidently demonstrated susceptibility to email fraud. However, such opportunities come with a cost - in terms of the inability to retrospectively capture the psychological influences of this susceptibility, specifically the relevant contextual influences at the time of the attack. This is reliant on the recall of the participant about the exact scenario and external factors that were in place at the time they received and responded to the email. Dependent on the period of time that has passed since the incident, this can prove difficult. Additional assessments of a participant's cognitive make-up may have changed as a result of the incident, making them less representative of the individual differences between users at the point when they became a victim. Finally, this methodology is reliant on the availability of a sample of past victims, as well as a comparable control group who have not demonstrated susceptibility. Ideally this control group will have been recipients of similar incoming emails as the victim, but this is very difficult to control for and unrealistic as a method for precisely comparing response behaviour between the two groups. In line with this approach, research has also analysed the content of genuine past phishing emails, to establish linguistic patterns and persuasion techniques that may encourage a response from the recipient (e.g. Freiermuth, 2011).

Some researchers have employed simulated phishing attacks as an assessment of susceptibility, in a manner comparable with penetration testing in industry assessments. These clearly provide the most ecologically valid behavioural assessment, but are also the most ethically challenging, in that recipients may feel upset or angered at being 'tricked' into responding, without having given consent prior to the attack. Unlike industry penetration testing, simulations as part of academic research are designed to assess the influence of specific factors, rather than a baseline measure of vulnerability. In order to do this, stimuli may be designed in a specific way to emulate persuasive techniques that might be employed in a phishing email, such as authority (Guéguen & Jacob, 2002) or familiarity (Jagatic, Johnson, Jakobsson, & Menczer, 2005). Alternatively, these may include additional measures to assess influences such as security knowledge (Wright & Marett, 2010).

As with industry penetration testing, one major limitation of these simulated attacks is the inability to control or monitor the context in which an email is received. This means that little insight can be gained, directly, about the situational factors influencing response behaviour, as this is reliant on the recall of the user themselves. It also becomes difficult to assess how the effect of different persuasive techniques varies between users, as sending a multitude of target messages, which assess each of these, to the same person may raise suspicion. On the other hand, if a single target email is sent, sample sizes would need to be large enough to account for individual differences between users. This type of methodology requires some further development in order to address these issues and provide a useful assessment of response behaviour.

In order to demonstrate how experimental design and consent issues may interact with the potential validity of a research study, it is worth describing an undergraduate student research project from our lab (Mack, 2014). One of the project objectives was to empirically study the consequences of informed consent about a phishing attack. The project, which had been approved by the institutional ethics committee as well as the institutional network support team, involved a modest sample size (N=30). Half the participants signed up to a study titled *"Reasoning and judgements made in an online capacity"*. These individuals provided informed consent to take part in the study, and as such, they were informed that they would be sent simulated phishing emails in the subsequent 7 days. The other participants signed up for a study, *"A study of human-computer interaction"*. They were sent the same simulated phishing emails, but prior to the study slot they signed up for, which was actually used to inform them of the study purpose and to then seek post-event consent for their involvement in the study.

Participants received two different emails from two bespoke email accounts created for study purposes with the knowledge of the institutional IT services. These emails came from "Lancaster" accounts (where the study was conducted), adopting a phisher's "spoofing" attack vector, and the sender was unfamiliar to participants. One email carried a warning message (account verification) and the other a competition incentive (win an iPad!). Both emails requested a reply response, though at that stage no confidential information was requested or retained. Later, only participants (both responders and non-responders) who agreed to have their data retained were retained in the study (although as it happened, no-one withdrew). The study showed that for those participants who provided informed consent, 40% showed some vulnerability in responding to one of the two phishing emails, whilst no-one responded to both. For those participants who had no prior warning via informed consent, 80% responded to at least one phishing email, and 20% responded to both. As well as revealing the extent of users' susceptibility to attack, these data suggests a dependency between the form of consent and response patterns. In other words, standard experimental design issues such as obtaining prior informed consent can have a material impact on how users will behave. This is in line with research from Parsons et al. (2013), reported above, which demonstrated similar effects as a result of gaining informed consent from participants for a role play study. Using an alternative research study as a mechanism for gaining partial consent is a concept supported by Resnik and Finn (2017). However, rather than opting in to participate, they argue that participants should be given the opportunity to opt-out of a study on email behaviour, avoiding a sample bias towards those who are more security conscious. Combined with privacy protection and appropriate debriefing, Resnik and Finn believe that simulated attacks can be conducted in an ethical manner, allowing for valuable data to be gathered.

Many ethical review boards are still reluctant to approve a simulated phishing attack without informed consent from the participant though, given the principle that participants should be fully informed before willingly volunteering to participate in research. Studies of this type also require the cooperation of relevant IT support, who need to be aware of the study and how to appropriately handle queries from individuals. It may be argued that seeking post-consent leads participants to feel under pressure to comply, given that the data has already been collected and it would otherwise be wasted. On the other hand, the study by Mack (2014) suggests that obtaining prior consent could compromise the integrity of a study. Although the evidence on the effect of priming is inconsistent to date, one alternative solution to the consent issue is to gain informed consent for a simulated phishing attack that will happen at some point in the future. With enough time between sign-up and the event, the effects of pre-warning may have dissipated, and thus the response behaviour elicited provides more naturalistic data. However, the authors are not aware of research that can pinpoint the delay period required for such a procedure to "work".

There have been a small number of studies that have used simulated attacks where the participants are naïve to the purpose of the study. Jagatic et al.'s (2005) study incorporated a simulation of a targeted phishing attack, using information gained about participants online without their consent. Following this study, Finn and Jakobsson (2007) reported that 30 out of the 1700 participants targeted complained about the research, with 7 asking for their data to be withdrawn. Although this is a small proportion of the overall sample size, disgruntlement amongst any number of participants is of concern to researchers ethically. A further example, although indirectly related, comes from a study conducted by Facebook, in which they manipulated newsfeed content to see if they could affect user's emotions in their own posts (Kramer, Guillory, & Hancock, 2014). Although there is a clause in the Terms and Conditions of having a Facebook account that legally allows this type of research, the organisation received extensive backlash from users and industry experts for the lack of informed consent (Arthur, 2014). If we wish to understand and model real-world fraud events, we need to consider how on-going genuine research and ethical issues can be accommodated without distorting the integrity of the study itself.

Key Insights and Usability

As mentioned above, the focus of academic research into susceptibility to phishing varies in terms of its aims and the theoretical implications of these, and as such the methodologies adopted vary as well. Most prominently, research considers three potential sources of influence – the content and persuasive techniques employed within the email itself, contextual factors at the time the email is received, and individual differences between the users who are receiving the email (see Jones, Towse, & Race, 2015, for a comprehensive overview).

It is becoming more common for sophisticated phishing emails to be targeted towards a specific recipient or group of recipients, in order to make the email more believable and thus increase response likelihood. This is a process that can be automated, with data gathered across a number of online sources to maximise the plausibility of the attack (Edwards, Larson, Green, Rashid, & Baron, 2017). Jagatic et al. (2005) used publicly available information from social media to develop emails that purported to come from someone known to the recipient and found an increased response rate to these, demonstrating the influence of familiarity and social compliance on response likelihood. Research into the link between social media usage and cyber crime victimisation (through phishing, as well as other attack methods), has demonstrated though that specific types of social networking sites are more likely to increase victimisation. Specifically, knowledge exchange sites, such as LinkedIn and Flickr, where users share a greater amount of personal information in order to maximise networking opportunities, are associated with higher levels of victimisation (Saridakis, Benson, Ezingeard, & Tennakoon, 2015).

Alternative considerations of persuasive techniques have examined the influence of authority. Guéguen and Jacob (2002) again used a simulated phishing attack, targeting users who signed on to network computers in a university building being monitored by the researchers. Participants were either sent an email from a low-status individual (another student) or a professor from the university, deemed to be of a higher authoritative status, with results demonstrating greater response likelihood for the email sent from the high-authority figure. These findings are in line with theoretical perspectives on the psychology of persuasion, outlining the influence of factors such as authority, social proof, and scarcity (Cialdini, 1993). This example is similar to whaling attacks, a type of phishing outlined earlier in the chapter, in which the fraudster sends an email from the hacked or imitated account of a senior executive within an organisation, to induce a response through a purported authoritative identity. Such persuasive factors are thought to lead users to overlook cues that would otherwise have indicated the illegitimacy of an email (Langenderfer & Shimp, 2001). Further support for this notion comes from Freiermuth (2011), who's analysis of email content demonstrated the presence of a number of mechanisms intended to invoke a response from the recipient. This research emphasises consistently used techniques in Nigerian 419 scams, such as building resonance with the scammer, offering rewards, and emulating a sense of urgency.

Additional contextual factors may lead to similar oversights in terms of the cues available within an email, for example when users are distracted or overly concerned with other tasks. Yan and Gozu (2012) demonstrated this when they asked participants to make email legitimacy judgments either as quickly as possible, or to take their time over decisions. When participants spent longer assessing the emails they demonstrated lower susceptibility. Further to this, Jones (2016) demonstrated that when participants were asked to complete a secondary verbal task (counting backwards aloud) simultaneously with an email legitimacy task, their accuracy was lower than a control and a secondary motor task condition. This study intended to emulate a scenario where users are multi-tasking whilst managing emails, typical of a daily office scenario, such as talking on the phone with a colleague or client.

An alternative, or complimentary, approach to understanding response behaviour considers whether individual differences between users may make some more susceptible than others (Williams, Beardmore, & Joinson, 2017). Factors that indicate a reliance on intuitive responses have been shown to increase susceptibility to fraud, such as self-control (Holtfreter, Reisig, Piquero, & Piquero, 2010), cognitive reflection, and inhibition (Jones et al., submitted). The influence of cognitive reflection was replicated across email legitimacy tasks, as well as an office simulation task in which participants were naïve to the true nature of the research (Jones, 2016), supporting the validity of this finding.

It is possible that there is a crossover between these different explanations of susceptibility, for example, users may be more inclined to rely on intuitive decision-making, thus demonstrating higher susceptibility in certain scenarios and in response to certain persuasive techniques that are employed. At this point though, this is an area that requires further exploration.

All of the insights highlighted here are currently limited by the unknown validity of the measures taken to assess susceptibility. It is therefore important that on-going work considers the development of an assessment tool and method that allows for control of factors being measured, whilst also ensuring maximum possible validity in measuring real world susceptibility. Below, the authors describe some potential directions that could unify approaches taken across industry and academic research in an attempt to reach this goal.

BUILDING A UNITED FRONT

Research gathered under controlled conditions in a lab setting provides valuable knowledge on how specified factors can influence perceptions of phishing emails. However, the methodologies employed in these settings mean that it is hard to know to what extent these factors relate to real world response behaviour and susceptibility. Ultimately – just because an influencing factor is significant in the lab doesn't mean that it is having the same effect in the real world.

Practical and ethical constraints in research make it difficult to assess susceptibility in a naturalistic environment. By enhancing collaborations between industry and academia, we will be one step closer to understanding how user decisions are influenced in the real world. Whilst industry approaches focus on appraising the vulnerability within an organisation, highlighting potential threats and identifying users that are more likely to respond, academic approaches take a more in depth look at why certain users respond whilst others do not. Ultimately, the combination of these approaches can allow for the development of novel techniques and effective training mechanisms to reduce susceptibility.

Psychological research has much to offer in addressing methodological and validity concerns associated with lab-based studies, but there are a number of inconsistencies still to be ironed out. For example, across a series of studies conducted by the authors, cognitive and situational influences were assessed through both an explicit judgment task, and an office simulation where email responses were monitored without participants being aware of the study purpose (Jones, 2016). Results were partially replicated across these, demonstrating the influence of cognitive reflection. However, a number of factors (e.g. inhibition, time pressure) were not replicated, bringing into question the alignment of the two methodologies in terms of how well they are assessing susceptibility. Without further investigation, it is difficult to establish which methodology provides a better representation of real world response behaviour, and as such which influential factors should be acted upon.

One of the potential ways in which research can be harnessed to interact more closely with real-world security concerns is to focus on the development of risk mitigation strategies that incorporate research insights on user behaviour. At the present time, as discussed, behavioural models of fraud vulnerability are not well developed. For this reason, a lot of the training currently available focuses on issues such as improving the ability to differentiate between genuine and fraudulent web sites and images, based on generic visual cues (Moreno-Fernandez, Blanco, Garaizar, & Malute, 2017). Whilst there is no evidence for or against the effectiveness of such training mechanisms in an organisational setting, some empirical research has demonstrated that priming (Jones, 2016; Junger, Montoya, & Overink, 2017) and knowledge of basic security cues (Downs, Holbrook, & Cranor, 2006) alone is not enough to reduce response likelihood to phishing emails. Even if an improvement were seen shortly after training on these cues, the saliency of these in an actual phishing email during a moment of regular day-to-day behaviour is unlikely to replicate this. Bullée, Montoya Morales, Junger, and Hartel (2016) examined the effectiveness of priming in relation to telephone-based social engineering attacks. Although an improvement in detection was seen one week after the intervention, this effect was lost when participants were tested again two weeks later, and in fact susceptibility was shown to increase.

The increasing sophistication of phishing emails means that generic visual cues that users are told to look out for, such as spelling mistakes and fake email addresses (as seen on the Citizen's Advice Bureau website, 2016), are often irrelevant in many cases. The more generic phishing emails are often picked up by spam filters these days, and so focus needs to be drawn to the more advanced emails designed to trick even the most security conscious user.

By understanding the factors that influence susceptibility, training programmes could be tailored to educate users about these, and to target the most susceptible individuals within an organisation, as part of a broader cyber risk mitigation programme. Therefore, the authors would advocate a gradual transition towards more empirically grounded and theoretically inspired training techniques, which can draw from a greater body of research knowledge in the design of interventions. Moreover, the authors emphasise the importance of assessing the effectiveness of these training methods over multiple time scales and contexts. The continued advancement in the techniques used by fraudsters means that training methods must do more than tell users what cues to look out for. Training programmes must be designed to transition alongside these changes in order to maintain their effectiveness. At the most advanced level, this may mean training users to understand the underlying mechanisms and motivations behind the development of phishing emails, to help users see through the malicious intentions of a sender when they are reading emails. But at its most basic level, this might simply mean that training programmes are kept as up to date as possible with the most sophisticated techniques and persuasive mechanisms used to manipulate the user. In line with current trends in social engineering attacks, one example might be to incorporate advice and information about the unseen harm on both a personal and an organisational level that can result from an employee posting information publicly on social media.

CONCLUSION

As outlined here, it is clear that there are differences in the approaches taken to tackling email fraud between industry and academia, although both are working towards the same goal of tackling the threat posed by email fraud. Whilst industry is concerned with managing risk to protect valuable assets, with immediate solutions to address the issue and prevent future financial loss for organisations, academic research is more focused on understanding the theoretical principles underlying response behaviour in order to develop long-term solutions. Although the process may be more drawn out, given the unknowns that require examination, this more in-depth understanding will benefit all invested parties in the future. For solutions to have an on-going impact on secure behaviour, these must ensure users are able to transition their knowledge in line with the development and increased sophistication of phishing attacks.

There are clear parallels between these two approaches, both of which have advantages and disadvantages in terms of the methods currently employed. Collaborations between industry and academia are becoming more common, and the authors believe that further progression in this direction can only benefit on-going efforts to build a united front against persistent cyber security threats. Whilst industry offers access to a real-world sample that can be studied in a naturalistic environment, academia works towards the most ethical and theoretically grounded methods to harness the potential from this. It is hoped that consideration of industry impact will help academic researchers orient their research to elicit maximum benefit for industry partners, whilst also demonstrating to industry the importance of considering the impact human decision-making can have on cyber security. The transition within research settings to use more naturalistic assessments of email response behaviour will allow for the development of more effective training solutions that are relevant to real world behaviour, have a long-term effect on susceptibility, and as such can decrease the risk of victimisation for organisations and individual users.

ACKNOWLEDGMENT

This research received no specific grant from any funding agency in the public, commercial, or not-for-profit sectors. However, the authors would like to acknowledge the cooperation of Lancaster University Information Systems Services for enabling and facilitating the undergraduate student project described in this chapter (Mack, 2014).

REFERENCES

Abu-Nimeh, S., Nappa, D., Wang, X., & Nair, S. (2007). A comparison of machine learning techniques for phishing detection. *Proceedings of The Anti-Phishing Working Group's Second Annual eCrime Researchers Summit*, 60-69. doi:10.1145/1299015.1299021

Arthur, C. (2014). Facebook study breached ethical guidelines, researchers say. *The Guardian*. Retrieved June 19, 2017, from: https://www.theguardian.com/technology/2014/jun/30/facebook-emotion-study-breached-ethical-guidelines-researchers-say

Barrett, N. (2003). Penetration testing and social engineering: Hacking the weakest link. *Information Security Technical Report, 8*(4), 56–64. doi:10.1016/S1363-4127(03)00007-4

Bullée, J. H., Montoya Morales, A. L., Junger, M., & Hartel, P. H. (2016). Telephone-based social engineering attacks: An experiment testing the success and time decay of an intervention. In *Proceedings of the Singapore Cyber-Security Conference (SG-CRC) 2016* (pp. 107-114). IOS Press.

Button, M., Nicholls, C. M., Kerr, J., & Owen, R. (2014). Online frauds: Learning from victims why they fall for these scams. *Australian and New Zealand Journal of Criminology, 47*(3), 391–408. doi:10.1177/0004865814521224

Cialdini, R. B. (1993). *Influence: The Psychology of Persuasion.* New York: Quill William Morrow.

Citizen's Advice Bureau. (2016). *Phishing – spam emails and fake websites.* Retrieved August 1, 2016, from: https://www.citizensadvice.org.uk/consumer/scams/scams/common-scams/computer-and-online-scams/phishing-spam-emails-and-fake-websites/

Downs, J. S., Holbrook, M., & Cranor, L. F. (2006). Decision strategies and susceptibility to phishing. In *Proceedings of the Second Symposium on Usable Privacy and Security* (pp. 79-90). ACM. doi:10.1145/1143120.1143131

Downs, J. S., Holbrook, M., & Cranor, L. F. (2007). Behavioural response to phishing risk. *Proceedings of the Anti-Phishing Working Groups Second Annual eCrime Researchers Summit*, 37-44. doi:10.1145/1299015.1299019

Duke, D. (2002). Ethical hackers – can we trust them? *Network Security, 3*, 3.

Edwards, M., Larson, R., Green, B., Rashid, A., & Baron, A. (2017). Panning for gold: Automatically analysing online social engineering attack surfaces. *Computers & Security, 69*, 18–34. doi:10.1016/j.cose.2016.12.013

Finn, P., & Jakobsson, M. (2007). Designing ethical phishing experiments. *Technology and Society Magazine, IEEE, 26*(1), 46–58. doi:10.1109/MTAS.2007.335565

Fischer, P., Lea, S. E., & Evans, K. M. (2013). Why do individuals respond to fraudulent scam communications and lose money? The psychological determinants of scam compliance. *Journal of Applied Social Psychology, 43*(10), 2060–2072. doi:10.1111/jasp.12158

Freiermuth, M. R. (2011). Text, lies, and electronic bait: An analysis of email fraud and the decisions of the unsuspecting. *Discourse & Communication, 5*(2), 123–145. doi:10.1177/1750481310395448

Garera, S., Provos, N., Chew, M., & Rubin, A. D. (2007). A framework for detection and measurement of phishing attacks. *Proceedings of the 2007 ACM Workshop on Recurring Malcode*, 1-8. doi:10.1145/1314389.1314391

Guéguen, N., & Jacob, C. (2002). Solicitation by e-mail and solicitor's status: A field study of social influence on the web. *Cyberpsychology & Behavior, 5*(4), 377–383. doi:10.1089/109493102760275626 PMID:12216702

Harrison, B., Vishwanath, A., & Rao, R. (2016). A user-centered approach to phishing susceptibility: The role of a suspicious personality in protecting against phishing. In *2016 49th Hawaii International Conference on System Sciences (HICSS)* (pp. 5628-5634). IEEE.

Holtfreter, K., Reisig, M. D., Piquero, N. L., & Piquero, A. R. (2010). Low self-control and fraud offending, victimization, and their overlap. *Criminal Justice and Behavior, 37*(2), 188–203. doi:10.1177/0093854809354977

Hong, K. W., Kelley, C. M., Tembe, R., Murphy-Hill, E., & Mayhorn, C. B. (2013, September). Keeping up with the Joneses: Assessing phishing susceptibility in an email task. *Proceedings of the Human Factors and Ergonomics Society Annual Meeting, 57*(1), 1012–1016. doi:10.1177/1541931213571226

Hudic, A., Zechner, L., Islam, S., Krieg, C., Weippl, E. R., Winkler, S., & Hable, R. (2012). Towards a unified penetration testing taxonomy. *Privacy, Security, Risk and Trust (PASSAT), 2012 International Conference on Social Computing,* 811-812.

Islam, R., & Abawajy, J. (2013). A multi-tier phishing detection and filtering approach. *Journal of Network and Computer Applications, 36*(1), 324–335. doi:10.1016/j.jnca.2012.05.009

Jagatic, T. N., Johnson, N. A., Jakobsson, M., & Menczer, F. (2005). Social phishing. *Communications of the ACM, 50*(10), 94–100. doi:10.1145/1290958.1290968

Jones, H., Towse, J., & Race, N. (2015). Susceptibility to email fraud: A review of psychological perspectives, data-collection methods, and ethical considerations. *International Journal of Cyber Behavior, Psychology and Learning, 5*(3), 13–29. doi:10.4018/IJCBPL.2015070102

Jones, H. S. (2016). *What makes people click: Assessing individual differences in susceptibility to email fraud* (Unpublished doctoral thesis). Lancaster University, UK.

Jones, H. S., Towse, J., Race, N., & Harrison, T. (submitted). *Email fraud – the search for psychological markers of susceptibility.*

Junger, M., Montoya, L., & Overink, F. J. (2017). Priming and warnings are not effective to prevent social engineering attacks. *Computers in Human Behavior, 66,* 75–87. doi:10.1016/j.chb.2016.09.012

Kramer, A. D. I., Guillory, J. E., & Hancock, J. T. (2014). Experimental evidence of massive-scale emotional contagion through social networks. *Proceedings of the National Academy of Sciences of the United States of America, 111*(24), 8788–8790. doi:10.1073/pnas.1320040111 PMID:24889601

Langenderfer, J., & Shimp, T. A. (2001). Consumer vulnerability to scams, swindles, and fraud: A new theory of visceral influences on persuasion. *Psychology and Marketing, 18*(7), 763–783. doi:10.1002/mar.1029

Mack, S. (2014). *Reasoning and judgements made in an online capacity. An exploration of how phishing emails influence decision making strategies* (Unpublished undergraduate dissertation). Lancaster University, Lancaster, UK.

Mitnick, K. D., & Simon, W. L. (2002). *The Art of Deception.* Indianapolis, IN: Wiley Publishing, Inc.

Modic, D., & Lea, S. E. G. (2011). *How neurotic are scam victims, really? The big five and Internet scams.* Paper presented at the 2011 Conference of the International Confederation for the Advancement of Behavioral Economics and Economic Psychology, Exeter, UK.

Moreno-Fernández, M. M., Blanco, F., Garaizar, P., & Matute, H. (2017). Fishing for phishers. Improving Internet users' sensitivity to visual deception cues to prevent electronic fraud. *Computers in Human Behavior*, *69*, 421–436. doi:10.1016/j.chb.2016.12.044

Murdoch, S. J., & Sasse, M. A. (2017). Should you really phish your own employees. *NS Tech*. Retrieved September 28, 2017, from http://tech.newstatesman.com/guest-opinion/phishing-employees

Myers, S. (2007). Introduction to phishing. In M. Jakobsson & S. Myers (Eds.), *Phishing and Countermeasures* (pp. 1–29). John Wiley & Sons, Inc.

National Institute of Standards and Technology (NIST). (2012). *Guide for conducting risk assessments*. NIST Special Publication 800-30, Revision 1. Retrieved September 28, 2017, from http://nvlpubs.nist.gov/nistpubs/Legacy/SP/nistspecialpublication800-30r1.pdf

Nicholson, J., Coventry, L., & Briggs, P. (2017). Can we fight social engineering attacks by social means? Assessing social salience as a means to improve phish detection. In *Proceedings of the Thirteenth Symposium on Usable Privacy and Security (SOUPS 2017)*. Santa Clara, CA: USENIX.

Norton. (2014). *Online fraud: Phishing*. Retrieved July 12, 2014, from http://uk.norton.com/cybercrime-phishing

Parsons, K., McCormac, A., Pattinson, M., Butavicius, M., & Jerram, C. (2013). Phishing for the truth: A scenario-based study of users' behavioural response to emails. In *Proceedings of IFIP International Information Security Conference* (pp. 366-378). Berlin: Springer.

Peterson, H. (2014). Target's massive data breach originated with a single phishing email. *Business Insider*. Retrieved May 18, 2017, from: http://www.businessinsider.com/target-hack-traced-to-phishing-email-2014-2?IR=T

Picchi, A. (2014). Target breach may have started with email phishing. *CBS News*. Retrieved May 18, 2017, from: http://www.cbsnews.com/news/target-breach-may-have-started-with-email-phishing/

Resnik, D. B., & Finn, P. R. (2017). Ethics and phishing experiments. *Science and Engineering Ethics*. doi:10.1007/s11948-017-9952-9 PMID:28812222

Roberts, J. J. (2017, April 27). Exclusive: Facebook and Google were victims of $100, payment scam. *Fortune*. Retrieved May 16, 2017, from: http://fortune.com/2017/04/27/facebook- google-rimasauskas/

Salah, K., Alcaraz Calero, J. M., Zeadally, S., Al-Mulla, S., & Alzaabi, M. (2013). Using cloud computing to implement a security overlay network. *IEEE Security and Privacy*, *11*(1), 44–53.

Saridakis, G., Benson, V., Ezingeard, J., & Tennakoon, H. (2015). Individual information security, user behaviour and cyber victimisation: An empirical study of social networking users. *Technological Forecasting and Social Change*, *102*, 320–330. doi:10.1016/j.techfore.2015.08.012

Schneier, B. (2000). *Secrets & Lies: Digital Security in a Networked World*. Indianapolis, IN: Wiley Publishing Inc.

Smith, D. (2016, November 6). WikiLeaks emails: What they revealed about the Clinton campaign's mechanics. *The Guardian*. Retrieved May 16, 2017, from: https://www.theguardian.com/us-news/2016/nov/06/wikileaks-emails-hillary-clinton-campaign-john-podesta

Verizon. (2017). *2017 Data Breach Investigations Report*. Retrieved May 18, 2017, from: http://www.verizonenterprise.com/verizon-insights-lab/dbir/2017/

Whitty, M. T., & Buchanan, T. (2012). The online romance scam: A serious cybercrime. *Cyberpsychology, Behavior, and Social Networking*, *15*(3), 181–183. doi:10.1089/cyber.2011.0352 PMID:22304401

Williams, E. J., Beardmore, A., & Joinson, A. N. (2017). Individual differences in susceptibility to online influence: A theoretical review. *Computers in Human Behavior*, *72*, 412–421. doi:10.1016/j.chb.2017.03.002

Wright, R. T., & Marett, K. (2010). The influence of experiential and dispositional factors in phishing: An empirical investigation of the deceived. *Journal of Management Information Systems*, *27*(1), 273–303. doi:10.2753/MIS0742-1222270111

Yan, Z., & Gozu, H. Y. (2012). Online decision-making in receiving spam emails among college students. *International Journal of Cyber Behavior, Psychology and Learning*, *2*(1), 1–12. doi:10.4018/ijcbpl.2012010101

Yeo, J. (2013). Using penetration testing to enhance your company's security. *Computer Fraud & Security*, *4*(4), 17–20. doi:10.1016/S1361-3723(13)70039-3

Yuhas, A. (2017, March 22). Lithuanian man's phishing tricked US tech companies into wiring over $100m. *The Guardian*. Retrieved May 16, 2017, from: https://www.theguardian.com/technology/2017/mar/22/phishing-scam-us-tech-companies-tricked-100-million-lithuanian-man

KEY TERMS AND DEFINITIONS

Collaboration: Bringing together alternative approaches and perspectives to develop novel ideas and solutions.

Email Fraud: The use of email as a means of deceiving users for personal or financial gain.

Individual Differences: Variations in human behaviour as a result of a specific trait or traits.

Informed Consent: The participant agrees to participate in research, with a full understanding of the research purpose and tasks involved.

Penetration Testing: Assessment of vulnerabilities within an organisation's computer system or network, including human users.

Persuasive Techniques: Factors that can be manipulated to influence human behaviour.

Susceptibility: A likelihood to be more easily affected or influenced by a specific thing.

Chapter 6
Introducing Psychological Concepts and Methods to Cybersecurity Students

Jacqui Taylor
Bournemouth University, UK

Helen Thackray
Bournemouth University, UK

Sarah E. Hodge
Bournemouth University, UK

John McAlaney
Bournemouth University, UK

ABSTRACT

This chapter begins with a brief review of the literature that highlights what psychology research and practice can offer to cybersecurity education. The authors draw on their wide-ranging inter-disciplinary teaching experience, and in this chapter, they discuss their observations gained from teaching psychological principles and methods to undergraduate and postgraduate cybersecurity students. The authors pay special attention to the consideration of the characteristics of cybersecurity students so that psychology is taught in a way that is accessible and engaging. Finally, the authors offer some practical suggestions for academics to help them incorporate psychology into the cybersecurity curriculum.

WHAT CAN PSYCHOLOGY OFFER TO CYBERSECURITY EDUCATION AND TRAINING?

There is a symbiotic relationship between the disciplines of computing and psychology: psychologists have helped in many ways to understand the way that computer systems are developed and used, but also an understanding of computers has helped psychologists to model and investigate human cognitive and social processes. This chapter will focus on the former; over the past 60 years, psychologists have

DOI: 10.4018/978-1-5225-4053-3.ch006

tracked and researched the development and impact of computers and they have also been instrumental in their design and evolution. To design, develop, implement and evaluate secure sociotechnical systems students need to understand concepts and research methods in psychology. To understand the potential risks of sociotechnical systems, cybersecurity students need to understand and consider how people perceive, remember, feel, think and solve problems, i.e. the domain of cognitive psychology. It is also important for students to consider individual differences and social behavior if effective interaction between people and computer systems is to be achieved, i.e. the domain of social psychology and individual differences. An understanding of these psychological topics enables students in cybersecurity to consider the potential capabilities and limitations of computer users and helps them to design computer systems that are more effective (usable) for a variety of user types. In addition to covering the foundation areas of Psychology, it is also important that cybersecurity students are taught evaluation methods and that they are able to consider the social impacts and ethical issues regarding the implementation and use of computer systems in organisations and society.

A review of the literature and media commentary on cybersecurity attacks shows that increasingly they involve social engineering techniques; where psychological principles are used to manipulate people into disclosing sensitive information or allowing others to access a secure system (Tetri & Vuorinen, 2013). For example, phishing emails and phone scams utilize many psychological principles relating to social influence to persuade users to open a link, such as appeals based on fear or invoking a sense of scarcity or urgency (Cialdini, 2008). However, despite the psychological nature of such cybersecurity attacks, research into the role of psychology in cybersecurity is still limited (McAlaney, Thackray and Taylor, 2016). Also, often research into the closely linked area of social engineering is conducted from the discipline of computing rather than psychology. Indeed, the call for papers for a recent conference organized in the UK by the Higher Education Academy on learning and teaching in cybersecurity listed relevant disciplines as 'STEM' and 'Computing' and the eventual program of abstracts contained no mention of psychology. Similarly, curricular guidance for the field of cybersecurity education produced by the ACM (McGettrick, 2013), contained just two uses of the word psychology and no further detail. However, within the last year the importance of psychology has begun to be recognized in the academic literature (McAlaney, Thackray and Taylor, 2016). For example, a recent article (Hamman, Hopkinson, Markham, Chaplik & Metzler, 2017) suggests the teaching of game theory in cybersecurity courses and links this to the psychological nature of many incidents. Hamman et al. propose that one of the benefits of game theory is that it fundamentally alters the way students view the practice of cybersecurity, and state that it helps to sensitize them to the human adversary element inherent in cybersecurity in addition to technology-focused best practices (p1).

The majority of psychological research that has been conducted so far in this area has focused on prevention and mitigation strategies for the targets of cybersecurity incidents with little focus on the motivation of the perpetrators (Rogers, 2010). Psychology can offer much in helping to understand the motivations of individual hackers or scammers, for example drawing on the research into individual differences, looking at factors such as self-esteem, introversion, openness to experience and social anxiety (Fullwood, 2015). Other work has shown that individual's motivations are not always related to financial gain but can be purely for entertainment or social status reasons (Rogers, 2010). In contrast, large scale cybersecurity incidents are often instigated by groups, as opposed to individuals acting alone. As such these incidents can be regarded as the result of group actions and group processes; theories from Psychology are used to help understand the formation, operation and influence of groups on their members, and these can be usefully applied to online groups (McAlaney, Thackray and Taylor, 2016). Many hacking incidents, especially those perpetrated by teenagers and young adults, have been strongly related to social group pressure and social psychological influences. For example, individuals involved in the 2015 TalkTalk and 2011 Paypal hacks were instructed on how to do this by members of Anonymous, the hacktivist collective.

Psychological theories relating to disinhibition and deindividuation have been used to explain a number of behaviors online and can also be used to understand cybersecurity incidents. The perception of anonymity afforded by online communications allows individuals to take actions that would otherwise result in legal or social sanctions. Disinhibition refers to the sense that actions conducted online do not feel as real as those conducted offline which, it has been argued, can lead individuals to lose self-control (Taylor & MacDonald, 2002). Deindividuation, in which individuals lose their sense of self-awareness when they interact within a group, has been applied to online groups where individuals are often less identifiable and separated by space and time (Taylor & MacDonald, 2002). This is an under-researched area, but it would seem that in line with Social Identity Theory some individuals become engaged with online groups to an extent which would seem to be particularly intense and where they lose some sense of personal identity to social identity. In summary, theories from psychology can be helpful to understand and help to predict online behavior.

OBSERVATIONS FROM TEACHING PSYCHOLOGY TO CYBERSECURITY STUDENTS

In this section, the authors will review their experiences teaching psychological principles to a wide variety of cybersecurity students. The authors have experience teaching at undergraduate and postgraduate level (full-time and part-time) and developing cybersecurity training tools for industry. Foundation areas in Psychology which the authors consider important to introduce to students prior to discussing their application in cybersecurity are: social processes (e.g. group-working and communication); cognitive processes (e.g. perception, attention and memory), and individual differences (e.g. life experiences, gender, personality, cognitive style). Once these areas of psychology are covered, then it is easier to show how the authors apply psychological principles to cybersecurity.

Social Psychology and Cognition

The work of social psychologists can help understand the ways that technology affects social interaction, attitudes and behaviour. The authors ensure that there is a strong focus on how students can make practical use of the research findings and cover the major topics within Social Psychology (conversation and communication; group processes; interpersonal perception and attraction; social influence; attitudes, and conflict) and Cognitive Psychology (perception, attention and memory). Then the authors apply this understanding of social cognition to cybersecurity contexts and example topics covered include:

1. How an analysis of online language and communication can be used to identify fraudulent communication and how persuasive language can influence faulty decision-making regarding judgments of trust;

2. Group dynamics in cybersecurity incidents are reviewed, for example the group processes that shape the actions of both the cyber attackers and their intended target, including how group dynamics may lead to risky decisions and overestimations of skill and ability;

3. The psychological basis of social engineering techniques, and how these may be mitigated and prevented;

4. The role of emotion when users engage with sociotechnical systems, e.g. Frustration experienced with the technical components of a secure system have been linked to poor decision making and subsequent risky behaviour;

5. The link between cognitive load and poor online decision making;

6. New technology and organisational change is highlighted, covering issues such as the management of staff working remotely online and selection and technology enhanced training of cybersecurity personnel; and

7. The psychological elements of computer games are covered, in terms of the way gamification is used to motivate and persuade potential victims of a scam and also the authors highlight elements of addiction that may lead to poor decision-making.

Assessment and practical activities are varied and three examples are included here. The ways that online groups can influence the way their members interact and behave is addressed by asking students to devise their own scam website which aims to adopt new members to a fictitious online community. Students design experimental materials to study the links between working memory and online search strategies. Thirdly, students use and evaluate an online training package to highlight cognitive biases in cybersecurity.

Individual Differences

To illustrate individual differences in susceptibility to scams, the authors cover the following topics:

1. A psychological understanding of the cognitive deterioration in older adults and how this knowledge can be used to understand how, when and why older adults are vulnerable to financial scams;

2. How gender and personality can affect levels of online susceptibility in relation to internet dating scams;

3. How stress and cognitive style can influence poor decision making; and

4. Research from consumer psychology related to e-commerce, e.g. Individual consumer behaviour and trust in e-commerce exchanges and relations between company and consumer.

In seminars, cybersecurity undergraduates engaged well in tasks where they were asked to think from both the defence and attack perspectives. One seminar involved asking students to identify the most at-risk groups and then tailor the advice they would give to that specific group. For example, if they are advising an older adult who is unfamiliar with technology, they must think of how to explain this using simple terminology. If explaining to a child how to stay safe online, they need to use examples that children can identify with. Students were also asked to design a cyberattack that would circumnavigate their advice. The most successful exercises were highly interactive; recapping information from the most recent lecture, discussing in groups and then presenting their viewpoints to the class as a whole. It was interesting to see that despite beginning the module with a somewhat cynical attitude to the importance of psychology, after a few seminars there was an increase in interest and participation. One large consensus from the students was that there needs to be greater emphasis on education about cybersecurity at all ages and levels of experience.

Research Methods

Cybersecurity students may have limited understanding regarding the way empirical methods (an integral part of all Psychology degrees) can be used to evaluate computer systems. To address this, topics such as Experimental Design and Internet-Mediated Research are covered. Ideally students need to experience or apply methods, therefore it is helpful if the teaching experience includes case studies and practical workshops and assessed scientific reports. The authors have run workshops which compare qualitative methods (e.g. observation, focus groups) and quantitative methods (e.g. questionnaires and performance scores) to evaluate the individual's perceived vulnerabilities and this has contrasted the different methodological approaches well.

Designing an Internet-based experiment or survey requires careful consideration. Although cybersecurity students clearly have the technical skills to conduct online surveys, they often have less understanding of experimental design and what can be done with the data. There are many benefits of Internet-mediated research (for example, access to a larger population), however, many psychological and methodological issues need to be addressed by cybersecurity students and researchers. Issues the authors cover include:

1. The difficulty in ensuring that the participant is who they say they are and that they are answering in an honest way;
2. How to gain a representative sample;
3. How to construct questionnaire items to avoid bias;
4. Issues of data screening and sample attrition rates need to be considered;
5. The demographic profiles and questionnaire scores of those who did and did not take part in online experiments or surveys need consideration, and finally
6. Ethical issues, e.g. Whether informed consent can be gained online and how debriefing will take place.

Ethics

The teaching of ethics to cybersecurity students is not new. For some time, the teaching of ethics has been a requirement on degrees accredited by the British Computer Society (BCS). Since the classic text on computer ethics (Johnson, 1985), coverage of ethics has increased as computer systems become more pervasive in daily life. For example, issues of information security such as privacy, ownership, access and liability and reliability have become more important. These advances have led to the most recent edition of computer ethics (Johnson, 2009) including much work drawing on Psychology, e.g. covering the psychological and social implications of Internet use. However, despite the increasing need for ethics teaching sometimes there can be pressure on Computing departments in meeting this requirement. This is mainly due to it being a difficult area for computing staff to teach which, according to Dark & Winstead (2005), is because the area of ethics is not positivistic in nature. As psychologists the authors have been able to offer a different perspective on teaching ethics to cybersecurity students, based on the work of Dark & Winstead (2005), who discuss the use of educational theory and moral psychology to inform the teaching of ethics in computing-related fields. In their paper, they discuss ideas on moral development and the nature of morality, specifically as it relates to changes that educators may be trying to elicit within computing students when teaching ethics. The ways that a computer scientist and a psychologist teach ethics can be quite different, with the former more likely to use a positivist approach and the latter an approach based on educational theories. For example, a positivist approach would define what is right and what is not right (i.e. define truth) and then address what happens if one does not do what is right or does what is wrong. However, many Psychologists would disagree, saying that you cannot teach right and wrong and that although there are many laws which computing students need to know about, regarding what is wrong/right in society, there are not many things that are ethically questionable that are not illegal (and possibly vice versa!). In summary, philosophers have long recognized that it is almost impossible to 'teach' a student ethics, rather teachers need to advance students' sense of moral development and reasoning (Kohlberg & Kramer, 1969), something covered on all Psychology degrees. With this in mind, it is also important to consider the age and experience of students when designing teaching materials on ethics (covered further later). In summary, Psychologists have a lot to offer in the teaching of ethics to cybersecurity students. Some academics (Greene & Hiadt, 2002) go as far as discussing ethics purely in psychological terms, regarding the cognitive, affective and social aspects, when they state that the origins of human morality are emotions linked to expanding cognitive abilities that make people care about the welfare of others, about cooperation, cheating and norm following.

Considering the importance of individual's own behaviour around security and their understanding of the implications and consequences of behaviour, the behavioural component of morality could be of great value to teaching psychological principles to cybersecurity students; especially as learning has been shown to be aided by doing (Reese, 2011). Utilising educational games such as the Cyber Security Challenge UK has been of great value; such games set challenges for students to complete such as finding hidden data within a spread sheet. Additionally, the authors draw on students' life experiences to aid learning of the psychological materials; discussed further in the next section.

CONSIDERATION OF THE PROFILE OF CYBERSECURITY STUDENTS IN DEVELOPING PSYCHOLOGY MATERIALS

The variation between students studying different disciplines has been well documented regarding life experiences, gender and approaches to studying (Richardson, 1994). It is proposed that some of the following factors may affect the way that psychology teaching materials are perceived and understood by cybersecurity students and their level of engagement with the materials. Without wishing to generalize and stereotype students, these factors were considered in the way that materials were designed and presented with the over-arching aim to produce materials that considered and embraced individual differences.

Gender

The composition of most Psychology and Computing degree courses are significantly skewed, with females making up the majority of psychology degrees (79%) and males making up the majority (82%)

of computing degrees (Higher Education Statistical Agency, 2014). There have been many attempts to explain the reasons why males and females are attracted to different disciplines and a review of these studies shows very little support for cognitive abilities being the differentiating factor; for example, similar abilities have been found when comparing students studying social with physical sciences (Halpern, 1992). Recent research has looked at personal values, interests or motivation factors to investigate what Radford and Holdstock (1995) term, 'what people want to do rather than what they can do'. Wilson (2003) used quantitative and qualitative methods to further understanding of how Computing is perceived. In her paper she argues from a constructionist approach that, rather than any real difference in skill, female and male differences are a product of historical and cultural construction of technology as masculine (p. 128). For example, she notes that girls at school have been shown to be superior to boys in some areas of programming, but that they lack encouragement and interest so that by the time they reach 18 years of age they have already opted out. Wilson (2003) identifies teaching styles which appeal to female students as those with an emphasis on relational and contextual issues and co-operative learning through teamwork and group projects. While styles preferred by males are those that emphasize the formal and abstract and independent learning. Therefore, when teaching psychology to cybersecurity students (where there are usually more male students) traditional methods used in Psychology classes such as seminar discussions have not always been the most effective method. The authors have tried to use a broad range of methods, but recognize that some are more effective with the majority male cybersecurity students.

Life Experiences

Cybersecurity postgraduate courses tend to attract a significant number of mature entrants who have frequently been employed in other careers, have many life experiences or are currently working in a related industry and studying part-time. It is important for the contextual examples to link to real security incidents and to draw on the experiences of students. While undergraduate cybersecurity courses are more likely to attract direct-entry students, therefore the examples may be more closely linked to incidents publicized in the media.

It is important to consider stage of moral development and life experience of students when presenting materials on the topic of ethics. For example, an environment needs to be created that allows students to safely reflect on and explore their moral beliefs relative to the current issues in cybersecurity. The authors found that postgraduate students are more interested in the philosophical debates regarding the psychological and legal implications of Internet use, compared to undergraduate students. Issues that students have debated include: whether deviance online is different from deviance in face-to-face contexts; whether online addiction is similar in process to other addictions and how it might impact security vulnerabilities, and how a person's face-to-face and online identity might differ.

Gibbs, Basinger and Fuller (1992) suggest undergraduates' moral development is not fully developed; they are still developing an understanding of how moral issues may relate more generally to societal functioning. This could explain differences in debates between undergraduates and postgraduates. The postgraduate students were more open to different perspectives than undergraduates and his could be due to being older, and therefore having stronger convictions formed, or life experience within the industry. Thus, this could also be informative to the types of materials used to teach psychological principles; the postgraduates may find it easier to consider the bigger picture and societal implications of cybersecurity. While undergraduates may need more support in understanding the wider societal implications.

Motivation to Study and Learning Style

The motivation of students to study a particular course will clearly affect their engagement and there may be some initial resentment of cybersecurity students toward the topic of psychology; this needs to be considered and addressed. Many students choose psychology to help develop an understanding of themselves and others and to develop 'people' skills useful later in a range of careers. In contrast, from our observations many cybersecurity students see the course as a stepping stone to gaining almost immediate employment in the security industry or as CPD to gain promotion.

Radford and Holdstock (1995) investigated differences between reasons why students chose Computing and Psychology degrees. Students were given a list of 60 items on the 'outcomes or benefits of Higher Education' to rank. These ranged from passing exams, learning to work with others, development as a person, develop problem solving skills etc. The results showed that the most important items differentiating the two fields were that computing students chose the development of problem-solving skills, logical thinking and increasing future earning power. While for psychology students, development as a person was important as was understanding other people, oneself and greater personal independence. They identified two key factors related to a student's choice of discipline: (i) personal development versus social relationships and (ii) thinking about and directly dealing with people versus things. The implications of this for teaching psychology to cyber students are twofold: (i) that cybersecurity students may be less open to thinking about people problems when considering online threats and security, and (ii) that it is important that students are aware of the way people use technology and their interactions with others can be as important as functionality.

A considerable amount of work has been published on the relationship between personality type and learning in Further and Higher Education, although there is relatively little focusing on students from specific disciplines. Layman et al (2006) collected personality types of students studying a software engineering course using the Myers-Briggs Type Indicator (MBTI). the authors considered this when adapting our psychology materials from those designed for psychology students, in terms of: groupwork and individual work; using lectures to emphasize concepts as opposed to factual data, and materials presented objectively as matters of fact with concise, concrete explanations.

It is important to recognize that students studying for cybersecurity courses are likely to have been taught in different ways and may approach studying in different ways, compared to those studying for Psychology degrees. From personal observation, cybersecurity students are generally more familiar with assessments which have definitive answers, while Psychology students are more accustomed to discussing the relative merits of both sides of a debate and to provide a balanced view rather than a definitive answer. This would support the extensive work by Kolb (1981) investigating learning styles and subject discipline. Depending on their background it has also been our experience that cybersecurity students can find the methodological approaches used in Psychology to be quite different from what they have previously experienced. Students from a cybersecurity background may be more accustomed to an epistemological and ontological stance which posits that understanding of phenomena is reached though objective study and experimental methods, and there is a finite set of solutions to any problem. In contrast the sub-disciplines of Psychology range from those which take a very positivist approach to those which are based largely on ideographic knowledge and social constructionism. Whilst the psychology topics that the authors have taught cybersecurity students do tend to lean more towards those which take a positivistic approach there is in general more subjectivity and uncertainty embedded with the teaching materials than they may be accustomed too. A comment that the authors frequently receive from cybersecurity students is that they find it strange that many areas of psychology have no single theory that is widely accepted as being the 'correct' one, and that instead there appears to be often be a multitude of, at times mutually exclusive, theories for any given psychological phenomenon.

CONCLUSION

We would like to conclude by reflecting on our experiences to offer some general tips for those about to embark on teaching psychological principles to cybersecurity students.

As with all interdisciplinary teaching, materials need to be adapted effectively to provide appropriate links to the other discipline. In the case of cybersecurity, psychology materials need to be linked to topics taught on other units within the cybersecurity course and to show an awareness of the professional context of cybersecurity. It is important to deliver the materials at the correct level, taking into account the relevant intended learning outcomes and educational stage. At the first year of an undergraduate degree, the emphasis needs to be on practical activities and workshops can be used to demonstrate how recommendations based on Psychology can be put into practice. Indeed, examples can be used to illustrate where Psychology has *not* been considered to great effect! At final year undergraduate level, the authors found that students appreciate more detail as to *how* research was conducted and they need to develop skills to allow them to consider different psychological methods to evaluate the security of online systems. At postgraduate level, students are interested in hearing about ground-breaking research where psychology is being applied to inform cybersecurity, but also they appreciate discussing the philosophical debates. It is important not to overwhelm students (at any level) with psychological content but to provide case studies and references to support the concepts being covered. Similar to being prepared regarding the curriculum and educational level of your intended learners, some understanding of the profile of your intended learners can assist in developing Psychology materials for cybersecurity students. For example, the style of presentation of Psychology activities can be adapted to better match the approaches to studying of cybersecurity students.

Finally, it is important to recognize that students will have a certain perception of what Psychology covers. It is common for some cybersecurity students to think Psychology is only concerned with treating psychological disorders or that it is an 'un-scientific' way of explaining human behavior. As a result, it is useful at the start of any contact with cybersecurity students to briefly cover what is Psychology and what is not Psychology and to differentiate between academic Psychology and 'popular' Psychology. This helps to contextualize the wider role of Psychologists in the many areas of modern life relating to computing and technology. This has been helped recently with TV programs such as 'Hunted' (2015) employing forensic psychologists and cybersecurity experts to hunt escapees.

REFERENCES

Cialdini, R. B. (2008). *Influence: science and practice* (5th ed.). Englewood Cliffs, NJ: Prentice Hall.

Dark, M., & Winstead, J. (2005). Using educational theory and moral psychology to inform the teaching of ethics in computing. In *Proceedings of the 2nd Annual Conference on Information Security Curriculum Development* (pp. 27-31). New York: ACM Press. doi:10.1145/1107622.1107630

Fullwood, C. (2015). The role of personality in online self-presentation. In A. Attrill (Ed.), *Cyberpsychology* (pp. 9–28). Oxford, UK: Oxford University Press.

Gibbs, J. C., Basinger, K. S., & Fuller, D. (1992). *Moral maturity: Measuring the development of sociomoral reflection*. Hillsdale, NJ: Erlbaum.

Greene, J., & Hiadt, J. (2002). How (and where) does moral judgement work? *Trends in Cognitive Sciences*, *6*(12), 517–523. doi:10.1016/S1364-6613(02)02011-9 PMID:12475712

Halpern, D. F. (1992). *Sex differences in cognitive abilities* (2nd ed.). Hillsdale, NJ: Erlbaum.

Hamman, S. T., Hopkinson, K. M., Markham, R. L., Chaplik, A. M., & Metzler, G. E. (2017). Teaching game theory to improve adversarial thinking in cybersecurity students. *IEEE Transactions on Education*, *99*, 1–7.

Higher Education Statistical Agency. (2014). *Qualifications obtained by students on HE courses at HEIs in the UK by level of qualification obtained, gender and subject area, 2012 to 2013*. Accessed on 16/12/16 from https://www.hesa.ac.uk/data-and-analysis/publications/students-2012-13/introduction

Hunted. (2015). *Channel 4 programme*. Retrieved May 30, 2017, from http://www.channel4.com/programmes/hunted

Johnson, D. (1985). *Computer ethics* (1st ed.). Englewood Cliffs, NJ: Prentice Hall.

Johnson, D. (2009). *Computer ethics* (4th ed.). Englewood Cliffs, NJ: Prentice Hall.

Kohlberg, L. & Kramer, R. (1969). Continuities and discontinuities in childhood and adult moral development. *Human Development*, *12*, 93-120.

Kolb, D. A. (1981). Learning styles and disciplinary differences. In A. W. Chickering (Ed.), *The Modern American College*. San Francisco, CA: Jossey-Bass.

Layman, L., Cornwell, T., & Williams, L. (2006). Personality types, learning styles, and an agile approach to software engineering education. *ACM SIGCSE Bulletin*, *38*(1), 428–432. doi:10.1145/1124706.1121474

McAlaney, J., Thackray, H., & Taylor, J. (2016). The social psychology of cybersecurity. *The Psychologist*, *29*(9), 686–689.

McGettrick, A. (2013). *Toward curricular guidelines for cybersecurity*. Retrieved May 30, 2017, from https://www.acm.org/education/TowardCurricularGuidelinesCybersec.pdf

Radford, J., & Holdstock, L. (1995). Gender differences in Higher Education aims between computing and psychology students. *Research in Science & Technological Education*, *13*(2), 163–176. doi:10.1080/0263514950130206

Reese, H. W. (2011). The learning-by-doing principle. *Behavioral Development Bulletin*, *17*(1), 1–19. doi:10.1037/h0100597

Richardson, J. T. E. (1994). Mature students in higher education: A literature survey on approaches to studying. *Studies in Higher Education*, *19*(3), 309–325. doi:10.1080/03075079412331381900

Rogers, M. K. (2010). The psyche of cybercriminals: A psycho-social perspective. In G. Ghosh & E. Turrini (Eds.), *Cybercrimes: a multidisciplinary analysis*. Berlin: Springer-Verlag.

Taylor, J., & MacDonald, J. (2002). The effects of asynchronous computer-mediated group interaction on group processes. *Social Science Computer Review*, *20*(3), 260–274. doi:10.1177/089443930202000304

Tetri, P., & Vuorinen, J. (2013). Dissecting social engineering. *Behaviour & Information Technology*, *32*(10), 1014–1023. doi:10.1080/0144929X.2013.763860

Wilson, F. (2003). Can compute, won't compute: Women's participation in the culture of computing. *New Technology, Work and Employment*, *18*(2), 127–142. doi:10.1111/1468-005X.00115

Chapter 7
The Role of Psychology in Understanding Online Trust

Helen S. Jones
University of Dundee, UK

Wendy Moncur
University of Dundee, UK

ABSTRACT

Across many online contexts, internet users are required to make judgments of trustworthiness in the systems or other users that they are connecting with. But how can a user know that the interactions they engage in are legitimate? In cases where trust is manipulated, there can be severe consequences for the user both economically and psychologically. In this chapter, the authors outline key psychological litera-ture to date that has addressed the question of how trust develops in online environments. Specifically, three use cases in which trust relationships emerge are discussed: crowdfunding, online health forums, and online dating. By including examples of different types of online interaction, the authors aim to demonstrate the need for advanced security measures that ensure valid trust judgments and minimise the risk of fraud victimisation.

INTRODUCTION

As our lives transition further into the digital world, the role of trust in day-to-day interactions is trans-forming. Internet users are required to make judgments about others without any of the emotional and behavioural cues that would be available in a face-to-face interaction (Rocco, 1998; Cheshire, 2011; Hancock & Guillory, 2015). Where interactions involve risk, through the disclosure of personal or fi-nancial information, a need for trust in other users and systems emerges. Although the development of trusting relationships online can benefit the user, both economically and personally, anonymity and the lack of accountability on the internet (Friedman, Kahn, & Howe, 2000) mean that this trust can also be manipulated more readily.

In cases where trust is misplaced or manipulated, users can suffer both financial loss and psychologi-cal trauma, depending on the nature of the relationship. Online fraud costs the UK almost £11 billion

DOI: 10.4018/978-1-5225-4053-3.ch007

per year (Action Fraud, 2016), and often results from abuse of a user's natural inclination to trust others. Examples include the theft of money through online transactions where the item never arrives or, on a more personal level, romance fraud where a user is manipulated into sending money to a fraudster posing as a potential romantic partner in need of financial assistance. In extreme cases, misplaced trust online may lead to physical harm, for example if a user makes the decision to meet with someone from a dating website whose motives turn out to be malicious. At the same time, legitimate organisations are impeded by a lack of trust from users who are overcautious and unwilling to divulge information online (Wang & Emurian, 2005). This means that withholding trust where it is warranted can result in missed opportunities for both the user and the organisations that are losing custom (Friedman, Khan, & Howe, 2000). It is therefore crucial that an optimal balance is reached to encourage users to make effective and accurate trust judgments online.

In this chapter, the authors will consider existing models of trust behaviour alongside insights from psychology and information systems that inform our understanding of the formation of trust beliefs and influence behaviour. The chapter will go on to consider three specific online scenarios in which trust is a prerequisite to successful interaction: crowdfunding, health forums, and online dating. These three scenarios cover a range of relationship types, from business-like investments through crowdfunding platforms, to personal and intimate relationship building through online dating. The commonality between all three though is that they emphasise a current trend towards a collaborative society and economy. Moving away from a need for institutional trust, these examples emphasise the need to understand how trust dynamics work between users and how social information can influence trust. By choosing to focus on these varying scenarios, the authors hope to demonstrate the diversity of risk faced online, whilst highlighting fairly underexplored examples of peer-to-peer interactions that are rapidly becoming the cornerstone to our digital lives.

There are parallels that can be drawn between crowdfunding and more traditional e-commerce transactions online, although the lack of legal regulation around crowdfunding means that this is an inherently riskier form of transaction. As an investment, rather than purchase, the funder has no guarantee that the product or organisation will be delivered as advertised. Similarly, engagement with health forums and online dating sites may be compared to traditional chat forum conversations in that they are computer mediated interactions between strangers. However, the personal and often intimate nature of these conversations means that users are likely to divulge information that can leave them in a more vulnerable position. As such there is an even more crucial need to ensure that the information people are sharing in such scenarios online is done so in a secure manner, and only with individuals who warrant trust. The potential to manipulate trust in these scenarios will be discussed, providing an overview of the central issues to be addressed in future research and security tools that are designed to encourage secure online connectivity.

BACKGROUND

What Is Trust?

Trust is an essential construct to the maintenance of a functioning society (Rotter, 1980). Without it, friendships and relationships would not exist, whilst organisations would not be able to establish and maintain a customer following. As such, definitions of trust are widespread and vary across disciplines, including psychology, economics, and information systems. However, across these disciplines, there is consistency in the emphasis on risk and uncertainty as underlying prerequisites for the development of trust (Cheshire, 2011). In relation to online behaviour, this risk may be created by a request to divulge personal or financial information to an unknown website, or through interaction with strangers whose intentions are unverified. An appropriate definition of trust is often dependent on the type of relationship being described, for example definitions may differ across interpersonal, societal, or systems-based interactions. One definition that encapsulates the positions taken across disciplines suggests that "trust is a psychological state comprising the intention to accept vulnerability based upon positive expectations of the intentions or behaviours of another" (Rousseau, Sitkin, Burt, & Camerer, 1998). In this sense, trust exists alongside risk, where a person accepts that the other party may or may not act in the expected manner, but believes that their intentions are good.

As well as understanding *what* trust is on a conceptual level, much research has considered *how* this develops. This is crucial to understanding situations where trust is misplaced, or when distrust in another person or system is displayed. Some propose that a disposition to trust exists as a static trait that differs between people and is maintained across contexts (Gurtman, 1992; Sorrentino, Holmes, Hanna, & Sharp, 1995). In particular, this trait is thought to encapsulate trust decisions in novel scenarios, when interacting with a stranger or when there is little additional information available to inform behaviour. Rotter (1980) suggests that a predisposition to trust builds from early childhood experiences relating to trust that result in generalised beliefs about other people and the honesty of their intentions. However, trust is a complex construct and later explanations combine this predisposition into more substantial models that take into account factors specific to a given situation, as discussed in more detail below.

Modelling Trust Behaviour

Mayer, Davis, and Schoorman (1995) provide a comprehensive model of trust with three core beliefs that are incorporated into many later definitions and explanations: ability, benevolence, and integrity. *Ability* refers to the perceived skills and knowledge of the trustee, based on available information or prior knowledge about them. If a person believes someone to be highly capable of completing the task in question, they will likely be more willing to disclose information to this person (Gillespie, 2003). *Benevolence* accounts for the extent to which a person perceives the intentions of another to be positive and good-natured. Finally, *integrity* refers to the perceived adherence to personal and moral principles on the part of the trustee. These latter two constructs are thought to influence a person's willingness to rely on the trustee, which in turn informs decisions about trust related behaviours such as co-operation and business transactions (Gillespie, 2003).

Models such as that proposed by Mayer, Davis, and Schoorman (1995), which are commonly used across the trust literature, were proposed in relation to interpersonal or organisational trust in an offline capacity, before the emergence of the internet as a platform for social interaction and e-commerce, amongst other activities. Therefore, it is necessary to consider how such explanations translate into an online environment, and whether these are in fact still applicable. The core beliefs outlined for human interaction may still hold in the online environment (Lankton & McKnight, 2011), but there are a number of additional factors to consider that may hinder trust development, such as anonymity and lack of accountability online, unknown vulnerabilities, and lack of regulations in place to provide assurance in case of harm (Friedman, Kahn, & Howe, 2000). Interactions with online systems, rather than other users, may again be considered differently. Cheshire (2011) argues that there are fundamental differences in the mechanisms underlying interactions between humans and systems, and that in many cases the need for trust is overridden by the security assurances available online, such as privacy icons. In these cases, the uncertainty and risk that underpins the need for trust is eradicated. Although this has potential positive consequences for secure behaviour, it does limit the potential for developing on-going trusting relationships. Cheshire (2011) does conclude though that the perceived humanness of some computer systems may blur the distinction between interpersonal and systems-based interactions.

Similarly, Lankton, McKnight, and Tripp (2015) suggest that different technologies elicit a different level of perceived humanness based on the social presence and affordances of a given system. Existing trust models, such as that proposed by Mayer, Davis, and Schoorman (1995) have been adapted to reflect the differing nature of interactions between a human user and a system, compared to interacting with another human. Functionality, helpfulness, and reliability replace ability, benevolence, and integrity, as the core beliefs associated with trust behaviour (McKnight, Carter, Thatcher, & Harrison, 2011). In some cases though there may be an interaction between the two sets of beliefs, for example in social networking sites where users display trust in the platform itself, as well as in the other users they are interacting with through the site. This is demonstrated in a study looking at trust on Facebook where the two sets of belief constructs were shown to conceptually relate (ability-functionality, benevolence-helpfulness, and integrity-reliability) in a model that outperformed either distinct set of beliefs in explaining trust attribution (Lankton & McKnight, 2011).

The research discussed in this chapter demonstrates the underlying constructs that support the development of trust in both interpersonal and systems based interactions. As mentioned above, an element of risk and uncertainty is a precursor for trust, as is the case in many online interactions where we are unfamiliar with the user or organisation we are interacting with. In the scope of this chapter, the authors are interested in understanding situations where trust is misplaced and the intentions of the 'other' turn out to be malicious. In order to do this, psychological mechanisms that inform beliefs about ability, benevolence, and integrity, in turn influencing trust behaviour, are considered.

Psychological Mechanisms in Trust Behaviour Online

Trust is recognised as a fundamental construct underpinning stability within society (Rotter, 1980), yet there is a disparity of literature drawing upon the psychology underlying trust behaviour (Dunning, Anderson, Schlösser, Ehlebracht, & Fetchenhauer, 2014). However, there are a number of constructs and mechanisms from the field of psychology that show clear relevance to the development of relationships through online interaction, and which may act as pre-cursors to the trust beliefs discussed above (ability, benevolence, and integrity). These fit into two main areas: the psychology of persuasion, which considers the role of social influences in trust development; and individual differences between users, which include cognitive and personality traits that may impact trust behaviour. Each of these will be discussed in more detail below.

Psychology of Persuasion

Literature on the psychology of persuasion and social influence outlines core factors that can elicit behaviour change. Cialdini (2001) outlines six principles of influence: reciprocation, commitment and consistency, social proof, liking, authority, and scarcity. A number of these can be linked to patterns of online behaviour (Guadagno & Cialdini, 2005), and demonstrate potential vulnerabilities that might be manipulated by fraudsters trying to deceptively gain the trust of users online for personal gain. Social proof, which provides insight on how to act in a given situation based on the behaviour of others and a desire to be liked, has been show to influence compliance online (Guadagno, Muscanell, Rice, & Roberts, 2013). Although compliance suggests only a surface-level change in behaviour, rather than a permanent attitude change (Turner, 1991), this is enough to have severe consequences for a user if they divulge security-related information as a result. Pee (2012) also demonstrated the influence of the majority in the context of social media, suggesting that the behaviour of others has a greater effect on willingness to trust in false information online than the information quality or source credibility does.

Reciprocation, another of Cialdini's principles, and one of the fundamental norms of human society, suggests an obligation to repay the good will of others. In this sense, by giving through an act of kindness, a person is assured that the recipient will return the favour at some point in the future. There is potential for this perceived obligation to be used as a bargaining tool against a person, and thus be used to manipulate behaviour. The notion of reciprocation is amplified when there is a shared sense of social identity between those involved, as the distinction between personal and group welfare is blurred (Abrams & Hogg, 2010). Shared identities often develop in online environments, and so it is possible that the notion of reciprocation could be used to persuade a user to engage unwillingly in a financial transaction as a return favour, for example, putting them at risk of fraud victimisation.

Aside from the notion of reciprocation, social identity alone may influence behaviour as a result of compliance with the norms of the group (Reynolds, Subašić, & Tindall, 2014), for fear of rejection or social out-casting. Originally developed to explore intergroup conflict and harmony (Tajfel & Turner, 1979), social identity theory is now commonly cited in understanding how group consensus on appropriate behaviour in a given situation can overcome uncertainty (Abrams & Hogg, 2010). In relation to trust, to which uncertainty is a precursor, people may rely on factors such as shared social identity to inform beliefs about ability and integrity during an interaction. There is a consensus that people have multiple social identities, and a specific context will influence which of these prevails (Turner, Hogg, Oakes, Reicher, & Wetherell, 1987). In addition, Goffman (1959) likens social identity to a theatrical performance, whereby the audience in a given scenario influences the character portrayed. In line with social proof, social identity theory implies that behaviour and beliefs are influenced by the actions and expectations of others, in particular those with whom we share a common identity. This human inclination to comply with the norms of a group may be used to manipulate behaviour by making a person feel obligated to act in a given way or divulge certain information that they may not otherwise do.

Within the context of a social group with a shared identity, a set of norms is established that orient the behaviour of group members (Neville, 2015). These arise through interaction and relationship building within the group (Turner, 1991), and often result from a compromise between the personal or alternate social norms of those in the group. Although there is some speculation on the exact process by which norms influence behaviour change (Reynolds, Subašić, & Tindall, 2014), it is acknowledged that social identity and norms interact to govern how a person should feel and act in a given situation (Turner et al., 1987). For example, a person who identifies as a football supporter may act in a rowdy manner at a match, but they would be unlikely to act this way in the workplace, where instead they adopt the identity of a reliable employee. There has also been some speculation on the motivations of compliance with social norms, with some arguing that this is purely a tactic employed to enhance personal self-image and give the impression of a moral lifestyle (Krueger, Massey, & DiDonato, 2008). Alternate research though has demonstrated that the adoption of social norms and associated group identity can result in long-term attitude change (Newcomb, 1943). Despite their importance in maintaining an orderly society

(Turner, 1991), social norms have been shown to lead to an excess of trust, which has clear consequences in light of cyber security threats, such as those associated with the example scenarios that are discussed later in this chapter. One example of such an impact comes from a study on privacy concerns in social networking sites, which demonstrated that perception of social norms about what data should be visible to others influenced security behaviour (Utz & Krämer, 2009). Dunning et al. (2014) suggest that fear of the negative consequences associated with disobeying social norms, such as guilt and anxiety, can lead people to comply and behave in ways that leave them vulnerable to the malicious intentions of others through unwarranted trust.

Individual Differences

Alternative accounts of behaviour online suggest that individual differences between users may be influential. Although the empirical evidence to support this is less convincing than that of social identity and social norms theories, it should be noted none the less in providing a comprehensive overview of the perspectives that psychology offers. In the broad context of trust behaviour, gender studies show that men are more trusting than women (Buchan, Croson, & Solnick, 2008), whilst women are viewed as more trustworthy (Dollar et al., 2001). Whilst these findings are replicated in relation to online shopping behaviour (Garbarino & Strahilevitz, 2004; Van Slyke, Comunale, & Belanger, 2002), the authors are unaware of any evidence to indicate that this is the case in online interpersonal interactions such as those described later in the chapter. That is not to say that these differences do not exist, simply that there is a dearth in literature to support this currently. Similarly, whilst there is a common conception that older users are more vulnerable online, the evidence for this is not clear cut, and in any case research in relation to the examples outlined below is lacking.

Kaptein and Eckles (2012) report findings that the success of persuasion techniques in an online context can be partially explained by individual differences in personality constructs, such as the need for cognition (i.e. the inclination to engage more rational cognitive processing techniques), and that this was consistent across multiple trials. In this sense, they propose that these differences are static rather than transient traits, and imply that some users are more susceptible to persuasion than others. The exact individual differences are not outlined though, and instead a broad heterogeneity in response between users is reported. More research would be necessary to establish if there are specific constructs that influence response to persuasion techniques in order to understand the nature and implications of these findings.

The notion of individual differences does link with a disposition to trust, discussed above, which may act as a static trait between users making some more likely to trust than others. Roghanizad and Neufeld (2015) on the other hand propose that trust behaviour is situation specific. This work taps in to dual-process theories of reasoning, which suggest that individual differences (Kyllonen & Christal, 1990; Markovits, Doyon, & Simoneau, 2002) or situational factors (Stanovich, 1999; Kahneman, 2000; Evans, 2003) might influence engagement in either rational or intuitive processing. When processing rationally, a person takes in all aspects of the information available to them in order to make an informed decision about how to behave or respond. Intuitive responses on the other hand rely on surface level information and pre-existing heuristics. When faced with risk, such as the requirement to disclose personal information online, Roghanizad and Neufeld (2015) propose that users rely on intuitive responses rather than engaging in rational contemplation about the trustworthiness of a given website or user.

The mechanisms discussed in this section have all been shown to influence behaviour in social situations, and by analogy relate to how users interact with one another online, and how relationships develop. Decisions surrounding the three beliefs associated with trust behaviour (ability, benevolence, and integrity) are likely to be informed by these mechanisms. By outlining the factors that influence and inform trust decisions and behaviour, the authors are also highlighting a number of vulnerabilities that might be used to manipulate impressions of trustworthiness made in an online environment, and thus deceive a user by eliciting trust where it is not warranted. This provides insight when considering fraud victimisation, and demonstrates core considerations in the development of tools to tackle cyber security issues surrounding human vulnerability.

Information Systems Approaches to Trust Behaviour Online

Although this chapter will focus predominantly on the human factors influencing the development of trust between users, it is worth also mentioning a complimentary approach, which considers the relationship between the user and the system they are engaging with. In both unidirectional and bidirectional interactions online, the platform on which these take place can have an important role in how the user perceives the trustworthiness of a site, but also of the other users that they might interact with on that site. Lindgaard, Fernandes, Dudek, and Brown (2006) suggest that people form an opinion about the visual appeal of a website within the first 50ms, and this may have a crucial impact on perceived trustworthiness (Lindgaard, Dudek, Sen, Sumegi, & Noonan, 2011). Factors such as errors making the site look unprofessional, the colour scheme adopted (Cyr, Head, & Larios, 2010), and the design of the site can have a crucial impact. The influence of these systems-based factors may depend on the type of site though, with ease of navigation viewed as important to informational sites (including online communities) whilst the presence and strength of brand placement is deemed more influential on sites with which the user is highly invested, such as financial services (Bart, Shankar, Sultan, & Urban, 2005).

Security assurances are regularly incorporated within web pages, although empirical data on the value of these is varied, with some suggesting that these have a positive impact on trust development (Odom, Kumar, & Saunders, 2002; Rifon, LaRose, & Choi, 2005; Wu, Hu, & Wu, 2010), whilst others report no effect (Hui, Teo, & Lee, 2007; McKnight, Kacmar, & Choudhury, 2004). The presence of security cues may contribute to the normative appearance of a website though, and in turn reflect whether information is presented as the user would expect it to be. This expectation of normality can act as a precursor to trusting beliefs about the authenticity of a web site (Li, Hess, & Valacich, 2008). The impact of these assurance cues may also be dependent of the level of risk involved in the interaction, with objective assessments such as these playing more of a role in trust development under low risk (Raghanizad & Neufeld, 2015).

Contrary to Cheshire's (2011) opinion that trust cannot exist between a human and a system, this research suggests that the assurances provided by the presence or absence of certain cues on a website can provide insight at least into the initial trustworthiness of an organisation or group. However, the development of ongoing relationships is reliant on more than this. In combination with interpersonal trust, these approaches seem to work together in explaining how users can decide which sites/platforms to interact with. They may then engage only with those perceived most trustworthy to develop on going relationships and interactions, which most often become reliant on interpersonal trust to succeed long term.

APPLIED ONLINE SCENARIOS

In this section, the authors explore the existing literature around user decision-making across three different example scenarios. As discussed above, these examples provide insight into a range of interaction types, from the business-like transaction of crowdfunding investment, to the intimate relationship building through online dating platforms. These highlight interesting new areas of interest in terms of trust in peer-to-peer interactions, which have perhaps been less extensively explored than more traditional business-to-peer scenarios such as e-commerce. It is hoped that this section highlights the valuable opportunities, and need to consider these three scenarios in the design of security solutions to protect users.

Crowdfunding

Crowdfunding acts as an alternative source of funding for small businesses that may be unable to gain financial backing through traditional means, such as bank loans and venture capital (Gerber & Hui, 2013). This inability to attain backing is often due to poor financial history, or simply because the business is new and therefore does not have the financial record to warrant support from corporate investors (Song & van Boeschoten, 2015). Crowdfunding platforms, such as Kickstarter and IndieGoGo, allow creators and business owners to design a campaign and collect money through small pledges made by funders. Two common models of crowdfunding are outlined here, although it should be recognised that these are not the only models in existence – with others including peer-to-peer lending, and charitable donations. The first to be discussed though – *reward-based* – generally generates smaller pledges, and provides funders with some form of non-monetary reward for their contribution (Belleflamme & Lambert, 2014; Lukkarinen, Teich, Wallenius, & Wallenius, 2016). Rewards range from an acknowledgement in the credits of a film being produced from the funding, to a discounted pre-order version of a product being launched as a result of the campaign (Mollick, 2014). The second model to consider is *equity-based*, whereby funders receive partial equity in the business they are supporting, and as such their contribution is acknowledged through on-going financial recuperation (Rakesh, Choo, & Reddy, 2015; Beier & Wagner, 2016). In addition to different campaign models, there are also two distinct investment structures for crowdfunding (as described in Gerber, Hui, & Kuo, 2012). The 'all-or-nothing' approach, adopted by Kickstarter, means that if a project does not reach its funding target, the investments are returned to the funders. The alternative is the 'all-and-more' approach, as employed by IndieGoGo, whereby the creator receives all of the contributions given to the campaign, regardless of whether the target sum is reached. The nature of these approaches means that 'all-or-more' generates higher risk for the funder, as they may lose their money and not receive any form of reward, financial or otherwise, if the project does not progress due to lack of funding.

The alternative forms of fundraising elicit differing theoretical approaches in terms of considering funder motivations and decisions to support a campaign, and as such, to place trust in the creator. Uncertainty and risk are at the core of participation in crowdfunding, given the lack of legal regulation in place, meaning that there is no guarantee a product will be delivered, or promise of financial security if a business fails to succeed (Kim, Shaw, Zhang, & Gerber, 2017). Although the lack of regulation is consistent across all types of crowdfunding, this has greater consequences in equity-based investments, as funders often put forward larger sums of money, and are reliant on the ongoing success of a business. As well as cases where the creators successfully launch a product, but this is not well received by the public, there are also situations where creators may be fraudulently collecting money, with no intention of giving back to the funders. These creators develop a misleading campaign, collecting money from funders for a non-existent concept or business. Given the evident risk factors and uncertainty involved in crowdfunding, it is important to understand how funders make decisions about which projects to support, in order to reduce risk of financial loss and potential fraud victimisation.

Aside from the financial benefits, creators on crowdfunding platforms report being motivated by the increased awareness they raise for their product or business, the community that develops from the support of numerous funders sharing their knowledge and experience, and the ability to maintain control over their business. For the funders, key motivators across campaign types include a sense of online philanthropy and becoming part of a community of supporters. On the other hand, participation is deterred by a lack of trust in how the creators will spend the money, as well as the potential downfalls in success as a result of creators' limited business experience (Gerber & Hui, 2013).

A majority of the research in the field of crowdfunding has focused on investment patterns and trends in the success of campaigns. Within reward-based campaigns, there is a trend for an inverted bell curve pattern of funding behaviour, whereby support peaks at the beginning of the campaign and rapidly declines until the deadline approaches, when a surge in funding activity occurs in successful campaigns (Kuppuswamy & Bayus, 2013; Beier & Wagner, 2016; Agrawal, Catalini, & Goldfarb, 2014). The initial peak in funding at the early stages of the campaign often comes from friends and family of the creator (Horvát, Uparna, & Uzzi, 2015), which is evidenced by geographical patterns in the location of funders (Agrawal, Goldfarb, & Catalini, 2011). Although funding from friends and family is not of interest here, given our aim of understanding how trust develops between strangers, it *is* of interest that this initial peak in funding is shown to predict overall campaign success, by encouraging additional funders in the latter stages (Colombo, Franzoni, & Rossi-Lamastra, 2015). The lull in funding activity in the central period may be explained by a diffusion of responsibility, whereby funders are less inclined to support the project as it already has support, so they make an assumption that other investors will continue to contribute (Kuppuswamy & Bayus, 2013; Fischer et al., 2011). The increase in activity as a project nears its closing date may indicate a deadline effect, something which has been acknowledged by researchers considering bidding in online auctions (Ariely & Simonson, 2003). Alternative explanations consider that risk averse funders wait until later in the campaign as they can identify whether a project will meet its funding target (Beier & Wagner, 2016), or that funders feel contributions at this stage are more meaningful, as they are pushing the campaign closer to its target, enhancing the philanthropic nature of their support (Kuppuswamy & Bayus, 2017).

Equity-based campaigns demonstrate a different pattern of support, with evidence of herding behaviour amongst investors (Kuppuswamy & Bayus, 2013). The behaviour of other investors is considered information assurance, on the assumption that if others are doing something, it must be the rational thing to do (Cialdini, 2001). In peer-to-peer lending platforms, where peers fund each other on a loan basis and the money is repaid with interest, a similar pattern is seen, with investors basing decisions on those who have already contributed, in place of more traditional cues such as the credit rating score of the creator (Zhang & Lui, 2012). In particular, research has demonstrated that the identity of early investors as experts in product development or financial investment encourages less-expert funders to contribute at a later stage (Kim & Viswanathan, 2014). This is supported by Burtch, Ghose, and Wattal (2016), who demonstrated that masking the identity of the earlier funders, and the amounts given, made others less inclined to contribute to the campaign. This behaviour indicates a reliance on social proof, with funders basing decisions on the behaviour of other funders, in both types of crowdfunding and links in with the principles of persuasion outlined above (Cialdini, 2001). Herding behaviour may leave funders at risk of fraud (Kuppuswamy & Bayus, 2013), as their funding decisions are being motivated by the behaviour of others (information about which may have been falsified; Wessel, Thies, & Benlian, 2016) rather than on the merit of the campaign itself. In extreme cases, where creators may have used fake accounts to exaggerate the apparent support for their campaign, funders may be falsely drawn into believing the worth of the project, and as such leave themselves in a vulnerable position if this is not successful. As mentioned earlier, a lack of legal regulation surrounding crowdfunding and the limited resolution resources available from crowdfunding platforms themselves make this an even greater risk.

Aside from the funding patterns observed most commonly in crowdfunding, researchers have considered alternative factors that may also influence funding behaviour, many of which relate to the social engagement of the creator. As a campaign progresses, funding is increased when the creator provides valuable updates (Hornuf & Schwienbacher, 2015; Kuppuswamy & Bayus, 2013), reassuring a potential funder that the project is progressing, and the creator is engaged in the fundraising process. In equity-based crowdfunding, project updates are particularly influential when they relate to new business developments and information about additional promotional campaigns being run by the creator (Block, Hornuf, & Moritz, 2016). Openness about prior financial history (Lukkarinen, Teich, Wallenius, & Wallenius, 2016) and linking social media accounts (Vismara, 2016) also encourages funders, as they likely feel that the creator has nothing to hide. In addition, the availability of social media information may elicit support through funders who feel they have a shared social identity with the creator (Kromidha & Robson, 2016). This openness to share as much information as possible with potential funders and demonstrate a robust social identity may also act as a reassurance that the creator did not just set up an account yesterday for the purpose of fraudulently gathering money. The extent and mechanisms by which wider online behaviour elicits trust in a creator is yet to be explored in the academic literature though.

A reliance on social information is further demonstrated through the influence of prior social capital gained on the crowdfunding platform. Creators who have established social capital through funding prior projects, completing successful projects in the past, and contributing to the crowdfunding community are more likely to receive funding in the early stages of a project, and more likely to reach their funding target (Colombo, Franzoni, & Rossi-Lamastra, 2014; Zvilichovsky, Inbar, & Barzilay, 2015). This demonstrates the importance of reciprocation (Cialdini, 2001) to trust behaviour in crowdfunding. Prior behaviour on the platform generates a community spirit amongst funders and creators, which often crosses over to external social networking sites (Skirnevskiy, Bendig, & Brettel, 2017; Rakesh, Choo, & Reddy, 2015). The positive impact of this on campaign success seems to link to social identity theory, discussed earlier, whereby a shared identity as a fellow crowdfunder or successful creator, encourages the development of trusting relationships between platform users.

However, there is potential for a fraudster to manipulate this reliance on social identity in order to attract funders to a campaign. By giving a sense of community and shared identity through the information published via the campaign, trust may develop under false pretences. Additional social information may be manipulated to attract further funders, as demonstrated by Wessel, Thies, and Benlian (2016) who report that 1.6 per cent of campaigns analysed incorporated a faked Facebook 'like' count. The effect of this fake information was an initial spike in funding, followed by a sharp decline, which was put down to the lack of actual social media coverage for the campaign, as the majority of this was faked, so genuine distribution was minimal. In an 'all-or-more' campaign, this means that initial investors who were tricked by fake social information will lose their money due to the consequential lack of funding later in the campaign. Although the intentions of the creator in this case may not be fraudulent, misleading the funder through false information remains unethical and highlights additional concerns for funders to consider when they are making decisions about campaign funding.

In outlining the key motivators and influential factors for crowdfunding campaigns, this section also highlights mechanisms that might be manipulated by a fraudster to elicit trust from a potential funder and falsely encourage their participation. Social behaviours, such as herding and reliance on demonstration of shared identity as an indicator of trustworthiness, leave the funder vulnerable. The lack of quality cues available to funders, when a product is yet to be manufactured and a business is in its infancy, makes it difficult to engage rational decision-making. This emphasises a need for solutions that provide validated assurances about creator legitimacy to encourage secure online behaviour and reduce fraud victimisation in this domain.

Health Forums

Engagement with online health information continues to increase, with estimates of between 50 (Office for National Statistics, 2016) and 70 (Gandhi, & Wang, 2015) per cent of people using the internet as a source of medical advice in 2015-16. One element of the search for information online involves connecting with online health forums, where users come together to discuss their own personal experiences (Rozmovits, & Ziebland, 2004; Zhao, Abrahamson, Anderson, Ha, & Widdows, 2013), to develop friendships (Leitner, Wolkerstorfer, & Tscheligi, 2008), and form support networks with others experiencing the same health issues (Kummervold et al., 2002; Zhao et al., 2013). The internet provides an opportunity for forum users to anonymously disclose information that they might otherwise be too embarrassed to share (Jones et al., 2011; Coulson, 2005; Kummervold et al., 2002). Such interactions can lead to reduced fear and isolation (Rozmovits, & Ziebland, 2004), and a more effective adaptive response to diagnosis that has in some cases improved patient quality of life as well as increasing survival time (Coulson, 2005). At the same time, reports demonstrate that users of online health information still have a higher level of trust in medical professionals than they do in online information (Li, James, & McKibben, 2016), suggesting that they are not influenced solely by the subjective contributions of other users.

On the other hand, there are two core concerns associated with forum use that will be discussed here: the quality of information provided in these, and the authenticity of the group members engaging in conversation. Although there is evidence that overall, users still trust medical advice from their doctors, this is not to say that the contributions of forum users do not also have some level of influence. There are movements in existence that have formed and continue to be promoted through online groups that actually advise against common medical practise. For example, the 'pro-anorexia' movement that supports the disease, and discourages recovery efforts (Fox, Ward, & O'Rourke, 2005), or a network of chronic fatigue sufferers who promote rest and inactivity, contrary to typical medical advice (Wright, Partridge, & Williams, 2000). The social power behind such movements poses a risk to the health of those that become invested in it, if they are following advice based on social proof from peers, rather than scientific evidence.

Anonymity in online forums is viewed by many as a positive factor, allowing users to disclose information more freely without being embarrassed. However, this also makes it more difficult to assess the credibility of another user (Lederman, Fan, Smith, & Chang, 2014), with a lack of verifiable social information to base this judgment on. Without any measures in place to validate the medical information provided, users may be left reliant on inaccurate advice that in extreme cases may be dangerous to their health (Coulson, 2005; Sudau et al., 2014). Sudau and colleagues (2014) conducted analyses on user posts from a Multiple Sclerosis forum online to establish the quality of external links provided. This demonstrated that across 8628 posts analysed, only 31 contained links to scientific publication about the topic in question, whilst 2829 contained links to social media sources, such as YouTube and Facebook. This reliance on unverified and subjective information, especially in relation to health information with many users suffering from serious illnesses, raises concern for the risks associated with engaging in online health forums.

In order to reach a stage where the benefits outweigh the potential costs in these forums, some have called for systems to be put in place that can verify the claims made by other users (Lederman, Fan, Smith, & Chang, 2014) or allow for authentication of another user's credibility to provide information through mutual rating systems (Zhao, Ha, & Widdows, 2013). Alongside the risk of misinformation being communicated amongst forum users, there is a threat of emotional exploitation in cases where fraudulent accounts are used to spread fake stories (Lederman, Fan, Smith, & Chang, 2014). Cases of Munchausen's by Internet are well reported, whereby somebody extensively researches the symptoms and associated consequences of a condition, in order to give a convincing fake account of being a sufferer in an online forum (Feldman, 2000). The motivations behind this are not transparent, but a lot of the time this seems to stem from a desire for attention. Regardless of the intention, the consequences of such behaviour can damage the trusting relationships between members of a forum group. Once one person is outed as being a liar, the bond between other members rapidly declines, as they no longer know who to believe (Pulman & Taylor, 2012). This type of trolling behaviour is also used to provoke emotional arguments between users, as another way of disrupting the group dynamic. There are reported cases of users abusing such forum groups for financial gain as well, generating donation from sympathetic others. In order to address the issues highlighted here and ensure that users are able to safely engage with health forums online, the authors note that understanding how these communities develop and the factors that lead users to disclose personal information or act on advice that may put them at risk is important.

The sense of trust that often develops between users within patient communities can lead relationships to progress from anonymous interactions to the disclosure of personal information. This can leave the user vulnerable to a number of security threats, predominantly identity theft, and endanger their personal safety as a result if details such as location are disclosed. Ongoing interactions rely on continued exchange of such information though, and can lead users to share more information than they possibly should, in an effort to maintain the relationship. In order to prevent trust being misplaced and confidential information disclosed as a result, it is important to understand where this trust originates from in the development of communities. As mentioned above, anonymity online makes it difficult for users to assess the credibility of those providing information. However, users are often reliant on warrants, such as the quality of source information and evidence of a user's credentials to provide assurance for the trustworthiness of the person posting content, and the information provided (Richardson, 2003; Mun, Yoon, Davis, & Lee, 2013). Trust can also be influenced by the response rates of a user, with research suggesting that the more regularly a person posts in the group, the more trustworthy they are perceived (Ridings, Gefen, & Arinze, 2002). Once trust has been established, this then positively predicts the development of empathic relationships and likelihood that a user will share health information and their own personal experiences, and take on board that of others within the community (Zhao, Abrahamson, Anderson, Ha, & Widdows, 2013).

The development of empathy between users in online health forums may also be predicted by the presence of a shared social identity (Zhao, Ha, & Widdows, 2013; Zhao et al., 2013). Given the importance of personal experiences and ability to exchange knowledge, users report feeling a connection with those who are similar to them (Sillence & Briggs, 2015), with 41% of Americans who seek online health information reporting that they wanted to interact with someone like them (Fox & Jones, 2009). There is little research considering the specific aspects of social identity that users wish to relate to in the context of health forums and communities. In many scenarios it may be the case that the similarity extends no further than suffering from the same condtiion, but this is an interesting avenue for further exploration. Before engaging with a community, potential new users may utilise archived forum discussions to establish whether they share the same basic norms and beliefs as the community (Erickson, 1997).

In line with the other use cases outlined here, there is a clear link between the development of trusting relationships and social identity, which in turn can lead to increased information sharing and potential vulnerability, when anonymous community members turn out to be malicious. Other factors, such as reciprocation, may also influence behaviour within the forum. For example, if a user has received useful advice, they may feel the need to repay the favour, say if someone is raising money for treatment. In situations like this, there is potential for the strong bonds created between users to be manipulated by a fraudster. This highlights an on-going challenge to detect malicious intentions within group members, thus protecting other users from harm, but whilst also attempting to maintain the trust dynamic that benefits so many users on a day-to-day basis.

Online Dating

The use of online dating sites is now the second most common way to meet a new partner, preceded only by introduction through friends (Hagen-Rochester, 2012). Recent statistics suggest that around 40% of Americans use online dating, with 7% of marriages in 2015 resulting from relationships started through this medium (Thottam, 2017). The stigma associated with online dating is also decreasing, with a 15% increase between 2005 and 2013 in the number of people who view it as a good way to meet new people and potential partners (Thottam, 2017). Although these data come from one of the largest dating sites (www.eHarmony.com), and thus might be biased, acceptance of online dating is evident in daily society, with people talking more openly about their experiences. These sites provide unique opportunities, allowing people who may never previously have crossed paths to meet one another, and also allowing interaction in a novel social environment (Whitty, 2008), which may benefit certain users, for example those who are more introverted. Although users of traditional online dating sites find it difficult to judge personality over the internet (Zytko, Freeman, Grandhi, Herring, & Jones, 2015), chatting socially online has been shown to elicit similar levels of trust as a face-to-face meeting (Zheng, Veinott, Bos, Olson, & Olson, 2002). As such, the extent to which trust builds through dating sites may be considered comparable to that established in an offline meeting.

However, as with most interactions online, there are risks involved with online dating. The most heavily reported in research is the misrepresentation of personal attributes, such as weight and height statistics. Over half of online daters report feeling that someone they interacted with has seriously misrepresented themselves in their profile (Smith & Duggan, 2013). It seems that women are more prolific liars in this sense than men (Lo, Hsieh, & Chiu, 2013), and that this most often involves misrepresentation of physical appearance, whilst men more often misrepresent information about marital status, relationship goals, and height (Schmitz, Zillmann, & Blossfeld, 2013). As a result, many users report that they are concerned with the veracity of information given on a dating profile (Norcie, de Cristofaro, & Bellotti, 2013; Couch, Liamputtong, & Pitts, 2012). These misrepresentations often relate to minor, and seemingly superficial, concerns that the user may be exaggerating in order to attract a partner. While this may cause confusion or annoyance when meeting the person offline for the first time, the long-term impact is likely to be minimal. In some cases this falsification can be taken to the extreme though, with the use of photos and information taken from another person's profile to intentionally deceive another. Also know as 'catfishing', this behaviour usually stems from a lack of self-confidence and desire to portray a more attractive individual, or from a malicious motive to take revenge on someone by convincing them of a potential love interest, only to humiliate them later on.

There are also many cases of financial loss in relation to online dating though, with £39 million lost to online romance fraud in the UK alone in 2016 (Cacciottolo & Rees, 2017). This is an occurrence that is becoming increasingly common, with an increase of 33% in the number of instances reported between 2013 and 2014 (Action Fraud, 2015). In cases of fraud, the criminals will engage with a potential partner and develop a relationship with them, often declaring love early on in the encounter. They then progress to procure money from the victim, often with a cover story of a personal crisis or a lack of money to visit the partner. In some cases, victimisation can progress to sexual abuse, where the user is persuaded to engage in cyber sexual activities, such as sending naked photographs to the fraudster. This can leave them in a vulnerable position, if they have sent sensitive media to the perpetrator that can then be used against them (Whitty, 2015). One possible consequence is blackmail, which may lead not only to financial loss on the part of the victim, but also to emotional trauma. This emotional distress is seen to be more prominent with those who are particularly lonely (Buchanan & Whitty, 2014).

There are also risks involved at the point when relationships are taken offline and users agree to meet for the first time. Users themselves report feeling concern surrounding sexual risk (such as unplanned pregnancy, sexually transmitted diseases, and violence), emotional trauma, and the risk of encountering dangerous individuals when meeting up offline (Couch, Liamputtong, & Pitts, 2012). Although it is difficult to authenticate the attributes a user reports on their profile without meeting them offline (Zykto et al., 2015), a user is putting their personal safety at risk by choosing to do this. It is therefore essential for research to progress from considering how users misrepresent superficial information such as their height and income data, to focus on methods for combatting malicious behaviour. This could help to reduce instances of misplaced trust that result in financial fraud or physical abuse.

There are some newly developed apps that are designed to provide assurance about a user's identity before any interpersonal interaction has even begun. For example, Tinder requires users to login through Facebook as a way to authenticate identity. However, whilst this allows for common interests and mutual friends to be used as an indication of a shared normative identity (Duguay, 2017), there is potential for this to be manipulated, as a user can generate a fake Facebook account in the moment to access Tinder. An alternative example, Happn (https://www.happn.com/), uses location features to monitor the number of times you have crossed physical paths with a user, and showing the last location where this occurred. Users report that this gives them a perception of similarity with the other user, if they spend a lot of time going to the same types of places (Ma, Sun, & Naaman, 2017). In a sense, this demonstrates the importance of a shared social identity between two users before they have even begun to interact. So, it is apparent that across these apps there are elements of shared identity that influence the decision-making process at the point where the user is deciding whether to engage with a potential partner.

At the point where two users begin to interact, there are a number of additional uncertainty reduction strategies that may be employed to assess the trustworthiness of a potential partner. Users report asking specific questions, checking consistency in information across conversations, and even Googling the information that another user gives about themselves (Gibbs, Ellison, & Lai, 2011). Engagement with these types of strategic assessments is predicted by how concerned a user is about three issues: their personal safety, the likelihood of another user providing misrepresentative information, and fear of recognition by people they know (Gibbs, Ellison, & Lai, 2011). Further to this, concern about issues such as personal safety may depend upon the user's motivation for using the dating site in the first place. For example, Lutz and Ranzini (2017) report that Tinder users who are only interested in casual hook-ups are likely to be less concerned about their personal safety than users who are looking for friendship, or self-validation. This highlights not only a need to consider how security tools might help to protect the user, but also how to educate users of the need to conduct such due diligence in the realm of online dating.

Unlike the other use cases outlined here, the development of trust in online dating has a greater likelihood of progressing a relationship to the offline world, where the couple make the decision to meet in person. The addition of physical risk to the user and their wellbeing accentuates the need for accurate trust judgments to be made within the context of online dating. Whilst individual uncertainty reduction strategies go some way to reducing this threat, these are still subjective judgments for the most part and do not by any means provide a fool proof mechanism for the user to ensure the interactions and behaviour they engage in are secure. The research to date indicates a level of naivety in some users who are confident in meeting strangers without consideration of the risks. On the other hand, it highlights a number of users who want to gather further information as reassurance, but are reliant on Google or social media, where there is a distinct lack of due diligence provided from the dating platforms themselves.

CONCLUSION

In this chapter, the authors have highlighted the importance of accurate trust judgements in online interactions. Across the three example scenarios outlined, there are evident security threats that exist as a result of trust being misplaced or manipulated during interpersonal interactions with strangers. This supports the need to understand the underlying mechanisms that elicit such trust. As more and more day-to-day activities begin to transition into the digital world, the opportunities for malicious users to take advantage of the human inclination to trust others will only escalate. Statistics show year on year that instances of cybercrime and online fraud are increasing, with an 8% increase seen in 2016 (BBC News, 2017).

Whilst insights from existing theoretical perspectives provide some initial steps towards understanding trust in online contexts, it is evident that there is a need for much more comprehensive and explicit research in this area. Research has begun to demonstrate the importance of social psychological factors across the use cases outlined, including identity and shared norms. Human interaction is at the core of many online activities, in addition to those discussed, and it is therefore crucial that user-centric security tools are designed to address the existing vulnerabilities experienced by users. A solid theoretical grounding to explain how relationships develop through interaction across a range of online contexts would provide the building blocks that are necessary to enhance secure connectivity online and take important steps towards tackling the threats faced in an ever more digital age.

ACKNOWLEDGMENT

This research was supported by the EPSRC [grant reference: EP/N02799X/1].

REFERENCES

Abrams, D., & Hogg, M. A. (2010). Social identity and self categorization. In J. F. Dovidio, M. Hewstone, P. Glick, & V. M. Esses (Eds.), *The Sage handbook of prejudice, stereotyping and discrimination* (pp. 179–193). London: Sage. doi:10.4135/9781446200919.n11

Action Fraud. (2015). *Figures show online dating fraud is up by 33% last year.* Retrieved May 7, 2017, from http://www.actionfraud.police.uk/news/new-figures-show-online-dating-fraud-is-up-by-33percent-last-year-feb15

Action Fraud. (2016). *Fraud & cybercrime cost UK nearly £11bn in past year.* Retrieved May 5, 2017, from http://www.actionfraud.police.uk/news/fraud-and-cybercrime-cost-UK-nearly-11bn-in-past-year-oct16

Agrawal, A., Catalini, C., & Goldfarb, A. (2011). The geography of crowdfunding. *SSRN Electronic Journal.* Retrieved May 18, 2017, from http://ssrn.com/abstract=1692661

Agrawal, A., Catalini, C., & Goldfarb, A. (2014). Some simple economics of crowdfunding. *Innovation Policy and the Economy, 14*(1), 63–97. doi:10.1086/674021

Ariely, D., & Simonson, I. (2003). Buying, bidding, playing, or competing? Value assessment and decision dynamics in online auctions. *Journal of Consumer Psychology, 13*(1-2), 113–123. doi:10.1207/S15327663JCP13-1&2_10

Bart, Y., Shankar, V., Sultan, F., & Urban, G. L. (2005). Are the drivers and role of online trust the same for all web sites and consumers? A large-scale exploratory empirical study. *Journal of Marketing, 69*(4), 133–152. doi:10.1509/jmkg.2005.69.4.133

BBC News. (2017). *Cybercrime and fraud scales revealed in annual figures.* Retrieved May 11, 2017, from http://www.bbc.co.uk/news/uk-38675683

Beier, M., & Wagner, K. (2016). User Behavior in Crowdfunding Platforms--Exploratory Evidence from Switzerland. In *Proceedings from 49th Hawaii International Conference on System Sciences.* IEEE. doi:10.1109/HICSS.2016.448

Belleflamme, P., & Lambert, T. (2014). Crowdfunding: Some Empirical Findings and Microeconomic Underpinnings. *SSRN Electronic Journal.* Retrieved May 21, 2017, from https://papers.ssrn.com/sol3/papers.cfm?abstract_id=2437786

Block, J. H., Hornuf, L., & Moritz, A. (2016). Which updates during an equity crowdfunding campaign increase crowd participation? *SSRN Electronic Journal.* Retrieved June 1, 2017, from https://papers.ssrn.com/sol3/papers.cfm?abstract_id=2781715

Buchan, N. R., Croson, R. T. A., & Solnick, S. (2008). Trust and gender: An examination of behavior and beliefs in the Investment Game. *Journal of Economic Behavior & Organization, 68*(3-4), 466–476. doi:10.1016/j.jebo.2007.10.006

Buchanan, T., & Whitty, M. T. (2014). The online dating romance scam: Causes and consequences of victimhood. *Psychology, Crime & Law, 20*(3), 261–283. doi:10.1080/1068316X.2013.772180

Burtch, G., Ghose, A., & Wattal, S. (2016). Secret Admirers: An Empirical Examination of Information Hiding and Contribution Dynamics in Online Crowdfunding. *Information Systems Research, 27*(3), 478–496. doi:10.1287/isre.2016.0642

Cacciottolo, M., & Rees, N. (2017). Online dating fraud victim numbers at record high. *BBC News*. Retrieved May 5, 2017, from http://www.bbc.co.uk/news/uk-38678089

Cheshire, C. (2011). Online trust, trustworthiness, or assurance? *Daedalus, 140*(4), 49–58. doi:10.1162/DAED_a_00114 PMID:22167913

Cialdini, R. B. (2001). The science of persuasion. *Scientific American, 284*(2), 76–81. doi:10.1038/scientificamerican0201-76 PMID:11285825

Colombo, M. G., Franzoni, C., & Rossi-Lamastra, C. (2015). Internal social capital and the attraction of early contributions in crowdfunding. *Entrepreneurship Theory and Practice, 39*(1), 75–100. doi:10.1111/etap.12118

Couch, D., Liamputtong, P., & Pitts, M. (2012). What are the real and perceived risks and dangers of online dating? Perspectives from online daters: Health risks in the media. *Health Risk & Society, 14*(7-8), 697–714. doi:10.1080/13698575.2012.720964

Coulson, N. S. (2005). Receiving social support online: An analysis of a computer-mediated support group for individuals living with irritable bowel syndrome. *Cyberpsychology & Behavior, 8*(6), 580–584. doi:10.1089/cpb.2005.8.580 PMID:16332169

Cyr, D., Head, M., & Larios, H. (2010). Colour appeal in website design within and across cultures: A multi-method evaluation. *International Journal of Human-Computer Studies, 68*(1), 1–21. doi:10.1016/j.ijhcs.2009.08.005

Dollar, D., Fisman, R., & Gatti, R. (2001). Are women really the 'fairer' sex? Corruption and women in Government. *Journal of Economic Behavior & Organization, 46*(4), 423–429. doi:10.1016/S0167-2681(01)00169-X

Duguay, S. (2017). Dressing up Tinderella: Interrogating authenticity claims on the mobile dating app Tinder. *Information Communication and Society, 20*(3), 351–367. doi:10.1080/1369118X.2016.1168471

Dunning, D., Anderson, J. E., Schlösser, T., Ehlebracht, D., & Fetchenhauer, D. (2014). Trust at zero acquaintance: More a matter of respect than expectation of reward. *Journal of Personality and Social Psychology, 107*(1), 122–141. doi:10.1037/a0036673 PMID:24819869

Erickson, T. (1997). Social interaction on the net: Virtual community as participatory genre. In *Proceedings of the Thirtieth Hawaii International Conference on System Sciences* (Vol. 6, pp. 13-21). IEEE. doi:10.1109/HICSS.1997.665480

Evans, J. B. T. (2003). In two minds: Dual-process accounts of reasoning. *Trends in Cognitive Sciences, 7*(10), 454–459. doi:10.1016/j.tics.2003.08.012 PMID:14550493

Feldman, M. D. (2000). Munchausen by internet: Detecting factitious illness and crisis on the Internet. *Southern Medical Journal, 93*(7), 669–672. doi:10.1097/00007611-200007000-00005 PMID:10923952

Fischer, P., Krueger, J. I., Greitemeyer, T., Vogrincic, C., Kastenmüller, A., Frey, D., & Kainbacher, M. (2011). The bystander-effect: A meta-analytic review on bystander intervention in dangerous and non-dangerous emergencies. *Psychological Bulletin, 137*(4), 517–537. doi:10.1037/a0023304 PMID:21534650

Fox, N., Ward, K., & O'Rourke, A. (2005). Pro-anorexia, weight-loss drugs and the internet: An "anti-recovery" explanatory model of anorexia. *Sociology of Health & Illness, 27*(7), 944–971. doi:10.1111/j.1467-9566.2005.00465.x PMID:16313524

Fox, S., & Jones, S. (2009). The social life of health information. *Pew Research Center*. Retrieved May 18, 2017, from http://www.pewinternet.org/2009/06/11/the-social-life-of-health-information/

Friedman, B., Khan, P. H. Jr, & Howe, D. C. (2000). Trust online. *Communications of the ACM, 43*(12), 34–40. doi:10.1145/355112.355120

Gandhi, M., & Wang, T. (2015). Digital Health Consumer Adoption: 2015. *Rock Health*. Retrieved May 12, 2017, from https://rockhealth.com/reports/digital-health-consumer-adoption-2015/

Garbarino, E., & Strahilevitz, M. (2004). Gender differences in the perceived risk of buying online and the effects of receiving a site recommendation. *Journal of Business Research, 57*(7), 768–775. doi:10.1016/S0148-2963(02)00363-6

Gerber, E. M., & Hui, J. (2013). Crowdfunding: Motivations and deterrents for participation. *ACM Transactions on Computer-Human Interaction, 20*(6), 34. doi:10.1145/2530540

Gerber, E. M., Hui, J. S., & Kuo, P. Y. (2012). Crowdfunding: Why people are motivated to post and fund projects on crowdfunding platforms. In *Proceedings of the International Workshop on Design, Influence, and Social Technologies: Techniques, Impacts and Ethics* (Vol. 2, p. 11). Academic Press.

Gibbs, J. L., Ellison, N. B., & Lai, C. H. (2011). First comes love, then comes Google: An investigation of uncertainty reduction strategies and self-disclosure in online dating. *Communication Research, 38*(1), 70–100.

Gillespie, N. (2003). Measuring trust in working relationships: The behavioral trust inventory. *Proceedings from Academy of Management Conference*.

Goffman, E. (1959). The moral career of the mental patient. *Psychiatry, 22*(2), 123–142. doi:10.1080/00332747.1959.11023166 PMID:13658281

Guadagno, R. E., & Cialdini, R. B. (2005). Online persuasion and compliance: Social influence on the Internet and beyond. In Y. Amichai-Hamburger (Ed.), *The social net: The social psychology of the Internet* (pp. 91–113). New York: Oxford University Press.

Guadagno, R. E., Muscanell, N. L., Rice, L. M., & Roberts, N. (2013). Social influence online: The impact of social validation and likability on compliance. *Psychology of Popular Media Culture, 2*(1), 51–60. doi:10.1037/a0030592

Gurtman, M. B. (1992). Trust, distrust, and interpersonal problems: A circumplex analysis. *Journal of Personality and Social Psychology, 62*(6), 989–1002. doi:10.1037/0022-3514.62.6.989 PMID:1619552

Hagen-Rochester. (2012). Online dating dumps the stigma. *Futurity*. Retrieved June 1, 2017, from http://www.futurity.org/online-dating-dumps-the-stigma/

Hancock, J., & Guillory, J. (2015). Deception with technology. In S. Sundar (Ed.), *The handbook of the psychology of communication technology* (pp. 270–289). Malden, MA: Wiley-Blackwell.

Hornuf, L., & Schwienbacher, A. (2015). Portal Design and Funding Dynamics in Crowdinvesting. *SSRN Electronic Journal*. Retrieved June 2, 2017, from http://ssrn.com/abstract=2612998

Horvát, E. Á., Uparna, J., & Uzzi, B. (2015). Network vs market relations: The effect of friends in crowdfunding. In *Proceedings from 2015 IEEE/ACM International Conference on Advances in Social Networks Analysis and Mining (ASONAM)* (pp. 226-233). IEEE.

Hui, K. L., Teo, H. H., & Lee, S. Y. T. (2007). The value of privacy assurance: An exploratory field experiment. *Management Information Systems Quarterly*, 19–33.

Jones, R., Sharkey, S., Ford, T., Emmens, T., Hewis, E., Smithson, J., & Owens, C. (2011). Online discussion forums for young people who self-harm: User views. *The Psychiatrist*, *35*(10), 364–368. doi:10.1192/pb.bp.110.033449

Kahneman, D. (2000). A psychological point of view: Violations of rational rules as a diagnostic of mental processes. *Behavioral and Brain Sciences*, *23*(5), 681–683. doi:10.1017/S0140525X00403432

Kaptein, M., & Eckles, D. (2012). Heterogeneity in the effects of online persuasion. *Journal of Interactive Marketing*, *26*(3), 176–188. doi:10.1016/j.intmar.2012.02.002

Kim, K., & Viswanathan, S. (2014). *The Experts in the Crowd: The Role of Reputable Investors in a Crowdfunding Market*. Retrieved May 16, 2017, from https://accounting.eller.arizona.edu/sites/mis/files/ssrn-id2258243.pdf

Kim, Y., Shaw, A., Zhang, H., & Gerber, E. (2017). Understanding Trust amid Delays in Crowdfunding. In *Proceedings of the 2017 ACM Conference on Computer Supported Cooperative Work and Social Computing* (pp. 1982-1996). ACM.

Kromidha, E., & Robson, P. (2016). Social identity and signalling success factors in online crowdfunding. *Entrepreneurship and Regional Development*, *28*(9-10), 605–629. doi:10.1080/08985626.2016.1198425

Krueger, J. I., Massey, A. L., & DiDonato, T. E. (2008). A matter of trust: From social preferences to the strategic adherence to social norms. *Negotiation and Conflict Management Research*, *1*(1), 31–52. doi:10.1111/j.1750-4716.2007.00003.x

Kummervold, P. E., Gammon, D., Bergvik, S., Johnsen, J. A. K., Hasvold, T., & Rosenvinge, J. H. (2002). Social support in a wired world: Use of online mental health forums in Norway. *Nordic Journal of Psychiatry*, *56*(1), 59–65. doi:10.1080/08039480252803945 PMID:11869468

Kuppuswamy, V., & Bayus, B. L. (2013). Crowdfunding creative ideas: The dynamics of project backers in Kickstarter. *SSRN Electronic Journal*. Retrieved May 18, 2017, from https://papers.ssrn.com/sol3/papers.cfm?abstract_id=2234765

Kyllonen, P. C., & Christal, R. E. (1990). Reasoning ability is (little more than) working-memory capacity?! *Intelligence, 14*(4), 389–433. doi:10.1016/S0160-2896(05)80012-1

Lankton, N. K., & McKnight, D. H. (2011). What does it mean to trust Facebook?: Examining technology and interpersonal trust beliefs. *ACM SiGMiS Database, 42*(2), 32–54. doi:10.1145/1989098.1989101

Lankton, N. K., McKnight, D. H., & Tripp, J. (2015). Technology, humanness, and trust: Rethinking trust in technology. *Journal of the Association for Information Systems, 16*(10), 880.

Lederman, R., Fan, H., Smith, S., & Chang, S. (2014). Who can you trust? Credibility assessment in online health forums. *Health Policy and Technology, 3*(1), 13–25. doi:10.1016/j.hlpt.2013.11.003

Leitner, M., Wolkerstorfer, P., & Tscheligi, M. (2008). How online communities support human values. In *Proceedings of the 5th Nordic conference on Human-computer interaction: building bridges* (pp. 503-506). ACM.

Li, X., Hess, T. J., & Valacich, J. S. (2008). Why do we trust new technology? A study of initial trust formation with organizational information systems. *The Journal of Strategic Information Systems, 17*(1), 39–71. doi:10.1016/j.jsis.2008.01.001

Li, Y. B., James, L., & McKibben, J. (2016). Trust between physicians and patients in the e-health era. *Technology in Society, 46*, 28–34. doi:10.1016/j.techsoc.2016.02.004

Lindgaard, G., Dudek, C., Sen, D., Sumegi, L., & Noonan, P. (2011). An exploration of relations between visual appeal, trustworthiness and perceived usability of homepages. *ACM Transactions on Computer-Human Interaction, 18*(1), 1–30. doi:10.1145/1959022.1959023

Lindgaard, G., Fernandes, G., Dudek, C., & Brown, J. (2006). Attention web designers: You have 50 milliseconds to make a good first impression! *Behaviour & Information Technology, 25*(2), 115–126. doi:10.1080/01449290500330448

Lo, S. K., Hsieh, A. Y., & Chiu, Y. P. (2013). Contradictory deceptive behavior in online dating. *Computers in Human Behavior, 29*(4), 1755–1762. doi:10.1016/j.chb.2013.02.010

Lukkarinen, A., Teich, J. E., Wallenius, H., & Wallenius, J. (2016). Success drivers of online equity crowdfunding campaigns. *Decision Support Systems, 87*, 26–38. doi:10.1016/j.dss.2016.04.006

Lutz, C., & Ranzini, G. (2017). Where Dating Meets Data: Investigating Social and Institutional Privacy Concerns on Tinder. *Social Media and Society, 3*(1).

Ma, X., Sun, E., & Naaman, M. (2017). What Happens in happn: The Warranting Powers of Location History in Online Dating. In *Proceedings of ACM Conference on Computer Supported Cooperative Work and Social Computing* (pp. 41-50). ACM. doi:10.1145/2998181.2998241

Markovits, H., Doyon, C., & Simoneau, M. (2002). Individual differences in working memory and conditional reasoning with concrete and abstract content. *Thinking & Reasoning, 8*(2), 97–107. doi:10.1080/13546780143000143

Mayer, R. C., Davis, J. H., & Schoorman, F. D. (1995). An integrative model of organizational trust. *Academy of Management Review, 20*(3), 709–734.

McKnight, D. H., Carter, M., Thatcher, J. B., & Clay, P. F. (2011). Trust in a specific technology: An investigation of its components and measures. *ACM Transactions on Management Information Systems*, *2*(2), 12. doi:10.1145/1985347.1985353

McKnight, D. H., Kacmar, C. J., & Choudhury, V. (2004). Shifting Factors and the Ineffectiveness of Third Party Assurance Seals: A two-stage model of initial trust in a web business. *Electronic Markets*, *14*(3), 252–266. doi:10.1080/1019678042000245263

Mollick, E. (2014). The dynamics of crowdfunding: An exploratory study. *Journal of Business Venturing*, *29*(1), 1–16. doi:10.1016/j.jbusvent.2013.06.005

Mun, Y. Y., Yoon, J. J., Davis, J. M., & Lee, T. (2013). Untangling the antecedents of initial trust in Web-based health information: The roles of argument quality, source expertise, and user perceptions of information quality and risk. *Decision Support Systems*, *55*(1), 284–295. doi:10.1016/j.dss.2013.01.029

Neville, F. (2015). Preventing violence through changing social norms. In P. D. Donnelly & C. L. Ward (Eds.), *Oxford textbook of violence prevention: Epidemiology, evidence, and policy* (pp. 239–244). Oxford University Press.

Newcomb, T. M. (1943). *Personality and social change: Attitude formation in a student community*. New York: Dryden.

Norcie, G., De Cristofaro, E., & Bellotti, V. (2013). Bootstrapping trust in online dating: Social verification of online dating profiles. In *Proceedings of International Conference on Financial Cryptography and Data Security* (pp. 149-163). Springer. doi:10.1007/978-3-642-41320-9_10

Odom, M. D., Kumar, A., & Saunders, L. (2002). Web assurance seals: How and why they influence consumers' decisions. *Journal of Information Systems*, *16*(2), 231–250. doi:10.2308/jis.2002.16.2.231

Office for National Statistics. (2016). *Internet access – households and individuals: 2016*. Retrieved May 21, 2017, from https://www.ons.gov.uk/peoplepopulationandcommunity/householdcharacteristics/homeinternetandsocialmediausage/bulletins/internetaccesshouseholdsandindividuals/2016#activities-completed-on-the-internet

Pee, L. (2012). Trust of Information on Social Media: An Elaboration Likelihood Model. In *Proceedings of the International Conference on Information Resources Management (CONF-IRM)* (pp. 2-9). AIS.

Pulman, A., & Taylor, J. (2012). Munchausen by internet: Current research and future directions. *Journal of Medical Internet Research*, *14*(4), e115. doi:10.2196/jmir.2011 PMID:22914203

Rakesh, V., Choo, J., & Reddy, C. K. (2015). Project recommendation using heterogeneous traits in crowdfunding. *Proceedings of Ninth International Conference on Web and Social Media*, 337-346.

Reynolds, K. J., Subašić, E., & Tindall, K. (2015). The problem of behaviour change: From social norms to an ingroup focus. *Social and Personality Psychology Compass*, *9*(1), 45–56. doi:10.1111/spc3.12155

Richardson, K. (2003). Health risks on the internet: Establishing credibility on line. *Health Risk & Society*, *5*(2), 171–184. doi:10.1080/13698570310001123948

Ridings, C. M., Gefen, D., & Arinze, B. (2002). Some antecedents and effects of trust in virtual communities. *The Journal of Strategic Information Systems*, *11*(3), 271–295. doi:10.1016/S0963-8687(02)00021-5

Rifon, N. J., LaRose, R., & Choi, S. (2005). Your privacy is sealed: Effects of web privacy seals on trust and personal disclosures. *The Journal of Consumer Affairs*, *39*(2), 339–362. doi:10.1111/j.1745-6606.2005.00018.x

Rocco, E. (1998). Trust breaks down in electronic contexts but can be repaired by some initial face-to-face contact. In *Proceedings of the SIGCHI conference on Human factors in computing systems* (pp. 496-502). ACM Press. doi:10.1145/274644.274711

Roghanizad, M. M., & Neufeld, D. J. (2015). Intuition, risk, and the formation of online trust. *Computers in Human Behavior*, *50*, 489–498. doi:10.1016/j.chb.2015.04.025

Rotter, J. B. (1980). Interpersonal trust, trustworthiness, and gullibility. *The American Psychologist*, *35*(1), 1–7. doi:10.1037/0003-066X.35.1.1

Rousseau, D. M., Sitkin, S. B., Burt, R. S., & Camerer, C. (1998). Not so different after all: A cross-discipline view of trust. *Academy of Management Review*, *23*(3), 393–404. doi:10.5465/AMR.1998.926617

Rozmovits, L., & Ziebland, S. (2004). What do patients with prostate or breast cancer want from an Internet site? A qualitative study of information needs. *Patient Education and Counseling*, *53*(1), 57–64. doi:10.1016/S0738-3991(03)00116-2 PMID:15062905

Schmitz, A., Zillmann, D., & Blossfeld, H. P. (2013). Do women pick up lies before men? The association between gender, deception patterns, and detection modes in online dating. *Online Journal of Communication and Media Technologies*, *3*(3), 52.

Sillence, E., & Briggs, P. (2015). Trust and engagement in online health a timeline approach. In S. S. Sundar (Ed.), *The Handbook of the Psychology of Communication Technology* (pp. 469–487). Malden, MA: Wiley Blackwell.

Skirnevskiy, V., Bendig, D., & Brettel, M. (2017). The influence of internal social capital on serial creators' success in crowdfunding. *Entrepreneurship Theory and Practice*, *41*(2), 209–236. doi:10.1111/etap.12272

Smith, A., & Duggan, M. (2013). *Online dating & relationships*. Pew Research Center. Retrieved May 16, 2017, from http://www.pewinternet.org/2013/10/21/online-dating-relationships/

Song, Y., & van Boeschoten, R. (2015). Success factors for Crowdfunding founders and funders. *Proceedings of the 5th International Conference on Collaborative Innovation Networks COINs15*.

Sorrentino, R. M., Holmes, J. G., Hanna, S. E., & Sharp, A. (1995). Uncertainty orientation and trust in close relationships: Individual differences in cognitive styles. *Journal of Personality and Social Psychology*, *68*(2), 314–327. doi:10.1037/0022-3514.68.2.314

Stanovich, K. E. (1999). *Who is rational? Studies of individual differences in reasoning*. Mahwah, NJ: Erlbaum.

Sudau, F., Friede, T., Grabowski, J., Koschack, J., Makedonski, P., & Himmel, W. (2014). Sources of information and behavioral patterns in online health forums: Observational study. *Journal of Medical Internet Research*, *16*(1), e10. doi:10.2196/jmir.2875 PMID:24425598

Tajfel, H., & Turner, J. C. (1979). An integrative theory of intergroup conflict. *The Social Psychology of Intergroup Relations, 33*(47), 74.

Thottam, I. (2017). 10 Online dating statistics you should know. *eHarmony*. Retrieved June 1, 2017, from http://www.eharmony.com/online-dating-statistics/

Turner, J. C. (1991). *Social influence*. Milton Keynes, UK: Open University Press.

Turner, J. C., Hogg, M. A., Oakes, P. J., Reicher, S. D., & Wetherell, M. S. (1987). *Rediscovering the social group: A self-categorization theory*. Oxford, UK: Blackwell.

Utz, S., & Krämer, N. C. (2009). The privacy paradox on social network sites revisited: The role of individual characteristics and group norms. *Cyberpsychology (Brno), 3*(2).

Van Slyke, C., Comunale, C. L., & Belanger, F. (2002). Gender differences in perceptions of web-based shopping. *Communications of the ACM, 45*(7), 82–86. doi:10.1145/545151.545155

Vismara, S. (2016). Equity retention and social network theory in equity crowdfunding. *Small Business Economics, 46*(4), 579–590. doi:10.1007/s11187-016-9710-4

Wang, Y. D., & Emurian, H. H. (2005). An overview of online trust: Concepts, elements, and implications. *Computers in Human Behavior, 21*(1), 105–125. doi:10.1016/j.chb.2003.11.008

Wessel, M., Thies, F., & Benlian, A. (2016). The emergence and effects of fake social information: Evidence from crowdfunding. *Decision Support Systems, 90*, 75–85. doi:10.1016/j.dss.2016.06.021

Whitty, M. T. (2008). Liberating or debilitating? An examination of romantic relationships, sexual relationships and friendships on the Net. *Computers in Human Behavior, 24*(5), 1837–1850. doi:10.1016/j.chb.2008.02.009

Whitty, M. T. (2015). Anatomy of the online dating romance scam. *Security Journal, 28*(4), 443–455. doi:10.1057/sj.2012.57

Wright, B., Partridge, I., & Williams, C. (2000). Management of chronic fatigue syndrome in children. *Advances in Psychiatric Treatment, 6*(2), 145–152. doi:10.1192/apt.6.2.145

Wu, G., Hu, X., & Wu, Y. (2010). Effects of perceived interactivity, perceived web assurance and disposition to trust on initial online trust. *Journal of Computer-Mediated Communication, 16*(1), 1–26. doi:10.1111/j.1083-6101.2010.01528.x

Zhang, J., & Liu, P. (2012). Rational herding in microloan markets. *Management Science, 58*(5), 892–912. doi:10.1287/mnsc.1110.1459

Zhao, J., Abrahamson, K., Anderson, J. G., Ha, S., & Widdows, R. (2013). Trust, empathy, social identity, and contribution of knowledge within patient online communities. *Behaviour & Information Technology, 32*(10), 1041–1048. doi:10.1080/0144929X.2013.819529

Zhao, J., Ha, S., & Widdows, R. (2013). Building trusting relationships in online health communities. *Cyberpsychology, Behavior, and Social Networking*, *16*(9), 650–657. doi:10.1089/cyber.2012.0348 PMID:23786170

Zheng, J., Veinott, E., Bos, N., Olson, J. S., & Olson, G. M. (2002, April). Trust without touch: jump-starting long-distance trust with initial social activities. In *Proceedings of the SIGCHI conference on human factors in computing systems* (pp. 141-146). ACM. doi:10.1145/503376.503402

Zvilichovsky, D., Inbar, Y., & Barzilay, O. (2015). Playing both sides of the market: Success and reciprocity on crowdfunding platforms. *SSRN Electronic Journal*. Retrieved May 8, 2017, from https://papers.ssrn.com/sol3/papers.cfm?abstract_id=2304101

Zytko, D., Freeman, G., Grandhi, S. A., Herring, S. C., & Jones, Q. G. (2015, February). Enhancing evaluation of potential dates online through paired collaborative activities. In *Proceedings of the 18th ACM conference on computer supported cooperative work & social computing* (pp. 1849-1859). ACM. doi:10.1145/2675133.2675184

KEY TERMS AND DEFINITIONS

Crowdfunding: A campaign platform that allows creators and business owners to collect money for a project through small pledges made by funders.

Fraud: Deception for the purpose of personal of financial gain.

Health Forums: Discussion networks that support peer-to-peer discussion surrounding medical concerns as a source of information and community interaction.

Online Dating: Using sites and apps online as a way of meeting potential romantic partners.

Social Identity: The perception one has of their sense of belonging to certain societal groups.

Social Norms: An unwritten set of rules that inform how a person should behave in a certain social situation.

Trust: A belief in the good intentions of another under circumstances where a lack of knowledge or experience means that there is an element of risk and uncertainty in the interaction.

Chapter 8
Volunteered Surveillance

Subhi Can Sarıgöllü
Istanbul Bilgi University, Turkey

Erdem Aksakal
Istanbul Bilgi University, Turkey

Mine Galip Koca
Istanbul Bilgi University, Turkey

Ece Akten
Istanbul Bilgi University, Turkey

Yonca Aslanbay
Istanbul Bilgi University, Turkey

ABSTRACT

As the front end of the digitized commercial world, corporations, marketers, and advertisers are under the spotlight for taking advantage of some part of the big data provided by consumers via their digital presence and digital advertising. Now, collectors and users of that data have escalated the level of their asymmetric power with scope and depth of the instant and historical data on consumers. Since consumers have lost the ownership (control) over their own data, their reaction ranges from complete opposition to voluntary submission. This chapter investigates psychological and societal reasons for this variety in consumer behavior and proposes that a contractual solution could promote a beneficial end to all parties through transparency and mutual power.

INTRODUCTION

This chapter explores the human experience and cyber cognition aspects of cyber security from a consumer point of view with macro-micro transitions at various levels. It primarily focuses on some of the root causes and the cognitive dimensions of cyber security and explores the societal and psychological dimensions of cyber security from consumers' point of view. Then it concentrates on online consumer experience over the case of Ad Blocks, elaborating on the asymmetric positioning of the consumer on

DOI: 10.4018/978-1-5225-4053-3.ch008

the reallocation of power, and ownership aspects. The study proposes a potential approach of balancing the asymmetry by an alternate way of shared access to consumer data. Finally, it concludes by introducing further concerns on cyber security and security in general that comes with the transformed version of cyber cognition.

Danger and fear are very primordial and deeply embedded into human existence and reasoning in every context. As relatively interim solutions, social structures, systems and all varieties of mechanisms have been created to overcome the danger and fear along with their long-term repercussions that have been shaping human evolution, cognition, individual and collective behavior since the beginning of history. Armies, states, belief systems, concepts of ownership and possession, legal and financial systems are the solutions reasoned and created for this primordial urge of being safe, and away from danger. In that perspective ownership, privacy, security, and protection have always been services and products that are deeply rooted in the markets of minds which are in constant evolution. The notion of security comes with cognition of our physical being (Lakoff & Johnson, 1999; Heidegger, 1996) and very much linked to the notions of danger, threat, and fear. Heidegger interprets fear and dread as critical modes of disclosure of the being, as a tool to understand, clarify and deepen our understanding of being in time (Heidegger, 1996). While considering the dynamics amongst human psychology, physiology, behavior, cognition, sociology and cyber security, the perceptions of fear, danger, and security play a critical role.

The rapid transformation of living standards across the globe during modern and postmodern eras have shifted perception and thought patterns along with the dynamics and structures that are regulating them (Lakoff & Johnson, 1999; Belk, 1988; Massumi, 1993). Especially the latest developments in the ICT arena- increased access to the internet, mobile device usage, social media usage and the arrival of IoT, shift individual, societal, commercial, administrative, financial, legal, ecological and cognitive landscapes to another dimension (Lakoff & Johnson, 1999; Massumi, 1993; Prensky, 2009). These shifts deepening the crack in the digital divide, the gap between the speed of technological and digital advancements and the speed of social systems and mechanisms to adjust, to protect and to cope with misuse, frictions, crime, escalates the individuals and smaller enterprises to a more vulnerable position. On September 7th., 2017, Equifax, a more than a century old US consumer credit reporting agency, has declared a major data breach affecting more than 143 million US consumers (57% of adults in the USA), 100,000 Canadians and 200,000 UK citizens. Social security numbers, personal ID details, credit card details are amongst the types of data that were breached. The current state of cyberspace can create such major susceptibilities.

Our living/offline world and digital/online experiences and their contents play a very critical role in shaping our perceptions and cognition of reality, danger, safety and security and our capacity to reason (Lakoff, 2009; Varela, Thompson & Rosch, 2017). Developments in cognitive science converging with technological advancements in all fields from genetics to physiology, artificial intelligence to physics take place at such a speed that human cognition has not experienced, processed, and internalized before. The speed of these developments becoming a part of everyday life of individuals, societies, and masses and the speed of societies and individuals to fully comprehend and master these developments are not synchronized. On the contrary, with the emergence of big data, advanced analytics, and the full-grown information society, previous asymmetries among social members and stakeholders have been increasing more than ever. It can be easily presumed that as the speed of development increases, the time, energy, and investment required for adjustment of the growing masses will tend to increase. Clearly, this transformative meta-process from post-modern times to a new era has no patience to stop and wait for all stakeholders (individuals as consumers, workers, companies, and organizations of all sizes, governments, international bodies, and structures) to be fully informed and ready to adjust to its accelerated evolution.

As it is skillfully referred in Varela, Thompson & Rosch's seminal work, The Embodied Mind;

...we saw that these various forms of groundlessness are really one: organism and environment enfold into each other and unfold from one another in the fundamental circularity that is life itself. (Varela, Thompson & Rosch, 2017)

External objects become parts of the self as one can employ control and power on them (McClelland, 1951). Belk's seminal work on the extended self (Belk, 1988) and its expansion to the extended digital self (Belk, 2013) brought a whole new perspective to understanding and explaining consumer behavior after the postmodern era. The self, invested in objects and images in terms of time, energy, effort, attention, labor, affection was explained as versions of the extended self (Belk, 1983; Csikszentmihalyi & Rochberg-Halton, 1981). The notion of security is also extended to the concept of ownership and possession (Belk, 1988; Furby, 1978; Furby,1991). The shift and allocation of power, control, free will and free choice, ownership, the quest for security and their relation to the extended self in the digital era are the critical issues that this chapter will be addressing.

BACKGROUND

With the increased usage of the internet, mobile devices and social media, people are enjoying the benefits of technology. Every track and action in the digital world is being recorded, not as a spy technology; mainly so called transparently and with pre-declarations to the user. Users are in a trade-off between getting attractive online offers and providing personal information and preferences in return. The rising question is: are users under voluntary surveillance as claimed?

On the Verge of Transient Equilibria

Transactions of ordinary individuals are captured, recorded through technological devices on behalf of the governments. Telecommunication systems, sensors, CCTV, biometrics, navigational devices, applications, tagging and tracking technologies, and health checks allow direct access for authorities to collect and record data of the people. The main argument here is the delicate balance between privacy and security. The unlawful nature of life reflects itself on the digital world; unfortunate attacks and increasing criminality rise the demand for security by citizens at the cost of their privacy, indeed, both must matter. Similar tracking by commercial organizations further rises the complexity and sensitivity of the issue. Some banks, retailers, shops, shopping malls use their sensors and video information to create secondary data for customer traffic analysis, segmentation, customer density analysis and for advanced analytics to extract further value without the permission of individuals. Moreover, many of everyday human social activities such as shopping, communicating, career building, manufacturing, financial transactions, traveling, exercising, relaxing are also digitalized to a degree. This, allows mobile devices, networks, GSM lines to provide all kinds of data, including location data of customers to service providers, device manufacturers, GSM operators, authorities, and contracted third-parties "in order to provide better service". The whole process is further aided by the current level of ICT infrastructures, software, and interfaces. Social media providing extreme free benefits from sharing moments with friends to instant messaging, from building a career to becoming a phenomenon in cyber space is another critical tool for data collection. Human existence, bodies, movements, choices, non-choices are becoming first "objects of data", then "objects of information".

In this chapter, advertisers as the front end of the much larger mechanisms they represent, will be under the spotlight for extracting and tracing big data and utilizing the portions of it for the advantage of the corporations, brands they represent in order to reach corporate objectives and specifically marketing and advertising targets and goals. Online or mobile ads, purchase invitations have a significant role both in the accumulation and utilization of big data as a critical variable of the profit cycle. They specifically track and target consumers from digital platforms. Consumers, easily trapped within the spirals of digital shopping platforms, are stepping in a zone of the branded digitized world.

In the period of brick and mortar brands, corporations and advertisers for many years asked consumers kindly to provide information and data with forms, loyalty programs, subscriptions, satisfaction surveys. Consumers had the option to provide this data voluntarily or could opt out in a voluntary manner. As the world became more digitized, brands, advertisers increasingly targeted to exceed the expectations of consumers. In the name of exceeding their expectations, consumers were spoiled, mesmerized and sometimes partially blinded by the attractiveness of ever-evolving offers in exchange of their voluntary contribution of valuable personal and purchase data. Sometimes that mutual fulfillment cycle was secured by employing third parties (through contracts and SLR/SLA's). Service providers of service providers where aggregate data gets collected also plays an important role. With these latest developments in the ICT sector and the recent technological data collection methods by targeted digital and mobile ad calls and advanced consumer analytics, the consumer lost her/his own will-power, ownership, and the control of her/his data. The majority of the consumers/users are not aware of the real value of their data, besides 94% of all cloud applications used globally for big data cloud services are found incompatible by users, creates serious security and compliance problems (Netscope Report, 2017).These fragmented data powerhouses of the highest bidder or the technologically most advanced players accessing, collecting and utilizing the consumer data now have unparalleled asymmetric power with all the historical and instant data of consumers. For mutually rewarding and sustainable treatment of data ownership and utilization, these data powerhouses need to be transparent and take a position between exploiting or protecting individuals' data for mutual benefit.

Although the use of data requires permission of the customer, as a rule, many contracts, terms, and conditions, or new device service agreements automatically provide this permission to companies. Hence, consumers' perception is dangerously funneled and shaped to a direction and they get used to being recorded as part of their daily lives and become the volunteered players of this gloriously produced stage: the wonderlands of technology. Even though consumers seem to gain power every day, the balance of distribution of power, choice and freedom in this approval, access, and privacy setting is quite debatable. Foucault refers to Karl Marx to emphasize that surveillance has become "a key economic force both as an integrated part of the production set up and as a separate moderating and disciplinary power" (Foucault, 1977, p.175). Transparency, connection, ethics, and consumer rights are theoretically expected to help consumers to shape the products, companies and the marketplace as the consumer is the locus and one of the key stakeholders of the free market environment. Seemingly, privacy is becoming the new name of freedom. This chapter presents some of the future scenarios, elaborating on the sustainability and impossibility of such one-sided, unchangeable contracts and suggests a more flexible scenario for the two front-end players of the system; consumers and advertisers.

Is Volunteered Surveillance an Example of Stockholm Syndrome?

Today Internet, free access, and mobile connectedness empower consumers through increased information access, choice, and options to impose market sanctions through voice and exit (Labrecque, vor dem Esche, Mathwick, Novak, & Hofacker, 2013). Consumers can shape the products customized according to their preferences, they can choose and have flexibility with various payment methods, complain and be compensated for their unfulfilled expectations and purchases. As corporations and organizations from various domains try to learn, access, understand, and predict the customer behavior, data production in the backstage rises an important question about how the consumer using this technology becomes an exchange commodity extracted from own data (Thatcher, Sullivan, & Mahmoudi, 2016). In this hyper-connected and digitized era where many advertisers are trying to hide their messages more subtly and where digital media are trying to make more money from collecting data through exposing the ads, consumers are becoming the victims.

The data collected from consumers, has multiple values; it can be easily translated to demand creation and internalized as a tradable asset into the system by brands, retailers, corporations' IT analytics departments, marketers, and advertisers. It is a digital chain of footprints of users. The lock of this chain, is the "I read and accept all terms and conditions" contracts that users generally accept while subscribing and most of the time without reading. A consumer clicking an ad or visiting a website automatically accepts data collection. In many scenarios, there is no contract, terms and conditions for such situations. In the best cases, only a generic sentence is presented to the consumer, which the consumer then approves by a single click. These generic sentences are commonly far from being consumer-oriented, are usually as follows:

I agree to the Terms and Conditions

I agree to the Privacy Policy

I have read and agree to the Terms

I accept the Terms of Service

Through these asymmetric, non-negotiable "terms and conditions" contracts, consumers accept to provide almost unlimited information with very little forethought. This approval commonly extends to include continuous digital footprints alongside all potential consequences in exchange for services. Service providers may also reserve modification rights to these terms in the long-run. Consequently, consumers agree to enter exchanges that they have no control of, and in many cases with none or limited access to of their own data. At its core, consumers need to be legally pre-informed and must have a chance to view and analyze, discuss these terms and conditions and contracts. The current digital standards do not provide consumers with opportunity to review, negotiate, argue, or oppose to these pre-constructed documents eventually forming "agree-or-leave" scenarios. Partial or selective data collections are also not commonly available options. Practically, the majority of consumers do not even read these obscure "terms and conditions" contracts. Besides, these contracts might differ greatly due to variations in legal systems across countries. Great variance is also present across social networks and digital service providers with regards to their end-user contracts (Table 1).

Table 1. Terms and conditions of some well-known service providers

Facebook	"You grant us a non-exclusive, transferable, sub-licensable, royalty-free, worldwide license to use any IP content that you post on or about Facebook (IP License). This IP License ends when you delete your IP content or your account unless your content has been shared with others, and they have not deleted it." (Facebook, 2015)
Google	"When you upload, submit, store, send or receive content to or through our services, you give Google (and those we work with) a worldwide license to use, host, store, reproduce, modify, create derivative works (such as those resulting from translations, adaptations, or other changes that we make so that your content works better with our services), communicate, publish, publicly perform, publicly display and distribute such content." (Google, 2014)
Instagram	"We may share user content and your information (including but not limited to, information from cookies, log files, device identifiers, location data and usage data) with businesses that are legally part of the same group of companies that Instagram is part of, or that become part of that group." (Instagram, 2013)
WhatsApp	"We may use both your personally identifiable information and certain non-personally-identifiable information (such as anonymous user usage data, cookies IP addresses, browser type, clickstream data, etc.) to improve the quality and design of the WhatsApp Site and WhatsApp Service and to create new features, promotions, functionality, and services by storing, tracking, and analyzing user preferences and trends." (WhatsApp, 2012)
Apple	"We may collect information such as occupation, language, zip code, area code, unique device identifier, referrer URL, location, and the time zone where an Apple product is used so that we can better understand customer behavior and improve our products, services and advertising." (Apple, 2016)
Twitter	"We collect and use your information below to provide, understand, and improve our services. You send us information when you use our services on the web, via SMS, or from an application such as Twitter for Mac, Twitter for Android, or TweetDeck. When using any of our services you consent to the collection, transfer, storage, disclosure, and use of your information is described in this Privacy Policy. This includes any information you choose to provide that is deemed sensitive under applicable law." (Twitter, 2017)
Samsung	"We collect various types of information in connection with the services, including: information you provide directly to us, information we collect about your use of our services, information we obtain from third-party sources. We use the information we collect to, among other things: provide the services you request, understand the way you use the services so that we can improve your experience, provide customized content and advertising. We may share your information with affiliates, business partners, service providers." (Samsung, 2017)

In some cases, these service applications come embedded in the device and consumers need to click accept/agree boxes to activate the device without fully realizing that action automatically creates a secondary value as they keep digitally engaged with the application, service, or device. From there on, big data analytics, advanced algorithms and sometimes backdoor programs are in full force to utilize consumer data generated by the consumer but this time owned by the service or device providing companies, organizations and advertisers and other parties that they might see appropriate and feasible to create commercial value in the name of providing a better service. At the point and the moment of that authorization, the actual and potential commercial value of consumer data is not known to the consumer on both individual and aggregate levels. Consumers click these ads in the pursuit of a benefit in advance, but they give the full data rights without knowing the limits of the economic value of this data ownership exchange in markets. In mildest terms, at the point of contractual agreement parties of this transaction are not equally equipped to understand the consequences and potential backdrops of this deal.

As Walter Lippman argues that "the first principle of a civilized state is that power is legitimate only when it is under contract" (Lippmann, 1955, p.166). Contract law across countries and time has been characterized by similar principles; it recognizes many exceptions to the rule that courts should fully enforce bargains between capable actors (Eisenberg, 1995). Although the application of law can vary across countries and states, the realization of any legally binding contract can only take place between competent parties. A competent party, and if that is a natural person, is one who agrees to a transaction and has the complete legal capacity to become liable for duties under the contract unless he or she is an infant, insane, or intoxicated (Moore, 1985). Infant, insane, intoxicated are the keywords when it comes to full comprehension and cognition of the capabilities of exponentially emerging digital experiences, cyber universes, and the intention and capabilities of its users, facilitators, and promoters. When the capacity and the potential of the big data and advanced cloud computing is considered, the educational and comprehension level of an average consumer is not even close to fully comprehending potential risks when it comes to her/his digital footprints, details of transactions and much more detailed data provided in voluntary and involuntary digital transactions. From that perspective many consumers, individuals on the average can be considered as infants compared to their legal opponents, corporations, brands, and any ITC'ed extensions of the system. Furthermore, the dopamine intoxication experienced in online gaming and insaneness as psychological disorder amplified by an overexposure to digital world can be discussed among experts.

There is a strong paradox here; the "customer-centric" commercial brands construct their business models on the notion of "digital user asset" which they obtain relying on a one-sided contract. All these factors listed above makes these digitally agreed and accepted contracts questionably binding due to the legal incompetency and asymmetry of power between parties. In that perspective, the consumer on the average does not have the capacity to fully comprehend the consequences of these contracts unless they are extremely well-informed or have the specific personality or psychological traits that make them risk-averse (Shropshire, Warkentin, Johnston, & Schmidt, 2006). In terms of considering full range of potential consequences of their cyber behaviors and experiences, most consumers can be considered as cyber infants, especially when it comes to agreeing "terms and conditions" contracts. 2017 ITU Report indicates that 70% of the world's youth (15-24 years) and 48% of the world's adult population have access to the internet (ITU, 2017). E-Marketer reports, in the USA alone the adult population spends more than 5.6 hours a day on the social media and more than 3 hours of it with mobile devices. Seemingly, a significant crowd are out there in the cyberspace to sign these contracts, but not fully recognizing the potential threats.

Some personal beliefs and justifications support the legitimacy of this surveillance. brands. Consider statements "I have nothing to hide," "It's for my own good," "I support the goals," "I'm getting paid," "It's just the way they do things here," "They have to do it to . . . stay competitive, obtain insurance, stop crime, avoid risks" (Marx, 2003). These beliefs can be expanded to critical perceptions which creates invitation and incubation hubs of cyber security breaches; (1) I am not important, so why should anyone be looking for me, (2) I don't have anything that anyone would want, (3) If there is cyber security breach, I cannot stop them even if I wanted to do so (Anderson, 2017). All of these power deprived beliefs can be addressed as cyber cognitive dissonance examples (Festinger & Carlsmith, 1959). As some experts have addressed, cyber security is not about computers, systems, or devices, but it is about human behavior and its interaction with them (Anderson, 2017).

The nature of psychological components of cyber space carries critical importance in understanding cyber behaviors in relation with cyber security. Recently many studies are conducted in the field, focusing on 'cyber behavior in workplace'; the relationship between risky cyber security behaviors and attitudes towards cyber security in a business environment, Internet addiction, and impulsivity (Hadlington, 2017), the extent gender plays a role in mediating the factors that affect cyber security beliefs and behaviors of employees (Anwar et al., 2016), the impact of personality, deterrence and protection motivation factors on non-compliance among organizational insiders, as a model of cyber security violation intention (McBride, Carter, & Warkentin, 2012), the probability of employees falling victim to a cyber security breach and organizational, environmental and behavioral factors serving to influence the extent to which employees adhere to cyber security practices (Herath & Rao, 2009a, 2009b), effectiveness of emergent risk management practices that attempt to reduce and control employee Internet abuse and its potential for addiction (Young & Case 2004). Furthermore, there are also researches on 'cyber behavior in individual domain'; the motivation and security profile of end users that pick up and plug in dropped USB flash drives (Tischer et al., 2016), the factors leading to failure of cyber security awareness campaigns in changing the information security behaviors of consumers (Bada & Sasse, 2015), personality explaining variance in computer user behavior (Shropshire, Warkentin, & Sharma 2015), the comparative optimism regarding online privacy infringement (Baek, Kim, & Bae, 2014), the personality traits influencing the susceptibility to social engineering attacks (Uebelacker & Quiel, 2014), social network addiction (Karaiskos, Tzavellas, Balta & Paparrigopoulos, 2010), individual differences between those who are most likely to pose a security risk and those who will likely follow most organizational policies and procedures (Shropshire, Warkentin, Johnston, & Schmidt, 2006).

Researches show that cyberspace has its own set of rules, codes, and social norms. In that perspective, it offers a unique culture with such rules, codes and norms that are changing much faster than the offline world. As the culture we are experiencing our existence can build, shape, change the way we perceive and think (Prensky, 2009; Lakoff, 2012), high speed culture of cyberspace is transforming the ways in which digital natives are perceiving, experiencing, and making sense of life and the world. Nature of cyberspace is a virtual construct, lifeless and online. The user is the only living part of the cyber interaction and cyber experience (Suler, 2005). Therefore, cyber security, cyber surveillance, cybercrimes, cyber privacy cannot be evaluated only as technologically emerged phenomena, but as a dynamically evolving amalgamation of social, political, psychological, and cognitive reasoning and set of contracts.

Ad-Blocking: The Consumers Fight Back

Advertising and data collection go hand in hand, so to better analyze data based privacy concerns, it is mandatory to see where commercial messages drive consumer behavior in the modern society. Online advertising is one of the areas in which consumers take the most counteraction towards commercial parties in the form of ad-blocking software.

The first online advertising dates back to 1993 (Dinger, 2016). For a period, all parties were mutually content with the practice, outcomes, and benefits. The initial excitement in the commercial landscape created by online advertising, providing both the ability to cut down on media budgets, and the ability to reach consumers in an interactive environment were very appealing for all players in the marketplace. On the consumer side, accessing to all the information by just a click was in turn a great convenience. Today global online advertisement volume has matched the volume of the global TV advertisements. Online advertising is no more a means of marketing communications that only targets a selected few, but a powerful game setter like TV advertisements. The audience is now broad and relevant compared to audiences targeted over other media. This reach, thus data potential, coupled with the capacity of interaction and skill in precision targeting, makes up the reason online advertising industry could quickly become a multibillion-dollar industry over the relatively short period of time. The result is an overwhelming selection of methods in which marketing communications are done through, online. A non-exhaustive list of forms would include text, banner, flash, pop-up, pop-under, floating, wallpaper, expanding, mobile, video and map ad (Dinger, 2016). The ads appear within search results, in e-mails or often embedded in web pages (Singh & Potdar, 2009). Although more intrusive – and sometimes illegal – online advertising methods do exist (such as some "Ad-Wares" and "Mal-Wares"), they are out of our scope for this chapter.

As technology progresses many digital publishers are now providing arguably intrusive and non-skippable video advertising chunks (Ratcliffe, 2016). This is where the war begins! As advertisers try to force their messages and collect data, consumers fight back. The result is the birth of ad-blocking software. These third-party solutions, varying in use and effect, try, and block all digital advertising on the consumer end, while leaving the desired content untouched. The number of users actively using digital advertising blocking software is expected to exceed 400 million around the globe (Adobe Page-Fair Reports, 2017). Yet this number corresponds to a fraction of total internet users who would block all digital advertising if the option was simply prompted to them (McConnell, 2015). As consumers use ad-blockers, advertisers fight back in various ways to make sure their messages go through.

This war, is the perfect spot to analyze why, when, and how consumers react to commercial messages and data collection. There are many reported reasons why consumers say they avoid online advertising ranging from risk perceptions to personality traits (van Schaik et al., 2017), preventing malware infection, ethics of respect to privacy and most importantly preventing the theft of data are some examples (Singh & Potdar, 2009; Vratonjic, Manshaei, Grossklags, & Hubaux, 2012). In contrast, we commonly see the very same consumers sharing their data willingly in other digital platforms; such as personal lifelog applications like Swarm. Research indeed shows that individuals provide a greater amount of personal data than they say they would (Norberg, Horne, & Horne, 2007). Although it is understandable that people would be willing to share information for promised benefits, we also see significant effects of mood and other psychological variables in play. Sad, angry, and depressed people have found out to be a lot less likely to share their location data compared to those that are happy and excited. Besides, the amount of information shared were also found out to be varied depending on people's currently undertaken tasks. Exercising, for example, found out to be an activity which made them willing to disclose information (Consolvo et al., 2005).

One of the perspectives that might provide some explanations to these findings is that millennials and digital natives are usually very tech-literate, however frames, restraints and notions like security is constructed in our cognition through a constant stream of loadings such as family, culture, education, language, and personal experiences starting before our birth, mostly constructed in the living (offline) world and strengthened by repetition. Human infants very quickly learn and start to teach that one might fall from heights, burn from heat. These experiences are deeply coded in our daily lives (Schutz and Luckmann, 1973; Lakoff & Johnson, 2008). However, when it comes to transferring digitized experiences the knowledge, experience and codes of cyberspace is not that deeply rooted and tested and approved by cyber evolution yet. In that sense a majority of online/cyber human experiences can be considered at infancy stage.

Other factors affecting people's privacy concerns range from demographics, technology experience to political orientation (Bergström, 2015). Some of these factors are straightforward; such as tech-literacy. Even this spectrum contains complexities in it. While younger audiences, being more knowledgeable about the digital world, are found out to be less worried about privacy in social networking sites, the opposite is found out to be true for debit card usage (Bergström, 2015). Politically left oriented individuals are significantly more worried about privacy compared to right oriented ones (Bergström, 2015). Moreover, regardless of their orientation, consumers from societies of lower general trust scores are shown to express greater concern for privacy issues (Thomson, Yuki, & Ito, 2015). Awareness and personal experience play further role in privacy concerns. Research shows that consumers who report privacy invasions were much more likely to act about it compared to consumers who only heard about such issues (Debatin, Lovejoy, Horn, & Hughes, 2009). When it comes to ad-blocking software, however, tech-literacy, brings the most obvious effect leading to action, regardless of concern levels.

Being the first scream of consumers to this abuse of their data, first ever occurrences of ad-blocking software date back to the beginning of this millennium (Whiteside, 2015). Since then, ad-blocking has always been a controversial topic as online advertising itself (Dinger, 2016). Some people even called ad-blocking software as theft of resources (Vratonjic et al., 2012). The popularity of these tools increase, users demand better, faster, and more thorough software. Today we witness the evolution of ad-blocking software from semi-professional and free add-ons to a full blown competitive marketplace for paid products. There are many premium ad-blockers, that provide their users with a paid version to block advertising not only on PC's but also on mobile devices and even within entire networks. Many antivirus software included basic ad-blocking service within their paid products. In September 2016, they broadened the scope of the category further by introducing built-in filters for "acceptable ads"!

Yet, to understand more about the future of ad-blocking, one must see where and how the need for such software has risen in the past (Kastrenakes, 2016). The first form of Ad-Blockers were simple pop-up disablers in desktop computer browsers (Sabri & Geraldine, 2014). Back in the late 90's and early 2000's, pop-up advertising was a very popular online advertising method. These pop-up blockers simply disabled the opening of new browser windows, unless otherwise clicked on by users. These types of software did not damage online advertising that much, since exposure effects done through banner advertising were not interrupted (Chang-Hoan & Cheon, 2004). Even if viewers did not click on ads, they familiarized with the advertised product and developed opinions about it (Singh & Potdar, 2009). On the contrary, advertisers tried to publish their ads on as many sites as possible and started to use intrusive methods, trying to aim for attention rather than action (Whiteside, 2015). This action-reaction relationship has continued for a decade. Flash-based advertising gave birth to flash-blockers, rich media advertising gave birth to ad-host blockers and non-skippable video advertising gave birth to video-blockers (Ratcliffe, 2016). Every attack tried by advertisers after this initial battle, brought forth more means and methods of avoiding online advertising from consumers and software developers (Johnson, 2013). Yet, many marketing professionals are solely focused on finding better ways to intrude and to "shove down marketing communications messages down consumers' throats" (Ratcliffe, 2016).

The following is a categorization attempt at a non-exhaustive but comprehensive list of methods used by these companies are trying to overcome the issue of ad-blocking.

Forceful Methods

Most approaches to overcome ad-blocking can be listed under forceful methods. These methods are mostly intrusive and sometimes even invasive (Ratcliffe, 2016). From hidden tracking robots to hardcoded content-delaying chunks, there are many examples that lie within the forceful methods category. These methods are arguably worst, in terms of aggravating the underlying problem. There are both passive and active methods that lie within this category.

Active Forceful Methods

Active forceful methods generally aim to overcome the ad-blocking software itself. These methods usually include a reminder to consumers that access to content will be restricted unless ad-blocking software is de-activated. In 2015, Yahoo Mail declared that they won't be allowing users to log-in on browsers with ad-blocking software enabled (Whiteside, 2015). The result was an outrageous reaction from the consumers. Many immediately cancelled their mail accounts, switching over to competitors. However, there are more active and intrusive methods as well. A recent example is the non-skippable mobile video ads, named bumper-ads, introduced by YouTube (Ratcliffe, 2016). This sort of method does not give the consumer to choose whether to know if advertising will be forced upon them or not at all.

Passive Forceful Methods

Passive forceful methods aim to deliver advertising through disguise, overcoming technological ad-blocking measures. Many of the apparently innocent methods also fall under this category. Within the heat of the moment and the depth of the economic implications of ad-blocking, many content creators try to come up with ways to hide their message within better received and more enjoyable advertising content (Dinger, 2016). From product-placement, to content marketing and gamification, there are increasingly many new tools available to advertisers every day.

Hijacking

Hijacking is one of the most uncommon ways of overcoming ad-blocking software. Being mostly illegal, "Ad-Wares" and illegal viruses invading consumers' personal devices are amongst the many methods that fall under this category.

The current methods undertaken by advertisers do not seem sustainable for many reasons. A study shows that after a certain amount of exposure, consumers tend to have negative attitudes towards personalized mobile advertising (text message based), which, in turn, negatively impacts their behavior towards all forms of advertising that does not include prior permission (Tsang, Shu-Chun, & Liang, 2004). When advertising itself becomes an abuse to be avoided, the attitude leaks to other media, and more importantly towards brands and content providers themselves. The software for ad blocking is more advanced than ever, with no foreseeable halt in advancement. Thus, it becomes practically impossible to technologically by-pass the filters employed. This leaves content providers demanding users to turn off ad-blocking software to reach content. Users, on the other hand, get even more annoyed about advertising that is forced on them. According to a report by PageFair, 74% of users said that they simply left those websites rather than performing the steps required to white list them. The same report also notes that users of these tools are generally more educated. 45% of ad blocking software users in the survey had attained a bachelor's degree or higher – compared to 30% of users across the US Census (O'Reilly, 2017). Advertising becomes an unwanted guest, ruining, and exploiting even the daily endeavors, in turn making consumers react against advertisers with whatever force they can wield (Taylor, 2004). Indeed, consumers, try to get clear, unbiased, correct, and controllable information from the market on many fronts. PageFair states that the alternative for content providers is to listen to their audience and come up with solutions. Facebook has undertaken a strategy of this sort in 2016. Before making sure ad-blocking software no longer works properly on their desktop website, the company surveyed users, updated its advertising preference tools, giving more control over how ads are being served. They eventually circumvented ad-blocking software, however due to better control and less invasiveness, the company said their desktop ad revenue grew 18% in the same quarter they employed the policy (O'Reilly, 2017).

The issue of intrusive online advertising is clear from the consumer point of view. However, there are further security issues to consider also for the main opponent of the battle, advertisers. The problem, for this side of the war, goes deeper than just being able to convey messages to consumers. An example of these deeper concerns is ads being clicked by non-human entities (Whiteside, 2015). Content providers that get paid through CPC methods sometimes go through with fraudulent actions such as using web robots that automatically click on ads, providing them with illegal profit. The uncertainty brought forth with methods like these, undermine the collective effort of many advertising and marketing companies, damaging both sides of marketing communications – consumers and advertisers alike (Dinger, 2016). Online advertising fraud has been around for a long time. However, the profitability -thus the final damage- of these methods are on the rise as well. Some very complex and well-hidden ad fraud scheme cost advertisers around $3 to $5 million per day starting from October 2016. Collectively named "Methbot" by WhiteOps, an anti-ad fraud security firm, the bots defrauded content providers like the Huffington Post, The Economist, Fortune, ESPN, Vogue, CBS Sports, and Fox News alike. More than six thousand content providers, including the social media giant Facebook were also hit by the scammers. Methbot is just a warning that shows how big a security threat for all stakeholders online ad may end up being one day (Slefo, 2016).

Although people are much more receptive of advertising when provided with greater power and that control seems to be the main value of importance in terms of ad receptivity (Elms, 2016), the situation mostly ends up with further intrusions of brands. In a day where an otherwise scary term like "viral" is used to describe a very popular and cherished method of advertising, consumers also feel a new emotion towards the marketing community: fear (Dinger, 2016). It wouldn't be unfair to use the word "war" to describe what advertisers and consumers are going through. And there is no winner at all. With the advancement of technologies and with the advancement towards "prosumer" mentality, consumers' access to knowledge is unrivaled (Rezabakhsh, Bornemann, Hansen, & Schrader, 2006). Clear communication and conveyance of messages between consumers and advertisers is a prerequisite for a democratic, fair, secure market and business environment. Yet, if something has not been done soon enough and in cooperation, there won't be enough credibility for any brand to find any reception for their messages.

SOLUTIONS AND RECOMMENDATIONS

For a sustainable secure cyber eco system, full range of cyber stakeholders; institutions, corporations, governments, digital service providers, content providers, advertisers, NGO's, self-regulatory organizations and individuals must align their intentions, priorities, and actions to elevate the weaker chains of the system into a more compatible position. Of course, the first requirement is an ethical approach from the business side. This study proposes further that a legal contractual solution is the prerequisite of giving back individuals the power, control and the ability to access to their own data/information while regaining privacy and guaranteeing security.

Soon, the following will most likely be the valid model: consumer oriented and customized "terms and conditions" contracts that consumers are pre-informed. This will provide negotiation power to the consumer. World's biggest video platform YouTube, voluntarily (without a serious competitor pressure or a user movement) initiated a business model for content owners. Even though YouTube (2017) doesn't commit a payment for content; it basically makes a payment for the high quality/advertisement friendly content. This model, is an example and could likely be a widespread business model for all digital platforms where users voluntarily share their data and content. If the content (data) users provide to the platform, becomes an "intellectual property" of the content owner; platforms will tend to share their revenues. Today, video is easily accepted as an intellectual property of the owner; why shouldn't a Facebook status, a tweet, an Instagram post, a simple location update or even the "likes" in a social platform? This very novel concern requires a more sensitive and more transparent treatment of data which is continuously generated by users' and consumers' choices, actions, non-actions, and non-decisions. Technology should not only be developing just for the benefit of corporations. A prosumerist model must rise and consumers must take the power to control and shape the data driven market. Developments in technology, social enlightenment and consumer movements must yield to a more mutually benefitting, contractual relations between consumers and data collecting parties.

FUTURE RESEARCH DIRECTIONS

The realms, domains, paradoxes and concerns examined throughout this study builds itself to a next generation solution proposition for the currently practiced, malfunctioning set of methodologies towards a more sustainable and more fairly functioning infrastructure. The nature of this next generation solution proposition must foster a fair distribution of power, control, ownership and revenue sharing in a transparent and on a well debated, then mutually agreed manner. Digital traces and data generated from cyber activities of customers must be reachable by them, being the sole owner of that personal data. Moreover, as the individual agrees to share his/her personal or behavioral data/information with service, experience or product providers (in a well informed and fully transparent contractual process and manner), the potential earnings that are generated by using this data/information, fully or partially needs to be "fairly" shared. The degree of complexity of this next generation solution proposition must match the sophistication levels of the algorithms that are built to capture, extract and analyze the customer data that have been currently utilized by the service providers. This approach implies a breadth of multi-disciplinary, multi-dimensional researches.

CONCLUSION

Cyberspace is a virtual construct and individuals as users and consumers are the only truly living part of it, at least for now. It is an ecosystem that is heavily borrowing from the offline world. However, when it comes to transferring real world experiences, codes, frames into knowledge domain, building parallels are not that easy because cyberspace is not that deeply rooted, tested, and approved by cyber evolution yet. Previously attained behaviors, personal traits, gender, or work-related attributes are not fully transferable to cyberspace experiences.

With the rapidly changing informational power dynamics and increasing digital divide in the cyber space, intrusive online advertising and data collection puts consumers and users into a more vulnerable and insecure position. In terms of their cyber-cognitive legal capacity, the majority of online cyber human experience can be considered as at its infancy stage. In deed public / private distinction has been confusing throughout history. Individuals are aware of being a part of presentation every second and tend to act as being on a public stage in all domains of their daily life (Goffmann, 1990). The digitalization in life further brings a blurred area between the definitions what is public and what is private. Consumers may rationally decide to share their personal information with third parties because they expect to receive a net benefit from those transactions; however, they have only little knowledge or control upon how their data will be used. All through the transaction, they are not able to identify what is private and what is public on behalf of their very rich self-data. Furthermore the consumer may not only share any of that earnings, and may even be in danger or bear a cost, not only monetarily, but psychologically if a third-party abuses that data (Varian, 1996).

Although it involves many dimensions such as time, region and culture, consumers now are in a journey to seek for their rights of security and privacy; and to regain the control and ownership of their own data. This is a very critical macro and issue that consumers are also in the pursuit of their other rights that are wholly framed, thus simply to choose while being informed, educated, heard, redressed. The speed of evolution of mutually benefiting and sustainable next generation business models must match the speed of the transformations taking place in cyber space.

REFERENCES

Adobe. (2015). *Ad Blocking Report.* Retrieved from: https://pagefair.com/blog/2015/ad-blocking-report/

Anderson, A. (2017). *TEDx Talks.* Retrieved from: https://www.youtube.com/watch?v=c_2Ja-OTmGc

Anwar, M., He, W., Ash, I., Yuan, X., Li, L., & Xu, L. (2016). Gender difference and employees' cyber security behaviors. *Computers in Human Behavior, 69*, 437–443. doi:10.1016/j.chb.2016.12.040

Apple. (2016). *Privacy Policy.* Retrieved from: http://www.apple.com/privacy/privacy-policy/

Bada, M., & Sasse, A. (2015). Cyber Security Awareness Campaigns: Why do they fail to change behaviour? *International Conference on Cyber Security for Sustainable Society*

Baek, Y. M., Kim, E. M., & Bae, Y. (2014). My privacy is okay, but theirs is endangered: Why comparative optimism matters in online privacy concerns. *Computers in Human Behavior, 31*, 48–56. doi:10.1016/j.chb.2013.10.010

Belk, R. (1983). In R. P. Bagozzi, A. M. Tybout, & A. Abor (Eds.), *Worldly possessions: Issues and criticisms. In Advances in Consumer Research* (vol. 10, pp. 514–519). Association for Consumer Research.

Belk, R. (1988). Possessions and the extended self. *The Journal of Consumer Research, 15*(2), 139–168. doi:10.1086/209154

Belk, R. (2013). Extended self in a digital world. *The Journal of Consumer Research, 40*(3), 477–500. doi:10.1086/671052

Bergström, A. (2015). Online privacy concerns: A broad approach to understanding the concerns of different groups for different uses. *Computers in Human Behavior, 53*, 419–426. doi:10.1016/j.chb.2015.07.025

Consolvo, S., Smith, I. E., Matthews, T., LaMarca, A., Tabert, J., & Powledge, P. (2005). Location disclosure to social relations: why, when, & what people want to share. *Proceedings of the SIGCHI Conference on Human Factors in Computing Systems*, 81-90. doi:10.1145/1054972.1054985

Csikszentmihalyi, M., & Rochberg-Halton, E. (1981). *The meaning of things: Domestic symbols and the self.* Cambridge, UK: Cambridge University Press. doi:10.1017/CBO9781139167611

Debatin, B., Lovejoy, J. P., Horn, A. K., & Hughes, B. N. (2009). Facebook and online privacy: Attitudes, behaviors, and unintended consequences. *Journal of Computer-Mediated Communication*, *15*(1), 83–108. doi:10.1111/j.1083-6101.2009.01494.x

Dinger, R. (2016). Site unseen. *Association of National Advertisers Magazine*. Retrieved from: http://www.ana.net/magazines/show/id/ana-2016-jan-site-unseen

Eisenberg, M. A. (1995). The limits of cognition and the limits of contract. *Stanford Law Review*, *47*(2), 211–259. doi:10.2307/1229226

Elms, S. (2016). 7 steps to avoid ad blocking. *ADMAP*. Retrieved from: https://www.warc.com/

Facebook. (2015). *Terms of Service*. Retrieved from: https://www.facebook.com/terms

Festinger, L., & Carlsmith, J. M. (1959). Cognitive consequences of forced compliance. *Journal of Abnormal and Social Psychology*, *58*(2), 203–210. doi:10.1037/h0041593 PMID:13640824

Foucault, M. (1977). Discipline and Punish: The Birth of the Prison (A. Sheridan, Trans.). New York: Vintage.

Furby, L. (1978). Possession in humans: An exploratory study of its meaning and motivation. *Social Behavior and Personality*, *6*(1), 49–65. doi:10.2224/sbp.1978.6.1.49

Furby, L. (1991). Understanding the psychology of possession and ownership: A personal memoir and an appraisal of our progress. *Journal of Social Behavior and Personality*, *6*(6), 457.

Goffman, E. (1990). *The presentation of self in everyday life.* London: Penguin.

Google. (2014). *Terms of Service*. Retrieved from: https://www.google.com/intl/en-GB/policies/terms/

Hadlington, L. (2017). Human factors in cyber security: Examining the link between internet addiction, impulsivity, attitudes towards cyber security, and risky cyber security behaviours. *Heliyon (London)*, *3*(7), e00346. doi:10.1016/j.heliyon.2017.e00346 PMID:28725870

Heidegger, M. (1996). *Being and time [Sein und Zeit].* Albany, NY: SUNY press.

Herath, T., & Rao, H. R. (2009a). Encouraging information security behaviors in organizations: Role of penalties, pressures and perceived effectiveness. *Decision Support Systems*, *47*(2), 154–165. doi:10.1016/j.dss.2009.02.005

Herath, T., & Rao, H. R. (2009b). Protection motivation and deterrence: A framework for security policy compliance in organizations. *European Journal of Information Systems*, *18*(2), 106–125. doi:10.1057/ejis.2009.6

Instagram. (2013). *Privacy Policy*. Retrieved from: https://www.instagram.com/about/legal/privacy/

ITU. (2017). *ICT Report.* Retrieved from: http://www.itu.int/en/ITU-D/Statistics/Documents/facts/ICTFactsFigures2017.pdf

Karaiskos, D., Tzavellas, E., Balta, G., & Paparrigopoulos, T. (2010). Social network addiction: A new clinical disorder? *European Psychiatry, 25*(1), 855–855. doi:10.1016/S0924-9338(10)70846-4

Kastrenakes, J. (2016). *Adblock Plus now sells ads.* Retrieved from: http://www.theverge.com/2016/9/13/12890050/adblock-plus-now-sells-ads

Labrecque, L. I., vor dem Esche, J., Mathwick, C., Novak, T. P., & Hofacker, C. F. (2013). Consumer power: Evolution in the digital age. *Journal of Interactive Marketing, 27*(4), 257–269. doi:10.1016/j.intmar.2013.09.002

Lakoff, G. (2009). The neural theory of metaphor. In Cambridge Handbook of Metaphor and Thought. New York, NY: Cambridge University Press. doi:10.2139/ssrn.1437794

Lakoff, G. (2012). Explaining embodied cognition results. *Topics in Cognitive Science, 4*(4), 773–785. doi:10.1111/j.1756-8765.2012.01222.x PMID:22961950

Lakoff, G., & Johnson, M. (1999). *Philosophy in the Flesh* (Vol. 4). New York: Basic books.

Lakoff, G., & Johnson, M. (2008). *Metaphors we live by.* Chicago: University of Chicago Press.

Lippmann, W. (1955). *Essays in the Public Philosophy.* Boston: Little, Brown, and Company.

Marx, G. T. (2003). A tack in the shoe: Neutralizing and resisting the new surveillance. *The Journal of Social Issues, 59*(2), 369–390. doi:10.1111/1540-4560.00069

Massumi, B. (Ed.). (1993). *The Politics of Everyday Fear.* Minneapolis, MN: U of Minnesota Press.

McBride, M., Carter, L., & Warkentin, M. (2012). *Exploring the role of individual employee characteristics and personality on employee compliance with cyber security policies.* Prepared by RTI International – Institute for Homeland Security Solutions under contract 3-312-0212782.

McClelland, D. (1951). *Personality.* New York: Holt, Rinehart, & Winston. doi:10.1037/10790-000

McConnell, T. (2015). The programmatic primer: Ad verification and privacy in the online advertising ecosystem. *WARC Exclusive.* Retrieved from: https://www.warc.com/

Moore, M. S. (1985). Causation and the excuses. *California Law Review, 73*(4), 1091–1149. doi:10.2307/3480429

Norberg, P. A., Horne, D. R., & Horne, D. A. (2007). The privacy paradox: Personal information disclosure intentions versus behaviors. *The Journal of Consumer Affairs, 41*(1), 100–126. doi:10.1111/j.1745-6606.2006.00070.x

O'Reilly, L. (2017). *Ad blocker usage is up 30% — and a popular method publishers use to thwart it isn't working.* Retrieved from: http://www.businessinsider.com/pagefair-2017-ad-blocking-report-2017-1

Prensky, M. (2009). H. sapiens digital: From digital immigrants and digital natives to digital wisdom. *Journal of Online Education, 5*(3), 1.

Ratcliffe, W. (2016). Point of view: Ad blocking's wake-up call. *ADMAP*. Retrieved from: https://www.warc.com/

ReportN. (2017). Retrieved from: https://resources.netskope.com/h/i/340223988-april-2017-worldwide-cloud-report

Rezabakhsh, B., Bornemann, D., Hansen, U., & Schrader, U. (2006). Consumer power: A comparison of the old economy and the internet economy. *Journal of Consumer Policy*, 29–36.

Sabri, O., & Geraldine, M. (2014). When do advertising parodies hurt? The power of humor and credibility in viral spoof advertisements. *Journal of Advertising Research*, 18–24.

Samsung. (2017). *Privacy Policy*. Retrieved from: https://account.samsung.com/membership/pp

Schutz, A., & Luckmann, T. (1973). *The Structures of the Life-world* (Vol. 1). Evanston, IL: Northwestern University Press.

Shropshire, J., Warkentin, M., Johnston, A., & Schmidt, M. (2006). Personality and IT security: An application of the five-factor model. *AMCIS 2006 Proceedings*, 3443-3448.

Singh, A. K., & Potdar, V. (2009). Blocking online advertising – A state of the art. *International Conference on Industrial Technology, ICIT*, 1-10.

Slefo, G. (2016). *Next-Level 'MethBot' Ad-Fraud Scam Cost Advertisers At Least $3 Million Per Day, WhiteOps Says*. Retrieved from: http://adage.com/article/digital/ad-fraud-scheme-cost-advertisers-3-million-day/307235/

Suler, J. (2004). The online disinhibition effect. *Cyberpsychology & Behavior*, *7*(3), 321–326. doi:10.1089/1094931041291295 PMID:15257832

Taylor, C. (2004). Consumer privacy and the market for consumer information. *The Rand Journal of Economics*, *35*(4), 631–650. doi:10.2307/1593765

Thatcher, J., O'Sullivan, D., & Mahmoudi, D. (2016). Data colonialism through accumulation by dispossession: New metaphors for daily data. *Environment and Planning: Society and Space*, 1–17.

Thomson, R., Yuki, M., & Ito, N. (2015). A socio-ecological approach to national differences in online privacy concern: The role of relational mobility and trust. *Computers in Human Behavior*, *51*, 285–292. doi:10.1016/j.chb.2015.04.068

Tischer, M., Durumeric, Z., Foster, S., Duan, S., Mori, A., Bursztein, E., & Bailey, M. (2016) Users really do plug in USB drives they find. *Security and Privacy (SP), 2016 IEEE Symposium*, 306-319. doi:10.1109/SP.2016.26

Tsang, M. M., Shu-Chun, H., & Liang, T.-P. (2004). Consumer attitudes toward mobile advertising: An empirical study. *International Journal of Electronic Commerce*, 65–78.

Twitter. (2017). *Privacy Policy*. Retrieved from: https://cdn.cms-twdigitalassets.com/content/dam/legal-twitter/asset-download-files/TheTwitterUserAgreement-1.pdf

Uebelacker, S., & Quiel, S. (2014). The social engineering personality framework. *4th Workshop on Socio-Technical Aspects in Security and Trust (STAST)*, 24-30.

van Schaik, P., Jeske, D., Onibokun, J., Coventry, L., Jansen, J., & Kusev, P. (2017). Risk perceptions of cyber-security and precautionary behaviour. *Computers in Human Behavior, 75*, 547–559. doi:10.1016/j.chb.2017.05.038

Varela, F. J., Thompson, E., & Rosch, E. (2017). *The embodied mind: Cognitive science and human experience*. Cambridge, MA: MIT press.

Varian, H. R. (1996). *Economic Aspects of Personal Privacy. Technical report*. Berkeley, CA: University of California.

Vratonjic, N., Manshaei, M., Grossklags, J., & Hubaux, J.-P. (2012). ad-blocking games: monetizing online content under the threat of ad avoidance. *Workshop on the Economics of Information Security (WEIS)*, 14-16.

Whatsapp. (2012). *Privacy Policy*. Retrieved from: https://www.whatsapp.com/legal/#Privacy

Whiteside, S. (2015). *The impact of ad blocking on brand strategy: three expert perspectives*. Retrieved from: https://www.warc.com/

Young, K. S., & Case, C. J. (2004). Internet abuse in the workplace: New trends in risk management. *Cyberpsychology & Behavior, 7*(1), 105–111. doi:10.1089/109493104322820174 PMID:15006175

KEY TERMS AND DEFINITIONS

Ad-Blocking: The act of using software products that are specifically designed to block marketing communications messages while leaving the original content untouched in digital and mobile browsers.

Consumer Data Analytics: A process of using current and historical consumer data, statistical algorithms, machine learning techniques, and other tools to detect and identify patterns and trends in order to make improved business decisions.

Cyber Cognition: As cyberspace is becoming a part of everyday living, cyber cognition is expanding one's cognition and comprehension to include the nature and the governing dynamics of cyberspace.

Data Centrism: Culture and perception where data is the center of the enterprise, business, legal, and ethical constructs in which data becomes the primary and permanent asset.

Digitalization: Digitalization is the use of digital technologies to change a business model and provide new revenue and value-producing opportunities; it is the process of moving to a digital business.

Ownership: The state, act, or right of imposing power and control on something, possessing an object.

Surveillance: Use of recorded data to get deeper insight about an individual, group, or case.

Transparency: A mutual benefit situation where data owner and data keeper agree on data use and ownership.

Voluntary: Any proceeding or action done, made, or given willingly without being forced or paid to do it. Actions done and choices made from one's free will or under the conscious control of the brain.

Chapter 9
Psychological and Behavioral Examinations of Online Terrorism

Sheryl Prentice
Lancaster University, UK

Paul J. Taylor
Lancaster University, UK

ABSTRACT

It has long been recognised that terrorists make use of the internet as one of many means through which to further their cause. This use of the internet has fuelled a large number of studies seeking to understand terrorists' use of online environments. This chapter provides an overview of current understandings of online terrorist behavior, coupled with an outline of the qualitative and quantitative approaches that can and have been adopted to research this phenomenon. The chapter closes with a discussion of the contentious issue of ethics in online terrorism research. The aim of the chapter is to equip readers with the necessary knowledge and skills to conduct their own research into terrorists' online behavior, taking best ethical practices into consideration when doing so.

INTRODUCTION

This chapter is the first of its nature to bring together separate applied approaches to the study of online terrorist behavior, which all ultimately seek to establish patterns in and between the online behaviors of particular individuals and/or groups. These patterns are studied with a view to gaining insights into the terrorist mindset (or rather, the mindset of specific groups or individuals), their beliefs, motivations, and influence tactics. It is important to note that these approaches tend to rest on the theoretical assumption that one's behavior (such as the language one uses) reflects one's psychology, an approach advocated by scholars such as the social psychologist Michael Billig. However, this position is not without its critics, due to a concern that the relationship between cognition and behavior may not be as direct as is often assumed (Carruthers, 2002). Nevertheless, such approaches have value in the sphere of cyber security,

DOI: 10.4018/978-1-5225-4053-3.ch009

in that they aim to assist in the identification and tracking of behaviors associated with certain terrorist groups or individuals online for the purpose of monitoring risk and deploying targeted counter measures.

The internet has created a myriad of opportunities for both would-be and established terrorists. These opportunities range from communication, to dissemination, to fundraising, and online warfare. With the diversification in terrorists' use of the internet, it has become of paramount importance for both academics and practitioners alike to create, or have at their disposal, a range of approaches for tackling the threats posed by terrorists online. The aim of this chapter is to provide an overview of recent advances in both manual and automated approaches to examining terrorists' online behavior, drawing on work from a variety of disciplines, including psychology, linguistics, computing, criminology, religious studies, politics, and international relations. To fulfil this aim, the chapter will be split into two separate, yet complementary sections: one emphasising online terrorist behavior, and the other reviewing methods.

The section on terrorist behavior will begin by discussing varying definitions of terrorism and evaluating how well such definitions capture modern developments in online terrorism. This will be followed by a description of online terrorist users and their source and content preferences. The section on methods will begin with an overview of manual approaches to online terrorist behavior (including content, discourse, report and framing analyses), before moving to an outline of automated approaches (such as the corpus linguistic approach, the automated psycholinguistic approach, sentiment analysis, social network analysis and data mining approaches). The method section will include focused studies to give the reader a clearer understanding of how the manual and automated approaches are applied in practice. The chapter will conclude with a section on ethical considerations. The aim of the section will be to demonstrate best procedure in online terrorism research by highlighting the factors that individuals must consider when undertaking research of this nature. As such, the central objective of the chapter will be to equip researchers and practitioners with the tools to conduct their own research into online terrorist behavior.

BACKGROUND

Before turning to the main content of the chapter, it is first of importance to understand what is meant when one refers to online terrorism. With this in mind, this section of the chapter will explore differing definitions of terrorism and discuss their suitability for the description of contemporary online terrorist behavior. Numerous scholars have discussed the difficulty of arriving at one overarching definition of terrorism, given the complexity of this phenomenon (Dedeoglu, 2003; Schmid, 2004; Weinberg, Pedahzur & Hirsch-Hoefler, 2004). Indeed, according to Ruby (2002), this complexity is due, in part, as to whether one is attempting to define terrorism in legal, moral or behavioral terms. Defining terrorism in online environments suffers from the same inherent difficulty as defining terrorism in offline environments in this regard.

Terrorism is legally defined in the UK within the Terrorism Act 2000 as:

An action that endangers or causes serious violence to a person/people; causes serious damage to property; or seriously interferes or disrupts an electronic system. The use or threat must be designed to influence the government or to intimidate the public and is made for the purpose of advancing a political, religious or ideological cause. (HMG, 2011, p. 108).

The political, religious and ideological causes alluded to in the above definition are not well defined. However, examples of political causes include resorting to violence against non-combatants in order to bring about an independent republic (as in the case of the I.R.A), or due to another's political views (as in the murder of Labour MP Jo Cox). Religious causes include encouraging the use of violence on the grounds that one's interpretation of a religious scripture stipulates the use of violence, or encouraging violence towards a particular group on the grounds of their religion (such as extreme far-right anti-Islamism). Ideological causes might include the violent advancement of a nationalist or Salafist agenda, for instance. In reality, however, these factors can be heavily intertwined, in the sense that, for example, an ideology can be both religious and/or political in nature. Similarly, the United States' Federal Bureau of Investigation (FBI, 2002, p. iv) defines terrorism as "the unlawful use of force or violence against persons or property to intimidate or coerce a government, the civilian population, or any segment thereof, in furtherance of political or social objectives". Such definitions focus on the perpetrator of a physical action using force, and in relation to online terrorism, such definitions focus particularly on cyber hacking. However, given that these are legal definitions, legal usages such as conducting online learning on particular terrorist groups, places, or concepts by consulting, for example, online encyclopaedias, would not be covered by such definitions.

This returns to Ruby's (2002) point on the perspective one takes to defining the phenomenon. From a behavioral perspective, which is perhaps more useful given the focus of this chapter and the wider volume, Schmid (2011, p. 3) distinguishes between terror (which is referred to as a state of mind), and terrorism, which is "an activity, method or tactic which, as a psychological outcome, aims to produce 'terror'". Other behavioral definitions include that of Kirwan and Power (2013, p. 190), who refer to terrorism as "the use of violence or intimidation to evoke fear in a specific group, in order to achieve a desired goal, which is often political, ideological, or religious in nature". Kirwan and Power's (2013) definition would not cover a variety of online behaviors, such as online fundraising, data mining, or networking, none of which use intimidation or violence to evoke fear in a specific group. In this way, such a definition is geared towards the intended victims of terrorist activity, rather than activity among terrorists themselves, or terrorists' consumption. Schmid's (2011) definition again focuses on the receptor of terrorist activities.

It therefore appears that a more specialised definition is required to describe terrorism in online environments. Gordon and Ford (2002) differentiate between activities that are unique to online environments and traditional terrorist activities that are also carried out online. While one might argue that traditional terrorist activities are well covered by existing definitions of terrorism, those activities which are specific to online environments (such as data mining, for example), require more tailored, domain specific descriptions. However, defining online terrorism is itself fraught with problems. A clear example of this is in researchers' varying conceptions of the term 'cyberterrorism'. Some researchers conceive 'cyber-terrorism' in the narrower sense of terrorist attacks on computational systems with a political objective. As Kirwan and Power (2013) explain, these researchers and practitioners do not see planning or operational aspects as cyberterrorism, or indeed, as hactivism, and instead reserve this term to refer solely to attacks on systems that result in injury, death or severe disruption.

Colarik and Janczewski (2008, p. xiii), for example, define cyber terrorism as "premeditated, politically motivated attacks by sub national groups or clandestine agents, or individuals against information and computer systems, computer programs, and data that result in violence against non-combatant targets", while Rogers' (2003, p. 78) defines a cyber-terrorist as "an individual who uses computer/network technology to control, dominate, or coerce through the use of terror in furtherance of political or social objectives". These conceptions of cyberterrorism are to some degree based in legal definitions of terrorism, thereby viewing cyberterrorism as a form of cyber-crime geared towards inflicting terror on the recipient. Related to this, Bowman-Grieve (2015, p. 86) highlights the need to differentiate between "cyber-terrorism" and "cyber-crime", arguing that in differentiating between these concepts, one gains a better understanding of the threat of cyberterrorism and how it can be addressed.

Researchers such as Awan (2016, p. 33) conceive cyber-terrorism more broadly as "any form of electronic media, that is, recruitment, propaganda and communication used in order to cause death and injure innocent people". Such definitions are perhaps of more use in describing the multi-faceted nature of current online terrorist behavior. However, Awan's definition focuses more on the producers (e.g. distributors, recruiters) rather than consumers of terrorism related content and it does not provide motivation. Perhaps a more accurate description might be 'the use of online platforms and technologies to persuade, inform, or otherwise engage others *or oneself* in terrorist related activities for criminal, political, or warfaring purposes'.

However, any definition which moves away from the expression of violence introduces ethical implications as to who one defines as an online terrorist. No matter one's definition, as Schmid (2011) argues, terrorism and its contexts of use evolve and therefore definitions must remain fluid in order to reflect this constant evolution.

SECTION A: ONLINE TERRORIST BEHAVIOR

Having discussed definitions of (online) terrorism and (online) terrorist behavior, this section will focus on online terrorist actors, beginning with a description of the typical characteristics of terrorists online, before moving to their online preferences.

The Online Terrorist User

As Horgan and Taylor (2013) state, one will frequently encounter the argument that there is no single profile of a terrorist, given that differing groups and individuals hold differing motivations and beliefs (Rúbbelke, 2004). However, the authors also highlight that, while there might not be an overall profile of a terrorist, certain groups, settings or contexts can contain meaningful patterns. It is the purpose of this section of the chapter to provide an overview of patterns established in the characteristics of terrorist users in an online setting. While a number of studies have sought to establish patterns in the characteristics of groups of convicted terrorists more generally (i.e. the Bakker, 2011 survey of jihadis in Europe and the Sageman, 2004 survey of global jihadis), studies specifically focussed on the online environment are scarce in comparison.

Given the constantly changing nature of the online terrorist environment, it is difficult to derive up-to-date characteristics of online terrorist users. In addition, while some users have been found to provide information as to their identity on forums, for example, the majority of terrorist users tend to go by code names or anonymised identities (Lachow & Richardson, 2007), and therefore demographic information is seldom available. For this reason, the characteristics outlined in this chapter generally relate to individuals who have been convicted of terrorism related offences with an online element. An exception to this is a review of users of the French based Ansar-al-Haqq (jihadist) website, conducted by Hussain and Saltman (2014). The authors' examination of user profile information reveals that users are predominantly male, non-converts to Islam, in the 20-30 age range, with the majority of members classed as under 30.

In a Vox-Pol report by Gill et al. (2015), the authors review the online behaviors of 227 convicted UK terrorists. It should be noted, however, that Gill et al.'s (2015) survey is primarily based on UK media reports, and therefore does not represent (or claim to represent) online terrorist users not reported on in the UK media. Of the 227 terrorists surveyed, 96% were male and aged 16-58, with a mean age of 28. One third worked in an administrative or service sector, and one third were unemployed, while 22% of those studied had some form of university education (14% were university students at the time of their conviction). The authors also found that lone-actor terrorists were far more likely to use online sources than terrorists functioning within a cell, presumably due in large part to a lack of available information from co-conspirators.

In a related study, Gill, Horgan and Deckert (2014) outline differences in lone actor usage of the internet via a sample of 119 lone actors, finding that Al-Qa'ida lone actors are more likely to make use of online sources than right-wing lone actors, or lone actors with a single cause. Gill and Corner (2015) have also observed that young lone actor terrorists are more likely to make use of online sources than older lone actors, as are non-US based lone actors, while those who engage in communicative behaviors online with others are less likely to commit a violent attack than those who do not. Overall, the general consensus from the limited number of studies at this point in time is that online terrorist users tend to be young males, who conduct their online learning alone. However, this is a pattern that is subject to change and does not constitute a rule or definitive 'profile'. Rather, it is a set of observations based on particular populations of terrorist online users at a particular time.

Terrorists' Use of Online Environments

Having established who online terrorist users are, the question arises as to what terrorist users use online environments for. The internet has a number of applications for terrorist users, and the advent of new platforms presents ever changing possibilities. As Lachow and Richardson (2007, p. 100) have pointed out, "Similar to information age businesses, [terrorist] groups use the Internet to create a brand image, market themselves, recruit followers, raise capital, identify partners and suppliers, provide training materials, and even manage operations". The authors highlight three key factors that make the internet such an appealing prospect for terrorist users: i) it offers ease of communication between members of a group, and between group members and outsiders, ii) it offers a low cost operational environment by presenting a means of intelligence gathering, training, and maintaining a public presence, and iii) it enables groups to have a global reach.

One such example of groups creating and marketing a brand image for themselves is the so-called Islamic State's use of platforms such as Twitter to advertise their day to day activities via the sharing of photo and video content (see Klausen, 2015). Note that terrorists' use of particular platforms is subject to change over time in response to various factors, including law and intelligence authority crackdowns (though this does not always dissuade users), platform closure, the introduction of new platforms, the degree of security or anonymity offered, the platform preferences of target audiences and associates, declining platform popularity, and changing operational strategies and requirements. A range of platforms are utilised by terrorists, including (but not limited to) social media sites, forums, blogs, search engines, encyclopedias, file share sites, official terrorist group websites, directories, and encrypted messaging services. Differing types of site are used for differing purposes. Encrypted messaging services, for example, are used for operational planning and communication, official terrorist group websites are used for propaganda purposes, and directories are used to distribute terrorist materials. However, note that certain site types have multiple uses.

Weimann (2004) notes some similarities between terrorists' use of the internet and that of political organizations, including propaganda and fund raising, but notes more individualised uses, such as the hiding of information in encrypted files or coded messages. Weimann (2004, pp. 5-11) lists eight key uses of the internet by terrorists, which are outlined below.

- **Psychological Warfare:** Instilling fear or uncertainty via threats of cyberterrorism or physical attacks, the spread of disinformation, or the release of emotionally disturbing content.
- **Publicity and Propaganda:** The release of written, visual and audiovisual material to shape the image of a terrorist organization or its perceived enemies.
- **Data Mining:** Use of the internet as a 'digital library' to research physical or cyber (hacking) targets via online search engines, forums, journals, and newspapers.
- **Fundraising:** The publication of bank accounts to which sympathisers can contribute, website areas in which donations can be made, the targeting of individuals via questionnaires and follow-up emails, and the use of charities, non-governmental organizations or financial institutions to produce a seemingly legal front for fund raising activities.
- **Recruitment and Mobilization**: Contacting sympathetic website users both on their own and related sites before moving conversations to secure or encrypted channels, distributing training materials, and using online bulletin boards to advertise.
- **Networking:** Increasingly decentralised communication, either within groups, between groups (i.e. on designated intelligence sharing sites), between groups and outsiders, or between sympathising individuals.
- **Sharing Information:** The provision of access to bomb making manuals, handbooks and videos.
- **Planning and Coordination:** The use of encrypted messaging services, messages hidden within graphic files, or open coded messages for planning and coordination of attacks between operatives.

However, much of this work focuses on users seeking to influence others, rather than those being influenced (or otherwise reaffirming their beliefs). The work of Gill et al. (2015) provides insight into how would-be terrorists engage with online environments prior to their conviction for terrorism offences. The authors observe that would-be terrorists primarily use the internet for the purpose of online learning. Drawing on Neumann's (2013) distinction between terrorists' communicative and instrumental use of the internet (with communicative use relating to the use of online environments to forge or strengthen social networks, and instrumental use referring to use of the internet for aspects of attack planning and surveillance), the authors explain that instrumental usage is more prominent in their study of convicted individuals. The authors find that those intercepted in the process of planning attacks tend to have used the internet to learn the specifics of their attack and to explore the viability of particular targets, with harder targets facilitating online learning.

While existing literature points out particular trends in terrorists' use of the internet, it is important to bear in mind that each user is different, and therefore preferred usage will vary from individual to individual, and from group to group, depending on the user's motivation and, where applicable, their target complexity (as highlighted by Gill et al., 2015), or their position within an organization. Indeed, in a report by Prentice, Wattam and Moore (2017), the authors distinguish between three types of online user, with differing levels of knowledge of the online environment and differing motivations that shape their online behavior. This research develops on the work of Gill et al. (2015) by distinguishing between users at differing stages of their online learning process. The key point raised in this section is that terrorist usage of the internet is not homogenous (and, as raised in the previous section, nor are terrorist users).

SECTION B: OVERVIEW OF METHODS

This section will outline both the manual and automated methods that one can adopt to the study of online terrorist behavior, including example studies.

Content Analysis

Content analysis takes many forms, and is an approach that can be adopted for both text and image data. Content analysis generally involves i) reviewing literature according to one's research question in order to arrive at a set of meaningful content coding categories, ii) isolating or summarising the components of one's text (whether that be a written, visual or audio-visual text), and iii) coding these components according to one's derived content categories (see Neuendorf, 2016, pp. 40-41 for a detailed overview of a typical content analysis process). One might also examine the interaction between the different components of one's message.

Relating this approach to the study of online terrorist behavior, Prentice et al. (2011) employed content analysis on a set of online messages written by members of proscribed terrorist organizations. The authors conducted a review of literature in the field of persuasive language in order to derive a set of influence tactics that could be used to describe how terrorists attempt to persuade others of their cause. A set of online messages authored by proscribed terrorist organizations and associated individuals were split into phrasal units and each phrasal unit coded according to the derived influence tactics. The proportion of occurrence of each influence tactic in and across messages was established to allow for cross-individual and cross-group comparisons. The authors found that influence tactics varied from group to group, and from individual to individual within the same group. For example, Osama Bin Laden's messages were found to be characterised by moral and social arguments, while the messages of Al-Zawahiri were characterised by employing a wide range of persuasive levers.

In a more recent study by Klausen (2015), the author examined the Twitter usage of Western fighters affiliated with IS in Syria. As part of this research, the author and their research team coded a total of 563 tweets according to a predefined coding scheme drawn from previous studies of online jihadist forum content. The scheme contained five categories: religious instruction, reporting from battle, interpersonal communication, tourism, and threats against the west. Coders were asked to sum up the primary meaning of each tweet according to one of the categories. Klausen found that reporting from battle was the most prominent theme of the tweets, and that pictorial content supported the message of the textual content, often serving to display jihadist lifestyle in such a way as to emphasise its appeal (for example, by conveying a sense of camaraderie between IS fighters).

Discourse Analysis

Discourse analysis is an approach whereby one performs a detailed linguistic analysis of a set of texts. As Gee (2014, p. 8) explains, discourse analysis takes many forms, but generally speaking it can be described as "the study of language in use", a study that takes account of the interactions between "ways of saying (informing), doing (action), and being (identity)". For example, if one says 'Can you do that for me?', they are simultaneously informing you that they wish you to do something, asking you a question (doing), and identifying themselves as polite and relational. It is important to distinguish between discourse analysis and critical discourse analysis. While discourse analysis relates its examination of language in use to the social roles we inhabit, critical discourse analysis is politically driven.

There are many sub-disciplines of critical discourse analysis (see Wodak & Meyer, 2009), but all relate their study of language in use to the ideologies, power structures and hierarchies present within a given society. As such, discourse analysis is interested in how social roles in particular contexts shape our language use, while critical discourse analysis looks at how language use is influenced by macro societal systems of social inequality, power abuse, and dominance (see van Dijk 2001, p. 96). Consider, for example, the following Daily Mail headline (Johnson, 2017): "Muslim calls for Immigration Minister's head transplant". One might infer that calling for a head transplant is a somewhat extreme or outlandish statement, and this statement is linked to an individual who is identified as a Muslim. In perpetuating negative representations of Muslims, the media can be said to be both shaping, and being shaped by, a wider Islamaphobia within certain groups of society. In other words, there is a socio-political impact, outcome, or purpose of such language use.

(Critical) discourse analysis approaches have been employed in the field of online terrorist behavior. Chiluwa (2017), for example, used a critical discourse analysis approach to assess the discourse of online terror threats written by Nigerian terrorist groups. The analysis involved a careful reading of the texts and an identification of threats of varying forms, both explicit "we shall carry out a series of bombings" (p. 331), and implicit "a situation that we will not take lightly" (p. 328). The author then related these threats to the contexts of Nigerian and global terrorism to interpret their perceived purpose. Chiluwa examined seven online publications by the terrorist groups Boko Haram and Ansaru. The author found ideological (i.e. belief and value system) and intertextual (i.e. reference to other texts) links with Al Qaeda and their concepts of "just war" and "defensive jihad" (p. 329), as echoed in threats such as "We are informing the government of France that we would continue to attack its citizens anywhere in the world as long as the government does not retract on its policies" (p. 331). Methods from pragmatics, a form of discourse analysis concerned with what is implied by the use of particular linguistic structures in particular contexts, were also employed. It was found that the form of the threats formulated by such groups differed from conventional verbal threats, with examples such as "This is a message from jamaatu ahlis sunnah lil daawati wal jihad, and we wish to inform Nigerians our reasons for attacking some media houses" (p. 327), employing a formal announcement structure to instill a sense of authority, confidence and certainty. Overall, the threats of such groups were said to follow a "because you did this, I/we will do that" structure rather than a conventional "if you do this, I/we will do that" threat structure (p. 329).

Report Analysis

Report analysis refers to the use of primary (e.g. interview data, trial transcripts, etc.) or secondary source (e.g. media articles) reports of terrorist activity involving online environments to gain insights into online terrorist behavior. While there are few studies at present in this area (see, for example, von Behr, Reding, Edwards & Gribbon, 2013), psychologist Paul Gill has recently pioneered an approach using, in particular, mainstream news articles to build up biographical details of individuals who have been convicted of terrorist offences with an online element (see Corner & Gill, 2015; Gill, 2015; Gill et al., 2017; Gill, Horgan & Deckert, 2014). This is an approach that has been used to observe trends in the online use of terrorists.

For example, Gill et al. (2015) combined existing lists of individuals who had either been convicted of terrorism in the UK, or who had died during the process of carrying out a terrorist act in the UK. Individuals were sourced from existing studies (such as Gill et al., 2014; Simcox & Dyer, 2013), searches of the online newspaper repository LexisNexis, and START's Global Terrorism Database. Using this method, the authors identified 227 individuals. LexisNexis was used to collect the majority of the information on individuals in the study, including socio-demographic information (such as age and gender), network behaviors (such as location of training and co-offenders), event-specific behaviors (such as the method of attack used and the attack targets), and post-event behaviors (such as claiming responsibility and details of the individual's arrest and/or conviction). The authors further recorded whether or not a given individual had used virtual sources and whether they had engaged with others online, with additional records being made as to the type of learning and interaction involved. The method allowed the authors to provide insights into the types of media that convicted terrorists had consumed in the run up to their conviction (such as the passive consumption of particular websites and extremist texts) and how online media is used in preparation for an attack (for example, to assist with attack planning, target choice and overcoming obstacles).

Framing Analysis

Framing analysis involves an assessment of what is foregrounded or backgrounded in a text. It is concerned with the processes of selection and omission an author has adopted in the creation of their text(s). More specifically, authors are said to employ what Goffman (1974, p. 21) terms "schemata of interpretation" when constructing texts, which are fixed internal frameworks of representation that individuals use in order to give events meaning. While the approach is not commonly used at present for the purpose of gaining insights into online terrorist behavior, Page, Challita and Harris (2011) have examined the collective action frames utilized by Al Qaeda in the Arabian Peninsula in the group's e-magazine *Sada al-Malahim*.

Likewise, Berntzen and Sandberg (2014) employed a framing analysis on the online manifesto released by lone wolf terrorist Anders Behring Breivik. To conduct their analysis, the authors applied an existing framework devised by Snow and Benford (1992), which entails a close examination of the document for evidence of i) diagnostic framing, which identifies the problem and describes who is to blame; ii) prognostic framing, which discusses what can be done to resolve the problem; and iii) motivational framing, which describes one's rationale or motive (pp. 760-761). Applied to Breivik's manifesto, the authors found that Breivik's diagnostic frame foregrounded Islam as a threat via interpreting Islam as a threat to Western values, enforced by a multicultural elite (e.g. "You cannot reason with Islam. Islam consumes everything eventually unless it is stopped in a decisive manner", p. 767). Breivik's prognostic frame was said to foreground armed resistance and terrorism as a response (e.g. "The only way we can then prevent Sharia law from being implemented as the only standard will be to suppress the Muslim majority through military force", p. 770). Finally, Breivik's motivational frame was described as foregrounding a requirement for change with emotional and religious undertones (e.g. "Many brothers and sisters have fallen already, the pioneers, the brave heroes, and the first to pick up their guns. We are the legacy of these first "unknown" pioneers. We did not want this but we are left no choice", p. 771).

Corpus Linguistics

Corpus linguistics is the study of language patterns in (generally) large bodies of language data (referred to as corpora). Corpus linguists build corpora to represent the language use of a particular target population. Researchers then use specialised software (e.g. AntConc – Anthony, 2016; CQPweb – Hardie, 2016; SketchEngine - Lexical Computing, 2017; Wmatrix – Rayson, 2009) to examine patterns in a study corpus and/or to compare the language of a study corpus with an appropriate reference or comparison corpus. The purpose of examining patterns in a corpus or corpora is to ascertain what characterizes the language of one's target population. Tutorials on corpus linguistic methods are available on the websites of associated software (see, for example, Rayson, 2013 for a Wmatrix tool tutorial).

However, there are a number of corpus linguistic methods that are common to all corpus linguistic software. Typically, one begins one's analysis by producing a frequency list, which lists all words in one's corpus and the number of times each word appears. This gives one an overall impression of their study corpus, for example, by examining the types of content words that appear (observing the words 'kill', 'bomb' and 'maim' occurring with high frequency may, for example, suggest content of a highly violent nature). However, these initial impressions need to be confirmed or refuted with further investigation. Researchers typically then employ a method known as collocation, which allows one to establish the terms that are strongly associated with a particular word of interest. For example, if the word 'evil' was to strongly associate with a particular regime, then this may indicate a regime to which contempt is felt. To establish whether this interpretation is correct, one would conduct a concordance, which displays a particular search word or phrase within its context. Finally, to determine whether one's observations are unique to their study corpus and not also characteristic of similar forms of language use, one would compare one's study corpus with a suitable comparison corpus (for example, terrorist and counter-terrorist corpora) in a method known as a keyness comparison. This tells one whether particular words (and in some cases, semantically related groups of words) are overused or underused in one corpus compared to another, or whether there is no significant difference in usage.

Corpus linguistics has been deployed to examine the online language use of Islamic terrorist groups. Prentice et al. (2011), for example, combined corpus linguistic analysis with content analysis on a set of online messages authored by proscribed terrorist organizations both before and after the 2009 Gaza conflict. The authors compared before and after messages and found that direct statements to engage in violence increased as the conflict heightened. A related study by Prentice, Rayson and Taylor (2012) found that, when compared to a corpus of general English language use, the language of a corpus of 250 online terrorist messages authored by proscribed terrorist organizations was characterized by semantically opposing concepts (e.g. darkness and light, life and death, behaving ethically or unethically), indicative of a polarized world view.

Automated Psycholinguistics

The automated psycholinguistic approach is similar to the corpus linguistic approach in that it entails the use of specialized software to examine how language use can be indicative of various psychological states. As such, unlike corpus linguistic tools, automated psycholinguistic tools are informed by psychological theory and based on the premise that examining one's language use provides insight into, for example, one's emotions (see Pennebaker, Mehl & Niederhoffer, 2003). A popular tool in this field is Linguistic Inquiry and Word Count (LIWC) (Pennebaker Conglomerates, 2017). Texts are loaded into the tool, which uses a set of internal dictionaries to assign each running word in a text to one or more of its content themes. These themes include:

- **Language Metrics:** Measures of sentence and word length
- **Function Words:** Closed class terms performing a grammatical function, such as pronouns, articles, prepositions, auxiliary verbs, adverbs, conjunctions, negations
- **Grammar Other:** Other grammatical terms such as verbs, adjectives, comparatives, interrogatives (questions), numbers, and quantifiers
- **Affect Words:** Terms relating to positive or negative (anxiety, anger, sadness) emotion
- **Social Words:** Terms relating to family, friends, or gender
- **Cognitive Processes:** Terms relating to insight, cause, discrepancies, tentativeness, certainty, or differentiation
- **Perpetual:** Terms relating to seeing, hearing and feeling
- **Biological Processes:** Terms relating to the body, health/illness, sexuality, and ingestion
- **Core Drives and Needs:** Terms relating to affiliation, achievement, power, reward, risk/prevention
- **Time Orientation:** Terms relating to the past, present or future
- **Relativity:** Terms relating to motion, space, or time
- **Personal Concerns:** Terms relating to work, leisure, home, money, religion, or death
- **Informal Speech:** Including swear words, netspeak, assent, non-fluencies, and fillers
- **All Punctuation:** Including commas, colons, question marks, etc.

Within the field of online terrorist behavior studies, Vergani and Bliuc (2016) used LIWC to analyze the first 11 issues of IS' internet magazine Dabiq, covering the period from July 2014 to July 2015. The authors found, for example, that the content of the magazine throughout this period was characterized by increasing references to females, which the authors linked to IS' desire to attract female recruits, as well as an increased engagement with 'netspeak' or internet jargon (such as "btw" and "lol", p. 16), which the authors suggested could be linked to attempts to appeal to the younger generation. Likewise, Pennebaker (2011) used LIWC to examine the language of 296 speeches, articles and interviews from members of four extremist groups, finding that the two violent extremist groups studied demonstrated less cognitive complexity and divergent thinking in the month preceding and following violent acts. A similar tool, DICTION (Hart & Lind, 2011) was used to categorize Islamic terrorist documents according to five master variables (Certainty, Optimism, Activity, Realism and Commonality) with 40 subvariables. The authors found, for example, that the language of violent Islamists was more optimistic than that of a non-violent comparison group.

Sentiment Analysis

Sentiment analysis involves the deployment of specialist software to evaluate the attitude of a specific group of online users. Sentiment analysis tools generally work by labelling each content word in a sentence as either positive or negative, while non-content words (i.e. grammatical terms such as 'and', or 'or') are labelled as neutral. More positive than negative terms in a sentence would result in the sentence being evaluated as positively valenced, while more negative terms than positive terms would result in a negatively valenced evaluation. By measuring the difference between positive and negative term counts in a sentence, one can arrive at an evaluation of the degree to which a sentence is positively or negatively valenced. Sentence scores are averaged to arrive at an overall evaluation of a text's (i.e. blog post, forum post, tweet, etc.) sentiment. While typically used in the domain of marketing and branding, the approach has also been adopted by those seeking to understand online terrorist behavior.

Bermingham, Conway and McInerney (2009) identified a group on YouTube professing to be for the purpose of "conversion of infidels" (p. 232) and analyzed the sentiment associated with different topics within users' posts. The authors used web crawling techniques to collect both user profiles (for user demographics) and user channel comments. The authors then employed a system on the data that combined SentiWordNet (a lexicon with words assigned as positive or negative), a part-of-speech tagger (a tool that codes words for their part-of-speech to distinguish between, for example, *can* as a verb and *can* as a noun), and a stemmer (a tool that identifies groups of words that belong to the same root word, e.g., *walked*, *walking* and *walker(s)* belong to the same root word *walk*). The frequency of each term in the collected data was established and concepts of potential interest to jihadists were arrived at via studying the top 50 most frequent terms. User posts containing these concepts were extracted and subjected to sentiment analysis, revealing that female users were the most extreme and least tolerant. Compared to males, females demonstrated a greater degree of positive sentiment toward the topic of al-Qaeda than male users and a greater degree of negative sentiment toward the topic of Judaism than male users.

Social Network Analysis

Computational approaches to the examination of online terrorist behavior can take many forms. One popular computational approach in this area is social network analysis, in which researchers start with a set of user accounts linked to known terrorist groups or individuals and follow the links from these accounts to the accounts of others (followers, subscribers, etc.). These links are used to create visual representations of the social network(s) surrounding particular individuals or groups. User accounts are typically referred to as 'nodes', while the links between them are referred to as 'edges'.

Klausen et al. (2012), for example, used social network analysis to demonstrate how the YouTube channels of seemingly unaffiliated jihadist groups were in fact interconnected. The authors began with Sharia4 YouTube channels, following links to the channel subscribers and the subscribers of those subscribers in a method known as 'snowballing'. Using this method, the authors found, for example, that the majority of their starting nodes showed similar patterns in connections, which the authors suggested was demonstrative of a centrally managed network of channels, resistant to the removal of one or more of these channels. Likewise, as part of a study investigating the ecosystem of IS support on VKontakte (a Russian based social networking site), Johnson et al. (2017) conducted a link analysis on posts containing pro-IS hastags that could be traced to underlying aggregates. The aggregates were extended via snowballing and the number of followers connecting to the aggregates was examined. The authors found that the size of these aggregates (the number of links to them) increased in the lead up to campaigns such as IS' assault on Kobane in September 2014. The authors suggested such observations could be predictive of future attacks involving co-ordinated efforts.

Data Mining

Another popular computational approach to online terrorist behavior is data mining. Data mining involves the design and use of specialised algorithms to automatically collect data that meets a specified set of requirements. Researchers Rowe and Saif (2016) used data mining techniques on social media data to try to work out when supporters "begin to adopt pro-IS behavior" (p. 329). Using a set of Twitter ids linked to users who had discussed the conflict in Syria in their tweets, the authors collected the ids of their followers. They then used a gazetteer to extract the ids of users based in Europe using user profile information. Twitter's REST API was used to retrieve the tweets of users whose full timeline was available. The authors examined the tweets for the uptake of extremist language (i.e. the inclusion of terms matching pre-existing dictionaries of extremist language) and the sharing of extremist material (i.e. sharing tweets linked to known pro-IS accounts). The authors found that the uptake of these online behaviors coincided with real-world events (i.e. the peaks in frequency of behaviors coincided with the dates of, for example, IS executions or particular air strikes). The latter is a process known as event analysis.

Similarly, Magdy, Darwish and Ingmar (2015) used data mining to extract tweets from Twitter that were either pro-IS or anti-IS. The authors extracted tweets containing references to IS by their preferred full title (taken to be indicative of support) and tweets containing references to IS in abbreviated form (taken to be indicative of antipathy). User timelines were then used to identify tweets occurring prior to the formation of IS. The authors utilized this data to build a classifier to predict IS support or antipathy, using tweet content to identify common terms in the tweets of those classified as pro-IS or anti-IS. The research found that pro-IS supporters, for example, made a greater number of references to failed Arab Spring Uprisings.

SECTION C: ETHICAL CONSIDERATIONS

No matter the approach one adopts, when seeking to understand online terrorist behavior, one needs to carefully consider one's ethical procedures in carrying out research of this nature. There are a number of useful guides that can be consulted for this purpose, which include the following:

- **Association of Internet Researchers (2012):** These guidelines contain a useful summary of online data types and the domain specific considerations that researchers should make according to their chosen data source(s).
- **British Psychological Society (2017):** The Society's guidelines on internet mediated research are particularly useful for guidance on the subjects of online research, and the roles and responsibilities of researchers.
- **Bickson et al. (2007):** These guidelines, produced by RAND members, provide a summary and detailed transcripts of meetings between experts in differing areas of terrorism studies and ethics, and provide a set of recommendations for research within this domain.
- **Universities UK (2012):** These guidelines have been formulated for university based research on security sensitive topics in the UK. However, many of the guidelines are also applicable outside of this context. The guidelines provide a detailed view of the procedures one should adopt to protect security sensitive data, including the prevention of dissemination. The guidelines also supply a useful ethical checklist that researchers can use to guide their decision making.

- • **Specific institution guidelines:** Many university institutions have produced their own specialised guidelines on conducting security sensitive research (see, for example, University of Leicester, 2016).

This section will focus on the key factors from these collective guidelines that should be addressed in one's ethical decision making.

With regard to the subjects of one's research, given the increased usage of online data by researchers, companies and other organizations alike, and with the advent of big data studies, debates are emerging in both academic and non-academic communities as to how online data can and should be used. One such area of contention is over the issue of informed consent. Some researchers argue that informed consent is always required, regardless of the subject, while others argue that seeking informed consent in studies of terrorist behavior presents heightened risks to researcher safety. The latter might also argue that one cannot be sure of the identity of who they are gaining permission from and that, in the case of big data studies, this introduces practical issues. The former would argue that informed consent should be sought, unless a good reason can be provided as to why this consent could or should not be obtained.

One could argue that, if the data is of a broadcast nature (i.e. written, audio, visual or audio-visual content broadcasting terrorist statements or activities, or recruitment materials), terrorist authors are unlikely to have the expectation of privacy, given that such communications have been designed with the explicit desire of being seen. However, if one were hoping to deal with data of an encrypted or password protected nature, this would not be perceived in the same manner. In all cases, researchers should be mindful of any copyright information contained on the sites they wish to investigate and any information relating to a site's terms of use. For terrorist material on general (non-terrorist) sites, it may be possible to gain permissions from the site's administrators or hosting company. Likewise, if one is examining data from known terrorist groups or individuals, then one might argue that such individuals are already exposing themselves to a high degree of risk by being a member of a terrorist organization, or choosing to engage in physical warfare. However, if one were studying anonymous individuals of an unknown affiliation, then one might argue that the potential for harm is greater, in that the activities of that individual may put them at harm of arrest or at social harm, in a way they would not have otherwise been had the research not been carried out.

A further consideration relating to minimizing potential harm to subjects is the dissemination of research on online terrorist behavior. Again, in cases where the author has already officially been identified as a member of a terrorist organization and has revealed their identity in their broadcast, this may be considered less problematic. However, if a subject has not done so, then (in accordance with BPS guidelines), it might be advisable to avoid using such data, given the "non-trivial" (p. 19) risk of harm. Quantitative terrorist behavior approaches may be more advisable in such scenarios, given that data are normally considered on aggregate, making individual author identification difficult.

Dissemination of research in this area also carries with it the risk of further distribution of terrorist material. For this reason, quotations from such material should be kept to a minimum, paraphrased, or surrounded by a counter narrative or analysis. One should avoid signposting terrorist material where possible. While this presents issues with regard to transparency, data sharing agreements can be set up between institutions to ensure the controlled use of material.

Indeed, as stipulated in the Universities UK (2012) guide to the storing and dissemination of security sensitive data (such as terrorist material), in cases where such data is stored or circulated in a careless manner, researchers will be in danger of misinterpretation by authorities and may leave themselves open to arrest or prosecution under counter-terrorism legislation. As the guideline authors state, this is particularly the case if one is accessing sites that are subject to counter-terrorism legislation within one's jurisdiction, as these may be subject to monitoring and accessing these sites has legal implications. Institutions typically have procedures for research involving such sites, such as notifying the appropriate authorities that a particular piece of research will be taking place and when. It is important to note that any collection of such data may prompt an investigation into one's research activities and therefore appropriate reporting procedures should be followed and documentation relating to the research should be maintained. Universities UK guidelines further recommend that data is stored on "specially designated" (p. 2) servers, which are overseen by an institution's ethical officer(s), and are only accessible to project team members.

While the study of online terrorist behavior is an ethically complex area, provided research is conducted in a responsible manner, it can provide insights to aid the challenge of tackling such behaviors online.

FUTURE RESEARCH DIRECTIONS

There are multiple areas for likely development in the field of online terrorist behavior studies. Taylor, Holbrook and Joinson (2017), for example, discuss future implications of current understandings of online terrorist behavior for policy and practice. The constantly evolving nature of the online terrorist environment means that new methods, tools and techniques will inevitably be developed to aid researchers and investigators. One possible area that may see expansion in coming years is quantitative image analysis. As this chapter attests, quantitative language analysis has received a relatively large amount of attention in the field, and as a result, we are beginning to determine robust patterns in online terrorist language use. However, image analysis has not received the same amount of attention, and images tend to have been analyzed as part of manual content analyses of terrorist online content. It is possible that future studies will enlist image analysis software to detect patterns in terrorist imagery. Another area that has received relatively little attention in terms of online terrorist behavior is the use of audio (such as nasheeds) or audio-visual (video) material. There is scope for both manual and automated approaches to enhance our understanding of these types of material and their importance for terrorist propaganda, or indeed, other terrorist purposes. The rise of big data studies is likely to continue in coming years, affording the possibility of establishing more reliable patterns in online terrorist behavior that could aid efforts in more accurate detection and prediction (as begun by researchers such as Johnson et al., 2017). Given the predicted uptake of big data studies in this arena, the security versus privacy debate alluded to in the ethical considerations section of this chapter will likely continue to reassert itself. Finally, as a concern with far-right terrorism grows in response to terrorism inspired by groups such as IS, it is foreseeable that future studies will pay greater attention to emergent as well as existing forms of terrorism.

CONCLUSION

This chapter sought to provide an overview of current approaches to understanding online terrorist behavior. In doing so, the chapter began with a discussion of current definitions of (online) terrorism and their relative lack of applicability to modern online terrorism as a whole. It is concluded that this is largely due to the changing nature and diversity of online terrorism, including terrorists' changing and diverse characteristics and preferences. Nevertheless, the chapter observed current trends in characteristics, such as Gill et al.'s (2015) observation that online terrorists tend to be males in their 20s of a lone-actor persuasion. Further trends were observed in terrorists' use of the internet, with those seeking to influence others using the internet for the spreading of propaganda, fund-raising, and information sharing (amongst other uses), and those engaging in consumption rather than exchange tending to use the internet for online learning purposes.

While the various methods presented in this chapter offer the researcher a far-ranging insight into online terrorist behavior, it is important to note that there are aspects of behavior that such approaches cannot and do not cover. Manual approaches, on the whole, offer a more in-depth understanding of terrorist behavior, given that they tend to entail detailed analyses of a small number of texts. The results of such analyses are therefore not generalizable. Automated approaches, on the other hand, do offer a means to establish more reliable patterns in behavior by working with large data sets. Automated approaches may thereby assist researchers and investigators in the location and prediction of terrorist behaviors. They also allow the swift processing of large amounts of terrorist material. However, these approaches offer a breadth rather than a depth of coverage and as they tend to consider data on aggregate, they can miss more nuanced distinctions between individuals or groups. Therefore, it is recommended, where possible, to combine approaches (see Prentice et al., 2011, for example, where the authors combine the approaches of content analysis and corpus linguistics, or Klausen, 2015, in which the author combines multimodal content analysis with social network analysis). Combining approaches can give one a more rounded understanding of terrorist behavior within a particular online space.

In conducting research of this nature, there can be a tendency for researchers to infer the effects that online terrorist content may have on those it is seeking to persuade, without asking target audience members whether such material appeals to them and in what sense it does so. One must be wary of attempting to read the mind of terrorists, and instead focus on what their content and patterns of online use can realistically tell us about their behavior. In doing so, the online behavioral researcher must be mindful of their legal and ethical obligations, maintain an awareness that the online terrorist environment is subject to change, and consider that the online environment is just one aspect of many that shapes a terrorist's behavior.

REFERENCES

Anthony, L. (2016). *AntConc*. Retrieved from http://www.laurenceanthony.net/software/antconc/

Association of Internet Researchers. (2012). Ethical decision making and internet research. Chicago, IL: Association of Internet Researchers (AoIR).

Awan, I. (2016). Cyber threats and cyber terrorism: The internet as a tool for extremism. In I. Awan & B. Blakemore (Eds.), *Policing cyber hate, cyber threats and cyber terrorism* (pp. 21–38). Abingdon, UK: Routledge.

Bakker, E. (2011). Characteristics of jihadi terrorists in Europe (2001-2009). In R. Coolsaet (Ed.), *Jihadi Terrorism and the Radicalisation Challenge: European and American Experiences* (pp. 131–144). Aldershot, UK: Ashgate.

Bermingham, A., Conway, M., McInerney, L., O'Hare, N., & Smeaton, A. F. (2009). Combining social network analysis and sentiment analysis to explore the potential for online radicalisation. In *International Conference on Advances in Social Network Analysis and Mining* (pp. 231-236). Athens, Greece: IEEE. doi:10.1109/ASONAM.2009.31

Berntzen, L. E., & Sandberg, S. (2014). The collective nature of lone wolf terrorism: Anders Behring Breivik and the anti-Islamic social movement. *Terrorism and Political Violence, 26*(5), 759–779. doi:10.1080/09546553.2013.767245

Bikson, T. K., Bluthenthal, R. N., Eden, R., & Gunn, P. P. (2007). *Ethical principles in social behavioral research on terrorism: Probing the parameters.* London: RAND.

Bowman-Grieve, L. (2015). Cyberterrorism and moral panics: A reflection on the discourse of cyberterrorism. In L. Jarvis, S. Macdonald, & T. M. Chen (Eds.), *Terrorism online: Politics, law and technology* (pp. 86–106). London: Routledge.

British Psychological Society. (2017). *Ethics Guidelines for Internet-mediated Research.* Leicester, UK: British Psychological Society.

Carruthers, P. (2002). The cognitive functions of language. *Behavioral and Brain Sciences, 25*(06), 657–674. doi:10.1017/S0140525X02000122 PMID:14598623

Chiluwa, I. (2017). The Discourse of Terror Threats: Assessing Online Written Threats by Nigerian Terrorist Groups. *Studies in Conflict and Terrorism, 40*(4), 318–338. doi:10.1080/1057610X.2016.1194025

Colarik, A. M., & Janczewski, L. J. (2008). Introduction to cyber warfare and cyber terrorism. In L. J. Janczewski & A. M. Colarik (Eds.), *Cyber warfare and cyber terrorism* (pp. xiii–xxx). New York: Information Science Reference.

Corner, E., & Gill, P. (2015). A false dichotomy? Mental illness and lone-actor terrorism. *Law and Human Behavior, 39*(1), 23–34. doi:10.1037/lhb0000102 PMID:25133916

Dedeoglu, B. (2003). Bermuda triangle: Comparing official definitions of terrorist activity. *Terrorism and Political Violence, 15*(3), 81–110. doi:10.1080/09546550312331293147

FBI. (2002). *Terrorism 2002-2005.* Washington, DC: United States Department of Justice.

Gee, J. P. (2014). *An introduction to discourse analysis.* Abingdon, UK: Routledge.

Gill, P. (2015). *Lone-actor terrorists: A behavioral analysis.* Abingdon, UK: Routledge.

Gill, P., & Corner, E. (2015). Lone-Actor Terrorist Use of the Internet and Behavioral Correlates. In L. Jarvis, S. Macdonald, & T. Chen (Eds.), *Terrorism Online: Politics, Law, and Technology* (pp. 35–53). London: Routledge.

Gill, P., Corner, E., Conway, M., Thornton, A., Bloom, M., & Horgan, J. (2017). Terrorist Use of the Internet by the Numbers. *Criminology & Public Policy, 16*(1), 99–117. doi:10.1111/1745-9133.12249

Gill, P., Corner, E., Thornton, A., & Conway, M. (2015). *What are the roles of the internet in terrorism? Measuring online behaviors of convicted terrorists.* London: VOX-Pol.

Gill, P., Horgan, J., & Deckert, P. (2014). Bombing Alone: Tracing the motivations and antecedent behaviors of lone actor terrorists. *Journal of Forensic Sciences, 59*(2), 425–435. doi:10.1111/1556-4029.12312 PMID:24313297

Goffman, E. (1974). *Frame Analysis: An Essay on the Organization of Experience.* New York: Harper Colophon.

Gordon, S., & Ford, R. (2002). Cyberterrorism? *Computers & Security, 21*(7), 636–647. doi:10.1016/S0167-4048(02)01116-1

HardieA. (2016). *CQPweb.* Retrieved from https://cqpweb.lancs.ac.uk/

Hart, R. P., & Lind, C. J. (2011). The rhetoric of Islamic activism: A Diction study. *Dynamics of Asymmetric Conflict, 4*(2), 113–125. doi:10.1080/17467586.2011.627934

HMG. (2011). *Prevent strategy.* London: Crown.

Horgan, J., & Taylor, M. (2013). *Terrorist psychology: Separating facts from fictions.* Retrieved April 26, 2017, from http://sites.psu.edu/icst/2013/04/19/terrorist-psychology-separating-facts-from-fictions/

Hussain, G., & Saltman, E. M. (2014). *Jihad trending: A comprehensive analysis of online extremism and how to counter it.* London: Quilliam.

Jarvis, L., MacDonald, S., & Chen, T. M. (2015). *Terrorism Online: Politics, Law and Technology.* Abingdon, UK: Routledge.

Johnson, N. F., Zheng, M., Vorobyeva, Y., Gabriel, A., Qi, H., Velasquez, N., & Wuchty, S. et al. (2016). New online ecology of adversarial aggregates: ISIS and beyond. *Science, 352*(6292), 1459–1463. doi:10.1126/science.aaf0675 PMID:27313046

Johnson, S. (2017, June). Muslim calls for Immigration Minister's head transplant. *Daily Mail.* Retrieved from http://www.dailymail.co.uk/news/article-4599544/Muslim-calls-Immigration-Minister-s-head-transplant.html

Kirwan, G., & Power, A. (2013). *Cybercrime: The psychology of online offenders.* Cambridge, UK: Cambridge University Press. doi:10.1017/CBO9780511843846

Klausen, J. (2015). Tweeting the Jihad: Social media networks of Western foreign fighters in Syria and Iraq. *Studies in Conflict and Terrorism, 38*(1), 1–22. doi:10.1080/1057610X.2014.974948

Klausen, J., Barbieri, E. T., Reichlin-Melnick, A., & Zelin, A. Y. (2012). The YouTube Jihadists: A social network analysis of Al-Muhajiroun's propaganda campaign. *Perspectives on Terrorism, 6*(1), 36–53.

Lachow, I., & Richardson, C. (2007). The Terrorist Use of the Internet—The Real Story. *Joint Force Quarterly, 45*(2), 100–103.

Lexical Computing. (2017). *SketchEngine.* Retrieved from https://www.sketchengine.co.uk/

Magdy, W., Darwish, K., & Weber, I. (2015). *FailedRevolutions: Using Twitter to Study the Antecedents of ISIS Support.* Palo Alto, CA: Association for the Advancement of Artificial Intelligence.

Neuendorf, K. A. (2016). *The content analysis guidebook.* Thousand Oaks, CA: Sage.

Neumann, P. (2013). Options and Strategies for Countering Online Radicalization in the United States. *Studies in Conflict and Terrorism, 36*(6), 431–459. doi:10.1080/1057610X.2013.784568

Page, M., Challita, L., & Harris, A. (2011). Al Qaeda in the Arabian Peninsula: Framing narratives and prescriptions. *Terrorism and Political Violence, 23*(2), 150–172. doi:10.1080/09546553.2010.526039

Pennebaker, J. W. (2011). Using computer analyses to identify language style and aggressive intent: The secret life of function words. *Dynamics of Asymmetric Conflict, 4*(2), 92–102. doi:10.1080/17467 586.2011.627932

Pennebaker, J. W., Mehl, M. R., & Niederhoffer, K. G. (2003). Psychological aspects of natural language use: Our words, our selves. *Annual Review of Psychology, 54*(1), 547–577. doi:10.1146/annurev. psych.54.101601.145041 PMID:12185209

Pennebaker Conglomerates. (2017). *LIWC.* Retrieved from https://liwc.wpengine.com/

Prentice, S., Rayson, P., & Taylor, P. J. (2012). The language of Islamic extremism: Towards an automated identification of beliefs, motivations and justifications. *International Journal of Corpus Linguistics, 17*(2), 259–286. doi:10.1075/ijcl.17.2.05pre

Prentice, S., Taylor, P. J., Rayson, P., Hoskins, A., & O'Loughlin, B. (2011). Analyzing the semantic content and persuasive composition of extremist media: A case study of texts produced during the Gaza conflict. *Information Systems Frontiers, 13*(1), 61–73. doi:10.1007/s10796-010-9272-y

Prentice, S., Wattam, S., & Moore, A. (2017). *Identifying and assessing the risk of re-used terrorist material* (Unpublished report). WAP Academic Consultancy Limited, UK.

Rayson, P. (2009). *Wmatrix: A web-based corpus processing environment.* Computing Department, Lancaster University. Retrieved from http://ucrel.lancs.ac.uk/wmatrix/

Rayson, P. (2013). *Wmatrix tutorials.* Retrieved September 15, 2017, from http://ucrel.lancs.ac.uk/ wmatrix/tutorial/

Rogers, M. (2003). The Psychology of Cyber-Terrorism. In A. Silke (Ed.), *Terrorists, victims and society: psychological perspectives on terrorism and its consequences* (pp. 77–92). Chichester, UK: John Wiley & Sons. doi:10.1002/9780470713600.ch4

Rowe, M., & Saif, H. (2016). Mining pro-ISIS radicalisation signals from social media users. In *Proceedings of the Tenth International AAAI Conference on Web and Social Media* (pp. 329–338). Palo Alto, CA: AAAI Press.

Rubbelke, D. T. (2005). Differing motivations for terrorism. *Defence and Peace Economics, 16*(1), 19–27. doi:10.1080/1024269052000323524

Ruby, C. L. (2002). The definition of terrorism. *Analyses of Social Issues and Public Policy (ASAP), 2*(1), 9–14. doi:10.1111/j.1530-2415.2002.00021.x

Sageman, M. (2004). *Understanding terror networks.* Philadelphia: University of Pennsylvania Press. doi:10.9783/9780812206791

Schmid, A. (2004). Terrorism-the definitional problem. *Case Western Reserve Journal of International Law, 36*, 375–419.

Schmid, A. P. (2011). Introduction. In A. P. Schmid (Ed.), *The Routledge Handbook of Terrorism Research* (pp. 1–38). Abingdon, UK: Routledge.

Simcox, R., & Dyer, E. (2013). Terror data: US vs. UK. *World Affairs, 176*(2), 45–55.

Snow, D. A., & Benford, R. D. (1992). Master Frames and Cycles of Protest. In A. D. Morris & C. M. Mueller (Eds.), *Frontiers in Social Movement Theory* (pp. 133–155). New Haven, CT: Yale University Press.

Taylor, P. J., Holbrook, D., & Joinson, A. (2017). Same Kind of Different. *Criminology & Public Policy, 16*(1), 127–133. doi:10.1111/1745-9133.12285

UK Universities, . (2012). *Oversight of security-sensitive research material in UK universities: guidance*. London: Universities UK.

University of Leicester. (2016). *Policy on researching and handling sensitive, extreme, or radical material*. Leicester, UK: University of Leicester.

Van Dijk, T. A. (2001). Multidisciplinary CDA: A plea for diversity. In R. Wodak & M. Meyer (Eds.), *Methods of critical discourse analysis* (pp. 95–120). London: Sage.

Vergani, M., & Bliuc, A.-M. (2015). The evolution of ISIS' language: A quantitative analysis of the language of the first year of Dabiq magazine. *Security, Terrorism and Society, 2*, 7–20.

von Behr, I., Reding, A., Edwards, C., & Gribbon, L. (2013). *Radicalisation in the Digital Era: The Use of the Internet in 15 Cases of Terrorism and Extremism*. Cambridge, UK: RAND Europe.

Weimann, G. (2004). *How modern terrorism uses the Internet. Special Report 116*. Washington, DC: United States Institute of Peace. Retrieved from www. terror. net

Weinberg, L., Pedahzur, A., & Hirsch-Hoefler, S. (2004). The challenges of conceptualizing terrorism. *Terrorism and Political Violence, 16*(4), 777–794. doi:10.1080/095465590899768

Wodak, R., & Meyer, M. (2009). *Methods for critical discourse analysis*. London: Sage.

KEY TERMS AND DEFINITIONS

Behavior: The actions one engages in, whether written, verbal, or (audio)visual.

Extremism: The incitement of hatred against a particular individual or group based on their ethnic or cultural background, or their religious, social, or political beliefs. This may or may not entail a violent element. An *extremist* is defined as one who engages in extremism. Similarly, *extremist content* is defined as content advocating extremism.

Jihadi(st): Individuals or content advocating a version of jihad (struggle) that entails armed violence against non-combatants.

Online Terrorism: The use of online platforms and technologies to persuade, inform, or otherwise engage others or oneself in terrorist-related activities for criminal, political, or warfaring purposes. The term *cyberterrorism* is here regarded as equivalent to online terrorism. An *online terrorist* is defined as one who engages in online terrorism.

Online Terrorist Environment: The interaction between sites used by terrorists to achieve their goals and further their cause, and the interaction between these sites and those used to inform others about terrorists or terrorism.

Terrorism: The use or incitement of violence against non-combatants as a tool employed for a specific goal. A *terrorist* is defined as one who engages in terrorism, while *terrorist content* is defined as that which incites violence against non-combatants, again for a specific goal.

Violence: The use of physical force to inflict harm, injury, or death.

Chapter 10
The Role of Religiosity in Technology Acceptance:
The Case of Privacy in Saudi Arabia

Rami Mohammed Baazeem
Jeddah University, Saudi Arabia

ABSTRACT

Religion plays a major role in shaping individual behaviour, especially in the religious countries. This chapter sheds light on the effect of religiosity on the intention to use technology and privacy and will use Saudi Arabia as an example. Using the unified theory of acceptance and use of technology (UTAUT) will help explain the intention to use technology. Thus, it clarifies that the intention to use technology is affected by the user behaviour. The user's behaviour is shaped by their religious beliefs which also affect their privacy views. A systematic review of the privacy literature shows that there is a lack of study on the effect of the religious beliefs on privacy. After reading this chapter, policy makers and managers will understand that religious belief should be considered when making new laws and regulations.

INTRODUCTION

This chapter focuses on the effect of religion on user behaviour and acceptance of security measures. The impacts of religion on user behaviour will likely affect cyber security. Looking at the literature, it became apparent that religion is not an acceptable measurement scale; instead, religiosity should be used. Islamic religion will be the primary focus in this chapter, and it will be reviewed in the strict Islamic context of Saudi Arabia. According to the literature, people who strongly follow a religion, such as Muslims, tend to ignore the rules and regulations if they contradict their religious teaching. The evidence in this chapter supports this claim. Religion has an impact on individual cyber security through user behaviour, perception of online privacy and acceptance to use.

The need for secure information and communication systems has been dictated by governments, the private sector and by many people. Thus, policies had to be put in place to ensure the security of the information system. These policies have been made to regulate the use, behaviour, and handling

DOI: 10.4018/978-1-5225-4053-3.ch010

of the information system by users (i.e. employees or ordinary people). However, there is evidence to show that many people do not follow appropriate use and behaviours for various reasons, even if they are obligated to do so (Bada & Sasse, 2014). Securing systems by advising people what to do and not to do is enough. The users need to understand and agree to the policies and how to implement them. Often, they need to do this despite their established behaviours and beliefs. Technology by itself cannot help secure the information system without the cooperation of the people who use it. When changing security protocols, adding new security controls or changing policy, the users must work for or with the new security measure rather than against it (de Lange & von Solms, 2013). Thus, the user's behaviour should be changed.

Beliefs affect the change of behaviour, and the main guides for the personal mental acceptance for taking action are attitudes and intentions (Bada & Sasse, 2014). When attitudes and intentions change, the individual behaviour will follow. This concept has been used in several behaviour models, such as the theory of planned behaviour, protection motivation theory, and theory of reasoned action (Bada & Sasse, 2014). This leads to the importance of using a behavioural model to test the effect of behavioural change and acceptance to use the technology under the new changes. This chapter proposes to use the unified theory of acceptance and use of technology UTAUT2 model, which will be explained later in this chapter in relation to religiosity and privacy perception.

This chapter will focus on the role of religion in affecting the individual's online behaviour and cybersecurity. After reading this chapter, cybersecurity policy makers and managers will have a better understanding of the effect of religion on cybersecurity through user behaviour and their acceptance to use the technology that is needed for security. Consequently, they will be able to make policies that will respect and be applicable to their religious employees and users, which will help to increase security and reduce threats.

RELIGION

Religion is a major influence on human life. It plays a major role in the formation of behaviours and attitudes (Essoo & Dibb, 2010). Berger (1961) shows that religion is a causal part of social behaviour. Meanwhile, several researchers have argued that individual behaviours and attitudes are justified by their religious beliefs (Foxall, Goldsmith & Brown, 1998). Delener (1994) argued that religion comprises beliefs and values, performing the role which people follow or use as a guide to their behaviour.

There are 5.8 billion people who follow a religion such as Christianity, Judaism, Buddhism, and Islam, which is 84 percent of the world's population (Harper, 2012). Religion, to some extent, helps to shape individual personality, moral standards, social norms, and behaviours. Furthermore, religion plays a major role in human behaviours and attitudes (Essoo & Dibb, 2010). Cohen and Hill (2007) argued that the boundary of moral standards, thoughts, judgments, attitudes and action of human behaviour are affected by religion, personal level and type of religiosity. In addition, Delener (1994) shows that religion comprises beliefs and values, performing the rules which people follow or use as a guide to their behaviour. For example, In Saudi Arabia, a Muslim country, many people pray five times a day. Four of these prayers are conducted in the business hours. At these times, all businesses close to giving time to people to pray. It has become a social norm that all businesses, social gatherings, meetings and activities are postponed for the time of prayer. Religious practices change individual behaviours and attitudes (Foxall, Goldsmith & Brown, 1998), affecting their social norms and shaping new ones.

There is a habitual familiarity with religion between academics and the general public. However, according to Guthrie et al. (1980), a clear definition of religion has eluded philosophers and social scientists for centuries. The interaction between religion, traditions, and cultures are the main cause of this mix up (Hood Jr, Hill & Spilka, 2009). Durkheim (1912) defined religion as "a unified system of beliefs and practices relative to sacred things, that is to say, things set apart and forbidden—beliefs and practices which unite into a single moral community called a Church, all those who adhere to them." Durkheim shifted the focus of religion from history and doctrine to the social function. Durkheim considers religion as social facts that are made of the beliefs and practices which unite a community.

Tillich (2001, p. 5) concentrates on faith rather than religion in a border sense. He argues that faith is an act of the total personality that comes from the human mind. In his view, religion, as faith, helps humans cope existentially. Tillich viewed religion from a functional perspective. According to Khraim (2010), religion should be considered to be a major cultural factor due to its universality and its impact on human behaviour, attitudes and values, both socially and individually. Religion has also been seen as one of the basic elements of social behaviour (Berger, 1961). Religious values and beliefs affect human norms and behaviours in many different ways, such as shaping public opinion, dealing with others, using products and in other parts of everyday life.

Geertz (1973) also defines religion as a system of symbols that act to creates pervasive, powerful and long-lasting moods and motivations in people. Geertz (1973, p. 90) claims that religious samples are created by formulating conceptions of a general order of existence that are approved as factual. This definition is substantial and functional: it explains what religion consists of and what it does in its psychological, cognitive and emotional functions. Geertz emphasised that human culture and experience are shaped by religion.

A review of the literature shows that religion overlaps with some characteristics of socio-cultural life (Schwartz, 1995; Tarakeshwar, Stanton & Pargament, 2003; Cohen & Hill, 2007; Choi, 2010; Muhamad & Mizerski, 2013). Behaviours of individuals and relationships inside groups, not to mention communities, organisation and families are affected by religion (Tarakeshwar, Stanton, & Pargament, 2003; Fam, Waller & Erdogan, 2004; Choi, 2010). Religion contributes to forming and shaping the individual's norms, thoughts, opinions, beliefs, decisions making, moral standards, socialisations and attitudes directly or indirectly (Wilkes, Burnett, & Howell, 1986; Fam, Waller & Erdogan, 2004; Choi, 2010). According to Khraim (2010), religion is considered as a major cultural factor due to its universality and its impact on the human behaviour, attitudes and values both socially and individually. It is also one of the basic elements of social behaviour (Berger, 1961). Religious values and beliefs impact human norms and behaviours in many different ways, such as shaping public opinion, dealing with others, using products and in other parts of everyday life. Furthermore, Hannah, Avolio, & May (2011) stated that the scope of beliefs and norms justify only 20% of the variation in individual behaviour. In addition to understanding the direct impact of user's religious beliefs on cyber security measures, it is important to identify to what extent people will allow their religion to take effect.

Religiosity

Looking back to Geertz's (1973) definition of religion, it is a system of symbols that act to create pervasive, powerful and long-lasting moods and motivation in people. The attitudes and motivations that have been formed by the symbolic system of religion lead to distinct levels of commitment to obey the values and philosophy of any religion, which is termed religiosity. Religion cannot affect two different individuals similarly, which means that the effect of religion will differ from one person to another. Therefore, although religion by itself cannot be used as a measurement, the degree of people commitment, belief, practice and acceptance of that religion, known as religiosity, can be measured (Mukhtar & Butt, 2012). Khraim (2010) stated that religiosity is a strong predictor of consumer behaviour. In the current research, many disciplines consider religiosity rather than religion in studying behaviour.

By looking at the literature, it becomes apparent that many researchers are focusing on the concept of religiosity rather than religion because it reflects how an individual tailors religion, which converges with behaviour (e.g. Wilkes, Burnett, & Howell, 1986; McDaniel & Burnett, 1990; Vitell, 2009; Schneider, Krieger & Bayraktar, 2011; Swimberghe, Flurry & Parker, 2011). Dasti and Sitwat (2014) stated that there is no standardised definition for religiosity.

McDaniel & Burnett (1990, p. 103) define religiosity as a belief in a God which comes with a commitment to follow the principles that are believed to be set forth by that God. Meanwhile, Worthington et al. (2003, p. 85) stated that personal religiosity is the extent to which a person complies with his or her religious values and beliefs, and practices them openly. By looking at these two definitions, it is clear that religiosity differs from spirituality since spirituality engages in an exploration of "meaning, unity, connectedness to nature, humanity and the transcendent" (Vitell, 2009, p. 156) while religiosity provides faith that is devoted to beliefs, attitudes, and behaviours (Emmons, 2005; Vitell, 2009). Since religiosity is unique, it cannot be easily considered as a measurable variable, but any person may innately carry a certain degree of religiosity (Wilkes, Burnett, & Howell, 1986; Abou-Youssef *et al.*, 2011). People who practice religion highly are not necessarily religious because this practice might be a daily routine action rather than an act of devotion (Khraim, 2010). Although there is no standardised measure of religiosity, many researchers develop or adopt a measure that fits with their needs (Khraim, 2010). Their religiosity dimensions differ widely, and they sometimes depend on the nature of the research. Thus, it is essential to see how researchers have developed methods to assess people's religiosity.

According to Vitell and Paolillo (2003), religiosity represents a main determinant of values and human convictions. Previous studies have shown that an individual's level of religiosity has obvious effects on their attitudes and behaviours (McDaniel & Burnett, 1990; Weaver, 2002). Since the mid-1970s, some researchers have attempted to explain the relationships between personal religiosity and personal characteristics, and they aim to determine whether such relationships can provide a basis for examining individual decision making processes (e.g. Barton & Vaughan 1976; Choi 2010; Clark & Dawson 1996; Donahue 1985; Miller & Hoffmann 1995; Swimberghe et al. 2011; Wiebe & Fleck 1980; Wilkes et al. 1986; Smith et al. 1979; Welch 1981; Tate & Miller 1971). However, these studies have produced mixed results (McDaniel & Burnett, 1990).

For example, McDaniel and Burnett (1990) claim that some studies have shown that the more religious people are, the more emotional they become (e.g. Barton & Vaughan 1976; Slater 1947). From another perspective, Ranck (1961) argued that highly religious people usually have lower self-esteem. It was later shown by Smith et al. (1979) that there is a positive association between religiosity and self-esteem. Kohlberg (1981) found that religious reasoning was based on the revelations of religious authorities while morality was based upon rational opinions and was influenced by cognitive development. The emphasis that is placed on morality and religiosity was not linked from their perspective. Despite the prior evidence, other studies have confirmed that there is a powerful connection between religion and morality, and considered personal religiosity to be a platform for the moral nature of behaviour (Magill, 1992; Geyer & Baumeister, 2005). Regardless of the external influences, the mixed findings stipulate that religiosity is a subjective characteristic that is profoundly natural to the individual and its dimensions of expression, and they are no worse in different disciplines and contexts (Donahue, 1985b; Wilkes, Burnett, & Howell, 1986; McDaniel & Burnett, 1990; Vitell, 2009).

Conceptualising Religiosity

In every attempt to conceptualise and measure religiosity as a construct, the absence of a commonly accepted definition of religiosity is a vital challenge that must be addressed (McDaniel & Burnett, 1990). A large number of different types of measurement approaches have been developed throughout the literature. For example, one of the approaches is the belief in God and church attendance (Allport & Kramer, 1946; Adorno *et al.*, 1950; Gough, 1951; Stouffer, 1955; Rockeach, 1960). Another approach is religious affiliation (Thompson & Raine, 1976; Hirschman, 1981, 1983a, 1983b; Delener, 1987; Farah & Newman, 2010). Other approaches include church attendance, the importance of and confidence in the religious value and self-perceived religiousness (Wilkes, Burnett & Howell, 1986). Belief in God and attending church were considered by an earlier approach to be the only factors to distinguish highly religious people from the less religious (Allport & Kramer, 1946; Adorno *et al.*, 1950; Gough, 1951; Stouffer, 1955; Rockeach, 1960). Nevertheless, other studies have argued that believing in God and attending churches do not reflect the involvement and commitment to religious values (Allport & Ross, 1967). Some academics have tried to measure religiosity based on denominational membership or religious affiliation (e.g. Delener 1987; Farah & Newman 2010; Hirschman 1981; Hirschman 1983a; Hirschman 1983b; Thompson & Raine 1976). The primary assumption that they used is that the power of religious affiliation is constant across religious clusters (Swimberghe, Flurry & Parker, 2011). Nonetheless, this opinion can lead to some difficulties when trying to differentiate between the attribute effects of religious affiliation and those of actual religiousness (Swimberghe, Flurry & Parker, 2011). Additionally, in some cases, the believers may prefer a specific denomination but have an affiliation with another denomination (Roof, 1980; McDaniel & Burnett, 1990; Swimberghe, Flurry & Parker, 2011). On the other hand, some researchers criticise religious affiliation as a too common definition that does not show the actual commitment to and practice of a religion and its creeds (Himmelfarb, 1975; Muhamad & Mizerski, 2013).

The behavioural science concept of conformity has been used by Wilkes et al. (1986). The concept of conformity, according to Engel & Roger (1995), states that an individual's complete psychological makeup is built around the *self* concept. Therefore, it has been posited that religiosity is a highly individual and multidimensional nature rather than a unidirectional nature (De Jong, Faulkner & Warland, 1976). As a result, the following combined items have been developed by Wilkes et al. (1986) to evaluate religiosity: church attendance, the importance of religious values, confidence in religious values and self-perceived religiousness. Religiosity has again been conceptualised as a multidimensional construct by McDaniel and Burnett (1990), who identify two components of religiosity: religious affiliation and religious commitment. They applied an open-ended questionnaire to measure religious affiliation. They addressed religious commitment from both cognitive and conative perspectives. Worthington et al. (2003) developed this approach to include a six-item, five-point scale to measure religious commitment. Other studies have also viewed religiosity through religious commitment (e.g. Essoo & Dibb 2010; Fam et al. 2004; Sood & Nasu 1995; Swimberghe et al. 2011). However, other researchers have needed to explain the main motivation for religiosity in terms of the differentiation between intrinsic and extrinsic religiosity (Allport & Ross, 1967; Schaefer & Gorsuch, 1991) because it is an exceptionally suitable approach (Vitell, 2009).

Islamic Religiosity Measurement Scale

Some researchers (e.g. McFarland, 1984; Khraim, 2010) argued that scales designed for Christianity are useless to Islam due to the cultural differences between the two religions. Many researchers have tried to develop a unique measurement for Islamic religiosity (e.g. Taai, 1985; Albelaikhi, 1988; Alsanie, 1989; Wilde & Joseph, 1997; Khraim, 2010). Most of their attempts cannot be generalised for many reasons, including but not limited to customised dimensions to fit their topic, the reliability of the subscales, and the use of the holy Quran as a guideline for the scale. Thus, it cannot be used for other religions.

Taai (1985) developed a scale for Islamic religiosity that was derived from a theological Islamic teaching source. This scale treats both recommended practice and obligatory practice as one, which affects its reliability and validity. Albelaikhi (1988) designed a three dimensions scale that includes both Islamic belief and practice. The score of the main belief element measured with the other measures was not included in their study. This increases the question of the functionality of measuring this dimension. Another scale has been developed by Alsanie (1989), where he treated faith and practice as a unidimensional variable. In spite of the fact that faith and practice should be, according to Islam, part of the individual's daily routine, they are not totally indivisible. For example, a Muslim can have a strong faith but still miss some prayers. Khraim (2010) developed a scale that consists of four dimensions, which are: Islamic financial services, seeking religious education, current Islamic issue, and sensitive products. However, this scale only focuses on Islamic behaviour and does not measure belief. Furthermore, the dimensions are designed to fulfil the author's area of interest, which is consumer behaviour. Wilde and Joseph (1997) developed a measurement called MARS (Muslim attitudes towards religion scale). They focused on the experiential dimension in preference of beliefs and practices of Islam.

Many successful studies have applied Allport and Ross's (1967) religious orientation scale, which is a Christian scale to measure Islamic religiosity (e.g. Ghorbani *et al.*, 2002; Ji & Ibrahim, 2007; Essoo & Dibb, 2010; Schneider, Krieger & Bayraktar, 2011; Mukhtar & Butt, 2012). According to Donahue (1985a), religious orientation scale can be used for Christianity and other religions because of its absence of doctrinal subjects and unlimited definitions of religion. A summary of the adopted scales for Islam is given in Table 1. The next section will explain the ways in which intrinsic and extrinsic religiosity are used as a conceptual approach for religiosity.

Intrinsic and Extrinsic Religiosity

The concept of using intrinsic religiosity as the 'religious orientation scale' was introduced by Allport (1950). Extrinsic religiosity is personal and utilitarian, unlike intrinsic religiosity, which is defined by internalised beliefs despite external consequences (Allport & Ross, 1967; Schaefer & Gorsuch, 1991). Intrinsic religiosity simply looks at religion as a meaning-endowing structure in terms of which all of life is understood (Donahue, 1985a; Clark & Dawson, 1996). On the other hand, two sub-dimensions can be used to explain extrinsic religiosity, which is extrinsic social religiosity and personal extrinsic religiosity (Ghorbani *et al.*, 2002; Ji & Ibrahim, 2007; Chen & Tang, 2013). According to Chen and Tang (2013), extrinsic social religiosity aims to achieve normal social goals, such as making friends, promoting personal interests and gaining social standing and acceptance in the community (Chen & Tang, 2013). For example, local church services at some Christian communities after Sunday service announce promotions and invite the congregation to try their services or products (Chen & Tang, 2013). Muslims are strictly prohibited from promoting business inside the mosque, but they do promote their

Table 1. Islamic religiosity measurement scale

Author	Year	Scale
Ghorbani, N; Watson, P.J; Ghramalek, A	2002	Allport and Ross (1967): Religiosity orientation scale
Worthington, J et al.	2003	Religion commitment inventory
Essoo,N; Dibb, S	2004	Allport and Ross (1967): Religiosity orientation scale
Krauss, S; Hamzah, A; Juhari, R; Hamid, J	2005	Muslim religiosity personality inventory
Krauss, s et al.	2006	Muslim religiosity personality inventory
Ji,C; Ibrahim, Y	2007	Allport and Ross (1967): Religiosity orientation scale
Masri,A; Priester,P	2007	Religiosity of Islamic scale
Abu-Raiya, H	2008	Psychological Measure of Islamic Religiousness
Tiliouine, H; Cummins, R; Davern, M	2009	Islamic Religiosity scale
Tiliouine,H; Belgoomdi, A	2009	Comprehensive measure of Islamic religiosity
Rehman, A; Shabbir, M	2010	Glock and Stark's (1964) dimensions
Khraim, H	2010	Islamic practical behaviour
Abou-Yousef, M et al.	2011	Modified Islamic religiosity scale
Mukhtar, A; Butt, M	2011	Allport and Ross (1967): Religiosity orientation scale
Schneider, H; Krieger, J; Bayraktar, A	2011	Allport and Ross (1967): Religiosity orientation scale
Dasti,r; Sitwat, A	2014	Multidimensional Measurement Scale
Bachleda, C; Hamelin, N; Benachour, O	2014	Religious commitment inventory
El-Menouar, Y	2014	Glock and Stark's (1964) dimensions

products or services directly after prayers and near to the mosques. Chen and Tang (2013) explained that the concept of extrinsic social religiosity is more concerned about the use of religion as self-serving rather than practising religion purely to connect with God.

The private individual gains include happiness, relief, comfort and protection, which are the focus of extrinsic religiosity (Laufer & Solomon, 2011; Chen & Tang, 2013). For example, some Muslims fast during the month of Ramadan for personal gains, such as losing weight rather than fasting to follow the doctrine of their religion (El Ati, Beji & Danguir, 1995; Roky *et al.*, 2004). Personal and social extrinsic religiosity has always been combined by the researcher to investigate extrinsic religiosity as one overall construct (Chen & Tang, 2013) because personal extrinsic religiosity sometimes functions similarly to intrinsic religiosity. The dispute has arisen because gaining personal comfort and protection are the same as aiming for God's forgiveness and mercy by following religious doctrine. According to Chen and Tang (2013), this concept led to slender empirical research on personal extrinsic religiosity. Nevertheless, a research context should be considered before choosing to conceptualise extrinsic religiosity as one or two constructs.

Donahue (1985a) argued that participants are mostly classified by a fourfold typology that is created by median splits of scale scores when applying intrinsic and extrinsic religiosity as dimensions of religious motivation. Hence, a participant who gets high intrinsic and low extrinsic score is categorised as an intrinsically religious person. On the other hand, a participant who gets high extrinsic and low intrinsic score is categorised as extrinsically religious. Getting high scores in both intrinsic and extrinsic is considered to be 'indiscriminately pro-religious.' In contrast, a non-religious partisan receives low intrinsic and extrinsic scores (Clark & Dawson, 1996). According to Donahue (1985a), this religious motivation or orientation framework can be considered to be an influential and instructive tool in personality-social psychology. Yet, there is another opinion which states that all religious searches involve means and ends, a pathway and destination; therefore, defining religion as means (intrinsic) versus ends (extrinsic) is imperfect (Pargament, 1992; Slater, Hall & Edwards, 2001).

This religious orientation measurement approach has been one of the most efficient and extensively used measurements in the literature, despite the criticism and the rise of a multiplicity of religiosity measures (Donahue, 1985a; Vitell, 2009). In addition, more than one hundred studies supported this approach in terms of its reliability and validity of the concept and measures (Muhamad & Mizerski, 2013). Based on the perception of human motivation, intrinsic and extrinsic religiosity appear to be measures that are used for studies involving nearly all religions (Allport & Ross, 1967; Gorsuch & McPherson, 1989; Ji & Ibrahim, 2007; Muhamad & Mizerski, 2013). It has been clearly proven that this approach can be applied to Muslims (Ghorbani *et al.*, 2002; Ji & Ibrahim, 2007), Jews (Laufer & Solomon, 2011) as well as Christians (Chen & Tang, 2013; Putrevu & Swimberghek, 2013). Therefore, the religious motivation will be the approach to conceptualise and measure religiosity in this research.

Allport and Ross's Religious Orientation Scale

Allport and Ross (1967, p. 434) define an extrinsic and extrinsic person as an 'extrinsically motivated person uses his religion whereas the intrinsically motivated lives his religion.' In other words, a person who is extrinsically motivated uses religion as a means to ease his or her life, whereas the intrinsically motivated person sees religion as a guideline and rule on how to live.

Although Allport and Ross's (1967) original paper did not include the full religious orientation scale, Essoo and Dibb (2010) successfully used a full religious orientation scale. By using a Likert scale to assess the responses, the instrument consists of eleven items on extrinsic religiosity and nine items on intrinsic religiosity. This thesis will adopt the religious orientation scale on the Islamic perspective by making minor changes, such as changing Church to Masjid and Bible to wholly Quran. Hood (1970) classified Allport and Ross's (1967) religious orientation scale respondent by a fourfold typology on the median split, as follows:

- High intrinsic+ low extrinsic= intrinsic,
- Low intrinsic+ High extrinsic= extrinsic,
- High intrinsic+ high extrinsic= indiscriminately pro-religious,
- Low intrinsic+ low extrinsic= non-religious.

Religiosity and Ethics

One of the main sources for ethical norms, which influence ethical evaluation, is a religion (Clark & Dawson, 1996). The individual's religiosity explains the ethical nature of human behaviour (Magill, 1992). Huffman (1988) viewed the effect of religiosity on the personal ethics through the sociological functionalist theory. He found that religiosity is one of the main sources of human values. Bartels (1967) argued that religion influence the human culture and ethics. In addition, religion explains moral behaviours and can be used to evaluate the code of conduct (De George, 1986). According to Muncy and Vitell

(1992), consumer ethics are moral principles and standards that guide the behaviour of individuals or groups as they obtain, use, dispose of goods and services (p.586). Hence, religion has to be considered as a factor that affects the ethical norms.

Conceptual Differences Between Religion and Religiosity

Religion cannot affect two different individuals similarly, which means that the effect of religion will differ from one person to another. Therefore, religion by itself cannot be used as a measurement but the degree of people commitment, belief, practice and acceptance of that religion, known as religiosity, is what can be measured (Mukhtar & Butt, 2012).

According to Johnson *et al.* (2001), the individual's commitment to his or her religion is reflected in his or her attitude and behaviour and may be called religiosity. Religiosity includes a diverse range of components of religion, such as belief, practice, knowledge, and experience, and it includes their impact on daily routine (O'Connell, 1975). Hence, religiosity is not unidimensional (Glock, 1962; Allport & Ross, 1967; Stark & Glock, 1968; King & Hunt, 1972). Furthermore, religiosity has an influential role in value choices (Keng & Yang, 1993), and forming the attitudes of individuals (E. Hirschman, 1981). In addition, religiosity is a *continuous rather than a discrete variable* (Argyle & Beit-Hallahmi, 2014). Religious ideology moulds an individual's opinion of what is right and wrong (Magill, 1992; Rest, 1986); thus, it can be used to measure their personal judgments. According to Weaver and Agle (2002), religiosity has an influence on attitude and human behaviour. Moreover, religiosity shows how committed the individual is to the values, practice, and ideas of a certain religion (Nejdet Delener, 1990). Thus, the use of religiosity in measuring the effect of religion on online behaviour is inevitable.

Why Islam?

Islam (like Christianity and Judaism) is a monotheistic religion that originated in the Middle East (Ji & Ibrahim, 2007). It has been augured that 20 years from now, one-third of the world's population will be Muslim, with a rate of increase of 1.84 percent, and more than half of all Muslims will be aged 18 years old (Quelch, 2001). Compared to the followers of other religions, Muslims are more committed to their beliefs, practice, and teaching (Bailey & Sood, 1993). According to Muhamad and Mizerski (2013), when living in an Islamic country, social pressure is the main factor that affects consumer behaviour. For Arabs, religion plays a major part in their personal lives, and it is considered to be essential. There is no room for atheists or agnostics in the Arab world (Nydell, 2011, p. 81). This is one of the reasons why Islam has a dominant role in a conservative Islamic Arabic country like Saudi Arabia. Therefore, this chapter will test the effect of religion on the online behaviour in the Islamic context.

The Religious Context of Saudi Arabia

Saudi Arabia is a conservative Islamic country with a monarchy that is led by the Al Saud royal family. According to the Central Intelligence Agency (2016), Saudi Arabia's has a population of 28 million and only one religion, which is Islam. Saudi Arabia is the homeland of Islam and was where the Prophet Muhammed (PBUH) started his revelation 1,400 years ago. Furthermore, the country has two of the three most sacred sites for Muslims, which are Makkah and Medina. Makkah is the city of the first wholly masjid, and there is a requirement for every Muslim to visit the city on pilgrimage (Hajj) once in a lifetime and Muslims are required to face Makkah five times a day when praying. On the other hand, Medina is the second holy Masjid for Muslims and is where the Prophet Muhammed (PBUH) is buried. This is why most of the Islamic world looks up to Saudi Arabia. The country uses the Sharia law (adopted from the whole Quran and Sunnah) in its constitution (Al-Kandari & Dashti, 2014). Consequently, Islam is the heart of the cultural, political and social life of Saudi Arabia, which makes it the perfect population to use in this study.

PRIVACY

The topic of information privacy has attracted much research attention, particularly in the online and e-commerce settings. Studies of information privacy have been conducted in corporate and commercial environments (Dinev et al., 2005; S. Smith, 2010), while in recent years the focus has shifted to individual privacy levels (Vladlena, Saridakis, Tennakoon, & Ezingeard, 2015).

According to Westin (1968), information privacy is the ability to control the individual's private information in which they have the full power over their information, including whether or not to share it. Information privacy is considered as one of the top ethical, legal, social, and political issues of the information era (Culnan, 1993). The fast growth of Internet technology and the digitalization of private information has created many new challenges to information privacy (Anderson & Agarwal, 2011).

According to Mekovec and Hutinski (2012), online privacy perception refers to online shopping and e-banking service users' anxiety about how an online company or bank (which is providing the e-service) will handle the information that they collect about the user during their online interaction. Online users and e-commerce consumers have become the main information providers to social media, blogs, and websites, which makes their personal information vulnerable. Furthermore, personalised web services and business intelligence software all make use of the user's personal information (Li & Sarkar, 2006)

Smith, Dinev and Xu (2011) undertook a meta-analysis of 320 articles and 128 books on information privacy. They find that there are many theoretical developments in the body of normative and purely descriptive studies that have not been addressed in empirical research on privacy. They also find out that some analyses receive less attention and that researchers should focus on the antecedents to privacy concern and its outcomes. Similarly, Bélanger and Crossler (2011) performed metadata analyses on 142 Journals and 102 conference papers. They assert that information privacy is a multilevel concept but is rarely studied as such. Their paper also finds that information privacy research has been heavily reliant on student-based and US-centric samples, which results in findings of limited generalisability.

On the other hand, Lee, Ahn and Bang (2011) conducted a strategic analysis and privacy perceptions and found that firms can improve social welfare privacy at the expense of the personal welfare. They also find that regulation that enforces the implementation of fair information practices can be efficient from the social welfare perspective. From a different perspective, Grover and Purvis (2011) find that the most dominant stressor of the technostress is work overload and role ambiguity, and the characteristics of intrusive technology are the dominant predictors of the stressor. Sutanto *et al.* (2013) proposed an IT solution for information privacy by conducting a field experiment of 629 people and a survey study of 120. They aimed to reduce the user's perception, and this led to an increase in the process and content gratification.

Li and Sarkar (2006) found a new way to protect data privacy while preserving data quality. Venkatesh, Thong and Xu (2012) identified various conceptualisations of information privacy concerns. They also developed an integrated conceptualization of information privacy concern (IPC) that validated the reliability and validity.

Recently, Boss *et al.* (2015) conducted a comprehensive review on 125 users and a field experiment on 327 using PMT and fear appeal manipulation. They find that Information system Planned Motivation Theory (PMT)research should use PMT and fear appeal manipulation before adding non-PMT constructs. Furthermore, they said that ISec PMT research should model and measure users' behaviour. Posey, Roberts and Lowry (2013) conducted a semi-structured interview with 33 participants. They found out that using a systematic approach is the best way to understand protective information security behaviour. Smith (2010) found that a strategy based on organisation subunit size is helpful in motivating and assisting the organisation to move toward accreditation. They came up with this finding by conducting a survey, interviews, observations and focus groups on 89 users.

Siponen and Vance (2010) argued that fear appeal does impact the end user's behavioural intention to comply with recommended individual acts of security; however, the impact is not uniform across all end users. From another perspective, Siponen and Vance (2010) reviewed 174 ethical decisions making. Their results suggested that practitioners should work to counteract employees' use of neutralisation techniques. (Anderson & Agarwal, 2011) raised several concerns about practising safe computing. They suggested that a home computer user's intention is formed by a combination of the cognitive, social and psychological components. This intuition can be enhanced via self-view and goal-frame message manipulation. Spears and Barki (2010) published a paper conducting two studies: the first one is a survey that is based on a questionnaire of 228 participants, while the other interviews 11 participants. They find that the user's participation improves security control performance and improve control development. Johnston, Warkentin and Siponen (2015) used fear appeal theory and conducted a survey and interview of 559 participants and showed that using fear appeal will provide a significant positive influence on compliance intention.

Finally, Wang, Gupta and Rao (2015) observed the behaviour of 14,680 online users and argued that the result of their study support the empirical application of routine activity theory in comprehending insider threats and providing a vision of how various applications have a different level of exposure to threats.

Privacy is one of the measure concerns of cyber security, and none of these researchers considered the effect of religion on the privacy. They tried to protect privacy by changing technology, behaviour, and policies. However, an individual's beliefs can have a strong effect on their norms and behaviours. Religious people, especially Muslims, behave and act according to their religion. Consequently, when trying to change their behaviours and their views on privacy, policy makers and managers should consider religious factors.

TECHNOLOGY ACCEPTANCE

User behaviour and the acceptance of use have been successfully explained through psychological theories, such as the theory of reasoned action, the theory of planned behaviour and protection motivation theory. However, they could not explain more than 50 per cent of the behaviour. Venkatesh et al. (2003) designed a unified theory that explains more than 50 percent of the behaviour, which they called the unified theory of acceptance and use of technology (UTAUT). After nine years, they updated the theory (called UTAUT2), and it then explained 74% of the behavioural intentions and 56% of the technology use.

Venkatesh et al. (2003) designed a unified theory of user acceptance of information technology that helps to understand the success of technology and to what extent the users accept and adapt to the new technology. This allowed the authors to improve and develop the technology and to find what motivates users to accept or refuse technology. The UTAUT combines the theory of reasoned action, technology acceptance model, motivation model, the theory of planned behaviour, a combination model of TAM and TPB, PC utilisation model, innovation diffusion theory and the social cognitive theory. The UTAUT theory's initial contracts are:

1. **Performance Expectancy**: Which is defined as the perceived benefits that an individual obtains by using technology in a certain activity (Venkatesh et al., 2003).
2. **Effort Expectancy**: Which is associated with how easy it seems to be to use a certain technology activity (Venkatesh et al., 2003).
3. **Social Influence**: This is the effect that a person held to be important to an individual has on the decision of that individual to use a technology activity (Venkatesh et al., 2003).
4. **Facilitating Condition**: Which is defined as the individual perception of the support available in order to use a technology activity (Venkatesh et al., 2003).
5. **Behavioural Intention**.

Performance expectations, effort expectancy, and social influence are essential elements to influence behavioural intention to use technology, while the behavioural intention and facilitating conditions explain technology use.

Venkatesh et al. (2012) later improved the UTAUT and added three constructs and named it UTAUT2, claiming that the added variance will explain behavioural intention and technology use more sufficiently. By doing this, the theory explained 74% of the behavioural intentions and 56% of the technology use. The three constructs are:

1. **Hedonic Motivation or Perceived Enjoyment**: Which is defined as the intrinsic motivation of an individual to obtain fun or pleasure from using a technology activity (Venkatesh et al., 2012).
2. **Price Value**: Which is defined as the perceived benefits of using a technology given its costs (Venkatesh et al., 2012).
3. **Habit**: Which refers to the automation of behaviour resulting from learning (Venkatesh et al., 2012).

Consequently, the UTAUT2 theory will help link and explain the effect of the individual religion on the acceptance to use the cyber security protocol, policies, and measures.

Islam and Accepting New Technologies

Religion is considered to have a huge influence on the culture, attitude, behaviour and business manner of people (Samovar, Porter, McDaniel, & Roy, 2015). Muslims usually ask their clerics if the behaviour, action or products are Halal (permissible) or Haram (forbidden) and they then act accordingly (Al-Kandari & Dashti, 2014).When answering these questions, the Muslim clerics give their justification from the Holy Quran, Sunnah or opinion of other Muslim scholars. Innovations and new technologies in Western countries are a necessity to progress and follow the civilised world, but Arabs fear that this might spoil their culture and the religious standards of the younger generation (Nydell, 2011). Many of the new technologies that have been introduced from other cultures have been initially rejected or criticised by Muslim scholars in Saudi Arabia (Al-Kandari & Dashti, 2014). For example, in 1999 the Internet was introduced to the Saudis, and it was heavily criticised and sometimes prohibited by Muslim scholars due to the fear that it will carry Western negative values and imperialism (Al-Shohaib, Al-Kandari, & Abdulrahim, 2009).

Nowadays, Muslim scholars have changed their perspective of modern technologies from disapproving it to conditionally approving and sometimes totally approving due to education, social media, and globalisation (Al-Kandari & Dashti, 2014). Muslim scholars have adopted the new social media, and it has become the most popular channel for them to speak with the public (Schanzer & Miller, 2012, p. 62). However, they still believe that there is a certain level of privacy between females and males (based on Islamic religion) that should be addressed. This is a good example of how the perspective of the Saudi clerics has changed over time. Nevertheless, the new way of thinking for Muslim scholar still based on what is ethical, moral and acceptable in Islam.

For the case of Saudi Arabia, the dimensions of technology, privacy and religion (see Figure 1) are clearly illustrated in the case of the ban on technology on religious grounds. Each has an impact on the other, and they are interrelated. Religion has an impact on technology, as shown in the example of the Internet ban in Saudi Arabia. Some technologies have been banned by religious people for religious reasons, while others banned the bad use of the technology. Privacy is determined by religion. For example, in Islam, pictures of females are private, and it is prohibited for a female to show her face and hair to strangers. Thus, some privacy matters have been established by religious causes. Technology has affected privacy through cyber crime and other means of invading privacy. And vice versa, the fear of the invasion of privacy has affected the way that many people use technology. These three dimensions affect each other, and they cannot be addressed separately, especially in religious-oriented countries such as Saudi Arabia.

CONCLUSION

With the rapid growth of information systems and technology, many governments and private sector bodies are encouraging their people to use these new developments while they are trying to secure their information systems and assets (Kirlappos & Sasse, 2012). Nowadays, almost all daily life and business

Figure 1. Interrelated dimensions

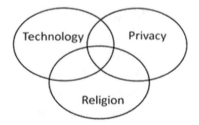

activities are computerised, and most transactions are digitalised. However, moving at high speed towards a digital world has come with a high-security risk. Thus, many governments and policy makers are trying to organise and protect online users and online business by making new legislation and policies. Training employees are one of the most popular protective measures that government and organisations use to increase the sufficiency of their cyber security—nevertheless, it is not working (Kirlappos, Parkin & Sasse, 2014). Therefore, the focus must be shifted to change people's behaviour and their capability to use and adapt to the new policies and security measures.

Religion has a considerable influence on people's behaviour and their relationship within families, groups, organization and communities where they act according to their religious beliefs and refuse anything that contradicts their beliefs, even if it is a compulsive policy or security measure (Tarakeshwar, Stanton, & Pargament, 2003; Fam, Waller & Erdogan, 2004; Choi, 2010). Furthermore, religion contributes to format and shape the individuals' norms, thoughts, opinions, beliefs, decisions making, moral standards, socialisations and attitudes directly or indirectly (Wilkes, Burnett, & Howell, 1986; Fam, Waller & Erdogan, 2004; Choi, 2010).

Giving information about risks and making new policies is not enough to change people's behaviour: they must also understand and accept them in order to change their behaviour, which will require a change in their attitude and intention (Bada & Sasse, 2014). The main influences on people skills, understanding, and knowledge of cyber security are beliefs, attitudes, perception and experience, which are the same influences on behaviour (Coventry, Briggs, Blythe, & Tran, 2014). Many awareness researchers have suggested that motivating people comes from linking their action to their values; thus, they will follow the security measures and accept the new policies without resistance (Bada & Sasse, 2014). People will work in a more productive way when their values are aligned with the new actions and policies to improve cyber security.

According to LaRose and Eastin (2004), when changing behaviour, cultural values and beliefs must be considered. Kirlappos et al. (2014) argued that cultural values should be considered when designing advertisement and warning messages. People's beliefs and behaviour present the main challenge to effectively apply policies and the security measures to protect information security. In the absence of instruction or procedure, people act according to their cultural beliefs and norms. Although many researchers have considered organisation culture, system updates, new policies that relate to cyber security, they did not consider the user's culture. Religion is one of the main effects on the user's culture, especially in religious countries such as Saudi Arabia.

As shown in the previous sections, religion is considered to be the main force that affects Muslim behaviour, acceptance and norms. A Muslim will not do anything that contradicts their religion, even if it is a state law or a company's policy and procedure. This is an important point that has largely been ignored by policy makers until now. However, it should be used as a strong tool to change people's behaviour to enhance cyber security and protect their information and assets.

REFERENCES

Abou-Youssef, M., Kortam, W., Abou-Aish, E., & El-Bassiouny, N. (2011). Measuring islamic-driven buyer behavioral implications: A proposed market-minded religiosity scale. *The Journal of American Science*, 7(8), 788–801. doi:10.1017/CBO9781107415324.004

Adorno, T. W., Frenkel-Brunswik, E., Levinson, D. J., & Sanford, R. N. (1950). *The authoritarian personality*. Academic Press.

Al-Kandari, A., & Dashti, A. (2014). Fatwa and the internet: A study of the influence of Muslim religious scholars on internet diffusion in Saudi Arabia. *Prometheus*, *32*(2), 127–144. doi:10.1080/08109 028.2014.998929

Al-Shohaib, K., Al-Kandari, A. A. J., & Abdulrahim, M. A. (2009). Internet adoption by Saudi public relations professionals. *Journal of Communication Management*, *13*(1), 21–36. doi:10.1108/13632540910931373

Albelaikhi, A. (1988). *Religious orientation and fear of death among Muslims and Christian individuals*. University of Rhode Island, Psychology Department.

Allport, G. W. (1950). *The individual and his religion: A psychological interpretation*. Academic Press.

Allport, G. W., & Kramer, B. M. (1946). Some roots of prejudice. *The Journal of Psychology*, *22*(1), 9–39. doi:10.1080/00223980.1946.9917293 PMID:20992067

Allport, G. W., & Ross, J. M. (1967). Personal religious orientation and prejudice. *Journal of Personality and Social Psychology*, *5*(4), 432–443. doi:10.1037/h0021212 PMID:6051769

Alsanie, S. I. (1989). *Relationship between level of Religiosity and Criminal Behavior* (Unpublished Doctoral Dissertation). Imam Ibn Suad Islamic University, Saudi Arabia.

Anderson, C., & Agarwal, R. (2011). Practicing Safe Computing: A Multimethod Empirical Examination of Home Computer User Security Behavioral Intentions. *Management Information Systems Quarterly*, *126*(2), 987–1027. doi:10.1093/qje/qjr008

Argyle, M., & Beit-Hallahmi, B. (2014). *The psychology of religious behaviour, belief and experience*. Routledge.

Bada, M., & Sasse, A. (2014). *Cyber Security Awareness Campaigns: Why do they fail to change behaviour?* Academic Press.

Bailey, J. M., & Sood, J. (1993). The effects of religious affiliation on consumer behavior: A preliminary investigation. *Journal of Managerial Issues*, 328–352.

Bartels, R. (1967). A model for ethics in marketing. *Journal of Marketing*, *31*(1), 20–26. doi:10.2307/1249296

Barton, K., & Vaughan, G. M. (1976). Church membership and personality: A longitudinal study. *Social Behavior and Personality*, *4*(1), 11–16. doi:10.2224/sbp.1976.4.1.11

Bélanger, F., & Crossler, R. E. (2011). Privacy in the Digital Age: A Review of Information Privacy Research in Information Systems. *Management Information Systems Quarterly*, *35*(4), 1017–1041. doi:10.1159/000360196

Berger, P. L. (1961). *Noise of Solemn Assemblies*. Bantam.

Boss, S. R., Galletta, D. F., Lowry, P. B., Moody, G. D., & Polak, P. (2015). What do users have to fear? Using fear appeals to engender threats and fear that motivate protective security behaviors. *Management Information Systems Quarterly*, *39*(4), 837–864. doi:10.25300/MISQ/2015/39.4.5

Chen, Y. J., & Tang, T. L. P. (2013). The Bright and Dark Sides of Religiosity Among University Students: Do Gender, College Major, and Income Matter? *Journal of Business Ethics, 115*(3), 531–553. doi:10.1007/s10551-012-1407-2

Choi, Y. (2010). Religion, religiosity, and South Korean consumer switching behaviors. *Journal of Consumer Behaviour, 9*(3), 157–171. doi:10.1002/cb.292

CIA. (2016). *The World Factbook — Central Intelligence Agency: Mozambique.* Retrieved January 9, 2017, from https://www.cia.gov/library/publications/resources/the-world-factbook/geos/sa.html

Clark, J. W., & Dawson, L. E. (1996). Personal religiousness and ethical judgements: An empirical analysis. *Journal of Business Ethics, 15*(3), 359–372. doi:10.1007/BF00382959

Cohen, A. B., & Hill, P. C. (2007). Religion as culture: Religious individualism and collectivism among American catholics, jews, and protestants. *Journal of Personality, 75*(4), 709–742. doi:10.1111/j.1467-6494.2007.00454.x PMID:17576356

Coventry, L., Briggs, P., Blythe, J., & Tran, M. (2014). *Using behavioural insights to improve the public's use of cyber security best practices.* Gov. Uk Report.

Culnan, M. J. (1993). "How Did They Get My Name?": An Exploratory Investigation of Consumer Attitudes Toward Secondary Information Use. *Management Information Systems Quarterly, 17*(3), 341–363. doi:10.2307/249775

Dasti, R., & Sitwat, A. (2014). Development of a multidimensional measure of islamic spirituality (MMIS). *The Journal of Muslim Mental Health, 8*(2). doi:10.3998/jmmh.10381607.0008.204

De George, R. T. (1986). Theological ethics and business ethics. *Journal of Business Ethics, 5*(6), 421–432. doi:10.1007/BF00380748

De Jong, G. F., Faulkner, J. E., & Warland, R. H. (1976). Dimensions of Religiosity Reconsidered; Evidence from a Cross-Cultural Study. *Social Forces, 54*(4), 866–889. doi:10.1093/sf/54.4.866

de Lange, M., & von Solms, R. (2013). An e - Safety Educational Framework in South Africa. *Southern Africa Telecommunication Networks and Applications Conference (SATNAC) 2013,* 497.

Delener, N. (1987). An exploratory study of values of Catholic and Jewish subcultures: Implications for consumer psychology. *World Marketing Congress, Proceedings of the Third Bi-Annual International Conference,* 151–155.

Delener, N. (1990). The effects of religious factors on perceived risk in durable goods purchase decisions. *Journal of Consumer Marketing, 7*(3), 27–38. doi:10.1108/EUM0000000002580

Delener, N. (1994). Religious contrasts in consumer decision behaviour patterns: Their dimensions and marketing implications. *European Journal of Marketing, 28*(5), 36–53. doi:10.1108/03090569410062023

Dinev, T., Bellotto, M., Hart, P., Colautti, C., Russo, V., Serra, I., … Madsen, T. L. (2005). Privacy trade-off factors in e-commerce - A study of Italy and the United States. In *Academy of Management Annual Meeting Proceedings* (pp. A1–A6). Academy of Management. Retrieved from http://10.0.21.89/AMBPP.2005.18781234

Donahue, M. J. (1985a). Intrinsic and extrinsic religiousness: Review and meta-analysis. *Journal of Personality and Social Psychology, 48*(2), 400–419. doi:10.1037/0022-3514.48.2.400

Donahue, M. J. (1985b). Intrinsic and Extrinsic Religiousness: The Empirical Research. *Journal for the Scientific Study of Religion, 24*(4), 418. doi:10.2307/1385995

Durkheim, É. (1912). *The Elementary Forms of the Religious Life.* Retrieved from https://books.google.com/books?hl=en&lr=&id=eEk1AwAAQBAJ&pgis=1

El Ati, J., Beji, C., & Danguir, J. (1995). Increased fat oxidation during Ramadan fasting in healthy women: An adaptative mechanism for body-weight maintenance. *The American Journal of Clinical Nutrition, 62*(2), 302–307. PMID:7625336

Emmons, R. A. (2005). Striving for the sacred: Personal goals, life meaning, and religion. *The Journal of Social Issues, 61*(4), 731–745. doi:10.1111/j.1540-4560.2005.00429.x

Engel, J. F., & Roger, D. (1995). *Consumer Behavior.* New York: Holt, Rinehart and Winston.

Essoo, N., & Dibb, S. (2010). Religious influences on shopping behaviour: An exploratory study. *Journal of Marketing Management, 20*(7–8), 683–712. doi:10.1362/0267257041838728

Fam, K. S., Waller, D. S., & Erdogan, B. Z. (2004). The influence of religion on attitudes towards the advertising of controversial products. *European Journal of Marketing, 38*(5/6), 537–555. doi:10.1108/03090560410529204

Farah, M. F., & Newman, A. J. (2010). Exploring consumer boycott intelligence using a socio-cognitive approach. *Journal of Business Research, 63*(4), 347–355. doi:10.1016/j.jbusres.2009.03.019

Foxall, G. R., Goldsmith, R. E., & Brown, S. (1998). *Consumer psychology for marketing* (Vol. 1). Cengage Learning EMEA.

Geertz, C. (1973). *The interpretation of cultures: Selected essays* (Vol. 5019). Basic books.

Geyer, A. L., & Baumeister, R. F. (2005). *Religion, Morality, and Self-Control: Values.* Virtues, and Vices.

Ghorbani, N., Watson, P. J., Ghramaleki, A. F., Morris, R. J., & Hood, R. W. Jr. (2002). Muslim-Christian Religious Orientation Scales: Distinctions, Correlations, and Cross-Cultural Analysis in Iran and the United States. *The International Journal for the Psychology of Religion, 12*(2), 69–91. doi:10.1207/S15327582IJPR1202_01

Glock, C. Y. (1962). *On the study of religious commitment.* Academic Press.

Gorsuch, R. L., & McPherson, S. E. (1989). Intrinsic/extrinsic measurement: I/E-revised and single-item scales. *Journal for the Scientific Study of Religion, 28*(3), 348–354. doi:10.2307/1386745

Gough, H. G. (1951). Studies of social intolerance: I. Some psychological and sociological correlates of anti-Semitism. *The Journal of Social Psychology, 33*(2), 237–246. doi:10.1080/00224545.1951.9921815

Grover, V., & Purvis, R. (2011). R Esearch a Rticle T Echnostress : T Echnological a Ntecedents. *Management Information Systems Quarterly, 35*(4), 831–858.

Guthrie, S., Agassi, J., Andriolo, K. R., Buchdahl, D., Earhart, H. B., Greenberg, M., & Sharpe, K. J. et al. (1980). A cognitive theory of religion. *Current Anthropology, 21*(2), 181–203. doi:10.1086/202429

Hannah, S. T., Avolio, B. J., & May, D. R. (2011). Moral maturation and moral conation: A capacity approach to explaining moral thought and action. *Academy of Management Review, 36*(4), 663–685. doi:10.5465/amr.2010.0128

Harper, J. (2012). *84 percent of the world population has faith: a third are Christian.* Retrieved January 4, 2017, from http://www.washingtontimes.com/blog/watercooler/2012/dec/23/84-percent-world-population-has-faith-third-are-ch/

Himmelfarb, H. S. (1975). Measuring religious involvement. *Social Forces, 53*(4), 606–618. doi:10.1093/sf/53.4.606

Hirschman, E. (1981). American Jewish Ethnicity: Its Relationship to Some Selected Aspects of Consumer Behavior. *Journal of Marketing, 45*(3), 102. doi:10.2307/1251545

Hirschman, E. C. (1983a). *Cognitive structure across consumer ethnic subcultures: A comparative analysis* (Vol. 10). NA-Advances in Consumer Research.

Hirschman, E. C. (1983b). Religious affiliation and consumption processes: An initial paradigm. *Research in Marketing, 6,* 131–170.

Hood, R. W. Jr. (1970). Religious orientation and the report of religious experience. *Journal for the Scientific Study of Religion, 9*(4), 285–291. doi:10.2307/1384573

Hood, R. W. Jr, Hill, P. C., & Spilka, B. (2009). *The psychology of religion: An empirical approach.* Guilford Press.

Huffman, T. E. (1988). *In the world but not of the world: Religiosity, alienation, and philosophy of human nature among Bible college and liberal arts college students.* Academic Press.

Ji, C.-H. C., & Ibrahim, Y. (2007). Islamic Doctrinal Orthodoxy and Religious Orientations: Scale Development and Validation. *The International Journal for the Psychology of Religion, 17*(3), 189–208. doi:10.1080/10508610701402192

Johnson, B. R., Jang, S. J., Larson, D. B., & De Li, S. (2001). Does adolescent religious commitment matter? A reexamination of the effects of religiosity on delinquency. *Journal of Research in Crime and Delinquency, 38*(1), 22–44. doi:10.1177/0022427801038001002

Johnston, A. C., Warkentin, M., & Siponen, M. (2015). an Enhanced Fear Appeal Rhetorical Framework: Leveraging Threats To the Human Asset Through Sanctioning Rhetoric 1. *Management Information Systems Quarterly, 39*(1), 113–134. doi:10.25300/MISQ/2015/39.1.06

Keng, K. A., & Yang, C. (1993). Value choice, demographics, and life satisfaction. *Psychology and Marketing, 10*(5), 413–432. doi:10.1002/mar.4220100505

Khraim, H. (2010). Measuring religiosity in consumer research from an Islamic perspective. *Journal of Economic & Administrative Sciences, 26*(1), 52–79. doi:10.1108/10264116201000003

King, M. B., & Hunt, R. A. (1972). Measuring the religious variable: Replication. *Journal for the Scientific Study of Religion*, *11*(3), 240–251. doi:10.2307/1384548

Kirlappos, I., Parkin, S., & Sasse, M. A. (2014). *Learning from "Shadow Security": Why understanding non-compliance provides the basis for effective security*. Academic Press.

Kirlappos, I., & Sasse, M. A. (2012). Security education against phishing: A modest proposal for a major rethink. *IEEE Security and Privacy*, *10*(2), 24–32. doi:10.1109/MSP.2011.179

Kohlberg, L. (1981). *The meaning and measurement of moral development*. Clark Univ Heinz Werner Inst.

LaRose, R., & Eastin, M. S. (2004). A social cognitive theory of Internet uses and gratifications: Toward a new model of media attendance. *Journal of Broadcasting & Electronic Media*, *48*(3), 358–377. doi:10.1207/s15506878jobem4803_2

Laufer, A., & Solomon, Z. (2011). The Role of Religious Orientations in Youth's Posttraumatic Symptoms After Exposure to Terror. *Journal of Religion and Health*, *50*(3), 687–699. doi:10.1007/s10943-009-9270-x PMID:19672716

Lee, D.-J., Ahn, J.-H., & Bang, Y. (2011). Managing Consumer Privacy Concerns in Personalization: A Strategic Analysis of Privacy Protection. *Management Information Systems Quarterly*, *35*(2), 423–A8. Retrieved from http://search.ebscohost.com/login.aspx?direct=true&db=bth&AN=60461925&site=ehost-live%5Cnhttp://content.ebscohost.com/ContentServer.asp?T=P&P=AN&K=60461925&S=R&D=bth&EbscoContent=dGJyMNXb4kSeqLc4v+bwOLCmr02eprNSr6q4SrSWxWXS&ContentCustomer=dGJyMPGps0i2q7J

Li, X.-B., & Sarkar, S. (2006). Privacy protection in data mining: A perturbation approach for categorical data. *Information Systems Research*, *17*(3), 254–270. doi:10.1287/isre.1060.0095

Magill, G. (1992). Theology in business ethics: Appealing to the religious imagination. *Journal of Business Ethics*, *11*(2), 129–135. doi:10.1007/BF00872320

McDaniel, S. W., & Burnett, J. J. (1990). Consumer religiosity and retail store evaluative criteria. *Journal of the Academy of Marketing Science*, *18*(2), 101–112. doi:10.1007/BF02726426

McFarland, S. (1984). Psychology of religion: A call for a broader paradigm. *The American Psychologist*, *39*(3), 321–324. doi:10.1037/0003-066X.39.3.321

Mekovec, R., & Hutinski, Ž. (2012). The role of perceived privacy and perceived security in online market. *MIPRO, 2012 Proceedings of the 35th International Convention*, 1883–1888.

Miller, A. S., & Hoffmann, J. P. (1995). Risk and Religion: An Explanation of Gender Differences in Religiosity. *Journal for the Scientific Study of Religion*, *34*(1), 63. doi:10.2307/1386523

Muhamad, N., & Mizerski, D. (2013). The effects of following islam in decisions about taboo products. *Psychology and Marketing*, *30*(4), 357–371. doi:10.1002/mar.20611

Mukhtar, A., & Butt, M. M. (2012). Intention to choose Halal products: The role of religiosity. *Journal of Islamic Marketing*, *3*(2), 108–120. doi:10.1108/17590831211232519

Muncy, J. A., & Vitell, S. J. (1992). Consumer ethics: An investigation of the ethical beliefs of the final consumer. *Journal of Business Research, 24*(4), 297–311. doi:10.1016/0148-2963(92)90036-B

Nydell, M. K. (2011). *Understanding Arabs: A guide for modern times*. Intercultural Press.

O'connell, B. J. (1975). Dimensions of religiosity among Catholics. *Review of Religious Research, 16*(3), 198–207. doi:10.2307/3510357

Pargament, K. I. (1992). Of Means and Ends: Religion and the Search for Significance. *The International Journal for the Psychology of Religion, 2*(4), 201–229. doi:10.1207/s15327582ijpr0204_1

Posey, C., Roberts, T., Lowry, P., Bennett, R. J., & Courtney, J. F. (2013). Insiders' protection of organizational information assets: Development of a systematics-based taxonomy and theory of diversity. *Management Information Systems Quarterly, 37*(4), 1189–1210. doi:10.25300/MISQ/2013/37.4.09

Putrevu, S., & Swimberghek, K. (2013). The influence of religiosity on consumer ethical judgments and responses toward sexual appeals. *Journal of Business Ethics, 115*(2), 351–365. doi:10.1007/s10551-012-1399-y

Quelch, J. A. (2001). *Cases in strategic marketing management: business strategies in Muslim countries*. Prentice Hall.

Ranck, J. G. (1961). Religious conservatism-liberalism and mental health. *Pastoral Psychology, 12*(2), 34–40. doi:10.1007/BF01784757

Rest, J. R. (1986). *Moral development: Advances in research and theory*. Praeger. Retrieved January 7, 2017, from https://books.google.co.uk/books?id=YDB-AAAAMAAJ

Rockeach, M. (1960). *The open and closed mind. Investigations into the nature of belief systems and personality systems*. New York: Basic Books. Actualidades en Psicología.

Roky, R., Houti, I., Moussamih, S., Qotbi, S., & Aadil, N. (2004). Physiological and chronobiological changes during Ramadan intermittent fasting. *Annals of Nutrition & Metabolism, 48*(4), 296–303. doi:10.1159/000081076 PMID:15452402

Roof, W. C. (1980). The Ambiguities of" Religious Preference" in Survey Research-A Methodological Note. *Public Opinion Quarterly, 44*(3), 403–407. doi:10.1086/268607

Samovar, L. A., Porter, R. E., McDaniel, E. R., & Roy, C. S. (2015). *Communication between cultures*. Nelson Education.

Schaefer, C. A., & Gorsuch, R. L. (1991). Psychological adjustment and religiousness: The multivariate belief-motivation theory of religiousness. *Journal for the Scientific Study of Religion, 30*(4), 448–461. doi:10.2307/1387279

Schanzer, J., & Miller, S. (2012). *Facebook Fatwa: Saudi Clerics*. Wahhabi Islam, and Social Media.

Schneider, H., Krieger, J., & Bayraktar, A. (2011). The Impact of Intrinsic Religiosity on Consumers' Ethical Beliefs: Does It Depend on the Type of Religion? A Comparison of Christian and Moslem Consumers in Germany and Turkey. *Journal of Business Ethics, 102*(2), 319–332. doi:10.1007/s10551-011-0816-y

Schwartz, S. H., & Huismans, S. (1995). Value Priorities and Religiosity in Four Western Religions. *Social Psychology Quarterly, 58*(2), 88–107. doi:10.2307/2787148

Siponen, M., & Vance, A. (2010). Neutralizaiton: New Insights into the Problem of Employee Information Systems Security. *Management Information Systems Quarterly, 34*(3), 487–502.

Slater, E. (1947). Neurosis and religious affiliation. *The British Journal of Psychiatry, 93*(391), 392–396. doi:10.1192/bjp.93.391.392 PMID:20265904

Slater, W., Hall, T. W., & Edwards, K. J. (2001). Measuring religion and spirituality: Where are we and where are we going? *Journal of Psychology and Theology, 29*(1), 4.

Smith, C. B., Weigert, A. J., & Thomas, D. L. (1979). Self-esteem and religiosity: An analysis of Catholic adolescents from five cultures. *Journal for the Scientific Study of Religion, 18*(1), 51–60. doi:10.2307/1385378

Smith, H. J., Dinev, T., & Xu, H. (2011). Theory and Review Information Privacy Research: An Interdisciplinary Review 1. *MIS QuarterlyInformation Privacy Research, 35*(4), 989–1015. doi:10.1126/science.1103618

Smith, S. (2010). Circuits of power: A study of mandated compliance to an information systems security de jure standard in a government organization. *MIS Quarterly, 34*(3), 463–486.

Sood, J., & Nasu, Y. (1995). Religiosity and nationality. An exploratory study of their effect on consumer behavior in Japan and the United States. *Journal of Business Research, 34*(1), 1–9. doi:10.1016/0148-2963(94)00015-7

Spears, J., & Barki, H. (2010). User participation in information systems security risk management. *Management Information Systems Quarterly, 34*(3), 503–522. doi:10.2337/dc10-0368

Stark, R., & Glock, C. Y. (1968). *American piety: The nature of religious commitment* (Vol. 1). Univ of California Press.

Stouffer, S. A. (1955). *Communism, conformity, and civil liberties: A cross-section of the nation speaks its mind.* Transaction Publishers.

Sutanto, J., Palme, E., Tan, C.-H., & Phang, C. W. (2013). Addressing the Personalization-Privacy Paradox: An Empirical Assessment on Smartphone Users. *Management Information Systems Quarterly, 37*(4), 1141–A5. doi:10.25300/MISQ/2013/37.4.07

Swimberghe, K., Flurry, L. A., & Parker, J. M. (2011). Consumer Religiosity: Consequences for Consumer Activism in the United States. *Journal of Business Ethics, 103*(3), 453–467. doi:10.1007/s10551-011-0873-2

Taai, N. M. (1985). *Religious Behavior Scale.* Arrobyaan Publishing.

Tarakeshwar, N., Stanton, J., & Pargament, K. I. (2003). Religion: An overlooked dimension in cross-cultural psychology. *Journal of Cross-Cultural Psychology, 34*(1), 377–394. doi:10.1177/0022022103034004001

Tate, E. D., & Miller, G. R. (1971). Differences in value systems of persons with varying religious orientations. *Journal for the Scientific Study of Religion, 10*(4), 357–365. doi:10.2307/1384781

Thompson, H., & Raine, J. (1976). Religious denomination preference as a basis for store location. *Journal of Retailing, 52*(2), 71–78.

Tillich, P. (2001). *Dynamics of faith* (Vol. 577). Zondervan.

Venkatesh, V., Morris, M. G., Davis, G. B., & Davis, F. D. (2003). User acceptance of information technology: Toward a unified view. *Management Information Systems Quarterly, 27*(3), 425–478. doi:10.2307/30036540

Venkatesh, V., Thong, J. Y. L., & Xu, X. (2012). Consumer Acceptance and Use of Information Technology : Extending the Unified Theory. *Management Information Systems Quarterly, 36*(1), 157–178.

Vitell, S. J. (2009). The role of religiosity in business and consumer ethics: A review of the literature. *Journal of Business Ethics, 90*(S2), 155–167. doi:10.1007/s10551-010-0382-8

Vitell, S. J., & Paolillo, J. G. P. (2003). Consumer Ethics: The Role of Religiosity. *Journal of Business Ethics, 46*(2), 151–162. doi:10.1023/A:1025081005272

Vladlena, B., Saridakis, G., Tennakoon, H., & Ezingeard, J. N. (2015). The role of security notices and online consumer behaviour: An empirical study of social networking users. *International Journal of Human-Computer Studies, 80*, 36–44. doi:10.1016/j.ijhcs.2015.03.004

Wang, J., Gupta, M., & Rao, H. R. (2015). Insider Threats in a Financial Institution: Analysis of Attack-Proneness of Information Systems Applications. *Management Information Systems Quarterly, 39*(1), 91–U491. doi:10.25300/MISQ/2015/39.1.05

Weaver, G. R. (2002). Religiosity and Ethical Behavior in Organizations : A Symbolic Interactionist Perspective. *Academy of Management Review, 27*(1), 77–97.

Weaver, G. R., & Agle, B. R. (2002). Religiosity and ethical behavior in organizations: A symbolic interactionist perspective. *Academy of Management Review, 27*(1), 77–97.

Welch, K. W. (1981). An interpersonal influence model of traditional religious commitment. *The Sociological Quarterly, 22*(1), 81–92. doi:10.1111/j.1533-8525.1981.tb02210.x

Westin, A. F. (1968). Privacy and freedom. *Washington and Lee Law Review, 25*(1), 166.

Wiebe, K. F., & Fleck, J. R. (1980). Personality Correlates of Intrinsic, Extrinsic, and Nonreligious Orientations. *The Journal of Psychology, 105*(2), 181–187. doi:10.1080/00223980.1980.9915149

Wilde, A., & Joseph, S. (1997). Religiosity and personality in a Moslem context. *Personality and Individual Differences, 23*(5), 899–900. doi:10.1016/S0191-8869(97)00098-6

Wilkes, R. E., Burnett, J. J., & Howell, R. D. (1986). On the meaning and measurement of religiosity in consumer research. *Journal of the Academy of Marketing Science, 14*(1), 47–56. doi:10.1007/BF02722112

Chapter 11
Groups Online:
Hacktivism and Social Protest

Helen Thackray
Bournemouth University, UK

John McAlaney
Bournemouth University, UK

ABSTRACT

This chapter provides a brief introduction to hacktivism and social protest online and highlights some of the socio-psychological and cognitive factors that can lead to individuals taking part in hacktivism groups. Hacktivism is an ill-defined area which some claim as a legitimate form of protest in the online world and others regard as illegal hacking; there is truth to both arguments, and those who believe it should be protected will continue to work for it to be recognised. The chapter explains how the depth of social ties and influence are still being examined, and whilst cognitive biases are recognised, strategies to mitigate and combat the vulnerability they present are still being developed.

INTRODUCTION

The internet is a significant aspect of global social change, and has greatly altered the nature of collective action and social movements (Jensen, 2015, Postmes & Brunsting, 2002). Hacktivism, a term combining 'hacking' and 'activism', is the use of various computer hacking tactics for political, social, and ideological motivations; hacktivists use nonviolent but often illegal digital tools to achieve these goals (Hampson, 2012, Krapp, 2005, Solomon, 2017). The common methods of hacktivism include defacing websites, using DDoS attacks, and other types of internet disruption (see Table 2, Hanna et al, 2016). The use of these tactics has led to challenges in distinguishing between hacktivism and hacking, as it can be that only the individuals' motivation is different. This chapter will discuss the current understanding and context surrounding hacktivism, before examining the cognitive and social psychological factors that can influence those involved in hacktivism and online social protest.

DOI: 10.4018/978-1-5225-4053-3.ch011

BACKGROUND

It is important to remember that cybersecurity incidents occur within a social context; even if it is not face to face, online interactions fulfil and rely on the same social or task needs as offline interaction with others (McKenna & Green, 2002). There remains, however, a lack of insight into the influence of psychological factors and social norms online, especially in the case of hacktivism. All actors within cybersecurity incidents interact with each other and within each group. Whilst hacktivism is regarded as a contested area, stuck between definitions of justified civil action and illegal hacking, there remains a strong need to challenge the stereotypes around it. The conflation of the terms "hacker" and "hacktivist", with "cybercriminal" and "cyberterrorist" adds to the confusion surrounding the different typologies identified (see Table 1). A divisive and complex issue, there are many governments and businesses see hacktivism as a threat, akin to cyber-terrorism and cybercrime (Drucker & Gumpert, 2000, Kubitschko, 2015, Manion & Goodrum, 2000, Shaw, 2006); others argue that social protest and change have always been a part of society (Scheuerman, 2016, Schrock, 2016), and that hacktivism is the progression of social protest (Kubitschko, 2015, Postill, 2014, Solomon, 2017).

Hacktivism is not a 21st century addition to the internet. The origins lie in computer based activism as early as the mid-1980s (Wray, 1998). One of the first known instances of a DDoS attack occurred in 1995, when a group of Italian artists blocked websites of the French government, in protest of the decision to undertake a series of nuclear tests (Milan & Atton, 2015). Hacktivism was not, however, a well-known phenomenon until the mid to late 2000s. One of the more predominant groups, Anonymous, began to use media attention as part of their strategy; previously activist groups had preferred to remain undetected in order to protect their projects from law enforcement (Milan & Atton, 2015). As such Anonymous is probably the most widely known hacktivist group by the general population.

Since the mid-1990s the continued rise of hacktivism has surprised and worried many; but its' growth in popularity can be attributed to several reasons. The ease of contributing from one's home or place of choice means that distance is no longer an issue in supporting a cause, even if it is quite literally the other side of the world. Hacktivism also comes with a lower level of risk when compared to physical public demonstrations, whilst still allowing their messages and protests to be seen by the public across the internet – although this is not to say that it is risk free as some once perceived it to be (see cognitive

Table 1. Key terms

(Computer) Hacker	One with the ability to access a computer or system without admission (Raymond, 1996).
Hacktivism	A method to express dissatisfaction with elements of political and social reality using online resources (Milan & Atton, 2015).
Slacktivism	Critical term for low-profile online activism, such as signing petitions and using online badges (Hanna et al, 2016).
Whistle-blowing	The leaking of confidential information to the public as a form of raising awareness about a contentious issue (Hanna et al, 2016).
Cybercriminal	A criminal who uses a computer or network to commit the crime (Anderson et al, 2013, Halder & Jaishankar, 2011, Moore, 2005, NCA, 2016).
Cyberterrorist	One who uses computer/network technology to terrorise opponents to further political or social objectives (Rogers, 2003).
Cyber delinquent	One who engages in illegal behaviours, such as verbal violence, hacking, and illegal copying of software in online environments (Hong & Kim, 2011).

factors). For many hacktivists now, there is also the motivation that state actors and law enforcement agencies have chosen to use electronic surveillance and hacking. As such the hacktivists regard their actions as a "means of levelling the playing field" (Solomon, 2017:3).

As a community, hacktivism is itself a social identity group, an "imagined community" (Anderson, 1983, Jordan & Taylor, 1998); a socially constructed community where there is no physical or geographical connection within the group, only the strong shared choice of interest and identity. It is known that hackers and hacktivists create social groups that provide expertise, support, and training within their communities (Jordan & Taylor, 1998:757). This being the case, the social psychological processes have a strong influence on the internal group behaviours, as well as their interaction with other groups. Studies investigating unifying identity traits have emphasised that the traditional stereotypes may not be as prevalent as previously believed (Jordan, 2001, Rogers, 2010, Tanczer, 2015). Along with these communities being divided by different aims and tasks, there are also cultural divisions to be acknowledged, although it is not as clear how big an impact these differences make. Groups with different cultural backgrounds and opposing causes will still use the same hacktivist techniques. For example the Syrian Electric Army, a group that supported the Assad Syrian government in 2011, used website defacements, spamming, and electronic surveillance against their opponents, such as the Western media (Perlroth, 2013), hijacking headlines and Twitter accounts to communicate their messages.

THEN AND NOW: MASS SOCIAL MOVEMENTS

Mass social movements were historically regarded as being negatively influenced by personal elements of self-esteem or satisfaction with life. It was believed that personality attributes such as "impotence, selfishness and boredom characterised the...individuals prone to join mass movements" (Travaligno, 2014:5). In the 20th century however, with the closer study of such movements, and the growth in popularity and public support, these activities became regarded as more of a symptom that something was wrong in society (Travaligno, 2014), for example the movements for civil rights and anti-war protests in the USA. These periods emphasised the differences between the academic explanations for mass

Table 2. Common Hacktivist tactics

Denial of Service attack (DoS attack)	Using one computer and one internet connection the targeted server is overloaded by repeated requests. This makes the server unreachable to others, thus blocking the website.
Distributed Denial of Service attack (DDoS attack)	Many computers and many connections from all over the world (sometimes in botnets) are used to overwhelm the server with requests.
Site redirects	Site redirects send visitors from the target website to another website of the hacktivists choosing.
Information theft	Involves unauthorised access to a computer or network and stealing data. The illegality of information theft is unambiguous despite its wide acceptance among hacktivists (Hampson, 2012).
Site defacements	With unauthorised access to a web server the hacktivist replaces or alters the web page to convey their message. This is the most common and usually least damaging form of hacktivism (Solomon, 2017).
Viruses and malware	Viruses and other malware can be used as a means of sabotage, infiltration or even making a political statement.

social movements, and the reality that was being witnessed. These significant contributions marked the departure from classic views of masses and crowds as irrational and disorganised (Gamson, 1975; Jenkins, 1985; cited in Travaligno, 2014). In fact, there developed socio-psychological models which showed that social movements were "more likely to emerge under conditions of structural stability, social connectedness and favourable mobilisation of resources" (Travaligno, 2014:5). Protesters came to be understood as rational actors, who weighed the cost and benefit of participating in such protests.

As such, it has been assumed that those involved in social movements, including hacktivism, will be equally rational actors. Within hacktivist groups, the entry requirements no longer entail elite computing knowledge, and those wanting to participate in hacking and hacktivism now can find multiple resources in seconds through search engines; it is similarly quick and easy to download computing tools written by others. Groups like Anonymous have been proponents of such techniques, making it simpler for people to be involved, and using strength in numbers rather than a smaller group of experts. The forms of hacktivist groups are dictated by the medium used; the internet allows them to exist in a decentralised "community without structure" (Leach, 2009:1059). As such, the most common feature across different groups is a consensus-based based approach to their activities. For the most part this means that through necessity hacktivist groupings are still relatively small, and regulated by trust and loyalty (Milan & Atton, 2015).

It has been suggested that some individuals, often adolescents and young adults, become involved in the activities of groups associated with cybersecurity incidents without a clear understanding of the risks involved (Olsen, 2012, Wolfradt & Doll, 2001); therefore they have not fully understood the relationship between the cost and benefit of their involvement in the groups. This participation and subsequent arrest of adolescents and young adults has continued with events such as the TalkTalk hack (Farrell, 2016) and the hacking collective "Crackas with Attitude" (Whitehead, 2016). It is now being recognised that cybercrime is a societal issue, with the UK's National Crime Agency running campaigns to educate young people about the dangers of getting involved in cybercrime (NCA, 2016). However the confusion surrounding the internet and international law, and the fact that many laws pre-date the widespread and versatile use of the internet, means that even those wishing to remain on the side of the law when engaging in hacktivism may struggle to find relevant legislation.

Social Protest or Hacking Crime?

Social movements can be defined as broad and informal networks of interaction, that participate independently in collective action which is "motivated by a shared concern about a particular set of political issues…but not separately from governmental institutions" (Meuleman & Boushel, 2014:50). Social movement organisations refer to many different types, ranging from formal, organised institutions to the radically informal, from the local to the global (Meuleman & Boushel, 2014). This in turn requires the recognition of the cultural differences that may be present between all those involved, whether participants or targets.

It is agreed that there must be certain characteristics in order for these networks to be categorised as a social movement; Although there is a wide diversity of forms of social protest, analysis of these forms by Hanna et al (2016) suggests they have only seven functions (purposes). The purposes overlap, and an individual protest action may seek to achieve several of these purposes. Most protests involve the coordination of many activities or forms of protest and exist in a nested hierarchy as part of a wider campaign within a social movement.

Table 3. Social movement characteristics

1. Information	To distribute information to the wider public in order to raise awareness about 'the cause' or the situation that is the subject of protest.
2. Fundraising	To raise funds to support the campaign.
3. Publicity	To gain publicity (media attention) through the undertaking of actions usually having a performative dimension.
4. Mobilization	To enlist participants for a specific protest event or campaign.
5. Solidarity building	To build solidarity (unity and commitment) and a sense of worth amongst protesters and toward the protest cause in general.
6. Political pressure	To apply pressure, through direct or indirect targeting, on authorities or decision-makers regarding their action/decision on a specific issue.
7. Direct action	To cause immediate disruption to a specific project (e.g. a blockade), usually performed as acts of civil disobedience.

(Hanna et al, 2016)

Bearing this in mind, hacktivist groups can claim to meet these criteria as a social movement. When using the internet for activism, Vegh et al. (2003) suggest that are two forms— internet-based and internet-enhanced. In internet-based activism, such as hacktivism or digital sit-ins, the internet is where the protest occurs. Internet-enhanced activism however is more about the organisation of the protest than any fundamental change to the protest itself. Solomon argues that there is "in reality little distinction between hacktivism and traditional protests" (2017:11), reasoning that hacktivists state similar motivations (a political or social cause), suggesting that hacktivists view themselves as working with more traditional protesters. An example of this was during the Arab Spring in 2011, where protesters physically present in Tunisia were aided via the internet by members of Anonymous when the government blocked access to the internet (Goode, 2015).

It has also been argued that hacktivism is the progression of social protest (Kubitschko, 2015, Postill, 2014, Solomon, 2017), with protest moving from the physical world into cyberspace, as are many other traditional activities, such as shopping and banking. Some hacktivists regard their work itself as comparable to a physical sit-in protest (Jordan, 2015), with others making their protests through social media sites (Tufekci & Wilson, 2012, Valenzuela, 2013). It is suggested that there is potentially a need to protect and legitimise to some of the less controversial forms of hacktivism (Douglas et al, 2017, Solomon, 2017), acknowledging that the right to protest is protected by international human rights. There are articles which protect freedom of opinion and expression and covers developments in ICT, interpreted to 'include all forms of audio-visual as well as electronic and Internet-based modes of expression.' (UN Assembly, 1966). For this to apply to hacktivism there must be features, such as clear communication, which distinguishes this type of civil disobedience from radical protest. Douglas et al (2017) state that the civil disobedience of hacktivism must achieve the following: 1) provoke a political or social response; 2) allow that change is possible within the existing social and political structure. In this way, they argue, even a controversial tactic of a DDoS attack may be classified an act of civil obedience, despite being an illegal action, as in some cases it has the aim of communicating dissent to the public conscientious motivation.

It has been noted that hackers seem to be less motivated by their values and more by what they dislike (Madarie, 2017); the same could be observed of social media website users (Tufekci & Wilson, 2012,

Valenzuela, 2013). Whilst hacktivism is primarily committed through individual action, such as coding and hacking, these actions gain meaning in the interaction with peers (Douglas et al, 2017).

Case Study: Anonymous and Lulzsec

Possibly the most infamous hacktivist group is the one known as Anonymous. With its origins on 4chan, the group started by pranking and "trolling" other online (and offline) communities, for entertainment. Over time this evolved in to people trying to use this group activity for "good" causes. This eventually led to a division in the group; those who wanted to prank and enjoy the "lulz", and those who wanted to be "white knights" (see Coleman (2014) for more details).

As participation within Anonymous became more about political and social causes, rather than just mischief making, many of those who became involved in hacktivism cited their motivation as a desire to counteract the increase in surveillance and repression of such activities (Coleman, 2014, Douglas et al, 2017). Anonymous has used these motivations as a recruitment tactic, manipulating publicity, both negative and positive, to draw attention and support. This policy however has attracted criticism, due to the imprisonment of a number of hacktivists who took part in large operations, as well as a general lack of transparency and poor accountability from the group (Douglas et al, 2017). This is an example of the problems in hacktivism where groups, Anonymous especially, have always maintained that they do not have leaders and hierarchy (Coleman, 2014).

The hacks or "operations" carried out by Anonymous have ranged from simple pranks to serious on going campaigns. For the past few years, the name or brand has almost exclusively been used for hacktivism; those who claim Anonymous involvement in causes that do not meet the criteria have been denounced publicly, often through official Twitter accounts. This has in turn led to a lot of in fighting, as some argue that there are no leaders, therefore no one can decide who is or is not a member of Anonymous. One of the methods the group uses to monitor and control group membership is assertive speech; it is the mode of communication not the speaker that matters; therefore by using and maintaining control via social media accounts, this is how they get the message across to others. The group has also been noted for their controversial control of group identity, and have doxed individuals (revealing their real life identity and personal information), revoking their Anonymous membership (Dobusch & Schoeneborn, 2015).

Anonymous are a contentious topic; some members feel they made serious contributions to bringing hacktivism to the fore of current activism and protest, other commentator and critics feel it was a group of children and "wannabes" causing trouble, meaning the Anonymous has, at one point or another, been categorised as being relevant to all the terms in Table 1. Regardless of which argument is supported, it cannot be denied that Anonymous did draw attention and awareness to the importance of cyber-security.

Case Study: The Chaos Computer Club (CCC)

The Chaos Computer Club (CCC) is Europe's oldest and one of the world's largest hacker organizations – and they have a very different approach to Anonymous. Created via a newspaper advert in 1981, the CCC started as a loose group of individuals, but formally became a not-for profit association in 1984, with continued interactions with institutions and political organisations (Kubitschko, 2015). This active decision to remain legal in the face of "anti-hacking" government legislation is one of the most interesting elements about this group. The group describes itself as a non-governmental, non-partisan, not-for-profit, and voluntary-based club that is sustained by membership fees and donations (Kubitschko, 2015). The CCC supports the principles hacker ethic (Levy, 2010) which stresses openness, sharing, decentralization, free access to computers and world improvement, as well as advocating more transparency in government, communication as a human right (Coleman, 2011, Kubitschko, 2015, Nissenbaum, 2004).

What makes the CCC significantly different to other hacker collectives is not their political dimension but their insistence on working as a legitimately recognised collective, even if they use illegitimate methods. One of the Club's aims is to teach the public to use technological skills and bring about political change. The groups hacks include exposing flaws in financial and political areas; for example in 1984, CCC members exploited a security flaw which allowed them to transfer 135,000 Deutschmark (ca. €68,000) from a German savings bank to their own (Kubitschko, 2015). The money was transferred back immediately and the flaw reported. The group has been involved in hacks which have either been a grey are or clearly illegal; this led to a period of decline in popularity in the 1990s. Within this group there appears to be the need to continue their legitimacy within the state of Germany, which struggled when members were conflicted about the group methods. The group rejuvenated itself in the 2000s, demonstrating flaws in a voting computer system that was in use in several countries and exposing the vulnerability of biometric identity systems. In 2011 they published an analysis of a malware program in use by the German police, which was used for surveillance; this highlighted the ability for the computer to be controlled remotely, as well as able to activate the microphone or camera (Kubitschko, 2015). It is emphasised that the CCC has a reputation for expertise, which they believe needs to be brought to the established centres of power by engaging with politicians, legislators and judges, (Kubitschko, 2015), because for the CCC, hacktivism is only one part of their purpose (Coleman, 2014, Kubischko, 2015).

SOCIO-PSYCHOLOGICAL FACTORS

As with all cyber-interactions, hacktivism occurs within a social context. As more individuals become involved in online communities relating to hacktivism, more groups develop and work together, and so the growth of potential online influence over individuals strengthens. This growth, especially in regard to social and ideological motivations, has been attributed in part to the fact that there is now a generation raised that has never known the world without the technology and innovation we have now (Seebruck, 2015), with increased user generated content increasing the confidence and perception of power individuals possess.

There are those who contend that online communication loses meaning and significance in understanding, due to the lack of visual face-to-face clues and prompts (Suler, 2004); this also however allows a group identity to develop, with its own language, and norms that group participants use to signal membership (Dobusch & Schoeneborn, 2015, McKenna & Green, 2002). These are strong contributors to the formation of an online collective identity and there is still a significant amount of social information available to help users decipher meaning that is not plainly stated. Similarly, Postmes & Brunsting dispute the statement that computers damage social ties (Turkle, 1999), arguing to the contrary, that it has been observed that the Internet "strengthens existing social movements, stimulates the formation of new ones, and mobilizes sizable numbers of people for collective action," (Postmes & Brunsting, 2002:294). There are various studies on the motivations of those who engage in hacking, ranging from financial gain, prestige, curiosity (Seebruck, 2015). These however have not found to be the strongest indicator of the occurrence of participation; when it comes to hacking related involvement it is the "social motivators (i.e., peer recognition/respect and team-play) and not the personal motivators (i.e., intellectual challenge/curiosity and justice) that are relevant to the frequency of involvement" (Madarie, 2017:93).

Intergroup attribution research (Branscombe & Wann, 1994, Cialdini et al, 1976, Hewstone & Jaspars, 1982, Ho & Lloyd, 1982, Tarrant & North, 2004) has shown that the achievements of group actions can strengthen individual members' beliefs that their group and members are highly skilled. It can also lead group members to attribute the success of opposing groups to external circumstances and luck. This has been thought to encourage online groups to carry out additional actions in hacktivism and against other cyber adversarial groups, especially if the group identity is reinforced, either by the actions involved (combining tactics shown in Tables 2 & 3) or by the subsequent media reporting. It has been observed that early news reports about Anonymous generally exaggerated the cohesiveness between members and the organisational structure of the group (Olson, 2012), which has then contributed to the group becoming more cohesive and organised.

The cohesiveness of newer hacking collectives was affected in 2012 by the exposure of a high profile member of Lulzsec, Sabu, as having been an informant for the FBI. His information led to the arrests of prominent group members in the USA, the UK and Ireland. There have been significant changes to the group behaviours since (Coleman, 2015), with greater antipathy of 'leader-fags', or those wanting to take charge, suspicion of new or unknown members, and of any one who seems to be desiring attention. This is despite repeated claims from groups such as Anonymous that they do not have an official leader or hierarchy (Coleman, 2014). This may or may not be the case, but regardless it is relevant that many members of such collectives believe this to be true, which potentially leaves them open to manipulation. After all, the creation of the internet was heavily influenced by those who wished to see technology move towards a "decentralised, and non-hierarchical version of society," (Rosenzweig, 1998:1552), and so those that follow these ideals may prefer to believe that a non-hierarchy has been achieved, a form of confirmation bias. It cannot be assumed that there is a complete lack of hierarchy in these communities, as there are obvious examples, especially in forums or Internet-Relay Chat (IRC) channels where it is necessary for administrators to moderate the content submitted by users (Dupont et al, 2016, Uitermark, 2016).

Another social element within these communities is the behavioural consequences of trust. Trusting behaviour requires the individual to relinquish control over valuable outcomes with the expectation that the other will reciprocate. On the internet many will openly talk about not trusting others, as there is no way to verify claims. Within hacktivism however, it has been shown that group membership is a strong predictor of trusting behaviour (Tanis & Postmes, 2005). Therefore, those who join a particular group or share a hacktivist identity are more inclined to trust other group members with no other influencing factor. Generalised trust is also believed to make a person more willing to engage in collective efforts and cooperate with other people (Sturgis et al, 2012, Van Lange, 2015), thereby encouraging individuals to take part in hacktivist tactics (see Table 2).

Online disinhibition effect is the removal or reduction of the social and psychological restraints that individuals experience in everyday face to face interaction (Suler, 2004, Hu et al, 2015, Joinson, 2007, Lapidot-Lefler & Barak, 2015). It could be argued that anonymity and online disinhibition can be positive, allowing the internet to be an open place where individuals can be honest on subjects that they may otherwise not wish to be identified with (McKenna & Green, 2002). This privacy combined with openness is what many involved in hacking and hacktivism claim to want to protect (Levy, 2010).

Within investigations into the elements that predict involvement or carrying out hacktivist actions, there is often a heavy focus on adolescents (Harris-McKoy & Cui, 2013, Wilcox et al, 2003, Wright et al, 2015). Unsurprisingly, one of the strongest factors predicting the change of cyber delinquency in young people was the amount of computer use (Wilcox et al, 2003, Wright, et al, 2015). This, combined with further studies, has led some to claim that there is a parental responsibility that needs to be acknowledged; a study in Korea concluded that to avoid computer delinquency parents should take responsibility for educating their children about the negative outcomes of illegal or criminal behaviours (Harris-McKoy & Cui, 2013). This is similar to an awareness raising campaign launched by the NCA (2015) in the UK, urging parents to be conscious of what their children might be doing online, and being aware of the legality of their actions.

Such studies as Harris-McKoy and Cui (2013) also highlight the importance of considering cultural differences and approaches. There has been a trend to place more importance on cognitive factors, looking at the cognitive influence on individual perception of risk, which has meant that cultural and social influences are sometimes neglected. The Cultural Theory of Risk however explains that social structures are associated with individual perceptions of societal dangers. Depending on the community and social structures people are used to and the values and social norms they have been taught, people understand risks differently. This means that the values of certain social or cultural contexts shape the individual's perception and evaluation of risks (Rippl, 2002). For example, at a higher level, Eastern cultures stress group solidarity and relationships with other people; Western cultures emphasize the self and autonomy (Wright et al, 2015). The extent to which this is evident in hacking groups is still not known but it must be considered as a factor.

Groupthink is another significant offline group phenomenon must be considered in the online group context (Packer, 2009). Janis (1972) defines groupthink as the psychological drive for consensus at any cost that suppresses is agreement and prevents the appraisal of alternatives in cohesive decision-making groups. He also identified the symptoms of Groupthink, which transpire when a group tries to make decisions. These include the illusion of invulnerability; collective rationalisation; stereotyped views of different groups; group pressure to conform; and self-censorship (Janis, 1972). Although groupthink does not always occur, it is more common when the groups are highly cohesive, especially in high-pressure situations. When there is pressure for agreement it has been found that group members can be more vulnerable to inaccurate and irrational thinking; as such decisions formed by groupthink have reduced probability of attaining successful outcomes (Janis, 1972). This has been seen in some hacktivist attempts, such as the manipulation of individuals to download and use software for DDoS attacks (The Paypal 14, see Coleman, 2014), with little information given and reassurance from other group members that this was a good and constructive action to take for the benefit of their cause. In the case of the PayPal 14, the individuals were later arrested and prosecuted by the US government (Coleman, 2014).

COGNITIVE FACTORS

As the significance of psychology becomes more widely acknowledged within the fields of computing and security, the cognitive factors influencing human behaviour must be re-examined. There are a number of acknowledged biases and heuristics that affect how individuals perceive and understand their surroundings. This section will discuss some of the more common ones that influence decision making and judgement.

There have been many concerns as computing and technology advanced that the "overuse of computers may have a deleterious effect on cognitive functioning" (Vujic, 2017:152). Theoretical-based predictions have so far supported the view that computer and Internet use can have a negative impact on short-term memory processing and sustained attention (Vujic, 2017). This has spread to the public perception that internet and computer use impair cognitive abilities, and encourage "lazy" patterns of thinking, particularly affecting memory and concentration (Nasi & Koivusilta, 2013). It has been identified that "the quality of computer use may be just as important as the measuring the quantity of computer use" (Vujic, 2017:159). This suggests that those who use computers over long periods of time daily are at greater risk of greater biased cognition, as well as lower attention (Tsohou et al, 2015, Vujic, 2017).

There have however also been studies that suggest evidence of a positive relationship between interactive computer use and cognitive performance (Small et al, 2009, Tun & Lachman, 2010, Vujic, 2017). Comparing a computer/internet "savvy" group and a net "naïve" group, the results revealed the internet "savvy" individuals experienced double the activity increase in the areas of the brain associated with complex reasoning, decision making and visual processing (Small et al., 2009). One explanation for these differences was the concept different "systems" of processing information. The first "System 1" or "bottom-up" is theorised to be automatic, unconscious, heuristic responses with minimal resources; "System 2" or "top-down" is considered resource-intensive and attention driven (Evans, 2003, Slovic et al, 2002, Vujic, 2017), requiring more mental effort, which is harder to sustain.

When it comes decision making and judgements, individuals have been found to over-rely on heuristics such as such as availability, and anchoring, therefore using simplified strategies to make choices (Tversky, 1972), without recognising the bias. The availability heuristic implies that in any decision-making process, easily remembered information is given greater weight by decision makers. In this way, recent events and vivid memories are given more importance by the individuals or groups as they are easier to recall (Tsohou et al, 2015), which allows potentially inaccurate information to be the basis of their decision. In a numerical comparison, anchoring is when an individual's numerical estimate is influenced toward an arbitrary value. Final estimations are strongly swayed by the initial value provided, making it easier to manipulate individuals when giving them initial information (Tsohou et al, 2015).

The affect heuristic is when an individual makes judgments and decisions quickly based on their emotional impressions. A common outcome of the affect heuristic is that people tend to underestimate risks and costs connected with things they like, and overestimate the risks and costs when they are related to things they dislike (Tsohou et al, 2015). Similarly, confirmation bias is where people tend to seek information that is consistent with their current hypothesis and are unlikely to seek information expected to be inconsistent with it (Chapman and Johnson, 2002, Tsohou et al, 2015). This is sometimes seen in social movement behaviours (see Table 3), where members will not look for external sources of information, trusting the other group members (as per generalised trust). Confirmation bias is considered to be one of the most prominent biases affecting decision making (Kahneman et al., 2011).

These attributes and biases are present in hacktivist groups, with many accounts from Anonymous members or former members having examples of optimism bias. Optimism bias leads individuals have a consistent tendency to believe that they are less at risk of experiencing a negative event themselves compared to others (Tsohou et al, 2015), therefore even if they did take part in an illegal activity they would be at less risk of being tracked by law enforcement agencies. This has been disproved through the arrests of those involved in Lulzsec, the PayPal 14, the TalkTalk hack, and Crackas with Attitude (Coleman, 2014, Farrell, 2016, Olsen, 2012, Whitehead, 2016). When recounting their individual experiences within the groups, the individuals stated that they were aware of the risk, aware that they were carrying out illegal actions but felt that they would not be caught, in part because they were aware of the risk and "it wouldn't happen to them" (Olsen, 2012, Coleman, 2014).

CONCLUSION

This chapter has provided a brief introduction to hacktivism and social protest online, and highlighted some of the socio-psychological and cognitive factors that can lead to individuals taking part in hacktivism groups. As stated, hacktivism is an ill-defined area which some people claim as a legitimate form of protest in the online world, and others regard as illegal hacking; there is truth to both arguments. Those who believe it should be protected will continue to work for it to be recognised. In terms of further study this area has a lot of potential for future research. The depth of social ties and influence is still being examined; and whilst cognitive biases are recognised, strategies to mitigate and combat the vulnerability they present are still being developed. What is clear from many studies and examples is that hackers are often skilled and intelligent individuals, who can offer a lot of knowledge and information. As the world continues to become more integrated with the online world, their knowledge and skill becomes even more valuable. The policies and laws that govern the internet need to be made with a greater awareness of the online world, and steps should be taken to protect the internet as the free, open and invaluable resource that it is.

REFERENCES

Anderson, B. (1983). *Imagined communities: Reflections on the origin and spread of nationalism*. London: Verso.

Anderson, R., Barton, C., Böhme, R., Clayton, R., Van Eeten, M. J., Levi, M., & Savage, S. (2013). Measuring the cost of cybercrime. In *The economics of information security and privacy* (pp. 265–300). Berlin: Springer. doi:10.1007/978-3-642-39498-0_12

Bae, S. M. (2017). The influence of strain factors, social control factors, self-control and computer use on adolescent cyber delinquency: Korean National Panel Study. *Children and Youth Services Review*, *78*, 74–80. doi:10.1016/j.childyouth.2017.05.008

Benjamin, V., Zhang, B., Nunamaker, J. F. Jr, & Chen, H. (2016). Examining Hacker Participation Length in Cybercriminal Internet-Relay-Chat Communities. *Journal of Management Information Systems*, *33*(2), 482–510. doi:10.1080/07421222.2016.1205918

Branscombe, N. R., & Wann, D. L. (1994). Collective self-esteem consequences of outgroup derogation when a valued social identity is on trial. *European Journal of Social Psychology*, *24*(6), 641–657. doi:10.1002/ejsp.2420240603

Cialdini, R. B., Borden, R. J., Thorne, A., Walker, M. R., Freeman, S., & Sloan, L. R. (1976). Basking in reflected glory: Three (football) field studies. *Journal of Personality and Social Psychology*, *34*(3), 366–375. doi:10.1037/0022-3514.34.3.366

Clough, J. (2010). Principles of Cybercrime. Cambridge University Press. doi:10.1017/CBO9780511845123

Coleman, G. (2011). Hacker politics and publics. *Public Culture, 23*(65), 511-516.

Coleman, G. (2014). *Hacker, hoaxer, whistleblower, spy: The Many Faces of Anonymous*. London: Verso.

Coleman, G. (2015). Epilogue: The State of Anonymous. In *Hacker, hoaxer, whistleblower, spy: The Many Faces of Anonymous* (pp. 401–461). London: Verso.

Dobusch, L., & Schoeneborn, D. (2015). Fluidity, Identity, and Organizationality: The Communicative Constitution of Anonymous. *Journal of Management Studies, 52*(8), 1005–1035. doi:10.1111/joms.12139

Douglas, D., Santanna, J.J., de Oliveira Schmidt, R., Granville, L.Z., & Pras, A. (2017). Booters: Can Anything Justify Distributed Denial-of-Service (DDoS) Attacks for Hire? *Journal of Information, Communication and Ethics in Society, 15*(1).

Drucker, S., & Gumpert, G. (2000). Cybercrime and punishment. *Critical Studies in Media Communication, 17*(2), 133–158. doi:10.1080/15295030009388387

Dupont, B., Côté, A., Savine, C., & Décary-Hétu, D. (2016). The ecology of trust among hackers. *Global Crime, 17*(2), 129–151. doi:10.1080/17440572.2016.1157480

Evans, J. S. B. (2003). In two minds: Dual-process accounts of reasoning. *Trends in Cognitive Sciences, 7*(10), 454–459. doi:10.1016/j.tics.2003.08.012 PMID:14550493

Farrell, S. (2016). TalkTalk counts costs of cyber-attack. *The Guardian*. Retrieved from https://www.theguardian.com/business/2016/feb/02/talktalk-cyberattack-costs-customers-leave accessed 24/09/16

Festinger, L. (1950). Informal social communication. *Psychological Review, 57*(5), 271–282. doi:10.1037/h0056932 PMID:14776174

Goode, L. (2015). Anonymous and the political ethos of hacktivism. *Popular Communication, 13*(1), 74–86. doi:10.1080/15405702.2014.978000

Halder, D., & Jaishankar, K. (2011). *Cyber crime and the Victimization of Women: Laws, Rights, and Regulations*. Hershey, PA: IGI Global.

Hampson, N. C. (2012). Hacktivism: A new breed of protest in a networked world. *BC Int'l & Comp. L. Rev., 35*, 511.

Hanna, P., Vanclay, F., Langdon, E. J., & Arts, J. (2016). Conceptualizing social protest and the significance of protest actions to large projects. *The Extractive Industries and Society, 3*(1), 217–239. doi:10.1016/j.exis.2015.10.006

Harris-McKoy, D., & Cui, M. (2013). Parental control, adolescent delinquency, and young adult criminal behavior. *Journal of Child and Family Studies, 22*(6), 836–843. doi:10.1007/s10826-012-9641-x

Hewstone, M., & Jaspars, J. M. F. (1982). Intergroup relations and attribution processes. In H. Tajfel (Ed.), *Social Identity and Intergroup Relations* (pp. 99–133). Cambridge, UK: Cambridge University Press.

Ho, R., & Lloyd, J. I. (1983). Intergroup attribution: The role of social categories in causal attribution for behaviour. *Australian Journal of Psychology, 35*(1), 49–59. doi:10.1080/00049538308255302

Hu, C., Zhao, L., & Huang, J. (2015). Achieving self-congruency? Examining why individuals reconstruct their virtual identity in communities of interest established within social network platforms. *Computers in Human Behavior, 50*, 465–475. doi:10.1016/j.chb.2015.04.027

Janis, I. L. (1972). *Victims of Groupthink*. New York: Houghton Mifflin.

Jensen, E. T. (2015). Cyber sovereignty: The way ahead. *Tex. Int'l LJ, 50*, 275.

Joinson, A. N. (2007). Disinhibition and the Internet. In J. Gackenbach (Ed.), *Psychology and the Internet: Intrapersonal, interpersonal, and transpersonal implications* (2nd ed.; pp. 75–92). San Diego, CA: Academic Press. doi:10.1016/B978-012369425-6/50023-0

Jordan, T. (2001). Mapping hacktivism: Mass virtual direct action (MVDA), individual virtual direct action (IVDA) and cyber-wars. *Computer Fraud & Security, 4*(4), 8–11. doi:10.1016/S1361-3723(01)00416-X

Jordan, T., & Taylor, P. (1998). A sociology of hackers. *The Sociological Review, 46*(4), 757–780. doi:10.1111/1467-954X.00139

Krapp, P. (2005). Terror and play; or what was hacktivism? *Grey Room MIT Press, 21*, 70–93. doi:10.1162/152638105774539770

Kubitschko, S. (2015). Hackers' media practices: Demonstrating and articulating expertise as interlocking arrangements. *Convergence, 21*(3), 388–402. doi:10.1177/1354856515579847

Lapidot-Lefler, N., & Barak, A. (2015). The benign online disinhibition effect: Could situational factors induce self-disclosure and prosocial behaviors? *Cyberpsychology: Journal of Psychosocial Research on Cyberspace, 9*(2), article 3.

Leach, D. K. (2009). An elusive 'we': Anti-dogmatism, democratic practice, and the contradictory identity of the German Autonomen. *The American Behavioral Scientist, 52*(7), 1042–1068. doi:10.1177/0002764208327674

Levy, S. (2010). *Hackers: Heroes of the Computer Revolution*. Sebastopol, CA: O'Reilly Media.

Madarie, R. (2017). Hackers' Motivations: Testing Schwartz's Theory of Motivational Types of Values in a Sample of Hackers. *International Journal of Cyber Criminology, 11*(1).

Manion, M., & Goodrum, A. (2000). Terrorism or civil disobedience: Toward a hacktivist ethic. *ACM SIGCAS Computers and Society, 30*(2), 14–19. doi:10.1145/572230.572232

Matusitz, J. (2005). Cyberterrorism: How Can American Foreign Policy Be Strengthened in the Information Age? *American Foreign Policy Interests, 27*(2), 137–147. doi:10.1080/10803920590935376

McKenna, K. Y., & Green, A. S. (2002). Virtual group dynamics. *Group Dynamics, 6*(1), 116–127. doi:10.1037/1089-2699.6.1.116

Meuleman, B., & Boushel, C. (2014). Hashtags, ruling relations and the everyday: Institutional ethnography insights on social movements. *Contemporary Social Science, 9*(1), 49–62. doi:10.1080/2158204 1.2013.851410

Milan, S., & Atton, C. (2015). Hacktivism as a radical media practice. *Routledge companion to alternative and community media*, 550-560.

Moore, R. (2005). *Cyber crime: Investigating High-Technology Computer Crime*. Cleveland, MI: Anderson Publishing.

Näsi, M., & Koivusilta, L. (2013). Internet and everyday life: The perceived implications of internet use on memory and ability to concentrate. *Cyberpsychology, Behavior, and Social Networking, 16*(2), 88–93. doi:10.1089/cyber.2012.0058 PMID:23113691

NCA. (2016). *Cyber crime: Preventing young people from getting involved*. National Crime Agency. Retrieved from http://www.nationalcrimeagency.gov.uk/crime-threats/cyber-crime/cyber-crime-preventing-young-people-from-getting-involved

Nissenbaum, H. (2004). Hackers and the contested ontology of cyberspace. *New Media & Society, 6*(2), 195–217. doi:10.1177/1461444804041445

Olsen, P. (2013). *We are Anonymous*. London: Random House.

Packer, D. J. (2009). Avoiding groupthink: Whereas weakly identified members remain silent, strongly identified members dissent about collective problems. *Psychological Science, 20*(5), 546–548. doi:10.1111/j.1467-9280.2009.02333.x PMID:19389133

Perlroth, N. (2013, May 17). Hunting for Syrian hackers' Chain of Command. *New York Times*. Retrieved from https://nyti.ms/2jPZmbx

Postill, J. (2014). Freedom technologists and the new protest movements: A theory of protest formulas. *Convergence, 20*(4), 402–418. doi:10.1177/1354856514541350

Postmes, T., & Brunsting, S. (2002). Collective action in the age of the Internet: Mass communication and online mobilization. *Social Science Computer Review, 20*(3), 290–301. doi:10.1177/089443930202000306

Raymond, E. (1996). *The New Hacker's Dictionary*. MIT Press.

Rippl, S. (2002). Cultural theory and risk perception: A proposal for a better measurement. *Journal of Risk Research, 5*(2), 147–165. doi:10.1080/13669870110042598

Rogers, M. (2003). The psychology of cyber-terrorism. Terrorists, Victims and Society: Psychological. *Perspectives on Terrorism and Its Consequences*, 75-92.

Rogers, M. K. (2006). A two-dimensional circumplex approach to the development of a hacker taxonomy. *Digital Investigation, 3*(2), 97–102. doi:10.1016/j.diin.2006.03.001

Rogers, M. K. (2011). The psyche of cybercriminals: A psycho-Social perspective. In Cybercrimes: A multidisciplinary analysis (pp. 217-235). Springer. doi:10.1007/978-3-642-13547-7_14

Rosenzweig, R. (1998). Wizards, Bureaucrats, Warriors, and Hackers: Writing the History of the Internet. *The American Historical Review, 103*(5), 1530–1552. doi:10.2307/2649970

Scheuerman, W. E. (2016). Digital disobedience and the law. *New Political Science, 38*(3), 299–314. doi:10.1080/07393148.2016.1189027

Schrock, A. R. (2016). Civic hacking as data activism and advocacy: A history from publicity to open government data. *New Media & Society, 18*(4), 581–599. doi:10.1177/1461444816629469

Seebruck, R. (2015). A typology of hackers: Classifying cyber malfeasance using a weighted arc circumplex model. *Digital Investigation, 14*, 36–45. doi:10.1016/j.diin.2015.07.002

Skinner, W. F., & Fream, A. M. (1997). A social learning theory analysis of computer crime among college students. *Journal of Research in Crime and Delinquency, 34*(4), 495–518. doi:10.1177/0022427897034004005

Slovic, P., Finucane, M., Peters, E., & MacGregor, D. G. (2002). Rational actors or rational fools: Implications of the affect heuristic for behavioural economics. *Journal of Socio-Economics, 31*(4), 329–342. doi:10.1016/S1053-5357(02)00174-9

Small, G. W., Moody, T. D., Siddarth, P., & Bookheimer, S. Y. (2009). Your brain on Google: Patterns of cerebral activation during internet searching. *The American Journal of Geriatric Psychiatry, 17*(2), 116–126. doi:10.1097/JGP.0b013e3181953a02 PMID:19155745

Solomon, R. (2017). Electronic protests: Hacktivism as a form of protest in Uganda. *Computer Law & Security Review, 33*(5), 718–728. doi:10.1016/j.clsr.2017.03.024

Sturgis, P., Patulny, R., Allum, N., & Buscha, F. (2012). Social connectedness and generalized trust: a longitudinal perspective. *ISER Working Paper Series*, 1-23.

Suler, J. (2004). The Online Disinhibition Effect. *Cyberpsychology & Behavior, 7*(3), 321–326. doi:10.1089/1094931041291295 PMID:15257832

Tanczer, L. M. (2016). Hacktivism and the male-only stereotype. *New Media & Society, 18*(8), 1599–1615. doi:10.1177/1461444814567983

Tanis, M., & Postmes, T. (2005). A social identity approach to trust: Interpersonal perception, group membership and trusting behaviour. *European Journal of Social Psychology, 35*(3), 413–424. doi:10.1002/ejsp.256

Tarrant, M., & North, A. C. (2004). Explanations for positive and negative behavior: The intergroup attribution bias in achieved groups. *Current Psychology (New Brunswick, N.J.), 23*(161). doi:10.1007/BF02903076

Travaglino, G. A. (2014). Social sciences and social movements: The theoretical context. *Contemporary Social Science, 9*(1), 1–14. doi:10.1080/21582041.2013.851406

Tsohou, A., Karyda, M., & Kokolakis, S. (2015). Analyzing the role of cognitive and cultural biases in the internalization of information security policies: Recommendations for information security awareness programs. *Computers & Security, 52*, 128–141. doi:10.1016/j.cose.2015.04.006

Tufekci, Z., & Wilson, C. (2012). Social media and the decision to participate in political protest: Observations from Tahrir Square. *Journal of Communication, 62*(2), 363–379. doi:10.1111/j.1460-2466.2012.01629.x

Tun, P. A., & Lachman, M. E. (2010). The association between computer use and cognition across adulthood: Use it so you won't lose it? *Psychology and Aging, 25*(3), 560–568. doi:10.1037/a0019543 PMID:20677884

Turkle, S. (1999). Cyberspace and Identity. *Contemporary Sociology, 28*(6), 643–648.

Tversky, A. (1972). Elimination by aspects: A theory of choice. *Psychological Review, 79*(4), 281–299. doi:10.1037/h0032955

Uitermark, J. (2017). Complex contention: Analyzing power dynamics within Anonymous. *Social Movement Studies*, *16*(4), 403–417. doi:10.1080/14742837.2016.1184136

UN General Assembly. (1966). *International Covenant on Civil and Political Rights*. Available at: http://www.refworld.org/docid/3ae6b3aa0.html

Valenzuela, S. (2013). Unpacking the use of social media for protest behavior: The roles of information, opinion expression, and activism. *The American Behavioral Scientist*, *57*(7), 920–942. doi:10.1177/0002764213479375

Van Lange, P. A. M. (2015). Generalized Trust: Four Lessons From Genetics and Culture. *Current Directions in Psychological Science*, *24*(1), 71–76. doi:10.1177/0963721414552473

Vegh, S., Ayers, M. D., & McCaughey, M. (2003). Classifying forms of online activism. In M. McCaughey & M. Ayers (Eds.), *Cyberactivism: Online Activism in Theory and Practice* (pp. 71–96). London: Routledge.

Vujic, A. (2017). Switching on or switching off? Everyday computer use as a predictor of sustained attention and cognitive reflection. *Computers in Human Behavior*, *72*, 152–162. doi:10.1016/j.chb.2017.02.040

Whitehead, T. (2016). British teenager suspected of being a mystery hacker who stole CIA boss emails. *The Telegraph*. Retrieved from http://www.telegraph.co.uk/news/uknews/crime/12154592/British-teenager-suspected-of-being-a-mystery-hacker-who-stole-CIA-boss-emails.html

Wilcox, P., Land, K., & Hunt, S. A. (2004). Criminal circumstance: A multicontextual criminal opportunity theory. *Symbolic Interaction*, *27*(1).

Wolfradt, U., & Doll, J. (2001). Motives of Adolescents to use the internet as a function of personality traits, personal and social factors. *Journal of Educational Computing Research*, *24*(1), 13–27. doi:10.2190/ANPM-LN97-AUT2-D2EJ

Wray, S. (1998). Electronic civil disobedience and the World Wide Web of hacktivism. *Switch New Media Journal*, *4*(2). Retrieved from http://switch.sjsu.edu/web/v4n2/stefan/

Wright, M. F., Kamble, S. V., & Soudi, S. P. (2015). Indian adolescents' cyber aggression involvement and cultural values: The moderation of peer attachment. *School Psychology International*, *36*(4), 410–427. doi:10.1177/0143034315584696

Chapter 12
A Cyber–Psychological and Behavioral Approach to Online Radicalization

Reyhan Topal
Bilkent University, Turkey

ABSTRACT

This chapter attempts to synthesize the mainstream theories of radicalization and the cyber-psychological and behavioral approaches with a view to identifying individuals' radicalization online. Based on the intersections of those two fields, this chapter first elaborates how radical groups use cyberspace with a specific concentration on the so-called cyber caliphate claimed by the Islamic State of Iraq and al-Sham (ISIS). Second, it revisits mainstream theories of radicalization and specifies the psychological and behavioral facets of the radicalization processes proposed by those theories. Following that, it integrates theories of radicalization with cyber-psychological and behavioral explanations of online radicalization to reveal how ISIS's use of cyberspace attracts individuals and facilitates online radicalization.

INTRODUCTION

Since 1990s, individuals and groups have been building new societies, spaces, and networks on the internet with their online identity bricks. Such experiences of digitalization have broadened the scope of social research, as scholars attempted to incorporate a new cyber dimension into their debates. Hence, recent research on terrorism and radicalization has moved beyond the classical theories of radicalization to empirical assessments of digital dynamics that may pave the way for online radicalization of individuals, which in turn culminate in acts of violence. In order to explain the contextual dynamics of online radicalization, scholars closely watch contemporary developments in cyberspace, and encompass the radical use of cyber tools in their research. Reiterating generally acknowledged facts about the internet, many of those studies dwell on the internet's facilitating role for individuals, who have radical ideas to some extent and who are already become radicalized, to socialize among other likeminded individuals, and for virtual radical groups to convey their messages to a larger audience by exceeding spatial and temporal limits.

DOI: 10.4018/978-1-5225-4053-3.ch012

Notwithstanding the increasing volume of publications that review online radicalization and terrorism, to date there have been very few scholarly efforts to expound on the cyber-psychological and behavioral dimensions of online radicalization. For the purpose of filling such a gap, this chapter aims to examine the intersections of radicalization theories and the cyber-psychological and behavioral approaches in order to identify how individuals become radicalized online. This chapter will first analyze how radicals use cyberspace with a specific concentration on the so-called cyber caliphate claimed by the Islamic State of Iraq and al-Sham (ISIS). Second, the chapter will elaborate on mainstream theories of radicalization in detail, and explore the psychological and behavioral facets of the radicalization processes referred by those theories. Finally, it will synthesize theories of radicalization with cyber-psychological and behavioral explanations of online radicalization in order to explain how ISIS' use of cyberspace attracts individuals and paves the way for online radicalization. Even though the utilization of online tools by radical groups might be traced back to the 1980s when members of those groups prepared propaganda movies on videotape and published sophisticated magazines to disseminate via mail (Stern and Berger, 2016), the use of cyberspace as an ideological battleground for radical groups occurred in the 2000s following the rise of social media as a phenomenon. Therefore, this chapter aims to reach a more comprehensive picture of contemporary developments in online radicalization by elaborating further on ISIS and the cyber-psychological and behavioral dimensions of the debate. Taking this into consideration, this chapter will specifically focus on the themes of *socialization, enculturation, cognitive opening, and anonymity* as psychological and behavioral dimensions to assess how cyberspace may play a facilitating role in radicalization.

ONLINE RADICALIZATION AND RADICALS' USE OF CYBERSPACE

Currently almost one-third of the world's population uses smart phones (Statista, 2017), Facebook has more than 2 billion active users (Statista, 2017), and Twitter has 328 million monthly users (Statista, 2017). Considering the transformative characteristic of internet technologies, and the facilitating role of social media platforms for communication and influence, it seems unsurprising that radical groups embraced those opportunities for the same reasons as other groups (Aly, et al., 2017). If one construes terrorism as a type of communication (Schmid and de Graaf, 1982) or as a form of "communicative violence" (Aly, et al., 2017), then disseminating propaganda messages to attract the masses and gain sympathizers/new recruits are central to it. Hence, this aspect of internet technologies which is prone to abuse became a golden opportunity for radical groups that hinge on communication due to the aforementioned reasons.

Research on online radicalization stemmed from concerns related to the dark side of the internet, which might facilitate the radicalization of individuals and furthermore their engagement with violent extremist activities. Before it was brought to light that al-Qaeda members shared the details of the planned terrorist attacks to be held on 9/11 through email drafts on a common email address, very few attempts had been made to address the possibility of online radicalization, although the inexorable progress and spread of internet technologies had already been a hot topic among social scientists. During 1990s, scholars expected diverse outcomes from the new digital age. On the one side, there were optimists who mostly cited the positive benefits of the internet, such as opening new channels for social relations by promoting pluralism and diversity (Rheingold, 1993), and providing a real medium for friendship (Katz & Aspden, 1997). On the other, there were pessimists who underscored the alarming side of the internet. According to those perspectives, the internet would create "a nation of strangers" (Turkle, 1995) by destroying social integration, and engender an "internet paradox" by reducing social involvement, psychological well-being, and emotional investment (Kraut et al., 1998). The truly interesting side of the debate was that online radicalization mostly used the internet's positive benefits such as providing a diverse and easily reachable mass, but then these aspects were twisted by potential radicals to reach like-minded individuals and groups, and to engage in violent extremism and terrorist acts.

The historical progress of how radical groups used cyberspace says a lot about how quickly they integrated their virtual goals and activities into a new cyber environment, though it is difficult to place each and every activity of those groups into chronological order. Despite Al Qaeda's early attempts to make use of the internet, Lebanon's Hezbollah emerged later on as a leading agent of radicalization in cyberspace. Today, Hezbollah has more than 20 websites in 7 languages (Arabic, Azeri, English, French, Hebrew, Persian, and Spanish), many television and radio channels as well as a quite complex social media network (The Meir Amit Intelligence and Terrorism Information Center, 2013), all of which provide the group with vast opportunities to establish networks, communicate, and spread propaganda. Among some of the cyber capabilities of Hezbollah are leaking planes' camera systems, organizing attacks on DoS (Denial of Service) and DDoS (Distributed Denial of Service), and hacking fiber optic cables (Richards, 2014). The group used most of those aforementioned capabilities during the Israel-Lebanon War of 2006 (Saad, Bazan & Varin, 2015). Founding the "Cyber Hezbollah", a branch of the group responsible for the group's cyber initiatives, Hezbollah holds regular cyber conferences with the participation of "Islamist hackers" and "cyber jihadists" in order to find new strategies in cyberspace (Wahdat-Hagh, 2011). Improved cyber skills give Hezbollah the opportunity to spread propaganda, communicate, win over the hearts and minds of potential radicals, and facilitate online radicalization.

As cyber technologies and online media sources gradually sophisticated, radical groups advanced their online strategies accordingly. A recent and staggering example was how members of Al Shabaab used the group's Twitter account during the terrorist attack at the Westgate Mall in Kenya in 2013 (Mair, 2017). During the four-day siege - which resulted in 67 fatalities and 175 wounded - the world watched closely while the group live-tweeted the terrorist attack on its Twitter feed. Considering that Kenya is one of the most active countries in Africa on Twitter, and President Uhuru Kenyatta is among the most-followed African leaders (Simon et al., 2014), Shabaab's use of Twitter as a communication channel seemed well-planned in attracting both domestic and international attention. Lashkar-e-Taiba, a Pakistan based militant organization, also has sophisticated cyber capabilities, and claimed to use Google Earth in order to gather intelligence and determine routes during its attacks on Mumbai in November 2008 (Glanz, Rotella and Sanger, 2014). What is more, Jamaat-ud-Dawah, the so-called charity arm of Lashkar-e-Taiba, allegedly held a two-day conference on social media for their future cyber initiatives, in Lahore, on December 26 and 27, 2015 (Sharma, 2016). In the light of those examples, the ability of radical groups to adopt and engage with a dynamic digital world is worth discussing.

Among other contemporary examples, ISIS is distinguished with its more sophisticated use of online platforms and its developed understanding of cyberspace in general. In order to draw a detailed picture of ISIS, one should undoubtedly consider its cyber dimension, which makes the group a cyber threat of modern times. Only through the use of social media and online communication was ISIS able to make its dramatic debut onto the global arena,claiming that it had founded a sharia-based sovereignty not only in Syria and Iraq but also across the world. ISIS is not unique in declaring war against non-believers, or in calling each and every Muslim to a global jihad. As an example, al Qaeda's members were mostly comprised of Arabs who fought against Soviet Russia during the "Afghan jihad" (Johnson and Mason, 2007) and went onto commit the 9/11 attacks against the US, and Lebanon's Hezbollah promised to continue fighting without recognizing any treaties, ceasefires, or peace agreements until the Muslims re-gained their rights and lands (Levitt, 2013). All these groups are of the same opinion about maintaining a global war against the Westand bringing the Muslims altogether under the same flag of Islam, like many other radical Islamist groups. What differentiates ISIS is that the group has been working to declare and promote those claims to the world online unlike the former examples, which remained relatively less salient and efficient in cyberspace. ISIS became the first radical group to claim a "cyber caliphate" when Cunaid Hussein, an ISIS militant from Britain, hacked the official Twitter and YouTube accounts of the U.S. Central Command, and published the following message online: "In the name of Allah, the Most Gracious, the Most Merciful, the Cyber Caliphate continues its Cyber Jihad" (CNN, 2015). By doing so, ISIS also became the first actor to conceptualize the "cyber jihad". So, why does ISIS persist on having supremacy in cyberspace?

Considering the spatial, financial, and legal obstacles in reaching a large audience and convincing others of ISIS' ongoing ideological battle, online radicalization appears to be the easiest and most efficient way to disseminate messages in order to gain new recruits. There are many facets to be discussed and understood about why the group claims a cyber caliphate, with persuasion and propaganda being the primary goals of ISIS in cyberspace. Their communication strategy attempts to persuade prospective recruits to do the following: Join the group, and fight in order to restore a caliphate for Islam (Farwell, 2014). If the target is non-believer, then persuade the target to accept Islam and move to Syria (*hijrah*). ISIS pursues complicated and well-planned communication strategies, particularly in social media, such as using the rhetoric of *takfir*, a very powerful doctrine of excommunication by pronouncing a Muslim an infidel (Zelin, 2014). Using the rhetoric of *takfir*, ISIS threatens Muslims with dismissal from Islam if they do not advocate what the group offers in the name of their peculiar interpretation of religion. Muslim youths, especially the ones who live in Western countries, facing discrimination, and isolation in small Muslim enclaves (Graham, 2015), pay great attention to ISIS' call, as the group's call for a global jihad and a universal caliphate under the flag of sharia on the borderless earth of Allah appears to promise limitless freedom, a utopia that those young people have long been yearning for. So, online propaganda and communication strategies of ISIS mostly address such a disgruntled group of youth easily prone to online radicalization.

The dissemination of knowledge plays a vital role for ISIS in online radicalization. Notwithstanding its extremist and irrational interpretation of the world and religion, the group's online media strategy stands as a modern and sophisticated one (Lesaca, 2015) that encompasses a wide spectrum of online magazines in different languages such as Dabiq in English and Konstantiniyye in Turkish, numerous social media platforms including Twitter, Facebook, and YouTube accounts, as well as blogs and forums to gather similar minds together. Through those platforms, the group has the opportunity of sharing high-quality photographs and videos, which reflect ISIS' growing violent political extremism (Conway, 2017). Hence, online media is an endless source for ISIS to simply reveal its tour de force. Apart from elaborating on the advanced skills of ISIS members, one should shed light on the reasons why and how ISIS uses cyberspace and online media so efficiently for online radicalization. Next chapter will problematize radicalization, and analyze mainstream theories of radicalization, and then be followed by another one that will integrate the cyber-psychological and behavioral approaches into radicalization theories to understand how cyberspace facilitates radical groups such as ISIS for online radicalization.

REVISITING THE THEORIES OF RADICALIZATION

Scholars of radicalization propose different types of models in order to explore the radicalization of individuals, as well as the decision to participate in radical groups, and engage in violent behavior. In each model, scholars underscore multifaceted social, economic, structural, psychological, circumstantial, and other types of determinants to dismantle the path towards radicalization. Therefore, there is not one strain of radicalization model that is agreed upon, giving the radicalization debate a lively characteristic. For example, the radicalization model proposed by some scholars concentrates on the theme of cognitive opening and attempts to analyze which material and non-material circumstances make individuals drift towards radicalization (Bjorgo & Horgan, 2009; Blee, 2002; Simi & Futrell, 2010). For others, the psychological wellbeing of individuals is of significance, so that emotions such as alienation, anger, disenfranchisement, and belief of being unjustly treated might pave the way for radicalization (Kimhi & Even, 2006). Peer dynamics (Bakker, 2006), motivation of group belonging (McCauley & Moskalenko, 2011), adventure-seeking (Gibson, 1994), seeking power and prestige (Stern, 2003), and demographic factors such as gender and age (Chermark & Gruenewald, 2015) are also usually considered significant factors among scholars.

Though there is a plethora of studies on why and how individuals become radicalized and join radical groups in the literature of radicalization and terrorism, there is almost no scholarly attempt to contextualize online radicalization within the radicalization theories. In order to examine the online radicalization process of individuals, one should carefully integrate those theories into the literature on radicals' use of cyberspace. Most of the radicalization theories regard the radicalization as a process, and attempt to analyze that process stage by stage. Among different types, there have been several established and widely-accepted models which try to examine the radicalization process. This chapter focuses on the mainstream models so as to contextualize online radicalization from a cyber-psychological and behavioral approach in those models.

Borum's model of radicalization in FBI Law Enforcement Bulletin is a prototypic psychological one (Borum, 2003). In his model, Borum proposes 4 stages: An initial stage where an individual notices that his/her conditions are not desirable, the second stage where the individual compares those undesirable conditions and comes to the conclusion that "it is not fair", the third stage where the individual blames a specific target for the unfair situation, and the last stage where the individual generates stereotypes and dehumanizes the enemy who seems responsible for the unfair situation (Borum, 2003). So, Borum's model of the process of radicalization focuses more on the ideological and psychological sides of the process.

Based on his ethnographic study among the members of Al-Muhajiroun, Wiktorowicz develops a 4-stage model of joining extremist groups, though he considers the term radicalization problematic: An initial stage where the "cognitive opening" of the individual occurs as a result of reverse life experiences such as discrimination or victimization, the second stage where those experiences lead the individual towards "religious seeking", the third stage where the individual regards the worldview of extremist Islamic groups as overlapping with his/her worldview and engages in a "frame alignment", and the last stage where the individual's "socialization and joining" the extremist Islamic groups occurs (Wiktorowicz, 2004). In spite of being a limited analysis of participation in extremist Islamic groups, Wiktorowicz's model offers significant insights about behavioral process of pre-participation.

Examining the radicalization process through a 5-floor staircase model, Moghaddam's model is also well-established (Moghaddam, 2005). On the ground floor, the individual experiences unfairness and relative deprivation, and if the individual believes that he/she cannot reach at greater justice through mobility or cannot influence the decision makers, he/she is more likely to climb onto the second floor where the anger and frustration with the deprivation is channeled towards the "enemy" mostly through physical force. On the third, the individual finds other like-minded individuals, and begins justifying terrorism. On the fourth, individual joins a terrorist group, and embraces the "us vs. them", and "good vs. evil" categorizations of the group. Finally, individual is trained for injuring and killing others, and sent to realize terrorist acts (Moghaddam, 2005). So, Moghaddam takes the process from a psychological/perceptional step, feeling of relative deprivation, and ends with physical act of violence.

Criticizing the gaps in the micro and macro approaches to the study of terrorism and radicalization, Sageman attempts to bridge both through a middle-range approach (Sageman, 2008). So, in contrast to the previously mentioned three models which explain radicalization process through sequential stages, Sageman puts forward the interplay of three cognitive and one situational factors to propose a non-linear radicalization process (Sageman, 2008). Among the cognitive factors are the sense of moral outrage which refers to feeling of being morally violated, the frame of interpretation which is used to justify the situation such as "war against Islam", and resonance with personal experiences such as discrimination (Sageman, 2008). According to Sageman, those cognitive factors reinforce each other, and in total, these factors may result in radicalization of the individual. As a situational factor, Sageman mentions "mobilization through networks", which refers to the individual's confirmation of his/her ideas through communication with other radicalized individuals (Sageman, 2008).

In the light of those established models, how could one explain online radicalization? The following chapter will integrate theories of radicalization into cyber-psychological and behavioral explanations of online radicalization so as to reveal how the ISIS' use of cyberspace attracts individuals and paves the way for online radicalization.

A CYBER-PSYCHOLOGICAL AND BEHAVIORAL APPROACH TO ONLINE RADICALIZATION

Throughout the previous chapters which reviewed the online presence of ISIS and the theories of radicalization, many aspects pertaining to the psychological and behavioral facets of the debate were covered. Both chapters referred to the psychological and behavioral dimensions of radicalization while addressing the reasons of ISIS' claims for a cyber caliphate and the main determinants of radicalization. With the purpose of contributing to the literature on online radicalization, this chapter elaborates on how internet technologies may facilitate online radicalization by providing favorable conditions for socialization, enculturation, cognitive opening, and anonymity. In doing so, this chapter tries to expand the scope of theories of radicalization by applying the aforementioned themes to explain online radicalization through the example of the ISIS' use of cyberspace.

Scholars generally argue that anonymity on the internet enables individuals to connect and socialize with others who share similar ideologies and values with themselves (Quinn and Forsyth, 2013). Such anonymity helps particularly lonely, marginalized, non-assertive, and asocial individuals socialize very quickly, since it is easier to communicate online without the pressure of face-to-face interaction, and online socialization helps individuals eliminate their socio-phobia. According to previous research, individuals experience lower social anxiety, more social desirability and higher self-esteem in the cyberspace than the virtual world due to the veil of anonymity. (Joinson, 1999). Such "positive" impact has several outcomes, according to McKenna and Bargh (2000):

The assurance of anonymity gives one far greater play in identity construction than is conceivable in face-to-face encounters. One can, for instance, change one's gender, one's way of relating to others, and literally everything about oneself [...] On the internet, where one can be anonymous, where one does not deal in face-to-face interactions, where one is simply responding to other anonymous people, the roles and characters one maintains for family, friends, and associates can be cast aside.

With regards to radicalization, it could be asserted that most people tend to behave in a harmonious way in the social environment, and the fear of legal ramifications and social rejection may prevent individuals from expressing their radical views and seeking other individuals with similar opinions (Holt, 2007; Quinn and Forsyth, 2013). Yet, anonymity allows individuals to socialize with others without those hesitations, and also diminish personal obstacles such as high social anxiety and low self esteem. This also explains why online platforms constitute the main basis of ISIS' attraction of sympathizers and new recruits. As previously mentioned, many Muslims living outside the Muslim-majority countries feel themselves excluded and unjustly treated in the societies they live in. The anonymity in the cyberspace gives them the opportunity of impersonation, and they easily meet and socialize with like-minded individuals who encourage them to engage in violent extremist activities and join ISIS. Therefore, the anonymity and socialization opportunities provided by the cyberspace address Wictorowicz's "socialization and joining," Moghaddam's "finding likely minds," and Sageman's "mobilization through networks" elements in the ISIS case.

Cognitive opening refers to the phenomenon in which personal crises or awakenings expose individuals to a new reality (Blee, 2002) such as radicalization or taking the decision to engage in violent acts. When individuals enter the process of cognitive opening, they seek ideas consistent with their own. In such a process, the internet, an endless source of ideological communication and messaging, might provide individuals easy access to networks and messages from the radical groups (Britz, 2010). What is more, cyberspace might be a source of cognitive opening following the previous steps of socialization with the help of anonymity. Therefore, internet accelerates the transition from cognitive opening to taking action, and individuals might easily end up participating in radical groups. To have a better understanding of cognitive opening and online radicalization, one should revise the ISIS case one more time. The ISIS' online media strategy is based on "convincing" others of anything the group claims, despite the irrationality of those claims, in order to accelerate the transition from cognitive opening to taking action. To exemplify, ISIS on its online platforms pretends to win its battle in Syria, and have already established a caliphate in the country where people are happily living. According to what ISIS claims online, new recruits will embrace real Islam by joining group, and they will be martyrs and go to the paradise if they die. Comparing their unjust situation with what ISIS promises, people decide to join the group more easily. Publishing online journals and photographs, and releasing videos which are professionally edited, ISIS disseminates those ideas with the help of cyberspace. Those aspects address Wictorowicz's "cognitive opening" and Moghaddam's "perception of fairness and feeling of relative deprivation" in the ISIS case.

Enculturation is one of the most significant aspects of online radicalization. When individuals experience cognitive opening, and find the ideology for which they have long been seeking, they enter into the process of enculturation where they learn the content of that ideology, its code of behavior, and the traditions that its followers embrace. The process of online enculturation is similar to how an individual embraces violent behavior on the streets in the real world. Forums, newsgroups, social media channels, and many other online platforms might facilitate the global transmission of knowledge (Rosenmann &

Safir, 2006), and radical groups get their share from such massive transmission. Once individuals who feel sympathy for radical groups socialize with other sympathizers and members online, they easily embrace the code of conduct and behavior patterns from members of these groups. So, they do not have to physically come together and spend time with one another for such enculturation to occur, as the internet melts the physical barriers of communication. ISIS' online media strategy appears to be a rich source of enculturation for anyone, as the group attempts to make a *jihadi* culture with its own jargon. To exemplify, the group uses the words *visit* (regular meetings of the group members), *invitation* (gaining new members), *migration* (participation to the ISIS), and *demonic* (anything in contrary with the ideology of the ISIS) in its online magazines. Once this jargon is embraced by people, even in the virtual absence of the ISIS in the life of radicals online, such *jihadi* culture will reproduce itself in different groups and in different times. Borum's "dehumanizing the enemy," Wictorowicz's "religious seeking," Moghaddam's "us versus them," and Sageman's "frame of interpretation" elements fit very well into such enculturation, and points to why scholars should integrate online radicalization into the literature on radicalization theories with respect to cyber-psychological and behavioral aspects of the debate.

CONCLUSION

Despite the increasing volume of publications that analyze online radicalization and terrorism, there have been almost no scholarly efforts that shed light on the cyber-psychological and behavioral dimensions of online radicalization. This chapter examines the intersections of radicalization theories and the cyber-psychological and behavioral approaches in order to identify how individuals get radicalized online through the ISIS case. Analyzing the online radicalization and radicals' use of cyberspace with a specific concentration on the ISIS' claim of a cyber caliphate, the chapter revisits the mainstream theories of radicalization, and specifies the psychological and behavioral facets of the radicalization processes proposed by those theories. Then, it integrates theories of radicalization with cyber-psychological and behavioral explanations of online radicalization so as to reveal how ISIS' use of cyberspace attracts individuals and paves the way for online radicalization. By doing so, it aims to reach a more comprehensive picture of contemporary developments in online radicalization by elaborating further on ISIS and the cyber-psychological and behavioral dimensions of its use of cyberspace by focusing on the themes of *socialization, enculturation, cognitive opening, and anonymity* as psychological and behavioral dimensions to assess how cyberspace may play a facilitating role for radicalization.

REFERENCES

Aly, A., Macdonald, S., Jarvis, L., & Chen, T. M. (2017). Introduction to the Special Issue: Terrorist Online Propaganda and Radicalization. *Studies in Conflict and Terrorism*, *40*(1), 1–9. doi:10.1080/10 57610X.2016.1157402

Bakker, E. (2006). *Jihadi Terrorists in Europe, Their Characteristics and the Circumstances in Which They Joined the Jihad: An Exploratory Study*. The Hague: Clingendael Institute.

Bjorgo, T., & Horgan, J. (2009). *Leaving Terrorism Behind: Individual and Collective Disengagement*. New York: Routledge.

Bjørgum, M. H. (2016). Jihadi Brides: Why do Western Muslim Girls Join ISIS? *Global Politics Review*, *2*(2), 91–102.

Blee, K. M. (2002). *Inside Organized Racism: Women and Men in the Hate Movement*. University of California Press.

Borum, R. (2003). Understanding the Terrorist Mindset. *FBI Law Enforcement Bulletin*, 7-10.

Britz, M. T. (2010). Terrorism and Technology: Operationalizing Cyberterrorism and Identifying Concepts. In T. J. Holt (Ed.), *Crime On-Line: Correlates, Causes, and Context* (pp. 193–220). Raleigh, NC: Carolina Academic Press.

Center, T. M. (2013). Terrorism in Cyberspace: Hezbollah's Internet Network. *Terrorism Info*. Retrieved 06 01, 2017, from http://www.terrorism-info.org.il/Data/articles/Art_20488/E_276_12_739632364.pdf

Chermak, S. D., & Gruenewald, J. (2015). Laying the Foundation for the Criminological Examination of Right-wing, Left-wing, and Al Qaeda Inspired Extremism in the United States. *Terrorism and Political Violence*, *27*(1), 133–159. doi:10.1080/09546553.2014.975646

CNN Staff. (n.d.). CENTCOM Twitter account hacked, suspended. *CNN*. Retrieved 20 10 2017, from http://www.cnn.com/2015/01/12/politics/centcom-twitter-hacked-suspended/index.html

Conway, M. (2017). Determining the Role of the Internet in Violent Extremism and Terrorism: Six Suggestions for Progressing Research. *Studies in Conflict and Terrorism*, *40*(1), 77–98. doi:10.1080/1 057610X.2016.1157408

Farwell, J. P. (2014). The Media Strategy of ISIS. *Survival: Global Politics and Strategy*, *56*(6), 49–55. doi:10.1080/00396338.2014.985436

Gibson, J. W. (1994). *Warrior Dreams: Violence and Manhood in Post-Vietnam America*. Louisville, KY: Hill & Wang.

Glanz, J., Rotella, S., & Sanger, D. E. (2014). Mumbai Attacks Piles of Spy Data, but an Uncompleted Puzzle. *New York Times*. Retrieved 04 16, 2017, from https://www.nytimes.com/2014/12/22/world/asia/in-2008-mumbai-attacks-piles-of-spy-data-but-an-uncompleted-puzzle.html?mcubz=2

Graham, J. (2015). Who Joins ISIS and Why? *Huffington Post*. Retrieved 06 10, 2017, from http://www.huffingtonpost.com/john-graham/who-joins-isis-and-why_b_8881810.html

Holt, T. J. (2007). Subcultural Evolution? Examining the Influence of on- and off-line Experiences on Deviant Subcultures. *Deviant Behavior*, *28*(1), 171–198. doi:10.1080/01639620601131065

Johnson, T. H., & Mason, M. C. (2007). Understanding the Taliban and Insurgency in Afghanistan. *Orbis*, *51*(1), 71–89. doi:10.1016/j.orbis.2006.10.006

Joinson, A. (1999). Social Desirability, Anonymity, and Internet-based Questionnaires. *Behavior Research Methods, Instruments, & Computers*, *31*(3), 433–438. doi:10.3758/BF03200723 PMID:10502866

Katz, J. E., & Aspden, P. (1997). A Nation of Strangers. *Communications of the ACM*, *40*(12), 81–86. doi:10.1145/265563.265575

Kimhi, S., & Even, S. (2006). The Palestinian Human Bombers. In J. Victoroff (Ed.), *Tangled Roots: Social and Psychological Factors in the Genesis of Terrorism* (pp. 308–322). Trenton, NJ: IOS Press.

Kraut, R., Mukhopadhyay, T., Szczypula, J., Kiesler, S., & Scherlis, W. (1998). Communication and Information: Alternative uses of the Internet in households. In *Proceedings of the CHI 98* (pp. 368-383). New York: ACM. doi:10.1145/274644.274695

Kruglanski, A. W., & Fishman, S. (2009). Psychological Factors in Terrorism and Counterterrorism: Individual, Group, and Organizational Levels of Analysis. *Social Issues and Policy Review*, *3*(1), 1–44. doi:10.1111/j.1751-2409.2009.01009.x

Lesaca, J. (2015). *On Social Media, ISIS Uses Modern Cultural Images to Spread Anti-modern Values*. Brookings Institute. Retrieved 05 30, 2017, from: https://www.brookings.edu/blog/techtank/2015/09/24/on-social-media-isis-uses-modern-cultural-images-to-spread-anti-modern-values/

Levitt, M. (2013). *Hezbollah: The Global Footprint of Lebanon's Party of God*. Washington, DC: Georgetown University Press.

Mair, D. (2017). #Westgate: A Case Study: How al-Shabaab Used Twitter During an Ongoing Attack. *Studies in Conflict and Terrorism*, *40*(1), 24–43. doi:10.1080/1057610X.2016.1157404

McCauley, C., & Moskalenko, S. (2008). Mechanisms of Political Radicalization: Pathways Toward Terrorism. *Terrorism and Political Violence*, *20*(3), 415–433. doi:10.1080/09546550802073367

McKenna, K. Y., & Bargh, J. A. (2000). Plan 9 From Cyberspace: The Implications of the Internet for Personality and Social Psychology. *Personality and Social Psychology Review*, *4*(1), 57–75. doi:10.1207/S15327957PSPR0401_6

Moghaddam, F. M. (2005). The Staircase to Terrorism: A Psychological Exploration. *The American Psychologist*, *60*(2), 161–169. doi:10.1037/0003-066X.60.2.161 PMID:15740448

Quinn, J. F., & Forsyth, C. J. (2005). Describing Sexual Behavior in the Era of the Internet: A Typology for Empirical Research. *Deviant Behavior*, *26*(3), 191–207. doi:10.1080/01639620590888285

Rheingold, H. (1993). *The Virtual Community: Homesteading on the Electronic Frontier*. MIT Press.

Richards, J. (2014). *Cyber-War: The Anatomy of the Global Security*. New York: Palgrave Macmillan. doi:10.1057/9781137399625

Rosenmann, A., & Safir, M. P. (2006). Forced Online: Pushed Factors of Internet Sexuality: A Preliminary Study of Paraphilic Empowerment. *Journal of Homosexuality*, *51*(3), 71–92. doi:10.1300/J082v51n03_05 PMID:17135116

Saad, S., Bazan, S., & Varin, C. (2015). Asymmetric Cyber-warfare between Israel and Hezbollah: The Web as a New Strategic Battlefield. *Webscience*. Retrieved 06 01, 2017, from: http://www.websci11.org/fileadmin/websci/Posters/96_paper.pdf

Sageman, M. (2008). *Leaderless Jihad: Terror Networks in the Twenty-First Century*. University of Pennsylvania Press. doi:10.9783/9780812206784

Schmid, A. P., & de Graaf, J. (1982). *Violence as Communication: Insurgent Terrorism and the Western News Media*. London: SAGE Publications.

Sharma, M. (2016). *Lashkar-e-Cyber of Hafiz Saeed*. Institute for Defense Studies and Analyses. Retrieved 06 01, 2017, from: http://www.idsa.in/idsacomments/lashkar-e-cyber-of-hafiz-saeed_msharma_310316#footnote1_amq1mz7

Simi, P., & Futrell, R. (2006). Cyberculture and the Endurance of Radical Racist Activism. *Journal of Political and Military Sociology, 34*(1), 115–142.

Simon, T., Goldberg, A., Aharonson-Daniel, L., Leykin, D., & Adini, B. (2014). Twitter in the Cross Fire—The Use of Social Media in the Westgate Mall Terror Attack in Kenya. *PLoS One, 9*(8), 1–11. doi:10.1371/journal.pone.0104136

Statista. (2017a). *Number of Smartphone Users Worldwide from 2014 to 2019 (in Millions)*. Retrieved 06 01, 2017, from: http://www.statista.com/statistics/330695/number-of-smartphone-users-worldwide/

Statista. (2017b). *Number of Monthly Active Facebook Users*. Retrieved 06 10, 2017, from https://www.statista.com/statistics/264810/number-of-monthly-active-facebook-users-worldwide/

Statista. (2017c). *Number of Monthly Active Twitter Users*. Retrieved 06 10, 2017, from https://www.statista.com/statistics/282087/number-of-monthly-active-twitter-users/

Statista. (2017d). *Number of Smartphone Users Worldwide*. Retrieved 06 10, 2017, from https://www.statista.com/statistics/330695/number-of-smartphone-users-worldwide/

Stern, J. (2003). *Terror in the Name of God: Why Religious Militants Kill*. New York: Harper Collins.

Stern, J., & Berger, J. M. (2016). *ISIS: The State of Terror*. New York: Harper Collins Publishers.

Taylor, M., & Horgan, J. (2006). A Conceptual Framework for Addressing Psychological Process in the Development of the Terrorist. *Terrorism and Political Violence, 18*(4), 585–601. doi:10.1080/09546550600897413

Turkle, S. (1996). Virtuality and Its Discontents: Searching for Community in Cyberspace. *The American Prospect, 24*(1), 50–57.

Usborne, D. (2015). Centcom 'Hacked' by ISIS Supporters: US Military Twitter Feed Publishes Personal Information of Senior Officers. *Independent*. Retrieved 05 03, 2017, from http://www.independent.co.uk/news/world/americas/us-central-command-hacked-by-islamic-state-supporters-9973615.html

Wahdat-Hagh, W. (2011). Iran And Cyber-Hezbollah Strategies: Killing Enemies In Hyperspace – Analysis. *Eurasia Review*. Retrieved 06 01, 2017, from: http://www.eurasiareview.com/25112011-iran-and-cyber-hezbollah-strategies-killing-enemies-in-hyperspace-analysis/

Wiktorowicz, Q. (2004). *Joining the Cause: Al-Muhajiroun and Radical Islam*. Paper presented at the Roots of Islamic Radicalism Conference, New Haven, CT.

Zelin, A. Y. (2014). *Al-Qaeda Disaffiliates with the Islamic State of Iraq and al-Sham*. Retrieved 05 30, 2017, from Washington Institute: http://www.washingtoninstitute.org/policy-analysis/view/al-qaeda-disaffiliates-with-the-islamic-state-of-iraq-and-al-sham

KEY TERMS AND DEFINITIONS

Anonymity: The condition in which someone's identity is unknown. It is the adjective of anonymous, which derived from the Greek word *anonymia*, meaning nameless.

Cognitive Opening: The state of mind in which an individual is eager to receive the message that mostly has an ideological characteristic.

Cyberspace: The virtual space where computer networks and internet exist.

Enculturation: The process in which an individual learns, internalizes, and applies the codes of a specific culture.

Internet: A worldwide platform that interconnects computer networks.

Online Radicalization: An aspect of radicalization where an individual begins or advances his/her radicalization process through cyberspace.

Chapter 13
Insider Attack Analysis in Building Effective Cyber Security for an Organization

Sunita Vikrant Dhavale
Defence Institute of Advanced Technology, India

ABSTRACT

Recent studies have shown that, despite being equipped with highly secure technical controls, a broad range of cyber security attacks were carried out successfully on many organizations to reveal confidential information. This shows that the technical advancements of cyber defence controls do not always guarantee organizational security. According to a recent survey carried out by IBM, 55% of these cyber-attacks involved insider threat. Controlling an insider who already has access to the company's highly protected data is a very challenging task. Insider attacks have great potential to severely damage the organization's finances as well as their social credibility. Hence, there is a need for reliable security frameworks that ensure confidentiality, integrity, authenticity, and availability of organizational information assets by including the comprehensive study of employee behaviour. This chapter provides a detailed study of insider behaviours that may hinder organization security. The chapter also analyzes the existing physical, technical, and administrative controls, their objectives, their limitations, insider behaviour analysis, and future challenges in handling insider threats.

INTRODUCTION

Technology is a fundamentally essential part for securing organizational information assets; however organization's employees are equally responsible for design, implementation and operation of these technological tools. A recent attack against Morgan Stanley, one of the world's largest financial services firms that exposed hundreds of thousands of customer accounts was carried out by one of the trusted employee of the same organization (Seth, 2015). The Computer Emergency Response Team (CERT) survey found that,insider attack cases made up 28% of all cybercrimes and more than 33% of organizations reported insider attacks in 2013 (Sangiri, & Dasgupta, 2016). ISACA conducted a research on cyber

DOI: 10.4018/978-1-5225-4053-3.ch013

security in 2016, which was based on the research among 2,920 security professionals in 121 countries (CIO&LEADER, 2017). The respondents in this survey listed the insider threats as one of the top threats, along with social engineering attacks. Recently, Edward Snowden's case highlighted the risky side of the insider threats in highly secure government institutions (BBC News, 2013).

Human elements representing as insiderssignificantly affect the efficiency of implemented cyber security program in any organization. Recent critical security incidents have shown that, the successful insider intrusions induce a fear of significant financial and credibility loss in an organization; and can be more damaging than the outsider threats. These insider attacks can be characterized in following ways: 1) they are carried out by our trusted employees; 2) they are carried out inside the boundaries of the organization; 3) they are hard to detect and may go undetected for years; 4) they don't happen often; and 5) they can damage the reputation of an organization severely. However, there is still a lack of awareness in many organizations regarding severity of the insider threats, while implementing organizational security controls. There is a need to urge cyber security professionals, policymakers, law enforcement, government and private organizations to share their knowledge and experience related to the recent insider based security incidents. A detailed study of the insider behaviour patterns need to be carried out in order to provide a reliable comprehensive solution for handling insider attacks.

This book chapter is organized as, 1) Section 1 gives general introduction of the subject; 2) Section 2 discusses characteristics of trusted malicious insiders; 3) Section 3 explains existing security controls and their limitations in detail; 4) Section 4 provides possible solutions for mitigating insider attacks; 5) Section 5 provides complex human behaviour analysis followed by the conclusion in Section 6.

TRUSTED MALICIOUS INSIDERS

The human element can compromise almost anything including the most intelligently designed security system (Infosec Institute, 2012). In addition, current research shows that the most common types of attack are carried out by disgruntled or angry insiders. The malicious insiders can be trusted employees (former/current), contractors, business partners, consultants, auditors, or vendors who intentionally misuse their authorized access to organizational assets. Here, trusted means the insiders to whom organization normally provide credentials (e.g. user name and password) to access organizational information resources. Hence, we can say, an insider is a person: 1) who is trusted by the organization and given a permission to work within the security perimeter of an organization; 2) who has authorized full/partial access to the organizational information systems; 3) who has partial/full knowledge about the design and working of organization's information systems; and 4) who has a potential to launch malicious attacks against organizational resources.

In an organization, an insider may have; 1) one or more roles along with; 2) certain responsibilities;3) technical expertise and 4) a hold on certain critical resources; which gives him 5) a number of opportunities; to harm informational assets in 6) intentional or unintentional way. Out of these factors, roles and responsibilities are granted by the organization itself in an overt manner; while technical capabilities or opportunities can be generated by an insider in an overt or covert manner. All these six factors are interrelated (Matt, et al. 2010). Fewer roles or less responsibilities lead to less workload and in turn may result in boredom, de-motivation or dissatisfaction. Higher responsibilities or more roles may lead to high workload; but in turn may result in stress and frustration. In case of dissatisfaction due to reasons including; less number of roles/less number of responsibilities/unfair rewards when compared with given responsibilities/poor treatment by the organization etc., insiders may suddenly turn to become an adversary. Techno savvy people may in particular pose more threat for any organization, if they become malicious. Access tocritical resources such as an insider having access to financial resources may create opportunities for theft. The greater the number of opportunities available to the insider, the greater the level of threat. .A famous example would be that of; Hanssen - the most damaging spy in FBI history (FAS, 2003). Hanssen's attacks involved hacking into his supervisor's workstation and compromising Foreign Intelligence Surveillance Act (FISA) wiretap applications in order to reveal the nation's most important counterintelligence and military secrets, including the identities of dozens of human assets. Hassen had both technical expertise as well as many opportunities to carry such malicious attacks silently.

Mmalicious insiders are generally involved in an unauthorized extraction, modification or destruction of sensitive corporate data; sometimes impersonating other user in order to escape safely from any kind of detection. They usually exploit their ready and immediate access along with their intimate knowledge about company's information resources to commit malicious, deliberate unauthorized acts. Here, while mentioning the term "malicious insiders", we do not refer to unintentional insiders. The threats arise from unintentional insiders are usually due to non-adherence or lack of security policy and non-conformance to security awareness and training programs such as poor passwords, poor coding practices, or falling prey to phishing attacks to share sensitive data with hackers etc. The attacks on Google in 2009 were initiated through phishing attacks carried out by exploiting non-awareness of unintentional insiders. Social engineering attacks become prevalent source of attacks against the unintentional insiders by luring them 1) to click on the malicious links, 2) to download malicious applications, 3) to share their credentials via phone/sms/email etc. Unintentional insiders can be treated as victims; but threats due to intentional insiders usually originate from malicious intentions and more damaging nature. Intentional malicious insiders can deliberately access valuable information in an unauthorized manner. Mostly they are technically capable and may use a combination of social engineering techniques along with sophisticated technical expertise to gain unauthorized access to organization's valuable information resources (Marwan, 2015). These malicious insiders can be active (perform a malicious act) or passive (help adversaries to perform a malicious act) with motivation affected by ideological, personal, economical, psychological or coercion reasons.

Intentional malicious insiders can also be classified into two categories – insider with authorized access but involved in carrying out illegal activities or insider having no legitimate access but trying to extend his/her privileges illegally to carry out malicious tasks (Zulkefli, & Jemal, 2014). Due to wider access and opportunities along with little/non-traceable evidence, intentional insider attacks become more damaging. Mitigation of these attacks pose more challenges than that of outsider attacks. In most of the cases of insider attacks, it is found that the attacker is a trusted techno-savvy employee who is capable of launching attacks. These types of insiders can leverage their assigned privileges to gather sensitive information. They adversely, deliberately, intentionally and inevitably misuse their trusted position in an organization to abuse, exploit and violate the information systems and services to compromise confidentiality, integrity and availability of organizations' assets (Zulkefli, & Jemal, 2014). They are well versed with the information systems handling critical data. They are aware of each and every minute detail about organization including mission, vision, policies, standard operating procedures, rules and regulations. However, in case of dissatisfaction due to reasons like unfair rewards/not well treatment by the organization, they may suddenly turn to be an adversary. They usually do not engage in rule breaking behavior and maintain their anonymity; hence they go undetected over a large time span. This makes it very challenging for organizational law practitioners to detect them. Further, unintentional involvement of legitimate users whose systems have been compromised by actual malicious insiders makes the detection even more challenging.

While studying the motives and intentions of malicious insiders, it is important to consider different categories of insiders such as full/part time employees, contract based workers, consultants, business partners, and vendors; as each of them may have different motives. Some of the common motives may be greed, revenge for perceived grievances, ego gratification, resolution of personal or professional problems, to protect/advance careers, to challenge skill, express anger, impress others, financial gains, secure future employment, and personal grievances from job termination/job dissatisfaction etc. The FBI report on Hanssen's attack states that his initial decision to commit espionage arose from a complex blend of factors including 1) low self-esteem 2) desire to demonstrate intellectual superiority 3) lack of conventional moral restraints 4) financial advantages, and 5) lack of deterrence etc. (FAS, 2003). The report also mentions that the personality flaws and the background that Hanssen brought with him into the FBI likely played a significant role in his decision to commit espionage (FAS, 2003). This example shows that malicious insiders are more dangerous than external attackers; as they are capable of carrying out malicious tasks in a very structured way that is smoother, faster, and less detectable and that might severely impact the organization (FAS, 2003). Hassen's attack incident also highlights the deficiencies in the FBI's protocol (FAS, 2003) in managing sensitive information. Due to longstanding systemic problems in the FBI's counterintelligence program and a deeply flawed FBI internal security program, Hassen had escaped from detection for a long time. This example also confirms the limitations of existing technological countermeasures in detecting malicious insider acts.

To combat complex natured insider attacks, organizations may need to implement a multi layered defensive approach targeted towards understanding motives/intentions of insiders, safeguarding sensitive business information, implementing effective security policy, logging and monitoring employee activity, conducting periodic and consistent insider vulnerability assessments, identifying and fixing any gaps in security controls etc. (MARWAN, 2015).

EXISTING ACCESS CONTROLS

Established studies on Information Security Management Systems (ISMS) focuses on many types of security access controls and categorizes them into three boarder categories named: Physical Controls, Technical Controls and Administrative Controls (REDHAT, 2016).

Physical Controls

Physical controls mainly focus on the physical protection of information, buildings, personnel, installations from man made threats like unauthorized physical access, theft, espionage, and terrorism as well as from natural disasters like fire, floods, hurricanes, earthquakes etc. Examples of physical controls are: Fences, Walls, Closed-circuit surveillance cameras, Motion or thermal alarm systems, Security guards, Picture IDs, Locked/dead-bolted steel doors, fire alarms, biometric recognition systems, secure properly grounded network/power connections, UPS (Uninterrupted Power Supplies) etc.

Some of the challenges with physical security controls are preventing employees entering facilities during unusual hours, unauthorized employees walking through an open door behind an authorized employee, and prohibiting employees to bring removable devices, Non-return of access badges after employee termination, physically entering another employee's office desk and accessing his machine, leaving personal laptops unattended/unlocked etc are additional issues. Many physical controls are targeted towards securing the organization from outsider attacker threats only.

Technical Controls

Technical controls are technological countermeasures for controlling the access and usage of sensitive data in an organization. Examples of Technical controls are Encryption, Smart cards, Network authentication, Access control lists (ACLs), File integrity auditing software, screen saver time lockout, identity management, authentication, authorization, firewall, Network Intrusion Detection System (NIDS), Host Intrusion Detection System (IDS), Intrusion Prevention System (IPS), Virtual Private Network (VPN), Secure Socket Layer (SSL), Transport Layer Security (TLS), Audits, Logs, HTTPS, Wireless Protected Access (WPA), Antivirus softwares, Log files, Event Manager, Port Scanner, and file access rights, Discretionary access control (DAC), Mandatory access controls (MAC), tape backupsetc.

Most of these controls are targeted towards securing the organization from outsider attacker threats. Few controls like audit logs, accountability, history etc. can be used for malicious insider detection.

Administrative Controls

Administrative controls define the human factors of security. It involves all levels of personnel within an organization and determines which users have access to what resources and information; Examples of Administrative controls are policies, security training, education and awareness, disaster recovery plans, personnel recruitment strategies, background verification, interview, rotation of jobs, mandatory vacations, personnel registration and accounting, risk analysis, business impact analysis etc.

Most of these administrative controls are targeted towards securing the organization from both inside and outside attacker threats. Policies form the foundation of administrative controls and should be communicated to all employees. Policies should convey message regarding what is and is not acceptable behavior and the consequences of behaving in unacceptable ways. Well-documented policies, standards, guidelines, and procedures provide employees with the capability to identify anomalous behavior in their peers, subordinates, and supervisors. Also training activity should not be treated as on time activity, instead it should be provided to employees on regular basis, in order to prepare them against any malicious events. To avoid fraudulent activities, countermeasures like job rotation, least privilege principle, need to know policy, mandatory vacations, peer review etc. will act as deterrent controls.

Physical, Technical and Administrative controls plays a vital role in implementation of an effective information system management system in an organization. Further depending upon the degree to which these controls can mitigate the risk, they are further categorized into three broader categories, namely preventive, detective and corrective controls.

1. **Preventive Controls:** Preventive controls minimize the possibility of loss by preventing the event from occurring. For example, Administrative controls such as segregation of duties/responsibilities (one person can submit a payment request, but a second person must authorize it), minimizes the chance an employee can issue fraudulent payments, Security Checks, Compartmentalization of sensitive information (i.e. dividing information into separately controlled parts to prevent insiders from collecting all the information necessary to attempt a malicious act), Implementation of career

enhancement policy with the goal of training all employees for the next higher position to create a pool of trained experts who may replace an incumbent leaving the organization even at short notice etc may also be beneficial.

2. **Detective Controls:** These controls monitor activity to identify instances where practices or procedures were not followed. For example, a business might reconcile the general ledger or review payment request audit logs to identify fraudulent payments. Depending on how soon the detective control is invoked after an event, a business may uncover a loss long after there is any opportunity to limit the amount of damages. Other detective controls are, alarms, sensors, surveillance, audit logs, event monitoring systems, location tracking (to determine throughout a facility by recording the locations/areas visited each day by the worker and the times that each location was visited) etc. To be effective, detection must be assessed.

3. **Corrective Controls:** Corrective controls restore the system or process back to the state prior to a harmful event. They minimize the impact of the loss by restoring the system to the point before the event. For example, a business may implement a full restoration of a system from backup tapes after evidence is found that someone has improperly altered the payment data, emergency response procedures, shifting processing on hotsite/alternate sites, business continuity, utilizing RAID (Redundant Array of Inexpensive Disks) systems. However, the restoration procedure may result in some degree of loss, like unavailability of systems and applications along with possible lost productivity, customer dissatisfaction, etc.

Further, these controls can be manual or automated (REDHAT, 2016). Manual controls help to minimize the chance of fraudulent payments, such as requiring an administrator and a manager to manually sign the applicable paperwork to indicate that the transaction was authorized and approved. As an alternative, the business can automate these controls by introducing a computer program with logical access, segregation of duties and maker/checker controls.

Based on these ISMS controls, it could be noted that many organizations invest their time, efforts and money in protecting their network against outside malicious attacks. However, they forget to focus on most damaging nature of insider generated threats.

COMPLEX HUMAN BEHAVIOUR ANALYSIS

While implementing effective countermeasures, it is important to note that the computer system controls cannot read human minds or their intent with perfect accuracy any more than humans can. Social engineer attackers carry out attacks successfully by studying human behavior, we as a defense side of this architecture also need to study complex human behavior and psychological factors in order to protect organizations from insider attacks. The effect of both personal factors (which cannot be changed and include biological characteristics, gender, culture, and age) and experiential factors (those which form an individual's personality based on past experiences) can be evaluated in these studies.

Within the psychology literature, there exist research that aims to characterise a person's mindset, such as the well-established OCEAN and the Dark Triad (Phillip et al. 2013). Immaturity, low self-esteem, amoral and unethical perspective, superficiality, proneness to fantasy, restlessness and impulsivity, and lack of conscientiousness are identified as important insider's personality traits by UK's Centre for the Protection of National Infrastructure (CPNI) (Jason et al. 2014). In order to judge the psychological risk levels, the author (Greitzer et al. 2010), studied psychological indicators such as 1) disgruntlement (dissatisfaction in current position, strong negative feelings regarding underpaid/undervalued etc.), 2) Not accepting feedback (e.g. unwilling to acknowledge errors, try to cover up mistakes by deceit), 3) anger management issues, 4) disengagement (For example, avoids meetings, remain detached, non-interaction with group), 5) disregard for authority, 6) poor performance, 7) More stressful, 8) Confrontation Behavior (For example, bullying), 8) Personal issues interfering in workplace, 9) Self centeredness, 10) untrustworthy characteristics, and 11) Unexplained absenteeism. The psychosocial indicators and the psychosocial risk were implemented as binary variable nodes in a Bayesian network model by the authors. The authors found that, self-centeredness is believed to be frequent as staff increase in seniority, some indicators such as lack of dependability, absenteeism acts as low risk while some indicators such as disregard for authority, disgruntlement, and anger management etc. act as high risk indicators (Greitzer et al. 2010). Besides this, insiders shorter term psychological states like stress, depression, anxiety and psychological disorders like gambling, drug addictions can also be considered as alarm indicators in insider threat detection.

MITRE researchers designed Elicit (Exploit Latent Information to Counter Insider Threats) prototype system for identifying insider threats (Caputo, Maloof, & Stephens, 2009). Contextual information related to user such as name, office location, organizational affiliation, seniority, projects, co-workers, job title, past activity, and organizational norms etc and related to information such as a document's producer, location, owner, and contents are used for detection of malicious insiders by the authors. After examination of user interaction with information, the gathered contextual information was used by Elicit to identify suspicious behaviours. Finally, a threat score is generated by Elicit by combining all observed behaviours in order to prioritize further investigations (Caputo, Maloof, & Stephens, 2009).

The authors in their work (James, & Janet, 2009) proposed a conceptual framework that captures the influence of the Big Five personality traits on some people who are more susceptible to the phishing attacks. The five broad personality domains are Neuroticism (tendency to have more depressed moods or suffer from feelings of guilt, envy, anger, and anxiety more frequently and more severely than other individuals), Extraversion (tendency to enjoy being with people and full of energy), Openness to experience (willingness to seek out new experiences/ideas), Agreeableness (kind, sympathetic, cooperative, warm, and considerate), and Conscientiousness (focuses on self-discipline, dutiful action, and a respect for standards and procedures) (James, & Janet, 2009). The study reveals that high score on Neuroticism, Extraversion, Openness to experience and Agreeableness were more inclined not to share their personal information in some circumstances. High score on Conscientiousness suggests resistance towards any social engineering and phishing attacks. The influence of the same traits can also be studied in case of malicious insider attacks.

Colwill in (2010) addressed criticality of insider threats and risks. Six personal characteristics believed to have direct implications for malicious insider risks: False sense of entitlement, personal and social frustrations, computer dependency, ethical flexibility, reduced loyalty and lack of empathy. Further the author emphasised on the fact that trust and loyalty can be transient and must no longer be assumed but supported by the appropriate demonstration and evidence of behaviour and understanding, in order to mitigate insider risks. Frank & Deborah in (2010) suggested a combination of traditional cyber security audit data with psychosocial data for insider threat detection and also stated the challenges/errors in evaluating predictive models for insider threats. Takayuki Takayuki in (2011) developed a framework that detects suspicious insiders using a psychological trigger that impels malicious insiders to behave suspiciously. In suggested architecture, first, the announcer creates triggering event that impels malicious insiders to behave suspiciously. These suspicious actions such as file/e-mail deletions are monitored to identify the suspicious insiders by analyzers. Greitzer et al. (2010) developed a prototype psychosocial model based on twelve behavioral indicators to predict the level of risks of insider threats. The author claims these easy to monitor indicators are capable of determining unstable individuals who, under the right circumstances, can break laws in anticipation of financial gain or revenge. A framework for characterizing insider attacks is proposed by authors in their work (Jason, 2011) to demonstrate how real-world cases can be mapped on to it to facilitate deeper understanding. Wiederhold, B. K. (2014) highlighted the need to involve psychologists in order better understand human behavior in cyber security space. He suggested identifying social situations in which individuals demonstrate a higher tendency to discount the risk of sharing private information, identifying patterns of malicious activities by observing deviations from normative behavior, adjusting people's perception by raising awareness of cyber security risks and also understanding the impact of cybercrime on victims'behavior throughout the stages of victimization etc. Bushra et al. (2015) suggests usage of internet browsing activity to predict the individual's psychological characteristics in order to detect potential insider-threats. Monica,et al. (2015) focused on the risky practice of sharing passwords and found that individuals who scored high on a lack of perseverance were more likely to share passwords. Identifying such individuals will help organizations improve their public awareness campaigns. The authors found that factors such age, self-monitoring, lack of premeditation, urgency, sensation seeking and lack of perseverance affect the tendency of insiders in sharing their passwords. For example, ounger people were more likely to share passwords compared with older people or highly impulsive person have greater tendency to disclose secret information due to lack of control on his/her emotions. In addition Hongmei et al. (2016) proposed linguistic analysis based predictive models as well as K-means to determine an employee's risk level through emails/social networking.

Social engineering attackers can gain advantage from the insiders who display by above mentioned personality traits/disorders. These attackers generally use following psychological tricks in order to influence insider victims to gain access to company's confidential information (Gragg, 2003; Lech, & Andrew, 2007).

1. They try to elevate the emotional state of victims, as victims are less likely to think through the presented arguments in heightened emotional states. For example, a fake mail sent to the victim by the attacker stating that he/she can no longer access particular system due to new security policies, may overwhelm the victim's ability to internally validate requests. There may be a threat of sharing password by the victim who is transitioned in this emotional state.

2. They overwhelm the victim by presenting a large amount of complex information, so that the insider victim may enter into a mentally passive state and start absorbing information without evaluating it. For example,, a fake telephonecall by the attacker explaining a complex tax refund policy may lead the victim to share his/her card/bank account details.

3. They exploit the human nature related to common psychological reaction to generosity (i.e. returning a favour). For example, the attacker may disconnect the victims machine from internet, make a telephone call to the victim by posing as technician, offering to restore the internet connection during the call. The victim may feel obliged to this attacker and in turn, he may carry out tasks which may be harmful to the organization. (such as installing any malicious software asked by attacker).

4. They may try to develop emotional trust from victims by pretending to have similar interests/ characteristics/ a common enemy to gain access to organizations information resources.

5. They coerce the victim to be part of some online survey (which may contain some malicious link), by succeeding in convincing victim that all of their colleagues had also taken part in similar kind of surveys.

6. They impersonate as an authority and ask for specific information by exploiting the fact that generally any employee is conditioned to respond to higher authorities.

All the mentioned study models are based on calculation of risk levels depending upon various insider characteristics. Most of these models target unintentional insiders and have limitations in case a security savvy person carries out malicious acts or if the malicious behaviour is not detected as an anomaly. The accuracy of these models can be verified successfully only after applying them in real cases/scenarios. The challenge in this case is most of the organizations may not report such insider related security incidents in order to avoid any damage to their reputation in the market.

We conducted a survey in our organization and observed the following factors related to insider behavior, as shown in Table 1. This survey was carried out as a part of a M.Tech. Course Security Standards and Audits. The students were asked to visit various departments, interview data center technicians/ employees of the organization and note down any findings.

During this survey, it is found if the employees believe that their actions can contribute to organizational betterment, it is likely to have a positive impact on their decision to adhere to the enforced strict security controls. Also perceived threat of sanctions influences their behaviour i.e., as punishment certainty/ severity are increased, the level of illegal behaviour decreases. If the employees are aware of existing monitoring and detection processes, they are more likely to follow the security policies with the fear of getting caught and penalized. Similarly, if the employees see their peers routinely following standard security practices, they are likely to be inclined to carry out similar behaviours. Long term permanent employees were less likely to become an insider threat, unless their job security was threatened by issues such as recessions or redundancy.

From the survey results, it can be seen that the security controls in many situations do not impede access. Also, such kind of surveys can reveal only unintentional insider attacks but not intentional malicious attacks. Hence, there is a need to study the complex human psychological behaviour while incorporating different countermeasures (Herath & Rao, 2009). Such comprehensive study incorporating proactive measures rather than based on reactive measures will benefit both employees and employer in building effective organization security.

Further, in these studies, we can also adopt white box and/or gray box penetration testing. White box testing generally simulates a scenario related to a person holding most privileges to access the system resources For example, system administrator and if he turns as an adversary, what level of attacks he can perform to cause damage. Gray box testing can simulate a scenario related to a person holding fewer privileges to access the system resources For example, normal user and if he turns as an adversary, what level of attacks he can perform to cause damage/how he will try to elevate his privilege levels etc.

Further during such studies,there is a need to analyze following important issues related to complex human behavior.

1. Capability to launch attack does not mean it will be used by an insider. Hence study and analysis on insiders who is likely to attack becomes a part of psychological domain.

Table 1. Analysis of organization security survey

Sr. No.	Task Carried out (intentionally/ unintentionally) by employee	Lack of Knowledge	Lack of Security control/policy
1	employees do disable antivirus software	thinking it is what slows their computer down	Disabling antivirus feature rights given to user
2	employees do often share passwords	So that other person can carry some task on behalf of him in case of his absence from duty on that day	Nonexistence of education/awareness/strict policy that prohibits sharing of passwords. Their blind trust on other colleagues.
3	employees stick password on their desks	complex passwords are assigned to each user which are difficult to remember	Users could have given the option to choose their own passwords with some controls like it should include special characters, symbols, numbers, minimum length should be=8chars, uppercase, not same as his/her name etc.
4	Sitting arrangement prone to shoulder surfing	Convenience and flexibility of working is valued more than information security, lack of awareness	Management should design sitting arrangements properly.
5	Users discussing corporate work related data/news with friends on social engineering websites	lack of awareness	Effective implementation of need to know policy required. Access to social engineering sites should be prohibited from office systems, users need to be educated through awareness programs.
6	Cash section staff knows the all financial details of other employees	The staff who was responsible for compiling statistics for financial/salary data, was also given read access to individual confidential data.	Effective implementation of need to know policy required. Data should be labeled and scope of access by staff should be defined.
7	Front desk staff person allowing guests/visitors in department without verifying their details	lack of awareness/training on how to deal with any visitor/ guest	Strict identity confirmation and verification policies need to be implemented at the front desk. Users involved in task of attending visitors, need to be educated through security awareness/training programs, CCTV monitoring systems, multiple level of checking before giving the access to visitors etc. may aid the situation.
8	Employees open any email attachment without any prior verification	Any malicious program (posing it as one of the genuine patches required by the system) can be sent as an e-mail attachment by attacker to a victim; to install it on user's machine to capture keystrokes or to overlay a fake window over the log-in window, to capture users log-in credentials	Effective spam detection email filters, strict email usage policies should be in place. User need to be educated through security awareness/training programs.
9	All records for the insider's department were maintained manually, on paper.	Records can be easily manipulated.	Awards can be distributed to motivate departments to become more online. Online docs should be stored securely on server. Most of the critical operations can be shifted online with digitization.
10	User can delete their email, files, browsing history, bookmarks, uninstall applications, stop execution of programs	There is no evidence keeping system in place in case of suspicious activities.	Un-installation/disabling of critical monitoring programs, deletion of history/email/files should be prohibited for users using strict security controls.
11	User allowed to download huge files	Malicious insiders may download malicious applications.	Increased/large sized downloads above normal should be alarmed/prohibited.
12	Users are encouraged to work after office hours.	Unusual/late hour works can attract many crimes.	There need to be strict policy/monitoring access system for late hour works.
13	User can send printing task to any printer in the network	If individual sends printing task to a printer other than the one closest to his/her office, raise suspicion.	A proper monitoring system must be employed to observe such unusual behaviors or such tasks can be prohibited by addition of strict controls.
14	Ex-employee had shown his old ID badge and security person gave him access to the premise.	Malicious ex-employees may be dangerous to the organization.	Strict physical security including CCTV surveillance needs to be implemented.
15	Employees use their smartphones for official works like email communication without any security. Their phones found to be in unlocked condition/not password or fingerprint protected.	If any malicious app is downloaded on to their phone sensitive email data can be leaked to outsider attackers. In addition of the phone is stolen then the data is also compromised.	Proper BYOD policies must be framed for the organization. MDM security solutions need to be implemented. Awareness should be created among users to lock their phone with password/biometric protections. Phones should be protected from threats like thefts and physical damage.
16	Biometric attendance system scans only in/out times.	As biometric attendance does not necessarily reflect a fact that person is in the premises or cannot track continually his presence in the premise, malicious insiders may use this opportunity to carry out malicious tasks.	Biometric attendance system along with CCTV monitoring may help in this case to track the presence of person within the premise/secure areas.
17	Users use the same passwords for longer time.	Easy to break such system when password remain static for longer time.	Mandatory password change should be enforced.
18	Contractors/Vendors are free to roam anywhere in the premises.	They can pose severe threats like theft of sensitive data.	Their access within the premise should be strictly restricted.

2. There is need of finding good tradeoffs between the individual's right to privacy and the organization's need to protect its assets.
3. Organization's intervention for security control may violate employee trust or legal guidelines. It may lead to misuse or false accusations.
4. Collection/monitoring of certain types of data may affect employee morale.
5. Non-malicious attacks or accidental loss of data by unintentional insiders can also cause major damage.
6. Challenges involved in spotting a lawful but suspicious user.
7. Uncertainty of employee actions as responsibility of whether to adhere to organizational security policies or ignore them is delegated to employees. Employees may choose to break security policies for malicious purposes or choose to evade security policies for mere convenience.
8. Monitoring every information security related action of each end-user is extremely costly and may not even be practically possible.
9. People may generally notice indications regarding abnormal behavioral pattern in their team member but fail to report it in timely manner; maybe they do not understand its significance, or felt that it is not their job to take any action or they do not know how to and whom to report it (Colwill, 2010).
10. Social influence in technology acceptance decisions is complex.

Besides these challenges, the study also suggested that instead of just implementing high level of security controls, it is better to train the insiders to follow good practices. An organization can use psychological tools to promote positive behavior on the part of employees. Hence, the psychological tools like motivation, punishment, certainty of detection and fear of being left out by peers etc. are found to play an important role in designing effective security policies for handling human behavior related issues.

POSSIBLE SOLUTIONS AGAINST INSIDER THREATS

As most of the security tools and techniques are designed for preventing or detecting intrusions and attacks from outside attackers; they fail to handle insider threats. These technological controls are not capable of preventing privileged system users such as system administrators from committing deliberate malicious actions. At the same time, limiting access for legitimate users to system informational resources may hamper their productivity and efficiency. Hence a good balanced solution is required.

Since insiders have legitimate and authorized access to system resources; it makes it even more difficult to identify malicious insiders because they are exposed to confidential organizational information as part of their daily tasks. Malicious insiders often abuse this privilege and use their knowledge of security controls to subvert defense measures and leak or steal mission critical data. Therefore; to combat this unique security threat, organizations need to implement their best security measures for detecting and responding to deliberate insider risks. After extensive literature survey and analysis, we have listed down following possible solutions for handling insider attacks. Most of these countermeasures falls under ISMS administrative controls, as they deals with human element.

1. There is need to enforce clear security policies, procedures and guidelines to employees at all levels of organization in order to mitigate suspicious employee's behaviours. The security policies must be communicated clearly to all. As malicious insiders are usually on the look out to exploit

any gaps in security policies, organizations should review the policies/procedures regularly and upgrade them as required to mitigate any security risks further.

2. Effective implementation of awareness programs is needed for training the insiders against security threats. Different modes of communication can be opted to promote security awareness amongst employees like, teleconferencing sessions, interactive video, training, web based training, videos, posters ("do and don't lists" or checklists), screensavers and warning banners/messages, instructor-led sessions, awards program etc. Irrespective of their role or function, every employee should be aware of the threats and potential consequences of malicious acts and of their own role in reducing the risks and in developing a comprehensive and effective security framework.

3. Robust access control mechanism with auditing capability is needed for all employees, which can provide access to only those who are authorized and keep track of their activities. Thus organization can make employees responsible for their own actions. Procedures supporting frequent and random auditing of employee system access can be adopted and confidentiality report can be generated.

4. Besides traditional authentication factors based on what you have, what you know and what you are, location tracking based factor called where you are can be used as part of insider threat prevention system (Sung & David, 2012).

5. Implementation of least privilege mechanism is required which allows any organizational employee to access only those information resources which are necessary to perform his daily tasks. Auditing for privilege over-entitlement should be carried out periodically.

6. Implementation of separation of duties policy is required which allows sharing of more than one individual in one single task in order to prevent fraud and error.

7. An auditing and securing security log is needed. Logs can contain detailed information which can be correlated with particular events happening within organization's information systems and networks. Security technologies such as firewalls, routers, intrusion detection systems, and antivirus software applications generate numerous logs; business organizations rely on those logs and analyze them for identifying any potential malicious insider activity, violations to security policies, and security incidents. Although logs can be very effective in capturing suspicious activity, timely analysis of huge amounts of logs is more challenging and in turn makes it difficult to identify and respond to potential malicious insider activity in a proactive manner. The presence of a centralized reporting program for security violations can be implemented.

8. Effective real-time event monitoring systems which can monitor insider activity and report any suspicious activities is required. Tracking of specific and critical events in real time should be supported.

9. Established security policies should be capable of determining what needs to be monitored and at what levels of system architecture.

10. Privileged users such as system administrators and IT managers should be monitored carefully as; they are aware of loosely enforced company's policies and procedures, system's security flaws and know how to exploit them to commit malicious actions. Therefore; business organizations need to pay additional attention to those advantageous individuals, like enforcing proactive and strict security measures following their termination such as account termination and ensuring that their access to any information resources is disabled.

11. Conducting insider threats vulnerability assessment is required in order to develop risk mitigation techniques. It's also important for organizations to incorporate vulnerability assessment plans into

a wide enterprise risk assessment strategy and identify the most critical information resources against both insiders and outsiders.

12. In case of sensitive job positions, regular or aperiodic/random counterintelligence polygraph examinations, background reinvestigations, regular interviews, frequent talks, meetings, discussions need to be adopted in order to prevent possible future unethical action/any accidental damage.

13. Mandatory periodic financial disclosure policy needs to be adopted by organization.

14. During hiring process of new workers, background investigations and police verifications, cross verification with suggested/related references, rigorous interview should be made mandatory in order to determine if a worker is vulnerable to becoming a potential threat in the future. The longer a person is observed the more accurate such predictions may be

15. Creating awareness amongst employee about handling classified materials, through repeated and regular interval training (both theoretical and practical oriented) in how to report and document security violations, role-playing scenarios to illustrate a specific situation, along with educating them on spotting suspicious behavior is essential.

16. Periodic personnel inspections/interviews/surveys may act as a preventive measure in every organization.

17. Implementation of effective job rotation policy adds the transparency in the work environment.

18. Being alert to individuals who are excessively negative about the organisation or their work.

19. Establishing formal organizational grievance procedure for staff to vent their feelings.

20. If an employee leaves the company, he or she should be escorted out of the company, shortly after returning the any and all company equipment. This will prevent the sabotage attempt made by a former employee.

21. Government agencies should attract talented civilian expertise in order to reduce rate of unintentional mistakes.

22. In the current era of social engineering, constant monitoring of presence of employee on social media sites is required to get useful information about his behavior/intentions. This data can be used as an alarm for the managers of organization. Any employee having knowledge of the physical and/or electronic set up of the organization's information system is vulnerable to social engineering attacks. Carrying out social engineering exploits is easier and far less time-consuming than that of any technical exploits to gain sensitive data. The mode of attacks may be in person, over telephone or via email. Social engineer attackers may pose as a high-ranking official in an organization, so that insider victim, intimidated by authority, may give out sensitive information. In such fake telephone calls, employees can be trained to handle call by using simple techniques like calling back to verify caller, asking some random questions and evaluating their answers, put callers on hold for some time in order to think more before passing any information.

23. Information flow can be observed at various stages via various controls. This may involve, prioritizing and constant monitoring information assets, observe baseline/normal behaviors on network, looking for anomalies etc.

24. Enumeration and audit of trust relationships with other organizations is required as their employees can be your insiders.

25. Preparation for data backup and recovery plan is important in order to survive any attacks.

26. Application of deterrent controls like, pop-up warnings indicating that employees are being monitored, signing company confidentiality agreement, addition of headers/footers indicating sensitiveness of document, mandatory training on safeguarding information etc. are important.

27. Decoy documents and honey pot techniques can be used to lure and identify malicious users.

28. To check the effectiveness of all controls, a feedback mechanism can be designed for assessment of implemented security program through evaluation forms, surveys, interviews, status reports, focus groups, independent observation, and bench marking etc.

29. Employees' suspicious behaviour, signs of vulnerability, unexplained wealth should be tracked time to time. Time to time, declaration can be taken from employees regarding their movable/immovable wealthy assets.

30. Anomaly-based detection methods which are capable of detecting the deviation between employee's current behaviour and his past normal activities may be used (Jason et al. 2016). Predictive models based on psychological profiling by asking set of questionnaires that cover user sophistication, pre-disposition and stress level etc. can be used (Jason et al. 2016). However, predicting the accuracy of these systems is difficult.

31. Directly-measured observables such ase working late, increased workload, web activity, phone logs, file server access and removable device usage can be used for insider threat detection (Phillip et al. 2013).

32. Generally, employees does not reveal their true nature in front of their boss. Hence, employee's peers can serve as monitoring tool. Training employees to watch for signs of discontent and encouraging them to anonymously report peers behavior to management may be used.

33. Escort temporary workers, contractors to make sure that they are in the right place while performing their duties. They should be reminded about their approved activities, including access to specific places and actions they should not perform

34. All access rights of terminated employee should be revoked immediately and same should be notified to the security guards/other concerned members in the organization who daily used to deal with this employee. Exit interviews can be conducted for terminated person to gain further hints regarding the purpose of leaving organization and to study his behavioural pattern/emotions at the time of exit etc.

35. In case of BYOD implementations, effective security measures like mobile data management solutions can be preferred to avoid any leakage of information to adversaries.

36. Periodic team interactions and frequent meetings with all employees may build the sense of trust on each other; spreading positive motivation towards organization.

37. People should report any sudden behavioural changes amongst the team members. Any display of potential betrayal characteristics should be reported immediately.

38. Finally, a team of psychologists working together with cyber security technicians should be implemented to study the characteristic behaviours of both insider and outsider attackers in order to safeguard organization against any kind of damage.

CONCLUSION

Malicious insiders' attacks against organizational resources pose a serious threat to organizations. Further the advancement and flexibility offered by technologies like Cloud environment, BYOD (Bring your own device), remote access systems, social media etc. makes the insider attack surface worse and broader. Insider threats have been extensively studied over last decade but still remains unsolvable. Although new technologies are being investigated to improve organizations' security postures to help understanding and mitigating insider attacks; there is a need to recognize this seemingly technical realm is actually a human problem. In most of the attacks, human behavior is the enabling factor. No technology solution is capable of preventing malicious insiders from carrying out attacks against organizational critical resources. A more comprehensive solution including support from psychological research may be devised to tackle this dynamic complex human behaviour based insider threat. Organizations need to study the psychological behaviour of insiders and continually upgrade their security solutions and employee training to tackle future attacks. Non-availability of sufficient real-world data and resistance of higher management to explore the risks of insider attack surface due to the legal implications involved adds more challenges in insider attack detection. Further, we cannot have 'one size fits all' solutions related to insider threats due to involved human behavioural complexities. However, such studies may lead a path for further investigation towards novel efficient mitigation strategies to overcome insider attacks.

ACKNOWLEDGMENT

The authors would like to thank Defence Institute of Advanced Technology, Pune for providing excellent infrastructure facilities to support this research study work.

REFERENCES

BBC News. (2013). *Profile: Edward Snowden.* Retrieved from http://www.bbc.co.uk/news/world-us-canada-22837100

Bushra, A. A., Philip, A. L., & Jason, R. C. & Nurse.(2015). Using Internet Activity Profiling for Insider-Threat Detection. In *Proceedings of 17th International Conference on Enterprise Information Systems* (pp. 709–720). Barcelona, Spain: Academic Press.

Caputo, D. D., Stephens, G. D., Stephenson, B., Cormier, M., & Kim, M. (2008). Lecture Notes in Computer Science: Vol. 5230. *An Empirical Approach to Identify Information Misuse by Insiders. Recent Advances in Intrusion Detection.* Springer.

Caputo, D. D., Maloof, M. A., & Stephens, G. D. (2009). Detecting the Theft of Trade Secrets by Insiders. A Summary of MITRE Insider Threat Research. *IEEE Security and Privacy*, 14–21.

CIO & Leader. (2017). *Cyber attack disrupting critical infrastructure in 2016 a likelihood, say security professionals.* Retrieved Apr 30, 2017, from http://www.cioandleader.com/article/2016/01/14/cyber-attack-disrupting-critical-infrastructure-2016-likelihood-say-security

Colwill, C. (2010). *Human factors in information security: The insider threat - Who can you trust these days? Information Security Technical Report.* Elsevier. doi:10.1016/j.istr.2010.04.004

Darkreading. (2012). *Five Significant Insider Attacks of 2012. Information Week: Dark Reading.* Retrieved Apr 30, 2017, from http://www.darkreading.com/vulnerabilities---threats/five-significant-insiderattacks-of-2012/d/d-id/1138865?

FAS. (2003). *A Review of the FBI's Performance in Deterring, Detecting, and Investigating the Espionage Activities of Robert Philip Hanssen*. Office of the Inspector General. Retrieved Apr 30, 2017, from https://fas.org/irp/agency/doj/oig/hanssen.html

Frank, L. G., & Deborah, A. F. (2010). Combining Traditional Cyber Security Audit Data with Psychosocial Data: Towards Predictive Modeling for Insider Threat Mitigation. Insider Threats in Cyber Security, 49, 85-114.

Gragg, D. (2003). *A multi-level defense against social engineering*. Retrieved Apr 30, 2017, from http://www.sans.org/rr/whitepapers/engineering/920.php

Greitzer, F. L., Noonan, C. F., Kangas, L. J., & Dalton, A. C. (2010). *Identifying at-Risk Employees: A Behavioral Model for Predicting Potential Insider Threats. A report published by Pacific Northwest National Laboratory on September 30, 2010*. U.S. Department of Energy.

Herath, T., & Rao, H. R. (2009). Encouraging Information Security Behaviors in Organizations: Role of Penalties, Pressures and Perceived Effectiveness. *Decision Support Systems*, *47*(2), 154–165. doi:10.1016/j.dss.2009.02.005

Hongmei, C., Carol, S., Zornitza, G. P., & Dominique, H. (2016). Determining Predisposition to Insider Threat Activities by using Text Analysis. In Proceedings of Future Technologies Conference (pp. 985-990). San Francisco, CA: Academic Press.

Infosec Institute. (2012). *Physical Access Control, 19 June 2012, Posted in General Security*. Retrieved Sep 12, 2017, from http://resources.infosecinstitute.com/physical-access-control/#gref

James, L. P., Janet, L. B., & James, F. C. (2009). *A Personality Based Model for Determining Susceptibility to Phishing Attacks*. University of Arkansas.

Jason, R. C., Nurse, O. B., Philip, A. L., Goldsmith, M., Sadie, C., Gordon, R.T., ... Whitty, M. (2014). Understanding Insider Threat: A Framework for Characterising Attacks. *Proceedings of IEEE Security and Privacy Workshops*, 214-228. doi:10.1109/SPW.2014.38

Jason, R. C., Nurse, P. A., Legg, O. B., Ioannis, A., Gordon, W., Monica, W., ... Sadie, C. (2014). A Critical Reflection on the Threat from Human Insiders – Its Nature, Industry Perceptions, and Detection Approaches. In *Lecture Notes in Computer Science: Vol. 8533. Proceedings of International Conference on Human Aspects of Information Security, Privacy, and Trust*. Springer. doi:10.1007/978-3-319-07620-1_24

Lech, J. J., & Andrew, M. C. (2007). Cyber Warfare and Cyber Terrorism. Information Science Reference.

Maloof, M. A., & Stephens, G. D. (2007). *Recent Advances in Intrusion Detection. In* Lecture Notes in Computer Science: Vol. 4637. *ELICIT: A System for Detecting Insiders Who Violate Need-to-Know* (pp. 146–166). Springer.

Marwan, O. (2015). Insider threats: Detecting and controlling malicious insiders. In *New Threats and Countermeasures in Digital Crime and Cyber Terrorism. IGI Global*. doi:10.4018/978-1-4666-8345-7.ch009

Matt, B., Engle, S., Deborah, A. F., Carrie, G., Frank, L. G., Sean, P., & Sean, W. (2010). *A Risk Management Approach to the "Insider Threat"*. Insider Threats in Cyber Security, e-scholarship, University of California. Retrieved Apr 30, 2017, from http://escholarship.org/uc/item/8sj9t023

Monica, W., Doodson, J., Sadie, C., & Duncan, H. (2015). Individual Differences in Cyber Security Behaviors: An Examination of Who Is Sharing Passwords. *Journal on Cyberpsychology, Behavious, and Social Networking, 18*(1), 2015. doi:10.1089/cyber.2014.0179

Philip, L., Nick, M., & Jason,, R.C., Jassim, H., Ioannis, A., Goldsmith, M., & Sadie, C. (2013). Towards a Conceptual Model and Reasoning Structure for Insider Threat Detection. *Journal of Wireless Mobile Networks, Ubiquitous Computing and Dependable Applications, 4*(4), 20–37.

Redhat. (2016). *Security Overview, Red Hat Enterprise Linux 3: Security Guide*. Retrieved Apr 30, 2017, from https://access.redhat.com/documentation/en-US/Red_Hat_Enterprise_Linux/3/html/Security_Guide/s1-sgs-ov-controls.html

Rose, R. N. (2016). *The Future of Insider Threats. Opinion-Cybersecurity*. Retrieved Apr 30, 2017, from https://www.forbes.com/sites/realspin/2016/08/30/the-future-of-insider-threats/#22e7a3d87dcb

Sanzgiri, A., & Dasgupta, D. (2016). Classification of Insider Threat Detection Techniques. In *Proceedings of the 11th Annual Cyber and Information Security Research Conference* (CISRC-2016). Oak Ridge, TN: ACM. doi:10.1145/2897795.2897799

Seth, R. (2015). *The biggest Cyberthreat to Companies could come from the Inside*. Retrieved Apr 30, 2017, from https://www.cnet.com/news/the-biggest-cyber-threat-to-companies-could-come-from-the-inside/

Sung, C., & David, Z. (2012). Addressing Insider Threat using Where You Are as Fourth Factor Authentication., In *Proceedings of IEEE International Carnahan Conference on Security Technology* (pp. 147-153). Boston: IEEE.

Takayuki, S. (2011). A Framework for Detecting Insider Threats using Psychological Triggers. *Journal of Wireless Mobile Networks, Ubiquitous Computing and Dependable Applications, 3*(1/2), 99–119.

Wiederhold, B. K. (2014). The Role of Psychology in Enhancing Cybersecurity. *Cyberpsychology, Behavior, and Social Networking, 17*(3), 131–132. doi:10.1089/cyber.2014.1502

Chapter 14
A Study of Good–Enough Security in the Context of Rural Business Process Outsourcing

Reena Singh
Manipal Institute of Technology, India

Hemant Jalota
DeepR Analytics, Canada

ABSTRACT

Data objects having low value like insurance or data-entry forms are shared between a client and rural business process outsourcing (RBPO) organisations for tasks like translation, proofreading, and data entry. These data objects are first decomposed into smaller parts and then assigned to RBPO users. Each user in a RBPO has access to only a few parts of a complete data object which he can leak to unauthorised users. But since the value of these parts is low, there is not enough incentive for the user to leak them. Such scenarios need good-enough security models that can provide reasonable security to an aggregate number of parts of low value data objects. In this chapter, the authors study the secure data assignment and leakage in RBPO by modeling it in the form of an optimisation problem. They discuss different scenarios of object decomposition and sharing, penalty assignment, and data leakage in the context of RBPO. They use LINGO toolbox to run their model and present insights.

INTRODUCTION

Information assets such as documents, audios, or videos are often shared between users. Scenarios where data sharing is across independent organizations make the issue of preventing data leakage more challenging. In recent years, an increasing number of data security breaches have surfaced. These events can not only have legal implications but also affect the brand image or business of an organization (Coopers, 2008). Thus organizations need to have a mechanism in place to prevent exposure of shared data to unauthorized users. Furthermore, recent studies have shown that internal employees of an organization

DOI: 10.4018/978-1-5225-4053-3.ch014

can also contribute to major security breaches. Many security professionals consider insider threats as an important challenge and better organizational policies and resources are needed for their management (Insider Attacks Industry Survey, 2017).

A resource may be shared by a group of people, with each person allowed access only to a part of the complete resource. For example, a user may be allowed access to only one section of a book. Restricting user access to a part of one complete resource helps in maintaining its security. The "need to know" principle restricts user access to only those resources (or their parts) which are necessary to carry out her responsibilities (Samarati, 1994). One way to achieve this is through a process of data distribution where each resource is decomposed into parts and distributed to the users, with each user getting access to one or more of these parts, based on the assigned task and the underlying security policy. This way of sharing data to business partners after decomposition is practiced by the Rural Business Process Outsourcing (RBPO) industry (Reena Singh, 2011).

In the recent years, there has been an increased awareness in India regarding the use of Information and Communication Technology (ICT) to promote socio-economic development of the rural population (Slaymaker, 2002). The RBPO industry in India has grown from USD 1.6 billion to USD 14.7 billion over a decade and this trend is expected to continue in the years to come (DSCI-KPMG, 2010). Some of the factors driving this rise of RBPOs in India are cost benefits from availability of cheap workforce, growing workload of repetitive tasks requiring simple skills, and increasing costs in cities (The stupendous rise of rural BPOs in India, 2016; Singh, 2010) . A detailed description of RBPO is given by Singh et al. (Reena Singh, 2011; Gonsalves, 2015). For clarity, we are reproducing it in the next section.

RBPO

Data and distribution is integral to the RBPO scenarios. The data includes documents, scanned images, associated audio files, videos etc. We refer to individual resources as data objects in the rest of the paper and use the terms resource, assets and data objects interchangeably. RBPOs distribute tasks across agents in different rural service delivery centres. The back offices of RBPO are distributed in several locations. RBPO organizations get orders from clients to perform tasks like data-entry, translation, proof-reading etc. They handle a large number of data objects (of reasonable sizes) on a daily basis. An RBPO organization has many small centres distributed in several locations and is organised hierarchically with a head office, a few regional offices and many local offices. The local office has a kiosk centre in a village or a cluster of villages, with computing and Internet facilities, shared by the operators to carry out the tasks assigned to them (Vaidyanathan, 2009).

A good-enough security measure adopted by RBPO is decomposing a data object into smaller parts before sharing with users (Reena Singh, 2011; Gonsalves, 2015). Sharing objects after decomposition has two benefits:

- Each part (or a set of parts) can be assigned to different users to carry out some task on it, independent from other users. Thus it decreases the total time required for task completion as many users can simultaneously work on different parts of the same data object.
- Each user has access to only a part (or a set of parts) of a data object. Thus, the overall object security is maintained.

Figure 1. Organization of a Rural BPO

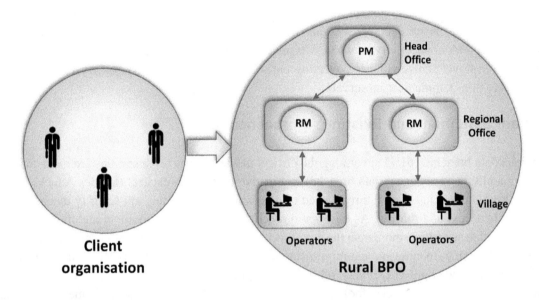

Further, given the low value and large number of resources, even if one user gets unauthorised access to some (say 10 out of 200 parts) which are more than he is assigned, even then the overall object is not fully compromised. Figure 1 shows the organization of an RBPO. One way of distributing data objects to RBPO involving object decomposition is:

1. A client assigns a task (e.g., translation) and sends the concerned data object to the Project Manager (PM) at the head office.
2. The PM decomposes the data object into smaller objects or doblets and distributes them to the lower levels (regional centers).
3. The next level comprises of Regional Managers (RM) at the regional centers who assign these doblets and task to the individual operators.
4. Operators at local centers form lowest level in the hierarchy. They perform tasks on the doblets assigned to them.
5. After task completion, doblets are send back to the RM for verification.
6. The RM checks quality of submissions and sends them to the PM.
7. If the level of RM is absent, then doblets are sent directly to the PM. PM approves the submission, composes the submitted doblets into a new data object and sends it back to the client.

The number of levels in an RBPO depends on whether it is a large or a small organization. A large RBPO organization generally has three levels with a head office in a city, regional offices in districts and local offices in villages (Vaidyanathan, 2009). A small RBPO organization can have two levels, head office in a city and local offices in villages. The client assigns tasks and data objects to the RBPO organization. Users in the RBPO carry out the assigned tasks on the shared object within the allotted time and return it back to the client after completion and necessary quality checks.

Samarati *et al.* recommend splitting of data over noncommunicating servers to give appropriate protection when outsourcing storage management and maintenance (Vimercati, 2010). In RBPO the low-value data objects are decomposed and shared with operators in different remote villages. In the absence of network connectivity between villages, since the value of data objects is low, the incentive of a person to travel across villages collecting parts of a data object is very low, hence this becomes analogous to non-communicating servers.

Problem Statement and Existing Approaches

Malicious data breaches (61%) are among the critical insider threats organizations are most concerned about (in addition to negligent data breaches and inadvertent data breaches) (Insider Attacks Industry Survey, 2017). These intentional threats need to be thwarted by adopting apt security mechanisms for internal data access and sharing. As information security begins to mature more and more companies are realising that security is more than the use of technical tools. It is about the process and practice with a focus on detecting, monitoring and minimising the effect of any security breach along with learning from the experience to prevent similar (related) ones in the future.

Security can never be perfect or foolproof. Sandhu proposes that a suitable security mechanism should be based on the cost of data ownership and ease of use, and that security should be "good-enough" and "business-driven" (Sandhu, 2003). A good example supporting this line of thought is the use of ATM card for bank transactions involving only a smart card with 4 digit pin number to secure the transactions which has worked very well till now.

A large number of digital objects are shared between users on a daily basis for carrying out different tasks in RBPO. Although organizations interacting with RBPO organizations desire their data to be secure, at the same time, given the limited skill set and remote distribution of users with less computing facilities, having extensive security mechanisms in place is both impractical and expensive given the less value of shared resources. To maintain a competitive edge, faster task completion is of prime concern in such scenarios. The value of each individual object is low. Some examples of such objects are insurance forms for proof-read or book-chapter for data entry. Since the data objects are decomposed into smaller parts before sharing with users, the value of each data object gets further reduced.

As mentioned earlier, a major risk security breaches in an organization can be attributed to both internal employees. Thus, modeling human behavior becomes a crucial factor in ensuring security of data assets in an organization (Mark Evans, 2016). The aim is to share resources in such a way that the employees having access to resources get less or no incentives for leaking them. This is ensured by - i) Keeping the value (cost) of the assigned data to be less, and ii) Adding penalty cost to the user in case the breach or leakage gets discovered. Associating penalty cost for data leakage is done to deter users from information misuse. Deterrence theory has a preventative effect that actual or threatened punishment has on potential offenders that affect an individual's decision about whether or not to commit a crime (Padayachee, 2012).

In RBPO workflow, different parts of a single data object, have different values and so the cost associated with leaking different parts varies. The objective of our "good-enough security" (GES) formalism is to find out the optimal number of object parts that can be leaked by users within the cost assigned by the organization. The number of parts leaked depend on the actual number of parts assigned to the users and the penalty associated with the leakage of each part. The cost that a user can incur for leaking a particular part differs across parts and data objects and it affects the user's decision whether she should leak that part or not. Thus, the higher the penalty, the lesser are the chances of leakage. Different applications have different security requirements based on a number of factors like the value of object being shared, task being carried on the shared object, or the trust on the users parts are being sent to.

Many existing approaches to modeling data leakage aim for leakage detection. They consider scenarios involving high value, sensitive data which is shared without decomposition. Few approaches modified the original data before sharing it with people. One such common technique is *watermarking*, where a unique code is inserted in the distributed object while sharing it with a person. Later on, if this particular data object is leaked, the leaker can be identified. Some approaches reduce the sensitivity of shared data by various techniques. One such technique is *perturbation* where data sensitivity is reduced by adding random noise to certain attributes, or by replacing exact values by ranges (Sweeney, 2002). White and Panda proposed a method to authomatically identify critical data items in databases to mitigate the influence of leakage using a statistical data relationship model (Panda, 2009).

Papadimitriou and Garcia-Molina proposed a model to identify the agent responsible for leaking the data which is distributed among the trusted agents. It is based on different data allocation schemes as well as distributing fake data among the agents (Garcia-Molina, 2011). Here the original data is not modified. Detecting misuse of data object via monitoring is resource intensive and time-consuming. Hence, careful selection of objects to be monitored is needed. Shabtai *et al.* proposed optimization models for selection of specific data objects for monitoring, such that the misuse detection is maximised and the monitoring effort is minimised (Asaf Shabtai, 2014). They assume that the original data cannot be modified before sharing and also fake data cannot be used.

Alfawaz *et al.* proposed a framework for understanding the behavior of organizational employees who perform authorised or unauthorised information security activities (Alfawaz Salahuddin, 2010). They conducted an exploratory study of organizations in Saudi Arabia, presented the observed information security practices and provided insights on the factors influencing human behavior regarding information security.

In this work we model good enough security for RBPO by modeling the object (and parts) assignment to user and leakage behavior so that the overall value (cost) associated with the data object is within the limit set by the organization.

MATHEMATICAL FORMULATION

We formalize "good-enough" security (GES) as an integer programming problem in this work. An integer programming problem is a mathematical optimization or feasibility program in which some or all of the variables are restricted to be integers. The system consists of a set of users with one or more parts of a data object (doblet) assigned to some user. The number of parts to be assigned to a user differs based on the value of the data object in question, reputation of the user etc. A penalty is associated for each combination of user and part being leaked. Every object is also assigned a threshold cost of leakage, which represents the maximum cost an organization can incur for leakage of this particular object.

In the remaining part of this section we first discuss the notations used in our mathematical formulation. Then, we define a model of GES for a single data object decomposed into a number of parts. Finally, we extend this model to a generic model suitable for more than one object.

Parameters Used in Our Formulation

We discuss the parameters used in our proposed models here.

- w_i: represents whether i^{th} part (doblet) is leaked or not. Thus,

$$w_i = \begin{cases} 0, & \text{if } w_i \text{ is not leaked,} \\ 1, & \text{otherwise.} \end{cases} \qquad (1)$$

- k_{ij}: represents whether user j received i^{th} part or not. Thus,

$$k_{ij} = \begin{cases} 0, & \text{if } doblet\ not\ received, \\ 1, & \text{otherwise.} \end{cases} \qquad (2)$$

- c_{ij}: represents penalty of user j for leaking i^{th} doblet.
- C_T: represents the threshold cost that the application can incur for leaking.
- U_j: represents the total number of parts that can be assigned to user j.
- w_{ik}: represents whether i^{th} part of kth data object is leaked or not. Thus,

$$w_i = \begin{cases} 0, & \text{if } w_i \text{ is not leaked,} \\ 1, & \text{otherwise.} \end{cases} \qquad (3)$$

- r_{ijk}: represents whether user j received i^{th} part of kth data object or not. Thus,

$$r_{ij} = \begin{cases} 0, & \text{if } part\ not\ received, \\ 1, & \text{otherwise.} \end{cases} \qquad (4)$$

- c_{ijk}: represents penalty of user j for leaking i^{th} part of kth data object
- C_{Tk}: represents the threshold cost that the application can incur for leaking k^{th} data object.
- U_{jk}: represents the total number of parts of kth data object that can be assigned to user j
- M: Number of users in the system
- N: Number of parts (doblets) of one data object
- L: Number of objects being shared

Model I

The aim of *Model I* is to maximise the sum of all leakages that can happen, subject to two constraints. The first constraint restricts the total leakage cost of the parts of a data object to be always less than or equal to the threshold cost allotted by an organization. This cost forms the upper bound on the leakage cost an organization can afford to incur. The second constraint restricts the number of parts leaked by a user to be always less than or equal to the parts she has actually been assigned. The mathematical formulation of the problem is as follows:

$$\text{Maximise } \sum_{i=1}^{N} w_i,$$

Subject to:

$$\sum_{j}^{M}\sum_{i=1}^{N} k_{ij} w_i c_{ij} \leq C_T, \tag{5}$$

$$\sum_{i}^{N} k_{ij} w_i \leq U_j, \quad j = 1, 2, ..., M. \tag{6}$$

$$w_i \in \{0,1\}, \quad i = 1, 2, ..., N. \tag{7}$$

Model II

In this model, the previous formulation of the problem is extended to more than one data object. Each object is decomposed into a number of parts and assigned to users. The aim of this model is to find the optimal value of parts that can be leaked across all the objects based on the leakage penalty and overall cost threshold set by the organization. The extended model is as follows:

$$\text{Maximise } \sum_{k=1}^{L}\sum_{i=1}^{N} w_i,$$

Subject to:

$$\sum_{j}^{M}\sum_{i=1}^{N} r_{ijk} w_{ik} c_{ijk} \leq C_{Tk}, \tag{8}$$

$$\sum_{i}^{N} r_{ijk} w_{ik} \leq N, \quad j = 1, 2, ..., M. \tag{9}$$

$$w_i \in \{0,1\}, \quad i = 1, 2, ..., N. \tag{10}$$

Both equations (8) and (9) are repeated for k = 1,.., L.

LINGO Model

We use LINGO toolbox to solve both Model I and Model II. LINGO is a software tool designed to efficiently build and solve linear, nonlinear, and integer optimization models (LINDO SYSTEMS INC, 1981). Figure 2 shows the LINGO model corresponding to the Model I. We extend this LINGO model corresponding to Model II. For simplicity, the extended model is not described in this paper. The values for different variables are based on the scenarios discussed in Section 3.

SCENARIOS

To validate the proposed models, we consider scenarios inspired from real life situations in the context of RBPO organizations. For Model I, these scenarios are considered with an assumption that single data object is shared between the client and RBPO organization. For Model II, L number of data objects are shared from the client to RBPO organization.

For this experiment, we consider the number of parts of a data object (N) is either equal to or greater than the number of users (M), i.e. $N \geq M$. There are three possible cases:

- If $N = M$ and duplication is not allowed. Here each user is assigned only one distinct part of a data object (doblet).
- If $N = M$ and duplication is allowed. Each doblet can be assigned to more than one users.
- If $N > M$ then some users are assigned more than one part of a data object.

To illustrate the difference between single and multiple data objects, we consider two examples. The *Example 1* demonstrates *Model I* and *Example 2* demonstrates *Model II* as follows:

Example 1: Let us consider that a *Project proposal* needs to be sent to an RBPO for proof-reading. The proposal comprises of 1) Executive summary, 2) Introduction, 3) Prior work, 4) Timeline, 5) Finance and budget, and 6) References sections. Section-wise decomposition is done to get 6 doblets, namely, *doblet-exec, doblet-intro, doblet-prior, doblet-timeline, doblet-budget, and doblet-ref.*

Example 2: Let us consider that 3 *Project proposals*, namely D1, D2 and D3 need to be sent to an RBPO for proof-reading. Each proposal comprises of 1) Executive summary, 2) Introduction, and 3) Budget sections. Section-wise decomposition of each proposal is done to get 3 doblets. For example, D1 is deomposed into *D1-exec, D1-intro, and D1-budget.* Similarly data objects D2 and D3 are decomposed to get *D2-exec, D2-intro, D2-budget* and *D3-exec, D3-intro, D3-budget* doblets respectively.

We now discuss the scenarios considered to validate our models based on Examples 1 and 2. Scenario 1, 2, 3 and 4 based on Example 1 apply to *Model I*. Scenarios 5 and 6 based on Example 2 apply to *Model II*.

Figure 2. LINGO model corresponding to the proposed Model I

```
SETS:
USERS / U1 U2 U3 U4 U5 U6/: PARTS_ASSIGNED;
PARTS / P1 P2 P3 P4 P5 P6/: LEAK;
ASSIGN(PARTS, USERS): RECEIVE, PENALTY;
ENDSETS
! Objective;
 MAX = @SUM(PARTS: LEAK);

! Leakage constraints;

 @SUM(ASSIGN(I,J) : RECEIVE( I, J) * LEAK(I) * PENALTY(I, J)) <=
 THRESHOLD_COST;

! Assignment constraints;
 @FOR(USERS(J) :
 @SUM(PARTS(I): RECEIVE( I, J) * LEAK(I)) <=
 PARTS_ASSIGNED(J));

! Here is the data;
DATA:
N_USERS = 6;
N_PARTS = 6;
THRESHOLD_COST = 5;
PARTS_ASSIGNED = 1 1 1 1 1 1;

RECEIVE = 1 0 0 0 0 0
 0 1 0 0 0 0
 0 0 1 0 0 0
 0 0 0 1 0 0
 0 0 0 0 1 0
 0 0 0 0 0 1 ;

PENALTY= 2 20 3 2 5 8
 2 20 3 2 5 8
 2 20 3 2 5 8
 2 20 3 2 5 8
 2 20 3 2 5 8
 1 20 3 2 5 8  ;

ENDDATA
@FOR(PARTS: @BIN(LEAK));
END
```

Scenario 1

Each operator is assigned a unique doblet, *operator 1, 2, 3, 4, 5, 6* are assigned *doblet-exec, doblet-intro, doblet-prior, doblet-timeline, doblet-budget, and doblet-ref* respectively. Further, we assume that the penalty of leaking any doblet is same for all operators, say *10.*

Scenario 2

As in Scenario 1, we consider that each data object is decomposed into 6 doblets and shared uniquely with 6 operators in RBPO. *Operators 1, 2, 3, 4, 5, 6* are assigned *doblet-exec, doblet-intro, doblet-prior, doblet-timeline, doblet-budget, and doblet-ref* respectively. Here, we change the penalty of a operator for different doblets. All users are assigned penalty of *2, 20, 3, 2, 5 and 8* on *doblet-exec, doblet-intro, doblet-prior, doblet-timeline, doblet-budget, and doblet-ref* respectively.

Scenario 3

In this scenario we allow for duplicate doblets. We consider that operator 1 is assigned *doblet-exec*, operator 2 is assigned *doblet-intro and doblet-prior*, operator 3 is assigned *doblet-prior*, operator 4 is assigned doblet-timeline and doblet-budget, operator 5 is assigned *doblet-budget* and operator 6 is assigned *doblet-ref*. The penalty assignment is the same as in Scenario 2.

Scenario 4

Here we assume that the object is decomposed into 10 doblets, namely *doblet-exec, doblet-intro1, doblet-intro2 doblet-prior, doblet-timeline, doblet-deliverable, doblet-budget1, doblet-budget2, doblet-signers and doblet-ref*. We consider that operator 1 is assigned *doblet-exec*, operator 2 is assigned *doblet-intro1 and doblet-intro2*, operator 3 is assigned *doblet-prior*, operator 4 is assigned *doblet-timeline and doblet-deliverable*, operator 5 is assigned *doblet-budget1* and operator 6 is assigned *doblet-budget2, doblet-signers and doblet-ref*. The penalty assignment is the same as in Scenario 2.

Scenario 5

Operator 1 is assigned *D1-exec, D1-intro, D2-exec, D3-exec and D3-budget*. Operator 2 is assigned *D1-budget, D2-intro, D2-budget and D3-intro*. The penalty of operator 1 on doblets of D1 are 2, 20, 2. The penalty of operator 2 on doblets of D2 are 20, 20, 2. The penalty of operator 1 on doblets of D3 are 20, 20, 2. The penalty of operator 2 on doblets of D1 are 2, 2, 20. The penalty of operator 1 on doblets of D2 are 20, 2, 2. The penalty of operator 2 on doblets of D3 are 20, 2, 20.

Scenario 6

Operator 1 is assigned *D1-exec, D1-intro, D2-exec, D2-intro, D2-budget, D3-exec and D3-budget*. Operator 2 is assigned doblets *D1-intro, D1-budget, D2-exec, D2-intro, D2-budget, D3-exec, D3-intro and D3-budget*. The penalty assignment is the same as Scenario 5.

RESULTS AND DISCUSSION

We executed our models in the LINGO toolbox. It provided optimal solutions for both Models I and II. We present the detailed results in this section.

Results of Model I

Table 1 shows the output w_i of the *Model I* for different values corresponding to input variables M, N, c_{ij}, C_T and k_{ij}. Rows 1-5 show the result of different threshold costs for cases where each user is assigned a unique part of an object ($N = M$). Out of these, rows 1 and 2 have the same penalty of leakage for any part of the object while rows 3-5 assign different penalties for different parts. Rows 6-8 show results for cases where a user can be assigned more than one part (i.e. duplication is allowed). Rows

Table 1. Result of Model I

S.No	k_{ij}	c_{ij}	C_T	Objective	Expected	w_i
1	1 1 1 1 1	10 10 10 10 10 10	10	1	Either	P6
2	1 1 1 1 1	10 10 10 10 10 10	15	1	Either	P4
3	1 1 1 1 1	2 20 3 2 5 8	5	2	P1, P4	P1, P4
4	1 1 1 1 1	2 20 3 2 5 8	10	3	P1, P3, P4	P1, P3, P4
5	1 1 1 1 1	2 20 3 2 5 8	20	5	P1, P3, P4, P5, P6	P1, P3, P4, P5, P6
6	2 1 2 1 1	2 20 3 20 5 8	5	1	P1	P1
7	2 1 2 1 1	2 20 3 20 5 8	10	2	P1, P6	P1, P6
8	2 1 2 1 1	2 20 3 20 5 8	20	2	P1, P6	P1, P6
9	2 1 2 1 3	2 20 3 20 5 8	5	2	P1, P4	P1, P4
10	2 1 2 1 3	2 20 3 20 5 8	10	3	P1, P4, P7	P1, P4, P7
11	2 1 2 1 3	2 20 3 20 5 8	20	4	P1, P4, P7, P10	P1, P4, P7, P10

9-11 show cases where the number of parts is more than the number of users, hence more than one part may be assigned to some users.

It can be seen that the values of leaked parts as given by the model (Column 6) agree with the expected results as checked manually (Column 5), thus validating the correctness of our model. Furthermore, we can see that as the threshold cost is increased for the same penalty assigned, more number of objects have chances to be leaked. For the same threshold cost, the number of objects leaked decrease with the increase in penalty.

Results of Model II

Table 2 shows the result of the lingo toolbox for *Model II* with $L = 3$ objects having $N = 2$ parts each, and $M = 2$ users. Different values are assigned to the input variables c_{ijk}, C_{Tk} and r_{ijk} and the value given by the model as output corresponding to w_{ik} is noted, where k ranges from *1* to *3* for the three objects we consider. Rows 1-3 show result for cases where duplicates are not allowed and each user is assigned a unique part. Rows 4-6 show cases where same parts are assigned to a user. Rows 7-9 have N = *3* parts of each object assigned to $M = 2$ users, i.e., $N > M$.

It can be seen that as in the earlier case, as expected, the increase in threshold cost allows more parts to get leaked and increase in penalty reduces the number of parts getting leaked for the same threshold cost.

Result Implications

Both the models show consistent results. We can see that the number (and value) of the resources that may get leaked depends on both the threshold cost set by the organization and penalty cost assigned to

Table 2. Result of Model II

S.No	$r_{ij1}/r_{ij2}/r_{ij3}$	c_{ij1}	c_{ij2}	c_{ij3}	$C_{T1}/C_{T2}/C_{T3}$	Objective	Expected	w_{ik}
1	1/1 1/1 1	2 20 2 2	20 2 20 20	20 20 2 20	5/ 5/ 5	2	X1, X2	X1, X2
2	1/1 1/1 1	2 20 2 2	20 2 20 20	20 20 2 20	20/ 20/ 20	4	X1, X2, Y1, Z1	X1, X2, Y1, Z1
3	1/1 1/1 1	2 20 2 2	20 2 20 20	20 20 2 20	40/ 40/ 40	6	All leaked	X1, X2, Y1, Y2, Z1, Z2
4	1/2 2/1 2	2 20 2 2	20 2 20 20	20 20 2 20	5/ 5/ 5	1	X1	X1
5	1/2 2/1 2	2 20 2 2	20 2 20 20	20 20 2 20	20/ 20/ 20	3	X1, X2, Z2	X1, X2, Z2
6	1/2 2/1 2	2 20 2 2	20 2 20 20	20 20 2 20	40/ 40/ 40	6	X1, X2, Y1, Y2	X1, X2, Y1, Y2
7	2/ 3 3/ 2 3	2 20 20 20 2 2	20 2 2 2 20 20	20 20 2 2 2 20	5/ 5/ 5	4	X1, X3, Y2, Z2	X1, X3, Y2, Z2
8	2/ 3 3/ 2 3	2 20 20 20 2 2	20 2 2 2 20 20	20 20 2 2 2 20	20/ 20/ 20	4	X1, X3, Y2, Z2	X1, X3, Y2, Z2
9	2/ 3 3/ 2 3	2 20 20 20 2 2	20 2 2 2 20 20	20 20 2 2 2 20	40/ 40/ 40	6	X1, X3, Y1, Y2, Z2, Z3	X1, X3, Y1, Y2, Z2, Z3

the users. The threshold cost depends on the value of the resource, thus scenarios where resources have higher value (important data) will have higher threshold cost. In such cases, if the penalty assignment of users is less, more number of resources may get leaked. Thus, for such cases, penalty cost of users should be set high to demotivate them from leaking the data. Furthermore, to reduce the leakage, less number of parts of the same object must be assigned to one particular user. Thus, the more the number of users with parts of a particular resource is being shared, the better the security (since a single user has low value of objects assigned which he may leak).

CONCLUSION AND FUTURE WORK

In this paper we present a formalization of good-enough security for Rural Business Process Outsourcing (RBPO) which involves sharing of resources of varied values, after decomposition. We use optimization techniques to find out the optimal number of parts (of one and multiple data objects) that can be leaked within the cost threshold assigned by an organization. The threshold an organization assigns for object leakage varies depending on the value of object as well as the reputation of the assigned user/ organization. Our analysis shows that more the penalty attached with a resource for leakage, lesser are the chances of its leakage. To reduce the leakage when the value of the object is high, less number of parts of the same object must be assigned to one particular user. The proposed models can be easily extended for different scenarios by changing values of different parameters. This will aid policy makers in studying different strategies for sharing data among employees and implementing the best one.

In future, we would analyze the proposed models in the presence of large number of users and data objects. We also plan to extend the proposed models to make them more dynamic, for example, incorporating dynamic penalty assignment based on the previous leakage behavior of a user.

REFERENCES

Alfawaz Salahuddin, K. N. (2010). Information security culture: a behaviour compliance conceptual framework. In *Proceedings of the 8th Australasian Conference on Information Security* (vol. 105, pp. 47-55). Australian Computer Society, Inc.

Asaf Shabtai, M. B. (2014). Optimizing data misuse detection. *ACM Transactions on Knowledge Discovery from Data*, *8*, 16.

Coopers, P. W. (2008). *Data Loss Prevention: Keeping sensitive data out of the wrong hands*. Retrieved 03 11, 2017, from https://www.pwc.com/us/en/increasing-it-effectiveness/assets/data_loss_prevention.pdf

DSCI-KPMG. (2010). *State of data security and privacy in Indian BPO industry (Tech. report)*. DSCI and KPMG.

Evans, M., Maglaras, L. A., He, Y., & Janicke, H. (2016). Human behaviour as an aspect of cybersecurity assurance. *Security and Communication Networks*, *9*(17), 4667–4679. doi:10.1002/sec.1657

Insider Attacks Industry Survey. (2017). Retrieved 09 09, 2017, from Haystax Technology: https://haystax.com/blog/ebook/insider-attacks-industry-survey

Lindo Systems Inc. (1981). Retrieved 03 11, 2017, from http://www.lindo.com

Padayachee, K. (2012). Taxonomy of compliant information security behavior. *Computers & Security*, *31*(5), 673–680. doi:10.1016/j.cose.2012.04.004

Panda, J. W. (2009). Automatic identification of critical data items in a database to mitigate the effects of malicious insiders. *Information Systems Security*, 208-221.

Papadimitriou, P., & Garcia-Molina, H. (2011). Data leakage detection. *IEEE Transactions on Knowledge and Data Engineering*, *23*(1), 51–63. doi:10.1109/TKDE.2010.100

Sandhu, R. (2003). Good-enough security. *IEEE Internet Computing*, *7*(1), 66–68. doi:10.1109/MIC.2003.1167341

Sandhu, R. S., & Samarati, P. (1994). Access control: Principle and practice. *IEEE Communications Magazine*, *32*(9), 40–48. doi:10.1109/35.312842

Singh, R., Divakaran, D. M., & Gonsalves, T. A. (2011). Taking rural BPO to new heights: an ACM for distributed and secure document sharing. *5th IEEE Conference on Advances in Networking and Telecommunication System*, 1-6.

Singh, R.,, & Gonsalves,, T. A. (2015). A pragmatic approach towards secure sharing of digital objects. *Security and Communication Networks*, *8*(18), 3914–3926. doi:10.1002/sec.1310

Singh, S. (2010). *Rural BPOs looking good to become a phenomenon in Indian outsourcing story.* Retrieved 11 21, 2016, from http://economictimes.indiatimes.com/tech/ites/rural-bpos-looking-good-to-become-a-phenomenon-in-indian-outsourcing-story/articleshow/6254294.cms

Slaymaker, R. C. (2002). *ICTs and rural development: review of the literature, current interventions and opportunities for action. Overseas Development Institute.* ODI.

Sweeney, L. (2002). Achieving k-anonymity privacy protection using generalization and suppression. *International Journal of Uncertainty, Fuzziness and Knowledge-based Systems, 10*(05), 571–588. doi:10.1142/S021848850200165X

The stupendous rise of rural BPOs in India. (2016). Retrieved 06 02, 2017, from https://www.outsource2india.com/why_india/articles/rise-of-rural-BPO-india.asp

Vaidyanathan, L. (2009). *Architectures for massively scalable, distributed rural service enterprises: requirements and models.* IITM-Rural Technology and Business Incubator (RTBI) and Xerox Corporation, Tech. Rep.

Vimercati, P. S. (2010). Data protection in outsourcing scenarios: Issues and directions. In *Proceedings of the 5th ACM Symposium on Information, Computer and Communications Security* (pp. 1-14). ACM.

Chapter 15
Online Research Methods

Linda K. Kaye
Edge Hill University, UK

ABSTRACT

With the advancement of technology and internet connectivity, the potential for alternative methods of research is vast. Whilst pen-and-paper questionnaires and laboratory studies still prevail within most scientific disciplines, many researchers are selecting more contemporary methods for undertaking research. This chapter provides an overview of a number of key online research methodologies to highlight their role in scientific investigation. In particular, it suggests how these may function to enhance our understanding of psychological issues, particularly within areas relating to cybersecurity.

INTRODUCTION

With the advancement of technology and Internet connectivity, the potential for alternative methods of research is vast, with many researchers selecting more contemporary methods for undertaking research. These include; online questionnaires, Smartphone-enabled applications (Apps), and online data mining, of which many can offer alternative research paradigms to that of traditional methodology. This chapter will provide an overview of a number of key online research methodologies such as those outlined previously, to highlight their role in scientific investigation. In particular, it will be suggested how these may function to enhance our understanding of psychological issues, particularly within areas relating to cybersecurity. Indeed, based on the prevalence of deviance which takes place in online environments, this calls for a focus upon the online arena itself as a platform to undertake research of this nature. In this way, we are ensuring our methods are ecologically valid as well as developing understanding of the digital skills necessary for practitioners to target cybersecurity-related issues.

Cybersecurity concerns are multidisciplinary and whilst the processing and computation of systems primarily resides in Computing fields, many issues may be considered to be psychological in nature. As such, cyberpsychology; a sub-domain of the Psychology discipline is becoming increasingly involved in cybersecurity policy and practice. However, even though many cybersecurity issues may consist a psychological underpinning, the efficacy of traditional psychological research methods may not be entirely sufficient to meet the demands of these issues. As such, cybersecurity researchers and practitioners

DOI: 10.4018/978-1-5225-4053-3.ch015

may be better placed to capitalising on alternative or modified methods from which to explore issues in cybersecurity. The Internet itself (comprising a multitude of domains), is therefore the central platform from which to obtain research data and opportunities. This considers the Internet both as a *mediator* from which to garner research data as well as the platform comprising the data itself.

Many methods described in this chapter fall under the umbrella of Internet-mediated research (IMR), in which the collection of research data is made possible by being connected through the Internet, to a functional online environment (e.g., online survey software, website, online forum, social networking site). The British Psychological Society (BPS) in their *Ethical Guidelines for Internet-mediated Research* define IMR as "any research involving the remote acquisition of data from or about human participants using the internet and its associated technologies." (BPS, 2017, pp3). In this sense, these specific methods would not exist in this form, in the absence of the Internet. As such, the advancement of Internet functionality and connectivity have been fundamental for the development of research methodology. BPS (2017) go on to define IMR further by making the distinction between reactive and non-reactive methodologies, whereby a reactive approach consists participants interacting with materials (e.g., online questionnaires, interviews) and a non-reactive one whereby researcher make use of data which is collected unobtrusively (data mining, observations). Online methods have been particularly popular for communication researchers within areas such as interpersonal, organisational or mass communication (Wright, 2005), although are also widely used in a range of disciplines. The next section focuses on online questionnaires as one form of IMR, with an account of their relative strengths and drawbacks as a data collection tool.

Online Questionnaires

Using online survey software to develop online questionnaires is becoming increasingly popular as a research tool. Survey software include; Survey Monkey, Survey Gizmo and Bristol Online Survey, although there are many others. These are not necessarily distinct from traditional pencil-and paper questionnaires but have been found to offer a number of additive benefits including:

- Time and resource efficiency.
- Relatively cheap (although pricing structures are typical and vary across different software packages).
- Access to diverse samples (Gosling, Vazire, Srivastava & John, 2004).
- Recruitment is not restricted geographically or physically.

However, with these benefits come a number of drawbacks including:

- Less intimacy in relationships with participants.
- Sample bias (Kraut, Olson, Banaji, Cohen & Couper, 2004).
- Less control in the recruitment and data collection process (Kraut et al., 2004)
- Lower response rate (Nulty, 2008).
- Some research measures may have restrictions on Copyright and Intellectual Property rights to publish online.

As researchers, it is first appropriate to determine whether online questionnaires are appropriate for the research questions, and more importantly, suitable for the target sample to elicit findings which will be representative of a given population. In some cases, online questionnaires can permit this process better than traditional pencil-and-paper questionnaires, as they can sometimes allow access to hard-to-reach samples (Gosling et al., 2004). However, it is worth noting that online methods such as questionnaires can be difficult to implement for those who are reluctant to engage in research. That is, without the physical presence of the researcher, this makes the research process more challenging than would be the case for pencil-and-paper questionnaires, and thus may not always be the most appropriate format through which to recruit research participants. However, conversely, the benefit of non-physical presence of the researcher can serve to highlight the anonymity of responding and thus may prompt responding on research exploring sensitive or moral issues, for example. There are also some ethical and practical considerations when developing online questionnaires, which researchers should adhere to. That is, although online research still follows the main principles outlined by the British Psychological Society (BPS) in its *Code of Ethics and Conduct* (2009) and *Code of Human Research Ethics* (2014), it is also strongly advised that researchers additionally consult the *Ethics Guidelines for Internet-mediated Research* (2017). This is relevant for most methods outlined in this chapter. Some of the key additional considerations are included in this resource, such as how to give consent online, dealing with withdrawal issues and online privacy.

One ethical issue which is often overlooked however, relates to mandatory reporting settings. With the exception of any consent statements which must be completed by participants who wish to take part, it is arguably an ethical violation to set questions as mandatory or compulsory. Namely, participants should not be "forced" to answer any given question if they do not wish to. Some survey software allow the option of "soft responding" (or something similar) which reminds participants if they have omitted any responses before proceeding to the next page. Using this option (if it is available) is the most advisable method when developing online questionnaires. If this function is not available, then researchers must ensure the questions are simply not set as compulsory.

However, in the context of cybersecurity, self-report questionnaires (online or otherwise) are not the most helpful as methods of detection or prevention of these concerns. Although they may garner data on users' psychological profiles or attitudes, they are limited in obtaining objective, real-time metrics relating to cybersecurity. As such, they may be best used to corroborate with other forms of (objective) data about users to be practically helpful in response to cybersecurity concerns (Halevi, Lewis & Memon, 2013).

Smartphone Applications (Apps)

With the advancement of mobile technology such as Smartphones and tablets, these are the platforms for which many Apps have been developed, which allow users to access Apps "on the go" within typical lifestyle behaviours. Researchers have started to take advantage of this opportunity by designing bespoke Apps which can garner data from participants within the context of their everyday behaviours (e.g., Andrews, Ellis, Shaw & Piwek, 2015; Kaye, Monk, Wall, Hamlin & Qureshi, 2018; Monk, Heim, Qureshi & Price, 2015). This can be operationalised in different formats; either as a data collection tool, similar to Experience Sampling Methodology (ESM), or as a "background" App which simply records Smartphone usage. The former of these as a form of ESM, is by no means a new phenomenon in psychological research (e.g., Csikszentmihalyi, Larson, & Prescott, 1977; Diener, & Emmons, 1985), yet the technological affordances of Apps provide additional benefits which traditional ESM research cannot. Namely, being able to obtain *real-time* data, which can provide contextually-relevant accounts of thoughts, feelings and/or behaviours. This may be particularly relevant as part of intervention or remedial strategies in research, in which in-vivo monitoring may permit researchers to intervene in a timely way rather than being otherwise restricted in this regard. In the context of cybersecurity, real-time data is particularly important on monitoring activity as-and-when it is taking place, and the functionality of Apps themselves may allow user identification and geo-location to be garnered; thus providing a mechanism through which individuals may be targeted in instances of deviant behaviour. Similarly, the latter format of App-enabled research in which a programme is installed to run in the background of a user's Smartphone, can be useful to gain usage behaviour such as number of times users check their phone, how long they use it for and how this may vary across time as well as context (if geo-location may be corroborated with these metrics). Indeed, this has been found to be a helpful addition to traditional self-reports in which Smartphone users grossly under-estimate the amount of times they check their Smartphones (Andrews et al., 2015). This "covert" approach to using Apps has merit in the context of cybersecurity given that users may be providing data inadvertently and be less aware of the impacts of their usage patterns on detection efficacy. The same may be said for Apps that users themselves may readily download from services such as Google Play or the App Store.

Additionally, the mobility of Apps also provide the opportunity for researchers to explore their research questions in a contextually-rich way, rather than being restricted by the laboratory or more traditional testing contexts (Kaye, Monk & Hamlin, in press). This holds a key theoretical benefit in which the phenomenon of interest can be explored in an ecologically valid context, whereby it is less likely to be prone to experimenter effects or demand characteristics. Further, given that contextual cues are known to play a key role in cognition, affect and behaviour (Kaye, Monk, Wall, Hamlin, & Qureshi, 2018; Monk & Heim, 2013a; 2013b, 2014; Monk et al., 2015), understanding how these work on a practical level is enabled within this type of research paradigm[1]. To make this type of methodology viable, researchers may find merit in collaborating with Computer Scientists, or alternatively, having development software which is freely available and offers a secure and user-friendly experience for non-specialised programmers (Piwek, Ellis & Andrews, 2016). With this established, there is great potential for this methodology to best capture "real-time, real-world" phenomena, across multiple participants simultaneously, in ways which have not been possible prior to functional Internet connectivity and mobile technology.

Like any other research method, however, this comes with its challenges and drawbacks. Namely, in respect of ESM-based App approaches, participant attrition is a key concern, in which requiring participants to respond to prompts within the context of their daily lives rather than within a controlled research setting can result in increased drop-out and withdrawal. The loss of participant control in this regard, is one key challenge of this type of research and whilst is immensely promising as a research tool, this may deter many researchers from attempting this type of approach. One way to bolster against likely drop-out, is to use the App system to maintain regular contact with participants throughout the research period, to ensure they are reminded of their participation and an ongoing relationship is maintained with the researcher. However, as App-enabled research is relatively new to the field of psychology, there is not yet sufficient evidence to suggest the extent to which this is effective as a strategy.

Online Immersive Environments

As well as IMR methods permitting connectivity to research tools such as questionnaires and Apps, there is also the potential of using immersive environments as research contexts themselves. This may be undertaken in multi-user virtual environments (MUVEs) such as Second Life or via other avatar-based interfaces.

Second Life, and other MUVEs can be useful research environments, particularly if researchers wish to explore a phenomenon associated with such a context. For example, Kleban and Kaye (2015) undertook interviews in the world of Second Life via Instant Messaging (IM) to explore the psychosocial affordances of Second Life for individuals with physical disabilities. Arguably, one may speculate that these interviews did not necessitate being undertaken in Second Life and could have simply been undertaken over email or IM. However, the role of context and salience is important here, as well as a sense of community which would be compromised otherwise, thus highlighting the utility of this approach for this sort of research. Although this approach is not appropriate for all research, it is indeed a novel means through which to explore individuals (or their alter egos, in some cases) within a meaningful context, and thus better investigate these issues as social phenomena rather than as independent entities. Within the context of cybersecurity or online deception, for example, this may be particularly useful as a way of understanding how users behave (or respond to questions) in certain contexts to explore the extent to which these environments may be suitable to prompt more accurate or enriched data compared to traditional interview formats. Indeed, evidence highlights the efficacy of avatar-mediated presence for accuracy of detecting truth and deception (Steptoe, Steed, Rovira & Rae, 2010), as well as on perceived intimateness and interpersonal trust (Bente, Rüggenberg, Krämer & Eschenburg, 2009), suggesting some potential of this technique over other methods such as purely text-based interactions.

MECHANICS ANALYSIS

One more novel means of undertaking research using online methods includes mechanics analysis. That is, when using touchscreen platforms such as tablets or Smartphones, there is the potential to obtain data on users' tactile responding such as temporal properties or intensity of touch or strokes and their correspondence with emotional states during screen-time activities such as gaming. That is, research has used this approach and established reasonable accuracy in discriminating emotional states as a product of finger strokes (Gao Bianchi-Berthouze, & Meng, 2012). Namely, states such as excitement, relaxation, frustration, boredom and arousal have been found to be discriminatory using this method (ibid). Although the efficacy of this method would appear to be largely restricted to touch-screen technology and perhaps more relevant for some online domains than others (e.g., gaming), the potential to extent this methodological approach to further explore psychological or emotional correlates of online experiences is promising.

Big Data

In recent years, "big data" has become a widely-used term and is generating interest in academics as well as industry representatives. Big data (often used interchangeably with "meta-data") refers to large-scale data sets which can be obtained from online sources and analysed in a quantitative way. In this way, it may transform pieces of qualitative data into a larger, contextualised quantitative form (Kunc, Malpass & White, 2016). Big data drawn from online sources may then be analysed in a number of different ways, including data mining or machine learning, through visualisation, optimisation and simulation.

There are a number of types of big data including:

- Online data- social networking sites, news feeds, web content.
- Consumed data- obtained from digital services.
- Actively supply data- obtained through crowdsourcing or respondent reporting.
- Data from objects- such as satellites or drones.

In respect of cybersecurity, the potential for gathering online data through social networking is vast, given the prevalence of the population who occupy these spaces. In this way, cybersecurity practitioners have a wealth of information they may access to gain insight into users' behaviours which may reveal something about mood, personality and intentions. Clearly this may be important information in cases of cyber deviance. For example, previous research has revealed that Facebook profiles are useful for enabling others to make accurate first impressions of others about their personality; namely in respect of their level of extraversion, conscientiousness and openness to experience (Darbyshire, Kirk, Wall & Kaye, 2016; Wall, Kaye & Malone, 2016). Big data which consolidates patterns across profiles, and combined this knowledge of the psychological correlates of these behaviours, is thus a valuable tool in the realm of cybersecurity.

Research in this regard has analysed social networking behaviour to explore issues such as information disclosure and cyber-victimisation (Benson, Saridakis & Tennakoon, 2015; Saridakis, Bendon, Ezingeard & Tennakoon, 2016). It has been found, for example, that it is possible to model social networking behaviour to explore how users' control over personal information is negatively related to their information disclosure (Benson et al., 2015), and that greater use of social networking sites is related to cyber-victimisation (Saradakis et al., 2016). These are just some examples of how researchers may capitalise on forms of online behaviour, such as social networking behaviours as a way of exploring issues relevant in cybersecurity.

Other methods typically used in cybersecurity include of those data visualisation methods (Staheli et al., 2014) and statistical language models (Zhou, Shi & Zhang, 2008). That is, data visualisation displays patterns of user behaviour such as logins and multiple account accessing from different devices to identify anomalies or vulnerabilities in behavioural patterns (Goodall, Radwan & Halseth, 2010). This approach has efficacy in its ability to draw global or indeed local analysis of user behaviour across networks which can support cybersecurity endeavours. Similarly, statistical language modelling garners words from text to categorise them as cues to detect behaviours such as online deception (Zhou et al., 2008). Clearly these large-scale, quantitative approaches have merit in the context of cybersecurity to model user behaviour as a proactive strategy to monitoring real-time concerns.

Finally, in the context of intrusion detection, there are additional ways of implementing cybersecurity practices using online data. For example, misuse detection-based systems apply knowledge from recognised attack patterns to identify current intrusion behaviour (Faysel & Haque, 2010). This can use signature-based approaches for example, which analyse the semantic characteristics of an attack from sources such as audit data logs in computing systems. Alternatively, a rule-based approach can be used whereby conditional rules are applied as detection techniques (Ning & Jajodia, 2003). There are also anomaly detection based systems which can apply statistical modelling, data mining or machine learning to highlight non-conformist behaviour and outliers (Faysel & Haque, 2010). Although most approaches here have been found to hold useful detection efficacy, there is greater degree of variability in their *prevention* potential (Faysel & Haque, 2010).

Netnography

The converse of big data is the potential to use online data to garner idiographic insight into psychological phenomena, rather than more nomothetic perspectives as is more the case for big data. As such, netnography is the way in which ethnographic research techniques may be applied within online contexts (Kozinets, 2002). Specifically, this approach uses ethnography as a way of understanding social interactions in digital communication contexts, from the perspective that the researcher is observing participant behaviour. Within this, the researcher discloses his or her presence and intentions within a given online community prior to the commencement of the research, and obtains copies of communications from members from which to make observations and developing coding strategies. Particularly, researchers should obtain specific permission from any member whose content is to be quoted in the research (Kozinets, 2002). As well as content analysis being highly regarded as a method of analysis (Langer & Beckman, 2005), obtaining online data can also permit other micro-analytic approaches such as conversation or discourse analysis (Giles, Stommel, Paulus, Lester & Reed, 2015). Indeed, conversation analysis has readily been used in respect of social media behaviours, particularly for exploring issues such as sequentiality in online posts (Reeves & Brown, 2016; Tolmie, Procter, Rouncefield, Liakata & Zubiaga, 2015). Additionally, other research has used Membership Categorisation Analysis as a means of exploring issues such as normative values and cultural practices in online communities (Simthson, Sharkey, Hewis, Jones, Emmens, Ford & Owens, 2011). These discursive methods are enlightening when exploring a range of research questions, including identity construction, lived experiences and user interaction, and are specifically useful for exploring sensitive topics (Langer & Beckman, 2005). Indeed, research for example, has identified how European politicians use Twitter for identity construction on both an individual and national level, through behaviours such as their linguistic strategies (De Cock & Roginsky, 2015). Alternatively, other research has found how obtaining screen-captures of online interaction can enable researchers gain access to the "lived experience" in context (Meredith, 2015). Understanding these sorts of interactions from a micro-perspective is noteworthy in light of the fact that online platforms are often a basis through which collective action is established and transformed to "real world" behaviours (Spears & Postmes, 2013). If political or radical action is a common feature in online environments, this provides data through which to understand these nuances and thus, the potential to develop strategies to intervene.

The key benefits of this approach is the largely "covert" role of the researcher within the research process. That is, although, as noted previously, their presence should be made apparent, there is less likelihood of them inadvertently impacting upon participant behaviour, as may be the case in experimental or self-report research. In the context of a real-world, meaningful context, the participant is in their more "natural" environment, and the presence of the researcher is more of a passive observer, than an active experimenter. As such, the likelihood of demand characteristics and social desirable responding is greatly reduced, in which more valid behaviour is expressed. Additionally, this also increases the likelihood of overall "participation" in the research as individuals are not so much "signing up" for research as is determined by the researcher, but more that they are allowing the researcher an insight into their behaviours, as and when they occur. As such, this is a highly useful approach from which to obtain lived accounts in a way which is not overly imposing or impactful on participants' usual behaviours.

However, in the context of cybersecurity this approach is a largely cumbersome means by which to monitor and assess threats for cybersecurity. That is, these approaches require researcher input in the analysis of extensive data which represents a time-consuming and resource-heavy pursuit. Further, these are unlikely to be representing real-time behaviours which calls into questions their applicability within proactive cybersecurity strategies.

GENERAL PRACTICAL AND ETHICAL PRINCIPLES FOR ONLINE RESEARCH

This chapter will now outline for additional principles which are relevant for conducting data using on-line research methods. This involves considerations at the participant pre-recruitment and recruitment stages, as well as issues surrounding researcher protection.

Pre-Recruitment

Prior to advertising research, researchers should be mindful of their role within a given online community. That is, this may require them to be active, known members of a community prior to undertaking research (e.g., for posting adverts to online questionnaires or requests for interviews). Online forums or networking sites for example, are often reluctant to permit research requests from member who have suddenly appeared with their advert without having first engaged with the community. Therefore, building relationships and engaging in community activities (discussions, forum threads) with members prior to recruiting is important. Within this, researchers should be engaging in the community with the identity of themselves as a researcher (and not an alter ego, or as an "undercover member"). Additionally, seeking permission from administrators, leaders or moderators of online communities to use the community as a place to undertake research should be a step all researchers should take prior to making research adverts available to members.

However, other online research may be undertaken by researchers which may reflect a form of "covert observation", a widely known approach in observational psychological research. For this, the researcher simply observes behaviour in its natural environment, without detailing their presence as a researcher. This may be relevant for research which uses online data from which to conduct analyses, such as micro-analysis or to undertake large-scale data mining. This is ONLY appropriate for publicly-available data. Although it is often tricky to establish the boundaries between public and private in online environments (see Kraut et al., 2004), public data would typically be any data which can be accessed without requiring authorisation, such as a log in to the host content provider. Any information which appears through a Google search and can be accessed fully would most likely be an example of public data. Should researchers require to access private participant online data (behaviours which have already taken place, and thus recorded digitally), this would be undertaken through requesting participant consent to obtain the data, detailing how it will be used and stored, in a similar way to other data gained in psychological research. It is also appropriate to allow participants to opportunity to remove or delete any details they would not wish the researcher to see prior to the data compilation process commencing.

Recruitment

Similarly to pre-recruitment, it is important for researchers to remain engaged within the given community to ensure that if members wish to ask questions about research or discuss issues (either on discussion boards or through private messages) that they have the opportunity to do so. Although it is standard practice for researchers to provide their contact details within the Briefing and Debriefing Stage of research, this will not necessarily be the only means by which participants may make contact. Researchers should be mindful of this, and therefore respond accordingly to queries and questions which may arise (either during or after the research has been undertaken). This is also important when returning after completion of the research to show thanks to participants and the community for their engagement or interest in the research.

Researcher Protection

Although much is discussed about ethical principles and practices in respect of participants, less is said about researchers and their potential vulnerability when recruiting in online worlds. Although this is not necessarily a new phenomenon in conducting research, the vastness of online environments which may be accessed by hundreds or thousands of users, means researchers may be vulnerable to threat or even harassment. This is a particular issue in respect of researchers needing to be identifiable in the research process, as previously mentioned. This may be particularly likely when researchers are studying controversial issues in which online members may send threatening messages based on their assumption about their position on such issues. There is no easy way of avoiding this possibility, except to have developed a good working relationship with the moderators of a given online community, and to remain professional in responding to any messages. If the community is well-maintained, the moderators should be supportive to any targets of such threats and take steps to remove any negative messages and in some cases, ban problematic members. However, this is not always the case. As a researcher, the best practice is to be familiar with the given community and its moderation processes prior to starting the research process (as previously mentioned, this is good practice anyway). This may help researchers decide on the nature of the community and how problematic behaviour is dealt with. If there is little evidence of any standardised practice in this regard, these communities are best to avoid.

E-Consent

Recent commentary has highlighting a number of opportunities and challenges associated with giving consent online (Grady, Cummings, Rowbotham, McConnell, Ashley & Kang, 2017). Namely, the advancement of Apps and Internet-based methods for enabling research has developed numerous complexities in the consent process which would traditionally be relatively straightforward. That is, consent principles such as ensuring participants understand the research and their rights is more difficult to control outside the traditional testing environment. For example, people do not readily read agreements or terms and conditions when on digital devices, and further, neither party is able to easily ask questions to gain assurance of understanding (Grady et al., 2017). Further in App-based methods, it may not always be possible to verify the identity of the participant. These are a number of challenges associated with giving consent online (e-consent), although there is development towards transforming e-consent practices, particularly in clinical research (Grady et al., 2017). For example, the interactive and multimedia affordances of mobile devices allow the possibility to provide consent information in the form of video clips or animation, with interactive quizzes to ensure understanding. Therefore, researchers should be mindful of the user-experience when developing research resources, including ethical information, given these are influential factors for engagement in these virtual environments.

CONCLUSION

Overall, the advancement of technology and functionality of the Internet has greatly developed the potential for new and extended methods of research enquiry beyond the traditional self-report or laboratory study. Arguably, one of the key benefits, as discussed within this chapter, is the potential to explore behaviour in a contextually-meaningful way, and additionally in respect of real-time occurrences, in some cases. Whilst utilising some of the methods outlined here are not necessarily relevant or appropriate for all research questions, researchers should consider the potential for these alternative methodologies which may not only hold new practical implications, but more importantly, be theoretically insightful.

From a practitioner perspective, it is important to understand that there is still much to learn about how our online behaviours and responses which may be garnered through these methods are truly representative of our "real world" behaviours. It should always be acknowledged that context (e.g., virtual versus face-to-face) can elucidate different characteristics and behaviours of users, and this can be largely idiosyncratic for different individuals. Therefore, this should be a critical consideration when using research data obtained from online formats, with a recommendation to remain vigilant of the ongoing work within the area of cyberpsychology and related disciplines which aim to establish further insight into these issues.

REFERENCES

Andrews, S., Ellis, D. A., Shaw, H., & Piwek, L. (2015). Beyond self report: Tools to compare estimated and real-world Smartphone use. *PLoS One*, *10*(10), e0139004. doi:10.1371/journal.pone.0139004 PMID:26509895

Benson, V., Saridakis, G., & Tennakoon, H. (2015). Information disclosure of social media users: Does control over personal information, user awareness and security notices matter? *Information Technology & People*, *28*(3), 426–441. doi:10.1108/ITP-10-2014-0232

Bente, G., Rüggenberg, S., Krämer, N. C., & Eschenburg, F. (2009). Avatar-Mediated Networking: Increasing Social Presence and Interpersonal Trust in Net-Based Collaborations. *Human Communication Research*, *34*(2), 287–318. doi:10.1111/j.1468-2958.2008.00322.x

BPS. (2009). *Code of Ethics and Conduct*. Leicester, UK: British Psychological Society.

BPS. (2014). *Code of Human Research Ethics*. Leicester, UK: British Psychological Society.

BPS. (2017). *Ethics Guidelines for Internet-mediated Research*. Leicester, UK: British Psychological Society.

Csikszentmihalyi, M., Larson, R., & Prescott, S. (1977). The ecology of adolescent activity and experience. *Journal of Youth and Adolescence*, *6*(3), 281–294. doi:10.1007/BF02138940 PMID:24408457

Darbyshire, D. E., Kirk, C., Wall, H. J., & Kaye, L. K. (2016). Don't Judge a (Face)Book by its Cover: Exploring Judgement Accuracy of Others' Personality on Facebook. *Computers in Human Behavior*, *58*, 380–387. doi:10.1016/j.chb.2016.01.021

De Cock, B., & Roginsky, S. (2015). Discursive identities on Twitter: Construction of the identity of MEP in pre-election period. Comparison between France, Spain and the United Kingdom. In F. Lienard & S. Zlitni (Eds.), *Electronic communication: challenges, opportunities and strategies* (pp. 137–148). Limoges: Lambert-Lucas.

Diener, E., & Emmons, R. A. (1985). The independence of positive and negative affect. *Journal of Personality and Social Psychology, 47*, 1108–1117. PMID:6520704

Faysel, M. A., & Haque, S. S. (2010). Towards Cyber Defence: Research in Intrusion Detection and Intrusion Prevention Systems. *International Journal of Computer Science and Network Security, 10*(7), 316–325.

Gao, Y., Bianchi-Berthouze, N., & Meng, H. (2012). What does touch tell us about emotions in touch-screen-based gameplay? *ACM Transactions on Computer-Human Interaction, 19*(4).

Giles, D. C., Stommel, W., Paulus, T., Lester, J., & Reed, D. (2015). The microanalysis of online data: The methodological development of 'digital CA'. *Discourse, Context and Media, 7*, 45–51. doi:10.1016/j.dcm.2014.12.002

Goodall, J. R., Radwan, H., & Halseth, L. (2010). Visual analysis of code security. In *Proceedings of the Seventh International Symposium on Visualisation for Cyber Security* (pp. 46-51). Ottawa, Ontario, Canada: Academic Press. doi:10.1145/1850795.1850800

Gosling, S. D., Vazire, S., Srivastava, S., & John, O. P. (2004). Should we trust web-based studies? A comparative analysis of seix preconceptions about Internet questionnaires. *The American Psychologist, 59*(2), 93–104. doi:10.1037/0003-066X.59.2.93 PMID:14992636

Grady, C., Cummings, S. R., Rowbotham, M. C., McConnell, M. V., Ashley, E. A., & Kang, G. (2017). Informed Consent. *The New England Journal of Medicine, 376*(9), 856–867. doi:10.1056/NEJMra1603773 PMID:28249147

Halevi, T., Lewis, J., & Memon, N. (2013). A pilot study of cyber security and privacy related behaviour and personality traits. In *Proceedings of WWW '13 Companion Proceedings of the 22nd international conference on World Wide Web companion* (pp. 737–744). Rio de Janeiro, Brazil: Academic Press.

Kaye, L. K., Monk, R. L., & Hamlin, I. (in press). "Feeling appy?": Using app-based methodology to explore contextual effects on real-time cognitions, affect and behaviours. In C. Costa & J. Condie (Eds.), *Doing research in and on the digital: Research methods across fields of inquiry*. Routledge.

Kleban, C., & Kaye, L. K. (2015). Psychosocial impacts of engaging in Second Life for individuals with physical disabilities. *Computers in Human Behavior, 45*, 59–68. doi:10.1016/j.chb.2014.12.004

Kaye, L. K., Monk, R. L., Wall, H. J., Hamlin, I., & Qureshi, A. W. (2018). The effect of flow and context on in-vivo positive mood in digital gaming. *International Journal of Human-Computer Studies, 110*, 45–52. doi:10.1016/j.ijhcs.2017.10.005

Kozinets, R. V. (2002). The field behind the screen: Using netnography for marketing research in online communities. *JMR, Journal of Marketing Research, 39*(1), 61–72. doi:10.1509/jmkr.39.1.61.18935

Kraut, R., Olson, J., Banaji, M., Cohen, J., & Couper, M. (2004). Psyhcological research online: Report of Board of Scienfitic Affairs' Advisory Group on the conduct of research on the internet. *The American Psychologist, 59*(2), 105–117. doi:10.1037/0003-066X.59.2.105 PMID:14992637

Kunc, M., Malpass, J., & White, L. (2016). *Behavioral Operational Research: Theory, Methodology and Practice*. Palgrave Macmillan. doi:10.1057/978-1-137-53551-1

Langer, R., & Beckman, S. C. (2005). Sensitive research topics: Netnography revisited. *Qualitative Market Research, 8*(2), 189–203. doi:10.1108/13522750510592454

Meredith, J. (2015). Getting access to lived experiences: Using screen-capture data for the analysis of online interaction. *Qualitative Methods in Psychology Bulletin, 20*.

Minocha, S., Tran, M. Q., & Reeves, A. J. (2010). Conducting empirical research in Virtual Worlds: Experiences from two projects in Second Life. *Journal of Virtual Worlds Research, 3*(1), 3–21.

Monk, R. L., & Heim, D. (2013a). Environmental context effects on alcohol-related outcome expectancies, efficacy and norms: A field study. *Psychology of Addictive Behaviors, 27*(3), 814–818. doi:10.1037/a0033948 PMID:24059833

Monk, R. L., & Heim, D. (2013b). Panoramic projection: Affording a wider view on contextual influences on alcohol-related cognitions. *Experimental and Clinical Psychopharmacology, 21*(1), 1–7. doi:10.1037/a0030772 PMID:23245196

Monk, R. L., & Heim, D. (2014). A real-time examination of context effects on alcohol cognitions. *Alcoholism, Clinical and Experimental Research, 38*(9), 2452–2459. doi:10.1111/acer.12504 PMID:25257294

Monk, R. L., Heim, D., Qureshi, A., & Price, A. (2015). "I have no clue what I drunk last night": Using Smartphone technology to compare in-vivo and retrospective self-reports of alcohol consumption. *PLoS One*. PMID:25992573

Ning, P., & Jajodia, S. (2003). Intrusion Detection Techniques. In H. Bidgoli (Ed.), *The Internet Encyclopedia* (pp. 355–367). Hoboken, NJ: John Wiley & Sons.

Nulty, D. D. (2008). The adequacy of response rates to online and paper surveys: What can be done? *Assessment & Evaluation in Higher Education, 33*(3), 301–314. doi:10.1080/02602930701293231

Piwek, L., Ellis, D. A., & Andrews, S. (2016). Can programming frameworks bring smartphones into the mainstream of psychological science? *Frontiers in Psychology, 7*, 1252. doi:10.3389/fpsyg.2016.01252 PMID:27602010

Reeves, S., & Brown, B. (2016, February). Embeddedness and sequentiality in social media. In *Proceedings of the 19th ACM Conference on Computer-Supported Cooperative Work & Social Computing* (pp. 1052--1064). New York, NY: ACM.

Saridakis, G., Benson, V., Ezingeard, J., & Tennakoon, H. (2016). Individual information security, user behaviour and cyber victimisation: An empirical study of social networking users. *Technological Forecasting and Social Change, 102*, 320–330. doi:10.1016/j.techfore.2015.08.012

Smithson, J., Sharkey, S., Hewis, E., Jones, R. B., Emmens, T., Ford, T., & Owens, C. (2011). Membership and boundary maintenance on an online self-harm forum. *Qualitative Health Research, 21*(11), 1567–1575. doi:10.1177/1049732311413784 PMID:21715606

Spears, R., & Postmes, T. (2013). Group identity, social influence and collective action online: Extensions and applications of the SIDE model. In S. S. Sundar (Ed.), *The Handbook of Psychology of Communication Technology*. Oxford, UK: Blackwell.

Staheli, D., Yu, T., Crouser, R. J., Damodaran, S., Nam, K., O'Gwynn, D., . . . Harrison, L. (2014). Visualization evaluation for cyber security: Trends and future directions. In *Proceedings of the Eleventh Workshop on Visualization for Cyber Security* (pp. 49-56). Paris, France: Academic Press. doi:10.1145/2671491.2671492

Steptoe, W., Steed, A., Rovira, A., & Rae, J. (2010). Lie Tracking: Social presence, truth and deception in avatar-mediated telecommunication. In *Proceedings of SIGCHI Conference on Human Factors in Computing Systems 2010* (pp.1039-1048). Atlanta, GA: Academic Press. doi:10.1145/1753326.1753481

Tolmie, P., Procter, R., Rouncefield, M., Liakata, M., & Zubiaga, A. (2015). *Microblog analysis as a programme of work*. arXiv preprint arXiv:1511.03193

Wall, H. J., Kaye, L. K., & Malone, S. A. (2016). An exploration of psychological factors on emoticon usage and implications for judgement accuracy. *Computers in Human Behavior, 62*, 70–78. doi:10.1016/j.chb.2016.03.040

Wright, K. B. (2005). Researching Internet-based populations: Advantages and Disadvantages of online survey research, online questionnaire authoring software packages and web survey services. *Journal of Computer-Mediated Communication, 10*(3). doi:10.1111/j.1083-6101.2005.tb00259.x

Zhou, L., Shi, Y., & Zhang, D. (2008). A statistical language modelling approach to online deception detection. *IEEE Transactions on Knowledge and Data Engineering, 20*(8), 1077–1081. doi:10.1109/TKDE.2007.190624

ENDNOTE

[1]   For a comprehensive overview of the ethical and practical considerations for App-based methods, see Kaye, Monk and Hamlin, in press.

Chapter 16
Emerging Threats for the Human Element and Countermeasures in Current Cyber Security Landscape

Vladlena Benson
University of West London, UK

John McAlaney
Bournemouth University, UK

Lara A. Frumkin
Open University, UK

ABSTRACT

The chapter presents an overview of emerging issues in the psychology of human behaviour and the evolving nature of cyber threats. It reflects on the role of social engineering as the entry point of many sophisticated attacks and highlights the relevance of the human element as the starting point of implementing cyber security programmes in organisations as well as securing individual online behaviour. Issues associated with the emerging trends in human behaviour research and ethics are presented for further discussion. The chapter concludes with a set of open research questions warranting immediate academic attention to avoid the exponential growth of information breaches in the future.

HUMAN ELEMENT: CYBER SECURITY STARTS HERE

Cybersecurity professionals agree that that security depends on people more than on technical controls and countermeasures. Recent reviews of the cyber security threat landscape show that no industry segment is immune to cyber-attacks and the public sector tops the list for targeted security incidents (Benson, 2017). This is largely attributed to the weaker cyber security mindset of employees. On the other hand, the financial sector year on year experiences the highest volume of cyber breaches aimed

DOI: 10.4018/978-1-5225-4053-3.ch016

at financial gain or espionage. What is common between these rather different sectors is that the attack vector by cyber criminals starts with social engineering the weakest link in their security chain. With the continuous loss of control over personal information exposed online (Benson et al., 2015) individuals present easy targets for non-technical attacks ranging from spear-fishing to whaling leading on to serious cyber victimisation.

Though human behaviour in online contexts has been addressed by researchers for some time, the cybersecurity industry, policymakers, law enforcement, public and private sector organizations are yet to realise the impact individual cyber behaviour has on security. It is important that this gap is addressed. A secure system is one which behaves in a predictable and rationale way; however as demonstrated by psychological research human behaviour and decision-making processes are multifaceted and often unpredictable. In order to improve cybersecurity practices there is a need for discussion that acknowledges that cybersecurity is inherently a complex socio-technical system. This concept is not new in psychological research. Indeed in 1951 Trist and Bamforth proposed the idea that changes to a technological system must be complemented by changes to social systems. To do one without the other could result in a systems failure. If one is concerned about cyber security, the human element must be investigated in depth. If the human element is not considered where human behaviour is involved, the system is doomed to failure before it begins.

To gain better insights in addressing evolving challenges of the digital world, Cybersecurity increasingly relies on advances in human behaviour research. Whilst technology may often form the core of cyber-attacks, these incidents are instigated and responded to by humans. As demonstrated in recent cybersecurity breaches, such as the WannaCry ransomware affecting 150 countries, cybersecurity incidents exploit the human element. Cyber threats are increasingly choosing psychological manipulation, known as social engineering, rather than hacking in the traditional technical sense. To effectively integrate technology with the human element, a number of fields can be looked to for guidance. The military and intelligence community have been dealing with this for some time; banking and financial industries as well. Both use aspects of psychology and the human element to better detect fissures in security. If we were to ignore basic psychological research would be doing a disservice to the cybersecurity field. Understanding decision making, vigilance, and sheer convenience which undoubtedly play a role in security are essential features to understanding how to keep ourselves safe in an increasingly cyber world. Making sure that the way that employees think about keeping company data secure should match habit and personality style. Requiring frequent password changes may not be an effective strategy as people are less likely to do that then come up with a single intricate password that they use for a year. Thinking about matching the behaviours with the person is an effective strategy, we look into aligning theory to existing experiences in order to answer the following questions:

1. Can psychological manipulation of a cyber victim be countered by technical controls? – current threats mitigation measures try to establish 'expected' user profiles and identify unusual behaviours.
2. Can lapses in decision making have a measured impact on organisational and individual vigilance? – establishing metrics around appropriate decision making can help reflect preparedness of organisations towards cyber-attacks, including those manipulating employees.
3. Will cultural differences and beliefs eventually lead to idiosyncratic cyber security mechanisms? – cyber security solutions, including authentication and detection mechanisms, follow a one-size-fit-all paradigm leading to varied effectiveness.

4. Can cybersecurity be better explained through the lens of a complex socio-technical system? – viewing a secure system as one which behaves in a predictable and rationale way creates issues when a human element is introduced into consideration.
5. What are the emerging ways to address the weaknesses of human behaviour? – achieving the secure state of mind requires more than technical countermeasures which rely not only on fear but on individual and collective human strengths.

The fight against cyber threats never stops and can be viewed as an arms race between malicious and benign actors. New areas have emerged in the field, such as the growth of commercial crimeware, the proliferation of open source hacking tools and social media enabled social engineering strategies which are worthy of attention. While for some cyber psychology is seen as a new way of doing old things, others highlight how differences in online behaviour warrant new methodological approaches to cyber security. For instance, the perceived anonymity and disinhibition effect offered by the internet is known to change human behaviour in several ways, such as altering perceptions of risk and willingness to engage in criminal behaviour.

WE ARE IN IT TOGETHER

We also need to consider not just the interaction between the individual and the machine, but also how the interaction between individuals shape their cybersecurity attitudes and behaviours. Individuals do not operate in a social vacuum; the actions of the attackers and the response of the targets are in part determined by the social worlds in which they operate. People will tend to alter their thoughts and behaviours to match the groups to which they belong (Kelman, 2006), which can include social groups, workplace group or groups of cybercriminals and hacktivists. Furthermore, emotions can spread throughout groups, even to individuals who were not involved in the incident that prompted the initial emotional response (Smith, Seger, & Mackie, 2007). In the case of hacktivism this may result in hacktivists engaging in attacks as a form of protest against targets that they have negative feelings towards, regardless of whether they have personally been affected by the actions of the target. In the case of employees within a company their response to cybersecurity threats may be influenced by the fear or stress experienced by colleagues who have fallen victim to attack such as phishing emails. In addition, the natural response of a company that has been the victim of a cyber-attack may be to hold group discussions about best to react. This is not surprising; after all humans have evolved as social creatures and we tend to draw closer together when our group is threatened. Yet it also known from psychological research that groups often make riskier decisions than an individual would alone (Wallach, Kogan, & Bem, 1962). This may apply not only to the targets of the attack but also the attackers, with both groups behaving in a riskier and possibly ultimately more damaging manner than they would have done as individuals. However, it has also been demonstrated within social psychological research that we often underestimate the extent to which we are influenced by those around us (Darley, 1992). This is an example of the type of irrationality and cognitive biases that can make the prediction of human behaviour especially challenging; not only may we misinterpret the behaviours and intentions of others we may fail to be aware of the factors that determine our own behaviour. A better understanding of how social processes influence the actions of all of the actors involved in a cybersecurity incident would improve threat prediction and help determine how to manage and optimise the response of the targets.

The importance of social norms and group identity vary between culture, ranging from those that value collectivism and acting for the good of the group to those which are individualistic and promote the success of the individual. Nevertheless, even in individualistic cultures such as the UK and USA a degree of interdependence with others is unavoidable. People working within an organisation have trust one another not to expose the organisation to cybersecurity threats through for example the opening of phishing emails. They place trust in IT services to protect them from cyber-attack, and in doing so may relegate their sense of responsibility for all computer related matters. Of course, this trust in IT services may be misplaced trust. As commented previously there is a limit to protection can be provided by technology if an individual persists in engaging in risky cyber behaviours. This relates to another well-known social psychological phenomenon known as diffusion of responsibility, in which individuals fail to take appropriate action, even in the face of impending danger, because they assume that others around them will act (Darley & Latané, 1968). These issue of trust and interdependence are not limited to the victims of cyber-attacks. Cybercrime is often a group exercise. Perpetrators rely on the skills and abilities of others to commit attacks, which requires the development and maintenance of trust. The importance of trust in such situations is arguably even more pertinent in cybercriminal gangs than in the victims they target. A betrayal by a group member may expose other group members to arrest and prosecution. The revelation that a member of the hacktivist collective Anonymous was an FBI informant could be argued to have caused more disruption within the group than did the efforts of their adversaries to dispel them. It is essential to explore these issues of group processes, trust and social identity, and how these influence the decision-making processes of individuals and groups within socio-technical systems.

Emerging Mitigation Measures

Psychologists have studied a range of topics about human behaviour and these findings must be applied to the cyber world to effectively keep people and their data secure. First, people within organisations need to be aware of the risks of cyber breaches and take them seriously. Research found that if someone has experienced a cyber threat, or has perceived such a threat, they are more likely to be vigilant (Chen & Zahedi, 2016). But, there may be ways to enhance vigilance before it comes to perceived or experienced threat. Gamification may be one way forward.

Users need to take steps to protect themselves and the data they are responsible for. Attitude may play a role. Being positive about the working environment could go a long way in increasing employee attentiveness to breaches. Trying to quell those who are disengaged with their offices or disgruntled employees who want to target the company are a worry. Corporations and employees must be vigilant and not let naivety at best and laziness or dissatisfaction with the work environment at worst come to the fore.

Behavioural nudge (Thaler & Sunstein, 2008) is another method to help ensure that company insiders are aware of the pitfalls of negligence to the very real risks of cyber breaches. Psychologists and other behaviourists have been using the concept of nudge for several years to see how it may help in altering a number of behaviours. Using these concepts for cybersecurity could be beneficial in eliciting more vigilant behaviours. Asking, and showing, employees how they could be responsible for security is essential. Changing risk taking or lackadaisical approaches could be done through nudge and yield behavioural change. If the corporations are expected to be responsible for cybersecurity and employees rely on that, there could be a breakdown in security. Creating awareness of how protection needs to be done by all users, especially in light of the incoming General Data Protection Regulations (GDPR) in May 2018, is a step in the right direction.

It will be interesting to see if the new GDPR alters the way companies deal with data protection and cybersecurity. Psychology can help with predictions as to whether the financial penalties that will be placed on companies make them more diligent. Or GDPR might encourage the company to nurture behaviour change on the part of its employees. It is believed that most people want to do the right thing so by using the regulations, nudge and by playing on aspects of personality, perhaps there will be positive changes in corporations and its employees working together to elicit secure cyber environments.

With the increasing global cyber dependency, international cyber security is not a uniform notion. In this respect aspects of psychological research show how an understanding of human behaviour can impact on keeping cyber systems secure. By considering the cultural contexts, maliciousness, personality and other such features of human behaviour, there are avenues to explore the intersection between cybersecurity and behaviour.

It is useful to review crime research as some aspects of cybercrime are similar or the same as more traditional forms of crime using new methods. Encrypting data through ransomware and requiring users to pay to have their data released is old fashioned extortion. Findings into how to deter extortion and other crimes like it may help to reduce the number of cyber breaches. Tapping into the psychology of fear may also help the victims understand what they are experiencing and how to cope with the infringement.

CONCLUSION

We started the discussion of key questions on psychological manipulation countermeasures and how organisational and individual vigilance can be affected by individual and collective decision making. We feel that much more research attention is necessary to help develop effective cyber security culture and address risk taking behavioural challenges.

We identified the challenges of globalisation in developing security technical solutions and opened the discussion on how culture, religion and social norms can impact controls effectiveness and taken into account when addressing the issues of cyber terrorism, propaganda and online radicalisation.

Evolving cyber threats warrant emerging ways to combat them; we see novel approaches to cyber security training, including gamification, nudging and attitude changing experiences, as the new methods facilitating collective appreciation of security objectives.

One final thought is about conducting research into cyber behaviour of individuals. As the access to data on individual digital behaviour has improved over the recent years, ethical questions became opaque. For instance, preserving anonymity of online research subjects presents issues of data 'scrubbing' and makes inferring identity straightforward. New methods are needed to ethically engage with individual users without exposing them to information breaches as shown in examples of NHS and AWS data sets exposures. As the cyber security landscape continuously changes, so are the challenges for cyber security researchers requiring agility in identifying counter mechanisms and innovation in understanding human decision-making.

REFERENCES

Benson, V. (2017). *The State of Global Cyber Security: Highlights and Key Findings*. London, UK: LT Inc; doi:10.13140/RG.2.2.22825.49761

Benson, V., Saridakis, G., & Tennakoon, H. (2015). Information disclosure of social media users: does control over personal information, user awareness and security notices matter? *Information Technology & People*, *28*(3), 426-441.

Chen, Y., & Zahedi, F. (2016). Individual's Internet Security Perceptions and Behaviors: Polycontextual Contrasts between the United States and China. *Management Information Systems Quarterly*, *40*(1), 205–222. doi:10.25300/MISQ/2016/40.1.09

Darley, J. M. (1992). Social organization for the production of evil. *Psychological Inquiry*, *3*(2), 199–218. doi:10.1207/s15327965pli0302_28

Darley, J. M., & Latané, B. (1968). Bystander intervention in emergencies: Diffusion of responsibility. *Journal of Personality and Social Psychology*, *8*(4), 377–383. doi:10.1037/h0025589 PMID:5645600

Kelman, H. C. (2006). Interests, relationships, identities: Three central issues for individuals and groups in negotiating their social environment. *Annual Review of Psychology*, *57*(1), 1–26. doi:10.1146/annurev.psych.57.102904.190156 PMID:16318587

Smith, E. R., Seger, C. R., & Mackie, D. A. (2007). Can emotions be truly group level? evidence regarding four conceptual criteria. *Journal of Personality and Social Psychology*, *93*(3), 431–446. doi:10.1037/0022-3514.93.3.431 PMID:17723058

Thaler, R. H., & Sunstein, C. R. (2008). *Nudge: Improving decisions about health, wealth, and happiness*. New Haven, CT: Yale University Press.

Trist, E. L., & Bamforth, K. W. (1951). Some social and psychological consequences of the Longwall Method of coal-getting: An examination of the psychological situation and defences of a work group in relation to the social structure and technological content of the work system. *Human Relations*, *4*(1), 3–38. doi:10.1177/001872675100400101

Compilation of References

Abou-Youssef, M., Kortam, W., Abou-Aish, E., & El-Bassiouny, N. (2011). Measuring islamic-driven buyer behavioral implications: A proposed market-minded religiosity scale. *The Journal of American Science, 7*(8), 788–801. doi:10.1017/CBO9781107415324.004

Abrams, D., & Hogg, M. A. (2010). Social identity and self categorization. In J. F. Dovidio, M. Hewstone, P. Glick, & V. M. Esses (Eds.), *The Sage handbook of prejudice, stereotyping and discrimination* (pp. 179–193). London: Sage. doi:10.4135/9781446200919.n11

Abu-Nimeh, S., Nappa, D., Wang, X., & Nair, S. (2007). A comparison of machine learning techniques for phishing detection. *Proceedings of The Anti-Phishing Working Group's Second Annual eCrime Researchers Summit*, 60-69. doi:10.1145/1299015.1299021

Action Fraud. (2015). *Figures show online dating fraud is up by 33% last year.* Retrieved May 7, 2017, from http://www.actionfraud.police.uk/news/new-figures-show-online-dating-fraud-is-up-by-33per-cent-last-year-feb15

Action Fraud. (2016). *Fraud & cybercrime cost UK nearly £11bn in past year.* Retrieved May 5, 2017, from http://www.actionfraud.police.uk/news/fraud-and-cybercrime-cost-UK-nearly-11bn-in-past-year-oct16

Adobe. (2015). *Ad Blocking Report.* Retrieved from: https://pagefair.com/blog/2015/ad-blocking-report/

Adorno, T. W., Frenkel-Brunswik, E., Levinson, D. J., & Sanford, R. N. (1950). *The authoritarian personality.* Academic Press.

Agrawal, A., Catalini, C., & Goldfarb, A. (2011). The geography of crowdfunding. *SSRN Electronic Journal.* Retrieved May 18, 2017, from http://ssrn.com/abstract=1692661

Agrawal, A., Catalini, C., & Goldfarb, A. (2014). Some simple economics of crowdfunding. *Innovation Policy and the Economy, 14*(1), 63–97. doi:10.1086/674021

Aguayo, D., Herman, K., Ojeda, L., & Flores, L. Y. (2011). Culture predicts Mexican Americans' college self-efficacy and college performance. *Journal of Diversity in Higher Education, 4*(2), 79–89. doi:10.1037/a0022504

Ajzen, I., & Fishbein, M. (1980). *Understanding attitudes and predicting social behaviour.* Academic Press.

Ajzen, I. (1991). The theory of planned behavior. *Organizational Behavior and Human Decision Processes, 50*(2), 179–211. doi:10.1016/0749-5978(91)90020-T

Albelaikhi, A. (1988). *Religious orientation and fear of death among Muslims and Christian individuals.* University of Rhode Island, Psychology Department.

Alfawaz Salahuddin, K. N. (2010). Information security culture: a behaviour compliance conceptual framework. In *Proceedings of the 8th Australasian Conference on Information Security* (vol. 105, pp. 47-55). Australian Computer Society, Inc.

Al-Gahtani, S. S., Hubona, G. S., & Wang, J. (2007). Information technology (IT) in Saudi Arabia: Culture and the acceptance and use of IT. *Information & Management, 44*(8), 681–691. doi:10.1016/j.im.2007.09.002

Al-Kandari, A., & Dashti, A. (2014). Fatwa and the internet: A study of the influence of Muslim religious scholars on internet diffusion in Saudi Arabia. *Prometheus, 32*(2), 127–144. doi:10.1080/08109028.2014.998929

Allport, G. W. (1950). *The individual and his religion: A psychological interpretation.* Academic Press.

Allport, G. W., & Kramer, B. M. (1946). Some roots of prejudice. *The Journal of Psychology, 22*(1), 9–39. doi:10.108 0/00223980.1946.9917293 PMID:20992067

Allport, G. W., & Ross, J. M. (1967). Personal religious orientation and prejudice. *Journal of Personality and Social Psychology, 5*(4), 432–443. doi:10.1037/h0021212 PMID:6051769

Almeshekah, M. H., & Spafford, E. H. (2014). Planning and integrating deception into computer security defenses. *Proceedings of the 2014 Workshop on New Security Paradigms Workshop*, 127–138. Retrieved from http://dl.acm.org/citation.cfm?id=2683482

Alsanie, S. I. (1989). *Relationship between level of Religiosity and Criminal Behavior* (Unpublished Doctoral Dissertation). Imam Ibn Suad Islamic University, Saudi Arabia.

Al-Shohaib, K., Al-Kandari, A. A. J., & Abdulrahim, M. A. (2009). Internet adoption by Saudi public relations professionals. *Journal of Communication Management, 13*(1), 21–36. doi:10.1108/13632540910931373

Aly, A., Macdonald, S., Jarvis, L., & Chen, T. M. (2017). Introduction to the Special Issue: Terrorist Online Propaganda and Radicalization. *Studies in Conflict and Terrorism, 40*(1), 1–9. doi:10.1080/1057610X.2016.1157402

Amichai-Hamburger, Y. (Ed.). (2013). *The social net: Understanding our online behavior.* OUP Oxford. doi:10.1093/acprof:oso/9780199639540.001.0001

Anderson, A. (2017). *TEDx Talks.* Retrieved from: https://www.youtube.com/watch?v=c_2Ja-OTmGc

Anderson, B. (1983). *Imagined communities: Reflections on the origin and spread of nationalism.* London: Verso.

Anderson, C., & Agarwal, R. (2011). Practicing Safe Computing: A Multimethod Empirical Examination of Home Computer User Security Behavioral Intentions. *Management Information Systems Quarterly, 126*(2), 987–1027. doi:10.1093/qje/qjr008

Anderson, R., Barton, C., Böhme, R., Clayton, R., Van Eeten, M. J., Levi, M., & Savage, S. (2013). Measuring the cost of cybercrime. In *The economics of information security and privacy* (pp. 265–300). Berlin: Springer. doi:10.1007/978-3-642-39498-0_12

Andrews, S., Ellis, D. A., Shaw, H., & Piwek, L. (2015). Beyond self report: Tools to compare estimated and real-world Smartphone use. *PLoS One, 10*(10), e0139004. doi:10.1371/journal.pone.0139004 PMID:26509895

Anthony, L. (2016). *AntConc.* Retrieved from http://www.laurenceanthony.net/software/antconc/

Anwar, M., He, W., Ash, I., Yuan, X., Li, L., & Xu, L. (2016). Gender difference and employees' cybersecurity behaviors. *Computers in Human Behavior, 69*, 437–443. doi:10.1016/j.chb.2016.12.040

Apple. (2016). *Privacy Policy.* Retrieved from: http://www.apple.com/privacy/privacy-policy/

Arends, R., Austein, R., Larson, M., Massey, D., & Rose, S. (2005). *DNS Security Introduction and Requirements.* Internet Engineering Task Force (IETF) RFC 4033.

Argyle, M., & Beit-Hallahmi, B. (2014). *The psychology of religious behaviour, belief and experience.* Routledge.

Ariely, D., & Simonson, I. (2003). Buying, bidding, playing, or competing? Value assessment and decision dynamics in online auctions. *Journal of Consumer Psychology, 13*(1-2), 113–123. doi:10.1207/S15327663JCP13-1&2_10

Armitage, C. J., & Conner, M. (2001). Efficacy of the theory of planned behaviour: A meta-analytic review. *British Journal of Social Psychology, 40*(4), 471–499. doi:10.1348/014466601164939 PMID:11795063

Arrindell, W. A., Hatzichristou, C., Wensink, J., Rosenberg, E., van Twillert, B., Sedema, J., & Meijer, D. (1997). Dimensions of national culture as predictors of cross-national differences in subjective well-being. *Personality and Individual Differences, 23*(1), 37–53. doi:10.1016/S0191-8869(97)00023-8

Arthur, C. (2014). Facebook study breached ethical guidelines, researchers say. *The Guardian*. Retrieved June 19, 2017, from: https://www.theguardian.com/technology/2014/jun/30/facebook-emotion-study-breached-ethical-guidelines-researchers-say

Asaf Shabtai, M. B. (2014). Optimizing data misuse detection. *ACM Transactions on Knowledge Discovery from Data, 8*, 16.

Association of Internet Researchers. (2012). Ethical decision making and internet research. Chicago, IL: Association of Internet Researchers (AoIR).

Attwell, G. (2007). Personal Learning Environments-the future of eLearning? *Elearning Papers, 2*(1), 1-8.

Awad, N. F., & Ragowsky, A. (2008). Establishing trust in electronic commerce through online word of mouth: An examination across genders. *Journal of Management Information Systems, 24*(4), 101–121. doi:10.2753/MIS0742-1222240404

Awan, I. (2016). Cyber threats and cyber terrorism: The internet as a tool for extremism. In I. Awan & B. Blakemore (Eds.), *Policing cyber hate, cyber threats and cyber terrorism* (pp. 21–38). Abingdon, UK: Routledge.

Bada, M., Sass, A. M., & Nurse, J. R. C. (2014). *Cyber Security Awareness Campaigns Why do they fail to change behaviour?* Academic Press.

Bada, M., & Sasse, A. (2014). *Cyber Security Awareness Campaigns: Why do they fail to change behaviour?* Academic Press.

Bada, M., & Sasse, A. (2015). Cyber Security Awareness Campaigns: Why do they fail to change behaviour? *International Conference on Cyber Security for Sustainable Society*

Baek, Y. M., Kim, E. M., & Bae, Y. (2014). My privacy is okay, but theirs is endangered: Why comparative optimism matters in online privacy concerns. *Computers in Human Behavior, 31*, 48–56. doi:10.1016/j.chb.2013.10.010

Bae, S. M. (2017). The influence of strain factors, social control factors, self-control and computer use on adolescent cyber delinquency: Korean National Panel Study. *Children and Youth Services Review, 78*, 74–80. doi:10.1016/j.childyouth.2017.05.008

Bailey, J. M., & Sood, J. (1993). The effects of religious affiliation on consumer behavior: A preliminary investigation. *Journal of Managerial Issues*, 328–352.

Bakker, E. (2006). *Jihadi Terrorists in Europe, Their Characteristics and the Circumstances in Which They Joined the Jihad: An Exploratory Study*. The Hague: Clingendael Institute.

Bakker, E. (2011). Characteristics of jihadi terrorists in Europe (2001-2009). In R. Coolsaet (Ed.), *Jihadi Terrorism and the Radicalisation Challenge: European and American Experiences* (pp. 131–144). Aldershot, UK: Ashgate.

Bandura, A. (1994). Social cognitive theory and exercise of control over HIV infection. In Preventing AIDS (pp. 25-59). Springer US. doi:10.1007/978-1-4899-1193-3_3

Bandura, A. (1977). Self-efficacy: Toward a unifying theory of behavioural change. *Psychological Review*, *84*(2), 191–215. doi:10.1037/0033-295X.84.2.191 PMID:847061

Bandura, A. (2004). Health promotion by social cognitive means. *Health Education & Behavior*, *31*(2), 143–164. doi:10.1177/1090198104263660 PMID:15090118

Barge, J. K., & Hirokawa, R. Y. (1989). Toward a communication competency model of group leadership. *Small Group Behavior*, *20*(2), 167–189. doi:10.1177/104649648902000203

Bargh, J., & Morsella, E. (2008). The Unconscious Mind. *Perspectives on Psychological Science*, *3*(1), 73–79. doi:10.1111/j.1745-6916.2008.00064.x PMID:18584056

Barrett, N. (2003). Penetration testing and social engineering: Hacking the weakest link. *Information Security Technical Report*, *8*(4), 56–64. doi:10.1016/S1363-4127(03)00007-4

Bartels, R. (1967). A model for ethics in marketing. *Journal of Marketing*, *31*(1), 20–26. doi:10.2307/1249296

Barton, K., & Vaughan, G. M. (1976). Church membership and personality: A longitudinal study. *Social Behavior and Personality*, *4*(1), 11–16. doi:10.2224/sbp.1976.4.1.11

Bart, Y., Shankar, V., Sultan, F., & Urban, G. L. (2005). Are the drivers and role of online trust the same for all web sites and consumers? A large-scale exploratory empirical study. *Journal of Marketing*, *69*(4), 133–152. doi:10.1509/jmkg.2005.69.4.133

Bauer, K., & Hein, S. E. (2006). The effect of heterogeneous risk on the early adoption of Internet banking technologies. *Journal of Banking & Finance*, *30*(6), 1713–1725. doi:10.1016/j.jbankfin.2005.09.004

Baumert, T., Buesa, M., & Lynch, T. (2013). The impact of terrorism on stock markets: The Boston bombing experience in comparison with previous terrorist events. *Institute of Industrial and Financial Analysis Complutense University of Madrid*, *88*, 1–24.

BBC News. (2013). *Profile: Edward Snowden*. Retrieved from http://www.bbc.co.uk/news/world-us-canada-22837100

BBC News. (2017). *Cybercrime and fraud scales revealed in annual figures*. Retrieved May 11, 2017, from http://www.bbc.co.uk/news/uk-38675683

Beier, M., & Wagner, K. (2016). User Behavior in Crowdfunding Platforms--Exploratory Evidence from Switzerland. In *Proceedings from 49th Hawaii International Conference on System Sciences*. IEEE. doi:10.1109/HICSS.2016.448

Bélanger, F., & Crossler, R. E. (2011). Privacy in the Digital Age: A Review of Information Privacy Research in Information Systems. *Management Information Systems Quarterly*, *35*(4), 1017–1041. doi:10.1159/000360196

Belk, R. (1983). In R. P. Bagozzi, A. M. Tybout, & A. Abor (Eds.), *Worldly possessions: Issues and criticisms. In Advances in Consumer Research* (vol. 10, pp. 514–519). Association for Consumer Research.

Belk, R. (1988). Possessions and the extended self. *The Journal of Consumer Research*, *15*(2), 139–168. doi:10.1086/209154

Belk, R. (2013). Extended self in a digital world. *The Journal of Consumer Research*, *40*(3), 477–500. doi:10.1086/671052

Belleflamme, P., & Lambert, T. (2014). Crowdfunding: Some Empirical Findings and Microeconomic Underpinnings. *SSRN Electronic Journal*. Retrieved May 21, 2017, from https://papers.ssrn.com/sol3/papers.cfm?abstract_id=2437786

Benjamin, V., Zhang, B., Nunamaker, J. F. Jr, & Chen, H. (2016). Examining Hacker Participation Length in Cybercriminal Internet-Relay-Chat Communities. *Journal of Management Information Systems*, *33*(2), 482–510. doi:10.1080/07421222.2016.1205918

Benson, V., Saridakis, G., & Tennakoon, H. (2015). Information disclosure of social media users: does control over personal information, user awareness and security notices matter? *Information Technology & People*, *28*(3), 426-441.

Benson, V. (2017). *The State of Global Cyber Security: Highlights and Key Findings*. London, UK: LT Inc; doi:10.13140/RG.2.2.22825.49761

Benson, V., Saridakis, G., & Tennakoon, H. (2015). Information disclosure of social media users: Does control over personal information, user awareness and security notices matter? *Information Technology & People*, *28*(3), 426–441. doi:10.1108/ITP-10-2014-0232

Bente, G., Rüggenberg, S., Krämer, N. C., & Eschenburg, F. (2009). Avatar-Mediated Networking: Increasing Social Presence and Interpersonal Trust in Net-Based Collaborations. *Human Communication Research*, *34*(2), 287–318. doi:10.1111/j.1468-2958.2008.00322.x

Beresford, B., & Sloper, P. (2008). *Understanding the dynamics of decision-making and choice: A scoping study of key psychological theories to inform the design and analysis of the Panel Study*. York, UK: Social Policy Research Unit, University of York.

Berger, P. L. (1961). *Noise of Solemn Assemblies*. Bantam.

Bergin, A. E. (2009). *Changing frontiers in the science of psychotherapy*. Aldine Transaction.

Bergström, A. (2015). Online privacy concerns: A broad approach to understanding the concerns of different groups for different uses. *Computers in Human Behavior*, *53*, 419–426. doi:10.1016/j.chb.2015.07.025

Bermingham, A., Conway, M., McInerney, L., O'Hare, N., & Smeaton, A. F. (2009). Combining social network analysis and sentiment analysis to explore the potential for online radicalisation. In *International Conference on Advances in Social Network Analysis and Mining* (pp. 231-236). Athens, Greece: IEEE. doi:10.1109/ASONAM.2009.31

Bernaards, F., Monsma, E. & Zinn, P. (2012). *High tech crime: Criminaliteitsbeeldanalyse 2012* [High-tech crime: Crime image analysis 2012]. Driebergen: Korps Landelijke Politiediensten.

Berntzen, L. E., & Sandberg, S. (2014). The collective nature of lone wolf terrorism: Anders Behring Breivik and the anti-Islamic social movement. *Terrorism and Political Violence*, *26*(5), 759–779. doi:10.1080/09546553.2013.767245

Bhabha, H. K. (1997). The world and the home. *Cultural Politics*, *11*, 445–455.

Bikson, T. K., Bluthenthal, R. N., Eden, R., & Gunn, P. P. (2007). *Ethical principles in social behavioral research on terrorism: Probing the parameters*. London: RAND.

Binford, L. R. (1962). Archaeology as anthropology. *American Antiquity*, *28*(02), 217–225. doi:10.2307/278380

Bishop, M., Gollmann, D., Hunker, J., & Probst, C. W. (2008). Countering insider threats. In *Dagstuhl Seminar Proceedings 08302* (pp. 1–18). Academic Press. Retrieved from http://vesta.informatik.rwth-aachen.de/opus/volltexte/2008/1793/pdf/08302.SWM.1793.pdf

Bishop, M., Butler, E., Butler, K., Gates, C., & Greenspan, S. (2012). Forgive and Forget. *21st EICAR Annual Conference Proceedings*, 151–159.

Bishop, M., & Gates, C. (2008). Defining the insider threat. In *Proceedings of the 4th annual workshop on Cyber security and information intelligence research* (pp. 12–14). New York: ACM Press. doi:10.1145/1413140.1413158

Bjorgo, T., & Horgan, J. (2009). *Leaving Terrorism Behind: Individual and Collective Disengagement*. New York: Routledge.

Bjørgum, M. H. (2016). Jihadi Brides: Why do Western Muslim Girls Join ISIS? *Global Politics Review*, *2*(2), 91–102.

Blackwood, L. M., Hopkins, N. P., & Reicher, S. D. (2012). *Divided by a common language?: conceptualising identity, discrimination, and alienation.* Restoring Civil Societies.

Blais, A.-R., & Weber, E. U. (2006). A Domain-Specific Risk-Taking (DOSPERT) scale for adult populations. *Judgment and Decision Making, 1*(1), 33–47. doi:10.1037/t13084-000

Blau, P. M. (1964). *Social exchange theory.* Academic Press.

Blee, K. M. (2002). *Inside Organized Racism: Women and Men in the Hate Movement.* University of California Press.

Block, J. H., Hornuf, L., & Moritz, A. (2016). Which updates during an equity crowdfunding campaign increase crowd participation? *SSRN Electronic Journal.* Retrieved June 1, 2017, from https://papers.ssrn.com/sol3/papers.cfm?abstract_id=2781715

Bloem, B., & Harteveld, A. (2012). *Horizontale fraude: Verslag van een onderzoek voor het Nationaal dreigingsbeeld 2012 [Horizontal fraud: Research report on the national threat assessment 2012].* Zoetermeer: Dienst IPOL.

Borum, R. (2003). Understanding the Terrorist Mindset. *FBI Law Enforcement Bulletin,* 7-10.

Bossler, A. M., & Holt, T. J. (2009). On-line activities, guardianship, and malware infection: An examination of routine activities theory. *International Journal of Cyber Criminology, 3*(1), 400–420.

Bossler, A. M., & Holt, T. J. (2010). The effect of self-control on victimization in the cyberworld. *Journal of Criminal Justice, 38*(3), 227–236. doi:10.1016/j.jcrimjus.2010.03.001

Boss, S. R., Galletta, D. F., Lowry, P. B., Moody, G. D., & Polak, P. (2015). What do users have to fear? Using fear appeals to engender threats and fear that motivate protective security behaviors. *Management Information Systems Quarterly, 39*(4), 837–864. doi:10.25300/MISQ/2015/39.4.5

Bowman-Grieve, L. (2015). Cyberterrorism and moral panics: A reflection on the discourse of cyberterrorism. In L. Jarvis, S. Macdonald, & T. M. Chen (Eds.), *Terrorism online: Politics, law and technology* (pp. 86–106). London: Routledge.

BPS. (2009). *Code of Ethics and Conduct.* Leicester, UK: British Psychological Society.

BPS. (2014). *Code of Human Research Ethics.* Leicester, UK: British Psychological Society.

Branscombe, N. R., & Wann, D. L. (1994). Collective self-esteem consequences of outgroup derogation when a valued social identity is on trial. *European Journal of Social Psychology, 24*(6), 641–657. doi:10.1002/ejsp.2420240603

Briggs, R., & Strugnell, A. (2011). *Radicalisation: The role of the internet.* Policy Planners' Network Working Paper. London: Institute for Strategic Dialogue.

Briggs, P., Jeske, D., & Coventry, L. (2016). Behaviour change interventions for cybersecurity. In L. Little, E. Sillence, & A. Joinson (Eds.), *Behaviour Change Research and Theory; Psychological and Technological Perspectives.* New York: Academic Press.

British Psychological Society. (2017). *Ethics Guidelines for Internet-mediated Research.* Leicester, UK: British Psychological Society.

Britz, M. T. (2010). Terrorism and Technology: Operationalizing Cyberterrorism and Identifying Concepts. In T. J. Holt (Ed.), *Crime On-Line: Correlates, Causes, and Context* (pp. 193–220). Raleigh, NC: Carolina Academic Press.

Brown, J. J., & Reingen, P. H. (1987). Social ties and word of mouth referral behavior. *The Journal of Consumer Research, 14*(3), 350–362. doi:10.1086/209118

Buchanan, T., & Whitty, M. T. (2014). The online dating romance scam: Causes and consequences of victimhood. *Psychology, Crime & Law*, *20*(3), 261–283. doi:10.1080/1068316X.2013.772180

Buchan, N. R., Croson, R. T. A., & Solnick, S. (2008). Trust and gender: An examination of behavior and beliefs in the Investment Game. *Journal of Economic Behavior & Organization*, *68*(3-4), 466–476. doi:10.1016/j.jebo.2007.10.006

Buchtel, E. E., & Norenzayan, A. (2009). *Thinking across cultures: Implications for dual processes*. J. St. BT Evans & K. Frankish.

Bullée, J. H., Montoya Morales, A. L., Junger, M., & Hartel, P. H. (2016). Telephone-based social engineering attacks: An experiment testing the success and time decay of an intervention. In *Proceedings of the Singapore Cyber-Security Conference (SG-CRC) 2016* (pp. 107-114). IOS Press.

Bullée, J. W. (2017). *Experimental social engineering investigation and prevention*. Enschede, The Netherlands: CTIT. doi:10.3990/1.9789036543972

Burger, Y., De Caluwé, L., & Jansen, P. (2010). *Mensen veranderen: Waarom, wanneer en hoe mensen (niet) veranderen [People change: Why, when and how people change or do not change]*. Deventer: Kluwer.

Burtch, G., Ghose, A., & Wattal, S. (2016). Secret Admirers: An Empirical Examination of Information Hiding and Contribution Dynamics in Online Crowdfunding. *Information Systems Research*, *27*(3), 478–496. doi:10.1287/isre.2016.0642

Bushra, A. A., Philip, A. L., & Jason, R. C. & Nurse.(2015). Using Internet Activity Profiling for Insider-Threat Detection. In *Proceedings of 17th International Conference on Enterprise Information Systems* (pp. 709–720). Barcelona, Spain: Academic Press.

Button, M., Nicholls, C. M., Kerr, J., & Owen, R. (2014). Online frauds: Learning from victims why they fall for these scams. *Australian and New Zealand Journal of Criminology*, *47*(3), 391–408. doi:10.1177/0004865814521224

Cacciottolo, M., & Rees, N. (2017). Online dating fraud victim numbers at record high. *BBC News*. Retrieved May 5, 2017, from http://www.bbc.co.uk/news/uk-38678089

Cacioppo, P., Petty, R., & Kao, F. C. (1984). The Efficient Assessment of Need for Cognition. *Journal of Personality Assessment*. doi:10.1001/archpsyc.64.10.1204

Cappelli, D., Moore, A., & Trzeciak, R. (2012). *The CERT Guide to Insider threats*. Academic Press.

Cappelli, D., Moore, A., & Silowash, G. (2012). *Common Sense Guide to Mitigating Insider Threats* (4th ed.). Academic Press. Retrieved from http://www.stormingmedia.us/00/0055/A005585.html

Caputo, D. D., Maloof, M. A., & Stephens, G. D. (2009). Detecting the Theft of Trade Secrets by Insiders. A Summary of MITRE Insider Threat Research. *IEEE Security and Privacy*, 14–21.

Caputo, D. D., Stephens, G. D., Stephenson, B., Cormier, M., & Kim, M. (2008). Lecture Notes in Computer Science: Vol. 5230. *An Empirical Approach to Identify Information Misuse by Insiders. Recent Advances in Intrusion Detection*. Springer.

Carmon, Z., Wertenbroch, K., & Zeelenberg, M. (2003). Option attachment: When deliberating makes choosing feel like losing. *The Journal of Consumer Research*, *30*(1), 15–29. doi:10.1086/374701

Carruthers, P. (2002). The cognitive functions of language. *Behavioral and Brain Sciences*, *25*(06), 657–674. doi:10.1017/S0140525X02000122 PMID:14598623

Cattell, H. E. P., & Mead, A. D. (2008). The sixteen personality factor questionnaire (16PF). In G. J. Boyle, G. Matthews, & D. H. Saklofske (Eds.), *The SAGE handbook of personality theory and assessment* (pp. 135–178). Los Angeles, CA: SAGE Publications.

Center, T. M. (2013). Terrorism in Cyberspace: Hezbollah's Internet Network. *Terrorism Info.* Retrieved 06 01, 2017, from http://www.terrorism-info.org.il/Data/articles/Art_20488/E_276_12_739632364.pdf

CERT. (2013). *Unintentional insider threats: A foundational study.* Retrieved from http://scholar.google.com/scholar?hl=en&btnG=Search&q=intitle:Unintentional+Insider+Threats+:+A+Foundational+Study#0

CERT. (2014). *Unintentional Insider Threats: Social Engineering.* Retrieved from http://oai.dtic.mil/oai/oai?verb=getRecord&metadataPrefix=html&identifier=ADA592507

Chen, Y. J., & Tang, T. L. P. (2013). The Bright and Dark Sides of Religiosity Among University Students: Do Gender, College Major, and Income Matter? *Journal of Business Ethics, 115*(3), 531–553. doi:10.1007/s10551-012-1407-2

Chen, Y., & Zahedi, F. (2016). Individual's Internet Security Perceptions and Behaviors: Polycontextual Contrasts between the United States and China. *Management Information Systems Quarterly, 40*(1), 205–222. doi:10.25300/MISQ/2016/40.1.09

Chermak, S. D., & Gruenewald, J. (2015). Laying the Foundation for the Criminological Examination of Right-wing, Left-wing, and Al Qaeda Inspired Extremism in the United States. *Terrorism and Political Violence, 27*(1), 133–159. doi:10.1080/09546553.2014.975646

Cheshire, C. (2011). Online trust, trustworthiness, or assurance? *Daedalus, 140*(4), 49–58. doi:10.1162/DAED_a_00114 PMID:22167913

Chiluwa, I. (2017). The Discourse of Terror Threats: Assessing Online Written Threats by Nigerian Terrorist Groups. *Studies in Conflict and Terrorism, 40*(4), 318–338. doi:10.1080/1057610X.2016.1194025

Choi, K. (2008). Computer crime victimization and integrated theory: An empirical assessment. *International Journal of Cyber Criminology, 2*(1), 308–333.

Choi, Y. (2010). Religion, religiosity, and South Korean consumer switching behaviors. *Journal of Consumer Behaviour, 9*(3), 157–171. doi:10.1002/cb.292

Christin, N., Egelman, S., Vidas, T., & Grossklags, J. (2011, February). It's all about the Benjamins: An empirical study on incentivizing users to ignore security advice. In *International Conference on Financial Cryptography and Data Security* (pp. 16-30). Springer.

Christin, N., Egelman, S., Vidas, T., & Grossklags, J. (2012). It's all about the Benjamins: an empirical study on incentivizing users to ignore security advice. In *Proceedings of the 15th international conference on Financial Cryptography and Data Security, FC'11* (pp 16–30). Springer-Verlag. doi:10.1007/978-3-642-27576-0_2

Chua, C. E. H., Wareham, J., & Robey, D. (2007). The role of online trading communities in managing internet auction fraud. *Management Information Systems Quarterly, 31*(4), 759–781.

CIA. (2016). *The World Factbook — Central Intelligence Agency: Mozambique.* Retrieved January 9, 2017, from https://www.cia.gov/library/publications/resources/the-world-factbook/geos/sa.html

Cialdini, R. B. (1993). *Influence: The Psychology of Persuasion.* New York: Quill William Morrow.

Cialdini, R. B. (2001). The science of persuasion. *Scientific American, 284*(2), 76–81. doi:10.1038/scientificamerican0201-76 PMID:11285825

Cialdini, R. B. (2008). *Influence: science and practice* (5th ed.). Englewood Cliffs, NJ: Prentice Hall.

Cialdini, R. B., Borden, R. J., Thorne, A., Walker, M. R., Freeman, S., & Sloan, L. R. (1976). Basking in reflected glory: Three (football) field studies. *Journal of Personality and Social Psychology, 34*(3), 366–375. doi:10.1037/0022-3514.34.3.366

Cialdini, R. B., & Goldstein, N. J. (2004). Social influence: Compliance and conformity. *Annual Review of Psychology, 55*(1), 591–621. doi:10.1146/annurev.psych.55.090902.142015 PMID:14744228

CIO & Leader. (2017). *Cyber attack disrupting critical infrastructure in 2016 a likelihood, say security professionals.* Retrieved Apr 30, 2017, from http://www.cioandleader.com/article/2016/01/14/cyber-attack-disrupting-critical-infra-structure-2016-likelihood-say-security

Citizen's Advice Bureau. (2016). *Phishing – spam emails and fake websites.* Retrieved August 1, 2016, from: https://www.citizensadvice.org.uk/consumer/scams/scams/common-scams/computer-and-online-scams/phishing-spam-emails-and-fake-websites/

Clark, J. W., & Dawson, L. E. (1996). Personal religiousness and ethical judgements: An empirical analysis. *Journal of Business Ethics, 15*(3), 359–372. doi:10.1007/BF00382959

Clough, J. (2010). Principles of Cybercrime. Cambridge University Press. doi:10.1017/CBO9780511845123

CNN Staff. (n.d.). CENTCOM Twitter account hacked, suspended. *CNN.* Retrieved 20 10 2017, from http://www.cnn.com/2015/01/12/politics/centcom-twitter-hacked-suspended/index.html

Cohen, A. B., & Hill, P. C. (2007). Religion as culture: Religious individualism and collectivism among American catholics, jews, and protestants. *Journal of Personality, 75*(4), 709–742. doi:10.1111/j.1467-6494.2007.00454.x PMID:17576356

Cohen, J. (1988). *Statistical Power Analysis for the Behavioural Sciences* (2nd ed.). Hillsdale, NJ: Lawrence Eribaum Associates.

Cohen, L. E., & Felson, M. (1979). Social change and crime rate trends: A routine activity approach. *American Sociological Review, 44*(4), 588–608. doi:10.2307/2094589

Colarik, A. M., & Janczewski, L. J. (2008). Introduction to cyber warfare and cyber terrorism. In L. J. Janczewski & A. M. Colarik (Eds.), *Cyber warfare and cyber terrorism* (pp. xiii–xxx). New York: Information Science Reference.

Coleman, G. (2011). Hacker politics and publics. *Public Culture, 23*(65), 511-516.

Coleman, G. (2014). *Hacker, hoaxer, whistleblower, spy: The Many Faces of Anonymous.* London: Verso.

Coleman, G. (2015). Epilogue: The State of Anonymous. In *Hacker, hoaxer, whistleblower, spy: The Many Faces of Anonymous* (pp. 401–461). London: Verso.

Colombo, M. G., Franzoni, C., & Rossi-Lamastra, C. (2015). Internal social capital and the attraction of early contributions in crowdfunding. *Entrepreneurship Theory and Practice, 39*(1), 75–100. doi:10.1111/etap.12118

Colwill, C. (2010). *Human factors in information security: The insider threat - Who can you trust these days? Information Security Technical Report.* Elsevier. doi:10.1016/j.istr.2010.04.004

Consolvo, S., Smith, I. E., Matthews, T., LaMarca, A., Tabert, J., & Powledge, P. (2005). Location disclosure to social relations: why, when, & what people want to share. *Proceedings of the SIGCHI Conference on Human Factors in Computing Systems*, 81-90. doi:10.1145/1054972.1054985

Conway, M. (2017). Determining the Role of the Internet in Violent Extremism and Terrorism: Six Suggestions for Progressing Research. *Studies in Conflict and Terrorism, 40*(1), 77–98. doi:10.1080/1057610X.2016.1157408

Cook, D. A., Levinson, A. J., Garside, S., Dupras, D. M., Erwin, P. J., & Montori, V. M. (2008). Internet-based learning in the health professions: A meta-analysis. *Journal of the American Medical Association, 300*(10), 1181–1196. doi:10.1001/jama.300.10.1181 PMID:18780847

Coopers, P. W. (2008). *Data Loss Prevention: Keeping sensitive data out of the wrong hands.* Retrieved 03 11, 2017, from https://www.pwc.com/us/en/increasing-it-effectiveness/assets/data_loss_prevention.pdf

Corner, E., & Gill, P. (2015). A false dichotomy? Mental illness and lone-actor terrorism. *Law and Human Behavior, 39*(1), 23–34. doi:10.1037/lhb0000102 PMID:25133916

Cotton, S. R., & Gupta, S. S. (2004). Characteristics of online and offline health information seekers and factors that discriminate between them. *Social Science & Medicine, 59*(9), 1795–1806. doi:10.1016/j.socscimed.2004.02.020 PMID:15312915

Couch, D., Liamputtong, P., & Pitts, M. (2012). What are the real and perceived risks and dangers of online dating? Perspectives from online daters: Health risks in the media. *Health Risk & Society, 14*(7-8), 697–714. doi:10.1080/136 98575.2012.720964

Coulson, N. S. (2005). Receiving social support online: An analysis of a computer-mediated support group for individuals living with irritable bowel syndrome. *Cyberpsychology & Behavior, 8*(6), 580–584. doi:10.1089/cpb.2005.8.580 PMID:16332169

Coventry, L., Briggs, P., Blythe, J., & Tran, M. (2014). *Using behavioural insights to improve the public's use of cyber security best practices.* Gov. Uk Report.

Coventry, L., Briggs, P., Jeske, D., & Van Moorsel, A. (2014). SCENE: A structured means for creating and evaluating behavioral nudges in a cyber security environment. Lecture Notes in Computer Science, 8517, 229–239. doi:10.1007/978-3-319-07668-3_23

CPNI. (2013). *CPNI Insider Data Collection Study: Report of Main Findings.* London: CPNI.

Cragan, J. F., & Wright, D. W. (1990). Small group communication research of the 1980s: A synthesis and critique. *Communication Studies, 41*(3), 212–236. doi:10.1080/10510979009368305

Csikszentmihalyi, M., Larson, R., & Prescott, S. (1977). The ecology of adolescent activity and experience. *Journal of Youth and Adolescence, 6*(3), 281–294. doi:10.1007/BF02138940 PMID:24408457

Csikszentmihalyi, M., & Rochberg-Halton, E. (1981). *The meaning of things: Domestic symbols and the self.* Cambridge, UK: Cambridge University Press. doi:10.1017/CBO9781139167611

Cullen, H. D. (1997). *A Comparison of the Decision Quality of Group Decisions Made in a Face-to-Face Environment with Decisions Made Using a Distributed Group Decision Support System (No. AFIT/GIR/LAS/97D-13).* Air Force Inst of Tech Wright-Patterson AFB OH.

Culnan, M. J. (1993). "How Did They Get My Name?": An Exploratory Investigation of Consumer Attitudes Toward Secondary Information Use. *Management Information Systems Quarterly, 17*(3), 341–363. doi:10.2307/249775

Cyr, D., Head, M., & Larios, H. (2010). Colour appeal in website design within and across cultures: A multi-method evaluation. *International Journal of Human-Computer Studies, 68*(1), 1–21. doi:10.1016/j.ijhcs.2009.08.005

Darbyshire, D. E., Kirk, C., Wall, H. J., & Kaye, L. K. (2016). Don't Judge a (Face)Book by its Cover: Exploring Judgement Accuracy of Others' Personality on Facebook. *Computers in Human Behavior, 58*, 380–387. doi:10.1016/j.chb.2016.01.021

Dark, M., & Winstead, J. (2005). Using educational theory and moral psychology to inform the teaching of ethics in computing. In *Proceedings of the 2nd Annual Conference on Information Security Curriculum Development* (pp. 27-31). New York: ACM Press. doi:10.1145/1107622.1107630

Darkreading. (2012). *Five Significant Insider Attacks of 2012. Information Week: Dark Reading.* Retrieved Apr 30, 2017, from http://www.darkreading.com/vulnerabilities---threats/five-significant-insiderattacks-of-2012/d/d-id/1138865?

Darley, J. M. (1992). Social organization for the production of evil. *Psychological Inquiry, 3*(2), 199–218. doi:10.1207/s15327965pli0302_28

Darley, J. M., & Latané, B. (1968). Bystander intervention in emergencies: Diffusion of responsibility. *Journal of Personality and Social Psychology, 8*(4), 377–383. doi:10.1037/h0025589 PMID:5645600

Darley, W. K., Blankson, C., & Luethge, D. J. (2010). Toward an integrated framework for online consumer behavior and decision making process: A review. *Psychology and Marketing, 27*(2), 94–116. doi:10.1002/mar.20322

Darwish, A., El Zarka, A., & Aloul, F. (2013). *Towards understanding phishing victims' profile.* Paper presented at the International Conference of Computer Systems and Industrial Informatics, Bochum, Germany.

Das, S., Kramer, A. D., Dabbish, L. A., & Hong, J. I. (2014). Increasing security sensitivity with social proof: A large-scale experimental confirmation. In *Proceedings of the 2014 ACM SIGSAC conference on computer and communications security* (pp. 739-749). ACM. doi:10.1145/2660267.2660271

Dasti, R., & Sitwat, A. (2014). Development of a multidimensional measure of islamic spirituality (MMIS). *The Journal of Muslim Mental Health, 8*(2). doi:10.3998/jmmh.10381607.0008.204

Dawar, N., Parker, P. M., & Price, L. J. (1996). A cross-cultural study of interpersonal information exchange. *Journal of International Business Studies, 27*(3), 497–516. doi:10.1057/palgrave.jibs.8490142

De Cock, B., & Roginsky, S. (2015). Discursive identities on Twitter: Construction of the identity of MEP in pre-election period. Comparison between France, Spain and the United Kingdom. In F. Lienard & S. Zlitni (Eds.), *Electronic communication: challenges, opportunities and strategies* (pp. 137–148). Limoges: Lambert-Lucas.

De George, R. T. (1986). Theological ethics and business ethics. *Journal of Business Ethics, 5*(6), 421–432. doi:10.1007/BF00380748

De Jong, G. F., Faulkner, J. E., & Warland, R. H. (1976). Dimensions of Religiosity Reconsidered; Evidence from a Cross-Cultural Study. *Social Forces, 54*(4), 866–889. doi:10.1093/sf/54.4.866

de Lange, M., & von Solms, R. (2013). An e - Safety Educational Framework in South Africa. *Southern Africa Telecommunication Networks and Applications Conference (SATNAC) 2013*, 497.

De Raad, B., & Perugini, M. (Eds.). (2002). *Big Five assessment.* Göttingen: Hogrefe & Huber Publishers.

Debatin, B., Lovejoy, J. P., Horn, A. K., & Hughes, B. N. (2009). Facebook and online privacy: Attitudes, behaviors, and unintended consequences. *Journal of Computer-Mediated Communication, 15*(1), 83–108. doi:10.1111/j.1083-6101.2009.01494.x

Dedeoglu, B. (2003). Bermuda triangle: Comparing official definitions of terrorist activity. *Terrorism and Political Violence, 15*(3), 81–110. doi:10.1080/09546550312331293147

Delener, N. (1987). An exploratory study of values of Catholic and Jewish subcultures: Implications for consumer psychology. *World Marketing Congress, Proceedings of the Third Bi-Annual International Conference,* 151–155.

Delener, N. (1990). The effects of religious factors on perceived risk in durable goods purchase decisions. *Journal of Consumer Marketing, 7*(3), 27–38. doi:10.1108/EUM0000000002580

Delener, N. (1994). Religious contrasts in consumer decision behaviour patterns: Their dimensions and marketing implications. *European Journal of Marketing, 28*(5), 36–53. doi:10.1108/03090569410062023

Diener, E., & Emmons, R. A. (1985). The independence of positive and negative affect. *Journal of Personality and Social Psychology, 47,* 1108–1117. PMID:6520704

Dietz-Uhler, B., & Bishop-Clark, C. (2001). The use of computer-mediated communication to enhance subsequent face-to-face discussions. *Computers in Human Behavior, 17*(3), 269–283. doi:10.1016/S0747-5632(01)00006-1

Dillard, J. P., & Nabi, R. L. (2006). The persuasive influence of emotion in cancer prevention and detection messages. *Journal of Communication, 56*(1), S123–S139. doi:10.1111/j.1460-2466.2006.00286.x

Dinev, T., Bellotto, M., Hart, P., Colautti, C., Russo, V., Serra, I., ... Madsen, T. L. (2005). Privacy trade-off factors in e-commerce - A study of Italy and the United States. In *Academy of Management Annual Meeting Proceedings* (pp. A1–A6). Academy of Management. Retrieved from http://10.0.21.89/AMBPP.2005.18781234

Dinger, R. (2016). Site unseen. *Association of National Advertisers Magazine.* Retrieved from: http://www.ana.net/magazines/show/id/ana-2016-jan-site-unseen

Dobusch, L., & Schoeneborn, D. (2015). Fluidity, Identity, and Organizationality: The Communicative Constitution of Anonymous. *Journal of Management Studies, 52*(8), 1005–1035. doi:10.1111/joms.12139

Dolan, P., Hallsworth, M., Halpern, D., King, D., Metcalfe, R., & Vlaev, I. (2012). Influencing behaviour: The mindspace way. *Journal of Economic Psychology, 33*(1), 264–277. doi:10.1016/j.joep.2011.10.009

Dollar, D., Fisman, R., & Gatti, R. (2001). Are women really the 'fairer' sex? Corruption and women in Government. *Journal of Economic Behavior & Organization, 46*(4), 423–429. doi:10.1016/S0167-2681(01)00169-X

Donahue, M. J. (1985a). Intrinsic and extrinsic religiousness: Review and meta-analysis. *Journal of Personality and Social Psychology, 48*(2), 400–419. doi:10.1037/0022-3514.48.2.400

Donahue, M. J. (1985b). Intrinsic and Extrinsic Religiousness: The Empirical Research. *Journal for the Scientific Study of Religion, 24*(4), 418. doi:10.2307/1385995

Doney, P. M., Cannon, J. P., & Mullen, M. R. (1998). Understanding the Influence of National Culture on the Development of Trust. *Academy of Management Review, 23*(3), 601–620.

Douglas, D., Santanna, J.J., de Oliveira Schmidt, R., Granville, L.Z., & Pras, A. (2017). Booters: Can Anything Justify Distributed Denial-of-Service (DDoS) Attacks for Hire? *Journal of Information, Communication and Ethics in Society, 15*(1).

Downs, J. S., Holbrook, M., & Cranor, L. F. (2006). Decision strategies and susceptibility to phishing. In *Proceedings of the Second Symposium on Usable Privacy and Security* (pp. 79-90). ACM. doi:10.1145/1143120.1143131

Downs, J. S., Holbrook, M., & Cranor, L. F. (2007). Behavioural response to phishing risk. *Proceedings of the Anti-Phishing Working Groups Second Annual eCrime Researchers Summit,* 37-44. doi:10.1145/1299015.1299019

Drucker, S., & Gumpert, G. (2000). Cybercrime and punishment. *Critical Studies in Media Communication, 17*(2), 133–158. doi:10.1080/15295030009388387

DSCI-KPMG. (2010). *State of data security and privacy in Indian BPO industry (Tech. report)*. DSCI and KPMG.

Dubrovsky, V. J., Kiesler, S., & Sethna, B. N. (1991). The equalization phenomenon: Status effects in computer-mediated and face-to-face decision-making groups. *Human-Computer Interaction, 6*(2), 119–146. doi:10.1207/s15327051hci0602_2

Duda, R. O., & Hart, P. E. (1973). *Pattern classification and scene analysis*. New York: John Wiley and Sons.

Duguay, S. (2017). Dressing up Tinderella: Interrogating authenticity claims on the mobile dating app Tinder. *Information Communication and Society, 20*(3), 351–367. doi:10.1080/1369118X.2016.1168471

Duke, D. (2002). Ethical hackers – can we trust them? *Network Security, 3*, 3.

Dunning, D., Anderson, J. E., Schlösser, T., Ehlebracht, D., & Fetchenhauer, D. (2014). Trust at zero acquaintance: More a matter of respect than expectation of reward. *Journal of Personality and Social Psychology, 107*(1), 122–141. doi:10.1037/a0036673 PMID:24819869

Dupont, B., Côté, A., Savine, C., & Décary-Hétu, D. (2016). The ecology of trust among hackers. *Global Crime, 17*(2), 129–151. doi:10.1080/17440572.2016.1157480

Durkheim, É. (1912). *The Elementary Forms of the Religious Life*. Retrieved from https://books.google.com/books?hl=en&lr=&id=eEk1AwAAQBAJ&pgis=1

Edwards, M., Larson, R., Green, B., Rashid, A., & Baron, A. (2017). Panning for gold: Automatically analysing online social engineering attack surfaces. *Computers & Security, 69*, 18–34. doi:10.1016/j.cose.2016.12.013

Edwards, W., & Fasolo, B. (2001). Decision technology. *Annual Review of Psychology, 52*(1), 581–606. doi:10.1146/annurev.psych.52.1.581 PMID:11148318

Egelman, S., & Schechter, S. (2013, April). The importance of being earnest (in security warnings). In *International Conference on Financial Cryptography and Data Security* (pp. 52-59). Springer Berlin Heidelberg. doi:10.1007/978-3-642-39884-1_5

Egelman, S., Cranor, L. F., & Hong, J. (2008, April). You've been warned: an empirical study of the effectiveness of web browser phishing warnings. In *Proceedings of the SIGCHI Conference on Human Factors in Computing Systems* (pp. 1065-1074). ACM. doi:10.1145/1357054.1357219

Egelman, S., & Peer, E. (2015a). Predicting Privacy and Security Attitudes. *Computers and Society: The Newletter of ACM SIGCAS, 45*(1), 22–28. doi:10.1145/2738210.2738215

Egelman, S., & Peer, E. (2015b). Scaling the Security Wall: Developing a Security Behavior Intentions Scale (SeBIS). *Proceedings of the ACM CHI'15 Conference on Human Factors in Computing Systems, 1*, 2873–2882. doi:10.1145/2702123.2702249

Eisenberg, M. A. (1995). The limits of cognition and the limits of contract. *Stanford Law Review, 47*(2), 211–259. doi:10.2307/1229226

El Ati, J., Beji, C., & Danguir, J. (1995). Increased fat oxidation during Ramadan fasting in healthy women: An adaptative mechanism for body-weight maintenance. *The American Journal of Clinical Nutrition, 62*(2), 302–307. PMID:7625336

Elmasry, M. H., Auter, P. I., & Peuchaud, S. R. (2014). *Facebook across culture: A cross-cultural content analysis of Egyptian, Qatari and American student Facebook pages* (PhD Dissertation). The American University in Cairo, Egypt.

Elms, S. (2016). 7 steps to avoid ad blocking. *ADMAP*. Retrieved from: https://www.warc.com/

Emmons, R. A. (2005). Striving for the sacred: Personal goals, life meaning, and religion. *The Journal of Social Issues*, *61*(4), 731–745. doi:10.1111/j.1540-4560.2005.00429.x

Engel, J. F., Blackwell, R. D., & Miniard, P. W. (1986). *Consumer behaviour*. Hinsdale, IL: Dryden.

Engel, J. F., Kollat, D. T., & Blackwell, R. D. (1978). *Consumer behavior*. Hinsdale, IL: Dryden.

Engel, J. F., & Roger, D. (1995). *Consumer Behavior*. New York: Holt, Rinehart and Winston.

Erickson, T. (1997). Social interaction on the net: Virtual community as participatory genre. In *Proceedings of the Thirtieth Hawaii International Conference on System Sciences* (Vol. 6, pp. 13-21). IEEE. doi:10.1109/HICSS.1997.665480

Essoo, N., & Dibb, S. (2010). Religious influences on shopping behaviour: An exploratory study. *Journal of Marketing Management*, *20*(7–8), 683–712. doi:10.1362/0267257041838728

Evans, J. B. T. (2003). In two minds: Dual-process accounts of reasoning. *Trends in Cognitive Sciences*, *7*(10), 454–459. doi:10.1016/j.tics.2003.08.012 PMID:14550493

Evans, J. S. (2008). Dual-processing accounts of reasoning, judgment, and social cognition. *Annual Review of Psychology*, *59*(1), 255–278. doi:10.1146/annurev.psych.59.103006.093629 PMID:18154502

Evans, M., Maglaras, L. A., He, Y., & Janicke, H. (2016). Human behaviour as an aspect of cybersecurity assurance. *Security and Communication Networks*, *9*(17), 4667–4679. doi:10.1002/sec.1657

Eysenbach, G. (2001). What is e-health? *Journal of Medical Internet Research*, *3*(2), e20. doi:10.2196/jmir.3.2.e20 PMID:11720962

Facebook. (2015). *Terms of Service*. Retrieved from: https://www.facebook.com/terms

Fam, K. S., Waller, D. S., & Erdogan, B. Z. (2004). The influence of religion on attitudes towards the advertising of controversial products. *European Journal of Marketing*, *38*(5/6), 537–555. doi:10.1108/03090560410529204

Farah, M. F., & Newman, A. J. (2010). Exploring consumer boycott intelligence using a socio-cognitive approach. *Journal of Business Research*, *63*(4), 347–355. doi:10.1016/j.jbusres.2009.03.019

Farajtabar, M., Yang, J., Ye, X., Xu, H., Trivedi, R., Khalil, E., . . . Zha, H. (2017). *Fake News Mitigation via Point Process Based Intervention*. Retrieved September 15, 2017 from http://proceedings.mlr.press/v70/farajtabar17a/farajtabar17a.pdf

Farrell, S. (2016). TalkTalk counts costs of cyber-attack. *The Guardian*. Retrieved from https://www.theguardian.com/business/2016/feb/02/talktalk-cyberattack-costs-customers-leave accessed 24/09/16

Farwell, J. P. (2014). The Media Strategy of ISIS. *Survival: Global Politics and Strategy*, *56*(6), 49–55. doi:10.1080/00396338.2014.985436

FAS. (2003). *A Review of the FBI's Performance in Deterring, Detecting, and Investigating the Espionage Activities of Robert Philip Hanssen*. Office of the Inspector General. Retrieved Apr 30, 2017, from https://fas.org/irp/agency/doj/oig/hanssen.html

Faysel, M. A., & Haque, S. S. (2010). Towards Cyber Defence: Research in Intrusion Detection and Intrusion Prevention Systems. *International Journal of Computer Science and Network Security*, *10*(7), 316–325.

FBI. (2002). *Terrorism 2002-2005*. Washington, DC: United States Department of Justice.

Feldman, M. D. (2000). Munchausen by internet: Detecting factitious illness and crisis on the Internet. *Southern Medical Journal*, *93*(7), 669–672. doi:10.1097/00007611-200007000-00005 PMID:10923952

Festinger, L. (1950). Informal social communication. *Psychological Review*, 57(5), 271–282. doi:10.1037/h0056932 PMID:14776174

Festinger, L., & Carlsmith, J. M. (1959). Cognitive consequences of forced compliance. *Journal of Abnormal and Social Psychology*, 58(2), 203–210. doi:10.1037/h0041593 PMID:13640824

Finn, P., & Jakobsson, M. (2007). Designing ethical phishing experiments. *Technology and Society Magazine, IEEE*, 26(1), 46–58. doi:10.1109/MTAS.2007.335565

Fischer, P., Krueger, J. I., Greitemeyer, T., Vogrincic, C., Kastenmüller, A., Frey, D., & Kainbacher, M. (2011). The bystander-effect: A meta-analytic review on bystander intervention in dangerous and non-dangerous emergencies. *Psychological Bulletin*, 137(4), 517–537. doi:10.1037/a0023304 PMID:21534650

Fischer, P., Lea, S. E., & Evans, K. M. (2013). Why do individuals respond to fraudulent scam communications and lose money? The psychological determinants of scam compliance. *Journal of Applied Social Psychology*, 43(10), 2060–2072. doi:10.1111/jasp.12158

Fiske, S. T., & Taylor, S. E. (2013). *Social cognition: From brains to culture*. Thousand Oaks, CA: Sage. doi:10.4135/9781446286395

Fogg, B. J. (2002). Persuasive technology: Using computers to change what we think and do. *Ubiquity*, 5.

Forgas, J. P., & East, R. (2008). On being happy and gullible: Mood effects on skepticism and the detection of deception. *Journal of Experimental Social Psychology*, 44(5), 1362–1367. doi:10.1016/j.jesp.2008.04.010

Foucault, M. (1977). Discipline and Punish: The Birth of the Prison (A. Sheridan, Trans.). New York: Vintage.

Fox, S., & Jones, S. (2009). The social life of health information. *Pew Research Center*. Retrieved May 18, 2017, from http://www.pewinternet.org/2009/06/11/the-social-life-of-health-information/

Foxall, G. R., Goldsmith, R. E., & Brown, S. (1998). *Consumer psychology for marketing* (Vol. 1). Cengage Learning EMEA.

Fox, N., Ward, K., & O'Rourke, A. (2005). Pro-anorexia, weight-loss drugs and the internet: An "anti-recovery" explanatory model of anorexia. *Sociology of Health & Illness*, 27(7), 944–971. doi:10.1111/j.1467-9566.2005.00465.x PMID:16313524

Frank, L. G., & Deborah, A. F. (2010). Combining Traditional Cyber Security Audit Data with Psychosocial Data: Towards Predictive Modeling for Insider Threat Mitigation. Insider Threats in Cyber Security, 49, 85-114.

Fredrickson, B. L., & Branigan, C. (2005). Positive emotions broaden the scope of attention and thought-action repertoires. *Cognition and Emotion*, 19(3), 313–332. doi:10.1080/02699930441000238 PMID:21852891

Freiermuth, M. R. (2011). Text, lies, and electronic bait: An analysis of email fraud and the decisions of the unsuspecting. *Discourse & Communication*, 5(2), 123–145. doi:10.1177/1750481310395448

Friedman, B., Khan, P. H. Jr, & Howe, D. C. (2000). Trust online. *Communications of the ACM*, 43(12), 34–40. doi:10.1145/355112.355120

Fullwood, C. (2015). The role of personality in online self-presentation. In A. Attrill (Ed.), *Cyberpsychology* (pp. 9–28). Oxford, UK: Oxford University Press.

Furby, L. (1978). Possession in humans: An exploratory study of its meaning and motivation. *Social Behavior and Personality*, 6(1), 49–65. doi:10.2224/sbp.1978.6.1.49

Furby, L. (1991). Understanding the psychology of possession and ownership: A personal memoir and an appraisal of our progress. *Journal of Social Behavior and Personality*, *6*(6), 457.

Furnell, S. M., Bryant, P., & Phippen, A. D. (2007). Assessing the security perceptions of personal internet users. *Computers & Security*, *26*(5), 410–417. doi:10.1016/j.cose.2007.03.001

Gandhi, M., & Wang, T. (2015). Digital Health Consumer Adoption: 2015. *Rock Health*. Retrieved May 12, 2017, from https://rockhealth.com/reports/digital-health-consumer-adoption-2015/

Gao, Y., Bianchi-Berthouze, N., & Meng, H. (2012). What does touch tell us about emotions in touchscreen-based gameplay? *ACM Transactions on Computer-Human Interaction, 19*(4).

Garbarino, E., & Strahilevitz, M. (2004). Gender differences in the perceived risk of buying online and the effects of receiving a site recommendation. *Journal of Business Research*, *57*(7), 768–775. doi:10.1016/S0148-2963(02)00363-6

Garera, S., Provos, N., Chew, M., & Rubin, A. D. (2007). A framework for detection and measurement of phishing attacks. *Proceedings of the 2007 ACM Workshop on Recurring Malcode*, 1-8. doi:10.1145/1314389.1314391

Gee, J. P. (2014). *An introduction to discourse analysis*. Abingdon, UK: Routledge.

Geert Hofstede. (n.d.). Retrieved from https://geert-hofstede.com/countries.html

Geert-Hofstede. (2015). Retrieved from: http://www.geert-hofstede.com

Geertz, C. (1973). *The interpretation of cultures: Selected essays* (Vol. 5019). Basic books.

Gerber, E. M., & Hui, J. (2013). Crowdfunding: Motivations and deterrents for participation. *ACM Transactions on Computer-Human Interaction*, *20*(6), 34. doi:10.1145/2530540

Gerber, E. M., Hui, J. S., & Kuo, P. Y. (2012). Crowdfunding: Why people are motivated to post and fund projects on crowdfunding platforms. In *Proceedings of the International Workshop on Design, Influence, and Social Technologies: Techniques, Impacts and Ethics* (Vol. 2, p. 11). Academic Press.

Geyer, A. L., & Baumeister, R. F. (2005). *Religion, Morality, and Self-Control: Values*. Virtues, and Vices.

Ghorbani, N., Watson, P. J., Ghramaleki, A. F., Morris, R. J., & Hood, R. W. Jr. (2002). Muslim-Christian Religious Orientation Scales: Distinctions, Correlations, and Cross-Cultural Analysis in Iran and the United States. *The International Journal for the Psychology of Religion*, *12*(2), 69–91. doi:10.1207/S15327582IJPR1202_01

Gibbs, J. C., Basinger, K. S., & Fuller, D. (1992). *Moral maturity: Measuring the development of sociomoral reflection*. Hillsdale, NJ: Erlbaum.

Gibbs, J. L., Ellison, N. B., & Lai, C. H. (2011). First comes love, then comes Google: An investigation of uncertainty reduction strategies and self-disclosure in online dating. *Communication Research*, *38*(1), 70–100.

Gibson, C. B., Huang, L., Kirkman, B. L., & Shapiro, D. L. (2014). Where global and virtual meet: The value of examining the intersection of these elements in twenty-first-century teams. *Annual Review of Organizational Psychology and Organizational Behavior*, *1*(1), 217–244. doi:10.1146/annurev-orgpsych-031413-091240

Gibson, J. W. (1994). *Warrior Dreams: Violence and Manhood in Post-Vietnam America*. Louisville, KY: Hill & Wang.

Giles, D. C., Stommel, W., Paulus, T., Lester, J., & Reed, D. (2015). The microanalysis of online data: The methodological development of 'digital CA'. *Discourse, Context and Media*, *7*, 45–51. doi:10.1016/j.dcm.2014.12.002

Gillespie, N. (2003). Measuring trust in working relationships: The behavioral trust inventory. *Proceedings from Academy of Management Conference*.

Gill, P. (2015). *Lone-actor terrorists: A behavioral analysis*. Abingdon, UK: Routledge.

Gill, P., & Corner, E. (2015). Lone-Actor Terrorist Use of the Internet and Behavioral Correlates. In L. Jarvis, S. Macdonald, & T. Chen (Eds.), *Terrorism Online: Politics, Law, and Technology* (pp. 35–53). London: Routledge.

Gill, P., Corner, E., Conway, M., Thornton, A., Bloom, M., & Horgan, J. (2017). Terrorist Use of the Internet by the Numbers. *Criminology & Public Policy, 16*(1), 99–117. doi:10.1111/1745-9133.12249

Gill, P., Corner, E., Thornton, A., & Conway, M. (2015). *What are the roles of the internet in terrorism? Measuring online behaviors of convicted terrorists*. London: VOX-Pol.

Gill, P., Horgan, J., & Deckert, P. (2014). Bombing Alone: Tracing the motivations and antecedent behaviors of lone actor terrorists. *Journal of Forensic Sciences, 59*(2), 425–435. doi:10.1111/1556-4029.12312 PMID:24313297

Glanz, J., Rotella, S., & Sanger, D. E. (2014). Mumbai Attacks Piles of Spy Data, but an Uncompleted Puzzle. *New York Times*. Retrieved 04 16, 2017, from https://www.nytimes.com/2014/12/22/world/asia/in-2008-mumbai-attacks-piles-of-spy-data-but-an-uncompleted-puzzle.html?mcubz=2

Glock, C. Y. (1962). *On the study of religious commitment*. Academic Press.

Godin, G., & Kok, G. (1996). The theory of planned behavior: A review of its applications to health-related behaviors. *American Journal of Health Promotion, 11*(2), 87–98. doi:10.4278/0890-1171-11.2.87 PMID:10163601

Goffman, E. (1959). The moral career of the mental patient. *Psychiatry, 22*(2), 123–142. doi:10.1080/00332747.1959.11023166 PMID:13658281

Goffman, E. (1974). *Frame Analysis: An Essay on the Organization of Experience*. New York: Harper Colophon.

Goffman, E. (1990). *The presentation of self in everyday life*. London: Penguin.

Goodall, J. R., Radwan, H., & Halseth, L. (2010). Visual analysis of code security. In *Proceedings of the Seventh International Symposium on Visualisation for Cyber Security* (pp. 46-51). Ottawa, Ontario, Canada: Academic Press. doi:10.1145/1850795.1850800

Goode, L. (2015). Anonymous and the political ethos of hacktivism. *Popular Communication, 13*(1), 74–86. doi:10.1080/15405702.2014.978000

Goodman, S., Morrongiello, B., & Meckling, K. (2016). A randomized, controlled trial evaluating the efficacy of an online intervention targeting vitamin D intake, knowledge and status among young adults. *The International Journal of Behavioral Nutrition and Physical Activity, 13*(1), 116. doi:10.1186/s12966-016-0443-1 PMID:27836017

Goodman, S., Morrongiello, B., Simpson, J. R., & Meckling, K. (2015). Vitamin D intake among young Canadian adults: Validation of a mobile vitamin D calculator app. *Journal of Nutrition Education and Behavior, 47*(3), 242–247. doi:10.1016/j.jneb.2014.11.006 PMID:25959447

Goodrich, K., & de Mooij, M. (2013). How 'social' are social media? A cross-cultural comparison of online and offline purchase decision influences. *Journal of Marketing Communications, 20*(1-2), 103–116. doi:10.1080/13527266.2013.797773

Google. (2014). *Terms of Service*. Retrieved from: https://www.google.com/intl/en-GB/policies/terms/

Gordon, S., & Ford, R. (2002). Cyberterrorism? *Computers & Security, 21*(7), 636–647. doi:10.1016/S0167-4048(02)01116-1

Gorsuch, R. L., & McPherson, S. E. (1989). Intrinsic/extrinsic measurement: I/E-revised and single-item scales. *Journal for the Scientific Study of Religion*, *28*(3), 348–354. doi:10.2307/1386745

Gosling, S. D., Vazire, S., Srivastava, S., & John, O. P. (2004). Should we trust web-based studies? A comparative analysis of seix preconceptions about Internet questionnaires. *The American Psychologist*, *59*(2), 93–104. doi:10.1037/0003-066X.59.2.93 PMID:14992636

Gough, H. G. (1951). Studies of social intolerance: I. Some psychological and sociological correlates of anti-Semitism. *The Journal of Social Psychology*, *33*(2), 237–246. doi:10.1080/00224545.1951.9921815

Gouran, D. S., & Hirokawa, R. Y. (1983). The role of communication in decision-making groups: A functional perspective. *Communications in Transition*, 168-185.

Gouran, D. S., & Hirokawa, R. Y. (1996). *Functional theory and communication in decision making and problem-solving groups. An expanded view. In Communication and group decision making* (pp. 55–80). Thousand Oaks, CA: Sage.

Grady, C., Cummings, S. R., Rowbotham, M. C., McConnell, M. V., Ashley, E. A., & Kang, G. (2017). Informed Consent. *The New England Journal of Medicine*, *376*(9), 856–867. doi:10.1056/NEJMra1603773 PMID:28249147

Gragg, D. (2003). *A multi-level defense against social engineering*. Retrieved Apr 30, 2017, from http://www.sans.org/rr/whitepapers/engineering/920.php

Graham, J. (2015). Who Joins ISIS and Why? *Huffington Post*. Retrieved 06 10, 2017, from http://www.huffingtonpost.com/john-graham/who-joins-isis-and-why_b_8881810.html

Graham, C. (2017). *NHS cyber-attack: Everything you need to know about "biggest ransomware" offensive in history*. The Telegraph.

Grazioli, S., & Wang, A. (2001). Looking without seeing: understanding unsophisticated consumers' success and failure to detect Internet deception. *ICIS 2001 Proceedings*, 23.

Greene, J., & Hiadt, J. (2002). How (and where) does moral judgement work? *Trends in Cognitive Sciences*, *6*(12), 517–523. doi:10.1016/S1364-6613(02)02011-9 PMID:12475712

Greitzer, F., Kangas, L., Noonan, C., & Dalton, A. (2010). *Identifying at-risk employees: A behavioral model for predicting potential insider threats*. Retrieved from http://www.pnl.gov/main/publications/external/technical_reports/PNNL-19665.pdf

Greitzer, F. L., Imran, M., Purl, J., Axelrad, E. T., Leong, Y. M., & Becker, D. E. ... Sticha, P. J. (2016). Developing an ontology for individual and organizational sociotechnical indicators of insider threat risk. *CEUR Workshop Proceedings*, 19–27.

Greitzer, F. L., Noonan, C. F., Kangas, L. J., & Dalton, A. C. (2010). *Identifying at-Risk Employees: A Behavioral Model for Predicting Potential Insider Threats. A report published by Pacific Northwest National Laboratory on September 30, 2010*. U.S. Department of Energy.

Grover, V., & Purvis, R. (2011). R Esearch a Rticle T Echnostress : T Echnological a Ntecedents. *Management Information Systems Quarterly*, *35*(4), 831–858.

Guadagno, R. E., & Cialdini, R. B. (2002). Online persuasion: An examination of gender differences in computer-mediated interpersonal influence. *Group Dynamics*, *6*(1), 38–51. doi:10.1037/1089-2699.6.1.38

Guadagno, R. E., & Cialdini, R. B. (2005). Online persuasion and compliance: Social influence on the Internet and beyond. In Y. Amichai-Hamburger (Ed.), *The social net: The social psychology of the Internet* (pp. 91–113). New York: Oxford University Press.

Guadagno, R. E., Muscanell, N. L., Rice, L. M., & Roberts, N. (2013). Social influence online: The impact of social validation and likability on compliance. *Psychology of Popular Media Culture*, 2(1), 51–60. doi:10.1037/a0030592

Guéguen, N., & Jacob, C. (2002). Solicitation by e-mail and solicitor's status: A field study of social influence on the web. *Cyberpsychology & Behavior*, 5(4), 377–383. doi:10.1089/109493102760275626 PMID:12216702

Guess, C. D. (2004). Decision-making in Individualistic and Collectivist Cultures. *Readings in Psychology and Culture, 4*. Retrieved from: http://scholarworks.gvsu.edu/cgi/viewcontent.cgi?article=1032&context=orpc

Gurtman, M. B. (1992). Trust, distrust, and interpersonal problems: A circumplex analysis. *Journal of Personality and Social Psychology*, 62(6), 989–1002. doi:10.1037/0022-3514.62.6.989 PMID:1619552

Guss, C. D., & Dorner, D. (2012). Cultural differences in dynamic decision-making strategies in a non-linear, time-delayed task. *Cognitive Systems Research*, 12(3), 365–376.

Guthrie, S., Agassi, J., Andriolo, K. R., Buchdahl, D., Earhart, H. B., Greenberg, M., & Sharpe, K. J. et al. (1980). A cognitive theory of religion. *Current Anthropology*, 21(2), 181–203. doi:10.1086/202429

Hadlington, L. (2017). Human factors in cybersecurity; examining the link between Internet addiction, impulsivity, attitudes towards cybersecurity, and risky cybersecurity behaviours. *Heliyon (London)*, 3(7), e00346. doi:10.1016/j.heliyon.2017.e00346 PMID:28725870

Hadlington, L., & Parsons, K. (2017). Can Cyberloafing and Internet Addiction Affect Organizational Information Security? *Cyberpsychology, Behavior, and Social Networking*, 20(9), 567–571.

Hagen-Rochester. (2012). Online dating dumps the stigma. *Futurity*. Retrieved June 1, 2017, from http://www.futurity.org/online-dating-dumps-the-stigma/

Halder, D., & Jaishankar, K. (2011). *Cyber crime and the Victimization of Women: Laws, Rights, and Regulations*. Hershey, PA: IGI Global.

Halevi, T., Lewis, J., & Memon, N. (2013). A pilot study of cyber security and privacy related behaviour and personality traits. In *Proceedings of WWW '13 Companion Proceedings of the 22nd international conference on World Wide Web companion* (pp. 737–744). Rio de Janeiro, Brazil: Academic Press.

Halevi, T., Lewis, J., & Memon, N. (2013). A pilot study of cyber security and privacy related behavior and personality traits. In *Proceedings of the 22nd International Conference on World Wide Web*. New York, NY: ACM. doi:10.1145/2487788.2488034

Halfond, W. G., & Orso, A. (2005, November). AMNESIA: Analysis and monitoring for neutralizing SQL-infection attacks. *Proceedings of the 20th IEEE/ACM International Conference on Automated Software Engineering*, 174–183. doi:10.1145/1101908.1101935

Hall, A. K., Bernhardt, J. M., & Dodd, V. (2015). Older adults' use of online and offline sources of health information and constructs of reliance and self-efficacy for medial decision making. *Journal of Health Communication*, 20(7), 751–758. doi:10.1080/10810730.2015.1018603 PMID:26054777

Halpern, D. F. (1992). *Sex differences in cognitive abilities* (2nd ed.). Hillsdale, NJ: Erlbaum.

Hamman, S. T., Hopkinson, K. M., Markham, R. L., Chaplik, A. M., & Metzler, G. E. (2017). Teaching game theory to improve adversarial thinking in cybersecurity students. *IEEE Transactions on Education*, *99*, 1–7.

Hampson, N. C. (2012). Hacktivism: A new breed of protest in a networked world. *BC Int'l & Comp. L. Rev.*, *35*, 511.

Hancock, J., & Guillory, J. (2015). Deception with technology. In S. Sundar (Ed.), *The handbook of the psychology of communication technology* (pp. 270–289). Malden, MA: Wiley-Blackwell.

Hannah, S. T., Avolio, B. J., & May, D. R. (2011). Moral maturation and moral conation: A capacity approach to explaining moral thought and action. *Academy of Management Review*, *36*(4), 663–685. doi:10.5465/amr.2010.0128

Hanna, P., Vanclay, F., Langdon, E. J., & Arts, J. (2016). Conceptualizing social protest and the significance of protest actions to large projects. *The Extractive Industries and Society*, *3*(1), 217–239. doi:10.1016/j.exis.2015.10.006

Hansen, T., Jensen, J. M., & Solgaard, H. S. (2004). Predicting online grocery buying intention: A comparison of the theory of reasoned action and the theory of planned behavior. *International Journal of Information Management*, *24*(6), 539–550. doi:10.1016/j.ijinfomgt.2004.08.004

HardieA. (2016). *CQPweb*. Retrieved from https://cqpweb.lancs.ac.uk/

Harper, J. (2012). *84 percent of the world population has faith: a third are Christian*. Retrieved January 4, 2017, from http://www.washingtontimes.com/blog/watercooler/2012/dec/23/84-percent-world-population-has-faith-third-are-ch/

Harrell, E., & Langton, L. (2013). *Victims of identity theft, 2012*. Washington, DC: Bureau of Justice Statistics.

Harris-McKoy, D., & Cui, M. (2013). Parental control, adolescent delinquency, and young adult criminal behavior. *Journal of Child and Family Studies*, *22*(6), 836–843. doi:10.1007/s10826-012-9641-x

Harrison, B., Vishwanath, A., & Rao, R. (2016). A user-centered approach to phishing susceptibility: The role of a suspicious personality in protecting against phishing. In *2016 49ᵗʰ Hawaii International Conference on System Sciences (HICSS)* (pp. 5628-5634). IEEE.

Hart, R. P., & Lind, C. J. (2011). The rhetoric of Islamic activism: A Diction study. *Dynamics of Asymmetric Conflict*, *4*(2), 113–125. doi:10.1080/17467586.2011.627934

Häubl, G., & Tifts, V. (2000). Consumer Decision Making in Online Shopping Environments: The Effects of Interactive Decision Aids. *Marketing Science*, *19*(1), 4–21. doi:10.1287/mksc.19.1.4.15178

Heidegger, M. (1996). *Being and time [Sein und Zeit]*. Albany, NY: SUNY press.

Henrich, J., Heine, S. J., & Norenzayan, A. (2010). The weirdest people in the world? *Behavioral and Brain Sciences*, *33*(3), 61-83.

Henshel, D., Sample, C., Cains, M. G., & Hoffman, B. (2016). Integrating Cultural Factors into Human Factors Framework for Cyber Attackers. *7th Annual Conference on Applied Human Factors and Ergonomics Conference*. doi:10.1007/978-3-319-41932-9_11

Herath, T., & Rao, H. R. (2009a). Encouraging information security behaviors in organizations: Role of penalties, pressures and perceived effectiveness. *Decision Support Systems*, *47*(2), 154–165. doi:10.1016/j.dss.2009.02.005

Herath, T., & Rao, H. R. (2009b). Protection motivation and deterrence: A framework for security policy compliance in organizations. *European Journal of Information Systems*, *18*(2), 106–125. doi:10.1057/ejis.2009.6

Hern, A., & Gibbs, S. (2017). *What is WannaCry ransomware and why is it attacking global computers?* Retrieved from https://www.theguardian.com/technology/2017/may/12/nhs-ransomware-cyber-attack-what-is-wanacrypt0r-20

Hewstone, M., & Jaspars, J. M. F. (1982). Intergroup relations and attribution processes. In H. Tajfel (Ed.), *Social Identity and Intergroup Relations* (pp. 99–133). Cambridge, UK: Cambridge University Press.

Higher Education Statistical Agency. (2014). *Qualifications obtained by students on HE courses at HEIs in the UK by level of qualification obtained, gender and subject area, 2012 to 2013*. Accessed on 16/12/16 from https://www.hesa.ac.uk/data-and-analysis/publications/students-2012-13/introduction

Himmelfarb, H. S. (1975). Measuring religious involvement. *Social Forces, 53*(4), 606–618. doi:10.1093/sf/53.4.606

Hirokawa, R. Y. (1985). Discussion procedures and decision-making performance. *Human Communication Research, 12*(2), 203–224. doi:10.1111/j.1468-2958.1985.tb00073.x

Hirokawa, R. Y. (1988). Group Communication and Decision-Making Performance A Continued Test of the Functional Perspective. *Human Communication Research, 14*(4), 487–515. doi:10.1111/j.1468-2958.1988.tb00165.x

Hirschman, E. (1981). American Jewish Ethnicity: Its Relationship to Some Selected Aspects of Consumer Behavior. *Journal of Marketing, 45*(3), 102. doi:10.2307/1251545

Hirschman, E. C. (1983a). *Cognitive structure across consumer ethnic subcultures: A comparative analysis* (Vol. 10). NA-Advances in Consumer Research.

Hirschman, E. C. (1983b). Religious affiliation and consumption processes: An initial paradigm. *Research in Marketing, 6*, 131–170.

HMG. (2011). *Prevent strategy*. London: Crown.

Ho, C., Lin, M., & Chen, H. (2012). Web users' behavioural patterns of tourism information search: From online to offline. *Tourism Management, 33*(6), 1468–1482. doi:10.1016/j.tourman.2012.01.016

Hoekstra, H., & De Fruyt, F. (2014). *NEO-PI-3 en NEO-FFI-3 persoonlijkheidsvragenlijsten: Handleiding [NEO-PI-3 and NEO-PI-3 personality questionnaires: Manual]*. Amsterdam: Hogrefe Uitgevers.

Hofstede, G. (1980). *Cultures Consequences: International Differences in Work-Related Values* (Vol. 5). Thousand Oaks, CA: Sage.

Hofstede, G., Hofstede, G. J., & Minkov, M. (2010). *Cultures and Organizations*. New York, NY: McGraw-Hill Publishing.

Hollander, Wolfe, & Chicken. (2014). *Nonparametric statistical methods* (3rd ed.). John Wiley & Sons.

Holtfreter, K., Reisig, M. D., Piquero, N. L., & Piquero, A. R. (2010). Low self-control and fraud offending, victimization, and their overlap. *Criminal Justice and Behavior, 37*(2), 188–203. doi:10.1177/0093854809354977

Holt, T. J. (2007). Subcultural Evolution? Examining the Influence of on- and off-line Experiences on Deviant Subcultures. *Deviant Behavior, 28*(1), 171–198. doi:10.1080/01639620601131065

Homans, G. C. (1974). *Social Behaviour: Its Elementary Forms*. New York: Harcourt Brace Jovanovich, Inc.

Hong, J. (2012). The state of phishing attacks. *Communications of the ACM, 55*(1), 74–81. doi:10.1145/2063176.2063197

Hong, K. W., Kelley, C. M., Tembe, R., Murphy-Hill, E., & Mayhorn, C. B. (2013, September). Keeping up with the Joneses: Assessing phishing susceptibility in an email task. *Proceedings of the Human Factors and Ergonomics Society Annual Meeting, 57*(1), 1012–1016. doi:10.1177/1541931213571226

Hongmei, C., Carol, S., Zornitza, G. P., & Dominique, H. (2016). Determining Predisposition to Insider Threat Activities by using Text Analysis. In Proceedings of Future Technologies Conference (pp. 985-990). San Francisco, CA: Academic Press.

Hood, R. W. Jr. (1970). Religious orientation and the report of religious experience. *Journal for the Scientific Study of Religion, 9*(4), 285–291. doi:10.2307/1384573

Hood, R. W. Jr, Hill, P. C., & Spilka, B. (2009). *The psychology of religion: An empirical approach.* Guilford Press.

Ho, R., & Lloyd, J. I. (1983). Intergroup attribution: The role of social categories in causal attribution for behaviour. *Australian Journal of Psychology, 35*(1), 49–59. doi:10.1080/00049538308255302

Horgan, J., & Taylor, M. (2013). *Terrorist psychology: Separating facts from fictions.* Retrieved April 26, 2017, from http://sites.psu.edu/icst/2013/04/19/terrorist-psychology-separating-facts-from-fictions/

Hornuf, L., & Schwienbacher, A. (2015). Portal Design and Funding Dynamics in Crowdinvesting. *SSRN Electronic Journal.* Retrieved June 2, 2017, from http://ssrn.com/abstract=2612998

Horvát, E. Á., Uparna, J., & Uzzi, B. (2015). Network vs market relations: The effect of friends in crowdfunding. In *Proceedings from 2015 IEEE/ACM International Conference on Advances in Social Networks Analysis and Mining (ASONAM)* (pp. 226-233). IEEE.

Howard, P. J., & Howard, J. M. (1995). *The Big Five quickstart: An introduction to the five-factor model of personality for human resource professionals.* Charlotte, NC: Center for Applied Cognitive Studies.

Huang, Y., & Bian, L. (2009). A Bayesian network and analytic hierarchy process based personalized recommendations for tourist attractions over the Internet. *Expert Systems with Applications, 36*(1), 933–943. doi:10.1016/j.eswa.2007.10.019

Hu, C., Zhao, L., & Huang, J. (2015). Achieving self-congruency? Examining why individuals reconstruct their virtual identity in communities of interest established within social network platforms. *Computers in Human Behavior, 50,* 465–475. doi:10.1016/j.chb.2015.04.027

Hudic, A., Zechner, L., Islam, S., Krieg, C., Weippl, E. R., Winkler, S., & Hable, R. (2012). Towards a unified penetration testing taxonomy. *Privacy, Security, Risk and Trust (PASSAT), 2012 International Conference on Social Computing,* 811-812.

Huff, L., & Kelley, L. (2003). Levels of organizational trust in individualist versus collectivist societies: A seven-nation study. *Organization Science, 14*(1), 81–90. doi:10.1287/orsc.14.1.81.12807

Huffman, T. E. (1988). *In the world but not of the world: Religiosity, alienation, and philosophy of human nature among Bible college and liberal arts college students.* Academic Press.

Hui, K. L., Teo, H. H., & Lee, S. Y. T. (2007). The value of privacy assurance: An exploratory field experiment. *Management Information Systems Quarterly,* 19–33.

Hunker, J., & Probst, C. (2011). Insiders and insider threats—an overview of definitions and mitigation techniques. *Journal of Wireless Mobile Networks, Ubiquitous Computing and Dependable Applications, 2*(1), 4–27. Retrieved from http://isyou.info/jowua/papers/jowua-v2n1-1.pdf

Hunted. (2015). *Channel 4 programme.* Retrieved May 30, 2017, from http://www.channel4.com/programmes/hunted

Hussain, G., & Saltman, E. M. (2014). *Jihad trending: A comprehensive analysis of online extremism and how to counter it.* London: Quilliam.

Hutchings, A., & Hayes, H. (2009). Routine activity theory and phishing victimisation: Who gets caught in the 'net'? *Current Issues in Criminal Justice, 20*(3), 1–20.

ICANN. (n.d.). Retrieved from http://www.icann.org

Information Security Forum. (2014). *From Promoting Awareness to Embedding Behaviours - Secure by choice, not by chance, Abstract*. Author.

Infosec Institute. (2012). *Physical Access Control, 19 June 2012, Posted in General Security*. Retrieved Sep 12, 2017, from http://resources.infosecinstitute.com/physical-access-control/#gref

Insider Attacks Industry Survey. (2017). Retrieved 09 09, 2017, from Haystax Technology: https://haystax.com/blog/ebook/insider-attacks-industry-survey

Instagram. (2013). *Privacy Policy*. Retrieved from: https://www.instagram.com/about/legal/privacy/

Işıklar, G., & Büyüközkan, G. (2007). Using a multi-criteria decision making approach to evaluate mobile phone alternatives. *Computer Standards & Interfaces*, 29(2), 265–274. doi:10.1016/j.csi.2006.05.002

Islam, R., & Abawajy, J. (2013). A multi-tier phishing detection and filtering approach. *Journal of Network and Computer Applications*, 36(1), 324–335. doi:10.1016/j.jnca.2012.05.009

ITU. (2017). *ICT Report*. Retrieved from: http://www.itu.int/en/ITU-D/Statistics/Documents/facts/ICTFactsFigures2017.pdf

Jackson, D. D., Ingram, L. A., Boyer, C. B., Robillard, A., & Huhns, M. N. (2016). Can Technology Decrease Sexual Risk Behaviors among Young People? Results of a Pilot Study Examining the Effectiveness of a Mobile Application Intervention. *American Journal of Sexuality Education*, 11(1), 41–60. doi:10.1080/15546128.2015.1123129

Jagatic, T. N., Johnson, N. A., Jakobsson, M., & Menczer, F. (2005). Social phishing. *Communications of the ACM*, 50(10), 94–100. doi:10.1145/1290958.1290968

James, L. P., Janet, L. B., & James, F. C. (2009). *A Personality Based Model for Determining Susceptibility to Phishing Attacks*. University of Arkansas.

Janis, I. L. (1972). *Victims of Groupthink*. New York: Houghton Mifflin.

Janis, I. L., & Mann, L. (1977). *Decision making: A psychological analysis of conflict, choice, and commitment*. Free Press.

Jansen, J., Junger, M., Kort, J., Leukfeldt, R., Veenstra, S., Van Wilsem, J., & Van der Zee, S. (2017). Victims. In R. Leukfeldt (Ed.), *Research agenda: The human factor in cybercrime and cybersecurity*. The Hague, The Netherlands: Eleven International Publishing.

Jansen, J., & Leukfeldt, E. R. (2015). How people help fraudsters steal their money: An analysis of 600 online banking fraud cases. In *Proceedings of the 2015 Workshop on Socio-Technical Aspects in Security and Trust (STAST)*, Washington, DC: IEEE Computer Society. doi:10.1109/STAST.2015.12

Jansen, J., & Leukfeldt, E. R. (2016). Phishing and malware attacks on online banking customers in the Netherlands: A qualitative analysis of factors leading to victimization. *International Journal of Cyber Criminology*, 10(1), 79–91.

Jansen, J., Leukfeldt, E. R., Van Wilsem, J. A., & Stol, W. Ph. (2013). *Onlinegedragingen: Een risico voor hacken en persoonsgerichte cyberdelicten?* (Online behaviour: A risk for hacking and person-oriented cybercrimes?). *Tijdschrift voor Criminologie*, 55(4), 394–408. doi:10.5553/TvC/0165182X2013055004005

Jarvis, L., MacDonald, S., & Chen, T. M. (2015). *Terrorism Online: Politics, Law and Technology*. Abingdon, UK: Routledge.

Jason, R. C., Nurse, O. B., Philip, A. L., Goldsmith, M., Sadie, C., Gordon, R.T., ... Whitty, M. (2014). Understanding Insider Threat: A Framework for Characterising Attacks. *Proceedings of IEEE Security and Privacy Workshops*, 214-228. doi:10.1109/SPW.2014.38

Jason, R. C., Nurse, P. A., Legg, O. B., Ioannis, A., Gordon, W., Monica, W., ... Sadie, C. (2014). A Critical Reflection on the Threat from Human Insiders – Its Nature, Industry Perceptions, and Detection Approaches. In *Lecture Notes in Computer Science: Vol. 8533. Proceedings of International Conference on Human Aspects of Information Security, Privacy, and Trust*. Springer. doi:10.1007/978-3-319-07620-1_24

Jensen, E. T. (2015). Cyber sovereignty: The way ahead. *Tex. Int'l LJ, 50*, 275.

Jeske, D., Coventry, L., & Briggs, P. (2013). Nudging whom how : IT proficiency, impulse control and secure behaviour. *CHI Workshop on Personalizing Behavior Change Technologies 2014*.

Ji, C.-H. C., & Ibrahim, Y. (2007). Islamic Doctrinal Orthodoxy and Religious Orientations: Scale Development and Validation. *The International Journal for the Psychology of Religion, 17*(3), 189–208. doi:10.1080/10508610701402192

John, O. P., & Srivastava, S. (1999). Big Five Inventory (Bfi). Handbook of Personality: Theory and Research, 2, 102–138. doi:10.1525/fq.1998.51.4.04a00260

Johnson, S. (2017, June). Muslim calls for Immigration Minister's head transplant. *Daily Mail*. Retrieved from http://www.dailymail.co.uk/news/article-4599544/Muslim-calls-Immigration-Minister-s-head-transplant.html

Johnson, B. R., Jang, S. J., Larson, D. B., & De Li, S. (2001). Does adolescent religious commitment matter? A reexamination of the effects of religiosity on delinquency. *Journal of Research in Crime and Delinquency, 38*(1), 22–44. doi:10.1177/0022427801038001002

Johnson, D. (1985). *Computer ethics* (1st ed.). Englewood Cliffs, NJ: Prentice Hall.

Johnson, E. J., & Payne, J. W. (1985). Effort and accuracy in choice. *Management Science, 31*(4), 395–414. doi:10.1287/mnsc.31.4.395

Johnson, N. F., Zheng, M., Vorobyeva, Y., Gabriel, A., Qi, H., Velasquez, N., & Wuchty, S. et al. (2016). New online ecology of adversarial aggregates: ISIS and beyond. *Science, 352*(6292), 1459–1463. doi:10.1126/science.aaf0675 PMID:27313046

Johnson, T. H., & Mason, M. C. (2007). Understanding the Taliban and Insurgency in Afghanistan. *Orbis, 51*(1), 71–89. doi:10.1016/j.orbis.2006.10.006

Johnston, A. C., Warkentin, M., McBride, M., & Carter, L. (2016). Dispositional and situational factors: Influences on information security policy violations. *European Journal of Information Systems, 25*(3), 231–251. doi:10.1057/ejis.2015.15

Johnston, A. C., Warkentin, M., & Siponen, M. (2015). an Enhanced Fear Appeal Rhetorical Framework: Leveraging Threats To the Human Asset Through Sanctioning Rhetoric 1. *Management Information Systems Quarterly, 39*(1), 113–134. doi:10.25300/MISQ/2015/39.1.06

Joinson, A. (1999). Social Desirability, Anonymity, and Internet-based Questionnaires. *Behavior Research Methods, Instruments, & Computers, 31*(3), 433–438. doi:10.3758/BF03200723 PMID:10502866

Joinson, A. N. (2007). Disinhibition and the Internet. In J. Gackenbach (Ed.), *Psychology and the Internet: Intrapersonal, interpersonal, and transpersonal implications* (2nd ed.; pp. 75–92). San Diego, CA: Academic Press. doi:10.1016/B978-012369425-6/50023-0

Joireman, J., Shaffer, M. J., Balliet, D., & Strathman, A. (2012). Promotion Orientation Explains Why Future-Oriented People Exercise and Eat Healthy: Evidence From the Two-Factor Consideration of Future Consequences-14 Scale. *Personality and Social Psychology Bulletin, 38*(10), 1272–1287. doi:10.1177/0146167212449362 PMID:22833533

Jonassen, D. H., & Kwon, H. II. (2001). Communication patterns in computer mediated versus face-to face group problem solving. *Educational Technology Research and Development, 49*(1), 35–51. doi:10.1007/BF02504505

Jones, H. S. (2016). *What makes people click: Assessing individual differences in susceptibility to email fraud* (Unpublished doctoral thesis). Lancaster University, UK.

Jones, H. S., Towse, J., Race, N., & Harrison, T. (submitted). *Email fraud – the search for psychological markers of susceptibility.*

Jones, C. S., & Hartley, N. T. (2013). Comparing correlations between four-quadrant and five-factor personality assessments. *American Journal of Business Education, 6*(4), 459–470. doi:10.19030/ajbe.v6i4.7945

Jones, H. S., Towse, J. N., & Race, N. (2015). Susceptibility to email fraud: A review of psychological perspectives, data-collection methods, and ethical considerations. *International Journal of Cyber Behavior, Psychology and Learning, 5*(3), 13–29. doi:10.4018/IJCBPL.2015070102

Jones, R., Sharkey, S., Ford, T., Emmens, T., Hewis, E., Smithson, J., & Owens, C. (2011). Online discussion forums for young people who self-harm: User views. *The Psychiatrist, 35*(10), 364–368. doi:10.1192/pb.bp.110.033449

Jordan, T. (2001). Mapping hacktivism: Mass virtual direct action (MVDA), individual virtual direct action (IVDA) and cyber-wars. *Computer Fraud & Security, 4*(4), 8–11. doi:10.1016/S1361-3723(01)00416-X

Jordan, T., & Taylor, P. (1998). A sociology of hackers. *The Sociological Review, 46*(4), 757–780. doi:10.1111/1467-954X.00139

Junger, M., Montoya, L., & Overink, F. J. (2017). Priming and warnings are not effective to prevent social engineering attacks. *Computers in Human Behavior, 66*, 75–87. doi:10.1016/j.chb.2016.09.012

Just, S., Premraj, R., & Zimmermann, T. (2008). Towards the next generation of bug tracking systems. *VL/HCC 2008 - IEEE Symposium on Visual Languages and Human-Centric Computing*, 82–85.

Kahneman, D. (2000). A psychological point of view: Violations of rational rules as a diagnostic of mental processes. *Behavioral and Brain Sciences, 23*(5), 681–683. doi:10.1017/S0140525X00403432

Kahneman, D. (2011). *Thinking, Fast and Slow*. Farrar, Straus and Giroux.

Kalichman, S. C., Benotsch, E. G., Weinhardt, L., Austin, J., Luke, W., & Cherry, C. (2003). Health-related Internet use, coping, social support, and health indicators in people living with HIV/AIDS: Preliminary results from a community survey. *Health Psychology, 22*(1), 111–116. doi:10.1037/0278-6133.22.1.111 PMID:12558209

Kaptein, M., & Eckles, D. (2012). Heterogeneity in the effects of online persuasion. *Journal of Interactive Marketing, 26*(3), 176–188. doi:10.1016/j.intmar.2012.02.002

Kaptein, M., Markopoulos, P., De Ruyter, B., & Aarts, E. (2015). Personalizing persuasive technologies: Explicit and implicit personalization using persuasion profiles. *International Journal of Human-Computer Studies, 77*, 38–51. doi:10.1016/j.ijhcs.2015.01.004

Karaiskos, D., Tzavellas, E., Balta, G., & Paparrigopoulos, T. (2010). Social network addiction: A new clinical disorder? *European Psychiatry, 25*(1), 855–855. doi:10.1016/S0924-9338(10)70846-4

Karamanian, A., Sample, C., & Kolenko, M. (2016). Hofstede's cultural markers in successful victim cyber exploitations. *11ᵗʰ International Conference on Cyber Warfare and Security*, 205-213.

Karni, E., & Vierø, M.-L. (2014). *Awareness of Unawareness: A Theory of Decision Making in the Face of Ignorance.* Queen's Economics Department Working Paper, No. 1322.

Kastrenakes, J. (2016). *Adblock Plus now sells ads.* Retrieved from: http://www.theverge.com/2016/9/13/12890050/adblock-plus-now-sells-ads

Katz, J. E., & Aspden, P. (1997). A Nation of Strangers. *Communications of the ACM, 40*(12), 81–86. doi:10.1145/265563.265575

Kaye, L. K., Monk, R. L., & Hamlin, I. (in press). "Feeling appy?": Using app-based methodology to explore contextual effects on real-time cognitions, affect and behaviours. In C. Costa & J. Condie (Eds.), *Doing research in and on the digital: Research methods across fields of inquiry.* Routledge.

Kaye, L. K., Monk, R. L., Wall, H. J., Hamlin, I., & Qureshi, A. W. (2018). The effect of flow and context on in-vivo positive mood in digital gaming. *International Journal of Human-Computer Studies, 110,* 45–52. doi:10.1016/j.ijhcs.2017.10.005

Keeney, M. (2005). *Insider threat study: Computer system sabotage in critical infrastructure sectors.* Retrieved from http://scholar.google.com/scholar?hl=en&btnG=Search&q=intitle:Insider+Threat+Study+:+Computer+System+Sabotage+in+Critical+Infrastructure+Sectors#0

Kelman, H. C. (2006). Interests, relationships, identities: Three central issues for individuals and groups in negotiating their social environment. *Annual Review of Psychology, 57*(1), 1–26. doi:10.1146/annurev.psych.57.102904.190156 PMID:16318587

Keng, K. A., & Yang, C. (1993). Value choice, demographics, and life satisfaction. *Psychology and Marketing, 10*(5), 413–432. doi:10.1002/mar.4220100505

Khan, B., Alghathbar, K. S., Nabi, S. I., & Khan, M. K. (2011). Effectiveness of information security awareness methods based on psychological theories. *African Journal of Business Management, 5*(26), 10862–10868. doi:10.5897/AJBM11.067

Khraim, H. (2010). Measuring religiosity in consumer research from an Islamic perspective. *Journal of Economic & Administrative Sciences, 26*(1), 52–79. doi:10.1108/10264116201000003

Kim, K., & Viswanathan, S. (2014). *The Experts in the Crowd: The Role of Reputable Investors in a Crowdfunding Market.* Retrieved May 16, 2017, from https://accounting.eller.arizona.edu/sites/mis/files/ssrn-id2258243.pdf

Kim, D. J., Ferrin, D. L., & Rao, H. R. (2008). A trust-based consumer decision-making model in electronic commerce: The role of trust, perceived risk, and their antecedents. *Decision Support Systems, 44*(2), 544–564. doi:10.1016/j.dss.2007.07.001

Kimhi, S., & Even, S. (2006). The Palestinian Human Bombers. In J. Victoroff (Ed.), *Tangled Roots: Social and Psychological Factors in the Genesis of Terrorism* (pp. 308–322). Trenton, NJ: IOS Press.

Kim, Y., Shaw, A., Zhang, H., & Gerber, E. (2017). Understanding Trust amid Delays in Crowdfunding. In *Proceedings of the 2017 ACM Conference on Computer Supported Cooperative Work and Social Computing* (pp. 1982-1996). ACM.

King, M. B., & Hunt, R. A. (1972). Measuring the religious variable: Replication. *Journal for the Scientific Study of Religion, 11*(3), 240–251. doi:10.2307/1384548

Kirkman, B. L., Lowe, K. B., & Gibson, C. B. (2006). A quarter century of culture's consequences: A review of empirical research incorporating Hofstede's cultural values framework. *Journal of International Business Studies, 37*(3), 285–320. doi:10.1057/palgrave.jibs.8400202

Kirlappos, I., Parkin, S., & Sasse, M. A. (2014). *Learning from "Shadow Security": Why understanding non-compliance provides the basis for effective security.* Academic Press.

Kirlappos, I., & Sasse, M. A. (2012). Security education against phishing: A modest proposal for a major rethink. *IEEE Security and Privacy, 10*(2), 24–32. doi:10.1109/MSP.2011.179

Kirwan, G., & Power, A. (2013). *Cybercrime: The psychology of online offenders*. Cambridge, UK: Cambridge University Press. doi:10.1017/CBO9780511843846

Klausen, J. (2015). Tweeting the Jihad: Social media networks of Western foreign fighters in Syria and Iraq. *Studies in Conflict and Terrorism, 38*(1), 1–22. doi:10.1080/1057610X.2014.974948

Klausen, J., Barbieri, E. T., Reichlin-Melnick, A., & Zelin, A. Y. (2012). The YouTube Jihadists: A social network analysis of Al-Muhajiroun's propaganda campaign. *Perspectives on Terrorism, 6*(1), 36–53.

Kleban, C., & Kaye, L. K. (2015). Psychosocial impacts of engaging in Second Life for individuals with physical disabilities. *Computers in Human Behavior, 45*, 59–68. doi:10.1016/j.chb.2014.12.004

Kohlberg, L. & Kramer, R. (1969). Continuities and discontinuities in childhood and adult moral development. *Human Development, 12*, 93-120.

Kohlberg, L. (1981). *The meaning and measurement of moral development*. Clark Univ Heinz Werner Inst.

Kohli, R., Devaraj, S., & Mahmood, A. (2014). Understanding Determinants of Online Consumer Satisfaction: A Decision Process Perspective. *Journal of Management Information Systems, 21*(1), 115–136. doi:10.1080/07421222.2004.11045796

Kolb, D. A. (1981). Learning styles and disciplinary differences. In A. W. Chickering (Ed.), *The Modern American College*. San Francisco, CA: Jossey-Bass.

Korzaan, M. L., & Boswell, K. T. (2008). The influence of personality traits and information privacy concerns on behavioral intentions. *Journal of Computer Information Systems, 48*(4), 15–24.

Kozinets, R. V. (2002). The field behind the screen: Using netnography for marketing research in online communities. *JMR, Journal of Marketing Research, 39*(1), 61–72. doi:10.1509/jmkr.39.1.61.18935

Kramer, A. D. I., Guillory, J. E., & Hancock, J. T. (2014). Experimental evidence of massive-scale emotional contagion through social networks. *Proceedings of the National Academy of Sciences of the United States of America, 111*(24), 8788–8790. doi:10.1073/pnas.1320040111 PMID:24889601

Krapp, P. (2005). Terror and play; or what was hacktivism? *Grey Room MIT Press, 21*, 70–93. doi:10.1162/152638105774539770

Kraut, R., Mukhopadhyay, T., Szczypula, J., Kiesler, S., & Scherlis, W. (1998). Communication and Information: Alternative uses of the Internet in households. In *Proceedings of the CHI 98* (pp. 368-383). New York: ACM. doi:10.1145/274644.274695

Kraut, R., Olson, J., Banaji, M., Cohen, J., & Couper, M. (2004). Psyhcological research online: Report of Board of Scienfitic Affairs' Advisory Group on the conduct of research on the internet. *The American Psychologist, 59*(2), 105–117. doi:10.1037/0003-066X.59.2.105 PMID:14992637

Kromidha, E., & Robson, P. (2016). Social identity and signalling success factors in online crowdfunding. *Entrepreneurship and Regional Development, 28*(9-10), 605–629. doi:10.1080/08985626.2016.1198425

Krueger, J. I., Massey, A. L., & DiDonato, T. E. (2008). A matter of trust: From social preferences to the strategic adherence to social norms. *Negotiation and Conflict Management Research, 1*(1), 31–52. doi:10.1111/j.1750-4716.2007.00003.x

Kruglanski, A. W., & Fishman, S. (2009). Psychological Factors in Terrorism and Counterterrorism: Individual, Group, and Organizational Levels of Analysis. *Social Issues and Policy Review, 3*(1), 1–44. doi:10.1111/j.1751-2409.2009.01009.x

Kubitschko, S. (2015). Hackers' media practices: Demonstrating and articulating expertise as interlocking arrangements. *Convergence*, *21*(3), 388–402. doi:10.1177/1354856515579847

Kummervold, P. E., Gammon, D., Bergvik, S., Johnsen, J. A. K., Hasvold, T., & Rosenvinge, J. H. (2002). Social support in a wired world: Use of online mental health forums in Norway. *Nordic Journal of Psychiatry*, *56*(1), 59–65. doi:10.1080/08039480252803945 PMID:11869468

Kunc, M., Malpass, J., & White, L. (2016). *Behavioral Operational Research: Theory, Methodology and Practice*. Palgrave Macmillan. doi:10.1057/978-1-137-53551-1

Kuppuswamy, V., & Bayus, B. L. (2013). Crowdfunding creative ideas: The dynamics of project backers in Kickstarter. *SSRN Electronic Journal*. Retrieved May 18, 2017, from https://papers.ssrn.com/sol3/papers.cfm?abstract_id=2234765

Kyllonen, P. C., & Christal, R. E. (1990). Reasoning ability is (little more than) working-memory capacity?! *Intelligence*, *14*(4), 389–433. doi:10.1016/S0160-2896(05)80012-1

Labrecque, L. I., vor dem Esche, J., Mathwick, C., Novak, T. P., & Hofacker, C. F. (2013). Consumer power: Evolution in the digital age. *Journal of Interactive Marketing*, *27*(4), 257–269. doi:10.1016/j.intmar.2013.09.002

Lachow, I., & Richardson, C. (2007). The Terrorist Use of the Internet—The Real Story. *Joint Force Quarterly*, *45*(2), 100–103.

Lakoff, G. (2009). The neural theory of metaphor. In Cambridge Handbook of Metaphor and Thought. New York, NY: Cambridge University Press. doi:10.2139/ssrn.1437794

Lakoff, G. (2012). Explaining embodied cognition results. *Topics in Cognitive Science*, *4*(4), 773–785. doi:10.1111/j.1756-8765.2012.01222.x PMID:22961950

Lakoff, G., & Johnson, M. (1999). *Philosophy in the Flesh* (Vol. 4). New York: Basic books.

Lakoff, G., & Johnson, M. (2008). *Metaphors we live by*. Chicago: University of Chicago Press.

Lambiotte, R., & Kosinski, M. (2014). Tracking the digital footprints of personality. *Proceedings of the IEEE*, *102*(12), 1934–1939. doi:10.1109/JPROC.2014.2359054

Langenderfer, J., & Shimp, T. A. (2001). Consumer vulnerability to scams, swindles, and fraud: A new theory of visceral influences on persuasion. *Psychology and Marketing*, *18*(7), 763–783. doi:10.1002/mar.1029

Langer, R., & Beckman, S. C. (2005). Sensitive research topics: Netnography revisited. *Qualitative Market Research*, *8*(2), 189–203. doi:10.1108/13522750510592454

Lankton, N. K., & McKnight, D. H. (2011). What does it mean to trust Facebook?: Examining technology and interpersonal trust beliefs. *ACM SiGMiS Database*, *42*(2), 32–54. doi:10.1145/1989098.1989101

Lankton, N. K., McKnight, D. H., & Tripp, J. (2015). Technology, humanness, and trust: Rethinking trust in technology. *Journal of the Association for Information Systems*, *16*(10), 880.

Lapidot-Lefler, N., & Barak, A. (2015). The benign online disinhibition effect: Could situational factors induce self-disclosure and prosocial behaviors? *Cyberpsychology: Journal of Psychosocial Research on Cyberspace*, *9*(2), article 3.

LaRose, R., & Eastin, M. S. (2004). A social cognitive theory of Internet uses and gratifications: Toward a new model of media attendance. *Journal of Broadcasting & Electronic Media*, *48*(3), 358–377. doi:10.1207/s15506878jobem4803_2

Lastdrager, E. E. H. (2014). Achieving a consensual definition of phishing based on a systematic review of the literature. *Crime Science*, *3*(1), 1–6. doi:10.1186/s40163-014-0009-y

Laufer, A., & Solomon, Z. (2011). The Role of Religious Orientations in Youth's Posttraumatic Symptoms After Exposure to Terror. *Journal of Religion and Health, 50*(3), 687–699. doi:10.1007/s10943-009-9270-x PMID:19672716

Layman, L., Cornwell, T., & Williams, L. (2006). Personality types, learning styles, and an agile approach to software engineering education. *ACM SIGCSE Bulletin, 38*(1), 428–432. doi:10.1145/1124706.1121474

Leach, D. K. (2009). An elusive 'we': Anti-dogmatism, democratic practice, and the contradictory identity of the German Autonomen. *The American Behavioral Scientist, 52*(7), 1042–1068. doi:10.1177/0002764208327674

Leach, J. (2003). Improving user security behaviour. *Computers & Security, 22*(8), 685–692. doi:10.1016/S0167-4048(03)00007-5

Lea, M., & Spears, R. (1991). Computer-mediated communication, de-individuation and group decision-making. *International Journal of Man-Machine Studies, 34*(2), 283–301. doi:10.1016/0020-7373(91)90045-9

Lech, J. J., & Andrew, M. C. (2007). Cyber Warfare and Cyber Terrorism. Information Science Reference.

Lederman, R., Fan, H., Smith, S., & Chang, S. (2014). Who can you trust? Credibility assessment in online health forums. *Health Policy and Technology, 3*(1), 13–25. doi:10.1016/j.hlpt.2013.11.003

Lee, D.-J., Ahn, J.-H., & Bang, Y. (2011). Managing Consumer Privacy Concerns in Personalization: A Strategic Analysis of Privacy Protection. *Management Information Systems Quarterly, 35*(2), 423–A8. Retrieved from http://search.ebscohost.com/login.aspx?direct=true&db=bth&AN=60461925&site=ehost-live%5Cnhttp://content.ebscohost.com/ContentServer.asp?T=P&P=AN&K=60461925&S=R&D=bth&EbscoContent=dGJyMNXb4kSeqLc4v+bwOLCmr02eprNSr6q4SrSWxWXS&ContentCustomer=dGJyMPGps0i2q7J

Leitner, M., Wolkerstorfer, P., & Tscheligi, M. (2008). How online communities support human values. In *Proceedings of the 5th Nordic conference on Human-computer interaction: building bridges* (pp. 503-506). ACM.

Lenhart, A., & Madden, M. (2007). *Teens, Privacy & Online Social Networks: How teens manage their online identities and personal information in the age of MySpace*. Academic Press.

Lesaca, J. (2015). *On Social Media, ISIS Uses Modern Cultural Images to Spread Anti-modern Values*. Brookings Institute. Retrieved 05 30, 2017, from: https://www.brookings.edu/blog/techtank/2015/09/24/on-social-media-isis-uses-modern-cultural-images-to-spread-anti-modern-values/

Leukfeldt, E. R. (2015). Comparing victims of phishing and malware attacks: Unravelling risk factors and possibilities for situational crime prevention. *International Journal of Advanced Studies in Computer Science and Engineering, 4*(5), 26–32.

Levitt, M. (2013). *Hezbollah: The Global Footprint of Lebanon's Party of God*. Washington, DC: Georgetown University Press.

Levy, S. (2010). *Hackers: Heroes of the Computer Revolution*. Sebastopol, CA: O'Reilly Media.

Lexical Computing. (2017). *SketchEngine*. Retrieved from https://www.sketchengine.co.uk/

Lindgaard, G., Dudek, C., Sen, D., Sumegi, L., & Noonan, P. (2011). An exploration of relations between visual appeal, trustworthiness and perceived usability of homepages. *ACM Transactions on Computer-Human Interaction, 18*(1), 1–30. doi:10.1145/1959022.1959023

Lindgaard, G., Fernandes, G., Dudek, C., & Brown, J. (2006). Attention web designers: You have 50 milliseconds to make a good first impression! *Behaviour & Information Technology, 25*(2), 115–126. doi:10.1080/01449290500330448

Lindo Systems Inc. (1981). Retrieved 03 11, 2017, from http://www.lindo.com

Lippmann, W. (1955). *Essays in the Public Philosophy*. Boston: Little, Brown, and Company.

Liu, Q. X., Fang, X. Y., Wan, J. J., & Zhou, Z. K. (2016). Need satisfaction and adolescent pathological internet use: Comparison of satisfaction perceived online and offline. *Computers in Human Behavior, 55*, 695–700. doi:10.1016/j.chb.2015.09.048

Li, W. C., & Harris, D. (2005). HFACS analysis of ROC Air Force aviation accidents: Reliability analysis and cross-cultural comparison. *International Journal of Applied Aviation Studies, 5*(1), 65–81.

Li, X.-B., & Sarkar, S. (2006). Privacy protection in data mining: A perturbation approach for categorical data. *Information Systems Research, 17*(3), 254–270. doi:10.1287/isre.1060.0095

Li, X., Hess, T. J., & Valacich, J. S. (2008). Why do we trust new technology? A study of initial trust formation with organizational information systems. *The Journal of Strategic Information Systems, 17*(1), 39–71. doi:10.1016/j.jsis.2008.01.001

Li, Y. B., James, L., & McKibben, J. (2016). Trust between physicians and patients in the e-health era. *Technology in Society, 46*, 28–34. doi:10.1016/j.techsoc.2016.02.004

Lo, S. K., Hsieh, A. Y., & Chiu, Y. P. (2013). Contradictory deceptive behavior in online dating. *Computers in Human Behavior, 29*(4), 1755–1762. doi:10.1016/j.chb.2013.02.010

Lucas, R. E. Jr, & Prescott, E. C. (1971). Investment under uncertainty. *Econometrica, 39*(5), 659–681. doi:10.2307/1909571

Lukkarinen, A., Teich, J. E., Wallenius, H., & Wallenius, J. (2016). Success drivers of online equity crowdfunding campaigns. *Decision Support Systems, 87*, 26–38. doi:10.1016/j.dss.2016.04.006

Lutz, C., & Ranzini, G. (2017). Where Dating Meets Data: Investigating Social and Institutional Privacy Concerns on Tinder. *Social Media and Society, 3*(1).

Lyons, S. L. (2015). *The Psychological Foundations of Homegrown Radicalization: An Immigrant Acculturation Perspective* (Doctoral dissertation).

Mack, S. (2014). *Reasoning and judgements made in an online capacity. An exploration of how phishing emails influence decision making strategies* (Unpublished undergraduate dissertation). Lancaster University, Lancaster, UK.

Madarie, R. (2017). Hackers' Motivations: Testing Schwartz's Theory of Motivational Types of Values in a Sample of Hackers. *International Journal of Cyber Criminology, 11*(1).

Magdy, W., Darwish, K., & Weber, I. (2015). *FailedRevolutions: Using Twitter to Study the Antecedents of ISIS Support*. Palo Alto, CA: Association for the Advancement of Artificial Intelligence.

Magill, G. (1992). Theology in business ethics: Appealing to the religious imagination. *Journal of Business Ethics, 11*(2), 129–135. doi:10.1007/BF00872320

Mair, D. (2017). #Westgate: A Case Study: How al-Shabaab Used Twitter During an Ongoing Attack. *Studies in Conflict and Terrorism, 40*(1), 24–43. doi:10.1080/1057610X.2016.1157404

Major, D. A., Turner, J. E., & Fletcher, T. D. (2006). Linking proactive personality and the Big Five to motivation to learn and development activity. *The Journal of Applied Psychology, 91*(4), 927–935. doi:10.1037/0021-9010.91.4.927 PMID:16834515

Malachowski, D. (2005). Wasted Time At Work Costing Companies Billions. *Asian Enterprise*, 14–16.

Maloof, M. A., & Stephens, G. D. (2007). *Recent Advances in Intrusion Detection. In* Lecture Notes in Computer Science: Vol. 4637. *ELICIT: A System for Detecting Insiders Who Violate Need-to-Know* (pp. 146–166). Springer.

Mandl, T. (2009). Comparing Chinese and German blogs. *HT '09 Proceedings of the 20th ACM Conference on Hypertext and Hypermedia*, 299–308. Retrieved from http://dl.acm.org/citation.cfm?id=1557964

Manion, M., & Goodrum, A. (2000). Terrorism or civil disobedience: Toward a hacktivist ethic. *ACM SIGCAS Computers and Society*, *30*(2), 14–19. doi:10.1145/572230.572232

Markovits, H., Doyon, C., & Simoneau, M. (2002). Individual differences in working memory and conditional reasoning with concrete and abstract content. *Thinking & Reasoning*, *8*(2), 97–107. doi:10.1080/13546780143000143

Martin, B., Brown, M., Paller, A. Kirby, D., & Christey, S. (2011) 2011 CWE/SANS top 25 most dangerous software errors. *Common Weakness Enumeration*, 7515.

Marwan, O. (2015). Insider threats: Detecting and controlling malicious insiders. In *New Threats and Countermeasures in Digital Crime and Cyber Terrorism*. IGI Global. doi:10.4018/978-1-4666-8345-7.ch009

Marx, G. T. (2003). A tack in the shoe: Neutralizing and resisting the new surveillance. *The Journal of Social Issues*, *59*(2), 369–390. doi:10.1111/1540-4560.00069

Massumi, B. (Ed.). (1993). *The Politics of Everyday Fear*. Minneapolis, MN: U of Minnesota Press.

Matheson, K., & Zanna, M. P. (1989). Persuasion as a function of self-awareness in computer mediated communication. *Social Behaviour*.

Matt, B., Engle, S., Deborah, A. F., Carrie, G., Frank, L. G., Sean, P., & Sean, W. (2010). *A Risk Management Approach to the "Insider Threat"*. Insider Threats in Cyber Security, e-scholarship, University of California. Retrieved Apr 30, 2017, from http://escholarship.org/uc/item/8sj9t023

Matusitz, J. (2005). Cyberterrorism: How Can American Foreign Policy Be Strengthened in the Information Age? *American Foreign Policy Interests*, *27*(2), 137–147. doi:10.1080/10803920590935376

Matusitz, J. (2014). The role of intercultural communication in cyberterrorism. *Journal of Human Behavior in the Social Environment*, *24*(7), 775–790. doi:10.1080/10911359.2013.876375

Ma, X., Sun, E., & Naaman, M. (2017). What Happens in happn: The Warranting Powers of Location History in Online Dating. In *Proceedings of ACM Conference on Computer Supported Cooperative Work and Social Computing* (pp. 41-50). ACM. doi:10.1145/2998181.2998241

Mayer, R. C., Davis, J. H., & Schoorman, F. D. (1995). An integrative model of organizational trust. *Academy of Management Review*, *20*(3), 709–734.

McAlaney, J., Thackray, H., & Taylor, J. (2016). The social psychology of cybersecurity. *The Psychologist*, *29*(9), 686–689.

McBride, M., Carter, L., & Warkentin, M. (2012). *Exploring the role of individual employee characteristics and personality on employee compliance with cyber security policies*. Prepared by RTI International – Institute for Homeland Security Solutions under contract 3-312-0212782.

McBride, M., Carter, L., & Warkentin, M. (2012). *Exploring the role of individual employee characteristics and personality on employee compliance with cybersecurity policies*. Washington, DC: RTI International.

McCauley, C., & Moskalenko, S. (2008). Mechanisms of political radicalization: Pathways toward terrorism. *Terrorism and Political Violence*, *20*(3), 415–433. doi:10.1080/09546550802073367

McClelland, D. (1951). *Personality*. New York: Holt, Rinehart, & Winston. doi:10.1037/10790-000

McConnell, T. (2015). The programmatic primer: Ad verification and privacy in the online advertising ecosystem. *WARC Exclusive*. Retrieved from: https://www.warc.com/

McCormac, A., Parsons, K., Zwaans, T., Butavicius, M., & Pattinson, M. (2016). *Test-retest reliability and internal consistency of the Human Aspects of Information Security Questionnaire* (HAIS-Q). Academic Press.

McCormac, A., Zwaans, T., Parsons, K., Calic, D., Butavicius, M., & Pattinson, M. (2016). Individual differences and Information Security Awareness. *Computers in Human Behavior*, *69*, 151–156. doi:10.1016/j.chb.2016.11.065

McCrae, R. R., & Costa, P. T. (1989). Reinterpreting the Myers-Briggs Type Indicator from the perspective of the five-factor model of personality. *Journal of Personality*, *57*(1), 17–40. doi:10.1111/j.1467-6494.1989.tb00759.x PMID:2709300

McCrae, R. R., & John, O. P. (1992). An introduction to the five-factor model and its applications. *Journal of Personality*, *60*(2), 175–215. doi:10.1111/j.1467-6494.1992.tb00970.x PMID:1635039

McDaniel, S. W., & Burnett, J. J. (1990). Consumer religiosity and retail store evaluative criteria. *Journal of the Academy of Marketing Science*, *18*(2), 101–112. doi:10.1007/BF02726426

McFarland, S. (1984). Psychology of religion: A call for a broader paradigm. *The American Psychologist*, *39*(3), 321–324. doi:10.1037/0003-066X.39.3.321

McGettrick, A. (2013). *Toward curricular guidelines for cybersecurity*. Retrieved May 30, 2017, from https://www.acm.org/education/TowardCurricularGuidelinesCybersec.pdf

McKenna, K. Y., & Bargh, J. A. (2000). Plan 9 From Cyberspace: The Implications of the Internet for Personality and Social Psychology. *Personality and Social Psychology Review*, *4*(1), 57–75. doi:10.1207/S15327957PSPR0401_6

McKenna, K. Y., & Green, A. S. (2002). Virtual group dynamics. *Group Dynamics*, *6*(1), 116–127. doi:10.1037/1089-2699.6.1.116

McKenzie, C. R. (2004). Framing effects in inference tasks—and why they are normatively defensible. *Memory & Cognition*, *32*(6), 874–885. doi:10.3758/BF03196866 PMID:15673176

McKnight, D. H., Carter, M., Thatcher, J. B., & Clay, P. F. (2011). Trust in a specific technology: An investigation of its components and measures. *ACM Transactions on Management Information Systems*, *2*(2), 12. doi:10.1145/1985347.1985353

McKnight, D. H., Kacmar, C. J., & Choudhury, V. (2004). Shifting Factors and the Ineffectiveness of Third Party Assurance Seals: A two-stage model of initial trust in a web business. *Electronic Markets*, *14*(3), 252–266. doi:10.1080/1019678042000245263

Mekovec, R., & Hutinski, Ž. (2012). The role of perceived privacy and perceived security in online market. *MIPRO, 2012 Proceedings of the 35th International Convention*, 1883–1888.

Meredith, J. (2015). Getting access to lived experiences: Using screen-capture data for the analysis of online interaction. *Qualitative Methods in Psychology Bulletin, 20*.

Meuleman, B., & Boushel, C. (2014). Hashtags, ruling relations and the everyday: Institutional ethnography insights on social movements. *Contemporary Social Science*, *9*(1), 49–62. doi:10.1080/21582041.2013.851410

Meuter, M. L., Ostrom, A. L., Roundtree, R. I., & Bitner, M. J. (2000). Self-service technologies: Understanding customer satisfaction with technology-based service encounters. *Journal of Marketing*, *64*(3), 50–64. doi:10.1509/jmkg.64.3.50.18024

Meyer, J. (2010). Representing risk preferences in expected utility based decision models. *Annals of Operations Research*, *176*(1), 179–190. doi:10.1007/s10479-008-0381-7

Milan, S., & Atton, C. (2015). Hacktivism as a radical media practice. *Routledge companion to alternative and community media*, 550-560.

Miller, A. S., & Hoffmann, J. P. (1995). Risk and Religion: An Explanation of Gender Differences in Religiosity. *Journal for the Scientific Study of Religion, 34*(1), 63. doi:10.2307/1386523

Minkov, M. (2011). *Cultural Differences in a Globalizing World*. Bingley, UK: Emerald Group Publishing Limited.

Minocha, S., Tran, M. Q., & Reeves, A. J. (2010). Conducting empirical research in Virtual Worlds: Experiences from two projects in Second Life. *Journal of Virtual Worlds Research, 3*(1), 3–21.

Mintz, A. (Ed.). (2016). *Integrating Cognitive and Rational Theories of Foreign Policy Decision Making: The Polyheuristic Theory of Decision*. Springer.

Mitnick, K. D., & Simon, W. L. (2002). *The Art of Deception*. Indianapolis, IN: Wiley Publishing, Inc.

Modic, D., & Lea, S. E. G. (2011). *How neurotic are scam victims, really? The big five and Internet scams*. Paper presented at the 2011 Conference of the International Confederation for the Advancement of Behavioral Economics and Economic Psychology, Exeter, UK.

Modic, D., & Lea, S. E. G. (2011). *How neurotic are scam victims, really? The Big Five and internet scams*. Paper presented at the 2011 Conference of the International Confederation for the Advancement of Behavioral Economics and Economic Psychology, Exeter, UK.

Moghaddam, F. M. (2005). The Staircase to Terrorism: A Psychological Exploration. *The American Psychologist, 60*(2), 161–169. doi:10.1037/0003-066X.60.2.161 PMID:15740448

Mollick, E. (2014). The dynamics of crowdfunding: An exploratory study. *Journal of Business Venturing, 29*(1), 1–16. doi:10.1016/j.jbusvent.2013.06.005

Monica, W., Doodson, J., Sadie, C., & Duncan, H. (2015). Individual Differences in Cyber Security Behaviors: An Examination of Who Is Sharing Passwords. *Journal on Cyberpsychology, Behavious, and Social Networking, 18*(1), 2015. doi:10.1089/cyber.2014.0179

Monk, R. L., & Heim, D. (2013a). Environmental context effects on alcohol-related outcome expectancies, efficacy and norms: A field study. *Psychology of Addictive Behaviors, 27*(3), 814–818. doi:10.1037/a0033948 PMID:24059833

Monk, R. L., & Heim, D. (2013b). Panoramic projection: Affording a wider view on contextual influences on alcohol-related cognitions. *Experimental and Clinical Psychopharmacology, 21*(1), 1–7. doi:10.1037/a0030772 PMID:23245196

Monk, R. L., & Heim, D. (2014). A real-time examination of context effects on alcohol cognitions. *Alcoholism, Clinical and Experimental Research, 38*(9), 2452–2459. doi:10.1111/acer.12504 PMID:25257294

Monk, R. L., Heim, D., Qureshi, A., & Price, A. (2015). "I have no clue what I drunk last night": Using Smartphone technology to compare in-vivo and retrospective self-reports of alcohol consumption. *PLoS One*. PMID:25992573

Montoya, L., Junger, M., & Hartel, P. (2013). How 'digital' is traditional crime? In *Proceedings of the 2013 European Intelligence and Security Informatics Conference (EISIC 2013)*. Washington, DC: IEEE Computer Society. doi:10.1109/EISIC.2013.12

Moore, M. S. (1985). Causation and the excuses. *California Law Review, 73*(4), 1091–1149. doi:10.2307/3480429

Moore, R. (2005). *Cyber crime: Investigating High-Technology Computer Crime*. Cleveland, MI: Anderson Publishing.

Moreno-Fernández, M. M., Blanco, F., Garaizar, P., & Matute, H. (2017). Fishing for phishers. Improving Internet users' sensitivity to visual deception cues to prevent electronic fraud. *Computers in Human Behavior, 69*, 421–436. doi:10.1016/j.chb.2016.12.044

Morgan, T. H., Cross, C. P., & Rendell, L. E. (2015). *Nothing in human behavior makes sense except in the light of culture: Shared interests of social psychology and cultural evolution. In Evolutionary Perspectives on Social Psychology* (pp. 215–228). Springer International Publishing.

Mouton, F., Leenen, L., Malan, M. M., & Venter, H. S. (2014, July). Towards an ontological model defining the social engineering domain. In *IFIP International Conference on Human Choice and Computers* (pp. 266-279). Springer Berlin Heidelberg. doi:10.1007/978-3-662-44208-1_22

Muhamad, N., & Mizerski, D. (2013). The effects of following islam in decisions about taboo products. *Psychology and Marketing, 30*(4), 357–371. doi:10.1002/mar.20611

Mukhtar, A., & Butt, M. M. (2012). Intention to choose Halal products: The role of religiosity. *Journal of Islamic Marketing, 3*(2), 108–120. doi:10.1108/17590831211232519

Muncy, J. A., & Vitell, S. J. (1992). Consumer ethics: An investigation of the ethical beliefs of the final consumer. *Journal of Business Research, 24*(4), 297–311. doi:10.1016/0148-2963(92)90036-B

Mun, Y. Y., Yoon, J. J., Davis, J. M., & Lee, T. (2013). Untangling the antecedents of initial trust in Web-based health information: The roles of argument quality, source expertise, and user perceptions of information quality and risk. *Decision Support Systems, 55*(1), 284–295. doi:10.1016/j.dss.2013.01.029

Murdoch, S. J., & Sasse, M. A. (2017). Should you really phish your own employees. *NS Tech*. Retrieved September 28, 2017, from http://tech.newstatesman.com/guest-opinion/phishing-employees

Muscanell, N. L., Guadagno, R. E., & Murphy, S. (2014). Weapons of influence misused: A social influence analysis of why people fall prey to internet scams. *Social and Personality Psychology Compass, 8*(7), 388–396. doi:10.1111/spc3.12115

Muth, J. F. (1961). Rational expectations and the theory of price movements. *Econometrica, 29*(3), 315–335. doi:10.2307/1909635

Myers, S. (2007). Introduction to phishing. In M. Jakobsson & S. Myers (Eds.), *Phishing and Countermeasures* (pp. 1–29). John Wiley & Sons, Inc.

Näsi, M., & Koivusilta, L. (2013). Internet and everyday life: The perceived implications of internet use on memory and ability to concentrate. *Cyberpsychology, Behavior, and Social Networking, 16*(2), 88–93. doi:10.1089/cyber.2012.0058 PMID:23113691

National Institute of Standards and Technology (NIST). (2012). *Guide for conducting risk assessments*. NIST Special Publication 800-30, Revision 1. Retrieved September 28, 2017, from http://nvlpubs.nist.gov/nistpubs/Legacy/SP/nistspecialpublication800-30r1.pdf

NCA. (2016). *Cyber crime: Preventing young people from getting involved*. National Crime Agency. Retrieved from http://www.nationalcrimeagency.gov.uk/crime-threats/cyber-crime/cyber-crime-preventing-young-people-from-getting-involved

NCSC. (2015). Cybersecuritybeeld Nederland (CSBN) 2015 [Cyber security assessment Netherlands (CSAN) 2015]. The Hague, The Netherlands: National Cyber Security Centre.

NCSC. (2016). *Cyber security assessment Netherlands (CSAN 2016)*. The Hague, The Netherlands: National Cyber Security Centre.

Neuendorf, K. A. (2016). *The content analysis guidebook*. Thousand Oaks, CA: Sage.

Neumann, P. (2013). Options and Strategies for Countering Online Radicalization in the United States. *Studies in Conflict and Terrorism, 36*(6), 431–459. doi:10.1080/1057610X.2013.784568

Neville, F. (2015). Preventing violence through changing social norms. In P. D. Donnelly & C. L. Ward (Eds.), *Oxford textbook of violence prevention: Epidemiology, evidence, and policy* (pp. 239–244). Oxford University Press.

Newcomb, T. M. (1943). *Personality and social change: Attitude formation in a student community*. New York: Dryden.

Ngo, F. T., & Paternoster, R. (2011). Cybercrime victimization: An examination of individual and situational level factors. *International Journal of Cyber Criminology, 5*(1), 773–793.

Nicholson, J., Coventry, L., & Briggs, P. (2017). Can we fight social engineering attacks by social means? Assessing social salience as a means to improve phish detection. In *Proceedings of the Thirteenth Symposium on Usable Privacy and Security (SOUPS 2017)*. Santa Clara, CA: USENIX.

Ning, P., & Jajodia, S. (2003). Intrusion Detection Techniques. In H. Bidgoli (Ed.), *The Internet Encyclopedia* (pp. 355–367). Hoboken, NJ: John Wiley & Sons.

Nisbett, R. (2010). *The geography of thought: how Asians and Westerners think differently... and why*. New York: Simon & Schuster.

Nissenbaum, H. (2004). Hackers and the contested ontology of cyberspace. *New Media & Society, 6*(2), 195–217. doi:10.1177/1461444804041445

Norberg, P. A., Horne, D. R., & Horne, D. A. (2007). The privacy paradox: Personal information disclosure intentions versus behaviors. *The Journal of Consumer Affairs, 41*(1), 100–126. doi:10.1111/j.1745-6606.2006.00070.x

Norcie, G., De Cristofaro, E., & Bellotti, V. (2013). Bootstrapping trust in online dating: Social verification of online dating profiles. In *Proceedings of International Conference on Financial Cryptography and Data Security* (pp. 149-163). Springer. doi:10.1007/978-3-642-41320-9_10

Norton. (2014). *Online fraud: Phishing*. Retrieved July 12, 2014, from http://uk.norton.com/cybercrime-phishing

Nulty, D. D. (2008). The adequacy of response rates to online and paper surveys: What can be done? *Assessment & Evaluation in Higher Education, 33*(3), 301–314. doi:10.1080/02602930701293231

Nurse, J. R. C., Creese, S., Goldsmith, M., & Lamberts, K. (2011). Trustworthy and effective communication of cybersecurity risks: A review. *Proceedings - 2011 1st Workshop on Socio-Technical Aspects in Security and Trust, STAST 2011*, 60–68. doi:10.1109/STAST.2011.6059257

Nydell, M. K. (2011). *Understanding Arabs: A guide for modern times*. Intercultural Press.

O'connell, B. J. (1975). Dimensions of religiosity among Catholics. *Review of Religious Research, 16*(3), 198–207. doi:10.2307/3510357

O'Neill, T. A., Hancock, S. E., Zivkov, K., Larson, N. L., & Law, S. J. (2016). Team Decision Making in Virtual and Face-to-Face Environments. *Group Decision and Negotiation, 25*(5), 995–1020. doi:10.1007/s10726-015-9465-3

O'Reilly, L. (2017). *Ad blocker usage is up 30% — and a popular method publishers use to thwart it isn't working*. Retrieved from: http://www.businessinsider.com/pagefair-2017-ad-blocking-report-2017-1

Odom, M. D., Kumar, A., & Saunders, L. (2002). Web assurance seals: How and why they influence consumers' decisions. *Journal of Information Systems, 16*(2), 231–250. doi:10.2308/jis.2002.16.2.231

Office for National Statistics. (2016). *Internet access – households and individuals: 2016.* Retrieved May 21, 2017, from https://www.ons.gov.uk/peoplepopulationandcommunity/householdcharacteristics/homeinternetandsocialmediausage/bulletins/internetaccesshouseholdsandindividuals/2016#activities-completed-on-the-internet

Olsen, P. (2013). *We are Anonymous.* London: Random House.

Over, D. (2004). Rationality and the normative/descriptive distinction. Blackwell handbook of judgment and decision making, 3-18.

Ozler, D. E., & Polat, G. (2012). Cyberloafing phenomenon in organizations: determinants and impacts. *International Journal of eBusiness and eGovernment Studies, 4*(2), 1–15. Retrieved from http://www.sobiad.org/eJOURNALS/journal_IJEBEG/arhieves/2012_2/derya_ergun.pdf

Packer, D. J. (2009). Avoiding groupthink: Whereas weakly identified members remain silent, strongly identified members dissent about collective problems. *Psychological Science, 20*(5), 546–548. doi:10.1111/j.1467-9280.2009.02333.x PMID:19389133

Padayachee, K. (2012). Taxonomy of compliant information security behavior. *Computers & Security, 31*(5), 673–680. doi:10.1016/j.cose.2012.04.004

Page, M., Challita, L., & Harris, A. (2011). Al Qaeda in the Arabian Peninsula: Framing narratives and prescriptions. *Terrorism and Political Violence, 23*(2), 150–172. doi:10.1080/09546553.2010.526039

Panda, J. W. (2009). Automatic identification of critical data items in a database to mitigate the effects of malicious insiders. *Information Systems Security*, 208-221.

Papadimitriou, P., & Garcia-Molina, H. (2011). Data leakage detection. *IEEE Transactions on Knowledge and Data Engineering, 23*(1), 51–63. doi:10.1109/TKDE.2010.100

Pargament, K. I. (1992). Of Means and Ends: Religion and the Search for Significance. *The International Journal for the Psychology of Religion, 2*(4), 201–229. doi:10.1207/s15327582ijpr0204_1

Parks-Leduc, L., Feldman, G., & Bardi, A. (2014). Personality traits and personal values: A meta-analysis. *Personality and Social Psychology Review, 19*(1), 3–29. doi:10.1177/1088868314538548 PMID:24963077

Parrish, J. L., Baily, J. L., & Courtney, J. F. (2009). A personality based model for determining susceptibility to phishing attacks. Decision Sciences Institute.

Parsons, K., Calic, D., Pattinson, M., Butavicius, M., McCormac, A., & Zwaans, T. (2017). The human aspects of information security questionnaire (HAIS-Q): Two further validation studies. *Computers & Security, 66*, 40–51. doi:10.1016/j.cose.2017.01.004

Parsons, K., McCormac, A., Butavicius, M., Pattinson, M., & Jerram, C. (2014). Determining employee awareness using the Human Aspects of Information Security Questionnaire (HAIS-Q). *Computers & Security, 42*, 165–176. doi:10.1016/j.cose.2013.12.003

Parsons, K., McCormac, A., Pattinson, M., Butavicius, M., & Jerram, C. (2013). Phishing for the truth: A scenario-based study of users' behavioural response to emails. In *Proceedings of IFIP International Information Security Conference* (pp. 366-378). Berlin: Springer.

Parsons, K., McCormac, A., Pattinson, M., Butavicius, M., & Jerram, C. (2015). The design of phishing studies: Challenges for researchers. *Computers & Security, 52*, 194–206. doi:10.1016/j.cose.2015.02.008

Patton, J. H., Stanford, M. S., & Barratt, E. S. (1995). Patton Factor Structure of the BIS.pdf. *Journal of Clinical Psychology.*

Payne, J. W. (1982). Contingent decision behavior. *Psychological Bulletin, 92*(2), 382–402. doi:10.1037/0033-2909.92.2.382

Payne, J. W., Bettman, J. R., & Johnson, E. J. (1988). Adaptive strategy selection in decision making. *Journal of Experimental Psychology. Learning, Memory, and Cognition, 14*(3), 534–552. doi:10.1037/0278-7393.14.3.534

Pee, L. (2012). Trust of Information on Social Media: An Elaboration Likelihood Model. In *Proceedings of the International Conference on Information Resources Management (CONF-IRM)* (pp. 2-9). AIS.

Pennebaker Conglomerates. (2017). *LIWC*. Retrieved from https://liwc.wpengine.com/

Pennebaker, J. W. (2011). Using computer analyses to identify language style and aggressive intent: The secret life of function words. *Dynamics of Asymmetric Conflict, 4*(2), 92–102. doi:10.1080/17467586.2011.627932

Pennebaker, J. W., Mehl, M. R., & Niederhoffer, K. G. (2003). Psychological aspects of natural language use: Our words, our selves. *Annual Review of Psychology, 54*(1), 547–577. doi:10.1146/annurev.psych.54.101601.145041 PMID:12185209

Perlroth, N. (2013, May 17). Hunting for Syrian hackers' Chain of Command. *New York Times*. Retrieved from https://nyti.ms/2jPZmbx

Peterson, H. (2014). Target's massive data breach originated with a single phishing email. *Business Insider*. Retrieved May 18, 2017, from: http://www.businessinsider.com/target-hack-traced-to-phishing-email-2014-2?IR=T

Petty, R. E., & Briñol, P. (2015). Emotion and persuasion: Cognitive and meta cognitive processes impact attitudes. *Cognition and Emotion, 29*(1), 1–26. doi:10.1080/02699931.2014.967183 PMID:25302943

Petty, R. E., & Cacioppo, J. T. (1986). The elaboration likelihood model of persuasion. *Advances in Experimental Social Psychology, 19*, 123–205. doi:10.1016/S0065-2601(08)60214-2

Pfleeger, S. L., & Caputo, D. (2012). Leveraging Behavioral Science to Mitigate Cyber Security Risk Security Risk. *Computers & Security, 31*(4), 597–611. doi:10.1016/j.cose.2011.12.010

Philip, L., Nick, M., & Jason, R.C., Jassim, H., Ioannis, A., Goldsmith, M., & Sadie, C. (2013). Towards a Conceptual Model and Reasoning Structure for Insider Threat Detection. *Journal of Wireless Mobile Networks, Ubiquitous Computing and Dependable Applications, 4*(4), 20–37.

Picchi, A. (2014). Target breach may have started with email phishing. *CBS News*. Retrieved May 18, 2017, from: http://www.cbsnews.com/news/target-breach-may-have-started-with-email-phishing/

Piwek, L., Ellis, D. A., & Andrews, S. (2016). Can programming frameworks bring smartphones into the mainstream of psychological science? *Frontiers in Psychology, 7*, 1252. doi:10.3389/fpsyg.2016.01252 PMID:27602010

Plous, S. (1993). *The psychology of judgment and decision making*. Mcgraw-Hill Book Company.

Posey, C., Roberts, T., Lowry, P., Bennett, R. J., & Courtney, J. F. (2013). Insiders' protection of organizational information assets: Development of a systematics-based taxonomy and theory of diversity. *Management Information Systems Quarterly, 37*(4), 1189–1210. doi:10.25300/MISQ/2013/37.4.09

Postill, J. (2014). Freedom technologists and the new protest movements: A theory of protest formulas. *Convergence, 20*(4), 402–418. doi:10.1177/1354856514541350

Postmes, T. (2007). The psychological dimensions of collective action, online. In A. Joinson, K. McKenna, T, Postmes, & U. Reips. (Eds.), The Oxford Handbook of Internet Psychology (pp. 165-184). Oxford, UK: Oxford University Press.

Postmes, T., & Brunsting, S. (2002). Collective action in the age of the Internet: Mass communication and online mobilization. *Social Science Computer Review, 20*(3), 290–301. doi:10.1177/089443930202000306

Postmes, T., Spears, R., & Lea, M. (1998). Breaching or building social boundaries? SIDE effects of computer-mediated communication. *Communication Research, 25*(6), 689–715. doi:10.1177/009365098025006006

Pratt, J. W. (1964). Risk Aversion in the Small and in the Large. *Econometrica, 32*(1/2), 122–136. doi:10.2307/1913738

Pratt, T. C., Holtfreter, K., & Reisig, M. D. (2010). Routine online activity and internet fraud targeting: Extending the generality of routine activity theory. *Journal of Research in Crime and Delinquency, 47*(3), 267–296. doi:10.1177/0022427810365903

Precht, T. (2007). *Home grown terrorism and Islamist radicalisation in Europe. From conversion to terrorism.* Academic Press.

Prensky, M. (2009). H. sapiens digital: From digital immigrants and digital natives to digital wisdom. *Journal of Online Education, 5*(3), 1.

Prentice, S., Wattam, S., & Moore, A. (2017). *Identifying and assessing the risk of re-used terrorist material* (Unpublished report). WAP Academic Consultancy Limited, UK.

Prentice, S., Rayson, P., & Taylor, P. J. (2012). The language of Islamic extremism: Towards an automated identification of beliefs, motivations and justifications. *International Journal of Corpus Linguistics, 17*(2), 259–286. doi:10.1075/ijcl.17.2.05pre

Prentice, S., Taylor, P. J., Rayson, P., Hoskins, A., & O'Loughlin, B. (2011). Analyzing the semantic content and persuasive composition of extremist media: A case study of texts produced during the Gaza conflict. *Information Systems Frontiers, 13*(1), 61–73. doi:10.1007/s10796-010-9272-y

Probst, C., Hunker, J., Gollmann, D., & Bishop, M. (2010). *Insider Threats in Cyber Security. Vasa.* New York: Springer. doi:10.1007/978-1-4419-7133-3

Pulman, A., & Taylor, J. (2012). Munchausen by internet: Current research and future directions. *Journal of Medical Internet Research, 14*(4), e115. doi:10.2196/jmir.2011 PMID:22914203

Purcell, M. (2013). Youtube and you. *Library Media Connection, 31*(4), 14–16.

Purkait, S. (2012). Phishing counter measures and their effectiveness–literature review. *Information Management & Computer Security, 20*(5), 382–420. doi:10.1108/09685221211286548

Putrevu, S., & Swimberghek, K. (2013). The influence of religiosity on consumer ethical judgments and responses toward sexual appeals. *Journal of Business Ethics, 115*(2), 351–365. doi:10.1007/s10551-012-1399-y

Pyrooz, D. C., Decker, S. H., & Moule, R. K. Jr. (2015). Criminal and routine activities in online settings: Gangs, offenders, and the Internet. *Justice Quarterly, 32*(3), 471–499. doi:10.1080/07418825.2013.778326

Quayle, E., & Taylor, M. (2011). Social networking as a nexus for engagement and exploitation of young people. *Information Security Technical Report, 16*(2), 44–50.

Quelch, J. A. (2001). *Cases in strategic marketing management: business strategies in Muslim countries.* Prentice Hall.

Quinn, J. F., & Forsyth, C. J. (2005). Describing Sexual Behavior in the Era of the Internet: A Typology for Empirical Research. *Deviant Behavior, 26*(3), 191–207. doi:10.1080/01639620590888285

Radford, J., & Holdstock, L. (1995). Gender differences in Higher Education aims between computing and psychology students. *Research in Science & Technological Education, 13*(2), 163–176. doi:10.1080/0263514950130206

Rains, S. A., & Karmikel, C. D. (2009). Health information-seeking and perceptions of website credibility: Examining Web-use orientation, message characteristics, and structural features of websites. *Computers in Human Behavior, 25*(2), 544–553. doi:10.1016/j.chb.2008.11.005

Rakesh, V., Choo, J., & Reddy, C. K. (2015). Project recommendation using heterogeneous traits in crowdfunding. *Proceedings of Ninth International Conference on Web and Social Media, 337-346.*

Ranck, J. G. (1961). Religious conservatism-liberalism and mental health. *Pastoral Psychology, 12*(2), 34–40. doi:10.1007/BF01784757

Ratcliffe, W. (2016). Point of view: Ad blocking's wake-up call. *ADMAP*. Retrieved from: https://www.warc.com/

Rathje, S. (2009). The definition of culture: An application-oriented overhaul. *Interculture Journal, 35–59.*

Raymond, E. (1996). *The New Hacker's Dictionary*. MIT Press.

Rayson, P. (2009). *Wmatrix: A web-based corpus processing environment*. Computing Department, Lancaster University. Retrieved from http://ucrel.lancs.ac.uk/wmatrix/

Rayson, P. (2013). *Wmatrix tutorials*. Retrieved September 15, 2017, from http://ucrel.lancs.ac.uk/wmatrix/tutorial/

Redhat. (2016). *Security Overview, Red Hat Enterprise Linux 3: Security Guide*. Retrieved Apr 30, 2017, from https://access.redhat.com/documentation/en-US/Red_Hat_Enterprise_Linux/3/html/Security_Guide/s1-sgs-ov-controls.html

Reese, H. W. (2011). The learning-by-doing principle. *Behavioral Development Bulletin, 17*(1), 1–19. doi:10.1037/h0100597

Reeves, S., & Brown, B. (2016, February). Embeddedness and sequentiality in social media. In *Proceedings of the 19th ACM Conference on Computer-Supported Cooperative Work & Social Computing* (pp. 1052--1064). New York, NY: ACM.

ReportN. (2017). Retrieved from: https://resources.netskope.com/h/i/340223988-april-2017-worldwide-cloud-report

Resnik, D. B., & Finn, P. R. (2017). Ethics and phishing experiments. *Science and Engineering Ethics*. doi:10.1007/s11948-017-9952-9 PMID:28812222

Rest, J. R. (1986). *Moral development: Advances in research and theory*. Praeger. Retrieved January 7, 2017, from https://books.google.co.uk/books?id=YDB-AAAAMAAJ

Reynolds, K. J., Subašić, E., & Tindall, K. (2015). The problem of behaviour change: From social norms to an ingroup focus. *Social and Personality Psychology Compass, 9*(1), 45–56. doi:10.1111/spc3.12155

Rezabakhsh, B., Bornemann, D., Hansen, U., & Schrader, U. (2006). Consumer power: A comparison of the old economy and the internet economy. *Journal of Consumer Policy, 29–36.*

Rheingold, H. (1993). *The Virtual Community: Homesteading on the Electronic Frontier*. MIT Press.

Richards, J. (2014). *Cyber-War: The Anatomy of the Global Security*. New York: Palgrave Macmillan. doi:10.1057/9781137399625

Richardson, J. T. E. (1994). Mature students in higher education: A literature survey on approaches to studying. *Studies in Higher Education, 19*(3), 309–325. doi:10.1080/03075079412331381900

Richardson, K. (2003). Health risks on the internet: Establishing credibility on line. *Health Risk & Society, 5*(2), 171–184. doi:10.1080/1369857031000123948

Ridings, C. M., Gefen, D., & Arinze, B. (2002). Some antecedents and effects of trust in virtual communities. *The Journal of Strategic Information Systems, 11*(3), 271–295. doi:10.1016/S0963-8687(02)00021-5

Rifon, N. J., Jiang, M., & Kim, S. (2016). Don't hate me because I am beautiful: Identifying the relative influence of celebrity attractiveness and character traits on credibility. In *Advances in Advertising Research* (Vol. 6, pp. 125–134). Springer Fachmedien Wiesbaden. doi:10.1007/978-3-658-10558-7_11

Rifon, N. J., LaRose, R., & Choi, S. (2005). Your privacy is sealed: Effects of web privacy seals on trust and personal disclosures. *The Journal of Consumer Affairs*, *39*(2), 339–362. doi:10.1111/j.1745-6606.2005.00018.x

Rippl, S. (2002). Cultural theory and risk perception: A proposal for a better measurement. *Journal of Risk Research*, *5*(2), 147–165. doi:10.1080/13669870110042598

Roberts, J. J. (2017, April 27). Exclusive: Facebook and Google were victims of $100, payment scam. *Fortune*. Retrieved May 16, 2017, from: http://fortune.com/2017/04/27/facebook- google-rimasauskas/

Roberts, J. M. Jr, Moore, C. C., Romney, A. K., Barbujani, G., Bellwood, P., Dunnell, R. C., & Terrell, J. (1995). Predicting similarity in material culture among New Guinea Villages from propinquity and language: A log-linear approach. *Current Anthropology*, *36*(5), 769–788. doi:10.1086/204431

Rocco, E. (1998). Trust breaks down in electronic contexts but can be repaired by some initial face-to-face contact. In *Proceedings of the SIGCHI conference on Human factors in computing systems* (pp. 496-502). ACM Press. doi:10.1145/274644.274711

Rockeach, M. (1960). *The open and closed mind. Investigations into the nature of belief systems and personality systems*. New York: Basic Books. Actualidades en Psicología.

Rogers, M. (2003). The psychology of cyber-terrorism. Terrorists, Victims and Society: Psychological. *Perspectives on Terrorism and Its Consequences*, 75-92.

Rogers, M. K. (2011). The psyche of cybercriminals: A psycho-Social perspective. In Cybercrimes: A multidisciplinary analysis (pp. 217-235). Springer. doi:10.1007/978-3-642-13547-7_14

Rogers, M. (2003). The Psychology of Cyber-Terrorism. In A. Silke (Ed.), *Terrorists, victims and society: psychological perspectives on terrorism and its consequences* (pp. 77–92). Chichester, UK: John Wiley & Sons. doi:10.1002/9780470713600.ch4

Rogers, M. K. (2006). A two-dimensional circumplex approach to the development of a hacker taxonomy. *Digital Investigation*, *3*(2), 97–102. doi:10.1016/j.diin.2006.03.001

Rogers, M. K. (2010). The psyche of cybercriminals: A psycho-social perspective. In G. Ghosh & E. Turrini (Eds.), *Cybercrimes: a multidisciplinary analysis*. Berlin: Springer-Verlag.

Roghanizad, M. M., & Neufeld, D. J. (2015). Intuition, risk, and the formation of online trust. *Computers in Human Behavior*, *50*, 489–498. doi:10.1016/j.chb.2015.04.025

Roky, R., Houti, I., Moussamih, S., Qotbi, S., & Aadil, N. (2004). Physiological and chronobiological changes during Ramadan intermittent fasting. *Annals of Nutrition & Metabolism*, *48*(4), 296–303. doi:10.1159/000081076 PMID:15452402

Roof, W. C. (1980). The Ambiguities of " Religious Preference" in Survey Research-A Methodological Note. *Public Opinion Quarterly*, *44*(3), 403–407. doi:10.1086/268607

Rose, R. N. (2016). *The Future of Insider Threats. Opinion-Cybersecurity*. Retrieved Apr 30, 2017, from https://www.forbes.com/sites/realspin/2016/08/30/the-future-of-insider-threats/#22e7a3d87dcb

Rosenmann, A., & Safir, M. P. (2006). Forced Online: Pushed Factors of Internet Sexuality: A Preliminary Study of Paraphilic Empowerment. *Journal of Homosexuality*, *51*(3), 71–92. doi:10.1300/J082v51n03_05 PMID:17135116

Rosenzweig, R. (1998). Wizards, Bureaucrats, Warriors, and Hackers: Writing the History of the Internet. *The American Historical Review, 103*(5), 1530–1552. doi:10.2307/2649970

Rotter, J. B. (1980). Interpersonal trust, trustworthiness, and gullibility. *The American Psychologist, 35*(1), 1–7. doi:10.1037/0003-066X.35.1.1

Rousseau, D. M., Sitkin, S. B., Burt, R. S., & Camerer, C. (1998). Not so different after all: A cross-discipline view of trust. *Academy of Management Review, 23*(3), 393–404. doi:10.5465/AMR.1998.926617

Rowe, M., & Saif, H. (2016). Mining pro-ISIS radicalisation signals from social media users. In *Proceedings of the Tenth International AAAI Conference on Web and Social Media* (pp. 329–338). Palo Alto, CA: AAAI Press.

Rozmovits, L., & Ziebland, S. (2004). What do patients with prostate or breast cancer want from an Internet site? A qualitative study of information needs. *Patient Education and Counseling, 53*(1), 57–64. doi:10.1016/S0738-3991(03)00116-2 PMID:15062905

Rubbelke, D. T. (2005). Differing motivations for terrorism. *Defence and Peace Economics, 16*(1), 19–27. doi:10.1080/1024269052000323524

Ruby, C. L. (2002). The definition of terrorism. *Analyses of Social Issues and Public Policy (ASAP), 2*(1), 9–14. doi:10.1111/j.1530-2415.2002.00021.x

Ruiter, R. A., Kessels, L. T., Peters, G. J. Y., & Kok, G. (2014). Sixty years of fear appeal research: Current state of the evidence. *International Journal of Psychology, 49*(2), 63–70. doi:10.1002/ijop.12042 PMID:24811876

Saad, S., Bazan, S., & Varin, C. (2015). Asymmetric Cyber-warfare between Israel and Hezbollah: The Web as a New Strategic Battlefield. *Webscience*. Retrieved 06 01, 2017, from: http://www.websci11.org/fileadmin/websci/Posters/96_paper.pdf

Sabri, O., & Geraldine, M. (2014). When do advertising parodies hurt? The power of humor and credibility in viral spoof advertisements. *Journal of Advertising Research*, 18–24.

Saddiq, M. A. (2010). *Whither e-jihad: evaluating the threat of internet radicalisation*. Academic Press.

Sagarin, B. J., Britt, M. A., Heider, J. D., Wood, S. E., & Lynch, J. E. (2003). *Bartering Our Attention: The Distraction and Persuasion Effects of On-Line Advertisements*. Cognitive Technology.

Sageman, M. (2004). *Understanding terror networks*. Philadelphia: University of Pennsylvania Press. doi:10.9783/9780812206791

Sageman, M. (2008). *Leaderless Jihad: Terror Networks in the Twenty-First Century*. University of Pennsylvania Press. doi:10.9783/9780812206784

Salah, K., Alcaraz Calero, J. M., Zeadally, S., Al-Mulla, S., & Alzaabi, M. (2013). Using cloud computing to implement a security overlay network. *IEEE Security and Privacy, 11*(1), 44–53.

Salam, A., Rao, R., & Pegels, C. (1998). An investigation of consumer-perceived risk on electronic commerce transactions: The role of institutional trust and economic incentive in a social exchange framework. *AMCIS 1998 Proceedings*, 114.

Samovar, L. A., Porter, R. E., McDaniel, E. R., & Roy, C. S. (2015). *Communication between cultures*. Nelson Education.

Sample, C., & Karamanian, A. (2015). Culture and Cyber Behaviours: DNS Defending. 14th ECCWS, 233–240.

Sample, C., Cowley, J., & Hutchinson, S. (2017a). Cultural Exploration of Attack Vector Preferences for Self-identified Attackers. *IEEE 11th International Conference on Research Challenges in Information Science*, 305–314. doi:10.1109/RCIS.2017.7956551

Sample, C. (2013). Applicability of Cultural Markers in Computer Network Attack Attribution. *Proceedings of the 12th European Conference on Cyber Warfare and Security*, 361–369.

Sample, C., Cowley, J., Watson, T., & Maple, C. (2016). Re-thinking threat intelligence. *International Conference on Cyber Conflict (CyCon US)*, 1–9.

Sample, C., Hutchinson, S., Karamanian, A., & Maple, C. (2017b). *Cultural Observations on Social Engineering Victims. 16th ECCWS*, 391–401.

Samsung. (2017). *Privacy Policy*. Retrieved from: https://account.samsung.com/membership/pp

Sanchez-Franco, M. J., Martinez-Lopez, F. J., & Martin-Velicia, F. A. (2009). Exploring the impact of individualism and uncertainty avoidance in Web-based training: An empirical analysis in European higher education. *Computers & Education*, *52*(3), 588–598. doi:10.1016/j.compedu.2008.11.006

Sandhu, R. (2003). Good-enough security. *IEEE Internet Computing*, *7*(1), 66–68. doi:10.1109/MIC.2003.1167341

Sandhu, R. S., & Samarati, P. (1994). Access control: Principle and practice. *IEEE Communications Magazine*, *32*(9), 40–48. doi:10.1109/35.312842

Sanzgiri, A., & Dasgupta, D. (2016). Classification of Insider Threat Detection Techniques. In *Proceedings of the 11th Annual Cyber and Information Security Research Conference* (CISRC-2016). Oak Ridge, TN: ACM. doi:10.1145/2897795.2897799

Saridakis, G., Benson, V., Ezingard, J., & Tennakoon, H. (2015). Individual information security, user behaviour and cyber victimization: An empirical study of social networking users. *Technological Forecasting and Social Change*. doi:10/1016/j.techfore.2015.08.012

Saridakis, G., Benson, V., Ezingeard, J. N., & Tennakoon, H. (2016). Individual information security, user behaviour and cyber victimisation: An empirical study of social networking users. *Technological Forecasting and Social Change*, *102*, 320–330. doi:10.1016/j.techfore.2015.08.012

Sasse, M., & Flechais, I. (2005). *Usable Security: Why Do We Need It? How Do We Get It?* Retrieved from http://discovery.ucl.ac.uk/20345/

Sasse, M., Brostoff, S., & Weirich, D. (2001). Transforming the "weakest link": A Human-Computer Interaction Approach for Usable and Effective Security. *BT Technology Journal*, *19*(3), 122–131. doi:10.1023/A:1011902718709

Schaefer, C. A., & Gorsuch, R. L. (1991). Psychological adjustment and religiousness: The multivariate belief-motivation theory of religiousness. *Journal for the Scientific Study of Religion*, *30*(4), 448–461. doi:10.2307/1387279

Schanzer, J., & Miller, S. (2012). *Facebook Fatwa: Saudi Clerics*. Wahhabi Islam, and Social Media.

Scheuerman, W. E. (2016). Digital disobedience and the law. *New Political Science*, *38*(3), 299–314. doi:10.1080/07393148.2016.1189027

Schmid, A. P. (2013). Radicalisation, de-radicalisation, counter-radicalisation: A conceptual discussion and literature review. *ICCT Research Paper, 97*, 22.

Schmid, A. (2004). Terrorism-the definitional problem. *Case Western Reserve Journal of International Law*, *36*, 375–419.

Schmid, A. P. (2011). Introduction. In A. P. Schmid (Ed.), *The Routledge Handbook of Terrorism Research* (pp. 1–38). Abingdon, UK: Routledge.

Schmid, A. P., & de Graaf, J. (1982). *Violence as Communication: Insurgent Terrorism and the Western News Media.* London: SAGE Publications.

Schmitz, A., Zillmann, D., & Blossfeld, H. P. (2013). Do women pick up lies before men? The association between gender, deception patterns, and detection modes in online dating. *Online Journal of Communication and Media Technologies, 3*(3), 52.

Schneider, H., Krieger, J., & Bayraktar, A. (2011). The Impact of Intrinsic Religiosity on Consumers' Ethical Beliefs: Does It Depend on the Type of Religion? A Comparison of Christian and Moslem Consumers in Germany and Turkey. *Journal of Business Ethics, 102*(2), 319–332. doi:10.1007/s10551-011-0816-y

Schneier, B. (2000). *Secrets & Lies: Digital Security in a Networked World.* Indianapolis, IN: Wiley Publishing Inc.

Schrock, A. R. (2016). Civic hacking as data activism and advocacy: A history from publicity to open government data. *New Media & Society, 18*(4), 581–599. doi:10.1177/1461444816629469

Schutz, A., & Luckmann, T. (1973). *The Structures of the Life-world* (Vol. 1). Evanston, IL: Northwestern University Press.

Schwartz, S. H. (2012). An overview of the Schwartz theory of basic values. *Online Readings in Psychology and Culture, 2*(1). doi:10.9707/2307-0919.1116

Schwartz, S. H., & Huismans, S. (1995). Value Priorities and Religiosity in Four Western Religions. *Social Psychology Quarterly, 58*(2), 88–107. doi:10.2307/2787148

Scott, S., & Bruce, R. (1995). Decision-making Style: The Development and Assessment of a New Measure. *Educational and Psychological Measurement, 55*(5), 818–831. doi:10.1177/0013164495055005017

Seebruck, R. (2015). A typology of hackers: Classifying cyber malfeasance using a weighted arc circumplex model. *Digital Investigation, 14*, 36–45. doi:10.1016/j.diin.2015.07.002

Senecal, S., Kalczynski, P. J., & Nantel, J. (2005). Consumers' decision-making process and their online shopping behavior: A clickstream analysis. *Journal of Business Research, 58*(11), 1599–1608. doi:10.1016/j.jbusres.2004.06.003

Seth, R. (2015). *The biggest Cyberthreat to Companies could come from the Inside.* Retrieved Apr 30, 2017, from https://www.cnet.com/news/the-biggest-cyber-threat-to-companies-could-come-from-the-inside/

Shafir, E., & LeBoeuf, R. A. (2002). Rationality. *Annual Review of Psychology, 53*(1), 491–517. doi:10.1146/annurev.psych.53.100901.135213 PMID:11752494

Shane, S. (1995). Uncertainty avoidance and the preference for innovation championing roles. *Journal of International Business Studies, 26*(1), 47–68. doi:10.1057/palgrave.jibs.8490165

Shankar, V., Smith, A. K., & Rangaswamy, A. (2003). Customer satisfaction and loyalty in online and offline environments. *International Journal of Research in Marketing, 20*(2), 153–175. doi:10.1016/S0167-8116(03)00016-8

Sharma, M. (2016). *Lashkar-e-Cyber of Hafiz Saeed.* Institute for Defense Studies and Analyses. Retrieved 06 01, 2017, from: http://www.idsa.in/idsacomments/lashkar-e-cyber-of-hafiz-saeed_msharma_310316#footnote1_amq1mz7

Shaw, R., Ruby, K., & Post, J. (1998). The Insider Threat to Information Sytems. *Security Awareness Bulletin*, 2–98.

Sheng, S., Holbrook, M., Kumaraguru, P., Cranor, L., & Downs, J. (2010). *Who falls for phish? A demographic analysis of phishing susceptibility and effectiveness of interventions.* Paper presented at The SIGCHI Conference on Human Factors in Computing Systems, Atlanta, GA.

Sher, S., & McKenzie, C. R. (2008). Framing effects and rationality. *The probabilistic mind: Prospects for Bayesian cognitive science*, 79-96.

Shetret, L. (2011). *Use of the Internet for Counter-Terrorist Purposes.* Center on Global Counterterrorism Cooperation. Retrieved May 25, 2017 from, http://www.globalct.org/wpcontent/uploads/2011/02/LS_policybrief_119.pdf

Shewder, R. A. (1999). Why cultural psychology. *Ethos (Berkeley, Calif.)*, 27(1), 62–73. doi:10.1525/eth.1999.27.1.62

Shiau, W. L., & Luo, M. M. (2012). Factors affecting online group buying intention and satisfaction: A social exchange theory perspective. *Computers in Human Behavior*, 28(6), 2431–2444. doi:10.1016/j.chb.2012.07.030

Shropshire, J., Warkentin, M., Johnston, A., & Schmidt, M. (2006). Personality and IT security: An application of the five-factor model. *AMCIS 2006 Proceedings*, 3443-3448.

Shugan, S. M. (1980). The cost of thinking. *The Journal of Consumer Research*, 7(2), 99–111. doi:10.1086/208799

Shu, K., Silva, A., Wang, S., Tang, J., & Liu, H. (2017). Fake news detection on socialmedia. A data mining perspective. *Proceedings of SIGKDD Explorations Newsletter*, 19(1), 22–36.

Silber, M. D., Bhatt, A., & Analysts, S. I. (2007). *Radicalization in the West: The homegrown threat.* New York: Police Department.

Silke, A. (2008). Research on terrorism. *Terrorism Informatics. Knowledge Management and Data Mining for Homeland Security*, 27-50.

Sillence, E., & Briggs, P. (2015). Trust and engagement in online health a timeline approach. In S. S. Sundar (Ed.), *The Handbook of the Psychology of Communication Technology* (pp. 469–487). Malden, MA: Wiley Blackwell.

Sillence, E., Briggs, P., Harris, P., & Fishwick, L. (2006). A framework for understanding trust factors in web-based health advice. *International Journal of Human-Computer Studies*, 64(8), 697–713. doi:10.1016/j.ijhcs.2006.02.007

Simcox, R., & Dyer, E. (2013). Terror data: US vs. UK. *World Affairs*, 176(2), 45–55.

Simi, P., & Futrell, R. (2006). Cyberculture and the Endurance of Radical Racist Activism. *Journal of Political and Military Sociology*, 34(1), 115–142.

Simon, T., Goldberg, A., Aharonson-Daniel, L., Leykin, D., & Adini, B. (2014). Twitter in the Cross Fire—The Use of Social Media in the Westgate Mall Terror Attack in Kenya. *PLoS One*, 9(8), 1–11. doi:10.1371/journal.pone.0104136

Singelis, T. M., & Brown, W. J. (1995). Culture, self, and collectivist communication linking culture to individual behavior. *Human Communication Research*, 21(3), 354–389. doi:10.1111/j.1468-2958.1995.tb00351.x PMID:12349710

Singh, S. (2010). *Rural BPOs looking good to become a phenomenon in Indian outsourcing story.* Retrieved 11 21, 2016, from http://economictimes.indiatimes.com/tech/ites/rural-bpos-looking-good-to-become-a-phenomenon-in-indian-outsourcing-story/articleshow/6254294.cms

Singh, A. K., & Potdar, V. (2009). Blocking online advertising – A state of the art. *International Conference on Industrial Technology, ICIT*, 1-10.

Singh, R.,, & Gonsalves,, T. A. (2015). A pragmatic approach towards secure sharing of digital objects. *Security and Communication Networks*, 8(18), 3914–3926. doi:10.1002/sec.1310

Singh, R., Divakaran, D. M., & Gonsalves, T. A. (2011). Taking rural BPO to new heights: an ACM for distributed and secure document sharing. *5th IEEE Conference on Advances in Networking and Telecommunication System*, 1-6.

Siponen, M., Pahnila, S., & Mahmood, M. A. (2010). Compliance with information security policies: An empirical investigation. *Computer*, *43*(2), 64–71. doi:10.1109/MC.2010.35

Siponen, M., & Vance, A. (2010). Neutralizaiton: New Insights into the Problem of Employee Information Systems Security. *Management Information Systems Quarterly*, *34*(3), 487–502.

Skinner, W. F., & Fream, A. M. (1997). A social learning theory analysis of computer crime among college students. *Journal of Research in Crime and Delinquency*, *34*(4), 495–518. doi:10.1177/0022427897034004005

Skirnevskiy, V., Bendig, D., & Brettel, M. (2017). The influence of internal social capital on serial creators' success in crowdfunding. *Entrepreneurship Theory and Practice*, *41*(2), 209–236. doi:10.1111/etap.12272

Slater, E. (1947). Neurosis and religious affiliation. *The British Journal of Psychiatry*, *93*(391), 392–396. doi:10.1192/bjp.93.391.392 PMID:20265904

Slater, W., Hall, T. W., & Edwards, K. J. (2001). Measuring religion and spirituality: Where are we and where are we going? *Journal of Psychology and Theology*, *29*(1), 4.

Slaymaker, R. C. (2002). *ICTs and rural development: review of the literature, current interventions and opportunities for action. Overseas Development Institute.* ODI.

Slefo, G. (2016). *Next-Level 'MethBot' Ad-Fraud Scam Cost Advertisers At Least $3 Million Per Day, WhiteOps Says.* Retrieved from: http://adage.com/article/digital/ad-fraud-scheme-cost-advertisers-3-million-day/307235/

Slovic, P., Finucane, M., Peters, E., & MacGregor, D. G. (2002). Rational actors or rational fools: Implications of the affect heuristic for behavioural economics. *Journal of Socio-Economics*, *31*(4), 329–342. doi:10.1016/S1053-5357(02)00174-9

Small, G. W., Moody, T. D., Siddarth, P., & Bookheimer, S. Y. (2009). Your brain on Google: Patterns of cerebral activation during internet searching. *The American Journal of Geriatric Psychiatry*, *17*(2), 116–126. doi:10.1097/JGP.0b013e3181953a02 PMID:19155745

Smith, A., & Duggan, M. (2013). *Online dating & relationships.* Pew Research Center. Retrieved May 16, 2017, from http://www.pewinternet.org/2013/10/21/online-dating-relationships/

Smith, D. (2016, November 6). WikiLeaks emails: What they revealed about the Clinton campaign's mechanics. *The Guardian.* Retrieved May 16, 2017, from: https://www.theguardian.com/us-news/2016/nov/06/wikileaks-emails-hillary-clinton-campaign-john-podesta

Smith, S. (2010). Circuits of power: A study of mandated compliance to an information systems security de jure standard in a government organization. *MIS Quarterly*, *34*(3), 463–486.

Smith, C. B., Weigert, A. J., & Thomas, D. L. (1979). Self-esteem and religiosity: An analysis of Catholic adolescents from five cultures. *Journal for the Scientific Study of Religion*, *18*(1), 51–60. doi:10.2307/1385378

Smith, E. R., Seger, C. R., & Mackie, D. A. (2007). Can emotions be truly group level? evidence regarding four conceptual criteria. *Journal of Personality and Social Psychology*, *93*(3), 431–446. doi:10.1037/0022-3514.93.3.431 PMID:17723058

Smith, H. J., Dinev, T., & Xu, H. (2011). Theory and Review Information Privacy Research: An Interdisciplinary Review 1. *MIS QuarterlyInformation Privacy Research*, *35*(4), 989–1015. doi:10.1126/science.1103618

Smithson, J., Sharkey, S., Hewis, E., Jones, R. B., Emmens, T., Ford, T., & Owens, C. (2011). Membership and boundary maintenance on an online self-harm forum. *Qualitative Health Research, 21*(11), 1567–1575. doi:10.1177/1049732311413784 PMID:21715606

Snow, D. A., & Benford, R. D. (1992). Master Frames and Cycles of Protest. In A. D. Morris & C. M. Mueller (Eds.), *Frontiers in Social Movement Theory* (pp. 133–155). New Haven, CT: Yale University Press.

Soeters, J. L., & Boer, P. C. (2000). Culture and flight safety in military aviation. *The International Journal of Aviation Psychology, 10*(2), 111–133. doi:10.1207/S15327108IJAP1002_1

Solomon, R. (2017). Electronic protests: Hacktivism as a form of protest in Uganda. *Computer Law & Security Review, 33*(5), 718–728. doi:10.1016/j.clsr.2017.03.024

Song, Y., & van Boeschoten, R. (2015). Success factors for Crowdfunding founders and funders. *Proceedings of the 5th International Conference on Collaborative Innovation Networks COINs15*.

Sood, J., & Nasu, Y. (1995). Religiosity and nationality. An exploratory study of their effect on consumer behavior in Japan and the United States. *Journal of Business Research, 34*(1), 1–9. doi:10.1016/0148-2963(94)00015-7

Sorrentino, R. M., Holmes, J. G., Hanna, S. E., & Sharp, A. (1995). Uncertainty orientation and trust in close relationships: Individual differences in cognitive styles. *Journal of Personality and Social Psychology, 68*(2), 314–327. doi:10.1037/0022-3514.68.2.314

Spears, J., & Barki, H. (2010). User participation in information systems security risk management. *Management Information Systems Quarterly, 34*(3), 503–522. doi:10.2337/dc10-0368

Spears, R., & Postmes, T. (2013). Group identity, social influence and collective action online: Extensions and applications of the SIDE model. In S. S. Sundar (Ed.), *The Handbook of Psychology of Communication Technology*. Oxford, UK: Blackwell.

Spook, J., Paulussen, T., Kok, G., & van Empelen, P. (2016). Evaluation of a serious self-regulation game intervention for overweight-related behaviors ("Balance It"): A pilot study. *Journal of Medical Internet Research, 18*(9), e225. doi:10.2196/jmir.4964 PMID:27670222

St. Johns, M. (2007). *Automated updates of DNS security (DNSSEC) trust anchors*. Internet Engineering Task Force.

Staheli, D., Yu, T., Crouser, R. J., Damodaran, S., Nam, K., O'Gwynn, D., . . . Harrison, L. (2014). Visualization evaluation for cyber security: Trends and future directions. In *Proceedings of the Eleventh Workshop on Visualization for Cyber Security* (pp. 49-56). Paris, France: Academic Press. doi:10.1145/2671491.2671492

Stanovich, K. E. (1999). *Who is rational? Studies of individual differences in reasoning*. Mahwah, NJ: Erlbaum.

Stark, R., & Glock, C. Y. (1968). *American piety: The nature of religious commitment* (Vol. 1). Univ of California Press.

Statista. (2017a). *Number of Smartphone Users Worldwide from 2014 to 2019 (in Millions)*. Retrieved 06 01, 2017, from: http://www.statista.com/statistics/330695/number-of-smartphone-users-worldwide/

Statista. (2017b). *Number of Monthly Active Facebook Users*. Retrieved 06 10, 2017, from https://www.statista.com/statistics/264810/number-of-monthly-active-facebook-users-worldwide/

Statista. (2017c). *Number of Monthly Active Twitter Users*. Retrieved 06 10, 2017, from https://www.statista.com/statistics/282087/number-of-monthly-active-twitter-users/

Statista. (2017d). *Number of Smartphone Users Worldwide*. Retrieved 06 10, 2017, from https://www.statista.com/statistics/330695/number-of-smartphone-users-worldwide/

Statline. (2016a). *Bevolking: Kerncijfers* [Population: Key figures]. Retrieved from http://statline.cbs.nl/StatWeb/publication/?VW=T&DM=SLNL&PA=37296ned&D1=a&D2=0,10,20,30,40,50,60,(l-1),l&HD=130605-0924&HDR=G1&STB=T.

Statline. (2016b). *Bevolking: Hoogst behaald onderwijsniveau* [Population: Highest attained level of education]. Retrieved from http://statline.cbs.nl/Statweb/publication/?DM=SLNL&PA=82275NED&D1=0&D2=0&D3=0&D4=0-1,4-5&D5=1,7,11&D6=64&VW=T

Statline. (2016c). *Inkomensklassen: Particuliere huishoudens naar diverse kenmerken* [Income brackets: Personal households according to various attributes]. Retrieved from http://statline.cbs.nl/Statweb/publication/?DM=SLNL&PA=70958ned&D1=0&D2=2&D3=1-8&D4=0,68-72,75-76&D5=l&HDR=T,G3,G4,G1&STB=G2&VW=T

Statline. (2016d). *Arbeidsdeelname: Kerncijfers* [Rate of employment: Key figures]. Retrieved from http://statline.cbs.nl/Statweb/publication/?DM=SLNL&PA=82309NED&D1=0-11,13-15,18-23&D2=0&D3=0-3,7-8&D4=0&D5=55-58,60-67&HDR=G4&STB=G1,G2,G3,T&VW=T

Steptoe, W., Steed, A., Rovira, A., & Rae, J. (2010). Lie Tracking: Social presence, truth and deception in avatar-mediated telecommunication. In *Proceedings of SIGCHI Conference on Human Factors in Computing Systems 2010* (pp.1039-1048). Atlanta, GA: Academic Press. doi:10.1145/1753326.1753481

Stern, J. (2003). *Terror in the Name of God: Why Religious Militants Kill.* New York: Harper Collins.

Stern, J., & Berger, J. M. (2016). *ISIS: The State of Terror.* New York: Harper Collins Publishers.

Stevens, T., & Neumann, P. R. (2009). *Countering online radicalisation: A strategy for action.* International Centre for the Study of Radicalisation and Political Violence.

Stol, W. Ph., Leukfeldt, E. R., & Klap, H. (2012). Cybercrime en politie: Een schets van de Nederlandse situatie anno 2012 [Cybercrime and the police: A sketch of the situation in the Netherlands anno 2012]. *Justitiële Verkenningen, 38*(1), 25–39.

Stouffer, S. A. (1955). *Communism, conformity, and civil liberties: A cross-section of the nation speaks its mind.* Transaction Publishers.

Sturgis, P., Patulny, R., Allum, N., & Buscha, F. (2012). Social connectedness and generalized trust: a longitudinal perspective. *ISER Working Paper Series*, 1-23.

Sudau, F., Friede, T., Grabowski, J., Koschack, J., Makedonski, P., & Himmel, W. (2014). Sources of information and behavioral patterns in online health forums: Observational study. *Journal of Medical Internet Research, 16*(1), e10. doi:10.2196/jmir.2875 PMID:24425598

Suler, J. (2004). The online disinhibition effect. *Cyberpsychology & Behavior, 7*(3), 321–326. doi:10.1089/1094931041291295 PMID:15257832

Sullivan, M. (2007). *Statistics: Informed decisions using data.* Upper Saddle River, NJ: Pearson Education Inc.

Sung, C., & David, Z. (2012). Addressing Insider Threat using Where You Are as Fourth Factor Authentication., In *Proceedings of IEEE International Carnahan Conference on Security Technology* (pp. 147-153). Boston: IEEE.

Sunstein, C. R. (2001). Why they hate us: The role of social dynamics. *Harv. JL & Pub. Pol'y, 25*, 429.

Sutanto, J., Palme, E., Tan, C.-H., & Phang, C. W. (2013). Addressing the Personalization-Privacy Paradox: An Empirical Assessment on Smartphone Users. *Management Information Systems Quarterly, 37*(4), 1141–A5. doi:10.25300/MISQ/2013/37.4.07

Sutton, M. (2009). Product design: CRAVED and VIVA. In B. S. Fisher & S. P. Lab (Eds.), *Encyclopedia of Victimology and Crime Prevention*. Thousand Oaks, CA: Sage.

Su, Z., & Wassermann, G. (2006, January). The essence of command injection attacks in web applications. *ACM SIG-PLAN Notices*, *41*(1), 372–382. doi:10.1145/1111320.1111070

Sweeney, L. (2002). Achieving k-anonymity privacy protection using generalization and suppression. *International Journal of Uncertainty, Fuzziness and Knowledge-based Systems*, *10*(05), 571–588. doi:10.1142/S021848850200165X

Swimberghe, K., Flurry, L. A., & Parker, J. M. (2011). Consumer Religiosity: Consequences for Consumer Activism in the United States. *Journal of Business Ethics*, *103*(3), 453–467. doi:10.1007/s10551-011-0873-2

Taai, N. M. (1985). *Religious Behavior Scale*. Arrobyaan Publishing.

Tajfel, H., & Turner, J. C. (1979). An integrative theory of intergroup conflict. *The Social Psychology of Intergroup Relations*, *33*(47), 74.

Tajfel, H. (1978). *Differentiation between social groups*. London: Academic Press.

Tajfel, H. (1979). Individuals and groups in social psychology. *The British Journal of Social and Clinical Psychology*, *18*, 183–190. doi:10.1111/j.20448260.1979.tb00324.x

Tajfel, H., & Turner, J. (1979). An integrative theory of inter-group conflict. In J. A. Williams & S. Worchel (Eds.), *The social psychology of inter-group relations* (pp. 33–47). Belmont, CA: Wadsworth.

Takayuki, S. (2011). A Framework for Detecting Insider Threats using Psychological Triggers. *Journal of Wireless Mobile Networks, Ubiquitous Computing and Dependable Applications*, *3*(1/2), 99–119.

Tanczer, L. M. (2016). Hacktivism and the male-only stereotype. *New Media & Society*, *18*(8), 1599–1615. doi:10.1177/1461444814567983

Tanis, M., & Postmes, T. (2005). A social identity approach to trust: Interpersonal perception, group membership and trusting behaviour. *European Journal of Social Psychology*, *35*(3), 413–424. doi:10.1002/ejsp.256

Tarakeshwar, N., Stanton, J., & Pargament, K. I. (2003). Religion: An overlooked dimension in cross-cultural psychology. *Journal of Cross-Cultural Psychology*, *34*(1), 377–394. doi:10.1177/0022022103034004001

Tarrant, M., & North, A. C. (2004). Explanations for positive and negative behavior: The intergroup attribution bias in achieved groups. *Current Psychology (New Brunswick, N.J.)*, *23*(161). doi:10.1007/BF02903076

Tate, E. D., & Miller, G. R. (1971). Differences in value systems of persons with varying religious orientations. *Journal for the Scientific Study of Religion*, *10*(4), 357–365. doi:10.2307/1384781

Tauber, E. M. (1972). Why do people shop? *Journal of Marketing*, *36*(4), 46–49. doi:10.2307/1250426

Taylor, C. (2004). Consumer privacy and the market for consumer information. *The Rand Journal of Economics*, *35*(4), 631–650. doi:10.2307/1593765

Taylor, J., & MacDonald, J. (2002). The effects of asynchronous computer-mediated group interaction on group processes. *Social Science Computer Review*, *20*(3), 260–274. doi:10.1177/089443930202000304

Taylor, M., & Horgan, J. (2006). A Conceptual Framework for Addressing Psychological Process in the Development of the Terrorist. *Terrorism and Political Violence*, *18*(4), 585–601. doi:10.1080/09546550600897413

Taylor, P. J., Holbrook, D., & Joinson, A. (2017). Same Kind of Different. *Criminology & Public Policy*, *16*(1), 127–133. doi:10.1111/1745-9133.12285

Tetri, P., & Vuorinen, J. (2013). Dissecting social engineering. *Behaviour & Information Technology, 32*(10), 1014–1023. doi:10.1080/0144929X.2013.763860

Thaler, R. H., & Sunstein, C. R. (2008). *Nudge: Improving decisions about health, wealth, and happiness.* New Haven, CT: Yale University Press.

Thatcher, J., O'Sullivan, D., & Mahmoudi, D. (2016). Data colonialism through accumulation by dispossession: New metaphors for daily data. *Environment and Planning: Society and Space*, 1–17.

The stupendous rise of rural BPOs in India. (2016). Retrieved 06 02, 2017, from https://www.outsource2india.com/why_india/articles/rise-of-rural-BPO-india.asp

Thompson, H., & Raine, J. (1976). Religious denomination preference as a basis for store location. *Journal of Retailing, 52*(2), 71–78.

Thomson, R., Yuki, M., & Ito, N. (2015). A socio-ecological approach to national differences in online privacy concern: The role of relational mobility and trust. *Computers in Human Behavior, 51*, 285–292. doi:10.1016/j.chb.2015.04.068

Thottam, I. (2017). 10 Online dating statistics you should know. *eHarmony*. Retrieved June 1, 2017, from http://www.eharmony.com/online-dating-statistics/

Tice, D. M., Bratslavsky, E., & Baumeister, R. F. (2001). Emotional distress regulation takes precedence over impulse control: If you feel bad, do it! *Journal of Personality and Social Psychology, 80*(1), 53–67. doi:10.1037/0022-3514.80.1.53 PMID:11195891

Tillich, P. (2001). *Dynamics of faith* (Vol. 577). Zondervan.

Tischer, M., Durumeric, Z., Foster, S., Duan, S., Mori, A., Bursztein, E., & Bailey, M. (2016). Users Really Do Plug in USB Drives They Find. *IEEE Symposium on Security and Privacy*, 1–14. doi:10.1109/SP.2016.26

Tolmie, P., Procter, R., Rouncefield, M., Liakata, M., & Zubiaga, A. (2015). *Microblog analysis as a programme of work.* arXiv preprint arXiv:1511.03193

Torok, R. (2010). *"Make A Bomb In Your Mums Kitchen": Cyber Recruiting And Socialisation of 'White Moors' and Home Grown Jihadists.* Academic Press.

Toronto Star. (2008, February 4). How Obama using tech to triumph. *Toronto Star*, p. B1.

Travaglino, G. A. (2014). Social sciences and social movements: The theoretical context. *Contemporary Social Science, 9*(1), 1–14. doi:10.1080/21582041.2013.851406

Trist, E. L., & Bamforth, K. W. (1951). Some social and psychological consequences of the Longwall Method of coal-getting: An examination of the psychological situation and defences of a work group in relation to the social structure and technological content of the work system. *Human Relations, 4*(1), 3–38. doi:10.1177/001872675100400101

Tsang, M. M., Shu-Chun, H., & Liang, T.-P. (2004). Consumer attitudes toward mobile advertising: An empirical study. *International Journal of Electronic Commerce*, 65–78.

Tsohou, A., Karyda, M., & Kokolakis, S. (2015). Analyzing the role of cognitive and cultural biases in the internalization of information security policies: Recommendations for information security awareness programs. *Computers & Security, 52*, 128–141. doi:10.1016/j.cose.2015.04.006

Tufekci, Z., & Wilson, C. (2012). Social media and the decision to participate in political protest: Observations from Tahrir Square. *Journal of Communication, 62*(2), 363–379. doi:10.1111/j.1460-2466.2012.01629.x

Tun, P. A., & Lachman, M. E. (2010). The association between computer use and cognition across adulthood: Use it so you won't lose it? *Psychology and Aging, 25*(3), 560–568. doi:10.1037/a0019543 PMID:20677884

Turkle, S. (1999). Cyberspace and Identity. *Contemporary Sociology, 28*(6), 643–648.

Turkle, S. (1996). Virtuality and Its Discontents: Searching for Community in Cyberspace. *The American Prospect, 24*(1), 50–57.

Turland, J., Coventry, L., Jeske, D., Briggs, P., & van Moorsel, A. (2015). Nudging Towards security: Developing an Application for Wireless Network Selection for Android Phones. *Proceedings of the 2015 British HCI Conference on - British HCI '15*, 193–201. doi:10.1145/2783446.2783588

Turner, J. C. (1991). *Social influence.* Milton Keynes, UK: Open University Press.

Turner, J. C., Hogg, M. A., Oakes, P. J., Reicher, S. D., & Wetherell, M. S. (1987). *Rediscovering the social group: A self-categorization theory.* Oxford, UK: Blackwell.

Tversky, A. (1972). Elimination by aspects: A theory of choice. *Psychological Review, 79*(4), 281–299. doi:10.1037/h0032955

Tversky, A., & Kahneman, D. (1981). *Evidential impact of base rates (No. TR-4).* Stanford Univ CA Dept of Psychology. doi:10.21236/ADA099501

Twitter. (2017). *Privacy Policy.* Retrieved from: https://cdn.cms-twdigitalassets.com/content/dam/legal-twitter/asset-download-files/TheTwitterUserAgreement-1.pdf

Uebelacker, S., & Quiel, S. (2014). The social engineering personality framework. *4th Workshop on Socio-Technical Aspects in Security and Trust (STAST)*, 24-30.

Uitermark, J. (2017). Complex contention: Analyzing power dynamics within Anonymous. *Social Movement Studies, 16*(4), 403–417. doi:10.1080/14742837.2016.1184136

UK Universities, . (2012). *Oversight of security-sensitive research material in UK universities: guidance.* London: Universities UK.

Ullmann-Margalit, E. (2006). Big decisions: Opting, converting, drifting. *Royal Institute of Philosophy, 58*(Supplement), 157–172. doi:10.1017/S1358246106058085

UN General Assembly. (1966). *International Covenant on Civil and Political Rights.* Available at: http://www.refworld.org/docid/3ae6b3aa0.html

University of Leicester. (2016). *Policy on researching and handling sensitive, extreme, or radical material.* Leicester, UK: University of Leicester.

Urbaniak, G. C., & Plous, S. (2015). Research Randomizer (Version 4.0) [software]. Retrieved via: http://www.randomizer.org/

Usborne, D. (2015). Centcom 'Hacked' by ISIS Supporters: US Military Twitter Feed Publishes Personal Information of Senior Officers. *Independent.* Retrieved 05 03, 2017, from http://www.independent.co.uk/news/world/americas/us-central-command-hacked-by-islamic-state-supporters-9973615.html

Utz, S., & Krämer, N. C. (2009). The privacy paradox on social network sites revisited: The role of individual characteristics and group norms. *Cyberpsychology (Brno), 3*(2).

Vaidyanathan, L. (2009). *Architectures for massively scalable, distributed rural service enterprises: requirements and models.* IITM-Rural Technology and Business Incubator (RTBI) and Xerox Corporation, Tech. Rep.

Valenzuela, S. (2013). Unpacking the use of social media for protest behavior: The roles of information, opinion expression, and activism. *The American Behavioral Scientist, 57*(7), 920–942. doi:10.1177/0002764213479375

Van de Vijver, F., & Leung, K. (1997). *Methods and Data Analysis for Cross-Cultural Research* (Vol. 1). Thousand Oaks, CA: Sage.

Van der Hulst, R. C., & Neve, R. J. M. (2008). *High tech crime, soorten criminaliteit en hun daders: Een literatuur-inventarisatie [High-tech crime, types of crimes and offenders: An inventory of literature].* The Hague, The Netherlands: Boom Juridische uitgevers.

Van Dijk, T. A. (2001). Multidisciplinary CDA: A plea for diversity. In R. Wodak & M. Meyer (Eds.), *Methods of critical discourse analysis* (pp. 95–120). London: Sage.

Van Kleek, M., Liccardi, I., Binns, R., Zhao, J., Weitzner, D. J., & Shadbolt, N. (2017, May). Better the devil you know: Exposing the data sharing practices of apps. In *Proceedings of the 2017 CHI Conference on Human Factors in Computing Systems* (pp. 5208-5220). ACM. doi:10.1145/3025453.3025556

Van Lange, P. A. M. (2015). Generalized Trust: Four Lessons From Genetics and Culture. *Current Directions in Psychological Science, 24*(1), 71–76. doi:10.1177/0963721414552473

van Schaik, P., Jeske, D., Onibokun, J., Coventry, L., Jansen, J., & Kusev, P. (2017). Risk perceptions of cyber-security and precautionary behaviour. *Computers in Human Behavior, 75*, 547–559. doi:10.1016/j.chb.2017.05.038

Van Slyke, C., Comunale, C. L., & Belanger, F. (2002). Gender differences in perceptions of web-based shopping. *Communications of the ACM, 45*(7), 82–86. doi:10.1145/545151.545155

Van Wilsem, J. (2011). Worlds tied together? Online and non-domestic routine activities and their impact on digital and traditional threat victimization. *European Journal of Criminology, 8*(2), 115–127. doi:10.1177/1477370810393156

Van Wilsem, J. (2013). 'Bought it, but never got it': Assessing risk factors for online consumer fraud victimization. *European Sociological Review, 29*(2), 168–178. doi:10.1093/esr/jcr053

Varela, F. J., Thompson, E., & Rosch, E. (2017). *The embodied mind: Cognitive science and human experience.* Cambridge, MA: MIT press.

Varian, H. R. (1996). *Economic Aspects of Personal Privacy. Technical report.* Berkeley, CA: University of California.

Vegh, S., Ayers, M. D., & McCaughey, M. (2003). Classifying forms of online activism. In M. McCaughey & M. Ayers (Eds.), *Cyberactivism: Online Activism in Theory and Practice* (pp. 71–96). London: Routledge.

Venkatesh, V., Morris, M. G., Davis, G. B., & Davis, F. D. (2003). User acceptance of information technology: Toward a unified view. *Management Information Systems Quarterly, 27*(3), 425–478. doi:10.2307/30036540

Venkatesh, V., Thong, J. Y. L., & Xu, X. (2012). Consumer Acceptance and Use of Information Technology : Extending the Unified Theory. *Management Information Systems Quarterly, 36*(1), 157–178.

Vergani, M., & Bliuc, A.-M. (2015). The evolution of ISIS' language: A quantitative analysis of the language of the first year of Dabiq magazine. *Security, Terrorism and Society, 2*, 7–20.

Verizon. (2017). *2017 Data Breach Investigations Report.* Retrieved May 18, 2017, from: http://www.verizonenterprise.com/verizon-insights-lab/dbir/2017/

Vimercati, P. S. (2010). Data protection in outsourcing scenarios: Issues and directions. In *Proceedings of the 5th ACM Symposium on Information, Computer and Communications Security* (pp. 1-14). ACM.

Vismara, S. (2016). Equity retention and social network theory in equity crowdfunding. *Small Business Economics*, *46*(4), 579–590. doi:10.1007/s11187-016-9710-4

Vitell, S. J. (2009). The role of religiosity in business and consumer ethics: A review of the literature. *Journal of Business Ethics*, *90*(S2), 155–167. doi:10.1007/s10551-010-0382-8

Vitell, S. J., Nwachukwu, S. L., & Barnes, J. H. (1993). The effects of culture on ethical decision-making: An application of Hofstede's typology. *Journal of Business Ethics*, *12*(10), 753–760. doi:10.1007/BF00881307

Vitell, S. J., & Paolillo, J. G. P. (2003). Consumer Ethics: The Role of Religiosity. *Journal of Business Ethics*, *46*(2), 151–162. doi:10.1023/A:1025081005272

Vladlena, B., Saridakis, G., Tennakoon, H., & Ezingeard, J. N. (2015). The role of security notices and online consumer behaviour: An empirical study of social networking users. *International Journal of Human-Computer Studies*, *80*, 36–44. doi:10.1016/j.ijhcs.2015.03.004

von Behr, I., Reding, A., Edwards, C., & Gribbon, L. (2013). *Radicalisation in the Digital Era: The Use of the Internet in 15 Cases of Terrorism and Extremism*. Cambridge, UK: RAND Europe.

Von Solms, R., & Van Niekerk, J. (2013). From information security to cyber security. *Computers & Security*, *38*, 97–102. doi:10.1016/j.cose.2013.04.004

Vratonjic, N., Manshaei, M., Grossklags, J., & Hubaux, J.-P. (2012). ad-blocking games: monetizing online content under the threat of ad avoidance. *Workshop on the Economics of Information Security (WEIS)*, 14-16.

Vujic, A. (2017). Switching on or switching off? Everyday computer use as a predictor of sustained attention and cognitive reflection. *Computers in Human Behavior*, *72*, 152–162. doi:10.1016/j.chb.2017.02.040

Wahdat-Hagh, W. (2011). Iran And Cyber-Hezbollah Strategies: Killing Enemies In Hyperspace – Analysis. *Eurasia Review*. Retrieved 06 01, 2017, from: http://www.eurasiareview.com/25112011-iran-and-cyber-hezbollah-strategies-killing-enemies-in-hyperspace-analysis/

Wallenius, J., Dyer, J. S., Fishburn, P. C., Steuer, R. E., Zionts, S., & Deb, K. (2008). Multiple criteria decision making, multiattribute utility theory: Recent accomplishments and what lies ahead. *Management Science*, *54*(7), 1336–1349. doi:10.1287/mnsc.1070.0838

Wall, H. J., Kaye, L. K., & Malone, S. A. (2016). An exploration of psychological factors on emoticon usage and implications for judgement accuracy. *Computers in Human Behavior*, *62*, 70–78. doi:10.1016/j.chb.2016.03.040

Wang, J., Gupta, M., & Rao, H. R. (2015). Insider Threats in a Financial Institution: Analysis of Attack-Proneness of Information Systems Applications. *Management Information Systems Quarterly*, *39*(1), 91–U491. doi:10.25300/MISQ/2015/39.1.05

Wang, Q. (2016). Why we should all be cultural psychologists? Lessons learned from the study of social cognition. *Perspectives on Psychological Science*, *11*(5), 583–596. doi:10.1177/1745691616645552 PMID:27694456

Wang, Y. D., & Emurian, H. H. (2005). An overview of online trust: Concepts, elements, and implications. *Computers in Human Behavior*, *21*(1), 105–125. doi:10.1016/j.chb.2003.11.008

Weaver, G. R. (2002). Religiosity and Ethical Behavior in Organizations : A Symbolic Interactionist Perspective. *Academy of Management Review*, *27*(1), 77–97.

Weaver, G. R., & Agle, B. R. (2002). Religiosity and ethical behavior in organizations: A symbolic interactionist perspective. *Academy of Management Review, 27*(1), 77–97.

Weimann, G. (2004). *How modern terrorism uses the Internet. Special Report 116.* Washington, DC: United States Institute of Peace. Retrieved from www. terror. net

Weinberg, L., Pedahzur, A., & Hirsch-Hoefler, S. (2004). The challenges of conceptualizing terrorism. *Terrorism and Political Violence, 16*(4), 777–794. doi:10.1080/095465590899768

Welch, K. W. (1981). An interpersonal influence model of traditional religious commitment. *The Sociological Quarterly, 22*(1), 81–92. doi:10.1111/j.1533-8525.1981.tb02210.x

Wessel, M., Thies, F., & Benlian, A. (2016). The emergence and effects of fake social information: Evidence from crowdfunding. *Decision Support Systems, 90*, 75–85. doi:10.1016/j.dss.2016.06.021

Westin, A. F. (1968). Privacy and freedom. *Washington and Lee Law Review, 25*(1), 166.

Whatsapp. (2012). *Privacy Policy.* Retrieved from: https://www.whatsapp.com/legal/#Privacy

Whitehead, T. (2016). British teenager suspected of being a mystery hacker who stole CIA boss emails. *The Telegraph.* Retrieved from http://www.telegraph.co.uk/news/uknews/crime/12154592/British-teenager-suspected-of-being-a-mystery-hacker-who-stole-CIA-boss-emails.html

Whiteside, S. (2015). *The impact of ad blocking on brand strategy: three expert perspectives.* Retrieved from: https://www.warc.com/

Whitten, A., & Tygar, J. D. (1998). *Usability of Security: A Case Study. Computer Science.* Retrieved from http://www.dtic.mil/cgi-bin/GetTRDoc?Location=U2&doc=GetTRDoc.pdf&AD=ADA361032

Whitty, M. T. (2008). Liberating or debilitating? An examination of romantic relationships, sexual relationships and friendships on the Net. *Computers in Human Behavior, 24*(5), 1837–1850. doi:10.1016/j.chb.2008.02.009

Whitty, M. T. (2015). Anatomy of the online dating romance scam. *Security Journal, 28*(4), 443–455. doi:10.1057/sj.2012.57

Whitty, M. T., & Buchanan, T. (2012). The online romance scam: A serious cybercrime. *Cyberpsychology, Behavior, and Social Networking, 15*(3), 181–183. doi:10.1089/cyber.2011.0352 PMID:22304401

Wiebe, K. F., & Fleck, J. R. (1980). Personality Correlates of Intrinsic, Extrinsic, and Nonreligious Orientations. *The Journal of Psychology, 105*(2), 181–187. doi:10.1080/00223980.1980.9915149

Wiederhold, B. K. (2014). The role of psychology in enhancing cybersecurity. *Cyberpsychology, Behavior, and Social Networking, 17*(3), 131–132. doi:10.1089/cyber.2014.1502 PMID:24592869

Wijn, R., Van den Berg, H., Wetzer, I. M., & Broekman, C. C. M. T. (2016). Supertargets: Verkenning naar voorspellende en verklarende factoren voor slachtofferschap van cybercriminaliteit [Super targets: Exploration of predictive and explanatory factors for cybercrime victimisation]. Soesterberg: Netherlands Organisation for Applied Scientific Research (TNO).

Wiktorowicz, Q. (2004). *Joining the Cause: Al-Muhajiroun and Radical Islam.* Paper presented at the Roots of Islamic Radicalism Conference, New Haven, CT.

Wilcox, P., Land, K., & Hunt, S. A. (2004). Criminal circumstance: A multicontextual criminal opportunity theory. *Symbolic Interaction, 27*(1).

Wilde, A., & Joseph, S. (1997). Religiosity and personality in a Moslem context. *Personality and Individual Differences*, *23*(5), 899–900. doi:10.1016/S0191-8869(97)00098-6

Wilkes, R. E., Burnett, J. J., & Howell, R. D. (1986). On the meaning and measurement of religiosity in consumer research. *Journal of the Academy of Marketing Science*, *14*(1), 47–56. doi:10.1007/BF02722112

Williams, E. J., Beardmore, A., & Joinson, A. N. (2017). Individual differences in susceptibility to online influence: A theoretical review. *Computers in Human Behavior*, *72*, 412–421. doi:10.1016/j.chb.2017.03.002

Wilson, F. (2003). Can compute, won't compute: Women's participation in the culture of computing. *New Technology, Work and Employment*, *18*(2), 127–142. doi:10.1111/1468-005X.00115

Wodak, R., & Meyer, M. (2009). *Methods for critical discourse analysis*. London: Sage.

Wogalter, M. S., Laughery, K. R., & Mayhorn, C. B. (2012). Warnings and hazard communications. Handbook of human factors and ergonomics, 4.

Wolfradt, U., & Doll, J. (2001). Motives of Adolescents to use the internet as a function of personality traits, personal and social factors. *Journal of Educational Computing Research*, *24*(1), 13–27. doi:10.2190/ANPM-LN97-AUT2-D2EJ

Wray, S. (1998). Electronic civil disobedience and the World Wide Web of hacktivism. *Switch New Media Journal*, *4*(2). Retrieved from http://switch.sjsu.edu/web/v4n2/stefan/

Wright, B., Partridge, I., & Williams, C. (2000). Management of chronic fatigue syndrome in children. *Advances in Psychiatric Treatment*, *6*(2), 145–152. doi:10.1192/apt.6.2.145

Wright, K. B. (2005). Researching Internet-based populations: Advantages and Disadvantages of online survey research, online questionnaire authoring software packages and web survey services. *Journal of Computer-Mediated Communication*, *10*(3). doi:10.1111/j.1083-6101.2005.tb00259.x

Wright, M. F., Kamble, S. V., & Soudi, S. P. (2015). Indian adolescents' cyber aggression involvement and cultural values: The moderation of peer attachment. *School Psychology International*, *36*(4), 410–427. doi:10.1177/0143034315584696

Wright, R. T., & Marett, K. (2010). The influence of experiential and dispositional factors in phishing: An empirical investigation of the deceived. *Journal of Management Information Systems*, *27*(1), 273–303. doi:10.2753/MIS0742-1222270111

Wu, G., Hu, X., & Wu, Y. (2010). Effects of perceived interactivity, perceived web assurance and disposition to trust on initial online trust. *Journal of Computer-Mediated Communication*, *16*(1), 1–26. doi:10.1111/j.1083-6101.2010.01528.x

Xiao, B., & Benbasat, I. (2015). Designing warning messages for detecting biased online product recommendations: An empirical investigation. *Information Systems Research*, *26*(4), 793–811. doi:10.1287/isre.2015.0592

Yan, Z., & Gozu, H. Y. (2012). Online decision-making in receiving spam emails among college students. *International Journal of Cyber Behavior, Psychology and Learning*, *2*(1), 1–12. doi:10.4018/ijcbpl.2012010101

Yar, M. (2005). The novelty of cybercrime: An assessment in light of routine activity theory. *European Journal of Criminology*, *2*(4), 407–427. doi:10.1177/147737080556056

Yeap, S. Y., & Park, J. (2010). *Countering internet radicalisation: A holistic approach*. Academic Press.

Yeo, J. (2013). Using penetration testing to enhance your company's security. *Computer Fraud & Security*, *4*(4), 17–20. doi:10.1016/S1361-3723(13)70039-3

Young, K. S., & Case, C. J. (2004). Internet abuse in the workplace: New trends in risk management. *Cyberpsychology & Behavior*, *7*(1), 105–111. doi:10.1089/109493104322820174 PMID:15006175

Yousafzai, S. Y., Foxall, G. R., & Pallister, J. G. (2010). Explaining internet banking behavior: Theory of reasoned action, theory of planned behavior, or technology acceptance model? *Journal of Applied Social Psychology*, *40*(5), 1172–1202. doi:10.1111/j.1559-1816.2010.00615.x

Yuhas, A. (2017, March 22). Lithuanian man's phishing tricked US tech companies into wiring over $100m. *The Guardian*. Retrieved May 16, 2017, from: https://www.theguardian.com/technology/2017/mar/22/phishing-scam-us-tech-companies-tricked-100-million-lithuanian-man

Zaheer, S., & Zaheer, A. (1997). Country Effects on Information Seeking in Global Electronic Networks. *Journal of International Business Studies*, *28*(1), 77–100. doi:10.1057/palgrave.jibs.8490094

Zelin, A. Y. (2014). *Al-Qaeda Disaffiliates with the Islamic State of Iraq and al-Sham.* Retrieved 05 30, 2017, from Washington Institute: http://www.washingtoninstitute.org/policy-analysis/view/al-qaeda-disaffiliates-with-the-islamic-state-of-iraq-and-al-sham

Zhang, B., & Xu, H. (2016, February). Privacy nudges for mobile Applications: Effects on the creepiness emotion and privacy attitudes. In *Proceedings of the 19th ACM conference on computer-supported cooperative work & social computing* (pp. 1676-1690). ACM. doi:10.1145/2818048.2820073

Zhang, J., Chen, C., Xiang, Y., Zhou, W., & Xiang, Y. (2013). Internet traffic classification by aggregating correlated naive bayes predictions. *IEEE Transactions on Information Forensics and Security*, *8*(1), 5–15. doi:10.1109/TIFS.2012.2223675

Zhang, J., & Liu, P. (2012). Rational herding in microloan markets. *Management Science*, *58*(5), 892–912. doi:10.1287/mnsc.1110.1459

Zhao, C., & Jiang, G. (2011). Cultural differences on visual self-presentation through social networking site profile images. *Proceedings of the ACM SIGCHI Conference on Human Factors in Computing Systems (CHI)*. doi:10.1145/1978942.1979110

Zhao, J., Abrahamson, K., Anderson, J. G., Ha, S., & Widdows, R. (2013). Trust, empathy, social identity, and contribution of knowledge within patient online communities. *Behaviour & Information Technology*, *32*(10), 1041–1048. doi:10.1080/0144929X.2013.819529

Zhao, J., Ha, S., & Widdows, R. (2013). Building trusting relationships in online health communities. *Cyberpsychology, Behavior, and Social Networking*, *16*(9), 650–657. doi:10.1089/cyber.2012.0348 PMID:23786170

Zheng, J., Veinott, E., Bos, N., Olson, J. S., & Olson, G. M. (2002, April). Trust without touch: jumpstarting long-distance trust with initial social activities. In *Proceedings of the SIGCHI conference on human factors in computing systems* (pp. 141-146). ACM. doi:10.1145/503376.503402

Zhou, L., Shi, Y., & Zhang, D. (2008). A statistical language modelling approach to online deception detection. *IEEE Transactions on Knowledge and Data Engineering*, *20*(8), 1077–1081. doi:10.1109/TKDE.2007.190624

Zvilichovsky, D., Inbar, Y., & Barzilay, O. (2015). Playing both sides of the market: Success and reciprocity on crowdfunding platforms. *SSRN Electronic Journal*. Retrieved May 8, 2017, from https://papers.ssrn.com/sol3/papers.cfm?abstract_id=2304101

Zytko, D., Freeman, G., Grandhi, S. A., Herring, S. C., & Jones, Q. G. (2015, February). Enhancing evaluation of potential dates online through paired collaborative activities. In *Proceedings of the 18th ACM conference on computer supported cooperative work & social computing* (pp. 1849-1859). ACM. doi:10.1145/2675133.2675184

About the Contributors

John McAlaney is a Chartered Psychologist, Chartered Scientist and Senior Lecturer in Psychology at Bournemouth University. He completed his undergraduate degree at the University of Stirling, his MSc at the University of Strathclyde and then his PhD at the University of West of Scotland in 2007. Dr McAlaney's PhD was on the topic of social psychology and substance use, looking particularly at misperceptions of peer norms. Following this he worked on an AERC funded post-doc position at London School of Hygiene and Tropical Medicine before moving onto a lecturing post at the University of Bradford in 2008. He joined the Department of Psychology at Bournemouth University in 2014. Since joining Bournemouth he has collaborated extensively with colleagues in the Department of Computing and Informatics to explore psychological factors of cyber security, including participation in hacking and hacktivism, group dynamics in cyber security actors and decision making processes in relation to phishing emails and other mediums.

Lara Frumkin is a chartered psychologist, fellow of the Higher Education Academy, and associate fellow of the British Psychological Society. She received her BS in psychology from Hobart and William Smith in the USA. She then completed an MA and PhD at the University of Maryland, both in social and community psychology. She worked at a non-profit association in Washington, DC prior to a role at the Justice Department with the US Federal Government. After moving to the UK, she worked at Middlesex University and the Institute of Education, coming to UEL in 2010. She has been the programme leader for the BSc Forensic Psychology degree and will be moving to the Open University in January 2018.

Vladlena Benson is Academic Relations and Research Director at ISACA LC and Professor of Cybersecurity at the University of West London. She is a specialist in technology governance, risk and compliance (GRC) and a Government Communications Headquarters (GCHQ)-certified Cyber Security Risk Management Frameworks practitioner. She is currently working with UK businesses on privacy and cyber security initiatives, such as the forthcoming General Data Protection Regulation (GDPR) and privacy compliance. Prof Benson's research areas cover: information privacy; cyber ecognizedon; gender and culture differences in online ecogniz; digital rights and the cyber vulnerability of young people. Her work also relates to religious orientation, digital ecogniz and privacy on social media. She is a strong advocate for increasing diversity in the cyber security work force, and actively endeavours to bring more female talent into the digital economy. As part of her research, she currently runs a number of projects to help target the digital skills crisis – developing tools for opening up cyberspace entrepreneurship opportunities from an early age. As a result of her work in this area, Prof Benson was ecognized at the Women in IT Awards 2017 for helping the development of career opportunities for women in cyber security.

* * *

Erdem Aksakal is a PhD marketing student at Bilgi University in the Management Department. He has been working in the technology industry since 2003, in many technical and management positions. He is a columnist and author on technology, urban life and people in work life. His focus is on writing and researching consumption culture and identities.

Ece Akten is a PhD student in communication at Istanbul Bilgi University. She has been working as a research assistant in the department of psychology and had been a psychodynamic psychotherapist. Her research focus is on the hierarchy, work-related stress and burnout of set (movie/tv series) workers.

Yonca Aslanbay is professor of marketing in the department of advertising in Istanbul Bilgi University. She received her Ph.D. degree in 1992. Her current teaching agenda and prior publications are in the domains of marketing and consumer behavior. Her recent research focuses on consumer culture, the new types of online collectivities and sustainability in markets.

Rami Baazim is a Saudi Citizen who is a second year PhD student at Kingston Business School. His major is information systems and his focus is on privacy, religiosity, online behaviour and the use of technology. He works in Jeddah University as a lecturer. He got his Master of IT/Business from Griffith University in Brisbane Australia.

Jonathan Z. Bakdash received the Ph.D. degree in psychology from the University of Virginia, Charlottesville, VA, USA, in 2010. He is a research psychologist with the Human Research and Engineering Directorate, U.S. Army Research Laboratory, Aberdeen Proving Ground, MD, USA. His research interests include human decision making, human–machine interaction, and cybersecurity.

Jildau Borwell is an analyst specializing in cybercrime at the Regional Intelligence Service in the Northern Netherlands police unit. Before her police education (Bachelor of Policing), she completed the Master of Sociology at the University of Groningen, with a specialisation in Crime and Safety.

Sunita Vikrant Dhavale, PhD (2015), is working as an Assistant Professor in Defence Institute of Advanced Technology (an autonomous institute under Ministry of Defence) in Pune, India. She received EC-Council's Certified Ethical Hacker (CEH-v9) certification in 2017. She has more than 20 publications in international journals, international conference proceedings and book chapters. Her research areas are steganography, multimedia forensics and penetration testing. She is member of many professional bodies including IEEE, ACM, ISTE, IETE, IAENG, and ISACA.

Lee Hadlington has been a Senior Lecturer at De Montfort University since 2006 after completing his PhD at Wolverhampton University. Originally coming from a background in applied cognitive psychology, he has developed a research profile in the area of cyber psychology. His main focus of interest is exploring the way in which humans use cognition in the online environment as well as the potential for digital technology to change the underlying processes that we use in daily life. Associated with his work in the area of cyberpsychology is a keen interest in exploring key aspects of technology-enabled crime. He has also worked extensively with a variety of external organisations in exploring aspects of insider threat, susceptibility to cybercrime and attitudes towards cybersecurity. The aim of this research is to help identify potential indicators that could highlight a susceptibility to cybercrime alongside an examination of how individual differences play a role in risky online behaviours.

Sarah Hodge is a Lecturer in Psychology at Bournemouth University. Her background is in psychology with her PhD focusing on the role of morality in video games. Her research interests span psychology and technology: with a particular interest in video games, cyber, social, moral, educational, and developmental psychology.

Hemant Jalota is currently working as a Machine Learning Researcher in DeepR Analytics, India. Before joining DeepR Analytics, he was assistant professor at Ansal University, Gurgaon for one year. He did PhD from Indian Institute of Technology Mandi and MSc from DAV Jalandhar. His areas of research are Operation Research, Fuzzy set theory, Portfolio optimization, Soft computing, Modelling and simulation (Engineering application).

Jurjen Jansen is a researcher at the Cybersafety Research Group (NHL University of Applied Sciences and the Dutch Police Academy) and an external PhD Candidate at the Open University of the Netherlands. His PhD project focusses on human aspects of the safety and security of online banking. More specifically on strengthening the online resilience of end users who make use of online banking services. Before starting his PhD, Jurjen contributed to research projects on youth and cyber safety, the nature and extent of cybercrime victimisation among Dutch citizens and the digital security of small and medium-sized enterprises.

Helen Jones is a postdoctoral research fellow at the University of Dundee, where she is working on a project that examines how users establish trust in different online contexts, and how this might be manipulated. Drawing on insights from the fields of human computer interaction and psychology, this research addresses some major concerns in cyber security – specifically, fraud and false identity. Helen previously completed her PhD at Lancaster University, which examined the psychological factors influencing susceptibility to email fraud. She has also worked at the University of Central Lancashire, researching the influence of behavioural and physiological factors in the detection of insider threats.

Linda Kaye is a Senior Lecturer in Psychology at Edge Hill University, who specialises in cyberpsychology. Her main interests surround the social contexts and processes of digital gaming, but she also is involved in research on the psychology of online behaviour. In particular, how individual-level and contextual-level factors interact in online environments.

Mine Galip Koca is a PhD marketing student in Bilgi University's Management Department. She has worked in credit card and mobile payments industries in various senior marketing management positions for more than 10 years. She is also a lecturer at the Boğaziçi University, Management Department. Her current research topics include sharing economy, time scarcity and consumer culture.

Sheryl Prentice is a postdoctoral researcher at Lancaster University working in the field of social science and security, and specialising in online terrorism. She is a Director of WAP Academic Consultancy Limited, a company delivering research and development projects relating to issues of online security.

Char Sample is research fellow employed for ICF at the US Army Research Laboratory in Adelphi, Maryland and with the University of Warwick, UK. Dr. Sample has over 20 years experience in the information security industry. Most recently Dr. Sample has been advancing the research into the role of national culture in cyber security events. Presently Dr. Sample is continuing research on modeling cyber behaviors by culture, other areas of research are information weaponization and data fidelity.

Subhi Can Sarıgöllü is a Ph.D. student in Business Administration-Marketing in Istanbul at Bilgi University. He is also employed as a marketing communications strategist since 2011, working with several advertising agencies. His current research focuses on corporate social responsibility, consumer behavior and privacy in the digital era.

Reena Singh is currently working as an Assistant Professor at Information and Communication Technology Department (I&CT), MIT, Manipal, India. She received PhD in Computer Science from Indian Institute of Technology Mandi, India in 2017. She has received M.Tech degree in Computer Science in 2009 and B. E. degree in Computer Science and Engineering in 2007. Her research interests include Access control, Distributed applications, Information security and Semantic web.

Wouter Stol received his doctorate on 'Police action and information technology' at the Vrije Universiteit of Amsterdam in 1996. He is currently professor of Cybersafety at NHL University of Applied Sciences and the Dutch Police Academy and professor of Police Studies at the Open University of the Netherlands. Main themes in his work include cybercrime, perpetratorship and victimisation of cybercrime, and measures against cybercrime (especially criminal law).

Jacqui Taylor is an Associate Professor in Psychology Education at Bournemouth University, UK. Jacqui is a Senior Fellow of the Higher Education Academy and has worked with the British Psychological Society on a number of committees and was previously the editor of their publication Psychology Teaching Review. Following a degree in psychology and a masters in information systems, Jacqui was awarded a PhD from the University of Portsmouth for her thesis, 'A social psychological analysis of computer mediated communication'. Jacqui has taught on the BSc (Hons) Psychology and Computing and BSc Psychology degrees and on Masters degrees in Cybersecurity. Jacqui is involved in all aspects of cyberpsychology teaching and research, including video-game use, online deviance, online addiction and social networking use by children and adolescents. She has developed innovative teaching practice regarding the development of student's online skills and is currently researching the role of positive psychology in e-learning and psychological literacy for employability.

Paul J. Taylor is Professor of Psychology at Lancaster University, UK, where he has led over £10M of projects in the areas of behavioural analytics and prediction. His work has, for example, developed a framework for understanding communicative sensemaking, developed novel ways of tracking social cohesion online, and built language-based tools for detecting insider threat. Paul directs the UK's national centre for behavioural and social science research on security threats (CREST). Involving over 100 researchers, CREST deliver synthetic and original research that helps the security and intelligence agencies better understand threat actors, gather better intelligence, make better decisions, and remain secure.

Helen Thackray is a PhD Candidate in Psychology and Computing. Her focus is social psychology within a cybersecurity context. Her research examines hacking communities, the group processes, and social identity.

Reyhan Topal is a PhD candidate in Political Science and Public Administration at Bilkent University, Ankara, Turkey. She previously received her MA from Middle East Technical University and BA from Bilkent University. Her academic interests concentrate on radicalisation, online radicalisation, non-violent extremism, conflict resolution and peacebuilding.

John Towse is an experimental psychologist, and senior lecturer in Psychology at Lancaster University. He obtained his BA in psychology from Oxford University and a PhD from Manchester University. He worked at Royal Holloway University of London prior to his appointment at Lancaster. His work focuses on a number of domains, including theoretical development of models in cognitive science, understanding the emergence of numerical cognition through childhood, and explanation for limits in behavioural regulation. He also has a focus on cybercognition, and is a member of Security Lancaster, with work in the field funded by DSTL and EPSRC.

Helen Wall is a Senior Lecturer at Edge Hill University with interests in the contextual and individual level factors that shape behavior in online and offline contexts." Dr Wall conducts research into the accuracy of personality judgements based on limited information cues to explore the social and cognitive process involved in interpersonal perception. Dr Wall's interests in personality, context and behaviour extend to the field of persuasion with a particular focus on individual differences in susceptibility to persuasion.

Index

Recommended Reference Books

ISBN: 978-1-4666-9661-7
© 2016; 308 pp.
List Price: $200

ISBN: 978-1-5225-1016-1
© 2017; 345 pp.
List Price: $200

ISBN: 978-1-5225-0983-7
© 2017; 1,852 pp.
List Price: $2,200

ISBN: 978-1-5225-0808-3
© 2017; 442 pp.
List Price: $345

ISBN: 978-1-4666-8793-6
© 2016; 548 pp.
List Price: $335

ISBN: 978-1-4666-8387-7
© 2015; 408 pp.
List Price: $325

Looking for free content, product updates, news, and special offers?
Join IGI Global's mailing list today and start enjoying exclusive perks sent only to IGI Global members.
Add your name to the list at **www.igi-global.com/newsletters.**

Publishing Information Science and Technology Research Since 1988

IGI Global
DISSEMINATOR OF KNOWLEDGE

www.igi-global.com   Sign up at www.igi-global.com/newsletters   f facebook.com/igiglobal   t twitter.com/igiglobal

Stay Current on the Latest Emerging Research Developments

Become an IGI Global Reviewer for Authored Book Projects

The overall success of an authored book project is dependent on quality and timely reviews.

In this competitive age of scholarly publishing, constructive and timely feedback significantly decreases the turnaround time of manuscripts from submission to acceptance, allowing the publication and discovery of progressive research at a much more expeditious rate. Several IGI Global authored book projects are currently seeking highly qualified experts in the field to fill vacancies on their respective editorial review boards:

Applications may be sent to:
development@igi-global.com

Applicants must have a doctorate (or an equivalent degree) as well as publishing and reviewing experience. Reviewers are asked to write reviews in a timely, collegial, and constructive manner. All reviewers will begin their role on an ad-hoc basis for a period of one year, and upon successful completion of this term can be considered for full editorial review board status, with the potential for a subsequent promotion to Associate Editor.

If you have a colleague that may be interested in this opportunity, we encourage you to share this information with them.

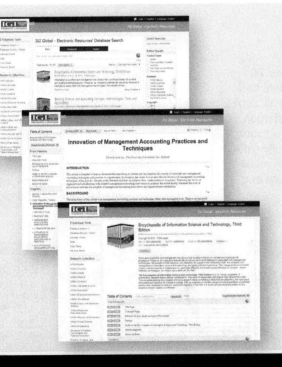